Abstracts of
Bristol County, Massachusetts
Probate Records

Abstracts of
BRISTOL COUNTY, MASSACHUSETTS
Probate Records

1687-1745

Compiled by
H.L. Peter Rounds, C.G.

CLEARFIELD

Reprinted for
Clearfield Company, Inc. by
Genealogical Publishing Co., Inc.
Baltimore, Maryland
1993, 1996, 2001

INTRODUCTION

The probate records for Bristol County, Massachusetts are located in the Registry of Probate in Taunton, Massachusetts. They commence with 1687, the county having been established in 1685. All volumes, up to 1870, are also available on microfilm from the Church of Jesus Christ of Latter Day Saints (Mormon), through its Salt Lake City depository. These can be ordered through any local branch LDS Genealogical Library.

Lengthy abstracts of Volume 1 were published many years ago by Lucy Hall Greenlaw. The first 49 pages appeared in the *Genealogical Advertiser*, Vols. 3 (1900) and 4 (1901). The remaining pages of Volume 1 (pp. 50-230) were published in the *New England Historic Genealogical Register*, Vols. 62, 63 & 64. Volume 2 (1698-1710), as abstracted by this present compiler, was published in the March 1985 issue of the *National Genealogical Society Quarterly*, Vol. 73.

In addition to the regular bound volumes, the Registry of Probate in Taunton also has most of the original probate documents themselves, from which these volumes were prepared. They are arranged alphabetically by surname, then by first name, and are grouped in envelopes with all papers relating to the estate of one particular decedent being put together in one envelope. Intensive research by this compiler and by other specialists demonstrates that there were often probate documents which were never copied into these bound volumes. As a result, these loose papers have even more genealogical details than are found in these volumes. The Mormons have also microfilmed these original probate documents of the period 1687 to 1870.

The compiler has here abstracted every item and entry, page by page, in all of Volumes 1-10, covering 1687-1745. Included are wills, inventories, administrators' accounts, receipts, divisions of estates, petitions, guardianships and other matters relating to the probate of estates. Every fact deemed to be of genealogical value has been included.

Abbreviations

abt. - about	comm. - committee
acct. - account	dau. - daughter
adm. - administrator	dcd. - deceased
agrmt. - agreement	div. - division
apprs. - appraisers	dtd. - dated
appt. - appointed	est. - estate
btwn. - between	exec. - executor
chldn. - children	grdau. - granddaughter

grson. - grandson
guard. - guardian
husb. - husband
incl. - including
intest. - intestate
inv. - inventory
paym. - payment

pres. - presented
prob. - probated
rcpt. - receipt
settl. - settlement
unmar. - unmarried
var. - various
witns. - witnesses

Town abbreviations:

Attl. - Attleborough	Lit. Compt. - Little Compton
Barr. - Barrington	Nort. - Norton
Berk. - Berkely	Rayn. - Raynham
Brist. - Bristol	Reho. - Rehoboth
Dart. - Dartmouth	Swan. - Swansea
Digh. - Dighton	Taun. - Taunton
East. - Easton	Tiv. - Tiverton
Free. - Freetown	Warr. - Warren

Names in capital letters in these abstracts are the names of those persons whose estates are the subjects of the entries.

Abstracts of
Bristol County, Massachusetts
Probate Records

VOLUME 1

1687-1698

Div. of Est. of JONATHAN BRIGGS of Taun., pres. 31 Jan. 1689/9
[sic]. Wife Experience. Son Jonathan (eldest). 7 sons & 5 daus.
not named [1:1].

Appt. of Samuel Howland as Adm. of Est. of his bro. JOHN HOW-
LAND of Free., dtd. 8 Aug. 1687 [1:2].

Inv. of Est. of JOHN HOWLAND, pres. 18 Aug. 1687. Apprs: Benjamin Chase & Mathew Boomer [1:2].

Appt. of William Carpenter, Sr. of Reho. as Adm. of ABIGAIL CAR-
PENTER, widow, of Reho., dtd. 7 Sept. 1687 [1:3].

Inv. of Est. of ABIGAIL CARPENTER, widow, of Reho., pres. 7 Sept.
1687. Mentions debts to Widow Sarah Carpenter. Apprs: John
Peck, Gilbert Brooks & Nicholas Peck [1:3].

Will of WILLIAM BROWN of Brist., Husbandman, dtd. 6 Aug. 1689,
prob. 20 Apr. 1697. The widow Jinnins [no relation stated].
Daus. Hannah Marshfield, Mary Backaway [or Barkaway], Susana
Hamond, Deliverance Corps. John Corps Exec. Witns: John Cary
John Smith & Richard Smith [1:4].

Notice to Exec. of Est. of JOHN HINTON of Brist., dtd. 14 Sept.
1687, John Gladding Exec. [1:5].

Will of JOHN HINTON of Brist., Carpenter, dtd. 29 May 1687, prob.
8 Sept. 1687. Only heir was Susannah Gladding, dau. of John
Gladding. John Gladding was Exec. Witns: Elizebeth Gladding
(38 yrs. old) & John Gladding, Jr. (16 yrs. old)[1:5].

Inv. of Est. of WILLIAM BROWN, dtd. 8 Aug. 1689, pres. by John
Corps. Apprs: George Waldron & Richard Smith [1:6].

Appt. of John Peck & William Carpenter as Adms. of Est. of WIL-
LIAM BOWEN of Reho., dtd. 7 Oct. 1686/7 [1:7].

Appt. of Thomas Lincolne, Jr. of Taun. as Adm. of Est. of RICH-
ARD STACY of Taun., dtd. 7 Dec. 1687 [1:9].

Appt. of Henery Harrison of Reho. as Adm. of Est. of JOHN MAR-
TIN of Reho., dtd. 7 Dec. 1687 [1:11].

Will of ELIZEBETH HOWLAND of Swan, 79 years old, dtd. 17 Dec.
1686, prob. 10 Jan. 1687/8. Sons: John (eldest), Joseph, Jabez & Isaack Howland. Son-in-law Mr. James Brown. Daus: Lidiah Browne, Elisebeth Dickenson & Hannah Bosworth. Grdau. Elisebeth Bursley. Grson. Nathaniel Howland son of Joseph Howland.
Grsons: James Browne & Jabez Browne. Grdaus: Dorothy Browne &
Desire Cushman. Witns: Hugh Cole, Samuel Vyall & John Browne
[1:13/4].

Rcpt. by Joseph Brown of Reho. for legacy from Est. of "my
Grandfather or Grandmother," paid by "my uncle James Browne"
of Swan., dtd. 30 Dec. 1691. Witns: John Brown, Mercy Heath
& James Brown, Jr. [1:14].

Rcpt. by William Parker of Seabrook, New London County, of legacy paid by "my uncle" James Browne of Swan., dtd. 2 July
1694. Witns: John Brown & James Brown, Jr. [1:14].

1

Will of DANIEL KING of Free., Shipwright, dtd. 21 Apr. 1688,
  prob. date not given. Sister Sarah Bixby. Esek Browne son
  of James Browne dcd. Samuel Gardiner son of Samuel Gardiner
  of Free. Witns.: John Shaw, Mathew Boomer, Jr., John Nor-
  cutt & Samuel Gardner [1:15].
Rcpt. by Lidia Brown, widow, for legacy from Est. of her husb.
  JOHN BROWN, Jr., dtd. 26 June 1663, paid by "my Brother James
  Brown" [1:15].
Rcpt. by Nathaniel Brown of Reho., Shipwright, of legacy from
  Est. of his grandmother, paid by "my uncle" James Browne of
  Swan., dtd, 6 Sept. 1694. Witns.: John Brown, John Brown,
  Jr. & Samuel Brown [1:15].
Rcpt. by John Brown, Jr. for legacy from Est. of his father who
  died 1661, which was held in trust by his uncle, Mr. James
  Brown, Sr. of Swan., dtd. 3 Sept. 1675, pres. 10 Oct. 1694.
  Witns.: John Cary & Abigail Cary [1:16].
Rcpt. by Anna Willit for legacy from Est. of her grandmother
  DOROTHY BROWN, held in trust by her uncle James Brown of Swan.
  dtd. 15 Dec. 1676, pres. 10 Oct. 1694 [1:16].
Appt. of Experience Briggs, widow, & Jonathan Briggs, eldest
  son (both of Taun.), as Adms. of Est. of JONATHAN BRIGGS of
  Taun., dtd. 6 March 1688/9 [1:16a].
Will of JOHN TITUS, Sr. of Rehoboth, dtd. 21 Feb. 1688/9, prob.
  20 Nov. 1689. Wife Abigail. Sons: Joseph (eldest), Silas &
  Samuel Titus. Daus.: Abigail, Mercy & Experience. Cousin
  Samuel Carpenter. Brother William Carpenter. Grchldn.: John
  Fuller, Abiall Fuller, John Titus, Silas Titus & Abigail Bow-
  en. Witns.: John Peck, Gilbert Brooks & William Carpenter
  [1:17/8].
Will of JOHN ALLEN of Swansea, in his 85th year, dtd. 12 March
  1689, prob. 27 May 1690. Wife Christiam. Sons: John (eldest),
  Isack & Daniel Allen. Dau. Deborah Buckland. Grchldn.: John
  Allen & Samuel Allen sons of Daniel Allen, Elisabeth dau. of
  Daniel Allen & Deborah Cole. Witns.: John Peck & Israel Peck
  [1:1920].
Blank page [1:21].
Will of SAMUEL HALL, Sr. of Taun., dtd. 25 Jan. 1698/9, prob.
  27 May 1690. Wife Elisabeth. Sons: Samuel, John, Nicholas,
  Ebenezer & George Hall. Daus.: Elisabeth, Mary, Sarah & Han-
  nah. Witns.: John Cowell, Samuel Page & Joseph Hall [1:22/3].
Blank pages [1:24/5].
Will of NATHANIEL BOSWORTH of Brist., Yeoman, dtd. 15 March 16-
  89/90, prob. 20 Nov. 1690. Wife Bridget. Sons: Nathaniel
  (eldest), Joseph, John, Jeremy, Bellamy & Edward Bosworth.
  Daus.: Mary, Bridgett & Hanah Jacob. Cousin Benjamin Jones.
  Mary Lobdell, Sarah Lobdell, John Lobdell & Nathaniel Lob-
  dell of unknown relationship. Mentions his lands in Hull.
  Witns.: William Throop & John Cary [1:26/7].
Blank page [1:28].

Will of WILLIAM BARTRUM of Swan., dtd. 10 Apr. 1688, prob. 19
Nov. 1690. Wife Sarah. Daus.: Mary, Elisabeth, Rebecca, Hes-
ter, Ellen, Hannah & Susannah. Witns.: Caleb Eddy, Cornelius
Edwards & Thomas Eastabrooke [1:29].
Blank page [1:30].
Will of BENJAMIN INGELL of Brist., Saylor, dtd. 4 Oct. 1690,
prob. 19 Nov. 1690. Wife Weightstill "who is now in child."
Son Benjamin (under 21). Witns.: John Cary, William Hoar &
Richard Smith [1:31].
Blank page [1:32].
Will of WILLIAM ROBINSON of Reho., Weaver, dtd. 10 July 1690,
prob. 19 May 1691. Brothers Benjamin, Samuel, George & John
Robinson. Brother William Carpenter. Sister Mary's chldn.
unnamed. Witns.: William Carpenter & Noah Carpenter [1:33].
Appt. of John Crossman & John Thresher, both of Taun., as Adms.
of Est. of ROBERT CROSSMAN of Taun., dtd. 26 Nov. 1692.
Blank page [1:35].
Will of JOSEPH WILBORE of Taun., dtd. 1 Apr. 1691, prob. 18 Nov.
1691. Dau. Anna Wilbore. Cousins: John Wilbore, Eliezer Wil-
bore, Samuel Wilbore, Joseph Wilbore, Shadrach Wilbore & Benjamin Wilbore (sons of my brother Shadrach Wilbore). Cousins
Sarah wife of Nathaniel Hoar & Rebekah wife of Abraham Hathaway. Hannah Briggs dau. of William Briggs of unknown relat.
Witns.: Nathaniel Williams, John Deane & Henry Hodges [1:36].
Blank page [1:37].
Will of JOHN COBB of Taun., Blacksmith, dtd. 25 Nov. 1690, prob.
18 Nov. 1691. Wife not named. Sons John, Morgan & Samuel
(all under 21). Dau. Elisabeth Woodward (under 21) & son Israel Woodward. Witns.: John Pollard, Sr., Mary Pollard & John
Pollard, Jr. [1:38/9].
Will of WILLIAM HARVEY, dtd. 12 June 1691, prob. date not giv-
en. Sons Thomas & Jonathan Harvey. Chldn. [unnamed] of my
son Joseph Harvey dcd. Nathaniel Thare [sic], Jr. [no relat.
stated]. Witns.: Joseph Willis, Henry Hodges & Samuel Danforth [1:40
Agrmt. btwn. Thomas Harvey, Sr. of Taun. (heir to Ests. of WIL-
LIAM HARVEY & JONATHAN HARVEY) and John Hathaway, Sr. & Sam-
uel Blake (both of Taun.), guards. of the chldn. of Joseph
Harvey dcd. Dtd. 18 Nov. 1691. Mentions: my sister-in-law
Hester Harvey & the children of my brother Joseph Harvey dcd.
Witns.: John Smith & Joseph French [1:41].
Agrmt. btwn. Thomas Harvey, Sr. of Taun. (heir of Ests. of WIL-
LIAM HARVEY & JONATHAN HARVEY) as one party, & Nathaniel Thay-
er (in behalf of his chldn.) & Thomas Harvey, Jr. (in behalf
of his wife) as the other party, dtd. 19 Nov. 1691. Witns.:
Nicholas Moorey & Richard Smith [1:41].
Will of SARAH STOUGHTON, wife of Nicholas Stoughton of Taun.,
dtd. 7 Aug. 1691, prob. 18 Nov. 1691. Husb. Nicholas Stough-
ton. Brother Edward Richmond & his chldn. [not named]. Sam-

uel Richmond son of brother John Richmond. Sarah Richmond
dau. of Edward Richmond. My sister Paul. Ebenezer & Benjamin sons of brother William Paul. Hanah wife of Peter Caswell. Edward son of Peter Caswell. Samuel son of my husb.
Nicholas Stoughton. Mr. Samuel Danforth, Pastor of Church
of Christ in Taun.   James Leonard, Jr. & Henry Hodges to be
Overseers. Witns.: Shadrach Wilbore, Samuel Wilbore & Anna
Wilbore [1:42/3].

Inv. of Est. of ANNA MILES of Swan., dtd. 1 Jan. 1693/4. Apprs.:
Samuel Luther, Caleb Eddy & Joseph Kent [1:43].

Agrmt. abt. Est. of JAMES LEONARD of Taun. btwn Isaac & Hannah
Dean, Joseph Leonard, Uriah Leonard, Thomas Leonard, Benjamin
Leonard, James Leonard, John & Abigail Kingsley & Isaac & Re-
becca Chapman. Mother-in-law Leonard, widow of their father
[probably step-mother]. Dtd. 5 Nov. 1691. Witns.: John
Thresher & Eliezer Carver [1:44].

Agrmt. btwn. Margaret Leonard late wife & now widow of JAMES
LEONARD, Jr. of Taun., and her husb's. chldn., agreeing to
terms written on the other side (see above). Dtd. 10 Nov.
1691. Witns.: John Thresher & Eliezer Carver [1:44].

Will of JOSEPH LEONARD of Taun., dtd. 15 Oct. 1692, prob. 30
March 1692/3. Wife Mary. My chldn. [minors, not named].
Brother Thomas Leonard & Deacon Henry Hodges to be Overseers.
Witns.: Joseph Grey, Uriah Leonard & Samuel Danforth [1:45].

Inv. of Est. of JOSEPH LEONARD of Taun., dtd. 18 Nov. 1692.
Apprs.: John Richmond & Joseph Willis [1:45].

Inv. of Est. of JOSEPH WILLIAMS of Taun., dtd. 17 March 1693.
Apprs.: Thomas Leonard, John Richmond & Benjamin Dean. Pres.
by his widow Elizabeth Williams [1:46].

Will of JOHN SMITH of Taun., dtd. 3 June 1690, prob. 12 Jan.
1691/2. Wife not named. Nicholas Joanes my wife's son.
Sons John (under 21) & Seth. 4 daus. not named. Thomas Leonard of Taun. & brother Samuel Smith of Medfield, Execs.Witns.:
Samuel Smith, Jr. & Samuel Barbur [1:47].

Will of RICHARD GODFREE of Taun., dtd. 4 Oct. 1691, prob. 17
Nov. 1691. Wife Mary. Sons: Robert, Richard & John Godfree.
Daus.: Jane wife of John Cobb, Alce wife of Peter Holbrook, Susannah wife of Edward Kettle. Witns.: Nathaniel Bunn, Shadrach Wilbore & Isack Negus [1:48].

Inv. of Est. of JOHN SMITH, Sr. of Taun., dtd. 16 Dec. 169(?),
pres. by Capt. Thomas Leonard of Taun., Exec. [1:49].

Will of WILLIAM WITHERELL, Sr. of Taun., dtd. 16 Dec. 1691,
prob. 4 Dec. 1691. Wife not named. Sons: William, John &
Ephraim (dcd.) Witherell. Jeremiah son of my son William.
Dau. Dorithy Wood. Witns.: Giles Gilbert, Joseph Gray & Samuel Danforth [1:50].

Will of JACOB BARNEY of Reho., Yeoman, dtd. 30 July 1692, prob.
10 Jan. 1692. Wife Ann. Sons: John (eldest) Joseph, Israell,
Jonathan & Samuel Barney (last 4 under 21). Daus.: Sarah

Hampton, Ruth Barney, Dorcas Throope, Abigail Marshall & Hannah Barney (under 21). Thomas Estabrooks, Sr. & Capt. Timothy Brooks & Samuel Bullock, Overseers. Witns.: the 3 Overseers & Richard Smith [1:51].

Inv. of Est. of GOODMAN WITHERILL, dtd. 13 Nov. 1691, pres. by his son William Witherill. Apprs.: Giles Gilbert, Joseph White & Anthony Newland [1:52].

Acct. of Joseph Kent, Adm. of Est. of ANNA MILES of Swan., dtd. 5 Feb. 1694 [1:52].

Rcpt. from Mary Tucker, dau. of Abraham Tucker of Dart., for legacy from Est. of her grandfather HENRY TUCKER, paid by her uncle John Tucker, dtd. 13 Nov. 1700. Witns.: Abraham Tucker & Hannah Tucker [1:53].

Rcpts. to their uncle John Tucker for legacies paid from the Est. of their grandfather HENRY TUCKER, from:
  Henry Tucker of Dart., dtd. 4 Apr. 1702
  Martha Tucker of Dart., dtd. 30 Apr. 1708
  Abigail Tucker of Dart., dtd. 7 Sept. 1708 [1:54].

Will of JOHN SMITH of Dart., dtd. 8 June 1691, prob. 12 Nov. 1692. Wife Ruhamah. Six sons: Judah, Gershom, Eliazer, Hezekiah, Deliverance Smith & one son not named. Daus. Hassadiah wife of Jonathan Russell, Mehitabel wife of John Russell, Hannah Smith, Sarah Smith & Deborah Smith. Grchldn.: James son of my son Eliazer Smith, James Russell son of Jonathan Russell & Mical son of my son Hezekiah Smith. Seth Pope & my brother-in-law Recompense Carby, Execs. Witns.: Benjamin Howland & Vallentine Hudelston [1:55].

Will of ANTHONY LOW, dtd. 6 Aug. 1692, prob. date not stated. Sons John (eldest) & Samuel Low. Dau. Elisabeth Low. My son Simon Davis. Mentions land in Warwick, in Swansea & "My Sloop Dulphin which now I am in." Wife is not named. Witns.: Richard Dean & John James [1:56].

Quitclaim by John Low of Warwick, R.I. to brother Samuel Low of Swan. of rights to Est. of their father ANTHONY LOW of Swan., dtd. 10 Nov. 1692. Witns.: William Brenton, Jeremiah Osborn & Richard Smith [1:56].

Will of MARY SISON of Dart., widow, dtd. 15 Apr. 1690, prob. 1 Dec. 1692. Husb. Richard Sison dcd. Sons: George, John & James Sison. Daus. Elisabeth wife of Caleb Allin & Ann wife of Peleg Tripp. Grchldn. John & Mary Sison chldn. of son John Sison; & Mary Sison dau. of son George Sison. Witns.: Joseph Tripp, George Cadman & John Anthony [1:57].

Inv. of Est. of Widow MARY SISON, dtd. 22 Sept. 1692, pres. by James Sison. Apprs.: George Cadman, James Trip & Valentine Hudeston [1:58].

Will of PETER HUNT of Reho., dtd. 19 June 1689, prob. 26 Dec. 1692. Wife Elisabeth. 4 sons: Enoch, John, Ephraim & Benjamin Hunt. Dau. Judeth Williams & her 2 sons Nathaniel Cooper & Thomas Cooper. Sons-in-law Samuel Peck & James Willett. Grdau. Sarah Peck. Witns.: Daniel Smith, Samuel Newman & Stephen Paine [1:59/60].

Agrmt. btwn. Rebecca Briggs, William Briggs (eldest son), John
Briggs & Nathaniel Thayer abt. div. of Est. of RICHARD BRIGGS
of Taun. Mentions widow, not named. Dtd. 13 Dec. 1692. Witns:
Jonah Linkon & James Woodward [1:60].

Will of WILLIAM HOAR of Brist., Baker, dtd. 23 July 1697, prob.
27 Dec. 1698. Wife Hannah, "The wife of my Youth & the Nat-
urall Mother of all the Children that Ever I had." Deacon
John Cary, John Birge & Nathaniel Blagrove, Overseers. Witns.:
John Cary, Thomas Walker & Nathaniel Blagrove [1:61].

Blank pages [1:62/3/4].

Agrmt. btwn. John Allen of Brist. & Thomas Read of Reho., Over-
seers of Est. of ISAAC ALLEN of Reho., as one party; & Daniel
Jencks of Attl. as the other party. Katheren widow of Isaac
Allen dcd. & now wife of Daniel Jencks. Only son Nehemiah
Allen. Dtd. 8 May 1695. Witns.: Stephen Paine, Joseph Brown
& John Cary [1:65].

Will of ISACC ALLEN of Reho., dtd. 3 Oct. 1692, prob. date not
stated; recorded 8 May 1695. Wife Katharine. Only son Nehemiah (minor). Daus. Katharine (eldest), Sarah & Deborah
(last 2 minors). Brother John Allen & Thomas Reed, Overseers.
Witns.: Jonathan Sprague, John Allen & Bethiah Allen [1:66].

Acct. of Est. of ISAACE ALLEN of Reho., pres. by Anthony Sprague of Reho., recorded 8 May 1695 [1:66].

Order for div. of Est. of ISAAC ALLEN, dtd. 5 Jan. 1693, btwn.
Anthony Sprague & chldn. of Isaac Allen [1:67].

Inv. of Est. of THOMAS BRENTNALL, dtd. Oct. 1692, pres. by Widow Ester Brentnall. Apprs.: John Ware & Thomas Skinner, Sr.
[1:67].

Inv. of Est. of ELIZABETH JANSON of Swan., widow, who died 31
May 1694, dtd. 10 July 1694, pres. by Elisha Davis, Adm.
Apprs.: William Salisbury & James Wheeler [1:68].

Div. of lands held in partner. by ISAAC ALLEN dcd. & Anthony
Sprague of Reho. Comm.: John Allen, Thomas Reed, Joseph Buckland, Sr. & Daniel Jencks, dtd. 16 July 1694 [1:68].

Inv. of Est. of PETER PITTS, dtd. 9 Jan. 1692. Mary Pitts widow, too old & infirm to travel to Court. Apprs.: John Pol-
lerd & Henry Hodges [1:69].

Will of PETER PITTS of Taun., dtd. 9 June 1692, prob. 12 Jan.
1692. Wife Mary. Sons: Samuel, Peter & Ebenezer. Daus.:
Alce, Mary & Sarah. John Hodges & Henry Hodges, Overseers.
Witns.: John Pollord, Samuel Thresher & Samuel Waldron [1:70].

Rcpts. by George Sison of Road Island; by Elisabeth Allen wife
of Caleb Allen of Sandwich, Barnstable County & by Ann Tripp
wife of Peleg Tripp of Road Island for legacies paid by their
brother, James Sison of Dart., from the Est. of their mother
MARY SISON, dtd. 17 Dec. 1692. Witns.: Valentine Hudelstun
& Richard Allen [1:71/2].

Rcpt. by Mary Sisson dau. of George Sisson of Road Island for

legacy from Est. of her grandmother MARY SISSON, paid by her
uncle James Sisson of Dart., dtd. 17 Dec. 1692 [1:72].

Prenuptial agrmt. btwn. ROBERT CROSSMAN of Taun., Carpenter, &
Martha Eatton of Brist., widow, dtd. 7 Dec. 1687. Witns.:Ed-
mond Ranger & Richard Smith [1:72].

Inv. of Est. of ROBERT CROSSMAN, Sr. of Taun., dtd. 17 Oct.
1692. Widow Martha Crossman too aged & infirm to come to
court. Apprs.: James Leonard & Thomas Dean [1:73].

Inv. of Est. of PHILIPE TABOR of Dart., dtd. 4 March 1692/3,
pres. by Mary Davice of Dart. Apprs.: Thomas Tabor & Joseph
Tripp, both of Dart. [1:74].

Will of JOHN BRIANT of Taun., dtd. 10 Feb. 1684, prob. 31 Aug.
1693. Wife Elisabeth. Son John Briant. Witns.: John Macumber, Sr., Joseph Wilbore & John Richmond [1:75].

Inv. of Est. of JOHN BRIANT of Taun. who died 11 Aug. 1693, dtd.
21 Aug. 1693, pres. by Elisabeth Briant, his widow. Apprs.:
John Richmond, Samuell Williams & Robert Crossman [1:76].

Will of Capt. GEORGE MACEY of Taun., dtd. 20 June 1693, prob.
5 Sept. 1693. Wife Susanna. Daus.: Elisabeth Hodges, Sarah
Black, Mary Williams, Rebeccah Williams & Deborah. Grchld.
Samuell Hodges. Friends John Hall & Joseph Willis, Overseers.
Witns.: Samuell Danforth, John Hoskins & Shadrach Wilbore,
all of Taun. [1:77/8].

Will of RICHARD WILLIAMS, aged abt. 80, dtd. 5 May 1786, prob.
10 Oct. 1693. Wife ffrauncis. Sons: Samuel, Nathanell, Joseph, Thomas & Benjamin. Daus.: Elisabeth & Hannah. Witns.:
James Walker, Thomas Leonard & James Leonard, Jr. [1:79/80].

Will of MARY WALKER of Reho., dtd. 15 May 1694, prob. 28 May
1694. Mother Jane Polles. 3 brothers: Samuel, Philip & Ebenezer Walker. Sisters Elisabeth Sweet & Martha Walker. Cousins Ann Perren, Abraham Perren & Sarah Perren. Patience dau.
of my sister Martha Walker. Unnamed chldn. of brothers Samuel & Philip. Witns.: Joseph Dogget, John Butterworth & William Carpenter [1:80].

Inv. of Est. of MARY WALKER of Reho., dtd. 25 May 1694. Apprs.
not named [1:81]

Inv. of Est. of JOHN PEREN of Reho., dtd. 23 May 1694, pres. by
Sarah Peren, his widow. Apprs.: Samuel Peck, Thomas Reed &
William Carpenter [1:81].

Will of THOMAS WILLMOUTH, Sr., dtd. 10 Dec. 1678, prob. 28 May
1694. Wife Rachell. 3 sons: Thomas, John & Jonathan. 2 daus.
Elisabeth & Mary. Brother-in-law Sgt. Jonathan Bliss & Sgt.
Thomas Reed, Overseers. Witns.: Daniel Smith & Joshua Smith
[1:82].

Inv. of Est. of Ensign THOMAS WILLMATH of Reho., dtd. 26 May
1694, pres. by Rachel Willmouth, his widow. Apprs.: William
Carpenter & John Butterworth [1:83].

Inv. of Est. of ABRAHAM PERIN of Reho., dtd. 24 May 1694, pres.
by Thos. Read & Saml. Walker, Adms. Apprs.: Samuel Peck, Wil-

liam Carpenter & Nicholas Ide [1:84].
Will of HENRY TUCKER of Dart., dtd. 1 March 1693/4, prob. 3 Ju-
ly 1694. Wife Martha. Sons John & Abraham Tucker. Dau. Sar-
ah Tucker. Sons-in-law Nathaniel Slocum & Samuel Perry. Gr-
chld. Henry Tucker son of Abraham. 4 daus. of my son Abraham
Tucker which his first wife Mary bore him, namely: Mary, Pa-
tience, Martha & Abigail. Witns.: John Akin, Thomas Briggs &
Eliazer Smith, all of Dart. [1:85].
Inv. of Est. of HENRY TUCKER of Dart., dtd. 1 May 1694. Apprs.:
Jonathan Russell & Thomas Briggs [1:86/7].
Will of JOSEPH FRENCH, Sr. of Taun., dtd. 24 Apr. 1694, prob. 3
July 1694. Wife Experience. Sons: Joseph, John, Nathaniel,
Jacob, Ebenezer & Jonathan. Dau. Elisabeth wife of James
Philips. Friends Deacon Henry Hodges & John Smith, Overseers.
Witns.: John Smith, John Spur, Thomas Richmond & Samuel Dan-
forth [1:88/9].
Inv. of Est. of JOSEPH FRENCH of Taun., dtd. 18 May 1694, pres.
by Experience French. Apprs.: John Smith, Henry Hodges & John
Pollard [1:90].
Rcpts. for legacies from Est. of Ensign THOMAS WILMOTH by Ra-
chel Wilmoth, his widow; by Jonathan Fuller in behalf of his
wife Elisabeth, eldest dau.; & by Mary Gilbert, dau., paid by
John & Jonathan Wilmoth, dtd. 4 June 1694. Witns.: Thomas
Read & Thomas Read, Jr. [1:90].
Div. of Est. of Ensign THOMAS WILMOTH, dtd. 4 June 1694, btwn.
Mary Wilmoth, widow of eldest son Thomas Wilmoth, as guard.
of their children; & George Robinson; & Jonathan & John Wil-
moth. Witns.: Thomas Read & Jonathan Fuller [1:91].
Acct. of small insolvent Est. of JETHRO, Negro of Swan., dtd.
21 July 1694, pres. by John Rogers of Brist., Adm. [1:91].
Inv. of Est. of JOHN MEDBERY of Swan., dtd. 15 May 1694, for
land which was Sarah Medbery's land before she married John
Medbery. Apprs.: Nicholas Tanner & Thomas Barnes [1:92].
Inv. of Est. of EPHRAIM HUNT of Reho. dtd. 8 June 1694, pres.
by Rebeccah Hunt his late wife. Apprs.: Samuel Peck, William
Carpenter & Thomas Read [1:93].
Acct. of Sarah Peren, Adm. of Est. of her husb. JOHN PEREN, Jr.
of Reho., dtd. 7 Aug. 1694 [1:94].
Div. of Est. of JOHN PEREN, Sr. of Reho. who died at Roxbury,
dtd. 3 Aug. 1694. 7 surviving chldn.: Samuel Peren, Noah
Peren (2nd surviv. son), Susanah Peren (youngest dau., under
18), Daniel Peren (3rd surviv. son), David Peren (4th surviv.
son), Mary Peren (eldest dau.), Mehettabell Peren (2nd dau.)
Son John now dcd. Thomas Read is uncle of all the chldn. Com-
mittee: William Carpenter, Samuel Peck, Thomas Read, Samuell
Walker & Nicholas Ide [1:94/5/6].
Acct. of Est. of JOHN PEREN, Sr., dtd. 7 Aug. 1694, pres. by
Thomas Read, Adm. [1:96].
Div. of land held in partner. by JOHN PEREN, Sr., John Peren,

Jr. & Abraham Peren, all late of Reho. dcd. Heirs of John
Peren, Sr.; widow & heirs of John Peren, Jr.; & heirs of Abraham Peren [all unnamed]. Dtd. 7 Aug. 1694. Comm. same as
above div. [1:97/8/9].

Div. of Est. of PHILIP TABER of Dart., dtd. 27 Nov. 1693. His
widow is not named. Sons Philip (eldest) & John Taber. Daus.:
Sarah, Lidiah, Abigail, Easter, Bethiah [no surnames] & Mary
Earle. Comm.: Jonathan Delano, Thomas Taber, Joseph Tripp,
Joseph Taber & George Cadman, all of Dart. [1:100/1].

Inv. of Est. of JOHN PEREN, Sr., dtd. 4 Nov. 1694, pres. by
John Peren, Adm. Apprs.: Thomas Read & Abraham Peren [1:101].

Rcpts. for legacies from Est. of PHILIP TABER of Dart. by Lidiah Taber dau., by Sarah Taber dau. & by Thomas Earl & wife
Mary Earl dau., paid by their mother Mary Davis, Adm., dtd.
16 Dec. 1693 [1:102].

Will of JOHN GREEN of Newport, Mariner, dtd. 4 Sept. 1694, prob.
4 Oct. 1694. No wife or children mentioned. Elizabeth Allen
of Boston. Nathaniel Allen, Sarah Allen, Dr. James Collins,
Benjamin Palmer & his sister Elisabeth, William Beho, Thomas
Lanford, Nicholas Peck, Dr. Huges, landlord Childs & chldn.
of Mr. Childs. The dcd. was taken in a fit & died before he
signed. Witns.: John Manchester, Joseph Cross & William Carpenter; Nicholas Peck & Ms. Martha Child [1:103/4].

Will of JOSEPH CHAFFEE of Swan., dtd. 22 Sept. 1694, prob. 13
Nov. 1694. Wife [not named]. Sons John & Joseph. Daus. [not
named]. Witns.: John Martin, Bamfield Capron & Nathaniel
Chaffee [1:105].

Inv. of Est. of JOSEPH CHAFFEE of Swan., dtd. 9 Nov. 1694, pres.
by widow Ann Chaffee. Apprs.: John Peck, Israel Peck & John
Ormsby [1:106].

Div. of Est. of JOHN MEADBERY of Swan. btwn. widow & chldn.,
dtd. 15 Oct. 1694. His widow Sarah Meadbery. Sons John (eldest), Benjamin (2nd), Thomas (3rd) & Nathaniel (youngest)(all
under 21). Daus. Hannah & Sarah [1:108].

Acct. of Philip Annadown, Adm. of Est. of his brother HENERY
ANNADOWN of Reho., dtd. 27 Dec. 1695. Sister [not named]
[1:108].

Inv. of Est. of NOAH SABIN, dtd. 13 Nov. 1691, pres. by James
Sabin, Adm. Apprs.: William Carpenter & Thomas Cooper, Sr.
[1:109].

Inv. of real est. of HEZEKIAH SABIN, dtd. 4 Dec. 1694. Apprs:
William Carpenter & Thomas Cooper, Sr. [1:109].

Inv. of Est. of HEZEKIAH SABIN, dtd. 3 July 1693, pres. by brother James Sabin of Reho. Brother John Sabin & sister [not
named]. Apprs: William Carpenter & John Read [1:110].

Inv. of Est. of JOHN GREEN, dtd. 10 Sept. 1694, pres. by Thomas Way of Newport, Exec. Apprs: Robert Little & Thomas
Brooks [1:110].

Inv. of Est. of JOHN HALL, Sr. of Taun., dtd. 2 Oct. 1693.
Apprs: Henry Hodges, Jonathan Pratt & Shadrach Wilbore [1:111].

Inv. of Est. of JOSEPH BOZWORTH of Reho, dtd. 2 Jan. 1694/5,
pres. by his widow Hester Bosworth. Apprs: William Carpenter & Enoch Hunt [1:112].

Inv. of Est. of JOHN RUSSELL of Dart., dtd. 21 Feb. 1694/5.
Apprs: John Shareman & Thomas Taber [1:113].

Will of JOHN RUSSELL of Dart, dtd. 19 Jan. 1687/8, prob. 2 Apr.
1695. No wife mentioned. Sons John Russell, Jonathan Russel & Joseph Russell. Grsons: Jonathan son of son Jonathan
Russell & John son of son Joseph Russell. Witns: Robert Dennis, William Woddell & Mary Garchel. On 2 Apr. 1695 Mary
Wodell, formerly Mary Garchel, made oath [1:114].

Inv. of Est. of JOHN STEVENSON, who died 16 Sept. 1695, dtd. 11
Oct. 1695, pres. by James Stevenson of Springfield, brother
& Adm. Apprs: David Freeman & Samuel Robinson [1:115].

Acct. of Thomas Way, Exec. of Est. of JOHN GREEN of Reho., dtd.
8 Apr. 1695. Mentions legacies to: Elisabeth Brooks, Robert
Little on the acct. of Benjamin Palmer, Henry Brightman, Jeremiah Childs of Reho., Dr. William Hughs of Boston, Robert Gardner of R.I. for William Beho, Elisabeth Collins wife of Dr.
Collins of Boston, Nicholas Peck Esq., Thomas Langford of R.I.
John Dave of R.I. & Benjamin Palmer [1:116].

Rcpt. by Thomas Brooks of Newport, R.I. for legacy his dau.
Elisabeth Brooks rcvd., paid by Thomas Way from Est. of JOHN
GREEN, dtd. 4 Sept. 1694. Witns: John Pocock & Arnold Collins
[1:116].

Rcpts. for legacies paid by Thomas Way out of Est. of JOHN GREEN
who died at Secunk in Sept. 1694, from:
    Robert Little of Newport, R.I. for Benjamin Palmer, dtd. 8
    Apr. 1695.
    Henry Brightman for his chldn., dtd. 8 Apr. 1695.
    Jeremiah Child for his chldn., dtd. 1 March 1694/5.
    William Hewes of Boston, dtd. 16 March 1694/5.
    Robert Gardner for William Beho, dtd. 27 Feb. 1694/5.
    Elisabeth Collins for her husb. James Collins.
    Nicholas Peck & his wife, dtd. 4 March 1694/5.
    John Davy of Newport, R.I., dtd. 15 Apr. 1695.
    Thomas Langford of Newport, R.I., dtd. 15 Apr. 1695 [1:117].

Inv. of Est. of RICHARD MARTEN of Reho., dtd. 7 May 1695, pres.
by son John Marten. Apprs: Samuel Newman, John Peck & William
Carpenter [1:119].

Acct. of Est. of RICHARD MARTEN by John Marten, son & Exec. Mentions Annis Chaffee, sister of John Marten, dtd. 9 May 1695
[1:119].

Will of RICHARD MARTEN of Reho., dtd. 2 June 1686, prob. 7 May
1695. 3 chldn. now in New Engl.: John Martin, Grace Ormsby &
Annis Chaffee. Sons Richard & Francis, both of whom are "now
in Old England." 2 sons [not named] of my son Francis, and
John eldest son of son Richard, if these grchldn. come over
from England to New England to live. John Ormsby eldest son

of dau. Grace. Friends Deacon Samuel Newman & William Carpenter, Overseers. Witns: William Carpenter, Thomas Read &
Stephen Paine [1:120].
Inv. of Est. of MATHEW ALLEN, Planter of Dart., dtd. 1 May 1695
pres. by his widow Sarah Allen. Apprs: John Sharman & John
Tucker [1:121].
Will of MATHEW ALLEN of Dart., dtd. 7 Feb. 1688, prob. 23 May
1695. Wife Sarah. Sons Samuel & Mathew Allen. Daus. Doro-
thy wife of John Calvin, Miriam Easton, Deborah Allen, Mary
Allen & Hassadyah Allen. Henry Tucker, John Russell & Nath-
aniel Howland, Overseers. Witns: John Russell, Thomas Taber
& Va. Hudleston [1:122].
Acct. of Est. of HENRY TUCKER of Dart., dtd. 2 July 1695, by
John Tucker, Exec. Legacies paid to: Sarah Tucker since mar-
ried & now Sarah Horrssee, Nathaniel Slocum, Samuel Perry, A-
braham Tucker & John Easton of Newport for society of Quakers
[1:123].
Rcpts. for legacies paid by John Tucker, Exec. of Est. of HENRY
TUCKER, to:
    Sarah Horssee of Sandwich, Barnstable Co., dau., signed by
        Sarah Haxse & Joseph Haxse, dtd. 1 March 1693.
    Nathaniel Slocum of Shrewsbury, Monmouth Co., East New Jer-
        sey, son-in-law of dcd., dtd. 12 March 1695.
    Samuel Perry of Sandwich, son-in-law, dtd. 4 March 1694/5.
    Abraham Tucker of Dart., son, dtd. 1 March 1695.
    John Easton of behalf of Society of Quakers, dtd. 27 Aug.
        1695 [1:123/4].
Acct. of Est. of JOSEPH FRENCH of Taunton, dtd. 2 July 1695 &
pres. by his widow, Experience French. Legacies to: sons Jo-
seph, John, Nathaniel, Jacob, Ebenezer & Jonathan French (last
3 under 21) [1:125].
Rcpts. by Joseph, John & Nathaniel French for legacies from Est.
of their father JOSEPH FRENCH, paid by their mother Experience
French, dtd. 7 March 1694/5. Witns: John Smith, Henry Hodges
& Robert Crossman [1:125].
Acct. of Experience French, Exec. of Est. of her husb. JOSEPH
FRENCH, dtd. 3 July 1695. Mentions her brother John Foster.
Dau. Elisabeth wife of James Phillips of Taun. [1:126].
Order for div. of lands in Free. of Est. of NICHOLAS WOODBERY
of Salem, dtd. 20 Aug. 1697. Sons Joseph & Isaace Woodbery,
both of Beverly. Hugh Woodbery of Brist., Adm. [1:126].
Div. of Est. of JOSEPH WILLIAMS of Taun., dtd. 5 July 1695. Wi-
dow Elisabeth Williams. Sons: Joseph (eldest), Benjamin (2nd)
Ebenezer (3rd), Richard (4th). Daus. Mahettabell Robinson
eldest) & Phebe (youngest). Comm: Thomas Leonard, Esq., Shadrach Wilbore, John Richmond, Henry Hodges & Samuel Williams,
all of Taun. [1:127/8].
Will of GILBERT BROOK of Reho., dtd. 6 June 1695, prob. 5 July
1695. Wife Sarah. Zachariah Carpenter that lives with me

[*no relat. stated*]. 9 daus. [*not named*]. Dau. Rachel's share
to Grson. Benony Wigin. Sons-in-law Robert Crossman & William
Manle, Execs. Grchldn. Basheba Walker & Brook Thresher. Witns:
Samuel Newman, Richard Bowen & Nathaniel Chaffee, all of Reho.
[1:128/9].

Inv. of Est. of GILBERT BROOKS of Reho., who died 13 June 1695,
dtd. 4 July 1695. Includes an "Appendix to the Will of Gilbert Brooks." Mentions "My children or Grandchildren as follows:" Mary Coleborn, Hannah Crossman, Bethiah Thresher, Rebeccah Horskins & Ester Stephen. Apprs: Nicholas Peck & Richard Bowen [1:129/30].

Acct. of Thomas Brintnall on his care of property of Thomas
Platts, dtd. 5 May 1690 [1:131].

Acct. of Ann Chaffee, widow, & sons John & Joseph Chaffee, Execs.
of Est. of JOSEPH CHAFFEE of Swan., dtd. 18 Dec. 1695 [1:132/3].

Will of ROBERT WHEATON of Reho, dtd. 2 Oct. 1687, prob. 24 Feb.
1695/6. Wife Alice. Sons: Joseph (eldest), Jeremiah, John,
Obadiah, Ephraim & Benjamin. 3 daus: Bethiah, Hannah & Mary.
Son Samuel's chldn. [*not named*]. Witns: John Peck, William
Carpenter & John Butterworth [1:133].

Inv. of Est. of ROBERT WHEATON, dtd. 11 Jan. 1695/6, pres. by
Alice Wheaton, his widow. Apprs: William Carpenter & Samuel
Millard [1:134].

Will of THOMAS READ of Reho., Tanner, dtd. 23 June 1695, prob.
24 Feb. 1695/6. Wife Hannah. Sons: James (eldest), Thomas &
Nathaniel. Daus: Sarah, Elisabeth, Mary, Hannah, Mehittabell
& Martha. Brothers William Carpenter, Moses Read & Daniel
Read, Overseers. Witn: Moses Read, John Wilmath & William Car-
penter [1:134/5/6].

Inv. of Est. of Ensign THOMAS READ of Reho., dtd. 12 Feb. 1695/6
pres. by Hannah Read his widow. Apprs: Capt. Nicholas Peck,
Esq., Deacon Samuel Peck & Lt. Preserved Abell [1:137].

Acct. of Susanah Macey, Exec. of Est. of her husb. GEORGE MACEY
of Taun., dtd. 16 Apr. 1696. Legacies to Elisabeth Hodges, to
Samuel Hodges, to Sarah Black, to Rebecca Williams, to Mary
Williams & to Deborah Macey [1:138].

Will of JOHN COOK of Dart., dtd. 9 Nov. 1694, prob. 16 Apr. 16-
96. Wife Sarah. Son-in-law Arthur Hathaway & wife Sarah my
dau.; son-in-law Stephen West & wife Mercey my dau.; Jonathan
Delano. Grson. Thomas Taber. Grdau. Hester Perry. Witns: Aaron Savory & Thomas Taber [1:139].

Inv. of Est. of JOHN COOK, dtd. 7 Dec. 1696 [*sic*], pres. by widow Sarah Cook. Apprs: Arther Hathaway & Thomas Taber [1:140].

Will of JOHN RUSSELL of Dart., dtd. 20 March 1695/6, prob. 16
Apr. 1696. Wife [*not named*]. Son John Russell (under 21). My
brother Jonathan's son Jonathan. Brother Joseph's son John.
Witns: John Sharman, Robert Havens & Thomas Taber [1:141].

Inv. of Est. of JOHN RUSSELL, dtd. 30 March 1696, pres. by Mehettabell Russell, his widow. Apprs: John Sharman & Thomas Taber [1:142].

Inv. of Est. of SAMUEL WILBORE of Taun., dtd. 21 Jan. 1695/6,
pres. by Sarah Willbore, his widow. Apprs: Stephen Marick,
Israel Thresher & Shadrack Willbore, Sr. [1:143].

Inv. of Est. of THOMAS BRIGGS of the North Purchase who died 1
Apr. 1696, dtd. 9 Apr. 1696, pres. by Samuel Briggs, youngest
son, Adm. The 2 other eldest sons refused Adm. Apprs: John
Witherel, Eliazer Carver, Uriah Leonard & Samuel Brentnall
[1:144].

Inv. of Est. of SAMUEL PITTS of Taun., dtd. 6 Feb. 1695/6, pres.
by Sarah Pitts his widow. Dcd. Samuel was eldest son of Peter
Pitts of Taun. Apprs: Richard Godfree & Edward Bobbit [1:145].

Inv. of Est. of JOHN EDDY of Taun., dtd. 11 Dec. 1695. Pres. by
Deliverance Eddy, his widow. Apprs: Henry Hodges, Uriah Leonard & Eliazer Carver [1:146].

Inv. of Est. of Capt. NATHAN HAYMAN of Brist., Mariner, dtd. 3
Feb. 1689, pres. by Nathaniel Blagrove of Brist., Merchant, &
Elizabeth Hayman his widow. Mentions parts of ships owned by
Nathan [1:147/8/9/50].

Div. of Est. of ROBERT CROSSMAN of Taun., btwn. his sons & daus.
dtd. 29 June 1696. John Crossman (eldest son); Robert Crossman (2nd son); Sarah Woodward (eldest dau.); Mary Gould (2nd
dau.); Elizabeth Hayward (3rd dau.); unnamed chldn. of Joseph
Crossman dcd. (3rd son); Samuel Crossman (youngest son) & Mercy Thresher (youngest dau.). Comm: Thomas Leonard, Esq., Philip King, Henry Hodges & James Leonard [1:151/2].

Acct. of debts of Est. of GILBERT BROOKS, who died 30 Dec. 1695,
dtd. 15 July 1696, pres. by Robert Crossman & William Manley
Execs. [1:153].

Acct. of legacies from Est. of GILBERT BROOKS, dtd. 6 July 1696
paid by Robert Crossman & William Manley, Execs. Widow not
named. Chldn: Bathshebe Walker, Bethiah Thresher, Saray Lyon,
Elisabeth Stevens' chldn. & Rachel (being in Long Island).
Mary Colebond shows dislike of the Will. Legacies also to:
Zachariah Carpenter, Benoni Wigins, Brooks Thresher & Rebecca Hoskins [1:154].

Will of JOHN SHAW of Swan., dtd. 24 Sept. 1696, prob. Oct. 16-
96. Wife Hannah. Son John Shaw (under 21). Land & house in
Boston to become John's. Witns: John Simmons, Ralph Earl, Martha Simmons, Thomas Earle & Samuel Gardner [1:155].

Inv. of Est. of JOHN SHAW, dtd. 8 Oct. 1696, pres. by Hannah
Shaw his widow. Apprs: John Hathaway, James Bell & Nicholas
Moorey [1:156].

Div. of Est. of EPHRAIM HUNT of Reho., dtd. 21, 22 & 25 May 16-
96, btwn. his widow & 4 chldn., incl. land he had in partner.
with his brother John Hunt. Wife Rebecca Hunt. 4 chldn: Daniel Hunt (eldest son), John Hunt (youngest son), Sarah Hunt &
Hannah Hunt. Comm: Samuel Peck, William Carpenter, Samuel Newman, Stephen Paine & Enoch Hunt [1:157/8/9].

Acct. of Rebecca Hunt, Adm. of Est. of her husb. EPHRAIM HUNT, dtd. 23 Oct. 1696. Mentions Sarah (eldest dau.), Hannah (young est dau.), sons Daniel & John Hunt [1:160].

Acct. of Deliverance Smith, Exec. of Est. of JOHN SMITH of Dart. dtd. 1 Dec. 1696. Mentions Wife Ruhamah, son Deliverance Smith, daus. Hassadiah wife of Jonathan Russell, Mehitabel wife of John Russell, Hannah Smith, Sarah Smith & Deborah Smith (under age) [1:161/2].

Rcpts. for legacies from Est. of JOHN SMITH, dtd. 10 Jan. 1693/4, by dau. Hassadiah Russel & husb. Jonathan Russell, by dau. Mehittabell & husb. John Russell and by daus. Hannah Smith & Sarah Smith [1:161/2].

Grant to widow Kathirine Newland from Est. of JERIMY NEWLAND, dtd. 12 July 1695.Widow Katherine had 4 small chldn. when her husb. died 15 years ago [1:163].

Inv. of Est. of Capt. EDWARD RICHMOND of Lit. Comp., dtd. 5 Dec. 1696, pres. by Edward Richmond, eldest son, Adm. Apprs: Daniel Eaton & Will Foabs [1:164].

Will of REMEMBER BRIGGS of Taun., dtd. 22 Apr. 1696, prob. 13 Jan. 1696/7. Wife Mary. Chldn. [*not named*]. Mentions land in Weymouth. Friends Maj. Ephraim Hunt of Weymouth & John Staples of Taunton, Overseers. Witns: Peter Reynolds, Priscilla Reynolds & Nathaniel Paine [1:165].

Inv. of Est. of REMEMBER BRIGGS of Taun., dtd. 22 May 1696, pres. by Mary Staple, his late widow. Apprs: Henry Andrews & Joseph Richmond [1:166].

Inv. of Est. of WILLIAM WOOD, Sr. of Dart., dtd. 4 Jan. 1696, pres. by William & George Wood, sons. Apprs: Aaron Davis, William Macumber, Jonathan Devil & Increase Allen [1:167/8].

Inv. of Est. of Lt. SAMUEL GARDNER of Swan., who died 8 Dec. 1696, dtd. 15 Feb. 1697, pres. by Elisabeth Gardner, his widow. Apprs: Hezekiah Luther, Ralph Chapman & James Cole [1:169 Blank page [1:179].

Div. of Ests. of HEZEKIAH SABIN & NOAH SABIN, both dcd. intest. who had land & chattels left to them by their father William Sabin of Reho., dtd. 12 March 1695/6, requested by James Sabin, "Eldest Brother of the Whole blood," Adm. Brothers & sisters: James Sabin, John Sabin, Lt. Preserved Abel guard. of Margaret Sabin youngest sister a minor, Joseph Buckland, Jr. in behalf of his wife Mehetable eldest sister, Mary Sabin (2nd sister) & Sarah Sabin (3rd sister) [1:171/2].

Acct. of Est. of HENRY ANNADOWN of Reho., dtd. 27 Dec. 1694. Mentions brother Philip Annadown [1:172].

Inv. of Est. of RICHARD BRIGGS of Taun., dtd. 8 July 1696, pres. by Rebecca Briggs, his widow. Apprs: Henry Hodges, Richard Stephens & Samuel Dean [1:173].

Div. of land of ELIAS IRISH of Taun., dcd., which he had in partner. with John Irish, dtd. 16 Apr. 1697. Land in Lit. Comp. Rebecca now wife of Jonathan Greenel of Lit. Comp. sole dau. of Elias Irish dcd. Comm: Philip King, Robert Crossman & Abel Burt of Taun.; & Lt. Joseph Tripp & Aron Davis of Dart. [1:173/4].

Acct. of Edward Richmond, Adm. of Est. of his father EDWARD RICHMOND of Lit. Comp., dtd. 19 May 1697 [1:175/6].

Div. of Est. of Capt. EDWARD RICHMOND among his chldn., dtd. 19 May 1697. Chldn: Edward Richmond, John Richmond, Abigail Rementon, William Palmer, John Palmer, Silvester Richmond, Sarah Richmond & Thomas Burge [1:176/7].

Div. of land of STEPHEN, an Indian, of Lit. Comp. who died 19 Dec. 1696, dtd. 14 Apr. 1697. Janoofas & Sue Codomuck, brother & sister of Stephen. Sue now dcd. Sons & daus. of Suncanawash, brother of Stephen, namely: Hezekiah, James, Sampson, Ester & Rebecca. Land was owned in partner. with Richard, also dcd. Heirs of Richard: Josiah & Sampson Borson and Zacheus the son of Sam & Sam Pauchachux. Comm: Maj. Benjamin Church, Joseph Church, Capt. William Southworth, Christopher Allen & William Foabs [1:177].

Div. of Est. of WILLIAM WOOD of Dart., dtd. 14 Apr. 1697. Ten chldn: William (eldest son), George, Josiah, Daniel, John & Joseph; & Mary "Mr. Mallets wife," Sarah Wood, Margaret Wood & Rebecca Wood. Apprs: Joseph Tripp, William Foabs & Joseph Taber [1:178/9].

Will of WILLIAM STONE of Bristol, Mariner, about to go to sea, dtd. 22 July 1697, prob. 29 May 1697. Wife Hannah. Chldn. Hannah & Abigail. Witns: Rebecca Blackman, Mary Jones & Edward Mills [1:180].

Inv. of Est. of WILLIAM STONE of Brist., dtd. 14 & 21 Nov. 1696. Est. now in Taunton. Apprs: Hugh Woodberree, John Glading, Jr., John Cary, Shadrach Wilbore & Henry Hodges [1:180/1].

Acct. of Est. of JOHN STEVENSON of Reho., dtd. 13 June 1697, pres. by James Stevenson of Springfield, Adm. [1:182].

Will of THOMAS DEAN of Taunton, dtd. 7 Aug. 1690, prob. 15 July 1697. Wife Katharine. Only son Thomas Dean. Daus: Hannah, Deborah, Katharine, Lidiah, Mercey & Elisabeth (all under age). Brothers John Dean & Isaac Dean, Overseers. Witns: Thomas Leonard, John Dean & Isaac Dean [1:183].

Inv. of Est. of THOMAS DEAN, dtd. 30 June 1697, pres. by Katharine Dean, his widow. Apprs: Thomas Leonard, John Dean, Richard Stephens & Isaace Dean [1:184/5].

Agrmt. btwn. Katherine Dean widow of THOMAS DEAN of Taun., & Thomas Dean only son of Thomas dcd., dtd. 13 July 1697. Daus: Hannah, Deborah, Katharine, Lidia, Mercey & Elisabeth. Witns: Thomas Leonard, Isaac Deane & Samuel Blake [1:185].

Acct. of Est. of JAMES LEONARD of Taun. dtd. 24 Aug. 1697, pres. by Thomas Leonard, his son & Adm. Ms. Margaret Leonard, mother-in-law of Thomas [*probably step-mother*]. Relatives of Thomas Leonard: brother James Leonard, brothers Joseph & Uriah Leonard, Executrix of Joseph [not named], brother Benjamin

Leonard, brother & sister John & Abigail Kinsley, brother &
sister Isaace & Rebecca Chapman, brother & sister Isaace &
Hannah Dean [1:187].
Acct. of Thomas Leonard, Adm. of Est. of JOHN SMITH of Taun.,
dtd. 24 Aug. 1694. The heirs are under age [1:188/9].
Grant of movables to Mary Chaplin, widow of WILLIAM CHAPLIN of
Swan., dtd. 10 Dec. 1697. There is no house or land [1:189].
Inv. of Est. of WIDOW BARTRAM, dtd. 6 Nov. 1694, pres. by William Hammond. Apprs: Hezekiah Luther & Zachariah Eddy [1:190].
Will of WILLIAM WODELL of Pocasset (Lit. Comp.), dtd. 8 Sept.
1692, prob. 2 May 1693. Grdau. Sarah Woddell. Priscilla & Isa-
bell Gatchel sisters of said Sarah Woddell. Dau. Mary Greenel
wife of Daniel Greenel. Grson. Richard Greenel. Grsons: Wil-
liam & Samuel Sanford. Grsons: John & Joseph Anthony sons of
my dau. Frances. Grdaus: Susannah, Elisabeth & Alice Anthony
daus. of my dau. Frances. Grson. William Woddell. Dau. Alice
Anthony. Grson. Richard Woddell. Grson. Return Woddell. Grson.
Gershom Wodell. Grson-in-law Robert Lawton. Friend John Green
of Warwick. Grson. Gershom Woddell & his mother Mary Woddell.
Neighbors Samson & Samuel Shearman, Oversees [1:191/2].
Acct. of Gershom Woddell & Mary Woddell, Adm. of Est. of WIL-
LIAM WODDELL, dtd. 8 Oct. 1697. Legacies to: William Anthony
son of John Anthony, Joseph Anthony, Susan Anthony, Daniel &
Mary Greenel, William & Samuel Sanford sons of Samuel Sanford
of Portsmouth & John Green of Warwick. Legacies as yet unpaid
to: Priscilla Gatchel & Isabel Gatchel; and Elizabeth Anthony
& Alice Anthony daus. of John Anthony of Portsmouth [1:194].
Agrmt. abt. land in Free. & Swan. of NICHOLAS WOODBERY of Bev-
erly & ISAACE WOODBERY of Salem, both dcd. intest. Chldn. of
Nicholas Woodbery: Isaace, Mary widow of son Nicholas dcd.,
Joseph, Emma widow of son Andrew dcd. late of Beverly, & Ben-
jamin Woodbery. Hugh Woodbery, Adm. of Isaace Woodbery [1:194].
Acct. of Hannah Shaw, widow & Exec. of Est. of her husb. JOHN
SHAW of Swan., dtd. 23 Oct. 1697 [1:195].
Will of THOMAS CASSWELL, Sr. of Taun., dtd. 28 Sept. 1691, prob.
14 Sept. 1697. Wife Mary. Sons: Stephen (eldest), Thomas (2nd)
Peter (3rd), John (4th), William (5th) & Samuel (6th) Casswell.
Daus: Mary, Sarah, Hannah, Elisabeth, Abigail & Hester. Dau.
Hannah wife of Daniel Ramsdell. Witns: Shadrach Wilbore, Sam-
uel Wilbore & Joseph Wilbore [1:196/7].
Inv. of Est. of THOMAS CASSWELL, dtd. 30 March 1696/7, pres. by
Samuel Casswell, Exec. Apprs: Israel Thresher, Joseph Richmond
& Henry Andrews [1:197/8].
Rcpt. by Thomas Mallet of Newport, R.I. to William Wood of Dart.
Exec. of Est. of his father WILLIAM WOOD of Dart., being a
legacy given in the Will to Daniel Wood & John Wood, Thomas
Mallet being their guard., dtd. 12 Feb. 1697/8 [1:198].
Acct. of Est. of JOHN FITCH of Reho., dtd. 21 Apr. 1699, pres.
by Mary Fitch, Exec. 4 daus. [not named][1:198].

Will of SAMUEL WILLIAMS of Taun., dtd. 6 Aug. 1697, prob. 9 Oct.
1697. Wife [not named]. Sons: Seth (eldest), Samuel & Daniel
(under 21) Williams. 3 daus: Sarah Dean, Mary Andros & Hannah.
Witns: John Richmond, Thomas Gilbert & Abigail Richmond[1:199].
Inv. of Est. of SAMUEL WILLIAMS of Taun., dtd. 31 Aug. 1697.
Apprs: John Richmond, Thomas Gilbert & Thomas Williams[1:200].
Acct. of Adm. of Est. of MARY SABIN, dtd. 3 Jan. 1698/9 [1:200].
Agrmt. btwn. Mrs. Ann Barney & her 4 sons abt. her rights in
Will of husb. JACOB BARNEY of Reho. Sons: Joseph, Israel, Jon-
athan & Samuel Barney, all of Reho. Solomon Curtice signed as
guard. of Jonathan Barney, & Samuel Bullock signed as guard.
of Samuel Barney. Witns: Nathaniel Paine, John West & John
Cary [1:201].
Div. of real est. of JACOB BARNEY of Reho. btwn. his 4 sons:
Joseph, Jonathan, Samuel & Israel Barney, dtd. 8 Dec. 1697.
Comm: Samuel Bullock, Thomas Ormsbe, John West, Solomon Cur-
tis & James Therber [1:202].
Inv. of Est. of PETER PAMPILLO, dtd. 26 Nov. 1697, pres. by Ms.
Joan Papillio, his widow. Apprs: Uzal Wardall & Jabez Gorham
[1:203].
Inv. of Est. of MARGARET SABIN, dtd. 6 Dec. 1697, pres. by James
Sabin. Apprs: William Carpenter & Samuel Peck [1:203].
Acct. of James Sabin, Adm. of Est. of MARGARET SABIN, dtd. 7
Dec. 1697 [1:203].
Inv. of Est. of WILLIAM BRENTON of Brist., late Master of Ship
Seaflower, recently home from Barbadus, dtd. 1 Apr. 1697,
pres. by Ebenezer Brenton, Adm. Apprs: Benjamin Funell, John
Jenkins, Samuel Pelton, John Cary, John Wilkins & Jabez How-
land [1:204].
Acct. of Est. of WILLIAM BRENTON of Brist., dtd. 22 Feb. 1697/8
pres. by Ebenezer Brenton, Adm. [1:205].
Acct. of legacies to chldn. of WILLIAM BRENTON of Brist. Sons:
William, Jr., Samuel, Benjamin & Jahleel Brenton, pres. by Eb-
enezer Brenton, Adm. [1:206/7].
Will of JOHN TITUS of Reho, dtd. 1 Nov. 1697, prob. 10 Jan.
1697/8. Wife Sarah. Sons: John (eldest), Samuel, Robert & Tim-
othy (last 3 under 21). Daus: Lidya, Hannah, Sarah, Elisabeth
& Abigail (last 3 under 18). Cousin John Fuller. My mother
Abigail Palmer. Brother Samuel Millard & brother Leonard New-
some, Overseers. Witns: Richard Bowen, Sr., Richard Bowen, Jr.
Samuel Carpenter & William Carpenter [1:206/7/8/9].
Inv. of Est. of JOHN TITUS of Reho., dtd. 8 Dec. 1697, pres. by
Sarah Titus & John Titus, Execs. Apprs: Jonah Palmer, William
Carpenter & Samuel Millard [1:209/10].
Will of JOHN FITCH of Reho., dtd. 20 June 1693, prob. 23 Feb.
1697/8. Wife Mary. 4 daus: Mary, Rebecca, Sarah & Hannah.
Friends Nicolas Peck, Esq. & Abraham Peren, Overseers. Witns:
Nicolas Peck, Christopher Sanders & William Carpenter[1:211/2].

Inv. of Est. of JOHN FITCH, dtd. 23 Feb. 1697/8, pres. by Mary
Fitch, his widow [1:212].
Will of SHADRACH WILBORE, Sr. of Taun., dtd. 12 Sept. 1696,
prob. 1 March 1697/8. Wife Hannah; her chldn. at Braintree.
My chldn: Samuel dcd. (eldest son), Joseph, John, Shadrach,
Eliazer, Benjamin, dau. Sarah wife of Nathaniel Hoar, dau.
Rebeckah wife of Abraham Hathaway & grson. Samuel Wilbore.
Witns: Henry Hodges, Israel Thresher & John Hoskins [1:213/4]
Inv. of Est. of SHADRACH WILBORE, dtd. 23 Feb. 1697/8, pres. by
Joseph & Shadrach Wilbore, sons. Apprs: Thomas Leonard, Henry
Hodges, Stephen Merick & John Hoskins [1:215].
Acct. of Est. of WILLIAM WOOD of Dart., dtd. 10 March 1697/8,
pres. by William & George Wood, Adms. Legacies to: William
Wood (eldest son), George Wood, Joseph Wood, Daniel Wood (to
his guard.), John Wood (to his guard. Thomas Mallet), Josiah
Wood (to his guard. David Lake), Mrs. Mary Mallet(signed by
Mallet), Sarah Wood, Margaret Wood (her guard. David Lake) &
Rebecah Wood (to her guard. David Lake) [1:216].
Rcpts. for legacies rcvd. from Est. of WILLIAM WOOD of Dart.,
paid by George & William Wood, Adms., from chldn:
  David Lake of Tiv. as guard. of Joseph Wood, dtd. 14 Mar.
    1697/8.
  David Lake of Tiv. as guard. of Margaret & Rebeccah Wood,
    dtd. 10 May 1697.
  David Lake of Tiv. as guard. of Josiah Wood, dtd. 8 Feb.
    1697/8.
  Sarah Wood, dtd. 14 Apr. 1697.
  Thomas Mallet of Newport, Linnen Draper, for his wife Mary
    Mallet, dtd. 14 Apr. 1697 [1:217/8].
Will of BENJAMIN PAINE now resident in Brist., dtd. 18 Apr. 16-
98, prob. 3 May 1698. Brother John Paine of Swan. Brother
Stephen Paine & brother-in-law Deacon Samuel Peck, Execs. My
landlady Ms. Jones. Witns: Benjamin Jones, Tristrem Bowerman
& Nathaniel Paine [1:218/9].
Inv. of Est. of BENJAMIN PAINE, dtd. 3 May 1698, pres. by Ste-
phen Paine & Deacon Samuel Peck. Apprs: Hugh Woodbery & Nath-
aniel Paine [1:219].
Inv. of Est. of MARY PRICE of Lit. Comp., dtd. 20 Apr. 1698,
pres. by John Price, son & Adm. Apprs: Christopher Allen &
William Foabs [1:220].
Will of JOSEPH WOOD of Taun., dtd. 12 Feb. 1697/8, prob. 19 May
1698. Wife Abigail. All my chldn: Joseph (eldest), John, Eph-
raim & that child my wife is with child of. Brother-in-law Jo-
seph Dean, Exec. Brothers-in-law Peter Walker & John Paul,
Overseers. Witns: Thomas Leonard, Silvanus Camball & Elkanah
Leonard [1:221].
Inv. of Est. of JOSEPH WOOD of Taun., who died 12 Feb. 1697/8,
pres. by Joseph Dean, Exec. Apprs: Abell Burt, John Crossman
& Robert Crossman [1:222].

Div. of Est. of NATHANIEL WILLIAMS of Taun., dtd. 25 July 1698.
Wife Elisabeth. Chldn: John (eldest son), Nathaniel (2nd son)
& Elisabeth (only dau., under 18), Comm: Thomas Leonard, James
Leonard, Henry Hodges, John Richmond, Sr. & Thomas Williams
[1:223/4].
Inv. of Est. of SAMUEL SMITH of Taun., dtd. 25 Aug. 1698, pres.
by his son Samuel Smith of Taun. Apprs: Robert Crossman &
Richard Stevens [1:224].
Additional inv. for Est. of SHADRACH WILBORE, dtd. 10 March 16-
98/9, pres. by Joseph Wilbore, Exec. Apprs: Henry Hodges &
Stephen Marick [1:224].
Acct. of Est. of THOMAS BRENTNALL who died 1692, dtd. 27 Dec.
1695, pres. by sons Samuel & Nathaniel Brentnall & by Hester
Brentnall, his widow [1:225].
Rcpt. by Jarvis Ballard, Exec. of Est. of John Jolliff for pay-
ment ordered by Mrs. Easter Smith, Exec. of Est. of her husb.
THOMAS BRENTNALL, dtd. 5 Feb. 1701 [1:226].
Blank pages [1:227/8/9].
John Saffin of Brist. puts "my Negro man Adam" in the custody
& service of Thomas Shepard my tennant in Brist. for 7 years,
after which he shall be free, dtd. 25 March 1694. Witns: Rachel Brown, Richard Smith & Samuel Galop [1:230].

End of Volume 1

Will of ELIASHIB ADAMS, Carpenter, of Brist., dtd. 12 May 1798, prob. 2 Aug. 1698. Wife Mehettabell. 4 minor chldn: William & Eliashib, Lidiah & Mehettabell. Witns: David Cary, Benjamin Jones & John Cary [2:1].

Inv. of Est. of ELIASHIB ADAMS of Brist., dtd. 27 July 1698, pres. 2 Aug. 1698. Apprs: Belamy Bosworth, David Cary & James Adams [2:2].

Will of ROBERT MILLERD of Reho., Tanner, dtd. 11 March 1698/9, prob. 29 March 1699. Wife Elizebeth. Sons: Solomon, Ephraim, Nathaniel, Nehemiah & Robert. Daus: Elizebeth, Mary & Experience. Grsons: John Bragg & Richard Bragg [2:3].

Inv. of Est. of ROBERT MILLERD, dtd. 21 March 1698/9. Apprs: Samuel Bullock, Jathniel Peck & Thomas Ormsbee [2:4].

Acct. of Est. of THOMAS READ of Reho., pres. 8 Aug. 1699. Sons Thomas Read & Nathaniel Read to be Execs., but now under guard. of Moses Read & David Read. Eldest son James Read. Daus. Sarah Read & Mary Read. Wife Hannah Read [2:5].

Acct. of Est. of JOHN TITUS of Reho., pres. 13 Sept. 1699. Widow Sarah Titus. Eldest son John Titus. Dau. Lidiah Titus. Minor chldn: Samuel Titus, Robert Titus, Timothey Titus, Hannah Titus, Sarah Titus, Elizebeth Titus & Abigail Titus [2:6].

Change of Exec. of Est. of SAMUEL SABIN of Reho. Wife Mary Sabin. Sons Samuel Sabin & Israel Sabin [2:7].

Inv. of Est. of SAMUEL SABIN of Reho., dtd. 2 Oct. 1699, pres. 16 Oct. 1699. Apprs: John Peck, Enoch Hunt & John Hunt [2:7].

Agrmt. abt. Est. of SAMUEL SABIN of Reho., dtd. 12 Oct. 1699, pres. 16 Oct. 1699. Samuel Sabin (eldest son) & son Israel Sabin mention "our Grandfather William Sabin" & "our Uncle John Martin." Witns: John Wilmarth, Thomas Chaffe & William Carpenter [2:8].

Inv. of Est. of NICHOLAS WHITE of Taun., dtd. 10 June 1699, pres. 14 Oct. 1699 by Nicholas White, son & Adm. Apprs: Increase Robinson, Thomas Harvey & Ezra Dean [2:9].

Schedule of Shares of Est. of NICHOLAS WHITE to go to sons John White & Joseph White, dtd. 28 Oct. 1698, pres. 14 Oct. 1699 [2:10].

Rcpt. & Accept. by Elizebeth Pratt, widow, of Taun., for legacy from Est. of her father NICHOLAS WHITE, dtd. 29 Oct. 1698, pres. 14 Oct. 1699 [2:11].

Acct. of Est. of NICHOLAS WHITE, pres. 14 Oct. 1699 by Nicholas White, son & Adm. Legacies to John White, to Joseph White & to Elizebeth Pratt, widow [2:11/2].

Rcpt. & Accept. by Sarah Read & Mary Read of legacies from Est. of their father Ensign THOMAS READ of Reho., paid by "our

Mother" Hannah Read, Exec. & by Moses Read & Daniel Read (guards. of "our brothers" Thomas Read & Nathaniel Read), dtd. 26 Feb. 1695/6, pres. 15 Dec. 1699 [2:12].

Acct. of Est. of ANNA TRANTOR sometime widow of John Bayly of Free. & since widow of Thomas Trantor of Free., pres. 12 Oct. 1699 by Joseph Waterman of Marshfield & William Makepeace of Free., Adms. Surviving chldn: Sarah Bayley dau. of John Bayley, & Mary Trantor & Anna Trantor daus. of Thomas Trantor. Eldest son John Bayley is dcd. [2:13].

Acct. of Est. of ELIZABETH JANSON, widow, of Swan., pres. 23 Dec. 1699 by Elisha Davis of Haverell, Co. of Essex, Adm. [2:14].

[Pages 15 & 16 torn out; probate index says it was will & Inv. of INCREASE ROBINSON].

Will of NOAH MASON of Reho., dtd. 15 Jan. 1699/1700, prob. 16 Apr. 1700. Wife Sarah. 4 sons: Noah, John, Daniel & Timothy Mason (all under 21). 4 daus: Mary Mason, Sarah Mason, Hannah Mason & Martha Mason (all under 21). Brothers Samuel Mason & Isaac Mason to be Overseers. Witns: Timothy Ide, Samuel Mason & Richard Bowen [2:17].

Inv. of Est. of NOAH MASON, dtd. 19 March 1699/1700, pres. 16 Apr. 1700. Apprs: John Butterworth, Moses Read & Jonathan Fuller [2:18].

Div. of Est. of ROBERT WHEATON of Reho., dtd. 31 May 1699, pres. 16 Apr. 1700. Sons: Jeremiah, John Ephraim, Obadiah & Benjamin Wheaton. Daus: Hannah wife of Ensign John Butterworth, Bethiah Plantin widow & Mary Man widow. Witns: Samuel Millerd & William Carpenter [2:19].

Inv. of Est. of RICHARD DURFIE of Tiv., pres. 10 Apr. 1700 by Anna Durfee, widow. Apprs: Daniel Howland & Job Manchester [2:20].

Div. of Est. of JOHN EDY of Taun., dtd. 12 Aug. 1696, pres. 11 Apr. 1700. Wife Deliverance Edy. Sons: Ebenezer (eldest), Eleazer (2nd), Joseph & Jonathan Edy. Daus: Mary Rude (eldest), Mercy Fisher (2nd), Hannah Edy, Susanna Edy & Patience Edy. Comm: Thomas Leonard, Shadrach Wilbore, James Leonard, Henry Hodges & Thomas Dean, all of Taun. [2:20/1].

Acct. of Est. of JOSEPH BOSWORTH of Reho., dtd. 28 Jan. 1694/5. pres. 24 Aug. 1697 by Hester Bosworth, Adm. [2:21].

Inv. of Est. of THOMAS ELLIOTT of Reho., dtd. 30 May 1700, pres. 12 July 1700 by Moses Read, Adm. Apprs: John Peck, William Carpenter & Daniel Smith [2:22].

Inv. of Est. of RICE LEONARD of Reho., dtd. 2 May 1700, pres. by Mary Leonard, Adm. Apprs: William Carpenter, Moses Read & Nicholas Ide [2:23].

Will of JOHN COCKBURN now resident in Brist., dtd. 21 Sept. 1699 prob. 9 Oct. 1700, in good health but now being bound to sea from Bristol to Cocoso in the Sloop Societie, Joseph Lord, Commander. To wife Mary Cockburn of the City of London the

residue of my estate in the Sloop Societie. John Borland & John
Maxwell merchants of Boston, & William Ralston of Newport to
be Execs. Witns: Nathaniel Blagrove, Richard Jenkins & John
Cary [2:24].

Acct. of Samuel Peck & Steven Paine, Execs. of Est. of BENJAMIN
PAINE of Brist., dtd. 11 Oct. 1700. Legacies to brothers:
Steven Paine, John Paine, Samuel Paine & Nathaniel Paine. Leg-
acies to bros.-in-law: Samuel Peck, Enoch Hunt, Jacob Pepper
& Daniel Aldis. Legacy to Benjamin Jones [no relation stated]
[2:25].

Rcpts. from John Paine, Swan., Samuel Paine & Nathaniel Paine
of Reho., for themselves; & rcpts. by Enoch Hunt of Reho., Jacob Pepper of Roxbury & Daniel Aldis of Deham for their wives,
sisters of dcd. Benjamin Paine, for legacies from Est. of said
BENJAMIN PAINE of Brist, dtd. 26 Sept. 1700. Witns: John Hunt
& Peter Hunt [2:26].

Will of ELIAZER WILBORE of Taun., dtd. 5 Sept. 1700, prob. 9
Oct. 1700. 4 bros.: Joseph, Shadrach, Benjamin & John Wilbor.
2 sisters: Sarah Hoar & Rebecka Hathaway. Sister-in-law Sarah
Wilbor. Cousins Anna Merrick & Samuel Wilbor. Witns: John
Dean, Morgan Cobb & Robert Crossman [2:27].

Inv. of Est. ELIAZER WILBORE of Taun., who died 11 Sept. 1700,
dtd. 3 Oct. 1700. Apprs: Henry Hodges & Robert Crossman [2:28].

Inv. of Est. of Capt. ISAAC NEGUS who died 29 Nov. 1700, dtd. 10
Dec. 1700. Hanah Negus widow & relict. Apprs: John Hathaway,
James Paul & Abell Burt [2:29].

Will of MARGARET LEONARD of Taun., widow, about the 68th year
of her age, dtd. 12 Nov. 1700, prob. 9 Apr. 1701. Son-in-law
Uriah Leonard's wife Elizebeth & his dau. Margaret. Dau.-in-
law Hanah Deane & her dau. Abigail Terry. Son-in-law James
Leonard's daus. Abigail & Prudence Lewis. Son-in-law Thomas
Leonard's daus. Elizebeth & Johanah. Cousin Eleazer Carver to
be Exec. [She was probably step-mother, not mother-in-law].
[2:30].

Will of DAVID CARPENTER of Reho., dtd. 12 May 1701, prob. 8 Sept.
1701. wife mentioned but not named. "The child my wife now
goes withall." Dau. Rebeckah (a minor). My grfather. Redway.
Brother Jacob. Brother Samuel Carpenter & John Ward to be
Execs. Witns: Enoch Hunt, John Hunt & Benjamin Hunt [2:31].

Inv. of Est. of DAVID CARPENTER of Reho., dtd. 25 Aug. 1701.
pres. by Rebecca Carpenter, widow. Apprs: William Carpenter,
Abiah Carpenter & Enoch Hunt [2:32].

Will of LAWRENCE SPRINGER of Lit. Comp., dtd. 4 Sept. 1701, prob.
24 Feb. 1701. Wife Martha. Sons: Thomas, Edward, John, Jona-
than, Joseph, Benjamin & Henry Springer. Daus: Mary Weaver,
Johanah Springer & Martha Springer. Dau. Mary's eldest dau.
Ann Dier. Dau. Johanah's son Jeremiah. John Wilbore, Sr. &
Joseph Wilbore to be Overseers. Witns: David Hillard, James
Bennet & Nathaniel Searls [2:33].

Inv. of Est. of BENJAMIN WILLIAMS of Taun., dtd. 11 Oct. 1701,
pres. by Rebeccah Leonard, Exec. & widow. Apprs: Thomas Leonard, Ezra Dean & Thomas Williams [2:34].

Inv. of Est. of ELIAZER GILBERT of Taun., who died 29 March 1701
dtd. 16 June 1701, pres. by Elizebeth Gilbert, widow. Apprs:
John Richmond, Thomas Gilbert & Robert Crossman [2:35].

Request by Adms. of Est. of LAWRENCE SPRINGER of Lit. Comp.,
dtd. 15 Nov. 1703. Wife dcd. 2 months ago. His 2 sons, who
were to receive land after his wife's decease, are not yet
of age. By John Wilbore & Joseph Wilbore, Execs. [2:35].

Inv. of Est. of JOHN WOODCOCK of Attl., dtd. 29 Oct. 1701, pres.
by John Woodcock & Samuel Guile both of Dedham, Adms. Apprs:
John Ware, Moses Reed & Anthony Sprague [2:36].

Agrmt. btwn. Joannah Woodcock, widow of JOHN WOODCOCK of Attl.
& his chldn. & heirs: John Woodcock, Israel Woodcock, Jonathan Woodcock, Thomas Woodcock, Thomas Eastabrook, Samuel
Guild & Benjamin Onion [2:37].

Acct. of Est. of JOHN COCKBORN of Brist., dtd. 5 Jan. 1701/2,
pres. by John Borland & John Maxwell, Execs. Mary Cockborn
widow [2:38].

Dismissal of John Borland & John Maxwell from all further respon-
sibility in Adm. Est. of JOHN COCKBORN, dtd. 5 Jan. 1701/2 [2:
38/9].

Will of ISAAC LEWES of Reho., Yeoman, dtd. 3 Dec. 1700, prob. 8
July 1701. Wife Hannah. Cousin Abraham Skinner of Malden. "I
have no children." Witns: William Dean, John Thomason & Nathaniel Millerd [2:39].

Agrmt. btwn. John Kennicut (eldest son) & Thomas Kennicut, both
of Swan., sons of ROGER KENNICUT, abt. settl. of land div.,
dtd. 19 May 1701 [2:40].

Settl. of land of Est. of JOHN CORPES of Brist. dcd. intest.
Eldest son John Corpes, aged near 22 years, with leave of
his father-in-law [stepfather] John Geriedi & Deliverance Geraedi[sic] his natural mother. Mentions there were 6 chldn.
[not named] of the dcd. John, dtd. 13 March 1701/2. Comm: Nathaniel Reynolds, Samuel Little & Capt. Samuel Gallope [2:41].

Agrmt. btwn. John Corpes, eldest son of JOHN CORPES of Brist.,
& his mother Deliverance Geraedi abt. paym. of John Corpes
to his mother Deliverance in settl. of Est. of said John
Corpes, dtd. 13 Apr. 1702 [2:41/2].

Acct. by Samuel Walker, Adm. of Est. of his father [not named],
dtd. 14 Apr. 1702. Mentions "my uncle Butterworth" & "my brother Philip Walker" [2:43].

Accept. by Court of above acct. for Est. of Deacon PHILIP WAL-
KER of Reho. (Court had ordered settl. & div. of this Est. in
1680). Jane relict of Philip. Samuel Walker eldest son [2:43].

Rcpts. by Henry Sweet of Swan. & his wife Elizebeth to his bro.-
in-law Samuel Walker of Reho. for legacy from Est. of PHILIP
WALKER, dtd. 15 Nov. 1687 & 29 Nov. 1688. Witns: William Carpenter & Josiah Carpenter [2:43/4].

Rcpt. by Henry Sweet of Swan. in behalf of his wife Elizebeth
to the comm. appt. to div. her father's Est., dtd. 31 March
1687. Comm: Daniel Peck, Esq., Capt. Hunt, Lt. Peck, Sgt.
Read & William Carpenter [2:44].

Rcpt. by Abraham Peren of Reho. on behalf of his wife [not
named] for a legacy from the Est. of his wife's father Deacon
WALKER, paid by "my Mother [probably mother-in-law] Jane Walker" & Samuel Walker, dtd. 31 Jan. 1682. Witns: William Carpenter, Sr. & Thomas Read [2:44].

Acct. of Lt. Samuel Walker of Reho. as guard. of Sarah Peren
his niece who is now above 20 years old but not yet able to
guide herself, dau. of ABRAHAM PEREN of Reho. dcd. He has
been her guard. since 28 May 1694. Dtd. 24 Feb. 1702 [2:45].

Rcpt. by Philip Walker & Ebenezer Walker sons of dcd. PHILIP
WALKER of Reho. for legacy paid by mother Jane Walker and brother Samuel Walker, Adms., dtd. 13 Apr. 1702 [2:45].

Inv. of Est. of Widow JANE POLLEY of Reho., formerly wife of
Philip Walker of Reho., dtd. 21 March 1702. Apprs: Samuel
Peck, Steven Paine & Daniel Smith. Pres. by her son Lt. Sam-
uel Walker [2:46].

Acct. of Rose Soul, widow & Adm of Est. of her husb. NATHANIEL
SOUL of Dart., dtd. 10 Oct. 1700 [2:47].

Acct. of Hannah Negus, Exec. of Est. of Capt. ISAACE NEGUS, dtd.
12 Sept. 1701 [2:47].

Inv. of Est. of HUGH WOODBERRY of Brist., dtd. 11 May 1702,
pres. by Mary Woodbery, widow & Adm. Apprs: David Cary &
James Adams [2:48].

Settl. of Est. of HUGH WOODBERY of Brist., Mariner, dtd. 15 June
1702. Wife Mary Woodbery. Son-in-law Edward Gross of Brist.,
Mariner. Mentions "Several children & grandchildren of the deceased," [not named]. Comm: Nathaniel Paine, Esq., Capt. Samuel Gallop, Lt. Samuel Little, Mr. John Birge & Mr. Peter Reynolds [2:49/50].

Appraisal of Est. of WILLIAM HODGE of Brist., dtd. 10 June 1702.
Comm: Nathaniel Paine, Samuel Gallop, Samuel Little, Peter
Reynolds & John Cary [2:51].

Settl. of Est. of WILLIAM HODGE of Brist., Mariner, dtd. 15
June 1702. Son William Hodge (arrived at age 21), Adm., &
other chldn: John Hodge, Sarah Hodge & Elizebeth Hodge [2:
51/2].

Acct. of Nathaniel Blagrove, Adm. of Est. of NATHAN HAYMAN of
Brist., dtd. 14 June 1702. Mentions his portion of ship "Richard & Michal," and the ketch "Betty" taken by the French. Eldest son [not named], son John, daus. Elizebeth, Sarah, Mary
& Grace. Acct. mentions var. debts to "Capt. Samuel Hayman,"
as well as many other persons [2:53/4].

Inv. of Est. of WILLIAM HOAR of Brist., Baker, dtd. 5 Jan. 1698/9
pres. by Hannah Hoard, widow & Exec. Apprs: Nathaniel Blagrove & John Cary [2:54/5/6].

Div. of Est. of NATHANIEL SOUL of Dart. btwn. his widow Rose
Soul & his chldn: Nathaniel Soul (eldest son), Silvanus Soul
(2nd son), Jacob Soul (3rd son) & Miles Soul (4th son). Comm:
William Southworth, Gershom Woodell & Job Winslow [2:56/7].

Agrmt. & div. of Est. of JANE POLLEY of Roxbury, mother of Samuel & Philip Walker of Rehoboth; Henry Sweet of Attl. in behalf of his wife Elizebeth; Ebenezer Walker & said Samuel Walker as guard. of chldn. of Abraham Peren of Reho. dcd. Witns
Hezekiah Luther, Thomas Bowen & Hugh Cole [2:57/8].

Will of DANIEL WILCOCK of Tiv., dtd. 9 June 1702, prob. 25 Aug.
1702. Wife Elizebeth. Sons: Daniel (eldest), Stephen, John,
Edward, Thomas & Samuel (dcd.) Wilcock. Daus: Mary wife of
John Earle, Lydia, Sarah wife of Edward Briggs, Susannah Wil-
cock (mentions "her grandfather John Cook"). Friends Thomas
Cornhil of Newport, Joseph Walker of Tiv. & John Coggeshall
of Portsmouth, Overseers. Witns: William Manchester, Edward
Briggs & Zachariah Allen [2:59/60/1].

Inv. of Est. of DANIEL WILCOCK of Tiv., who died 2 July 1702,
dtd. 16 July 1702, pres. by John & Edward Willcox. Apprs:
John Coggeshall & Zachariah Allen [2:62].

Acct. of Est. of SHADRACH WILBORE of Taun., dtd. 9 Dec. 1701,
pres. by Joseph Wilbore & Shadrach Wilbore, Execs. Legacies
to: Widow Wilbore [not named], Joseph Wilbore, John Wilbore,
Eliezer Wilbore, Sarah Hoar, Shadrach Wilbore, Benjamin Wilbore & Abraham Hathaway (his wife's legacy) [2:63/4].

Agrmt. of heirs of THOMAS BRIGGS of Taun., dtd. 5 May 1696,
signed by: sons Thomas Briggs (eldest), Daniel Briggs & Samuel Briggs; & by Uriah Leonard of Taun. (who purchased the
portion of Susannah Cobb, wife of John Cobb & dau. of the dcd.
Thomas Briggs). Samuel Briggs to take care of his aged mother
Witns: Samuel Hall & John Cary [2:64/5].

Accept. of terms of above agrmt. by Ann Briggs, relict of THO-
MAS BRIGGS, dtd. 25 Aug. 1697. She was unable to travel to
court. Witns: Samuel Leonard & Elkanah Leonard [2:65].

Div. of Est. of Lt. JOHN HALL of Taun., dtd. 29 Dec. 1694 btwn.
his widow [not named] & his chldn: John Hall (eldest son),
Joseph (2nd son), James (3rd son), Benjamin (4th son, under
21) & Jacob (5th son, under 21). Dau. Hannah (under 18). Comm
Thomas Leonard, Henry Hodges, John Cary & Increase Robinson
[2:66/7].

Acct. of Anthony Newland, Adm. of Est. of his father & mother
JEREMIAH & KATHERINE NEWLAND of Taun., dtd. 10 Jan. 1700/1.
Legacies to: Jerimy Newland, John Newland, Benjamin Newland,
William Witherly, John Witherly, William Cobb, Nicholas Smith
& Anthony Newland [2:67/8].

Rcpt. from Jerimy Newland, Benjamin Newland, John Newland, William Witherly, John Witherly, William Cobb & Nicholas Smith
to "our brother" Anthony Newland for legacies paid from Est.
of "our ffather & mother" JEREMIAH NEWLAND & KATHERINE NEW-

LAND of Taun., dtd. 10 Jan. 1700/1. [*Signers show "Witherel,"
not "Witherly"*][2:68].

Inv. of Est. of RICE LEONARD of Reho., dtd. 2 May 1700, pres.
by Mary Leonard, Adm. Apprs: William Carpenter, Moses Read
& Nicholas Ide [2:69].

Div. of Est. of SAMUEL PITTS of Taun. btwn. his widow Sarah
Pitts & his chldn: Samuel Pitts (eldest son), Henry (2nd son),
Peter (3rd son), Ebenezer (4th son), Sarah (eldest dau.), Mary
(2nd dau.) & Abigail (3rd dau.). Relict Sarah Pitts now Sarah Blake. Dtd. 6 June 1701. Comm: Thomas Leonard, Henry Hodges, Benjamin Dean, Richard Godfrey & Edward Bobbit[2:70a/71a]
[*page numbering error*].

Acct. of Est. of ELIASHIP [*sic*] ADAMS of Brist., dtd. 8 Oct. 17-
00, pres. by Mehettabel Adams, widow & Exec. Mentions "her
brother Daniels." "The children are all young & under the
guardianship of their Mother" [2:72a].

Inv. of Est. of SAMUEL BRIGGS of Taun., dtd. 6 Oct. 1704, pres.
by Mary Briggs, widow. Apprs: Philip King, Joseph Richmond &
Joseph Williams [2:72a].

Rcpt. from Nathan Hayman of Brist., Mariner, to Nathaniel Bla-
grove, Adm. of Est. of Nathan's father NATHAN HAYMAN, dtd. 25
May 1696. Witns: Richard Sterlin, Richard Horton & Joseph
Smith [2:74a].

Rcpt. from Thomas Church of Brist., Mariner, to Nathaniel Bla-
grove, Adm. of Est. of Capt. NATHAN HAYMAN, father of Sarah
Hayman now Sarah Church wife of Thomas, dtd. 2 May 1700. Witns:
Thomas Coram & Jabez Howland [2:74a/5a].

Rcpt. from John Hayman of Boston to Nathaniel Blagrove, Adm. of
Est. of Capt. NATHAN HAYMAN, John's father, dtd. 18 Jan. 1708/9
Witns: Timothy Ingraham & Sarah Ingraham [2:75a].

Rcpt. from William Brattle of Cambridge, Middlesex Co., Clerk,
to Nathaniel Blagrove, Adm. of Est. of Capt. NATHAN HAYMAN,
dtd. 28 Feb. 1708/9. William Brattle was son-in-law of dcd.
Nathan, signing in behalf of his wife [*not named*]. Signed at
Charlestown. Witns: Thomas Newton & Elisha Cooke, Jr. Approved
by Samuel Hayman, Justice of the Peace of Middlesex County[2:
76a].

Rcpt. from Grace Hayman of Brist., Spinster, to Nathaniel Blagrove, Adm. of Est. of her father Capt. NATHAN HAYMAN, dtd.
22 Jan. 1708/9. Witns: Nathan Hayman & John Birge [2:77a].

Rcpt. from George Brownell & his wife Easter, dau. of PHILIP TA-
BER of Dart., to her mother Mary Davis & her brother Philip
Taber, Execs., dtd. 1 May 1699 [2:77a].

Rcpt. from Abigail Taber dau. of PHILIP TABER of Dart., dcd.,
to her mother Mary Davis, Exec., dtd. 16 March 1696/7 [2:77a].

Rcpt. from Bethiah Taber dau. of PHILIP TABER of Dart. to her
mother Mary Davis & to her brother Philip Taber, Execs., dtd.
26 Apr. 1708 [2:78a].

Order for appraisal & div. of Est. of RICHARD SMITH of Brist.,

dtd. 10 June 1710. 5 chldn. [not named] & their mother Joyce
Smith. Comm: Capt. Samuel Gallop, Mr. Charles Church & Mr.
Samuel Ryall [2:78a].

Div. of Est. of RICHARD SMITH of Brist. btwn. his 5 chldn: Mercy Smith widow of eldest son John Smith on behalf of the 1
son & 2 daus. of John dcd.; Nathaniel Smith; Samuel Smith;
Daniel Smith & Hannah Eddy widow, dtd. 10 June 1710. Comm:
Samuel Gallop, Charles Church & Samuel Ryall [2:79a].

Commission of Nathaniel Byfield to be Judge of Probate for
Bristol from Queen Anne, signed by Gov. Joseph Dudley, dtd.
26 Oct. 1702 [2:70].

Will of THOMAS BUTT of Lit. Comp., Cooper, dtd. 28 Dec. 1702,
prob. 2 Feb. 1702/3. Wife Elizebeth. Sons: Zacheus (eldest
son), Idido & Moses Butt. Dau. Hiphzibah Earle. Sarah wife
of son Zacheus. Grchldn: Sarah Butt, John Butt & Elizebeth
Butt chldn. of son Zacheus. Maid servant Ann Dier. My Indian man called Pope. Friends Aaron Davis, Jr. & Joseph Wilbore, both of Lit. Comp., to be Overseers. Witns: John Briggs
Nicholas Hart, Jethro Jefferyes, Richard Craw & Thomas Townsend [2:71].

Inv. of Est. of THOMAS BUTT, dtd. 16 Jan. 1702/3, pres. by Elizebeth Butt, widow of Thomas. Apprs: Nathaniel Tompkins (aged
63) & Jonathan Thurston (aged 45) [2:73].

Will of WILLIAM CARPENTER of Reho., dtd. 10 Nov. 1702, prob.
20 Apr. 1703. Wife Miriam. Sons: John (eldest), William, Benjamin, Josiah, Nathaniel, Daniel, Noah, Obadiah & Ephraim
Carpenter. 4 daus: Priscilla, Miriam, Hannah & Abigail [no
surnames]. Timothy Titus shall serve out his time as obliged
to me. Witns: Enoch Hunt, John Butterworth & Samuel Walker
[2:74/5].

Inv. of Est. of WILLIAM CARPENTER of Reho., dtd. 5 Feb. 1702/3,
pres. by Miriam Carpenter, his widow. Apprs: John Butterworth, Moses Read & John Willmarth [2:76].

Inv. of Est. of NATHANIEL TOOGOOD of Swan., dtd. 31 March 1703,
pres. by Martha Toogood, his widow. Apprs: John Martin, John
Eddy & Edward Thurber [2:77/8].

Acct. of Rebecca Carpenter, Exec. of Est. of her husb. DAVID
CARPENTER of Reho., dtd. 16 June 1703 [2:78].

Inv. of Est. of NATHANIEL COOPER of Reho., dtd. 12 Feb. 1702/3,
pres. by Mary Cooper, his widow [2:79].

Inv. of Est. of THOMAS THURBER of Swan., dtd. 12 Apr. 1703,
pres. by Ruth Thurber, widow, & James Thurber, son. Apprs:
John Thurber, Robert Millerd & Richard Lee [2:80].

Inv. of Est. of NATHANIEL CHAFFEE of Reho., dtd. 2 March 1703/4
pres. by Mercey Chaffee, his widow. Apprs: Stephen Paine &
Samuel Walker [2:81].

Will of NOAH LLOYD of Swan., Citizen & Woolen Draper of the
City of London, dtd. 27 June 1700, prob. 4 Sept. 1703. Friend
Maj. Samuel Cranston, Esq., of Newport & his wife & chldn.

[*not named*]. My brother George Lloyd of England. My nephew
George Lloyd son of my bro. George Lloyd. Sons [*not named*]
of my younger bro. Thomas Lloyd of England. My bro. John
ffarers and his wife [*not named*] of Hamton in England of rents
due for my farm at Saule in Glocester Shire England. My Rev-
erend friend Mr. Nathaniel Clap, Minister. Mr. Thomas ffox
of Newport & his wife Elizebeth. Mr. William Allen of Newport & his dau. Mary. Friend Mary Cole of Newport. Mentions
his lands in Swan. & Secunk (Reho.). John Harwood & Henry
Cornish both of the City of London. Mr. Weston Clarke & Mr.
Benjamin Newbery both of Newport, Overseers. Witns: Latham
Clarke, James Clarke & John Adlin, Jr. [2:82/3/4].
Inv. of Est. of NOAH LLOYD of Swan., dtd. 6 Oct. 1703, pres.
by Samuel Cranston, Exec. Apprs: James Brown, Jr. & Thomas
Allin [2:85].
Inv. of Est. of EDWARD THURBER of Swan., dtd. 21 Oct. 1703,
pres. by Margret Thurber widow of Edward. Mentions, as an
asset, what Edward "is to have in reversion after his father
& mother decease." Apprs: John Martin & Samuel Bullock[2:86].
Agrmt. btwn. William Hatch of Swan., Yeoman & only son of WIL-
LIAM HATCH (one party) & John Barstow of Scituate County of
Plymouth, Mariner, in behalf of himself & Lidia his wife, only
dau. of said William Hatch dcd. (2nd party), dtd. 25 Feb. 17-
02. Witns: William Wood, John Cary & John Cary, Jr.[2:87/8].
Inv. of Est. of NATHANIEL WHITTICER of Reho., dtd. 8 June 1703,
pres. by Lt. John Hunt & John Whitticer, Adms. Apprs: Samuel
Newman, John Thomas & Francis Wilson [2:88].
Will of WILLIAM WOODCOCK of Attl., dtd. 15 June 1703, prob. 7
Feb. 1703/4. Wife Mary. Eldest dau. Mary Freeman. Youngest
dau. Mirriam Woodcock. Other 3 daus: Sarah Balkcume, Allice
Burkland & Ame Fuller. Witns: John Wilkinson, Anthony Sprague
& Mary Sprague [2:89].
Inv. of Est. of WILLIAM WOODCOCK of Attl., dtd. 1 Dec. 1703,
pres. by Mary Woodcock, widow. Apprs: Moses Read, Nicholas
Ide & Anthony Sprague [2:90].
Acct. of widow Mary Cooper of Reho., Adm. of Est. of her husb.
[*not named*], from 20 Apr. 1703 to 10 May 1704. Mentions "the
children [*not named*] being young" [2:91].
Acct. of Est. of NATHANIEL TOOGOOD of Swan., dtd. 29 May 1704,
pres. by Martha Toogood, widow, & John Toogood, son [2:92].
Will of GEORGE SOULE of Dart., dtd. 25 March 1697, prob. 30 June
1704. Wife Deborah. Sons: William (eldest), John & Nathan
Soule. Daus: Deborah Soule, Mary, Lidiah & Sarah Soule (all
under 18). Friends Joseph Tripp & George Cadman of Dart. to
be Overseers. Witns: Isaac Lawton, John Coggeshall & Elizebeth Coggeshall. On 22 March 1704 Deborah Soule, widow of
George, dcd., deposed that she was not capable of coming to
court & that she did not accept what was given to her in her
husband's will, but desired to have her thirds as by law[2:93].

Inv. of Est. of GEORGE SOULE of Dart., dtd. 17 May 1704, pres.
by William Soule, Exec. Apprs: Joseph Tripp, William Wood &
George Cadman [2:94].

Inv. of Est. of CALEB CORY of Dart., dtd. 19 Apr. 1704, pres.
by Sarah Cory, his widow. Apprs: William Earle & Jonathan
Tripp [2:95].

Inv. of land in Swan. to the right of WILLIAM SALSBERY of Swan.
sometime of Milton, dcd., dtd. 13 July 1704, pres. by William
Salsbery, son. Apprs: Joseph Mason & Thomas Bowen [2:96].

Additional Inv. of Est. of GEORGE SOULE of Dart., dtd. 17 Apr.
1705, pres. by William Soule, son & Adm. Apprs: Silvanus
Soule & Nathaniel Soule [2:96].

Will of DANIEL EATON of Lit. Comp., dtd. 29 Apr. 1704, prob.
21 Aug. 1704. Wife Rebeccah. Patience Emery, Rebecah Emery
& Daniel Emery [relat. not stated]. Cousin & kinswoman Mary
Calender my brother's dau. by marriage. Friends & neighbors
George Pearce & James Bennet both of Lit. Comp. to be Overseers. Witns: John Woodman, William Fobes & Joseph Willbore
[2:97/8].

Inv. of Est. of DANIEL EATON of Lit. Comp. who died 11 July 1704
dtd. 22 July 1704, pres. by Rebecah Eaton, his widow. Apprs:
Joseph Wilbur & Aron Davis [2:98/9].

Appt. of Deacon Samuel Newman of Reho. to be guard. of Susanah
Kent, dau. of Ensign JOSEPH KENT of Swan., dtd. 18 Sept. 1704
[2:99].

Inv. of Est. of JOSEPH KENT of Swan., dtd. 5 Sept. 1704, pres.
by Samuel Kent & Joshuah Kent, sons. Mentions Joseph Kent,
Jr. & Samuel Kent. Apprs: Samuel Newman, Enoch Hunt & John
Hunt [2:100].

Agrmt. for div. of Est. of Ens. JOSEPH KENT of Swan. btwn. his
widow Susannah Kent & her chldn., dtd. 15 Sept. 1704. Two
younger sons Samuel & Joshuah Kent. Eldest son Joseph Kent.
Susannah Kent, only dau., under guard. of Deacon Samuel Newman. Witns: John Saffin, John Smith & Richard Lee [2:101/2].

Acct. of Est. of WILLIAM CARPENTER of Reho.. dtd. 18 Sept. 1704,
pres. by Miriam Carpenter, his widow. Eldest son John Carpenter. Other chldn: Josiah, Nathaniel, Daniel, William, Obadiah, Noah & Ephraim Carpenter; Jonathan Bliss & his wife Miriam; Richard Sweet & his wife Priscilla; & Hannah Carpenter
[2:103].

Rcpt. by John Carpenter for legacy from Est. of his father WIL-
LIAM CARPENTER, paid by his mother Miriam Carpenter, dtd. 25
May 1703. Witns: Robert Martin, Ezekiel Read & Daniel Car-
penter [2:103].

Rcpt. by Hannah Carpenter for legacy from Est. of her father
WILLIAM CARPENTER, paid by her mother Miriam Carpenter, dtd.
29 Sept. 1703. Witns: Robert Martin & Daniel Carpenter [2:
104].

Rcpt. by Priscilla Sweet & her husb. Richard Sweet for her legacy from Est. of her father WILLIAM CARPENTER paid by her mother Miriam Carpenter, dtd. 6 March 1703/4 [2:104].
Rcpt. for legacies from Est. of their father WILLIAM CARPENTER,
paid by their mother Miriam Carpenter, signed by: Obadiah Car-
penter, Josiah Carpenter, Nathaniel Carpenter, Daniel Carpen-
ter, Jonathan Bliss, William Carpenter, Ephraim Carpenter &
Noah Carpenter, dtd. 15 May 1704 [2:105].
Acct. of Est. of THOMAS ELIOT of Reho., dtd. 2 Nov. 1704, pres.
by Moses Read, Adm. [2:105].
Order granting small Est. of THOMAS ELIOT of Reho. dcd. intest.
to eldest son Thomas Eliot, who is directed to make payms. to
the other 4 chldn. [not named], dtd. 30 Oct. 1704 [2:105/6].
Agrmt. btwn. Joanna ffowler, widow of JOHN WOODCOCK of Attl.,
& her chldn: John Woodcock (eldest son), Israel Woodcock, Jon-
athan Woodcock, Thomas Woodcock, Thomas Easterbrook, Samuel
Guild & Benjamin Onion. Joannah is now wife of James ffowler,
dtd. 6 March 1703, pres. by Capt. Samuel Guild, Adm. Witns:
James Browne, Christopher Hall & Mary Blackenton [2:106].
Acct. of John Woodcock of Dedham, Co. of Suffolk, & Samuel Guild,
Adms. of Est. of their late father JOHN WOODCOCK of Attl., dtd.
2 Nov. 1704 Mentions a paym. "to our mother upon Agreement"
[2:107].
Inv. of Est. of BENJAMIN STAR of Taun., dtd. 12 Feb. 1703/4,
pres. by Ruth Star [relat. not stated]. Apprs: Thomas Leonard & John Richmond [2:108].
Inv. of Est. of RICHARD JENKINS of Brist., dtd. 25 Feb. 1703/4,
pres. by Mary Jenkins, his widow. Incl. lengthy list of yard
goods, thread, ribbons, buttons, etc. Apprs: Nathaniel Paine
& Simon Davis [2:109/10].
Will of JOSEPH ALLEN of Dart., dtd. 1696 [day & month not listed]
prob. 11 Oct. 1704. Wife Sarah Allen, also called mother of
the chldn. Sons: Josiah, William, Joseph, Benjamin, Trustram,
Ralph, Daniel & Ruben Allen. Daus: Rose Howland, Abigail Allen, Sarah Allen & Hannah Allen. Friend William Earle & brother Increase Allen to be Overseers. Mentions lands in Barnstable & Dart. Witns: Robert Carr (of Newport), John Wilbur
(of Lit. Comp.) & John Smith [2:111/2].
Inv. of Est. of JOSEPH ALLEN of Dart. who died in Sept. 1704,
dtd. 18 Nov. 1704, pres. by Joseph Allen & Josiah Allen, sons
& Execs. Apprs: Increase Allen & Benjamin Allen [2:112/3].
Will of NATHANIEL POTTER of Dart., Yeoman or Husbandman, dtd.
18 Oct. 1704, prob. 20 Nov. 1704. Wife Elizebeth. Sons: Stokes,
Nathaniel, William, Benjamin, Samuel & Iccabode Potter. Daus:
Mary Willbor, Rebecca Kerby, Elizebeth Potter & Katherine Pot-
ter (who is under 18). Friends James Tripp & Hugh Mosher to
be Overseers. Witns: Stephen Wilcock, Thomas Lake & John
Lake [2:114].

Inv. of Est. of NATHANIEL POTTER of Dart., dtd. 25 Oct. 1704, pres. by Elizebeth Potter & Stokes Potter, Execs. Apprs: Jonathan Davil, Thomas Lake & Phillip Taber [2:115].

Will of JOHN RICKETSON of Dart., dtd. 4 Jan. 1704/5, prob. 26 Feb. 1704/5. Father William Ricketson. Father-in-law Mathew Wing. My 3 brethren William Ricketson, Jonathan Ricketson & Timothy Ricketson. Witns: Daniel Wood, William White & James Tripp [2:116].

Inv. of Est. of JOHN RICKETSON, dtd. 27 Jan. 1704/5, pres. by Mathew Wing, Exec. Apprs: Thomas Hathaway & William White [2:116].

Inv. of Est. of Deacon WILLIAM THROOPE of Brist., dtd. 1 Jan. 1704/5, pres. by Mrs. Mary Throope, his widow. Apprs: Thomas Walker & James Adames [2:117].

Inv. of Est. of MERCY COLE of Rehoboth, dtd. 6 Feb. 1704, pres. by John Brookes of Reho. Apprs: Benjamin Carpenter, John Thomas, John Kenicut & Ebenezer Luther [2:118].

Inv. of Est. of HENRY SWEET of Attl., dtd. 5 Jan. 1704/5, pres. by Elizebeth Sweet, his widow. Apprs: Nicholas Ide, Jonathan Fuller & Daniel Smith [2:119].

Will of STEPHEN MARICK of Taun., dtd. 29 March 1696, prob. 11 Apr. 1705. "In good health but purposeing to goe forth to War in the present Expedition on foot against the Indian Enemy." Wife Anna. Only son Isaac Marick. 3 daus: Mercy, Mary & Sarah (all under 18). Mentions his land in Taun., in Norwich & in Pacataqua (New Jerzey). Cousin Joseph Wilbore. John Smith "my prentice Boy." Father William Marick dcd. Pastor Samuel Danforth. Witns: Benjamin Church, Thomas Leonard & Mary Staple [or *Staphe*][2:120/1].

Inv. of Est. of STEPHEN MARICK, dtd. 3 March 1704/5, pres. by Anna Marick, his widow. Apprs: Ezra Dean, Israel Thresher & Benjamin Dean [2:122].

Will of MARY FITCH of Reho., dtd. 26 March 1702/3, prob. 13 Nov. 1704. 4 daus: Mercy Ormsby (eldest), Rebecah Read, Sarah Mason & Hannah Brown. Son-in-law Moses Read, Exec. Witns: Daniel Carpenter, Samuel Carpenter & Thomas Read, Jr. [2:123].

Inv. of Est. of MARY FITCH OF Reho., widow, dtd. 21 Nov. 1704, pres. by Moses Read, Exec. Mentions items "at Capt. Joseph Browns" & "at Thomas Ormsbys." Apprs: Samuel Walker, Daniel Smith & Daniel Carpenter [2:124].

Will of Deacon WILLIAM THROOPE of Brist., Yeoman, in his 67th year, dtd. 12 June 1704, prob. 1 Jan. 1704/5. Wife Mary. 3 sons: Dan, John & William Throope. 2 eldest daus. Mary Barney wife of John Barney, & Elizebeth Peck wife of Jonathan Peck. My youngest son Thomas Throope. 2 youngest daus. Mercy & Lidiah [*no signature or witns. included*][2:125/6].

Accept. by heirs of the above will of "our Honoured father WILLIAM THROOPE," dtd. 12 June 1704, signed by: Dan Throope, John Throope, William Throope & Thomas Throope, all of Brist. Men-

tions "our mother Mary Throope." Record of Court on 4 June
1705 mentions presence there also of: Mary Barney wife of John
Barney, Elizebeth Peck wife of Jonathan Peck & Lidiah Cary
wife of Eliazer Cary. Witns: Thomas Walker, James Adams &
John Cary [2:126/7].

Will of JOSIAH ROBINSON of Taun., "being pressed to goe forth
to the Eastward against the Indians," dtd. 16 Aug. 1703, prob.
4 June 1705. Brothers Increase Robinson & Ebenezer Robinson.
4 sisters: Sarah Dean, Hannah Williams, Bethia Pitts & Abigail
Robinson. My honoured mother [not named]. Mentions his lands
in Taun., in Dorchester & in the North Purchase. Witns: Samuel Danforth, Hannah Danforth & Thomas Briggs [2:128].

Inv. of Est. of JOSIAH ROBINSON, dtd. 2 June 1705, pres. by Ebenezer Robinson, Exec. Apprs: Thomas Wade & John White [2:
128/9].

Inv. of Est. of SAMUEL TITUS of Reho., dtd. 23 March 1703/4,
pres. by Richard Bowen of Reho., uncle. Apprs: Stephen Paine
& John Wilmarth [2:129].

Inv. of Est. of WILLIAM PHILLIPS of Taun., dtd. 15 [month not
given] 1705, pres. 2 July 1705 by Ensign Thomas Gilbert of
Taun. Apprs: Jared Talbut, Abram Hathway & John Paul[2:130/1].

Inv. of Est. of JOSEPH WILLIS of Taun., dtd. 31 Jan. 1704/5,
pres. by Joseph Willis. Apprs: Henry Hodges, Thomas Harvey &
Samuel Blake. Mentions land at Bridgewater [2:131].

Request by Sarah Willis, widow of JOSEPH WILLIS, that adm. on
his Est. be granted to her eldest son Joseph Willis of Taun.,
dtd. 2 July 1705 [2:131].

Will of JOSEPH HALL of Taun., dtd. 14 Apr. 1705, prob. 10 July
1705. Wife Mary. 3 sons: Joseph (eldest), Nathaniel & Nehemiah Hall. 3 daus: Mary, Mehettabel & Abigail. Cousin Joseph
Eliot. Mentions gift of Est. to his wife "for bringing up of
my young children....as they come of age." Witns: John Spur,
James Bell & Increase Robinson [2:132].

Inv. of Est. of JOSEPH HALL of Taun., dtd. 6 June 1705, pres.
by Mary Hall, his widow. Apprs: Thomas Leonard, James Leonard & Ezra Dean [2:133].

Acct. of Est. of DANIEL EATON of Lit. Comp., dtd. 4 Sept. 1705,
pres. by Rebecca Eaton, Exec. [2:134/5].

Appt. of Israel Nichols of Hingham, Co. of Suffolk, to be guard.
to his son Nathaniel Nichols, grson. of ANTHONY SHAW late of
Lit. Comp. [2:136].

Acct. of Est. of JOHN WILKINS of Brist., not dated, pres. 1 Oct.
1705 by Anstis Wilkins & Samuel Wilkins, Adms. Mentions eldest dau. Mary Jenkins [2:136].

Agrmt. abt. div. of Est. of JOHN WILKINS, dtd. 1 Oct. 1705. Anstis Wilkins, widow. Son Samuel Wilkins to rcv. double portion. Dau. Mary Jenkins. Benjamin Elleree & Abigail his wife,
dau. of the dcd. Youngest dau. Mehettabell Wilkins. Witns:
John Cary & Benjamin Coggeshall [2:136/7].

Acct. of Est. of BENJAMIN POTTER of Dart., dtd. 7 June 1710, pres. by Mary Potter, his widow [2:138/9].

Inv. of Est. of ANTHONY SHAW of Lit. Comp., who died 21 Aug. 1705, dtd. 3 Sept. 1705, pres. by Israel Shaw of Lit. Comp. Apprs: William Southworth & Joseph Wilbore [2:140].

Inv. of Est. of MARY TIMBERLAKE, widow sojourning in Lit. Comp. who died 10 Sept. 1705, dtd. 29 Sept. 1705, pres. by John Woodman, Adm. Apprs: Aron Davis, Jr. & William ffobes [2:140].

Inv. of Est. of JOHN WILKINS of Brist., dtd. 19 Oct. 1704, pres. by Mrs. Anstis Wilkins & Samuel Wilkins, Joint Adms. Apprs: John Cary, Samuel Little & Belamy Bosworth [2:141].

Will of JOSEPH PECK, Yeoman, of Reho., dtd. 5 July 1697, prob. 5 Dec. 1705. Daus: Patience wife of Richard Bowen, Mary wife of Benjamin Hunt, Elizebeth wife of Capt. Mason & Hannah wife of Daniel Read. Sons Jathnell Peck & Samuel Peck. Witns: John Peck, William Dean & Jonah Palmer [2:142/3].

Codicil to his Will by JOSEPH PECK, Sr., dtd. 11 March 1701, pres. 5 Dec. 1705. Witns: Thomas Ormsbee, William Blantine & Hannah Ormsbee [2:143].

Inv. of Est. of JOSEPH PECK, Sr., of Reho., dtd. 1 Dec. 1705, pres. by Samuel Peck of Palmers River in Reho., son & Exec. Apprs: Thomas Ormsbee & John Barney [2:144].

Inv. of Est. of RICHARD WHITTICER of Reho., dtd. 7 Jan. 1705/6, pres. by Noah Whitticer, son & Adm. Mentions right of land in North Purchase in Attl. Apprs: John Thomas & Benjamin Allen [2:145].

Inv. of Est. of THOMAS RICHMOND of Taun., who died 14 Dec. 1705, dtd. 19 Dec. 1705, pres. by John Richmond, Sr. & Richard Godfree, Adms. Mentions Mary Godfree, sister of Thomas dcd. Apprs: Benjamin Crane, Abrahm Hathaway & Peter Walker [2:146].

Will of CONSTANT SOUTHWORTH of Brist., being bound on a voyage to sea, dtd. 14 Jan. 1702, prob. 5 Feb. 1705. Brothers Nathaniel Southworth & Edward Southworth. Cousin Edward Grey, Jr. of Tiv., son of my uncle Edward Grey of Tiv. Brother Ichabod Southworth of Plimouth. Witns: Edward Grey of Tiv., Nathaniel Coddington & William Coddington, both of Newport [2:147].

Deposition by Nathaniel Bunn that he heard John Richmond, Sr. of Taun. say he had given a Deed to his son, Thomas Richmond, for 70 acres, dtd. 4 Feb. 1705 [2:147].

Inv. of Est. of JOHN FRY of Brist., dtd. 7 Feb. 1705, pres. by Deliverance Fry, his widow. Apprs: John Butterworth & John Archer [2:148].

Acct. of Est. of MERCY COLE of Reho., dtd. 7 Jan. 1705/6, pres. by John Brookes, Adm. 5 brothers & 5 sisters remaining: Capt. James Cole, Hugh Cole, John Cole, Ebenezer Cole, Benjamin Cole, Martha Sweeting, Ruth Luther, Anne Salisbury, Experience Brooks & Mary Kingsley. Mentions debts paid to many persons, incl. Henry Sweeting, & to both Jonathan Kingsley & John Brooks "for diet" [2:149].

Inv. of Est. of THOMAS MAKEPEACE of Taun., dtd. 4 Feb. 1705/6,
pres. by Mary Makepeace, his widow. Apprs: Thomas Jones,
Jared Talbut & James Tisdale. Mentions John Simmons, bro.-in-
law of Thomas dcd. [2:150].

Acct. of Est. of SAMUEL BRIGGS of Taun., dtd. 6 March 1705/6,
pres. by Mary Briggs, Adm. & his widow. Mentions paym. "to
brother John Hall" [2:151].

Appt. of Jonathan Woodbery of Brist., Mariner & eldest son, to
be Adm. of Est. of Capt. SAMUEL WOODBERY of Brist., Mariner,
dtd. 30 May 1706 [2:151].

Will of FRANCES WILLIAMS of Taun., widow of Deacon Richard Wil-
liams, dtd. 20 Oct. 1703, prob. 7 March 1705/6. My son Par-
meter. My son Nathaniel Williams his widow. My son Joseph
Williams widow. My son Benjamin Williams widow. My son Thomas
Williams of Taun. My dau. Elizebeth Bird of Dorchester. Witns:
Joseph Hall, John Hoskins & Ezra Dean [2:152].

Inv. of Est. of Widow FRANCES WILLIAMS of Taun., dtd. 8 Feb. 17-
05/6, pres. by Thomas Williams of Taun., Exec. Apprs: James
Hall & Ebenezer Robinson [2:152].

Inv. of Est. of RUTH HATHWAY, widow of John Hathway of Taun.,
dtd. 23 Jan. 1705/6, pres. by Benjamin Paul, Husbandman, of
Taun. Mentions son-in-law Samuel Talbut of Taun. Apprs: Benjamin Crane & Nathaniel French [2:153].

Inv. of Est. of THOMAS MAKEPEACE of Taun., dtd. 16 March 1706,
pres. by Mary Makepeace, his widow. Apprs: James Tisdale &
Samuel Talbut [2:154].

Will of THOMAS WILLIAMS of Taun., dtd. 17 Apr. 1706, prob. 12
June 1706. Wife Mary. Son Jonathan Williams. 6 daus: Mary,
Sarah, Hannah, Bethiah, Mehitabel & Dameris. Wife Mary is
called mother of son John. Witns: Thomas Leonard, Edward Cobb
& John Hall [2:155].

Inv. of Est. of THOMAS WILLIAMS of Taun., dtd. 12 June 1706,
pres. by Mrs. Mary Williams & Jonathan Williams, Execs. Apprs:
Thomas Leonard, Henry Hodges & Increase Robinson [2:156].

Inv. of Est. of EPHRAIM EMERSON of Taun. who died 8 Apr. 1706,
pres. by Elizebeth Emerson, his widow, recorded 18 June 1706.
Apprs: Robert Crossman & Richard Haskins [2:157].

Inv. of Est. of Capt. SAMUEL WOODBERY of Brist., Mariner, dtd.
28 May 1706, pres. by Jonathan Woodbery, eldest son. Apprs:
John Cary & James Adams [2:158].

Will of SAMUEL PERRY of Reho., dtd. 2 Nov. 1705, prob. 3 July
1706. Wife Mary. Eldest son Jesiel Perry. Daus: Elizebeth
Perry, Rebeccah Perry & Sarah Perry. Grson. Henry Amedown.
Youngest son Samuel Perry, who is to maintain his mother.
Samuel Mason & Daniel Smith of Reho. to be Overseers. Wife
Mary asked for will to be violated and that she rcv. her 3rds
as by law, instead. Witns: Stephen Paine, John Butterworth,
Timothy Ide & Daniel Smith [2:159/60].

Inv. of Est. of SAMUEL PERRY of Reho., dtd. 22 Apr. 1706, pres.

by Mary Perry, widow, & Samuel Perry, son. Apprs: John Butterworth, Samuel Walker & Daniel Smith [2:160].

Will of THOMAS BARNES of Swan., dtd. 7 May 1705, prob. 3 July
1706. Wife Elizebeth to rcv. "things that were hers before
Marriage." Mentions that "my wife shall Endeavor to make good
the agreement Concerning Mary Barnes according to Indenture."
Sons: Thomas (eldest), John, Peter & Samuel (youngest) Barnes.
Daus: Lidiah wife of Thomas Olney at Providence, Anne wife of
Thomas Allin of Swan., Sarah wife of Benjamin Wight of Provi-
dence, Elizebeth wife of John Bullick at Providence & Hannah
Barnes (youngest). Witns: Israel Peck, Nathaniel Peck & Jo-
seph Heath [2:161/2].

Inv. of Est. of THOMAS BARNES of Swan., who died 8 June 1706,
dtd. 14 June 1706, pres. by Elizebeth Barnes, widow, & Samuel Barnes, son [2:162/3].

Acct. of Est. of Mrs. MARY TIMBERLAKE of Lit. Comp., dtd. 3 July
1706, pres. by son-in-law John Woodman, Adm. Legacies: ¼ to
chldn. of Henry Timberlake, ¼ to Joseph Timberlake, ¼ to chldn.
of John Timberlake & ¼ to Hannah wife of John Woodman. "Mary
Timberlake had four sons and two daughters: William, Henry,
Joseph, John, Elizebeth, and Hannah. William hath a daughter
now Mrs. Mumford who had the greatest part of her fathers
Estate, Henry is Dead left a son Henry and two Daughters, Joseph remains alive, John is dead left three Daughters Elizebeth Mary & Hannah, Elizebeth Coggeshall is liveing hath had
of her mother before the Will a peice of land in Newport, Hannah Woodman is yet alive." The acct. mentions funeral charges
paid by John Coggeshall & money owed by Stephen Mumford of
Newport [2:164/5].

Inv. of Est. of JOHN THURBER of Swan., dtd. 8 Aug. 1706, pres.
by Priscilla Thurber, his widow. Apprs. not named [2:165].

Lt. John Hunt was granted more time to finish Adm. of Est. of
NATHANIEL WHITTICER, dtd. 6 Nov. 1706 [2:165].

Invs. of Est. of CONSTANT SOUTHWORTH of Tiv., dtd. 5 Feb. 1705
& 20 Aug. 1706, pres. by Nathaniel Southworth of Middleborough
Exec. Apprs: Samuel Little, Joseph Wanton, David Little & Constant Church [2:166].

Inv. of Est. of ANNA MARICK, widow of Stephen Marick of Taun.,
who died 4 March 1705, dtd. 4 Sept. 1706, pres. by Isace
Merick son-in-law [step-son?]. Apprs: Nathaniel Crossman &
John Mason [2:167].

Agrmt. abt. settl. of Est. of HUGH WOODBERY & MARY WOODBERY, his
wife, both dcd., signed by: William Fulton of Brist. Attorney
for Jonathan Woodbery of Brist. Mariner & guard. of Samuel &
Sarah Woodbery brother & sister of the said Jonathan who are
all chldn. of Capt. Samuel Woodbery Mariner dcd.; Mary Woodbery of Brist. widow of John Woodbery Mariner dcd. & guard.
of Nathaniel Woodbery son of the dcd. John; Joseph Pratt of
Brist., Sadler, & Elizebeth his wife; Edward Gross of Newport,

Mariner, & Mary his wife, dtd. 3 Oct. 1706 [2:168].

Inv. of Lt. THOMAS FRY of Brist., Mariner, dtd. 3 Oct. 1706,
pres. by Samuel Penfield & Hannah his wife, Adms. Consists
of personal est. "found to be with his mother Mrs. Hanah
Butterworth in Bristol." Apprs: Joseph Pratt & James Adames
[2:169].

Petition of Philip Walker of Reho. on behalf of his sister Elizebeth Sweet, widow of HENRY SWEET of Attl., requesting more time
to finish Adm. of her husband's Est. Not dated [2:169].

Inv. of Est. of JONATHAN TRIPP of Dart., dtd. 4 Dec. 1706, pres.
by Martha Hart, widow of Jonathan & now wife of Samuel Hart.
She requested that her father, William Brownell of Dart., be
made Adm. Apprs: Joseph Tripp & William Brownell [2:170].

Petition of Mary Perry, widow of SAMUEL PERRY, & her son Samuel
Perry, that the original terms of her husband's will stand,
withdrawing her request for thirds, dtd. 4 Dec. 1706 [2:170/1].

Rcpt. for legacies from Est.. "of our Honrd Mother" MARY FITCH
of Reho., paid by "our brother Ensigne Moses Read," dtd. 25
Nov. 1704 & signed by Thomas Ormsby, Mary Ormsby, Joseph
Brown, Hannah Brown & Sarah Mason [2:171].

Rcpt. for legacy from Est. of HENRY ANDREWES, dtd. 22 Jan. 1674
[sic], by "Samuel Richmond of Taunton...& Mehittable my wife."
signatures are given as Samuel Richmond & Mehittable Andrus.
Witns: James Reed, John Bagley & Nicholas Moorey. On 21 May
1706, two of the witnesses testified that they had seen the
paper signed & sealed by "Samuel Richmond and Mehitabel who
was then his wife (although she be called above Mehettabell
Andrus)" [2:172].

Rcpt. for legacy from Est. of "our honered ffather" HENRY AN-
DREWS of Taun., dtd. 15 July 1701, paid by "our brother Henry
Andrewes," signed by Joshua Tisdale & his wife Abigail Tisdale
of Free. Witns: Thomas Roberts, John Andrews & Joseph Tisdale [2:172].

Rcpt. for legacy from Est. of HENRY ANDREWES of Taun., paid by
"our Brother Henry Andrewes of Taunton," dtd. 12 Feb. 1706/7,
signed by William Corbit & his wife Hannah dau. of the dcd.
Henry. Brother Henry was called "only son" of dcd. Henry.
Witns: Samuel Humphrey & Joshua Tisdale [2:173].

Depostiion by Abram Hathaway & Isaace Hathaway that they lived
neard Thomas Richmond's farm in Taun. & knew he was in actual
possession of it for more than 20 yrs., dtd. 5 March 1706/7
[2:173].

Acct. of Est. of THOMAS RICHMOND of Taun., undated, pres. by
Richard Godfree of Taun. & "his father John Richmond," Adms.
Mentions Mary Godfree, wife of Richard Godfree, as being sis-
ter of dcd. Thomas [2:174].

Acct. of John Richmond of Taun., Adm. of Est. of THOMAS RICHMOND
of Taun., dtd. 6 March 1706. Mentions things belonging to the
Est. which are still in the hands of: "my son Ebenezer Rich-

mond," "my son Joseph Richmond," "my son Samuel Richmond, "my
son Edward Richmond," "my son in law Richard Godfree" & "my
son in law James Walker." Also mentions "my son John Richmond."
Mentions Mary Godfree wife of Richard Godfree of Taun. & Susannah Reed wife of James Reed of Middlebury, sisters & the
"only whole blood" survivors of the dcd. [2:174/5/6].
Order to div. real est. of NATHAN HAYMAN, Mariner, of Brist.,
dtd. 5 Feb. 1706 [2:177].
Div. of the real est. of NATHAN HAYMAN, Mariner, btwn. the widow [not named] (who is now wife of Nathaniel Blagrove) & his
6 chldn: Capt. Samuel Hayman (eldest son) & his wife Priscilla,
the Rev. William Brattle in the right of his wife Elizebeth,
Capt. Thomas Church in the right of his wife Sarah, Mrs. Mary
Hayman, Mrs. Grace Hayman & John Hayman. Comm: Simon Davis,
Samuel Little, John Allen & James Adames [2:177/8].
Inv. of Est. of WILLIAM DOWNS of Brist., Mariner, dtd. 26 Feb.
1706/7, pres. by Elezebeth Downs, his widow. Apprs: Samuel
Little & James Adams [2:178].
Inv. of Est. of WILLIAM RICKETSON of Dart., dtd. 4 June 1707,
pres. by Elizebeth Wing, widow of William & now wife of Mat-
thew Wing. Apprs: Joseph Tripp, Deliverance Smith & George
Cadman [2:179].
Acct. of Est. of EPHRAIM EMERSON of Taun., dtd. 6 Aug. 1707,
pres. by Elizebeth Emerson of Taun., his widow & Adm. Men-
tions her dau. [not named] who is about 6 yrs. old [2:180].
Will of JOHN DAGGETT of Reho., dtd. 11 Jan. 1703/4, prob. 1 Oct.
1707. Wife Ann. Sons Nathaniel & Joseph Daggett. Daus. Ann &
Elizebeth [no surnames]. Witns: Thomas Read, Noah Mason &
Jonathan Fuller. John was son of Joseph [2:181].
Inv. of Est. of JOHN DAGGETT of Reho, dtd. 12 Sept. 1707, pres.
by Nathaniel Daggett, son & Exec. Apprs: John Butterworth,
Daniel Smith & Samuel Mason [2:182].
Div. of Est. of WILLIAM RICKETSON of Dartmouth, Carpenter, dtd.
10 Oct. 1707. Elizebeth, widow of William & now wife of Mat-
thew Wing of Dart., Yeoman. Sons: William, Jonathan & Timothy
Ricketson. Daus: Elisebeth wife of Daniel Wood & Rebeccah wife
of John Russell. Calls Elizebeth Wing the mother of these
chldn. Apprs: Samuel Gallap & John Cary [2:183/4].
Inv. of Est. of RICHARD HEATH of Swan., dtd. 16 Sept. 1699,
pres. on 6 Aug. 1707 by Mercy Salsbery, widow of Richard &
now wife of Cornelius Salsbury of Swan. Apprs: John Hunt &
Ephraim Wheatton [2:185].
Rcpts. from Abel Burt & his wife Grace & from Joseph Richmond
& his wife Mary for legacies from Est. of "our honed father"
HENRY ANDREWS of Taun., as paid by "our Brother Henry Andrews
of Taunton." Mentions "our honed Mother Mrs. Mary Andrews
late of Taunton," dcd. Both dtd. 28 Marcy 1707. Witns:
Thomas Leonard, Israel Thrasher, Nathaniel Bunn & Abram Hathaway [2:186].

Will of RUBEN WAIT of Dart., dtd. 11 Oct. 1707, prob. 5 Nov. 1707.
Wife Tabitha. 5 sons: Thomas, Benjamin, Joseph, Ruben & Jeremiah (last 4 under age). Daus: Elinor Wait, Abigail Wait & Tabitha Wait. Witns: George Cadman, Joseph Tripp & John Tripp [2:187].

Inv. of Est. of RUBEN WAIT of Dart., dtd. 16 Oct. 1707, pres. by Tabitha Wait, his widow & Exec. Apprs: Joseph Tripp, James Tripp & George Cadman [2:188].

Agrmt. on settl. of Est. of RICHARD HEATH, Tailor, of Swan., signed by Cornelius Salisbury, by Mercy Salisbury widow of Richard Heath & now wife of Cornelius Salisbury, by Joseph Heath & by Hannah Heath, all of Swan. Mentions eldest son John Heath who is now at "sea and is not Returned nor is it known when he will," dtd. 6 Nov. 1707. Witns: John Cary & Martha Throope [2:189].

Inv. of Est. of THOMAS HIX of Portsmouth concerning his land in Tiv., dtd. 3 Dec. 1707, pres. by Thomas Hix, son & Adm. Apprs: Gershom Woodall & Richard Borden [2:190].

Refusal of Mary Hix to be Adm. of Est. of her late husb. THOMAS HIX of Portsmouth, & accept. by her of div. made or to be made by "my children," dtd. 3 Dec. 1707. Witns: Lot Tripp & Richard Borden [2:190].

Agrmt. by chldn. of THOMAS HICKS of Portsmouth abt. div. of his Est. in Tiv., dtd. 3 Dec. 1707. Signed by Thomas Hicks (eldest son), Samuel Hicks (2nd son), Ephraim Hicks (3rd & last son), Susannah & Abigail Hicks (2 eldest daus.) & Richard Borden as guard. of dau. Elizebeth Hicks (under 20). Mentions their mother Mary Hix of Portsmouth [2:190/1].

Acct. of Est. of Capt. SAMUEL WOODBURY of Brist. & request for a div., dtd. 3 Dec. 1707, pres. by Jonathan Woodbury, Adm. [2:191].

Acct. of Est. of RICHARD WHITTICER, dtd. 4 Feb. 1705/6, pres. by Noah Whitman, son [-in-law]. Lists debts paid to 34 people [2:192].

Will of WILLIAM PABODIE of Lit. Comp., dtd. 13 May 1707, prob. 27 Feb. 1707/8. Wife mentioned but not named. Son William Pabodie. Daus: Lidea Greenill & Mary, Mercy, Martha, Priscilla, Ruth, Sarah, Hannah, Elizebeth dcd. & Rebecca dcd. [no surnames]. 3 grsons: Stephen Southworth son of dau. Rebecca dcd.; & John & William Pabodie sons of my son William. Mentions son-in-law William Foabes & son-in-law Icabod Wiswall. Mentions lands in Lit. Comp., in Duxbury & west of Providence. Witns: John Woodman, Peter Taylor & Samuel Willbore [2:193/4].

Inv. of Est. of WILLIAM PABODIE of Lit. Comp. who died 13 Dec. 1707, dtd. 30 Dec. 1707, pres. by Mrs. Elizebeth Pabodie, widow, & her son William Pabodie, Execs. Apprs: John Palmer & Edward Richmond [2:195].

Will of Lt. SAMUEL LITTLE of Brist., dtd. 13 Jan. 1707/8, prob. 3 March 1707/8. Wife Sarah. Eldest son Samuel Little. Young-

est son Edward Little. Dau. Sarah Billings wife of Richard
Billings. Grchldn. Sarah Billings & Richard Billings, Jr.
Friends Capt. Samuel Gallap & Deacon John Cary of Brist. to
be Overseers. Witns: James Carpenter, Solomon Drowne & Mercy
Osborne [2:196/7].

Inv. of Est. of Lt. SAMUEL LITTLE of Brist., dtd. 4 Feb. 1707/8
pres. by Sarah Little, his widow & Exec. [2:198/9].

Inv. of Est. of DEBORAH JENKINS, widow, dtd. 15 March 1707/8,
pres. by Joseph Butterworth of Swan., Adm. Apprs: John Thurber & John Kinnicut [2:200].

Order that debts against Est. of THOMAS MAKEPEACE of Taun. be
paid by Mary Makepeace, his widow & Adm., dtd. 7 Apr. 1708
[2:200/1].

Div. of Est. of JOSEPH WOOD of Taun., dtd. 5 May 1708, pres. by
Peter Walker. It was found improper & a new div. was ordered
[2:201].

Will of JOSEPH JACOB, Carpenter, of Brist., dtd. 26 May 1703,
prob. 22 Apr. 1708. Wife Hannah. Nathaniel Jacob, only surviving son. Wife Hannah called Nathaniel's mother. Witns:
John Lobdill, William Gillman & John Cary [2:202].

Inv. of Est. of JOSEPH JACOBES of Brist., dtd. 2 March 1707/8,
pres. by Hannah Jacob, widow & Exec. Apprs: John Cary, Belamy Bosworth & John Throope [2:203].

Blank Page [2:204].

Will of NICHOLAS TANNER of Swan., dtd. 17 Oct. 1699, prob. 13
May 1708. Wife mentioned but not named. Cousins: Hannah Squire,
James Thomas, Margaret Squire & John Thomas. Cousins John Thomas & Margaret Squire to be Execs. Witns: Benjamin Carpenter & Benjamin Carpenter, Jr. [2:205].

The widow [not named] of NICHOLAS TANNER of Swan. appeared in
court on 13 May 1708 & asked more time to decide if she would
accept her husband's will. On 20 June 1708 she appeared again
& refused to accept the will, requesting her right as the law
allows [2:205].

Agrmt. btwn. John Thomas, Exec. of will of NICHOLAS TANNER of
Swan., & Mary Tanner, widow of Nicholas, dtd. 6 Oct. 1708,
for her to get her 3rds as the law allows. Witns: Thomas Wood
& John Cary [2:206].

Will of SAMUEL PECK of Reho, dtd. 11 June 1705, prob. 2 June
1708. No wife mentioned. Only son Noah Peck. Dau. Sarah Sabin.
son-in-law Nathaniel Samuel Paine [sic], who is later referred
to merely as Samuel Paine. Grdaus. Anne Paine & Sarah Paine.
Gives to son Noah "the time I have in Abigail Negro," and "the
time I have by Indenture in Joseph Paine." Refers to "the
Contract made with my wife before Mariage." Witns: John Butterworth, Daniel Smith & Daniel Carpenter [2:207].

Inv. of Est. of Deacon SAMUEL PECK of Reho., dtd. 10 May 1708,
pres. by Noah Peck, son & Exec. Apprs: John Butterworth, Moses
Read & Daniel Smith [2:208].

Inv. of Est. of SAMUEL WHEATON of Swan., dtd. 1 June 1708, pres.
by Hannah Wheaton, his widow. Apprs: John Allen of Brist. &
Edward Luther of Swan. On 4 May 1701 an addition of 3 items
was made to the Inv. [2:209].

Acct. of Est. of EDWARD THURBER of Swan., dtd. 5 May 1708, pres.
by Margaret Thurber, his widow & Adm. An order of the court
directed a div., parts to go to: his widow Margaret, his son
Richard Thurber & his unnamed dau. [2:210].

Inv. of Est. of NICHOLAS TANNER of Swan., dtd. 5 May 1708, pres.
by John Thomas of Swan., Exec. Apprs: Elisha May, John West
& Joseph Mason [2:211].

Inv. of Est. of JOHN BRIANT of Taun. "who dyed at Sippiran about
ten years ago," dtd. 5 Aug. 1707, pres. by Mary Briant, dau. of
John. Apprs: Henry Hodges, Nathaniel Thayer, Thomas Harvey
& Robert Crossman [2:212].

Order to Mary Makepeace, Adm. of Est. of THOMAS MAKEPEACE, that
she pay 10 shillings for every 20 shillings due to creditors
to settle the Est., which is near insolvency, dtd. 4 Aug.
1708 [2:213].

Acct. of William Brunell, Adm. of Est. of JONATHAN TRIPP of Dart.
dtd. 4 Aug. 1708. Mentions items in the Inv. set forth for the
widow & 4 unnamed chldn. Incl. debts paid to abt. 24 people
[2:213/4].

Acct. of Est. of JOHN BRYANT of Taun., dtd. 4 Aug. 1708, pres.
by John Briant, his son [2:214].

Acct. of Mary Derby (formerly Bryant), one of the Adms. of Est.
of JOHN BRYANT of Taun., dtd. 4 Aug. 1708. Mentions paym. of
debt to "Samuel Derby to Carry the citation to Rochester."
The court ordered div. of the remaining Est., making 5 shares
for 4 unnamed chldn. [2:214/5].

Acct. of Elizebeth Downes, widow & Adm. of Est. of her husb. WIL-
LIAM DOWNES of Brist., dtd. 18 Sept. 1708. Incl. item to Maj.
Walley for rent. Mentions that the widow Elizebeth has 3 young
chldn. to bring up, so the remaining small Est. was granted
to her [2:216].

Inv. of Est. of Deacon JOHN BUTTERWORTH of Brist., dtd. 6 Oct.
1708, pres. by John & Joseph Butterworth, sons & Adms. Apprs:
John Cary & James Adames [2:217].

Rcpt. by George Jenkins for legacy rcvd. from "my uncle Joseph
Butterworth of Swanzey Administrator to the Estate of my Hon[rd]
Grandfather John Butterworth & the Estate left by my late mother Deborah Jenkins and all the Estate of my late brother Ebenezer Jenkins all Deceased," dtd. 1 March 1713/4 [2:217].

Will of NATHANIEL REYNOLDS of Brist., dtd. 7 Oct. 1706, prob. 3
Nov. 1708. No wife mentioned. 5 sons: Nathaniel Reynolds of
Boston (eldest), John, Peter, Joseph & Benjamin (youngest)
Reynolds. Daus: Sarah ffosdick wife of John ffosdick of Bos-
ton, Mary Woodbery, Hannah Royall wife of Samuel Royall of
Boston & Ruth Reynolds. Sister Mary Sanger of Watertown.

Mentions his houses in Boston, his farm & house in Brist. &
his 500 acres in Quenepank. Witns: Samuel Penfield, Lidia
Cary & John Cary [2:218/9/20].

Inv. of Est. of JOHN PEARCE of Tiv., dtd. 20 Dec. 1707, pres.
by Mary Pearce, his widow. Apprs: William Willbor, George
Pearce & Richard Barden [2:221].

Inv. of Est. of JOHN HALL, Jr. of Taun., dtd. 17 June 1708, pres.
by Elizebeth Hall, his widow. Mentions his sister Hannah Hall
& his unnamed mother. Apprs: Thomas Leonard, Henry Hodges &
Edward Richmond [2:222].

Inv. of Est. of SAMUEL LEONARD of Reho., dtd. 26 Nov. 1708, pres.
by Mary Leonard, his widow. Apprs: Moses Read & Daniel Smith
[2:223].

Acct. of Moses Read, Adm. of Est. of NATHANIEL CHAFFEE of Reho.,
dtd. 5 July 1708. Mentions there is only one child left by Nathaniel: Dorothy Chaffee, abt. 6 yrs. old. The child's mother
is Mercy, now wife of James Read of Reho., Tanner. Said James
Read & wife Mercy appt. guard. of dau. Dorothy [2:224].

Inv. of Est. in Brist. of Capt. NATHANIEL REYNOLDS of Brist.,
dtd. 28 Dec. 1708, pres. by John Reynolds, Peter Reynolds,
Joseph Reynolds & Benjamin Reynolds, all : sons of Nathaniel.
Apprs: Dan Throope & William Throope [2:225].

Inv. of Est. in the south end of Boston of Capt. NATHANIEL REY-
NOLDS of Brist., dtd. at Boston 3 Nov. 1708. Apprs: Joseph
Hill & Josiah ffranklin [2:225].

Inv. of Est. of JOSHUA SMITH of Swan. who died 21 Jan. 1707/8,
dtd. 19 Feb. 1707/8, pres. by Zachariah Bicknell of Swan.,
Adm. Inv. requested by Rachel Smith, widow of Joshua, & by
Samuel Andross & Zachariah Bignall who married 2 of the sisters of Joshua & who are "Attorneys for the rest of the Daughters." Mentions land in Weymouth & in Swan. Apprs. in Weymouth: John Pratt & William Terrey; none listed for Swan. [2:
226/7].

Inv. of Est of ELIZEBETH BARNES of Swan. who died 27 Nov. 1708,
dtd. 27 Dec. 1708, pres. by John King of Providence, eldest
son. Apprs: Thomas Allen & Benony Price [2:228].

Inv. of Est. of JOHN SHEPERSON of Attl., dtd. 3 Dec. 1708, pres.
by Elizebeth Sheperson, his widow. Apprs: Daniel Jenckes &
Hezekiah Peck [2:229].

Acct. of Est. of HENRY STACEY, dtd. 5 Jan. 1708/9, pres. by William Crawford, Attorney in behalf of his mother, Mrs. Freelove
Crawford, Adm. for Henry. Court directed an Inv. of the insolvent Est. be taken [2:229/30].

Acct. of Est. of REMEMBER BRIGGS of Taun., dtd. 5 Jan. 1708,
pres. by Mary Staple, his widow & Exec. Contains "debts payd
out of s^d Estate in ye Year 1696/7" [2:231].

Inv. of Est. of Ensign HENRY STACEY of Reho., dtd. 10 Feb. 1708/9.
Apprs: John Butterworth, Moses Read & Daniel Smith [2:232].

Adm. of Est. of THOMAS NEWMAN granted to his son Thomas Newman,

it having been rcvd. by him from "the hands of his Brother
John Safford," previous Adm., dtd. 30 June 1691 at Salem, Essex County. Recorded at Brist. 27 Sept. 1701 [2:232].

Inv. of Est. of NATHANIEL DAGGETT of Reho., dtd. 30 Dec. 1708,
pres. by Rebekah, his widow & Exec. Apprs: John Butterworth,
Samuel Mason & Daniel Smith [2:233].

Inv. of Est. of NATHANIEL DAGGET left to him by his father JOHN
DAGGET in reversion after his mother's decease, dtd. 30 Dec.
1708. Same apprs. as above [2:233/4].

Inv. of Est. of NICHOLAS HOW of Lit. Comp. who died 30 Dec. 1708
dtd. 2 March 1708/9, pres. by Elenor How, his widow [2:234].

Acct. of Samuel Penfield, Adm. of Est. of Lt. THOMAS FRY, dtd.
2 March 1708/9 [2:234/5].

Agrmt. abt. settl. of Est. of Capt. SAMUEL WOODBURY, Mariner,
of Brist., dtd. 3 March 1708/9, signed by his widow & chldn:
William ffulton, "Chiriurgion" of Brist. & Mary ffulton his
wife & widow of Samuel Woodbury; Jonathan Woodbery (son), Mariner of Brist.; Samuel Woodbery (son), Shipwright of Newport;
& Doctor William ffulton as guard. of Sarah Woodbury (dau.).
Witns: Constant Church & John Cary [2:236].

Rcpt. by sisters of JOSHUA SMITH of Swan. for legacies from his
Est., he having "left no child but five sisters," namely: Mary
wife of Samuel Pettes of Weymouth, Elizebeth wife of Samuel
Andross of Milton, Joanna wife of Josiah Ripley, Hannah wife
of Zachariah Bicknell & Sarah wife of Joseph Orcut (all but
2nd "of Weymouth"). Legacies paid by Samuel Andross & Zachry
Becknel, dtd. 5 March 1707/8. Witns: Abial Whitman, Sr. &
Abiah Whitman [2:237].

Rcpt. by Rachel Smith of Swan., widow of JOSHUA SMITH, Yeoman,
for legacy paid by Samuel Andross, Carpenter of Milton, & by
Zachariah Bicknell, Yeoman of Weymouth, Adms.,dtd. 25 March
1708/9. Witns: Thomas Tiffany & Ebenezer Allin [2:238].

Rcpt. & release by Mary Smith, widow, of Weymouth, for a legacy
from Est. of her son JOSHUA SMITH of Swan., paid by Samuel
Andross of Milton & Zachry Bicknel of Weymouth, Adms., dtd.
10 Apr. 1708 in County of Suffolk. Witns: Steven ffrench &
William Pratt [2:239].

Rcpt. & release by Samuel Andross, Housewright, of Milton, for
legacy from Est. of his bro.-in-law JOSHUA SMITH of Swan.,
paid by his bro.-in-law Zachry Bicknell, Adm., dtd. 3 Aug.
1708. Witns: Stephen ffrench & Joseph Orcutt [2:239/40].

Acct. of Hannah Wheatton, Adm. of Est. of her husb. SAMUEL
WHEATTON, dtd. 3 May 1709. Mentions "her brother Nathaniel
Wheatton" [brother-in-law?]. Also mentions her only child Samuel Wheaton, who was abt. 2 mo. old when his father died. Hannah was appt. guard. of son Samuel [2:240/1].

Order for div. of real est. of JONATHAN BRIGGS, Husbandman, of
Taun., dcd. intest., dtd. 5 May 1708 [2:242].

Div. of real est. of JONATHAN BRIGGS of Taun. among his chldn:
sons Jonathan Briggs (eldest), David Briggs, John Briggs,

John Briggs, Thomas Briggs, Amos Briggs, Benjamin Briggs, Eb-
enezer Briggs & Nathaniel Briggs. Mentions son to make payms.
"to the sisters" [not named]. Comm: Ephraim Hathaway, Edward
Shove, Jared Talbut, Abram Hathaway & Ebenezer Pitts[2:242/3].
John Thomas, Exec. of Est. of NICHOLAS TANNER of Swan., is gran-
ted more time to finish his admin., dtd. 1 June 1709 [2:243].
Will of JERIMIAH OSBORN of Brist., dtd. 27 July 1708, prob. 6
Apr. 1709. Wife Mercey. Mentions "my young children." Son
John Osborn to recv. double portion, but other chldn. not
named. Witns: John Birge, Peter Reynolds & John Cary[2:244].
Inv. of Est. of JERIMIAH OSBORN of Brist., dtd. 24 March 1709,
pres. by Mercey Osborne, his widow. Apprs: Simon Davis & Wil-
liam ffulton [2:245/6].
Acct. of Est. of JOHN PEARCE of Tiv., dtd. 1 June 1709, pres. by
Mary Pearce, Adm. [2:246/7].
Request for div. of Est. of Capt. SAMUEL WOODBURY of Brist.,
dtd. 3 Dec. 1707, pres. by Jonathan Woodbury, Adm. [2:247].
Order for div. of real est. at Taun. among the 4 chldn. [not
named] of JOHN BRYANT, who dcd. at Rochester, dtd. 1 Dec. 1708
[2:248].
Div. of real est. of JOHN BRYANT of Rochester, dtd. 7 Apr. 1709.
Only son John Bryant. Daus: Mary Derby wife of Samuel Derbee,
Elizebeth Bryant & Experience Bryant. Comm: Thomas Leonard,
Henry Hodges, Thomas Harvey, Jared Talbut & John Andrewes
[2:248/9].
Acct. of John Thomas, nephew & Exec. of Est. of NICHOLAS TANNER
of Swan., dtd. 6 Sept. 1709 [2:249].
Release by Margarit Squire for legacy from Est. of NICHOLAS TAN-
NER, rcvd. from John Thomas, Exec., dtd. 10 Dec. 1709 [2:249].
Release by Hannah Squire for legacy from Est. of NICHOLAS TANNER
rcvd. from John Thomas, Exec., dtd. 18 March 1708/9 [2:249].
Will of NATHANIEL DAGGET of Reho., dtd. 14 Dec. 1708, prob. 5
Jan. 1708/9. Wife Rebecah. Sons: Nathaniel, John & Amos Dagget.
Daus: Rebecah Dagget, Jemima Dagget & Abigail Dagget (all un-
der age). Friends Samuel Mason & Daniel Smith of Reho. to be
Overseers. Witns: John Butterworth, Samuel Mason & Daniel
Smith [2:250].
Inv. of Est. of AARON CLARK of Swan., dtd. 15 March 1708/9, pres.
by Sarah Clark, his widow. Apprs: Benjamin Carpenter, ffran-
cis Willson & John Barney [2:251].
Acct. of Richard Bowen, Adm. of Est. of SAMUEL TITUS of Reho.,
dtd. 5 Jan. 1708/9 [2:252].
Debts due from Est. of HENRY STACEY, undated but reported by
John Butterworth & Daniel Smith [2:253].
Acct. of Est. of HENRY STACEY, dtd. 6 July 1709, pres. by Wil-
liam Crawford of Providence on behalf of his mother, ffreelove
Crawford, Adm. Incl. Inv. & paym. of debts. Est. now insolvent [2:253/4].

Will of JONAH PALMER, Sr., Husbandman, of Reho., dtd. 22 Sept.
1704, prob. 6 July 1709. Wife Abigail. Mentions agrmt. made
with her before their marriage. Sons: Samuel (eldest) & Jonah
Palmer. Eldest 3 daus: Hannah French, Mary Dagget & Martha
[*no surname*]. Also dau. Grace Carpenter. Grson. Samuel Palmer
son of son Samuel. 3 sons [*not named*] of my son Jonah. Grchldn.
Jonah & Joseph Titus. Grchldn. Stephen Carpenter, Lidia Carpenter & Gershom Carpenter. Ensign Moses Read to be Exec. &
he shared equally with son Samuel Palmer in receiving the
home lot. Cash to Joseph Ormsbee [*apparently hired man*].
Witns: Daniel Carpenter, John Ormsbee & Preserved Abell [2:
255/6].
Inv. of pers. est. of JONAH PALMER, Sr. of Reho., dtd. 5 July
1709, pres. by Samuel Palmer & Ensign Moses Read [2:256].
Will of THOMAS LEWIS of Brist., dtd. 11 Aug. 1708, prob. 6 July
1709. Aged wife Hannah. Mentions "my sons & daughters," but
only names dau. Hepzebath. Witns: David Cary, John Cary &
Abigail Howland [2:257].
Inv. of THOMAS LEWIS of Brist., dtd. 31 May 1709, pres. by Hannah Lewis, his widow. Apprs: Samuel Gallap & John Cary[2:258].
Agrmt. btwn. Elizebeth Fuller, widow of JONATHAN FULLER of Attl.
& their chldn: David Fuller of Attl.; Daniel Fuller & Nathaniel Fuller both of Windham, County of Hartford, Conn.; Thomas
Fuller, Robert Fuller & Noah Fuller of Attl.; Elizebeth Shepherdson, widow of John Sheperson late of Attl.; John Follett
& Sarah his wife of Attl.; & Stephen Cross of Mansfield, Co.
of Hartford & his wife Mary. Witns: Mary Weeks & John Fuller
[2:259/60/1].
Agrmt. abt. settl. of Est. of JOHN PEARCE of Tiv., dtd. 3 Aug.
1709, signed by chldn: John Pearce (only son) of Tiv.; John
Read, Jr. of Free. & Mary (eldest dau.) his wife; Samuel Sher-
men of Swan. & Sarah (4th dau.) his wife; Thomas Cooke, Jr.
of Tiv. & his wife Elizebeth (5th dau.), John Cook (son of
John Cooke) of Tiv. & Rachel (6th dau.) his wife; & Alice
Pearce (youngest) of Tiv. Mentions thirds to go to "our hon[d]
mother Mary Pearce" [*2nd & 3rd daus. not listed*][2:261/2].
Will of JOHN DEVEL, Jr. of Dart., dtd. 8 Aug. 1709, prob. 7
Sept. 1709. Wife Marah. Sons William & Jonathan Devel. Daus:
Hannah Devel (under 20), Abyah & Meribeth (both under 18).
Witns: Joseph Tripp, James Tripp & George Cadman [2:263].
Inv. of Est. of JOHN DEVEL of Dart., dtd. 13 Aug. 1709, pres.
by Marah Devel, his widow. Apprs: Joseph Tripp, James Tripp
& George Cadman [2:264].
Will of ROBERT MILLERD of Reho., Tanner, dtd. 4 May 1709, prob.
7 Sept. 1709. Wife Charity. Sons: John, Samuel, Robert & Ben-
jamin (all under age) Millerd. Daus: Charity, Rachel, Patience
& Mary (all under 18). Witns: Samuel Bulluck, William Wood
& Joseph Mason [2:265].
Inv. of Est. of ROBERT MILLERD of Reho. who died 7 Aug. 1709,

dtd. 22 Aug. 1709, pres. by Charity Millerd, his widow. Mentions land at Reho., Swan. & Attl. Apprs: Samuel Bullock, John Brooks, William Wood & Joseph Mason [2:266].

Noah Fuller of Attl. granted more time as Adm. of Est. of his father JONATHAN FULLER of Attl., dtd. 3 May 1710 [2:266].

Acct. of Mary Pearce, widow & Adm of Est. of her husb. JOHN PEARCE of Tiv., dtd. 7 Sept. 1709. Daus: Mary Read, Susanah Woodall dcd., Anne Sheffield dcd., Sarah Shearman, Elizebeth Cooke & Rachel Cooke. Only son John Pearce [2:267/8].

Acct. of William Pabodie, son & Adm. of Est. of his father WILLIAM PABODIE of Lit. Comp., dtd. 7 Sept. 1709. Legacies to: sisters Mary, Mercey, Martha, Priscilla, Sarah, Ruth, Hannah, Lidiah, heirs of sister Elizebeth & the husband [not named] of sister Rebecah [2:268/9].

Acct. of Est. of SAMUEL PERREY of Reho., dtd. 1 March 1709, pres. by Samuel Perrey, son & Exec., & by his guard. Timothy Ide, both of Reho. Mentions legacies to: my mother [not named] & my sisters Elizebeth Perrey & Rebecca Perrey [2:269].

Will of THOMAS BRAMAN of Taun. No. Purch., dtd. 19 June 1709, prob. 31 Aug. 1709. Wife Hannah. Mentions "my sons & daughters," but names only sons Daniel (to rcv. double portion) & John ("who is already bound out"). Witns: George Leonard, Robert Tucker & Nathaniel ffisher [2:270].

Inv. of Est. of BENJAMIN POTTER of Dart., dtd. 5 Dec. 1709, pres. by Mary Potter, his widow. Apprs: George Cadman, James Tripp & George Wood [2:271].

Inv. of Est. of JOSEPH HIX of Dart., dtd. 9 Aug. 1709, pres. by Mary Hix, his widow. Apprs: George Cadman, John Akin & William Wood [2:272].

Capt. John Butterworth & Joseph Butterworth granted more time to adm. the Est. of their father Deacon JOHN BUTTERWORTH, dtd. 6 Apr. 1710 [2:272].

Inv. of Est. of Capt. JOHN BROWN of Swan., dtd. 17 Dec. 1709, pres. by Anne Brown, his widow. Apprs: Thomas Allen, William Wood & Joseph Mason [2:273].

An order granting remaining Est. of WILLIAM BRENTON, Mariner, of Brist., to his eldest son Benjamin Brenton, with shares to be paid to the heirs of Maj. Ebenezer Brenton now dcd. (previous Adm.) & to bro. Jahleel Brenton, dtd. 30 Jan. 1709/10 [2:274].

Will of DEBORAH SOULE of Dart., widow of George Soule, Sr., dcd. dtd. 24 Jan. 1708/9, prob. 1 March 1709/10. Sons: William & Nathan Soule. Daus: Sarah Soule, Mary Devell & Lidiah Brownel. Grdau. Mary Soule dau. of my son George Soule dcd. Witns: Silvanus Soule, Jacob Soule & Nathaniel Soule [2:275].

Inv. of Est. of DEBORAH SOULE of Dart., dtd. 1 March 1709/10, pres. by Sarah Soule, dau. & Exec. [2:275].

Will of JOHN LAPHAM of Dart., dtd. 5 Dec. 1709, prob. 5 Apr. 1710. Wife Mary. 2 sons: John & Nicholas Lapham. Dau. Mary

Dyer. Witns: Judah Smith, John Tucker & Valentine Hudlestone [2:276].
Inv. of Est. of JOHN LAPHAM of Dart., dtd. 5 Apr. 1710, pres.
by Mary Lapham, his widow, & by John Lapham, son. Apprs: John Tucker & Valentine Hudelstone [2:277].
Will of STEPHEN PAINE of Reho., dtd. 13 Feb. 1709/10, prob. 6 Apr. 1710. Wife Mary. Sons: Stephen (eldest, under 21) & Edward Paine. Wife Mary & Lt. John Butterworth & Ens. Moses Read to be Execs. Witns: Nathaniel Chaffee, Daniel Chaffee & Daniel Carpenter [2:278/9].
Inv. of STEPHEN PAINE of Reho., dtd. 18 March 1709/10, pres. by Mary Paine, his widow. Apprs: Benjamin Hunt & Daniel Smith [2:279/80].
Acct. of Elizebeth Potter, widow & Adm. of Est. of her husb. NATHANIEL POTTER of Dart., dtd. 5 Apr. 1710. Legacies to: Mary Wilbore, Benjamin Potter, William Potter, Robert Kerbee, Benjamin Tripp & Samuel Potter [2:280].
Will of ISAACE DEAN of Taun., dtd. 15 Dec. 1709, prob. 11 Apr. 1710. Wife Hannah. Sons: Nathaniel & Jonathan Dean. Daus: Alice King, Abigail Terrey, Hannah Hodges, Mehettabel Dean, Abiah Dean & Deborah Dean. Witns: John Williams, Jonathan Williams & Seth Leonard [2:281].
Acct. of Lt. Noah Peck of Reho., son & Adm. of Est. of Deacon SAMUEL PECK of Reho., dtd. 4 Jan. 1709/10 [2:282].
Rcpts. for legacies from Est. of Deacon SAMUEL PECK, paid by Noah Peck, Exec. to: Moses Read Attorney for John Sabin & his wife Sarah dau. of Deacon Peck, & to John Butterworth Attorney for Samuel Paine & his chldn. that he had by Anne his wife dau. of Deacon Peck, dtd. 22 June 1709 [2:282].
Inv. of Est. of ISAAC DEANE of Taun., dtd. 2 Feb. 1709/10, pres. by Hannah Dean, his widow, & by Nathaniel Dean, son, Execs. Apprs: Thomas Leonard, Henry Hodges & Thomas Dean [2:283].
Inv. of Est. of NATHANIEL WHEATON of Swan. who died 20 Nov. 1709 dtd. 22 [no month] 1709/10, pres. 5 Apr. 1710 by John Wheaton of Swan., his father. Apprs: Joseph Mason & John Kenicut [2:284].
Inv. of Est. of ISAAC SPOONER of Dart. who died 27 Dec. 1709, dtd. 31 Dec. 1709, pres. by Alice Spooner, his widow. Apprs: Jonathan Dellano & Thomas Hathaway [2:284/5].
Order for div. of Est. of JOHN PEARCE, Yeoman, of Tiv. dcd. intest., dtd. 24 July 1709 [2:285].
Div. of Est. of JOHN PEARCE of Tiv. btwn. his widow Mary Pearce & his chldn: son John Pearce; Amos Sheffield as guard. of his chldn. [not named] by late wife Anne Sheffield dcd., dau. of John Pearce; Mary, Susanah & Sarah Woodall, daus. of Richard Woodall by Susanah his wife dcd., dau. of John Pearce, Amos Sheffield being guard. of said Mary, Susanah & Sarah Woodall. Comm: Edward Grey, Daniel Howland & William Manchester [2:285/6].
Will of AMOS SHEFFIELD, Blacksmith, of Tiv., dtd. 17 Apr. 1707,

prob. 9 June 1710. 4 chldn: son John Sheffield (under 16) &
3 daus. Susana, Mary & Ruth Sheffield (all under 16). My father-in-law John Pearce & Mary Pearce his now wife to be Execs. & to bring up my chldn. Mentions Elizebeth Cook as aunt
of said chldn. Witns: John Lindsay, Thomas Cory & Samuel Jennings. Will mentions no wife, but on 7 June 1710 appeared in
court Sarah Sheffield, widow of Amos & requested her rights
as the law allows for herself & her child Aron Sheffield [2:
287/8].

Inv. of Est. of AMOS SHEFFIELD of Tiv., dtd. 1 Apr. 1710, pres.
by Mary Pearce, Exec. Apprs: Edward Grey, Joseph Wanton &
John Reed, Jr. [2:289].

Will of OBADIAH BOWEN, Yeoman, of Swan., "being Grown Ancient,"
dtd. 11 Dec. 1708, prob. 14 Oct. 1710. No wife mentioned. Son
Samuel Bowen of Cohansey; grsons. Aron Bowen, Daniel Bowen &
Nathan Bowen sons of my son Obadiah Bowen dcd.; son Joseph
Bowen; James Bowen & Hezekiah Bowen [*relation not stated*] get
land recorded in land records as to William Bowen; son Thomas
Bowen to be Exec. Dau. Hannah Brooks. To Lidia Mason [*rela-
tion not stated*]. Grdaus. Katherine Bowen, Sarah Bowen, Allice
Bowen & Elizebeth Bowen. Mentions his lands in Attleborough,
Rehoboth & Swan.   Witns: Caleb Eddy, John Paddock & John De-
votion [2:290/1].

Inv. of Est. of OBADIAH BOWEN of Swan., dtd. 4 Oct. 1710, pres
by Thomas Bowen, Exec. Apprs: Caleb Eddy & John Cary [2:291].

End of Volume 2

Will of OBADIAH BOWEN of Swan, Yeoman, dtd. 11 Dec. 1708, prob.
14 Oct. 1710. Sons: Samuel Bowen of Cohanzey, Joseph Bowen,
[torn] Bowen, Hezekiah Bowen & Thomas Bowen. Dau. Hannah Brooks
Lidia Mason [dau.?]. Grsons: Aaron, Daniel & Nathan Bowen sons
of my son Obadiah dcd.; grdaus: Katherine Bowen, Sarah Bowen,
Allice Bowen & Mary Bowen. Witns: Job Eddy, John Paddock[3:1/2].
Will of NICHOLAS PECK of Reho., dtd. 2 Oct. 1707, prob. 22 Nov.
1710. Sons: Joseph, Hezekiah, Jonathan & Elisha Peck. Daus:
Mary Smith wife of Ensign [torn] Smith, Martha wife of [torn].
Witns: Samuel Peck, John Butterworth & Daniel Smith [3:3/4].
Inv. of NICHOLAS PECK, dtd. 25 Oct. 1710, pres. by Joseph & Jon-
athan Peck, sons. Apprs: John Butterworth, Moses Read & Daniel
Smith [3:5].
Will of JAMES BROWN of Swan., Gent., being about 71 years of age,
dtd. 25 Oct. 1694, prob. 11 Jan. 1710/1. Wife Lidia. Sons:
James & Jabez Brown. Dau. Dorothy Kent. Witns: Samuel Newman,
Samuel Viall & John Bullock [3:6/7].
Inv. of JAMES BROWN of Swan., dtd. 29 Oct. 1710, pres. by Lidia
Brown of Swan., widow & Exec. Apprs: Samuel Mason, Thomas Al-
len & Joseph Mason [3:8].
Will of DAVID WHIPPLE of Reho., dtd. 24 March 1709/10, prob. 8
Jan. 1710/1. Wife Hannah. Sons: David, Israel Jeremiah & Wil-
liam. Daus: Sarah Whipple, Abigail Whipple & Deborah Towers.
Witns: Wm. Jenckes, Tho. Whipple & Obadiah Jenckes [3:9/10].
Inv. of Est. of Ensign DAVID WHIPPLE of Reho., dtd. 1 Jan. 17-
10/11, pres. by Hannah Whipple, widow & Exec. Apprs: Daniel
Jenckes, Daniel Smith & Silvanous S[torn][3:11/2].
Inv. of Est. of DANIEL READ of Reho., dtd. 10 Nov. 1710, pres.
by Hannah Read, his widow, & Daniel Read, his son. Apprs: Mo-
ses Read, Daniel Smith & Benjamin Hunt [3:13].
Agrmt. btwn. Samuel Newman & David Newman, sons of SAMUEL NEW-
MAN of Reho., dtd. 2 Jan. 1710/1. Witns: Thomas Greenwood,
Preserved Abell & Elizebeth Greenwood [3:14].
Will of SAMUEL NEWMAN of Reho., dtd. 25 Feb. 1702, prob. 5 Feb.
1710/1. Wife Theodosha. Sons: Samuel & David Newman, Grson.
Daniel Smith (under age). Witns: Nathaniel Paine, John Spar-
hawk & Joseph Pratt [3:15].
Inv. of Est. of SAMUEL NEWMAN of Reho., dtd. 28 Dec. 1710, pres.
by Dea. Sam. Newman, Exec. Apprs: Benj. Hunt & Dan. Smith[3:16].
Rcpt. by Daniel Smith for legacy from Est. of his grfath. SAMUEL
NEWMAN, paid by Samuel & David Newman, Execs., dtd. 8 Nov. 1714
Witns: Dan. Carpenter & Jabez Carpenter [3:17].
Inv. of JOSIAH WOOD, dtd. Dart. 26 June 1710, pres. by Philip Ta-
ber, Adm. Apprs: Ebenezer P[illegible] & Icabod Potter [3:18].

Inv. of Est. of JOHN JENNINGS, dtd. 4 Jan. 1710/1, pres. 5 Feb. 1710/1 by Joseph Jennings, his father. Witns: George Pearce & Samuel Tompkins [3:18].

Quit claim granted by Hezekiah Luther, Jr. & his wife Martha "whose maiden name was Gardner Daughter of Mr Samuel Gardner of Swanzey," to "our brother" Samuel Gardner of Swan., giving up all right to the Est. of their father SAMUEL GARDNER of Swan., dtd. 16 Jan. 1710/1. Witns: William Anthony & Edward Luther [3:19].

Acct. of Sarah Soule, Exec. of Est. of DEBORAH SOULE of Dart., dtd. 7 March 1710/1. Sarah mentions "my brother William Soule," "Mary Devil my sister," "Lidia Brown my sister," "Mary Soule daughter of my late brother George Soule" & "my brother Nathan Soule" [3:20].

Will of JOSEPH CHURCH, Esq., of Lit. Comp., dtd. 15 Feb. 1710/1, prob. 12 March 1710/1. Wife ment. but not named. Sons: Joseph (eldest) & John Church. Daus: Elizabeth Blackman wife of Joseph Blackman, Mary Wood wife of John Wood, Deborah Grey wife of Samuel Grey & Abigail Simons wife of William Simons. Mary Tocockono, employed by dcd. "My Indian boy Amos." Friends Thomas Church & John Palmer to be Overseers. Witns: John Palmer, Jonathan Davenport & Edward Thurston [3:21/2/3].

Inv. of Est. of JOSEPH CHURCH of Lit. Comp. who died the 5th of March 1711, dtd. 12 March 1711, pres. by Joseph & John Church, sons & Execs., recorded 13 March 1710/1. Apprs: Thomas Church John Palmer, Joseph Wilbore & Edward Richmond [3:24/5/6].

Inv. of Est. of NATHANIEL TOOGOOD of Swan. who died 8 Feb. 1709/10, dtd. 27 May 1710, pres. 7 June 1710 by John Toogood, brother & Adm. Apprs: Joseph Mason & John Kenicut [3:26/7].

Claim of Benjamin Carpenter on the Est. of NATHANIEL TOOGOOD, made as guard. of "the children of his now wife (by her former Husband Mr Nathaniel Toogood Senr)," dtd. 7 May 1711 [3:27].

Acct. of John Hunt & John Whitticer, Adms. of Est. of NATHANIEL WHITTICER of Reho., pres. 4 March 1710/1. Mentions an item to pay for the funeral of Elizabeth Whitticer; an item for "Sundry Cloathing for the children;" "an item for linen for the Infant Child;" and item "to ffrancis Wilson to help bring up one of the Little Child:;" next item "to Samuel Whitticer for Ditto;" "a "Camlet Coate" to Philip Whittaker & items "to John Whitticer;" Nathaniel Whittaker (eldest son of the dcd.); "the rest of them: Philip, Experience, Margaret, Hannah & Rebecca" [3:28/9/30].

Copy of Will of JOHN MACKINTOSHE, dtd. 11 May 1708 at Paramarib in Suriname, registered in the secretary's office in Suriname, entered in Bristol records 26 Apr. 1711. To the "poor of ye beneath division of Comamma in the Collony Sirriname." To "my Uncle Henry Mackintosh." Abraham Kinkbnysen, Secy. of the Colony Surinam, called the dcd. "John Mackintosh young man." Witns: Isais Montzingh & Adrian Debruanne [3:31/2].

Will of PHILIP KING of Taun., dtd. 12 [torn], 1706/7, prob. 7
May 1711. Wife Judith. Daus: Mary Leonard, Elizabeth Hall,
Experience White, Hannah Paddlefoot [sic], Lidia King & Judith King. Son John King. Witns: Benjamin Dyar, Samuel Bad-
lam & Stephen ffrench [3:32½/32].

Inv. of Est. of Ensign PHILIP KING who died in Taun. 26 Dec. 17-
10, dtd. 20 Jan. 171/1, pres. 7 May 1711 by John King, Exec.
[3:32/33].

Acct. of Est. of JOHN LAPHAM of Dart. by son John Lapham in behalf of his mother Mary Lapham, pres. 7 May 1711 [3:33].

Acct. by Elizabeth Sheppeson, widow & Adm. of JOHN SHEPPESON,
recorded 16 May 1711 [3:34].

Inv. of Est. of ROBERT FULLER of Attl., dtd. 17 Jan. 1710/1,
pres. by Mary ffuller his widow. Mentions debts owed to David ffuller & to John ffuller. Apprs: Jonathan Freeman, Thomas Tingley & John ffollett [3:35].

Will of EDWARD BISHOP of Reho., Innkeeper, dtd. 10 May 1711,
prob. 28 May 1711. Wife Sarah. Sons: Edward (eldest), Samuel,
William, Jonathan, Joseph, David, Benjamin ("if he lives to
come home"), John & Ebenezer Bishop. Daus: Priscilla Day wife
of Samuel Day & Sarah Jorden. Son-in-law Samuel Day. Grsons:
Edward Day & John Day sons (under 21) of Samuel Day. Witns:
Deacon Samuel Newman, Moses Read & Daniel Carpenter [3:36/7-
8/9].

Inv. of Est. of EDWARD BISHOP of Reho., dtd. 22 May 1711, pres.
28 May 1711 by Mrs. Sarah Bishop, his widow & Exec. [3:40].

Acct. of John Butterworth & Joseph Butterworth, Adms. of the
Est. of their father JOHN BUTTERWORTH of Brist., pres. 2 Apr.
1711. Mentions cash paid to "Mrs. Butterworth for her part of
her dower in s^d Estate" [3:41/2].

Div. of remainder of Est. of Deacon JOHN BUTTERWORTH, dtd. 2 Apr.
1711. To John Butterworth eldest son 2 shares; to Joseph Butterworth 1 share; to heirs of Benjamin Butterworth dcd. 1
share; to heirs of Sarah Howard dcd. 1 share; to heirs of Deborah Jenkins dcd. 1 share; and 1 share each to Mercy Blood,
Hopstill Edy wife of John Edy & Mary Thayer wife of Samuel
Thayer [3:42].

Order for div. of lands left to his six daus. by THOMAS WILLIAMS
of Taun., dtd. 16 Oct. 1710 [3:43].

Div. of lands of THOMAS WILLIAMS among his 6 daus., dtd. 28 Feb.
1710/1. Daus: Mary Robinson (eldest), Sarah Williams (2nd),
Hannah Williams (3rd), Bethiah (4th), Mehettabel (5th) & Da-
mareis (6th)[no surnames for last 3]. Comm: Thomas Leonard,
Henry Hodges, Thomas Harvey, James Leonard & John White[3:43/4].

Discharge from William Wood of Taun. & his wife [not named] to
John Wetherel & William Wetherel, Execs. of "the Estate of
our Brother EPHRAIM WETHEREL deceased," dtd. 20 March 1702/3.
Witns: John Richmond & Sarah Stasey. Notation that on 4 June
1710 "Sarah formerly Stasey now the wife of John Edy Took
Oath" [3:45].

Will of PETER WALKER of Taun., dtd. 3 Apr. 1711, prob. 2 July
1711. Sons: Peter (eldest), Edward & James Walker. Daus: Abi-
gail Walker (eldest), Katherine Walker (under 21) & Hannah
Walker (under 21). To "Thomas Eliot who did live with me."
Brother James Walker, where said Eliot now dwells. Paul Dud-
ley, Esq., Robert Crossman, Joseph Wood "and my Brother Eli-
azer Walker" to be Overseers. Witns: James Walker, Abel Burt
& Timothy Holloway [3:46/7].
Inv. of Est. of PETER WALKER of Taun., dtd. 24 Apr. 1711, pres.
2 July 1711 by Peter Walker, Exec. Apprs: John Smith, John
Crossman & Samuel Waldron [3:47/8].
Will of ABEL BURT of Taun., "being under sore sickness of bo-
dy," dtd. 31 May 1711, prob. 30 June 1711. No wife mentioned.
Sons: Seth, Abel, Joseph, Josiah & Jotham (last 4 under age).
Daus: Priscilla Burt & Miriam Burt. My sister Mary Burt (un-
mar.). Elder Hodges, my brother John Burt & brother Henry An-
drewes to be Overseers. Witns: Joseph ffrench, Benjamin Ter-
rey & Jonathan ffrench [3:49].
Inv. of Est. of ABEL BURT of Taun., dtd. 28 June 1711, pres.
30 June 1711 by Seth Burt, Exec. Apprs: John Crane, John Tisdale & Thomas Terrey [3:50].
Will of WILLIAM MACUMBER of Dart., dtd. 1 Apr. 1711, prob. 2
July 1711. Wife Mary. Sons: William, Thomas, Abiel, John &
Ephraim Macumber. Daus: Elizabeth (unmar.) & Mary Macumber.
Witns: Jonathan Daval, George Cadman & Nathan Soul [3:51/2].
Inv. of Est. of WILLIAM MACUMBER of Dart., dtd. 5 June 1711,
pres. by Mary Macumber, his widow & Exec. Apprs: Jonathan Da-
vel, William Wood & George Cadman [3:53].
Inv. of Est. of Widow REBECCA DAGGET of Reho., dtd. 27 Apr. 17-
11, pres. by George Wood of Reho., her son-in-law [3:54].
Will of Capt. NATHAN HAYMAN, Mariner, of Brist., "being in Good
health...being Called to hazard my frail life upon the Great
waters," dtd. 7 Jan. 1709, prob. 13 July 1711. Wife Priscilla.
Witns: Jonathan Woodbery, Peter Reynolds & John Cary [3:55].
Inv. of Est. of EDWARD ROBINSON of Dart., dtd. 10 Aug. 1711,
pres. by Joanna Robinson, his widow & Adm. Apprs: James Tripp,
Joseph Tripp & George Cadman [3:56].
Letter of Attorney granted to "my trusty friend Isaac Ayars of
Cohanze" (late of Rhode Island) by Samuel Bowen of Cohanze,
County of Salem, Province of West New Jersey, to be lawful at-
torney to receive from Thomas Bowen of Swan. a legacy from
the Est. of "his & my Hon^rd ffather OBADIAH BOWEN Senr," dtd.
16 Oct. 1711 at County of Glocester, Prov. of New Jersey.
Witns: Will: Parker & Sarah Wheaton [3:57].
Rcpt. by Isaac Ayars of Cohanze, County of Salem, Prov. of West
Jersey, for a legacy of money he rcvd., as attorney for Samuel Bowen of Cohanze, from Thomas Bowen of Swan., Adm. of Est.
of OBADIAH BOWEN, their father, dtd. 16 Nov. 1711. Witns: Nathaniel Millerd & John Cary [3:57/8].

Will of NATHANIEL BRIGGS of Taun., "bound forth on ye Expedition Against Canada," dtd. 9 July 1711, prob. 19 Nov. 1711. Brothers: Thomas, Benjamin, Ebenezer, John & David Briggs. Sister Experience Merrick. Cousin Damaris Bobit eldest dau. of Elkanah Bobit. David Briggs eldest son of my brother David Briggs. Witns: Sarah Blake, Benjamin Harvey & Dorothy Wood [3:58].

Inv. of Est. of NATHANIEL BRIGGS of Taun., dtd. 16 Nov. 1711, pres. by Thomas Briggs of Taun., his brother & Adm. Apprs. not named [3:58¼].

Rcpt. by Pardon Tillinghast for money rcvd. from Philip Walker of Reho. upon the acct. of HENRY SWEET of Attl., referring to acct. of Elizabeth Sweet, dtd. "about the year 1706," recorded 5 March 1711 [3:58¼].

Acct. of Est. of HENRY SWEET of Attl., by Elizabeth Sweet, his widow & Adm., dtd. 3 Nov. 1711 [3:58½].

Inv. of JOHN TERREY of Free., Blacksmith, dtd. 6 Nov. 1711, pres. by Remember Terrey, his widow & Adm. Apprs: Jonathan Dodson & John Read, Jr. [3:59/60].

Inv. of Est. of DANIEL HOWLAND of Tiv., dtd. 26 Jan. 1711/2, pres. by Mary Howland, his widow & Adm. Apprs: Joseph Wanton & Robert Dennice [3:61/2].

Inv. of Est. of NATHANIEL BRIGGS of Taun., dtd. 16 Nov. 1711, pres. by Thomas Briggs, brother & Exec. Apprs: Jared Tallbut, Abram Hathway & Isaac Hathway [*Same inv. as on p. 58¼, above*] [3:62].

Rcpts. by Thomas Eliot & Joseph Eliot on behalf of themselves & their sisters Elizabeth & Abigail Eliot for legacies from Est. of "ouf honrd ffather" THOMAS ELIOT, paid by Ensign Moses Read of Reho., dtd. 3 Aug. 1711 [3:63].

Antenuptial agrmt. & promise of engagement btwn. BENJAMIN FULLER of Reho. & Judith Smith, dtd. 3 Jan. 1698/9, pres. same day, recorded 29 Feb. 1711/2. Witns: Thomas Smith & Henry Smith [3:64].

Inv. of Est. of BENJAMIN FULLER of Reho., dtd. 23 Jan. 1711/2, pres. by Judith Fuller, his widow & Adm. Apprs: Moses Read, Abiah Carpenter & Daniel Smith [3:64/5].

Inv. of Est. of CHRISTOPHER HALL who died 3 July 1711, dtd. 16 Nov. 1711, pres. by Mary Hall of Attl., his widow. Apprs: John Fuller, Jonathan Fuller & Benjamin Robinson [3:66].

Inv. of Est. of ARTHUR HATHAWAY of Dart., who died 11 Dec. 1711, dtd. 17 Dec. 1711, pres. by John Hathaway, his son & Exec. Apprs: Thomas Taber & Jonathan Delano [3:67].

Will of ARTHUR HATHAWAY of Dart., dtd. 9 Feb. 1709/10, prob. 6 Feb. 1711/2. Wife Sarah. Sons: John, Thomas & Jonathan Hathaway. Daus: Mary Hammond, Lidia Sisson & Hannah Cadman. Witns: John Cannon, Jr., Isaac Howland & Jonathan Delano [3:68].

Authorization to Samuel Walker of Reho. to sell land owned by Sarah Perrum dau. of his sister, said Sarah being non compos mentis, and it being nec. to provide for her, dtd. 2nd Tue. of Sept. 1702, recorded 1 March 1711/2 [3:69].

Rcpt. by Anne Perrin & Ruth Perrin for legacies from the Ests. of theirfather ABRAHAM PERRIN of Reho. & their grandmother JANE POLLEY of Roxbury, paid by their guard. Cornet Samuel Walker of Reho., dtd. 13 Apr. 1708. Witns: Samuel Peck & Daniel Smith [3:69].

Rcpt. by Isaac Perren for legacy from the Ests. of his father ABRAHAM PERRIN of Reho. & his grandmother JANE POLLEY of Roxbury, paid by his guard. Capt. Samuel Walker of Reho., dtd. 29 Dec. 1711. Witns: Daniel Smith & Abigail Smith[3:71][*page 70 was omitted in numbering*].

Order for appraisal of real est. left by NATHANIEL WHITTACER of Reho., Husbandman, to be taken by Lt. John Hunt, Lt. Moses Read & Joseph Peck, dtd. 13 March 1710/1 [3:71/2].

Order that the real est. left by NATHANIEL WHITTAKER of Reho. be granted to Nathaniel Whitaker, eldest son. Also mentions son Nathaniel's duty to pay other "several children" their full shares., dtd. 5 Feb. 1711/2 [3:72].

Inv. of Est. of JOHN GOLD of Taun. who died 24 Dec. 1711, dtd. 29 Feb. 1711/2, pres. 5 March 1711/2 by John Gold, his eldest son & Adm. Notation made that in his will dtd. 11 Apr. 1692, John Gold named as Execs. his wife Mary Gold & Robert Crossman, Jr. Adm. granted 5 March 1711 to eldest son John since said Mary Gold is dead & Robert Crossman renounced Adm. Apprs. not listed [3:73].

Will of JAMES BURRILL of Dart., dtd. 7 Aug. 1711, prob. 3 March 1711/2. Sons James (under age) & ffrancis Burrill. Mentions eldest son [*not named*] "who follows the Sea." Daus: Elizabeth Dinah, Hannah, Jane & Sarah. My "sister Ward." Mentions Joseph Nicholson as being grandfather of "my children." Brother Joseph Burrill. Mentions paym. to be made "after my Mothers Decease." States that he disposed of his household goods to his daughters "after the Decease of my first wife." [*No subsequent wife mentioned*]. Nathaniel Howland & William Soul to be Adms. Witns: Joshua Sherman, Eliashib Smith, John Allen & George Howland [3:74].

Inv. of Est. of JAMES BURRILL of Dart., dtd. 7 Feb. 1711/2, pres. by Nathaniel Howland, Exec. Apprs: Philip Shearman & Joshua Shearman [3:75].

Power of Attorney granted to "Our well beloved Brother John Brooks" of Reho. by Timothy Brooks & Hannah Brooks his wife of Cohanse, County of Salem, Prov. of West New Jersey, that said John might rcv. the legacy to be paid by Thomas Bowen of Swan. "from his and our Hon[rd] ffather OBADIAH BOWEN Sen[r]," dtd. 16 Oct. 1711 at County of Glocester, Prov. of New Jersey. Witns: Samuel Bowen & Isaac Ayars [3:76].

Rcpt. by John Brooks of Swan., attorney for Timothy Brooks & Hannah his wife of Cohanze, County of Salem, Prov. of West

New Jersey, for legacy to said Hannah Brooks paid by Thomas
Bowen of Swan., Exec. of Est. of his father OBADIAH BOWEN of
Swan., dtd. 10 March 1711/2 [3:76/7].
Inv. of Est. of THOMAS COOPER of Reho., dtd. 12 Feb. 1711/2,
pres. by Thomas Cooper, his eldest son & Adm, Apprs: Moses
Read & Daniel Smith [3:77].
Agrmt. abt. settl. of Est. of THOMAS COOPER of Reho., btwn.
sons & daus. & sons-in-law: Thomas Cooper, Samuel Cooper,
Mary Cooper, Timothy Ide, Elizabeth Ide, Hezekiah Peck, Deb-
orah Peck, John Humphrey, Sarah Humphrey, John Robinson, Judith Robinson & James Read "in behalf of his children which
he had of his wife Mercey," all of Reho. & Attl., dtd. 8 Feb.
1711/2. Witns: Moses Read & Daniel Smith [3:78/9].
Agrmt. of distrib. of Est. of EDWARD BAYLEY of Tiv. btwn. his
widow & chldn., dtd. 7 Apr. 1712. Mentions a will he wrote 18
Aug. 1711 which could not be proved because of only 2 witns.
Widow ffrances Bayley. Chldn: Edward Bayley (eldest son), Sarah Bayley (dau.), John Bayley (son) & Elizabeth Manchester
(dau.) wife of George Manchester. Witns: Joseph Ginnings &
John Cary [3:80/1].
Will of JABEZ HOWLAND of Brist., Blacksmith, dtd. 14 May 1708,
prob. 21 Feb. 1711/2. Wife Bethiah. Son Jabez is Exec.with
his mother. Mentions "my four sons" [not named]. Witns: Dan
Throop, William Martin & John Cary [3:82].
Will of JOHN THURSTON of Reho., Blacksmith, dtd. 22 Nov. 1711,
prob. 7 Apr. 1712. Wife Hannah. Son David Thurston. 7 daus:
Sarah, Hannah, Bethiah, Rebeccah, Mehittabel, Pheebe & Jane.
Witns: Leonard Newsum, Philip Walker & Daniel Carpenter[3:83].
Inv. of JOHN THURSTON of Reho., dtd. 17 Jan. 1711/2, pres. by
Hannah Thurston, his widow & Exec., & by David Thurston, his
son. Apprs: John Butterworth & Moses Read [3:84].
Will of ROBERT HAVENS of Dart., dtd. 30 March 1708, prob. 7
Apr. 1712. Wife Elizabeth. Sons: Robert, William, George &
Joseph Havens (last 3 under age). Daus: Ruth & Elizabeth Ha-
vens. Witns: Isaac Shearman, Joshua Shearman & John Tucker
[3:85].
Inv. of Est. of ROBERT HAVENS of Dart., Planter, dtd. 3 Aug. 17-
08, prob. 7 Apr. 1712 by Elizabeth Havens his widow & Exec.
Apprs: Joshua Shearman & Isaac Shearman [3:86].
Inv. of Est. in Lit. Comp. of JAMES PECKHAM of Newport, dtd.
21 March 1711/2, pres. by William Peckham of Newport & Capt.
Thomas Grey of Lit. Comp., Adms. Apprs: William Wilbore, William Pabodie & Jonathan Head [3:87].
Will of SAMUEL GREY of Lit. Comp., Yeoman, dtd. 20 March 1712,
prob. 7 Apr. 1712. Wife Deborah. Sons: Samuel (eldest), Simeon & Ignatious Grey. Daus: Dorothy & Lidiah Grey. Brother
Thomas Grey, Exec. Friends William Pabodie & John Palmer &
my brother John Church to be Overseers. Witns: Edward Gray,
Jonathan Head & Richard Billings [3:88/9].

Inv. of SAMUEL GREY of Lit. Comp., dtd. 2 Apr. 1712, pres. by
Mrs. Deborah Grey, his widow, & by Thomas Grey, his brother,
Execs. Apprs: John Palmer, John Church & William Pabodie
[3:89/90].
Inv. of Est. of EBENEZER SMITH of Reho., dcd. intest., dtd. 2
March 1710/1, pres. by Priscilla Smith, his widow & Adm.
Apprs: William Dean, Jathniel Peck & Jonathan Bliss [3:91].
Will of ENOCH HUNT of Reho., Yeoman, dtd. 28 Nov. 1711, prob.
5 May 1712. Wife not mentioned. Sons Nathaniel & Stephen Hunt.
Grson. Enoch Hunt. Grdau. Mary Hunt. Witns: Joseph Peck, Sr.
Ephraim May & Joseph Peck, Jr. [3:92/3].
Inv. of Est. of Capt. ENOCH HUNT of Reho., dtd. 3 Apr. 1712,
pres. by Stephen & Nathaniel Hunt, his sons & Execs. Apprs.
not named [3:93].
Inv. of JOSEPH AMORY of Lit. Comp., dtd. 7 Feb. 1711/2, pres.
by Elizabeth Amory, his widow & Adm. Apprs: Nathaniel Searls
& Joseph Willbur [3:94].
Acct. of Thomas Bowen of Swan., son & Exec. of Est. of OBADIAH
BOWEN of Swan., dtd. 12 May 1712. Legacies: to Isaac Ayars
for Samuel Bowen of Cohanse; to John Brooks for Timothy Brooks
& Hannah his wife; to Joseph & Lidia Mason; to Allice wife of
Jacob Chase; to Joseph Bowen; to James & Hezekiah Bowen; to
Daniel & Aron Bowen; to Mary Bowen alias Bush; to Abigail Bow-
en for use of her dau. Sarah Bowen; to Ephraim Smith for use
of his wife Mary [3:95].
Rcpt. by Joseph Mason & Lidia Mason for one cow given by will
of "my Honrd ffather," paid by Thomas Bowen of Swan., dtd. 1
Jan. 1710 [3:96].
Rcpt. by Jacob Chase for pewter platter given to his wife Allice
Chase by the will of her "Honorable grandfather," paid by
Thomas Bowen of Swan., dtd. 6 Jan. 1711 [3:96].
Rcpt. by Mary Bowen alias Mary Bush for pewter platter given to
her by "her hon^d Grandfather," from the hands of Thomas Bowen
[3:96].
Inv. of Est. of JOSEPH BISHOP late resident of Reho., late dcd.
at sea, dtd. 1 Apr. 1712, pres. by Samuel Bishop & Samuel Day
Adms. Apprs: Moses Read, Samuel Newman & Daniel Carpenter
[3:96].
Order that since Mrs. Hannah Randall, widow of THOMAS RANDALL
of Taun. North Purchase, through infirmity of old age, could
not appear, & since Thomas Randall, eldest son, refused adm.,
that therefore Adm. be granted to Israel Randall, 2nd son of
dcd., dtd. 6 Oct. 1712 [3:97].
Experience Whittaker chose her uncle James Wheeler to be her
guard. Also, Ens. Joshua Smith was appt. guard. of Rebecah,
and Mr. Francis Wilson was appt. guard. of Hanah & Margaret
Whittacer, all chldn. of NATHANIEL WHITTICER of Reho., dtd.
4 Aug. 1712 [3:97].
Appt. of Timothy Walker, "the Eldest Son Surviving" to be Adm.

of Est. of Capt. SAMUEL WALKER, since Mrs. Elizabeth Walker
   the widow, renounced adm., dtd. 20 Oct. 1712 [3:98].
Inv. of Capt. SAMUEL WALKER, Gent., of Reho., dtd. 5 Sept. 1712,
   pres. by Mrs. Elizabeth Walker, his widow, & by Timothy Walker, his son & Adm. Apprs: Abiah Carpenter, Daniel Smith &
   Daniel Carpenter [3:98/9].
Inv. of SAMUEL WALKER, Jr. of Reho., dtd. 9 Sept. 1712, pres.
   by Mrs. Ruth Walker, his widow. Apprs: Daniel Smith & Eben-
   ezer Walker [3:100].
Will of JONAH LINKON of Brist., Yeoman, "being at this time un-
   der some dissettlement & disquietment by Reason of my wives
   Remouving from me and not Expecting her Return," dtd. 22 Mar.
   1708/9, prob. 3 Nov. 1712. To my wife [not named]. To William
   Caswell & Lidiah Caswell, son & dau. of "my Brother William
   Caswell & my Sister Mercey his wife of Taunton." Friend John
   Throope of Brist. as Exec. Witns: John Cary, Abigail Howland
   & Lidia Cary [3:101/2].
Codicil to his will by JONAH LINKON, dtd. 4 Apr. 1709, adding
   to land bequeathed to William & Lidiah Caswell, chldn. of sis-
   ter Mercy Caswell [3:102].
Inv. of Est. of JONAH LINKON, dtd. 31 Oct. 1712, pres. by John
   Throope of Brist., Exec. Apprs: John Cary & Robert Jolls
   [3:103].
Acct. of Daniel Smith & Priscilla Smith, Adms. of Est. of EBEN-
   EZER SMITH of Reho., brother of Daniel, recorded 10 Nov. 1712.
   Incl. debts paid to abt. 13 persons [3:104/5].
Rcpts. by Joseph Dagget, Richard Bowen & Thomas Bowen for money paid to them by Daniel Smith, Adm. of Est. of his brother
   EBENEZER SMITH, dtd. 1711, 6 Oct. 1712 & 4 Nov. 1712 [3:105].
Agrmt. on settl. of Est. of JOSEPH LEONARD of Taun. btwn. Jo-
   seph Willis & his wife Mary Willis (formerly her first husband
   was said Joseph Leonard), with the chldn. of dcd. Joseph Leonard: Edward Leonard, William Leonard, Samuel Hodges & Exper-
   ience (dau.) his wife, Mehetabel Leonard & Silence Leonard,
   all of Taun. Mentions Joseph Willis son of said Mary Willis.
   Dtd. 2 Apr. 1712. Witns: James Leonard, Joseph Wilson, Sam-
   uel Danforth & Dorothy Wood. Notation made on 5 Apr. 1712 of
   "Mehetable Leonard now Harvey" [3:106/7/8].
Will of THOMAS WILLCOX of Tiv., dtd. 9 Aug. 1712, prob. 2 Sept.
   1712. Brother Edward Willcox. Also mentions "to my Brothers &
   Sisters" [not named]. Witns: Nicholas Howland, John Briggs
   & Zachariah Howland [3:109].
Inv. of Est. of THOMAS WILLCOX of Tiv., dtd. 9 Sept. 1712, pres.
   by Edward Willcox, brother & Exec. Apprs: William Manchester
   & Job Briggs [3:110].
Objections against proving will of WILLIAM FOBES of Lit. Comp.,
   registered by Edward Southworth Of Lit. Comp. "in behalfe of
   himself and Fobes Southworth and Rebeccah Southworth," his
   chldn. & grchldn. of said William Fobes, dtd. 12 Nov. 1712
   [3:111/2].

Will of WILLIAM FOBES of Lit. Comp., dtd. 4 Nov. 1712, prob. 4
Dec. 1712. My son-in-law Joseph Seabery & son-in-law Josiah
Sawyer & his wife Martha. My dau. Elizabeth Briggs wife of
William Briggs, & her eldest son Lovet Briggs. My dau. Con-
stant Little wife of John Little. My grsons. Fobes Southworth
(under 21), Samuel Seabery & John Sawyer. Grdau. Rebeccah
Southworth (under 21). Justice Thomas Church to be guard. of
grson. Fobes Southworth. Son-in-law Joseph Seabery & Silves-
ter Richmond to be Overseers. Witns: Capt. Thomas Gray, Jo-
seph Blackman & Thomas Church [3:112/3/4].
Inv. of Est. of Lt. WILLIAM FOBES who died 6 Nov. 1712, dtd. 12
Nov. 1712, pres. by Thomas Church & John Little, Execs. Apprs:
Thomas Grey, Edward Richmond & John Wood [3:115/6].
Appt. of Benjamin Hunt of Reho. as guard. of Peter Cooper of Re-
ho., son of NATHANIEL COOPER, dtd. 9 Feb. 1712/3 [3:117].
Appt. of Nathaniel Carpenter of Attl. as guard. of Nathaniel
Cooper & Judith Cooper, son & dau. of NATHANIEL COOPER of Reho., dtd. 9 Feb. 1712/3 [3:117].
Rcpt by Anne Perren, dau. of ABRAHAM PERREN of Reho., for legacy paid by Thomas Read & Nathaniel Read, being the money "my
Unkle Insign Thomas Read," Adm. to her father, was supposed
to have paid her, dtd. 25 Feb. 1705/6. Witns: Elizabeth Carpenter & Josiah Carpenter [3:117].
Rcpts. by Ephraim Carpenter, Hannah Carpenter & Mehetabel Read
for legacies paid by our brothers Thomas & Nathaniel Read
from the will of "our ffather THOMAS READ," dtd. 5 Feb. 17-
12/3 [3:117].
Rcpt. by Samuel Perrin for money from Moses Read which Thomas
was to pay to Mehittabel Perren, dtd. 6 Apr. 1699 [3:118].
Rcpt. by Pierson Richardson to Moses Read for "all the goods
of Mehetabel Perrens that was left in Thomas Reads hands,"
dtd. 20 Oct. 1699 [3:118].
Rcpt. by Nathaniel Brewer to Moses Read "for money by order of
Mehittabel Richardson," dtd. 9 May 1700 [3:118].
Inv. of Est. of JOHN CRABTREE of Attl., dtd. 22 Dec. 1712, pres.
by Hannah Crabtree, his widow. Apprs: Jonathan ffuller, Thomas Tingle & John ffollett [3:118].
Acct. of John Hathaway Adm. of Est. of ARTHUR HATHAWAY of Dart.
dtd. 2 March 1712. Mentions paym. to 9 persons, incl. Jonathan Hathaway & Thomas Hathaway [3:119].
Inv. of Est. of TRISTRAM BOWERMAN of Brist., dtd. 9 March 1712/3
pres. by Mrs. Joan Bowerman, his widow, & by Samuel Bowerman,
eldest son. Apprs: Peter Reynolds & William Throope[3:120/1/2
Will of CALEB EDDY of Swan., Husbandman, dtd. 18 May 1710, prob.
6 Apr. 1713. Wife Elizabeth. Sons: Caleb (eldest), Samuel &
Benjamin. Daus: Elizabeth, Hannah, Hopestill & Mary (under
age) Eddy. Request that Samuel take care of his mother. Witns:
Thomas Eastabrook, Lidiah Mason & Joseph Mason [3:123/4].

Inv. of Est. of Deacon CALEB EDDY of Swan. who died 23 March
1712/3, dtd. 15 Apr. 1713, pres. by Elizabeth Eddy & Samuel
Eddy, Execs. [3:124/5].

Inv. of Est. of JOB MANCHESTER of Dart., dtd. 8 Jan. 1712, pres.
by Hannah Manchester, his widow [3:125].

Will of JOHN MARTIN of Swan., Weaver, dtd. 28 Aug. 1711, prob. 6
Apr. 1713. Wife Joana Martin. Sons: Melatiah, John, Ephraim,
Manasseth & Ebenezer Martin. Daus: Joanna & Judith (mentions
"my four daughters," but only these 2 are named). Witns: John
Bosworth, Jabez Bosworth & Philip Short [3:126/7].

Inv. of Est. of JOHN MARTIN of Swan. who died 21 March 1712/3,
dtd. 3 Apr. 1713, pres. by Mrs. Joanna Martin, his widow, &
son Ebenezer Martin, Execs. Apprs: Joseph Mason & John West
[3:128/9].

Inv. of Est. of THOMAS READ, Sr. of Taun. who died 11 June 1711
pres. 7 Jan. 1712/3 by Israel Randall of Taun. No. Purchase,
Adm. Apprs: Thomas Pratt, Samuel Cary & John Daly [3:129].

Inv. of Est. of ANTHONY NEWLAND of Taun., dtd. 19 June 1712,
pres. by Hester Newland, his widow & Exec. Apprs: Benjamin
Leonard, James Leonard, Jr. & John Austin [3:130].

Will of ANTHONY NEWLAND of Taun., "being very sick," dtd. 12
May 1712, prob. 7 July 1712. Wife Hester. Mentions "my chil-
dren yet in Minority," but does not name them. Witns: John
Austin, Joseph Grey & Simeon Wetherel [3:131].

Will of THOMAS EASTABROOK of Swan., Yeoman, dtd. 4 Nov. 1710,
prob. 4 May 1713. Wife not mentioned. Sons John & Thomas
Eastabrook. Daus. Elizabeth Bozworth & Sarah Eddy. "My grand-
sons," & "my Grand Daughters" were left money but not named.
Witns: Hezekiah Bowen, Samuel Mason & Joseph Mason [3:132].

Inv. of Est. of Insigne THOMAS EASTABROOK of Swan., dtd. 11
Apr. 1713, pres. by John & Thomas Eastabrook, Execs. & sons.
Apprs: Joseph Butterworth, William Wood & Joseph Mason[3:133].

Will of JOHN LANE of Nort., "being very sick and weak," dtd. 21
Nov. 1712, prob. 9 Apr. 1713. Wife mentioned by not named.
Sons: John, Ebenezer, Ephraim, Benjamin, Samuel & Asaphe.
Daus. Mary & Prissilla. Son John is "to maintain my wife &
bring up the smale Children." Witns: Joseph Avery, Capt. John
Leonard & Anna Leonard [3:134].

Inv. of Est. of JOHN LANE of Norton, dtd. 3 Dec. 1712, pres.
by Sarah Lane, his widow, & by John Lane, Execs. Apprs: John
Smith, George Leonard & Robert Tucker [3:135].

Acct. of Timothy Walker, Adm. of Est. of Capt. SAMUEL WALKER
of Reho., dtd. 6 Dec. 1712. Mentions paym. to 29 people [3:
136/7].

Acct. of Judith Fuller, Adm. of Est. of her husband BENJAMIN
FULLER of Reho., pres. 6 Apr. 1713. Mentions paym. to 24
diff. people, incl. one to John Fuller [3:136/7].

Acct. of George Wood of Reho., Adm. of Est. of his mother-in-
law Widow REBECAH DAGGET of Reho., pres. 9 Apr. 1713. Incl.

paym. of items: "To Dr Wood for my Grandmother," "shoes for my Grandmother," "cloath for my Grandmother" & "Brother John Dagget" [3:137/8].

Order for div. of Est. of SAMUEL WALKER of Reho., dtd. 9 March 1712/3 [3:139].

Div. of Est. of Capt. SAMUEL WALKER of Reho., Yeoman, btwn. his widow Mrs. Elizabeth Walker, & his chldn: Samuel, Jr. dcd. (eldest son), Timothy (2nd son), Peter (3rd son), Noah Perrin in the right of his wife Patience, Ephraim (4th son), Martha (2nd dau.) & Benjamin (youngest son) Walker, dtd. 9 Apr. 1713. Comm: Daniel Smith, Benjamin Hunt, Abiah Carpenter, David Newman & Daniel Carpenter [3:139/40/1/2].

Acct. of Philip Taber, Adm. of Est. of JOSIAH WOOD of Dart., dtd. 1 Oct. 1711. George & Daniel Wood, brothers of Josiah dcd. [3:143].

Jabez Gold of Taun., Cordwainer, chosen by his brother & sister Benjamin & Elizabeth Gold, to be their guard., dtd. 26 June 1713 [3:143].

Div. of Est. of BENJAMIN FULLER of Reho. btwn. his widow Judith Fuller & his chldn: Benjamin (eldest son), John (2nd son), Joseph Martin in the right of his wife Mary, Ezekiah (3rd son), Amos (4th son), Joshua (5th son) & Abiel (6th son) Fuller, dtd. 12 May 1713. Comm: John Butterworth, Moses Read, Abiah Carpenter & Daniel Newman [3:144/5/6].

Order that an agrmt. to settl. the Est. of JOHN WOODMAN of Lit. Comp. & of his late wife HANNAH WOODMAN be prepared prior to proceeding with proving his will, dtd. 1 June 1713[3:147].

Will of JOHN WOODMAN of Lit. Comp., dtd. 16 June 1710, prob. 2 June 1713. Wife Hannah. Sons: Robert (eldest), John & Edward Woodman. Daus: Hannah wife of Nicholas Howland, Edith Woodman, Rebecah Woodman, Elizabeth Woodman & Silvia Woodman. Mentions lands in Lit. Comp., Tiv. & Newport. Witns: Peter Horsewel, Josiah Sawyer & Elizabeth Horswel [3:148/9].

Inv. of Est. of JOHN WOODMAN of Lit. Comp., dtd. 1 May 1714, pres. by Robert & John Woodman, sons. Apprs: Joseph Wanton, Aaron Davis, Jr. & William Pabodie [3:150/1].

Agrmt. btwn. chldn. of JOHN & HANNAH WOODMAN, both dcd., abt. settl. of Est., dtd. 16 June 1713. Chldn: Robert Woodman; John Woodman; Edward Woodman; Hannah Howland wife of Nicolas Howland of Dart., Cordwainer; Edith Church wife of Capt. Thomas Church of Lit. Comp.; Rebeccah Woodman; Elizabeth Woodman & Silvia Woodman. Witns: Joseph Wanton, Peter Horswell & John Cary [3:152/3].

Inv. of Est. of JABEZ HOWLAND of Brist., dtd. 6 Feb. 1711/2, pres. by Mrs. Bethiah Howland, his widow, & by Jabez Howland, son, Execs. Apprs: Simon Davis, Samuel Gallap & John Cary [3:154/5].

Rcpt. by Increase Robinson, Jr. of Taun. for money rcvd. from his mother-in-law Elizabeth Williams, Adm. of Est. of JOSEPH

WILLIAMS of Taun., for legacy to his wife Mehettabel Robinson, dau. of Joseph Williams, dtd. 1 July 1695. Witns: John
Richmond, Shadrach Willbore & Thomas Leonard [3:155].

Acct. of John Gold, son & Adm. of Est. of JOHN GOLD of Taun.,
dtd. 7 July 1713. Inc. an item for "Hannah Gold for her Tending her Parents in the time of their sickness." Mentions funeral expenses for his mother Mary Gold as well as for his father John Gold [3:156].

Acct. of Bethiah Howland & Jabez Howland of Brist., Execs. of
Est. of JABEZ HOWLAND of Brist., dtd. 24 July 1713[3:157/8].

Satisfaction expressed by Silvia Woodman abt. the agrmt. by her
brothers & sisters "during her nonage" abt. settl. of Est. of
their father, dtd. 20 March 1717/8 [3:158].

Rcpt. by Silvia Woodman for legacy from Est. of her father JOHN
WOODMAN, paid by her brothers Robert & John Woodman, Adms.,
dtd. 20 March 1717/8. Witns: Thomas Church & Samuel Howland
[3:158].

Inv. of Est. of JOHN BRIGGS of Tiv. who died 2 July 1713, pres.
30 July 1713 by Hannah Briggs of Tiv., his widow. Apprs: William Southworth, Job Briggs & Robert Dennis [3:159].

Inv. of JONATHAN PECK of Brist., dtd. 23 July 1713, pres. by
Mrs. Elizabeth Peck of Brist., his widow. Apprs: James Adames
& Peter Reynolds [3:160].

Acct. of Joanah Robinson, Adm. of Est. of her husb. EDWARD ROB-
INSON of Dart. who dcd. intest., pres. 3 Aug. 1713. Mentions
"money paid mother Hall" [3:161/2].

Will of JOHN PECK of Reho., "being aged," dtd. 26 May 1708,
prob. 5 Cot. 1713. No wife mentioned. Son Nathan Peck. Daus:
Hester Willmath, Dorothy Glover wife of Edward Glover, Ann
Peck & Abigail Peck. Witns: John Butterworth, Samuel Carpenter & Daniel Smith [3:163/4].

Inv. of Est. of JOHN PECK of Rehoboth, dtd. 2 Oct. 1713, pres.
by Nathan Peck of Reho., Exec. Apprs. not named [3:164].

Order for div. of est. of JOHN GOLD of Taun., dtd. 15 July 1713
[3:165].

Div. of real est. of Mr. JOHN GOLD of Taun. btwn. his chldn:
John (eldest son), Joseph, Nathaniel, Jabez, Benjamin & Hannah Gold, Ebenezer Bishop in the right of his wife Mary, &
Elizabeth Gold. Comm: Samuel Williams, John White & John Mason [3:165/6].

Accts. of Deborah Throope formerly Deborah Grey, & of Capt.
Thomas Grey, Execs. of Est. of Mr. SAMUEL GREY of Lit. Comp.,
dtd. 3 Nov. 1713. Hers mentions paym. to some 35 diff. people,
incl. acknowledgement of Deborah's rcpt. of money due "by my
Husbands Will." Thomas' acct mentions "to my Brother Deceased"
& incl. paym. to 16 diff. people, one of whom was "Widow Mary
Pearce Adm^trix to ye Estate of Capt Amos Sheffield"[3:167/8/9].

Rcpt. by Dan Throope & Deborah Throope late wife of SAMUEL GREY
& now wife of Dan Throope of Brist., Shipwright, for money

rcvd. from Capt. Thomas Grey of Lit. Comp., Exec., dtd. 3 June
1713. Witns: William Pabodie & Judith Pabodie [3:170].
Will of HUGH MOSHER of Newport, dtd. 12 Oct. 1709, prob. 7 Dec.
1713. Wife Sarah rcvd. only "all the moveable Estate I had
with her in Marriage." Sons: James, Nicholas, John, Joseph &
Daniel Mosher. Grson. Hugh Mosher son of son Nicholas. Mentions his grsons. "of my surname Mosher," but does not name
them. Also mentions "my Grand Children not of my Name," without naming them. Son James & friend Daniel Sabeere of Newport
Execs. Friend Jeremiah Clarke my kinsman & Capt. John Stanton
of Newport to be Overseers. Mentions lands in Dart. & in Newport. Witns: John Sabeer, John Bayley, Jr. & Samuel Rhoades
[3:171/2].
Inv. of Est. of HUGH MOSHER of Dart., Yeoman, dtd. 10 Nov. 1713,
pres. by James Mosher & Daniel Sabeer, Execs. Apprs: Jonathan
Davel & Ebenezer Tripp [3:173].
Acct. of Mary Hall, Adm. of Est. of her husb. CHRISTOPHER HALL
of Attl., dtd. 1 Nov. 1713 [3:174].
Acct. by Ruth Walker, Adm. of Est. of her husb. SAMUEL WALKER,
dtd. 7 Dec. 1713. Mentions paym. to 29 diff. people, incl. Eb-
enezer Walker [3:175/6].
Div. of Est. of SAMUEL WALKER, Jr. of Reho., made by widow Ruth
Walker, by Lt. Moses Read guard. of Oliver (eldest son) & Moses (son) Walker, & by Daniel Carpenter guard. of Ruth Walker
(dau.); div. made btwn. widow & above 3 chldn., dtd. 7 Dec.
1713 [3:176].
Inv. of Est. of THOMAS BRAYMAN of Taun. North Purch., dtd. 21
July 1709, pres. by Hannah Brayman & Daniel Brayman of Taun.
Apprs: John Lane, George Leonard & Samuel Hodges [3:1777/8].
Will of THOMAS LEONARD "the Eldest of yͤ Name in Taunton," being in his 71st year of age, dtd. 29 Jan. 1711/2, prob. 5 Feb.
1713/4. Wife Mary. Mentions Mary's "father Watson." Sons: Tho-
mas (eldest), John, George, Samuel & Elkanah. Daus. Mary Tis-
dale wife of John Tisdale & Elizabeth Williams. Grson. Thomas
Leonard son of my son John. My brothers Benjamin & James Leon-
ard. Mentions lands in Middlebury, Taun., Reho. & Taun. North
Purchase. Friends Elder Henry Hodges, Deacon Ezra Deane, Deacon Israel Thresher & Seth Williams to be Overseers. Witns:
Samuel Danforth, Hannah Danforth widow of Isaac Deane, Stephen
Leonard & Eliazer Carpenter, Jr. [3:179-185].
Will of WILLIAM HILLIARD of Lit. Comp., Cooper, dtd. 15 Dec. 17-
13, prob. 1 Feb. 1713/4. Wife Deborah. Sons David & Jonathan.
Daus: Deborah wife of John Paddock, Esther wife of Jerimy
Gears, Mary wife of John Palmer, Abigail Hilliard & Sarah Hil-
liard. Witns: Benjamin Head, Joseph Willbore & Richard Bill-
ings [3:186/7].
Inv. of Est. of Mr. WILLIAM HILLIARD of Lit. Comp. who died 24
Jan. 1713/4, dts. 26 Jan. 1713/4, pres. by Mrs. Deborah Hil-
liard, his widow. Apprs: John Palmer, John Church & William

Pabodie [3:187/8].
Order for inv. of Est. of WILLIAM FOBES of Lit. Comp., dtd. 10
  Jan. 1713/4, mentions Adms. John Little & Thomas Church guard.
  of Fobes Southworth [3:187][*page numbering error*].
Acct. of Robert Woodman & John Woodman, Execs. of Est. of JOHN
  WOODMAN of Lit. Comp., dtd. 3 Apr. 1714. Mentions paym. to:
  Nicholas Howland & Hannah Howland, to Thomas Church & Edith
  Church, to Rebecah Woodman & to Edward Woodman [3:187/8].
Rcpts. for legacies paid by Robert & John Woodman, sons & Execs.
  of Est. of JOHN WOODMAN of Lit. Comp., as signed by:
    Nicholas Howland & Hannah Howland, 11 March 1713/4.
    Thomas Church & Edith Church, 23 Dec. 1713.
    Rebeccah Woodman, 28 Dec. 1713.
    Elizabeth Woodman, 28 Dec. 1713.
    Edward Woodman, 16 Jan. 1713/4 [3:188].
Acct. of Hannah Crabtree, Adm. of Est. of her husb. JOHN CRAB-
  TREE, Jr., recorded 14 Apr. 1714 [3:189].
Inv. of Est. of SAMUEL ALLEN who died 15 Nov. 1713, pres. 5 Apr.
  1714 by Mary Allen of Taun., his widow. Mentions debts owed
  to 22 people, incl. "my mother Mary King." Apprs: Henry Hod-
  ges, John Andrewes & William Hodges [3:190/1].
Inv. of Est. of JOHN CASWELL of Norton, dtd. 20 March 1713/4,
  pres. by Elizabeth Caswell, his widow. Apprs: George Leonard,
  Nicholas White & Benjamin Williams [3:191¼].
Inv. of Est. of the Rev. Mr. JOHN WILSON of Swan., dtd. 13 Jan.
  1713/4, pres. by Mrs. Margaret Willson, his widow. Apprs:
  Samuel Low, Samuel Kent & Ebenezer Allen [3:191 3/4].
Will of JOSEPH SALISBURY of Lit. Comp., Cordwainer, dtd. 26
  March 1714, prob. 5 July 1714. Wife Mary Salisbury. Sons:
  John, Joseph & William. Daus: Mary, Hope & Susannah Salis-
  bury. Wife Mary & kinsman Icabode Williston, Execs. Witns:
  Samuel Tompkins, Esek Carr & Richard Billings [3:191 3/4-192].
Inv. of Est. of JOSEPH SALISBURY, Cordwainer, dtd. 25 June 1714,
  pres. by Mary Salisbury, his widow. Apprs: Thomas Brownel &
  John Palmer [3:192/3].
Inv. of SAMUEL KINGSLEY, Sr. of Taun. No. Purch. who died 17 Dec.
  1713, dtd. 19 Feb. 1713/4, pres. by Samuel Kingsley of Taun.
  No. Purch., eldest son. A notation from Mary Kingsley, widow
  of Samuel, declining Adm. & asking that her son Samuel be
  made Adm. Apprs: Edward ffobs, John Phillips & Thomas Pratt
  [3:194].
Acct. of Elizabeth Amory, Adm. of Est. of her husb. JOSEPH AM-
  ORY of Lit. Comp., dtd. 3 May 1714. Mentions paym. to 15 diff.
  people [3:195].
Will of SAMUEL LUTHER, Jr. of Swan., Husbandman, "being sick &
  weak in body," dtd. 16 July 1714, prob. 2 Aug. 1714. Wife mentioned but not named. Sons: Samuel (eldest), James Caleb, Con-
  sider, Benjamin, Jabez & Eliazer Luther. Daus: Elizabeth &
  Sarah Luther. Friends Nathaniel Luther & Joseph Mason & brother Theophilus Luther, Overseers. Witns: Hugh Cole, Deborah
  Cole & Lidia Mason [3:196/7].

Inv. of Est. of SAMUEL LUTHER, Jr. of Swan., dtd. 27 July 1714, pres. by Sarah Luther, his widow. Apprs: Joseph Butterworth & Joseph Mason [3:197/8].

Rcpt. by John Robinson & Judith Robinson for legacy from Est. of "our hon^d father" THOMAS COOPER of Reho., paid by our brothers Thomas Cooper & Samuel Cooper, Adms., dtd. 11 Dec. 1712. Witns: Noah Sabin & Miriam Carpenter [3:198].

Rcpt. by Hezekiah Peck & Deborah Peck for legacy from Est. of "our Hon^rd father" THOMAS COOPER of Reho., paid by "our brothers" Thomas & Samuel Cooper, Adms., dtd. 22 Dec. 1712. Witns: Abiah Carpenter & George Bersto [3:198].

Rcpt. by Mary Cooper, John Humphrey & Sara Humphrey for legacies from Est. of "our hon^rd ffather" THOMAS COOPER of Reho., paid by "our brothers" Thomas & Samuel Cooper, Adms., dtd. 17 Dec. 1712. Witns: Thomas Smith & Tabitha Headly [3:199].

Rcpt. by Timothy Ide & Elizabeth Ide for legacy from Est. of "our hon^rd father" THOMAS COOPER of Reho., paid by "our brothers" Thomas & Samuel Cooper, Adms., dtd. 11 Dec. 1712. Witns; Timothy Walker & Timothy Ide, Jr. [3:199].

Inv. of Est. of RICHARD BRAGG of Attl., dtd. 15 Dec. 1713, pres. by Thomas Bragg of Reh., his brother & Adm. Apprs: Nicholas Ide & John ffrench [3:199].

Inv. of Est. of Maj. THOMAS LEONARD of Taun., Gent., dtd. 3 Dec. 1713, pres. by John & Samuel Leonard, his sons & Execs. Apprs: Capt. Henry Hodges, Deacon Israel Thresher & John King. Mentions lands in Middlebury, Taun., in Nort. & in North Purch. [3:200/1/2/3].

Inv. of Est. of JOSHUA FINNEY of Swan., dtd. 29 Sept. 1714, pres. by Mercey Phinney, his widow. Apprs: John Rogers, John Devotion & Richard Harding [3:204].

Will of MARY MASON of Reho., widow, "being aged," dtd. 28 Jan. 1712/3, prob. 6 Dec. 1714. Sons: Pellatia, Benjamin, Noah dcd., Samuel, Joseph & Sampson Mason. Daus: Mary wife of Ephraim Wheaton, Sarah [no surname], Bethiah Wood dcd. & Thankful Bowen. Daus. of my dau. Bethiah dcd. Witns: Samuel Whitaker, John Wheaton & Samuel Bullock [3:205/6].

Inv. of Est. of widow MARY MASON of Reho., dtd. Oct. 1714. Apprs: ffrancis Wilson & James Wheeler [3:206].

Order for div. of real est. of TRISTRAM BOWERMAN of Brist., dcd. intest. [3:207].

Appt. of Martha Church, widow, to be Adm. of Est. of her husb. EDWARD CHURCH of Brist., dtd. 2 Apr. 1707 [3:207].

Rcpt. by John Barnes for legacy in will of his father [not named], dtd. 6 July 1706 [3:208].

Rcpt. by John Stone & Hannah Stone of Warwick for legacy from "Our Hon^rd father" THOMAS BARNES of Swan., paid by Elizabeth Barnes & Samuel Barnes, Execs., dtd. 19 Aug. 1706. Witns: Nathaniel Peck & Joanna Renells [3:208].

Rcpt. by Henry Sweeting for money paid by Samuel Barnes, owed by his father THOMAS BARNES, dtd. 17 Apr. 1707 [3:208].

Rcpt. by Peter Barnes in behalf of Sarah Wight wife of Benjamin
Wight for a legacy given by her father THOMAS BARNES, paid by
Samuel Barnes & Elizabeth Barnes, Adms., dtd. 16 Sept. 1706.
Witns: John Paine & Stephen Paine [3:208].

Rcpt. by John Bullock for legacy from "my Honrd father" THOMAS
BARNES of Swan., paid by Samuel Barnes & Elizabeth Barnes,
Adms., dtd. 7 Nov. 1706 [3:208].

Rcpt. by Peter Barnes for legacy from "my hon^d father" THOMAS
BARNES, paid by Samuel Barnes & Elizabeth Barnes, dtd. 16
Sept. 1706 [3:208].

Rcpt. by Thomas Allin for legacy from "my Honrd father" THOMAS
BARNES, paid by Samuel Barnes & Elizabeth Barnes, Adms., dtd.
12 Nov. 1706 [3:209].

Rcpt. by Ann Keese of Portsmouth for money owed her husb. John
Keese dcd. by THOMAS BARNES, paid by Elizabeth Barnes & Samuel Barnes, Adms., recorded 18 March 1720/1 [3:209].

Rcpt. by Thomas Olney, Jr. for legacy to Lidia Olney wife of
Thomas from THOMAS BARNES, paid by Samuel Barnes, Exec., recorded 23 March 1720/1 [sic] [3:209].

Rcpt. by Thomas Barnes for legacy from THOMAS BARNES, paid by
Elizabeth Barnes & Samuel Barnes, Adms., dtd. 21 Sept. 1706
[3:209].

Blank pages [3:210/1].

Will of JOHN BROOKS of Swan., Yeoman, "very sick & weak," dtd.
9 Apr. 1713, prob. 20 Dec. 1714. Wife Tabitha. Sisters: Eliz-
abeth Lewis, Hepsabeth Mason, Rebecca Martin, Abigail Press
"Liveing in West Jersey," & Anna Right. Elder brother Timothy
Brooks "liveing at said West Jersey." Brother Josiah Brooks
"Liveing at West Jersey." Cousin Mary Salisbury dau. of my
sister Mary Salisbury dcd. Cousin Samuel Salisbury brother
of said Mary Salisbury. Cousin James Lewis son of my sister
Elizabeth Lewis of Swan. Cousin Job Mason son of my sister
Hipzabath Mason of Swan. Cousin Mary Lewis dau. of my sister
Lewis. Brother-in-law Palatiah Mason of Swan. Brother-in-law
Melatiah Martin of Reho. Christian Kingsley wife of Nathaniel
Kingsley of Swan. Mary Cole & Lidia Cole daus. of Hugh Cole
of Swan. Mary Brown dau. of Lt. John Brown of Swan. & grdau.
of Capt. James Cole. "My first wifes Relations that is to say
the Coles." Witns: William Wood, Samuel Gardner & Joseph Ma-
son [3:212/3].

Inv. of Est. of JOHN BROOKS who died 22 Nov. 1714, dtd. 7 Dec.
1714, pres. by Thomas Lewis & Pelatiah Mason, Execs. Apprs:
Joseph Mason, William Wood & William Anthony [3:214/5].

Joseph Sabeers granted longer time to finish Adm. of Est. of
HUGH MOSHER, to report 11 Jan. 1714 [3:213][page numbering
error].

Will of JAMES TISDALE, Sr. of Digh., dtd. 2 Oct. 1713, prob.
7 March 1714. Wife not mentioned. Only son James Tisdale, Jr.
Daus: Mary Haskins, Martha Hodges wife of John Hodges, Jr.,
Margaret wife of Josiah Winslow & Sarah Johnson. Grdau. Mary

Haskines who hath nursed me. Grsons. Ebenezer Winslow, Eliphalet Hodges & Mearrick Johnson. Brother Joseph Tisdale to
be overseer. Witns: Joseph Deane, Peter Pitts & Mary Burt
[3:211][*page numbering error*].

Codicil of JAMES TISDALE, Sr. of Digh., dtd. 24 Feb. 1713/4,
prob. 7 March 1714. Sons-in-law Josiah Winslow of Free., John
Hodges of Nort. & John Johnson of Lebanon. Grchldn. Ebenezer
Winslow, Eliphalet Hodges & Marrik Johnson. Grdau. Mary Haskins who nurses me. Witns: Edward Shaw, John Clemens & Benjamin Smith [3:212].

Adm. of Est. of GREENFIELD HANNOVER of Taun. granted to Joseph
Wood [*should be Atwood, see p. 94*] of Digh. at request of Mary
Hannover the widow. Mention made abt. said Joseph [At]Wood,
"him being a Relation and knowing the Estate" [3:212].

Inv. of Est. of GREENFIELD HANNOVER of Taun. who died 15 Jan.
1714/5, dtd. 8 March 1714/5, pres. by Mary Hannover his widow. Apprs: Thomas Gilbert, Robert Crossman & Jonathan ffrench
[3:214¼].

Will of SAMUEL CORNELL of Dart., dtd. 15 May 1699, prob. 7 Feb.
1714/5. Wife not mentioned. Sons: Thomas (eldest) & Samuel.
Dau. Comfort Cornel. Cousin Thomas Cornel of Portsmouth & cousin George Cadman of Dart. to be Execs. & also to be guards.
to "take care of the bringing upp of my Children." Witns: Robert Lawton, Daniel Willbore & John Anthony [3:214/5].

Agrmt. btwn. Thomas & Samuel Cornell, brothers, abt. Est. of
their father SAMUEL CORNELL of Dart., dtd. 27 Jan. 1714/5.
Witns: George Cadman & James Tripp [3:215/6].

Inv. of Est. of SAMUEL CORNELL of Dart., dtd. 20 Jan. 1714/5,
pres. by George Cadman, Exec. Mentions "the Homestead ffarme
where the s^d Samuel Cornel lived" & "ye farm at Peskechuet
where Samuel Cornell Junr liveth." Apprs: George Cadman, Nicholas Howland & John Russell [3:217].

Will of JOHN TOOGOOD of Swan., Weaver, "being very low & weak
in body," dtd. 22 Feb. 1714/5, prob. 2 May 1715. Wife Hannah.
"My children" are not named. Witns: William Tickner, Peleg
Willbore & Edward Luther [3:218].

Inv. of Est. of JOHN TOOGOOD of Swan., dtd. 20 Apr. 1715, pres.
by Mrs. Hannah Toogood, his widow. Apprs: Edward Luther &
Thomas Turner [3:219].

Acct. of James Mosher of Dart. & Daniel Sabeers of Newport, Execs. of Est. of HUGH MOSHER of Dart., dtd. 6 June 1715. Mentions paym. to abt. 18 persons, incl. John Mosher bro. of
James [3:220/1].

Inv. of Est. of NATHANIEL PERRY of Reho., dtd. 22 Apr. 1715,
pres. by Sarah Perry, his widow. Incl. lands in Attl., Reho.
& Swan. Apprs: Abiah Carpenter & Daniel Carpenter [3:222].

Inv. of Est. of GEORGE GOODING of Digh., dtd. 8 Cot. 1712, pres.
by Mrs. Deborah Gooding, his widow. Apprs: Richard Haskins,
Samuel Waldron & Edward Shove [3:223].

Will of THOMAS PERRY, Jr. of Reho., Yeoman, "being very sick &
weak in Body," dtd. 18 May 1715, prob. 4 July 1715. Wife Ruth
Perry. "My children" are not named. Friends Capt. Samuel Peck
& Daniel Carpenter to advise my wife. Witns: Jonathan Cushing, Thomas Bowen & Adam Cushing [3:224].

Inv. of Est. of THOMAS PERRY, Jr. of Reho., dtd. 1 July 1715,
pres. by Mrs. Ruth Perry, his widow. Mentions lands in Attl.,
Reho. & Swan. Apprs: Samuel Peck & Daniel Carpenter [3:225].

Inv. of Est. of JOSHUA ORMSBE of Reho., dtd. 1 July 1715, pres.
by Mehettabell Ormsbe, his widow & Adm. Apprs: David Newman
& Daniel Smith [3:226].

Acct. of Margaret Willson late of Swan. now of Mendon, Adm. of
Est. of her husb. the Rev. Mr. JOHN WILLSON of Swan., dtd. 20
Apr. 1715 [3:227/8].

Will of STEPHEN TEOMAN, Mariner, "being sick & weak," dtd. in
Barbados 15 May 1715, prob. there 21 May 1715, pres. at Brist.
1 Aug. 1715. Wife Martha Teoman "now liveing in Redderisse In
the Kingdom of Great Brittain." Father-in-law Thomas Newton
"of New Bristol in New England" & "my mate Daniel Thurston"
to be Execs. with my wife. Mentions his vessel was at anchor
in Carlisle Bay. Witns: ffred ffeals, Silvanus Weastqutt &
John Downing [3:229/30].

Will of WILLIAM BROWNEL of Dart., "being very sick," dtd. 16
Nov. 1714, prob. 1 Aug. 1715. Wife Sarah. Sons: Smiton,
George, Thomas, William, Benjamin & Robert Brownel. Daus:
Martha, Anne & Mary [no surnames given]. Mentions lands in
Lit. Comp. Friend Nathaniel Soule to be Overseer with son
Smiton. Witns: Nathaniel Soule & Joseph Mosher [3:230/1].

Inv. of Est. of WILLIAM BROWNEL of Dart., dtd. 21 March 1714,
taken "by Sarah Brownel his last wife," pres. by Mrs. Sarah
Brownel, his widow. Apprs: Nathaniel Soule & Benjamin Gifford
[3:231].

Inv. of Est. of JOHN KNAP, Sr. of Taun., dtd. 18 June 1715,
pres. by John Knap, his son. Apprs: Samuel Prat, William Rice
& John Crossman [3:232].

Agrmt. btwn. Mrs. Mary Leonard & her 2 sons, John & Samuel Leon-
ard, all Execs. of Maj. JOHN LEONARD of Taun., with Jonathan
Williams of Taun. & his wife Elizabeth Williams dau. of John
Leonard dcd., dtd. 21 Dec. 1714. Mentions that the father of
Jonathan Williams was Thomas Williams of Taun., dcd. Witns:
Abraham Jones & John White, Jr. [3:234/5].

Acct. of Mercey ffinney & Joshua ffinney, Adms. of JOSHUA FIN-
NEY of Swan. dtd. 14 Sept. 1715 [3:235].

Will of JOHN BORDEN of Free., Yeoman, dtd. 5 July 1715, prob. 1
Aug. 1715. Wife not mentioned. Sons: Stephen (eldest), William, George & Joseph Borden (last 3 under 21). Daus. not
mentioned. "My honor[d] father John Borden of Portsmouth,"
still living. My brother Richard Borden of Tiv. Witns: Samuel Forman, Elizabeth Carter & Jonathan Stoder [3:236/7].

Codicil to Will of JOHN BORDEN of Free., dtd. 16 July 1715. "My
loving Wife" is not named. Witns: Benjamin Durffee, Mathew
Boomer & Samuel fforman [3:237].

Agrmt. btwn. Jabez, Josiah, Samuel & Joseph (youngest) Howland,
all of Brist., sons of JABEZ HOWLAND of Brist., abt. div. of
Est., excepting for what their mother Bethiah Howland keeps
in her own hands. Nathan Townsend, only son of our only sister Elizabeth Townsend dcd., late wife of Nathan Townsend of
Newport. Dtd. 26 Nov. 1714. Witns: William Munrow & Joseph
Wardall [3:238/9/40].

Will of PENTECOST BLACKINTON of Attl., Yeoman, dtd. 23 Sept. 17-
15, prob. 1 Nov. 1715. Wife mentioned but not named. Sons:
Benjamin (eldest) & Pentecost. Dau. Elizabeth. Mentions without names "all my other children." Witns: John Dagget, John
Bennet & John ffoster [3:241/3][page numbering omission].

Rcpt. & release signed by Joseph, Benjamin, Ebenezer, Richard &
Phebe Williams, all chldn. of JOSEPH WILLIAMS of Taun., dtd.
20 Sept. 1715. Mentions "our Hon^d mother Elizabeth Philips
the present wife of Samuel Philips Senr of Taunton." Witns:
Samuel Danforth & Benjamin Muston [3:243].

Acct. of Sarah Perry, Adm. of Est. of her husb. NATHANIEL PERRY
of Reho., dtd. 7 Nov. 1715. Mentions paym. to abt. 15 people,
incl. one for "cloathing for the children" [3:244].

Inv. of Est. of WILLIAM MACUMBER of Taun., dtd. 26 Oct. 1714,
pres. by Sarah Macumber, his widow. Apprs: Henry Hodges &
Seth Williams [3:245].

Div. of Est. of WILLIAM MACUMBER of Taun. btwn. his widow Sarah
Macumber & his chldn: Abiall (eldest son), William, Annah &
Sarah Macumber, dtd. 8 Nov. 1715 [3:245].

Acct. of Sarah Macumber, Adm. of Est. of her husb. WILLIAM MAC-
UMBER of Taun., dtd. 6 Nov. 1715 [3:246/7].

Acct. of Samuel Kingsley of Taun. North Purch., son & Adm. of
SAMUEL KINGSLEY of said North Purch. who dcd. intest., dtd.
10 Nov. 1715 [3:247/8].

Will of JOSEPH CHURCH of Lit. Comp., dtd. 11 Jan. 1714/5, recorded 3 Jan. 1715/6. Wife Grace. Sons: Nathaniel, Caleb (under 21), Richard & Israel (last 2 called "my two youngest
sons"). 4 daus: Sarah, Alce, Deborah & Elizabeth [no surnames
given]. Grdau. Grace Church (under 18). Grson. Joseph Church
(under 23). Bro-in-law Israel Shaw & friend Deacon Pabodie to
be Overseers. Witns: Richard Thomas, Benjamin Southworth &
Edward Richmond [3:249/50/1].

Accept. by Grace Church, widow of JOSEPH CHURCH, of terms of
his will, dtd. 11 Jan. 1714/5. Witns: Richard Thomas, Benjamin Southworth & Edward Richmond [3:252].

Order for Inv. of Est. of JOSEPH CHURCH of Lit. Comp., dtd. 2
Jan 1715 [3:253].

Inv. of Est. of JOSEPH CHURCH of Lit. Comp. who died 19 Dec.
1715, dtd. 27 Dec. 1715. Apprs: John Wood, William Peabody,
Edward Richmond & Israel Shaw [3:254/5].

Commission of Nathaniel Byfield to be Judge of Probate, granted by King George, dtd. 24 Dec. 1715 [3:256].

Appt. of Ebenezer Brenton to be Register of Probate, by King George, dtd. 24 Dec. 1715 [3:257].

Inv. of Est. of EXPERIENCE HOLMES of Dart., recorded 27 Jan. 1714, pres. by Patience Holmes, his widow. Apprs: Edward Winslow & William Wittaredge [3:258/9].

Order for div. of Est. of BENJAMIN WILLIAMS of Taun., dtd. 2 Oct. 1711 [3:259].

Div. of Est. of BENJAMIN WILLIAMS of Taun. Widow mentioned but not named. Sons:Josiah (eldest), Benjamin & John Williams. Dau. Rebecca Pitts wife of Samuel Pitts, dtd. 3 Sept. 1714. Comm: Henry Hodges, John Williams, Samuel Williams & Ebenezer Robinson, all of Taun [3:260/1].

Div. of Est. of SAMUEL BRIGGS of Taun., dtd. 4 Aug. 1703. Widow Mary Caswell now wife of Benjamin Caswell. Chldn: Thomas (eldest son) Briggs, Elida Briggs, Hannah Briggs, Elizabeth Briggs & Mary the wife of "Jnº Fo[illegible]s. Comm: Thomas Harvey, Jnº King, Samuel Hodges & Thomas Seamans [3:262/3/4].

Div. of Est. of NATHANIEL PERRY of Reho, recorded 16 Feb. 1715. Widow Sarah Perry. Nathaniel Perry (eldest son), Jacob Perry (2nd son), John Perry (3rd son), Jacob Ide in right of his wife Sarah (eldest dau.) & Patience Perry (youngest dau.). Comm: Daniel Smith, Benjamin Hunt, Daniel Carpenter, John Robinson & Ebenezer Walker [3:264/5/6/7].

Appt. of Rachel Fuller, widow, as Adm. of Est. of her husb. NOAH FULLER of Attl., dtd. 5 March 1715 [3:268].

Inv. of Est. of NOAH FULLER of Attl., dtd. 31 Jan. 1715, pres. by Rachel Fuller, his widow & Adm. Apprs: Daniel Smith, Thomas Tingley & Noe Carpenter [3:268/9].

Appt. of John Horton of Reho., eldest son, to be Adm. of Est. of his father THOMAS HORTON of Reho., dtd. 2 Apr. 1716 [3:270].

Appt. of Remembrance Dye, widow, as Adm. of Est. of her husb. JOHN DYE of Lit. Comp., dtd. 2 Apr. 1716 [3:270/1].

Appt. of Edward Richmond of Lit. Comp. to be Adm. of Est. of JAMES RIDER of Lit. Comp., dtd. 2 Apr. 1716 [3:271].

Inv. of Est. of PENTECOST BLACKINGTON of Attl., dtd. 18 Oct. 1715, pres. by Mary Blackington his widow. Apprs: John Daggett, Jonathan Fuller & John Follett [3:272].

Inv. of Est. of THOMAS HORTON of Reho., dtd. 28 March 1716, pres. by John Horton, Eldest son. Apprs: John West & James Bowen [3:273].

Inv. of Est. of JOHN DYE of Lit. Comp., dtd. 28 Feb. 1715/6, pres. by Remembrance Dye, his widow. Apprs: Edward Richmond & Jonathan Thurston [3:274].

Inv. of Est. of JAMES RIDER of Lit. Comp. who died intest. 17 Feb. 1715/6, dtd. 23 March 1715/6, pres. by Mr. Edward Richmond, a Select Man of Lit. Comp. [3:276].

Will of SAMUEL HOWLAND, Sr. of Free., Yeoman, "being aged,"
dtd. 4 Feb. 1714/5, prob. 7 May 1716. Wife Mary. Daus: Mary
Rounsevall, Alce Howland & Content Sandford. Sons: Samuel,
John, Abraham, Joshua & Gershom Howland. Grdau. Mary Martin.
The chldn. of my son Isaac dcd. who are surviving. Witns: Eb-
enezer Sherman, Benjamin Sherman & John Read, Jr. [3:276/7].
Inv. of Est. of SAMUEL HOWLAND of Free., dtd. 18 Apr. 1716,
pres. by John Howland, his son [3:277/8].
Will of WILLIAM BRIGGS of Lit. Comp., Yeoman, dtd. 3 Apr. 1716,
prob. 2 July 1716. Wife mentioned but not named. Sons Job &
William. Daus: Susanah Dennis, Deborah Head & Elizabeth Wood-
man. 2 mulatto girls Hope & Mercy. My servant lad Jerem[a]
Springer (under 21). Robert Dennis, John Woodman & Benjamin
Head, Overseers. Witns: Edward Pelham, Jonathan Davenport,
Jr. & Joseph Wilbur. Notation that the widow was not content
with the Will & asks what the law allows [3:278/9/80].
Order of Inv. of Est. of WILLIAM BRIGGS of Lit. Comp., dtd. 2
July 1716 [3:281].
Inv. of Est. of WILLIAM BRIGGS of Lit. Comp. who died 12 May
1716, dtd. 17 May 1716, pres. by Job Briggs, his son & Exec.
Apprs: William Wilbore & Job Briggs [3:281/2/3].
Inv. of Est. of EDWARD LEONARD of Taun., dtd. 25 June 1716.
Apprs: John Wilbore, Seth Williams & Samuel Deane [3:283/4].
Appt. of Benjamin Munroe of Brist. & Sarah Bennett, widow, to be
Adms. of Est. of her husb. RICHARD BENNETT of Brist., dtd. 3
Sept. 1716 [3:284/5].
Inv. of Est. of Mr. RICHARD BENNETT of Brist. dtd. 18 Aug. 1716.
Apprs: Samuel Gallup, Thomas Walker & Ural Wardwel [3:285/6].
Will of HENRY HEAD of Lit. Comp., dtd. 24 March 1708, prob. 20
Aug. 1716. Wife Elizabeth. Sons: Jonathan, Henry & Benjamin.
Daus: Elizabeth Head, Mary & Innocent. Negro man Jeffery. Ne-
gro woman Rose. Little negro boy Scipio. Witns: John Peckham,
John Winslow & Elias Williams [3:286/7/8].
Inv. of Est. of HENRY HEAD of Lit. Comp., pres. 20 Aug. 1716 by
Elizabeth Head, his widow. Apprs: William Wilbore & John Peck-
ham [3:288/9].
Will of GEORGE LEONARD, Sr. of Nort., in the 44th year of his
age, dtd. 30 Aug. 1716, recorded 10 Sept. 1716 [date of probate not noted]. Wife Anna. 5 daus: Phebe, Anna, Abigail, Marcy & Mary Leonard. 3 sons: George, Nathaniel (2nd son) & Ephraim (3rd son)(all under age). My grandfather Watson. My uncle
James Leonard. My man Caleminco. My boy Dick. My sisters Elizabeth Williams & Mary Tisdal. Witns: John Leonard, Benjamin
Ware & Ephraim Lane [3:289/90/1/2/3].
Will of MARGARET THURBER of Swan., widow, "being very sick," dtd.
20 March 1716, prob. 4 Nov. 1716. Dau. Margaret Thurber (under 18). Richard Harding of Swan. as Exec. Witns: Joshua Kent,
Solomon Curtis & Edward Luther [3:294].
Inv. of Est. of MARGARET THURBER, dtd. 18 Aug. 1716, pres. by
Richard Harding, Exec. Apprs: John Rogers, Elisha May & John

Devotion [3:295].

Will of JOHN HOSKINS of Digh., Weaver, dtd. 1 May 1715, prob. 3 Sept. 1716. Wife Elizabeth. Sons-in-law Ebenezer Pits & Henry Gossett. My brother Richard Hoskins. Witns: Jared Talbut, Nathaniel Fisher & John Reed [3:296/7].

Acct. of Sarah Brownel, Exec. of Est. of her husb. WILLIAM BROWNEL of Dart., dtd. 3 Sept. 1716. Mentions paym. to numerous persons, incl: my dau. Alce; my son-in-law Wm. Potter; my son Thomas Brownel; my dau-in-law Margaret Brownel; my son Smiton Brownel [3:298/9].

Will of JOHN ROUND of Swan., Yeoman, "being weak of Body," dtd. 16 Oct. 1710, recorded 10 Nov. 1716 [date of probate not indicated]. Wife Elizabeth. Sons: John, Richard & George. 5 daus: Elizabeth Bowen wife of Joseph Bowen, Ruth Mason wife of Benjamin Mason, Sarah Bozworth wife of Jonathan Bozworth, Judith Round & Susannah Read wife of John Read. Job Winslow, Sr. & Samuel Bullock, Sr., Overseers. Witns: John West, Henry West & William West [3:299/300].

Inv. of Est. of JOHN ROUND of Swan. who died 7 Oct. 1716, recorded 10 Nov. 1716, pres. by Elizabeth Round, his widow, & by John Round, son. Apprs: Samuel Bullock, John West & Richard Harding [3:301].

Order for acct. by Elizabeth Round & John Round, Adms. of Est. of JOHN ROUND of Swan., dtd. 10 Nov. 1716 [3:302].

Appt. of Hannah Carpenter of Reho., widow, to be Adm. of Est. of her husb. JONATHAN CARPENTER of Reho., dtd. 23 Oct. 1716 [3:302].

Inv. of Est. of JONATHAN CARPENTER of Reho., dtd. 20 Sept. 1716, pres. by Hannah Carpenter, his widow. Apprs: Daniel Carpenter & Ebenezer Walker [3:303/4].

Inv. of Est. of JOHN MASON of Reho., dtd. 25 Sept. 1716, pres. by Noah Mason. Apprs: John Butterworth, Moses Read & Daniel Smith [3:304].

Agrmt. on div. of Est. of JOHN MASON of Reho. by his brothers, sisters & bros.-in-law: Noah Mason (eldest), Daniel Mason, Timothy Mason, Mary Mason, George Bearsto, Jr., Martha Bearsto, all of Reho., & Daniel Brown & Sarah Brown of Swan., dtd. 23 Oct. 1716. To our mother Sarah Mason. Witns: John Butterworth & Joseph Brown [3:305/6].

Will of SAMUEL HALL of Taun., dtd. 21 Aug. 1716, recorded 26 Nov. 1716. Wife Abigail. Sons Jonathan (eldest) & Samuel (youngest). Daus: Esther Blake & Hannah Hall (youngest). "The lad who lives with Me, namely Ebenezer Pratt" (under 21). "The girl who lives with me Elizabeth Pratt" (under 17). Witns: Abraham Jones, Samuel White & Jabez Prat [3:307/8/9].

Inv. of Est. of SAMUEL HALL of Taun. who died 30 Aug. 1716, dtd. 27 Sept. 1716, pres. by Jonathan Hall, eldest son & by Abigail Hall, his widow. Mentions lands in Taun. & in Bridge-

water. Apprs: Henry Hodges, Samuel Leonard & Stephen Leonard
[3:309/10].

Appt. of Henry Smith of Reho. & Rebecca Perry, widow, as Adms.
of Est. of her husb. DAVID PERRY, dtd. 5 Nov. 1716[3:311/2].

Inv. of Est. of DAVID PERRY of Reho., dtd. 26 Sept. 1716, pres.
by Rebecca Perry, his widow. Apprs: Daniel Smith, Jathniel
Peck & Jonathan Bliss [3:312/3].

Will of JONATHAN BLACKMAN of Lit. Comp., "being very sick," dtd.
4 Oct. 1716, recorded 2 Dec. 1716. Wife mentioned but not
named. "My child which is already [female], and that which is
not yet born...which my wife is big with." "My Honered mother
& my Uncle John Church" to be Execs. Witns: Thomas Gray, Edward Richmond & William Pabodie [3:313/4]

Inv. of Est. of JONATHAN BLACKMAN of Lit. Comp. who died 8 Oct.
1716, recorded 10 Dec. 1717, pres. by Leah Blackman & John
Church. Apprs: John Wood & Edward Richmond [3:315/6].

Will of THOMAS ORMSBEE of Reho., Yeoman, dtd. 3 March 1715/6,
recorded 10 Dec. 1716. Wife Mary. 5 sons: Thomas, Jeremiah,
Jacob, Ezra & Daniel Ormsbee. 4 daus: Mary Salsbury wife of
William Salsbury, Hannah Thompson wife of John Thompson, Bethiah Shaw wife of Thomas Shaw & Esther Redway wife of Preserved Redway. Witns: Nathaniel Luther, Richard Harding & John
West [3:316/7].

Inv. of Est. of THOMAS ORMSBEE of Reho., dtd. 1 Nov. 1716, pres.
by Jacob Ormsbee. Apprs: John West, Jathniel Peck & James Bow-
en [3:318].

Will of JOHN HUNT, Sr. of Rehoboth, "being Sick & weak in Body,"
dtd. 7 July 1712, recorded 22 Dec. 1716. Wife Mary. Sons: Peter (eldest) & Ephraim (under 21) Hunt. Daus: Deborah Hunt
(eldest), Hannah Hunt (2nd), Martha Hunt, Mary Hunt & Elizabeth Hunt. My servant Wade Sabin (indentured). Witns: Moses
Read, Joseph Peck & Daniel Carpenter [3:319/20/1/2].

Inv. of Est. of Lt. JOHN HUNT of Reho., dtd. 7 Dec. 1716, pres.
by Peter Hunt, son. Mentions lands in Reho., Swan. & Attl.
Apprs: Daniel Smith, Elisha May & Daniel Carpenter [3:323/4].

Appt. of Abigail Williams, widow. as Adm. of Est. of her husb.
JOSEPH WILLIAMS of Taun., dtd. 7 Jan. 1716/7, recorded 8 Jan.
1716/7 [3:324].

Inv. of Est. of JOSEPH WILLIAMS of Taun., dtd. 6 Nov. 1716,
pres. by Abigail Williams, his widow. Apprs: Seth Williams,
John Witherel & John Briggs [3:325].

Acct. of Mercy Finney, widow, & Joshua Finney, son, Adms. of
Est. of her husb. JOSHUA FINNEY of Swan., dtd. 7 Jan. 1716/7.
Incl. paym. to abt. 11 persons [3:326/7].

Order for Inv. of Est. of SAMUEL LUTHER of Swan. to Mary Luther
his widow & to Theophilus Luther, his son, Execs., dtd. 14
Jan. 1716/7 [3:327].

Rcpt. by Nathaniel Peck for legacy from Est. of his father JOHN
PECK, paid by Nathaniel's bro.-in-law Edward Glover. Witns:

Jonathan Carpenter & Daniel Carpenter [3:327].

Order for Inv. of Est. of MOSES READ of Reho., to Ezekiel Read, Exec., dtd. 4 Feb. 1716/7 [3:328].

Rcpt. by Mary Hunt of legacy from Est. of JOSEPH PECK of Reho., paid by Samuel Peck, Exec., dtd. 8 Dec. 1715 [3:328].

Rcpt. by Richard Bowen & Patience Bowen of legacy from Est. of JOSEPH PECK of Reho., paid by Samuel Peck, Exec., dtd. 8 Dec. 1715 [3:328].

Will of SAMUEL LUTHER of Swan., "Elder of ye Church of Christ in Swanzey," dtd. 2 May 1714, recorded 8 Feb. 1716/7. Wife Mary. Sons: Samuel (eldest), Theophilus, Joshua & Ebenezer. 4 daus: Mary Luther, Mehitabel Cole, Susannah Luther & Martha Cole. Grsons: Martin Luther & Theophilus Luther. Grdau. Johannah Willmarth. Witns: Samuel Bullock, Thomas Eastabrook & Joseph Mason [3:329/30/1].

Inv. of Est. of Mr. SAMUEL LUTHER of Swan., dtd. 31 Dec. 1716, pres. by Mary & Theophilus Luther. Apprs: Joseph Mason, John Thomas & Joseph Butterworth [3:332].

Will of MOSES READ of Reho., dtd. 28 May 1716, prob. 4 Feb. 1716/7. Wife Rebeckah. Sons: Zachariah (eldest) & Ezekiel (youngest). Dau. Rebeckah Mason wife of Samuel Mason. Grsons. Oliver Walker & Moses Walker (both under 21), sons of dau. & son-in-law Bethiah & Samuel Walker, both dcd. Grson. John Bishop son of John Bishop & dau. Mary Bishop dcd. Cousins Joshua Read & Elizabeth Read, both of whom I have brought up from a child. My servant John Robinson (under 21), son of John Robinson, Cordwinder. Witns: Timothy Ide, Thomas Lindley & Daniel Carpenter [3:333/4/5/6].

Inv of Est. of Capt. MOSES READ of Reho., dtd. 15 Jan. 1716/7, pres. by Ezekiel Read, son. Apprs: Daniel Smith & Daniel Carpenter [3:337].

End of Volume 3, Part 1

VOLUME 3 (PART 2)

1717-1721

Volume 3 of Bristol County probate records is bound in two
separate volumes. The first volume is called Part 1, and consists of pages 1-337. Part 2 contains pages 338-736. When
these records were microfilmed in Taunton in 1967 by the Church
of Jesus Christ of Latter Day Saints (Mormon), Part 2 was not
done. The microfilm on which Volume 3 appears jumps from page
337 of Part 1 directly to the first page of Volume 4.

This compiler contacted the office of the Probate Register in
Taunton in 1985 and was assured that there is in existence Part
2 of Volume 3. However, for some years it has been at a bind-
ery, where it is being painstakingly restored and re-bound. It
can be examined only by special arrangements made through the
Probate Register's office in Taunton.

In the front of Part 1 there is a hand-written index of the
contents of both Parts 1 and 2. Thus, it is possible to recon-
struct at least a skeleton of the subjects which are on the un-
microfilmed pages, 338-736. Presented below is a near-literal
transcription of the index entries for those pages in Part 2.
This listing does *not* index contents of Part 1.

. . . .

Inventory of Mr Jonathan Bliss 595
John ffoster Guardian to Hipzaba Blackenton 599
Administration granted to Samuel Blake upon his fathers person-
   al Estate 599
Mr Samuel Blakes Inventory 601
William Briggs his Receipt to his mother for Sixty pounds mon-
   ey 358
Samuel Bliss allowed to be Guardian to Ephraim Bliss 633
Abraham Carpenter allowed to be Guardian to Daniel Bliss 633
Widow Mary Bliss allowed guardian to her foure daughers minors
   to wit Mary Hannah Bethiah & Rachel 633
Thomas Brigg his Will 645 his Inventory 646
Accompts of Jonathan & Jacob Bliss 660 661 662
Devision Together about ye order of Estate of Jonathan Bliss
   662 663 664 665 666 667 668 669
Devision of s^d Blises personal Estate about ye order 669 670
   671 672
Jonathan & Jacob Bliss Receipts 673 674 675
Bosworth Elizabeth Letter of Administration Recorded 714
Bosworth Jno Inventory 714
Bowen Hezekiah Daniel Aron Nathan Agreem^t 715
Buckland Deborah Lett of Administration foll 719
[torn]eca Bliss widdow to James Bliss Resigns her
[torn]dministration with Thomas Bliss ye Eldest
[torn] foll 691
[torn] Inventory foll 692
[torn]on Granted to ye Second Son and
[torn]ly Sam^{ll} & Abraham foll 691

Mrs Alice Church Letter of Administration 380
Co^l Benjamin Churchs Inventory 381 382
The Agreement of the Children of Co^l Church 384
Joseph Carpenter Inventory 404
Zachariah Carpenters Inventory 423
The Accompt of Hannah Carpenter Administra^x of the Estate of
   her Husband deceased 424
   Her Receipts for money paid 423 424
Madam Church her Letter of Administration 380
Silvanus Cambels Will 461 Inventory 462
David Cary his Will 484 his Inventory 486
Henry Cranes Release & Quit Claim 487 488
George Cadmans Will 501 his inventory 502
John Cranes Will 503 504 his Inventory 50[torn]
Abiah Carpenters accompt of his mothers Est[torn]
   his Receipts 507
John Chaffe Allowed Guardian to Jonath[torn]
William Carpenters Will 524 his I[torn]
The Widow Cadmans Receipts [torn]
Silvanus Cambell his Will 6[torn]

Devision of Samuel Gallaps personal Estate 626 627 628
   order for ye Devision of s^d Estate 648
Pheby Greys acquittance foll 731
Thomas Grey & Edward Grey Letter of Administration

Hoskins Amee her acquittance to Richard Hoskins 350
Hoskins Rich^{d}s Release 351
The Will of Henry Hodges Es^q 365
   his Inventory 366
Mrs Deborah Hilliard Receipts 379 & 380
The Will of Deborah Hilliard 385   her In[torn]
Inventory of John Haile 393
Inventory of Richard Haile J^r[torn]
The Will of Bartholomew Hunt 3[torn]
Will of Joseph Hicks 402   his Inv[torn]
Nathaniel Hunt his Inventory [torn]
Stephen Hunt his Inventory [torn]
Benjamin Head 361   invent[torn]
Capt Henry Hodges his [torn]
Hilliard Richard [torn]
Deborah Hilliard Will 385   her Inventory 386
Ephraim Hathways Inventory 446
Josiah Howlands Inventory 454
The Accompt of Peter Hunt 474
John Hathway Jn^r Inventory 491
David Hilliards Receipts 518 519 520
   his allowance for further time to finish Administration 520
Mary Hix her accompt 561   also 559
Joseph Allens power of Attorney to Nath Howland 476
Samuel Hills his Inventory 574
The Accompt of Elizabeth Hathway 577
Mr John Hodges his Will folio 584 585
   Inventory 578
Hayman John his Will 621   his Inventory 622
Hannour Greenfyeld 213[or 713?]
Edward Halls Letter of Administration foll 734
Jno Halls Inventory 734

Jaret Ingraham Will 376   his Inventory 377
Mrs Priscilla Irish Letter of Administration 383
John Irish his Will 387   his Inventory 389
Joseph Jennings his Will 421
Samuel Jenne his Inventory 437
Benj^a Jones his Will 469
The Accompt of Hannah Jenne 588 & Receipts 589
David Irish his accompt 684 685 686

The accompt of John Knap Adminstrator upon the Estate of his
   father 364

End of Index of Vol. 3, Part 2

VOLUME 4

1721-1723

Appt. of John Summers of Rochester, Co. of Plym., as Adm. of
Est. of his brother NATHAN SUMMERS of Dart. dcd. intest.,
dtd. 5 Jan. 1721/2 [4:1].
Petition by Mary Carpenter, widow of DANIEL CARPENTER of Reho.
& by Daniel Carpenter, eldest son, that Adm. be granted to
Jabez Carpenter, 2nd son, dtd. 24 Oct. 1721 [4:2].
Appt. of Jabez Carpenter as Adm. of Est. of his father DANIEL
CARPENTER, dtd. 16 Nov. 1721 [4:2].
Inv. of Est. of DANIEL CARPENTER of Reho., dtd. 24 Oct. 1721,
pres. by Daniel Carpenter, his son. Apprs: Daniel Smith, Abi-
all Carpenter & Thomas Read, Jr. [4:3/4/5].
Order to Hannah Read, widow, for inv. of Est. of her husb. John
Read of Free., dtd. 5 Feb. 1721/2 [4:5/6].
Will of JOHN READ of Free., Yeoman, dtd. 5 March 1713/4, prob.
6 Feb. 1721/2. Wife Hannah. Sons: John (eldest) & Joseph Read.
Grchldn: Benjamin, John, Joseph, Oliver & Thomas Sherman, (all
under 21), chldn. of my dau. Hannah Sherman dcd. Witns: Con-
stant Church, John Peirce & Nathan   Classon [4:6/7/8].
Order to William Winslow, eldest son, for inv. of Est. of his
father JOABE WINSLOW of Free., dtd. 19 Feb. 1721/2 [4:9].
Will of JOABE WINSLOW of Free., Yeoman, dtd. 12 Nov. 1717, prob.
19 Feb. 1721/2. Wife Ruth. Sons: William, Richard, James,
George, Jonathan, Joseph (of Swan.) & John Winslow. Dau. Elizabeth Winslow. Witns: Daniel Whitehead, Samuel Allen & John
Read [4:9/10/1].
Will of EPHRAIM MAY of Reho., Cordwainer, "being sick & weake
in Body,"Dtd. 1 Sept. 1721, prob. 16 Nov. 1721. To wife Deliverance "all the Household Stuff which She brough to mee
when wee were first married." Son Ephraim (under 21). Daus:
Hannah May, Deliverance May, Naomy May & Bethia May (all under 20). "My Honored Father Israel Peck" Witns: Joseph Peck,
Nicholas Peck & Elisha May [4:12/3].
Inv. of Est. of EPHRAIM MAY of Reho. dtd. 15 Nov. 1721, pres.
by Deliverance May, widow & Exec. Apprs: Thomas Ormsbery, Joseph Peck & Jabez Bozworth [4:13/4].
Will of JOHN INGOLS of Reho., Yeoman, dtd. 16 Apr. 1718, prob.
5 Feb. 1721/2. Sons John Ingols who "hath been a disobedient
and undutifull son to me." "Well beloved Son Edmund Ingols."
2 daus. Elizabeth Crabtree wife of Benjamin Crabtree, & Sarah
Howard wife of William Hayward [sic]. No wife mentioned, except mention of his daus. includes "divide their mothers
cloathes." Witns: John West & Hennery West [4:15.
Inv. of Est. of JOHN INGOLS, Yeoman, dtd. 26 Jan. 1721/2, pres.
5 Feb. 1721/2 by Edmund Ingols, son & Exec. Apprs: John West,
James Hix & John Horton [4:16].

83

Rcpt. by Elisha May & Elizabeth May of Taun. for legacy to Elizabeth in will of her father JAMES WALKER of Taun., paid by
"our Brother Nehemiah Walker" of Taun., Exec. dtd. 2 Apr. 1722.
Witns: Joseph Allen & Hannah May [4:16/7].

Rcpt. by Cornelius White & Mehitabel White of Taun. for legacy
from Her father JAMES WALKER of Taun., paid by "our Brother
Nehemiah Walker," Exec., dtd. 24 FEb. 1721/2. Witns: James
Walker & Eliakim Walker [*Also see entry below for Cornelius &
Mehitable Wight*][4:17].

Rcpt. by John Gilbert & Mary Gilbert of Taun. for legacy from
her father, JAMES WALKER of Taun., paid by "our Brother Nehemiah Walker," Exec., dtd. 6 March 1721/2. Witns: Timothy
Smith & Seth Makefpeace [4:17].

Rcpt. by Cornelius Wight & Mehittable Wight [*In diff. handwriting,
but is identical to entry above for Cornelius & Mehitabell
White*]. Relating to JAMES WALKER of Taun. [4:18].

Rcpt. by Richard Godfree, Jr. & Barsheba Godfrey of Taun. for
legacy from her father JAMES WALKER of Taun., paid by "our
Brother Nehemiah Walker," dtd. 7 Feb. 1721/2. Witns: John
Godfree & Sary Hancum [4:18].

Rcpt. by William Linkon & Rebeckah Linkon of Taun. for a legacy
from her father JAMES WALKER of Taun., paid by "our Brother
Nehemiah Walker," dtd. 24 Feb. 1721/2. Witns: Josiah Walker
& Abigail Walker [4:19].

Will of THOMAS GRAY of Lit. Comp., Yeoman, "being sicke &weak,"
dtd. 21 Sept. 1721, prob. 23 Nov. 1721. Wife Pheby. 2 sons:
Thomas & Edward Gray. Daus: Anna Richmond & Rebeccah Gray.
Grchldn. Barzeller Richmond, Mary Gray & Anstes Gray. Warren
Gibs, son of my kinsman Nathaniel Gibs. Mentions; my negro
maid Peg, negro woman Sarah, negro man Will, mulatto girl Al-
mey & mulatto boys Solomon & Jefery. Mentions his land in
Lit. Comp. & Tiv. & house lots in "Plimouth Town." Witns:
Capt. John Palmer, William Simmonds & Nathaniel Searles[4:19/
20/1/2/3].

Codicil to will by THOMAS GRAY of Lit. Comp., dtd. 21 Oct. 1721.
Wife Pheby. Sons Thomas & Edward. Witns: Silvester Richmond,
Jonathan Davenport, Jr. & Nathaniel Searles [4:24/5].

Inv. of Est. of Capt. THOMAS GRAY of Lit. Comp., dtd. 7 Nov.
1721, pres. by Thomas & Edward Gray, sons & Execs. Apprs:
Thomas Church, William Pabody & John Wood [4:25/6/7/8].

Will of JOSEPH TISDALE of Taun., "being very Sicke," dtd. 12
Feb. 1721/2, prob. 2 March 1721/2. Wife Mary. 2 sons: Joseph
& Elkanah Tisdale. Daus: Mary dcd. who married Joseph Winslow
of Swan., Hannah dcd. who married William Hodges, Sarah wife
of Thomas Read of Digh., Abigail wife of Ephraim Hayward of
Bridgewater, Elizabeth Tisdale yet unmar. To the chldn. [5?]
of my dau. Mary dcd. To George & Abigail Hodges, chldn. of
my dau. Hannah dcd. Witns: Thomas Harvey, Thomas Macomber &
Samuel Hacket, Jr. [4:29/30].

Appt. of Mary Burr, widow, to be Adm. of Est. of her husb. SY-
MOND BURR of Reho., dtd. 16 Apr. 1722 [4:31/2].
Petition by Sarah Garnsey, widow of JOHN GARNSEY dcd. intest.,
declining Adm. & asking that Adm. be granted to "some of my
Husbands children," dtd. 5 Apr. 1722. Witns: Joseph Garnsey
& Francis Wilson [4:33].
Appt. of Seth Garnsey, son, & James Bowen, son-in-law, as Adms.
of Est. of JOHN GARNSEY of Reho., dtd. 16 Apr. 1722 [4:33].
Order to Seth Garnsey, son, & James Bowen, son-in-law, to have
inv. of Est. of JOHN GARNSEY of Reho.,dtd. 16 Apr. 1722 [4:
33/4].
Will of SYMOND BURR, Sr. of Reho., Cooper, "Being In a week &
Languishing Condition," dtd. 14 Dec. 1721, prob. 16 Apr. 1722.
Wife Mary. Sons: Symond, Isaac, David & Samuel Burr. Daus: Han-
nah Burr, Mary Burr, Ruth wife of Hennery Smith & Rachel Burr.
Grson. Symond Smith son of my dau. Ruth Smith. Friends Lt.Jon-
athan Kingsley & James Bowen to apprize my Est. Witns: Jona-
than Kingsley, James Brown & Elisha Bisbe [4:35/6].
Inv. of Est. of DANIEL BLANDING of Reho., dcd. intest., dtd. 20
Oct. 1721, pres. by Mary Blanden [sic], his widow. Apprs: Sam-
uel Fuller, Nathaniel Willmarth & John Willmarth [4:37].
Inv. of Est. of NATHANIEL SUMMERS of Dart., dtd. 10 Feb. 1721/2,
pres. by John Summers, his brother & Adm. Apprs: Elisha Wing,
Ebenezer Holmes & Edward Winslow [4:38].
Inv. of Est. of JOSEPH PECK of Reho., dtd. 28 Oct. 1720, pres.
by Joseph & Nicholas Peck, his sons. Apprs: Jathniel Peck,
Ephraim May & Jabez Bozworth [4:39].
Acct. of Joseph Peck & Nicholas Peck, Adms. of Est. of their
father JOSEPH PECK of Reho., dtd. 23 Feb. 1721/2. Mentions
paym. to abt. 25 people, incl. an item "To Household Goods
advanced to mary Butterworth upon her marriage" [4:40/1].
Order for div. of Est. of Mr. JOSEPH PECK of Reho. dcd. intest.
dtd. 22 Feb. 1721/2 [4:41].
Div. of Est. of Mr. JOSEPH PECK of Reho., dtd. 24 Feb. 1721/2,
among his chldn: Joseph Peck (eldest son), Nicholas Peck (2nd
son), Israel Peck (3rd son), Stephen Peck (youngest son), Mary
Butterworth (eldest dau.), Lydiah Peck (2nd dau.) & Margaret
(youngest dau.). Comm: Daniel Smith, Abiall Carpenter, Samuel
Mason & Peter Hunt [4:42/3/4].
Appt. of Samuel Kingsley of Taun. North Purch. as guard. of
Bethia Kingsley & Abigail Kingsley, daus. of SAMUEL KINGSLEY
of Taun. No. Pur. dcd., dtd. 5 March 1721/2 [4:44].
Elizabeth Whitaker, dau. of Mr. SAMUEL WHITAKER of Reho. dcd.,
chose Joshua Smith of Reho. as her guard. [4:44].
Order to Hannah Howland, widow & Exec. of NICHOLAS HOWLAND of
Dart. to obtain inv., dtd. 7 May 1722 [4:45].
Margaret Peck, dau. of JOSEPH PECK of Reho. dcd., chose John
Butterworth, Jr. of Reho. as her guard., dtd. 21 Feb. 1721/2
[4:46].

Appt. of Rebecca Bliss, widow of SAMUEL BLISS dcd., as guard. of
her son John Bliss, dtd. 21 Feb. 1721/2 [4:46].

Lydia Peck, dau. of JOSEPH PECK of Reho. dcd., chose Peter Hunt
of Reho as her guard., dtd. 21 Feb. 1721/2 [4:46].

Jonathan Perry, son of THOMAS PERRY, Jr. dcd. chose Jathniel
Peck of Reho. to be his guard., dtd. 21 Feb. 1721/2 [4:46].

Zachariah Briggs, son of CLEMENT BRIGGS dcd., chose Thomas Manley of Taun. No. Purch. as his guard., dtd. 5 March 1721/2
[4:46].

Lidiah Briggs, dau. of CLEMENT BRIGGS of Taun. No. Purch. dcd.,
chose Ephraim Randall as her guard., dtd. 5 March 1721/2[4:46].

Appt. of Ephraim Randall of Taun. No. Pur. as guard. of John
Briggs, son of CLEMENT BRIGGS of Taun. No. Pur., dtd. 5 March
1721/2 [4:46].

Thomas Manly of Taun. No. Pur. allowed to be guard. of Hannah
Briggs, dau. of CLEMENT BRIGGS, dtd. 5 March 1721/2 [4:46].

Appt. of Sarah Wilcox as Adm. of Est. of her husb. DANIEL WIL-
COX of Dart. dcd. intest., dtd. 7 May 1722 [4:47].

Order for inv. to Mary Tisdell, widow, & to Joseph Tisdell, son,
& to Elkanah Tisdell, son of JOSEPH TISDELL of Taun., dtd. 2
March 1721/2 [4:48].

Inv. of Est. of Mr. JOHN GARNSEY of Reho., Carpenter, dtd. 20
Apr. 1722, pres. by Seth Garnsey & James Bowen, Adms. Apprs:
William Salisbury, Francis Wilson & John Thompson [4:49/50].

Acct. of Remembrance Cory, Adm. of Est. of her husb. JOHN DYE
of Lit. Comp. dcd. intest., dtd. 7 May 1722. Incl. paym. to
abt. 16 persons [4:51/2].

Inv. of Est. of CLEMENT BRIGGS of Taun. No. Pur. East Precinct
of Norton dcd. intest., dtd. 3 FEb. 1720/1, pres. by Clement
Briggs, his son & Adm. Apprs: Thomas Randoll, Josiah Keith &
Ephraim Randoll [4:52/3].

Acct. of Clement Briggs, son & Adm. of Est. of his father CLEM-
ENT BRIGGS of East Precinct of Nort., dtd. 5 Sept. 1721[4:53/4].

Acct. of Francis Wilson & Thomas Ormsbery, Adms. of Est. of
NATHANIEL WHITAKER of Reho. dcd. intest., dtd. 15 Jan. 1721/2.
Mentions: Christopher Bowen & Rebecca his wife, sister to the
dcd., Aron Bowen & Experience his wife, another of said sisters, Samuel Millard & Hannah his wife another of said sisters
& Margaret another sister to said dcd. [4:55][*Apparently this
entry refers to Nathaniel Whitaker, son of Nathaniel Whitaker,
With the death of the son, his portion of his father's Est.
was then divided btwn. his surviving sisters, as noted in the
rcpts. below*].

Rcpt. by Aron Bowen & Experience his wife for legacy on her own
behalf & in behalf of her bro. Phillip dcd., Experience being
sister of NATHANIEL WHITAKER of Reho. dcd., from Est. of their
father, paid by Francis Wilson & Thomas Ormsbery, Adms., dtd.
18 Dec. 1721. Witns: Samuel Miller & Stephen Bowen [4:56].

Rcpt. by Samuel Millard & Hannah his wife for legacies in her own behalf & in behalf of her bro. Phillip dcd., Hannah being sister of dcd. NATHANIEL WHITAKER of Reho., said legacies from Est. of her father, paid by Francis Wilson & Thomas Ormsbery, Adms., dtd. 9 Dec. 1721. Witns: James Bowen & Jonathan Wilcox [4:56].

Rcpt. by Christopher Bowen & Rebecah Bowen his wife for her own & part of her brother Phillip's (dcd.) legacies, Rebecah being sister of dcd. NATHANIEL WHITAKER of Reho., said legacies from her father's Est., paid by Francis Wilson & Thomas Ormsbery, Adms., dtd. 11 Dec. 1722. Witns: John Carpenter & Margaret Whitaker [4:56].

Rcpt. by Francis Wilson, guard. of Margaret Whitaker, for her own & part of her brother Phillip's (dcd.) legacies, Margaret being sister of dcd. NATHANIEL WHITAKER of Reho., said legacies from her father's Est., paid by Thomas Ormsbery, Adm., dtd. 18 Dec. 1722. Witns: James Bowen & Jane Whitaker [4:56].

Inv. of Est. of JOHN READ of Digh. who died 13 Jan. 1721/2, dtd. 30 Apr. 1722, pres. by Bethiah Read, widow, & by George Read, son, Execs. Apprs: Daniel King & Ephraim Emerson[4:56½].

Inv. of Est. of BENJAMIN CRANE of Digh. who died 13 Oct. 1721, dtd. 2 Nov. 1721, pres. by Mary Crane, his widow. Apprs: Deacon Abraham Hathaway, Gershom Crane & Capt. Jared Talbut [4:56½/7/7½].

Div. of Est. of NATHANIEL COOPER of Reho., dtd. 2 Apr. 1722, btwn. his chldn: Peter (eldest son), Nathaniel (2nd son) & Judith Cooper (dau.). Comm: Daniel Smith, Daniel Carpenter, Thomas Cooper & Thomas Read [4:58/9].

Will of NICHOLAS HOWLAND of Dartmouth, dtd. 9 March 1721/2, prob. 7 May 1722. Wife Hannah. Sons: Samuel (eldest), Nicholas (2nd), Joseph, Daniel, Joab & Benjamin Howland. Daus: Abigail Russell (eldest), Mary Tucker (2nd), Rebeccah Howland (3rd), Hannah Howland (4th) & Edith Howland (5th)(last 2 are under 18). Witns: John Tucker, Hennery Howland & William Soule [4:59/60/1].

Inv. of Est. of NICHOLAS HOWLAND of Dart., Cord Winder [sic], dtd. 18, 20 & 24 Apr. 1722, pres. by Hannah Howland, his widow & Exec. Apprs: John Tucker, Hennery Howland & William Soule [4:61/2/3/4].

Order for inv. of Est. of EBENEZER PAUL of Digh. to Edward Paul of Digh., brother & Exec., dtd. 4 June 1722 [4:64].

Will of EBENEZER PAULL of Taun., "being in the 26th year of my age and in Good Health...whereas I am now about going forth in an expedition against ye Common Enemy and under the Command of Capt Thomas Church of Bristol," dtd. 4 Jan. 1702, prob. 4 June 1722. Wife Sarah, to whom is also given "The Householde Stuff which She brought with her." Brother Edward Paull. Witns: Thomas Leonard, Benjamin Crane, Thomas Robberts & Joseph Tisdell [4:65].

Bond given by Hannah Read, Exec. of Est. of her husb. JOHN READ of Free., dtd. 4 June 1722 [4:66].

Inv. of Est. of Mr. JOSEPH TISDELL of Taun., dtd. 26 FEb. 1721/2, pres. by Joseph Tisdail & Elkanah Tisdail, sons & Execs. Apprs: Seth Williams, John Andross & Samuel Leonard [4:66/7/8].

Acct. of John Reed of Free., Adm. of Est. of Mrs. MARY PEIRCE of Tiv., dtd. 4 June 1722. Mentions paym. to abt. 20 persons, incl: "Susannah Sheffield being a Legacy," "John Wilcoks being a Legacy to his wife," "The Administrator being a Legacy to his wife," & "John Pearce being a Legacy [4:68/9].

Acct. of Jabez Carpenter, Adm. of Est. of his father DANIEL CARPENTER of Reho. dcd. intest., dtd. 16 March 1721/2. Mentions money paid by and to abt. 50 diff. persons, incl: Nathaniel Carpenter, Josiah Carpenter, Insigne Abiell Carpenter, Ephraim Carpenter, James Carpenter & Jabez Carpenter [4:69½/70].

Order for div. of Est. of DANIEL CARPENTER of Reho., dtd. 16 March 1721/2 [4:70].

Div. of Est. of DANIEL CARPENTER of Reho. btwn. his widow Mary Carpenter & his chldn: Daniel (eldest son), Jabez (2nd son), Eleazer (youngest son) & Bethiah Carpenter (dau.), dtd. 29 March 1721/2. Comm: Daniel Smith, Abiall Carpenter, John Robinson & Thomas Read [4:70/1/2/3/4].

Rcpt. by Mary Carpenter for legacy from Est. of DANIEL CARPENTER of Reho., paid by Jabez Carpenter, Adm., dtd. 30 March 1721/2. Witns: Abiell Carpenter & Mary Hunt [4:74].

Rcpt. by Daniel Carpenter for legacy from Est. of DANIEL CARPENTER of Reho. paid by Jabez Carpenter, Adm., dtd. 30 March 1721/2. Witns: Mary Carpenter & Mary Hunt [4:74].

Rcpt. by Obediah Carpenter, guard. of Eleazer & Bethiah Carpenter, son & dau. of DANIEL CARPENTER of Reho., for legacy paid by Jabez Carpenter, Adm., dtd. 30 March 1721/2. Witns: Mary Carpenter & Daniel Carpenter [4:75].

Acct. of Elisha Bliss, Adm. of Est. of his bro. JACOB BLISS of Reho dcd. intest., dtd. 1 Jan. 1721/2. Mentions paym. to abt. 8 persons, incl. "To Docter Squire Allen for Phissick & time in visiting the Deceased" [4:75/6].

Acct. of Samuel Bliss & Abraham Bliss of Reho., Adms. of Est. of their father SAMUEL BLISS of Reho. dcd. intest., dtd. 13 Feb. 1721/2. Mentions paym. to Rebecca Bliss widow of Samuel [4:76/76½/77].

Order for div. of Est. of SAMUEL BLISS of Reho., dtd. 22 Feb. 1721/2 [4:77/8].

Div. of Est. of SAMUEL BLISS of Reho. btwn. his widow Rebecah Bliss & chldn: Thomas (eldest son), Samuel (2nd son), Abraham (3rd son), Nathaniel (4th son) & John (youngest son); Ruth Sabin (eldest dau.) & Mary Bliss (youngest dau.), dtd. 7 March 1721/2. Comm: Daniel Smith, Abiah Carpenter, Josiah Carpenter & John Willmouth [4:78/9/80/1].

Will of ABRAHAM HOLMES of Dart., "being well Stricken In years,"
dtd. 3 Aug. 1714, prob. 8 July 1722. No wife mentioned. Son
Experience Holmes. Daus: Elisabeth Bowrne, Bersheba Dogged,
Rose Blancker & Susanah Whitman dcd. Witns: William Rayment,
Mary Mallard & Timothy Ruggles [4:81/2/3].

Acct. of Seth Garnsey & James Bowen, Adms. of Est. of JOHN GARN-
SEY of Reho., dtd. 9 May 1722. Remaining balance div. btwn.
widow Sarah Garnsey & chldn: Hennery (eldest son), Ebenezer,
Joseph, John, Seth & Beriah Garnsey; Mehetibell wife of John
Horton, Hannah wife of Thomas Horton, Elesebeth wife of James
Bowen, Mary wife of Samuel Hicks & Waitstill wife of Timothy
Titus [4:83/4].

Order for div. pers. Est. of JOHN GARNSEY of Reho., dtd. 12 May
1722 [4:85].

Div. of pers. Est. of JOHN GARNSEY of Reho. btwn. widow Sarah
Garnsey & chldn: Hennery (eldest son), Ebenezer, Joseph, John
& Seth Garnsey; Mehetible Horton wife of John Horton, Hannah
Horton wife of Thomas Horton, Elizabeth Bowen wife of James
Bowen, Mary Hix wife of Samuel Hix, Waitstill Titus wife of
Timothy Titus & Beriah Garnsey (son) whose guard. is Jacob
Ormsbery, dtd. 13 July 1722. Comm: John West, Francis Wilson
& Jonathan Kingsley [4:85/6/7/8].

Inv. of Est. of SIMON BURR of Reho., dtd. 23 Apr. 1722, pres.
by Mary Burr, widow, & by Samuel Burr, son, Execs. Apprs: Jonathan Kingsley & James Bowen [4:89/90].

Acct. of Mary Whitaker & Richard Whitaker of Reho., Adms. of
Est. of her husb. & his father, SAMUEL WHITAKER of Reho. dcd.
intest., dtd. 22 Feb. 1721/2 [4:91/2].

Order for div. of Est. of SAMUEL WHITACER of Reho., dtd. 22
Feb. 1721/2 [4:93].

Div. of Est. of SAMUEL WHITAKER of Reho. btwn. widow Mary Whit-
aker & chldn: Richard (eldest son) & Samuel (youngest son)
Whitaker; Sarah Briggs (eldest dau.), Mary Smith (2nd dau.),
Jane Whitaker (3rd dau.), Elizabeth Whitaker (4th dau.), Gris-
sel Whitaker (5th dau.) Rachel Whitaker (6th dau.) & Ruth
Whitaker (youngest dau.), dtd. 16 March 1721/2. Comm: Daniel
Smith, John Wilmarth & Samuel Fuller [4:93/4/5].

Acct. of Joseph Southworth & Samuel Southworth, sons & Execs.
of Est. of Capt. WILLIAM SOUTHWORTH of Lit. Comp., dtd. 7
Feb. 1721/2. Mentions: "To the Gardian of Samuel Blangue" &
legacies paid to Edward Southworth, to Benjamin Southworth,
to Thomas Southworth, to Joseph Southworth, to Stephen Southworth & to Andrew Southworth per will [4:96/7/8/9/100].

Rcpt. by Robert Jolls of Brist., Yeoman, guard. to Thomas Martin of Brist. dcd., son of John Martin, Jr., for a legacy
paid by Joseph Martin, Exec. of Est. of his father JOHN MAR-
TIN of Lebenon Connecticut, said money left to Thomas Martin
by his grandfather John Martin of Lebenon, dtd. 26 Oct. 1722
[4:100].

Appt. of Stephen Tabby as Adm. of Est. of his mother Mrs. PRIS-
CILLA IRISH, widow of John Irish of Lit. Comp., dtd. 3 Sept.
1722 [4:101].
Appt. of Jonathan Taber as sole Exec. of Est. of his father THO-
MAS TABER, Jr., since Joseph Taber brother of the dcd. Thomas
declined to be Exec., dtd. 4 Sept. 1722 [4:102].
Satisfaction by Rebecca Taber with will of her husb., dtd. 1
Sept. 1722 [4:102].
Order to Jonathan Taber to execute will of his father THOMAS TA-
BER, Jr. of Dart., dtd. 4 Sept. 1722 [4:102/3].
Will of THOMAS TABER, Jr. of Dart., Tanner, "Being Weake in
Body," dtd. 2 Aug. 1722, prob. 4 Sept. 1722. Wife Rebecca.
Sons: Jonathan & Seth Taber. Daus: Prissillah Taber, Easter
Taber & Mary Taber (all under 23 years). Son Jonathan Taber &
brother Joseph Taber to be Execs. Witns: Jonathan Delano, Sam-
uel Spanner & Thomas Lenney [4:103/4/5].
Inv. of Est. of EBENEZER PAUL of Digh., Yeoman, dtd. 8 Aug. 1722,
pres. by Edward Paul, brother & Exec. Apprs: Deacon Joseph
Dean, Deacon Abraham Hathaway & Daniel Axtell [4:106].
Inv. of Est. of DANIEL WILCOX of Dart. who died 22 Feb. 1721/2,
dtd. 2 March 1721/2, pres. by Mrs. Sarah Wilcox, his widow.
Apprs: George Lawton, Samuel Cornell & Capt. John Akin [4:
107/8].
Appt. of Elesebeth Kenikett as Adm. of Est. of her husb. JOHN
KENIKETT of Swan., dtd. 10 Sept. 1722 [4:109].
Rcpt. by Thomas Cook of legacy from Est. of "our Honoured Moth-
er MARY PEARCE of Tiverton," paid by John Read, Adm., dtd. 24
July 1722 [4:110].
Rcpt. by Samuel Sherman of legacy from Est. of "our Honoured
Mother MARY PEARCE" of Tiv., paid by John Read, Adm., dtd.
24 July 1722 [4:110].
Rcpt. by John Cook of legacy from Est. of "our Honoured Mother"
MARY PEARCE of Tiv., paid by John Read, Adm., dtd. 24 July
1722 [4:110].
Rcpt. by Black [?] Perry from Est. of "our Honoured Mother" MARY
PEARCE of Tiv., paid by John Read, Adm., dtd. 24 July 1722
[4:110].
Inv. of Est. of Mrs. PRICILLA IRISH of Lit. Comp. who died 11
June 1722, dtd. 8 Sept. 1722, pres. by Stephen Tabbey, son.
Apprs: Jonathan Wood, Peter Horsewell & William Pabodie [4:
111/2].
Inv. of Est. of Ens. JOHN KENICET of Swan. who died 23 Aug.
1722, dtd. 29 Aug. 1722, pres. by Elesebeth Kenniket, his widow. Apprs: Joseph Mason, Thomas Eastarbrooke & Edward Luther
[4:113/4].
Rcpts. by Eleazer Gilbert late of Taun. but now of Norton, for
legacy from Est. of his father ELEAZER GILBERT of Taun., paid
by Elizabeth Townsen of Taun., his widow & Adm. & also mother
of this son Eleazer. Elizabeth is now also widow of George

Townsen dcd., dtd. 4 Feb. 1717/8 & 13 Jan. 1719/20. Witns:
John Gilbert & Elizabeth Willis; & Mary Williams & James Williams [4:115/6].

Rcpt. by Stephen Gary & Mercy Gary of Taun. for legacy from
Est. of Mercy's father ELEAZER GILBERT of Taun., as paid by
"our father in law [stepfather] George Townsen & mother Elizabeth Townsen," Adm. of Eleazer, dtd. 4 May 1717. Witns: Seth
Williams & Elnathan Thrasher [4:116].

Acct. of Elizabeth Townsen of Taun., Exec. of Est. of her husb.
GEORGE TOWNSEN of Taun., dtd. 1 Oct. 1722 [4:117/8].

Ratification of earlier agrmt. abt. settl. of Est. of RICHARD
KERBY of Dart., "somtime more y^n Ninteen years since Died
Intestate," said agrmt. having been btwn. Richard's chldn:
Richard & Recompense Kerby; Sarah Allen & Ruhamath Smith
(both of Dart. & both widows) & Jane Leander of Sandwich (now
dcd.), dtd. 21 July 1707, recorded 9 Oct. 1722. Witns: Henery
Howland & Samuel Marehu [4:119].

Accept. of settl. of Est. of RICHARD KERBY of Dart. by his gr-
chldn: Tabatha Waite, Deborah Leander, Sarah Leander & Joseph
Leander, chldn. of Jane Leander late of Sandwich dcd., dtd. 9
Oct. 1707, 29 March 1708 & 31 March 1708. Witns: Joseph Tripp
& John Tripp; John Lapham, Jr. & Judah Smith; William Soule
& Samuel Merehou [4:120].

Appt. of Hannah Carr as Adm. to Est. of her husb. ROBERT CARR
of Swan. dcd. intest., dtd. 22 Oct. 1722 [4:121].

Inv. of Est. of Mr. ROBERT CARR of Swan., Merchant, dtd. 20
Oct. 1722, pres. by Mrs. Hannah Carr, his widow. Mentions his
lands in Swan., Reho., Barrington, Newport & in Ashford, Ct.
Apprs: John Devotion, Barnard Haile & Aron Bowen [4:122/3].

Appt. of Patience Holmes, as Adm. of Ests. of her husb. EXPER-
IENCE HOLMES & of ABRAHAM HOLMES, both of Dart., said Experience having been son & Exec. of Abraham dcd., dtd. 27 Oct.
7122 [4:124].

Acct. of John Summers of Rochester, Adm. of Est. of his brother
NATHAN SUMMERS of Dart., dtd. 30 Oct. 1722 [4:125/6].

Agrmt. abt. settl. of Est. of NATHAN SUMMERS of Dart. by his
brothers & sisters: John Summers, Stephen Wing & Elizabeth
his wife, John Walker & Sarah his wife, Jeneverah (female)
Summers, Keziah Summers & Nathan DAvis & Elizabeth Davis in
the right of their mother Mary Davis dcd. who was sister to
Nathan Summers, dtd. 31 Oct. 1722 [4:126/7].

Acct. of Patience Holmes, Adm. of Est. of her husb. EXPERIENCE
HOLMES of Dart., dtd. 30 Oct. 1722. Mentions an item "To
charges for and about a posthumus child" [4:128/9].

Inv. of Est. of Deacon ABRAHAM HOLMES of Dart., dtd. 17 July
1722, pres. 30 Oct. 1722 by Patience Holmes, widow of Experience Holmes son of Abraham & Adm. of both Ests. Apprs: Joseph Sampson & John Walker [4:129/30].

More time granted to Mrs. Mary Rosier [?[, Adm. of Est. of her
   former husb. Mr. SETH DEANE of Taun., her father Mr. Edward
   Cobb appearing to inform court she cannot come due to sickness, dtd. 5 Nov. 1722 [4:130].
Petition of Francis Wilson, John West, Thomas Shaw & Joseph
   Garnsey (son) abt. land & housing left by JOHN GARNSEY of Re-
   ho., dtd. 8 Oct. 1722 [4:130].
Petition by Hennery, Ebenezer, Joseph & John Garnsey (eldest,
   2nd, 3rd & 4th sons of JOHN GARNSEY dcd.), asking that land
   left by their father be granted to their brother Seth Garn-
   sey, dtd. 9 Oct. 1722 [4:131].
Order for appraisal of above land & housing left by JOHN GARN-
   SEY of Reho., dtd. 2 Nov. 1722 [4:131].
Appraisal & granting of above land & housing left by JOHN GARN-
   SEY to Seth Garnsey (5th son), with Seth to pay his brothers &
   sisters: Hennery (eldest son), Ebenezer, Joseph, John & Ber-
   iah Garnsey; Mehitabell wife of John Horton, Hannah wife of
   Thomas Horton, Elizabeth wife of James Bowen, Mary wife of
   Samuel Hicks & Waitstill wife of Timothy Titus. Also mentions
   Sarah Garnsey, widow of John. Comm: Francis Wilson, William
   Salsbery & John Thompson [4:132/3].
Order for div. of Est. of CLEMENT BRIGGS of Taun. No. Purch.,
   dtd. 6 March 1721/2 [4:133].
Div. of Est. of CLEMENT BRIGGS of Taun. No. Purch. among his
   chldn: Clement (eldest son), Zachariah (2nd son) & John (3rd
   son); Elizabeth Briggs (eldest dau.), Hannah Briggs (2nd dau.)
   & Lidiah Briggs (3rd & youngest dau.), dtd. 5 Oct. 1722. Comm:
   Ephraim Randell, John Phillips, Thomas Manley, Samuel Kings-
   ley & Benjamin Drake [4:134-140].
Order for div. of Est. of SAMUEL KINGSLEY of Taun. No. Purch.,
   dtd. 5 Marche 1721/2 [4:141].
Div. of Est. of SAMUEL KINGSLEY of Taun. No. Purch. dcd. intest.
   btwn. widow [not named] & the chldn: Samuel (eldest son) &
   Benjamin (2nd son) Kingsley; Hannah Hayward (eldest dau.),
   Sarah Hayward (2nd dau.), Mary Willis (3rd dau.), Susanah
   Kingsley (4th dau.), Abigail Kingsley (5th dau.) & Bethiah
   Kingsley (6th & youngest dau.), dtd. 5 Oct. 1722. Comm: Ben-
   jamin Drake, Thomas Manley, Ephraim Randell & John Phillips
   [4:141-147].
Appt. of Edward Gray as Adm. of Est. of his son EDWARD GRAY,
   Jr. of Tiv. dcd. intest., dtd. 3 Dec. 1722 [4:148].
Inv. of Est. of THOMAS TABER, Jr. of Dart., Tanner, dtd. 30
   Nov. 1722, pres. by Jonathan Taber, his son & Exec. Apprs:
   Philip Taber & Stephen West [4:149].
Inv. of Est. of EDWARD GRAY, Jr. of Tiv., Yeoman, dtd. 19 Nov.
   1722, pres. by Rebecca Gray, his widow. Apprs: Joseph Seabery,
   Samuel Sandford & Benjamin Earll [4:150/1].
Acct. of Bridget Pampalion of Brist., Exec. of Est. of her
   husb. Mr. JOHN PAMPELION of Brist., dtd. 9 Nov. 1722. Mentions

paym. to abt. 21 persons, incl. "To Benj: Pamelion for Wager
dew to him." Ordered that the balance of Est. be div. btwn.
"the Widow & Child of the deceased," naming "Mrs Bridgett y^e
Widoww," & "Ebenezer Pampelion the Son" [4:152/3].
Appt. of William Whipple, Husbandman of Attl., as Adm. of Est.
of his mother HANNAH WHIPPLE of Attl. Mentions son Israel
Whipple who dcd. before his mother. Dtd. 8 Dec. 1722[4:154/5].
Will of HANNAH WHIPPLE of Attl., widow, "being aged and Weak,"
dtd. 8 May 1720, prob. 8 Dec. 1722. Chldn: Joseph Cornell [or
Cowell?], Jeremiah Whipple, Israel Whipple, William Whipple,
Deborah Tower & Sarah Razey. Witns: Anthony Sprague, Sarah
Whiteman & Lydia Sprague [4:155/6].
Inv. of Est. of Mrs. HANNAH WHIPPLE of Attl., widow, dtd. 25
Oct. 1722, pres. 8 Dec. 1722 by William Whipple, son & Adm.
Apprs: Silvanus Scott, Daniel Jenckes & Gilbert Grant[4:156/7].
Order for inv. to Joseph Peckcom of Lit. Comp., Yeoman, Adm. of
Est. of his father JOHN PECKCOM of Lit. Comp., dtd. 7 Jan.
1722/3 [4:158].
Will of JOHN PECKUM of Lit. Comp., Yeoman, dtd. 1 Dec. 1722,
prob. 7 Jan. 1722/3. Wife Mary. Sons: John, Joseph & Ruben
Peckum. Daus: Lydia, Margaret & Ruth (later mentions daus. as
unmar.). Mentions a bedroom for "my mother in Law Margarat
Bennit." Friends Joseph Wanton of Tiv. & John Tayler of Lit.
Comp. as Overseers. Witns: David Hillard, William Wilbur &
Edward Richmond [4:159/60/1].
Acct. of Mary Fuller, widow, Adm. of Est. of her husb. JONATHAN
FULLER of Attl. dcd. intest., dtd. 19 Jan. 1722/3 [4:161/2].
Requests by Francis Fuller & Mary Fuller, son & dau. of JONA-
THAN FULLER of Attl. that their mother Mrs. Mary Fuller be
their guard., dtd. 19 Jan. 1722/3 [4:162/3].
Petition by Margaret Terry, formerly widow & Adm. of Est. of
her former husb. the Rev. JOHN WILSON of Swan., & by her
present husb. Samuel Terry. Mentions allowance "for Beareing
a Posthumus Child." Dtd. 13 Sept. 1722 [4:164].
Notice of Appt. of Mrs. John Deane of Groton, New London Co.,
Ct. to be guard. of Mary Douglas, dau. of Mary Douglas dcd.,
who was dau. of GRINDFIELD HANNOVER dcd. of Taun., dtd. 4
March 1722/3 [4:165].
Request of Jane Hannover that "my Brother Edward Blake" be her
guard., in relation to Est. of her late father GRINDFIELD
HANNOVER of Taun., dtd. 5 March 1722/3 [4:165].
Appt. of John Martin, eldest son, as Adm. of Est. of his father
JOHN MARTIN of Reho., dtd. 4 March 1722/3 [4:166].
Inv. of Est. of JOHN MARTIN, Sr. of Reho., dtd. 6 Sept. 1720,
pres. by John Martin, son & Adm. Apprs: Daniel Smith & Daniel
Carpenter [4:167].
Affirmation by Isack Hathaway of Digh., Yeoman & only son of
ISACK HATHAWAY of Digh. dcd. Mentions his "mother Mary Hath-

away;" his brother-in-law & sister Elkanah Bobbet & wife Mary;
& his sister Hopeful Wood wife of Richard Wood, dtd. 8 Feb.
1722/3. Witns: Nathaniel Fisher & Ebenezer Pitts [4:168].

Acct. of Joseph Atwood, Adm. of Est. of GREENFIELD HANNOVER of
Taun., dtd. 15 Jan. 1714 [sic][4:169].

Acct. of Ebenezer Mahurim, son & Adm. of Est. of his father
HUGH MAHURIM of Taun. dcd. intest., dtd. 4 Feb. 1722/3[4:170/1]

Petition by Jonathan, Elisha & Ephraim Bliss, eldest, 2nd & 3rd
brothers of JACOB BLISS of Reho. Mentions their younger brother Daniel Bliss, dtd. 1 March 1722/3 [4:171].

Petition by Jathniel Peck, John Thompson, Jacob Ormsbe, Henry
Smith, Thomas Ormsbe & Ezra Ormsbe re Est. of JACOB BLISS of
Reho., their former neighbor, dtd. 2 March 1722/3 [4:171].

Order for appraisal of Est. of JACOB BLISS of Reho. dcd. intest.
dtd. 11 March 1722/3 [4:172].

Appraisal of Est. of JACOB BLISS of Reho., dtd. 11 March 1722/3.
Apprs: Jathniel Peck, Abiall Carpenter & James Bowen[4:172].

Div. of Est. of JACOB BLISS of Reho., dtd. 20 March 1722/3. Brothers: Jonathan, Elisha, Ephraim & Daniel Bliss. Sisters: Myr-
iam, Mary, Hannah, Bethiah & Rachel [4:173].

Order for inv. to Richard Bowen & John Bowen of Reho., sons &
Adms. of Mr. RICHARD BOWEN of Reho., dtd. 25 March 1722/3 [4:
174].

Will of RICHARD BOWEN, Sr. of Reho., Yeoman, "Being aged & In-
firmed," dtd. 12 Apr. 1718, prob. 25 March 1722/3. Wife Martha. 2 sons: Richard & John Bowen. Chldn. of my dau. Sarah
Able; chldn. of my dau. Easther Millerd; chldn. of my dau.
Mary Walker. Grson. Dan Bowen. Grdau. Sarah Walker. Mentions
covenant he had with Martha before marriage, with date of 20
Dec. 1689. Witns: Benjamin Hunt, Edward Glover & Daniel Smith
[4:175/6].

Inv. of Est. of RICHARD BOWEN of Reho., dtd. 28 March 1722/3,
pres. by Richard & John Bowen, sons & Execs. Apprs: Abiall
Carpenter & Edward Glover [4:177].

Inv. of Est. of JOHN PECKOM of Lit. Comp. who died 4 ec. 1722,
dtd. 113 Dec. 1722, pres. by John Peckcom, son & Exec. Apprs:
David Hillard, Jonathan Head & Edward Richmond [4:178/9/80].

Hannah Sole, widow of WILLIAM SOLE of Dart. declines to adm. the
Est. & asks that her 2 sons William & George Sole be appt.
Adms., also asking that these sons be made guards. "To my
orfian Children which are under age," dtd. 6 May 1723[4:180].

Appt. of William Sole & George Sole, sons, as Adms. of Est. of
their father WILLIAM SOLE of Dart., dtd. 6 May 1723 [4:181].

Inv. of Est. of WILLIAM SOULE of Dart., Yeoman, dtd. 25 Apr.
1723, pres. by William Soule & George Soule, sons & Adms.
Apprs: Jonathan Davill, Benjamin Wilbur & Phillip Allen [4:
182/3].

Order for inv. to Hannah Shaw, widow, & to Benjamin Shaw, eldest son, Adms. of Est of their husb. & father BENJAMIN SHAW
of Taun., dtd. 10 July 1723 [4:184].

Will of BENJAMIN SHAW "the Eldest of that Name in Taunton," dtd.
7 March 1719/20, prob. 10 July 1723. Wife Hannah. Sons: Benjamin (eldest), Samuel, Jonathan & Ebenezer Shaw (last 2 under
21). Daus: Hannah Hathaway, Sarah Shaw, Abigail Shaw & Susanah Shaw (last 3 under 18 & unmar.). Witns: Stephen Leonard,
Ebenezer Robinson & Thomas Leonard, Jr. [4:185/6/7/8/9].
Order for inv. to John Ide of Attl., Husbandman, Exec. of Est.
of NICHOLAS IDE of Attl., dtd. 10 July 1723 [4:189/90].
Will of NICHOLAS IDE of Attl., Weaver, "Bring Sick and very
weak," dtd. 18 Feb. 1722/3, prob. 3 July 1723. Wife Elisebeth.
Sons: Jacob (eldest), John, Benjamin, Nathaniel [dcd?] & Nicholas [dcd?] Ide. Dau. Martha Carpenter. Grsons: Benjamin
Ingraham & Nicholas Ide. Witns: Samuel Tingley, Ebenezer Free-
man & Noah Carpenter [4:190/1/2].
Inv. of Est. of Lt. NICHOLAS IDE of Attl., dtd. 28 June 1723,
pres. by John Ide, son & Exec. Apprs: Thomas Tingley & Noah
Carpenter [4:192/3].
Acct. of Elizabeth Richmond, widow & Adm. of Est. of her former
husb. JOHN HAULE of Taun., dtd. 8 July 1723. Mentions rcpts.
& paym. to abt. 12 persons, incl. Hannah Hall [4:194].
Order for inv. to Edward Gray of Lit. Comp., Yeoman, Exec. of
Est. of his brother Dr. THOMAS GRAY of Lit. Comp., dtd. 10
Aug. 1723 [4:195].
Will of THOMAS GRAY of Lit. Comp., Doctor, "being Sicke and
Weake," dtd. 8 July 1723, prob. 1 Aug. 1723. Mother-in-law
Phebe Gray [stepmother?]. Brother Edward Gray. Nephew Thomas
Gray (under 21) son of my brother Edward. Bro.-in-law William
Richmond & his wife my sister Anna. Sister Rebecca wife of
· John Pabodie. My negro boy Solomon; my negro woman Sarah.
Witns: John Church, John Tomlin & Richard Billings [4:196/7].
Inv. of Est. of Dr. THOMAS GRAY of Lit. Comp., dtd. 17 July 17-
23, pres. by Edward Gray, Jr., brother & Exec. Apprs: Thomas
Church, William Pabodie & Peter Taylour [4:197/8/9].
Order for inv. to Hezekiah Luther of Swan., Husbandman, Exec.
of Est. of his father HEZEKIAH LUTHER of Swan., dtd. 4 Aug.
1723 [4:200].
Will of HEZEKIAH LUTHER of Swan., Yeoman, dtd. 4 March 1722/3,
prob. 5 Aug. 1723. No wife mentioned. Sons: Edward, Hezekiah
& Joseph Luther. Daus: Elisebeth Kennicut & Hannah Winslow.
My "Indian Slave Called Sarah alias Pegge." Witns: William
Anthoney, Joseph Hix & Abraham Anthony [4:201/2].
Appt. of Mary Pullin, widow, as Adm. of Est. of her husb. NI-
CHOLAS PULLIN of Reho. dcd. intest., dtd. 11 Sept. 1723 [4:
202/3].
Inv. of Est. of NICHOLAS PULLIN of Reho., dtd. 24 June 1723,
pres. by Mary Pullin, his widow. Apprs: Abiah Carpenter, John
Robinson & John Bishup [4:203/4].
Acct. of Mary Blanding, widow & Adm. of Est. of her husb. DAN-
IEL BLANDING of Reho., dtd. 11 Sept. 1723. Incl. small paym.
to Noah Blanding [4:204/5].

Rcpt. by Sarah Church of Lit. Comp. for legacy from Est. of her
father JOSEPH CHURCH, paid by her brother Nathaniel Church of
Lit. Comp., Exec., dtd. 25 Dec. 1717. Witns: Benjamin Southworth & [torn] Palmer [4:205].

Appt. of Mrs. Deborah Peck, widow, & Hezekiah Peck, eldest son,
to be Adms. of Est. of HEZEKIAH PECK of Attl. dcd. intest.,
dtd. 16 Sept. 1723 [4:206].

Acct. of Est. of CLEMENT BRIGGS of Taun. No. Purch., dtd. 9
Oct. 1722 [4:207].

Div. of Est. of CLEMENT BRIGGS of Taun. No. Purch. btwn. his
chldn. Sons: Clement (eldest), Zachariah (2nd) & John (3rd)
Briggs. Daus: Elizabeth Briggs (eldest), Hannah Briggs (2nd)
& Lydia Briggs (youngest), dtd. 9 Dec. 1722. Comm: Benjamin
Drake, Ephraim Randell, Samuel Kingsley, Thomas Manley & John
Phillips [4:208].

Appt. of Mrs. Hannah Thompson, widow, & George Thompson, son,
as Adms. of Est. of their husb. & father JOHN THOMPSON dcd.
intest., dtd. 7 Oct. 1723 [4:209].

Inv. of Est. of BENJAMIN SHAW of Taun., dtd. 3 Sept. 1723, pres.
by Benjamin Shaw, son & Exec. Apprs: John Andrews & Ebenezer
Robinson [4:210].

Appt. of John Caswell to be Adm. of Est. of his brother JOSIAH
CASWELL of Norton, dcd. intest., dtd. 11 Oct. 1723 [4:211].

Appt. of Edward Paul of Digh. as Adm. of Est. of his son EDWARD
PAUL, Jr. of Digh. dcd. intest., dtd. 9 Oct. 1723 [4:212].

Order for div. of Est. of JONATHAN FULLER of Atttl. dtd. 19 Jan.
1722/3 [4:213].

Div. of Est. of JOHN [sic; but later references call him "Jona-
than] FULLER of Attl. btwn. his widow [not named] & chldn.:
Jonathan Fuller (eldest son), Elizabeth Fuller, Peleg Fuller,
Jeremiah Fuller, Francis (son) Fuller, Mary Fuller & Mehetible
Swettland, dtd. 2 Oct. 1723. Comm: Thomas Tingley, John Fos-
ter & Samuel Day [4:214/5/6/7].

Inv. of Est. of JOHN THOMPSON of Reho., dtd. 8 Oct. 1723, pres.
by Hannah Thompson, his widow. Apprs: John West, William Salisbury & Samuel Bullock [4:217/8].

Will of ISRAEL PECK of Swan. alias Barrington, Yeoman, "Being
in the seventy six year of my age," dtd. 8 Aug. 1718, prob.
10 Oct. 1723. No wife mentioned. Only son Nathaniel Peck.
Daus: the wife [not named] of Josiah Dean, Mary the wife of
Ephraim May, Mehittabel Whittaker dcd. Grdau. Mehetibell dau.
of my dau. Mehitabel. Chldn. [not named] of my dau. Mehetibell dcd. Mentions his lands in Barr. & in Reho. Witns: Zac-
ariah Bicknell, Elisha May & John Cary [4:219/20].

Appt. of Mrs. Abigail Tisdell, widow, as Adm. of Est. of her
husb. ELKANAH TISDELL of Taun., dtd. 21 Oct. 1723 [4:221/2].

Agrmt. abt. div. of Est. of JOHN MACOMBER, Sr. of Taun. (as his
desire was in writing expressed and attested by John Richmond,
Abigall Richmond & Anna Marick before Justice Thomas Leonard

on 31 March 1694), btwn. his son John Macomber, his dau. widow Mary Staples & his grson. John Staples son of dau. Mary,
dtd. 2 Apr. 1723. Mentions "land in Taunton where Thomas Macomber Now Dwells which was the Homestead of his Grandfather
Macomber." Witns: Thomas Macomber & John Smith [4:223/3½/4].
Appt. of Deacon Samuel Dean of Taun. as Adm. of Est. of his
mother Mrs. SARAH DEANE of Taun. dcd. intest., dtd. 29 Oct.
1723 [4:224/5].
Order for inv. to Hugh Coale of Swan. & Joseph Buckland of Reho.
Execs. of Est. of JOHN ALLEN of Swan., dtd. 1 Nov. 1723 [4:
225/6].
Will of JOHN ALLEN of Swan., Yeoman, dtd. 1 Jan. 1722/3, prob.
1 Nov. 1723. Disposes of his Est. in Barrington. John Fare-
wather, James Farewather, Elizabeth Winslow & Christian Sim-
son chldn. of my sister Elisebeth Farewather of Boston dcd.
Chldn. [not named] of "my Kinswoman Sarah Guin that was the
Wife of Thomas Guin of Boston Deceased." The Church in Barr.
called Elder Wheaton's Church, formerly called Elder Luther's
Church. Daniel, Ebenezer, Samuel & Joseph Allen sons of my
brother Daniel Allen. James Addoms son of James Addoms of
Barr. Sons [not named] of my kinswoman Christian Peck dcd.
James Bucklin, Joseph Bucklin, Baruch Bucklin, Isaac Bucklin
& Lydia Barrow chldn. of my sister Deborah Bucklin. Nehemiah
Allen & Deborah Hopkins chldn. of my brother Isaac Allen dcd.
Grchldn. of my brother Isaac Allen dcd., namely his dau. Beth-
iah's 2 chldn. & his dau. Sarah's one child. Kinswoman Debor-
ah Cole wife of Hugh Cole of Swan.; James Cole son of Hugh
Cole. Daus. of my kinswoman Deborah Cole, namely Deborah Cole,
Christian Kingsley, Mary Cole, Lidia Sisson, Bethiah Luther
Anna Cole & Hannah Cole. Kinsman Hugh Cole of Swan., House
Carpenter, & Joseph Bucklin of Reho., Yeoman, as Execs. along
with my kinsman Ebenezer Allen of Barr. Witns: Joseph Butter-
worth, Jonathan Kingsley & Benjamin Kingsley [4:226/7/8].
Appt. of Henery Bragg of Brist. as Adm. of Est. of Mr. HENERY
BRAGG of Attl. dcd. intest., dtd. 4 Nov. 1723 [4:229].
Inv. of Est. of HENERY BRAGG of Attl., dtd. 18 Oct. 1723, pres.
by Mrs. Sarah Bragg, widow of Henery. Mentions "his son Wil-
liam Bragg." Apprs: John Foster, John French & Samuel Fuller
[4:230].
Order for inv. to Mrs. Bethiah Macomber, widow & Exec. of Est.
of her husb. JOHN MACOMBER of Dart., dtd. 4 Nov. 1723[4:231].
Will of JOHN MACOMBER of Dart., Yeoman, "Being Very Sick and
Weake," dtd. 7 Oct. 1723, prob. 4 Nov. 1723. Wife Bethiah.
Sons: Phillip (eldest), Abiall, John & William Macomber (all
under 21). Daus: Marcy & Mary (both under 18). To my mother
Mary Macomber; my sister Elizabeth, my father William Macomber dcd. Also mentions his wife now being with child. My brother Phillip Taber and friends William Wood & Nathaniel Sole,

all of Dart., to be overseers. Witns: William Macomber, William Wood, Jedediah Wood & Nathaniel Sole [4:232/3/4/5].

Acct. of Rebecca Wilcox, Adm. of Est. of her hus. JOHN WILCOX of Lit. Comp. dcd. intest., dtd. 4 Nov. 1723 [4:236/7].

Appt. of Abigail Maxcee, widow, & Elexander Maxcee, son, as Adms. of Est. of their husb. & father ELEXANDER MAXCEE of Attl. dcd. intest., dtd. 9 Nov. 1723 [4:237/8].

Inv. of Est. of JOHN MACOMBER of Dart., dtd. 28 Oct. 1723, pres. by Bethiah Macomber, his widow. Apprs: William Wood, Thomas Cory & Nathaniel Sole [4:238/9/40].

Div. of Est. of Capt. SAMUEL WALKER of Reho. btwn. his widow Elesebeth Walker & his chldn: chldn. of Samuel Walker, Jr. dcd. (eldest son); Timothy Walker (2nd son); Peter Walker (3rd son); Ephraim (4th son); Benjamin Walker (5th son); Patience Perin (eldest dau.) & Martha Bowen (youngest dau.), dtd. 7 Jan. 1722/3. Comm: Josiah Carpenter, Phillip Walker & Samuel Brown [4:241/2/3].

Inv. of Est. of HEZEKIAH PECK of Attl., pres. 6 Dec. 1723 by Deborah Peck & Hezekiah Peck, Adms. Apprs: George Leonard, Ebenezer Tiler & Seth Richerson [4:244/5].

Inv. of Est. of HEZEKIAH LUTHER of Swan., dtd. 8 Aug. 1723, pres. by Hezekiah Luther, son & Exec. Apprs: Thomas Estabrooke & William Anthony [4:245/6].

Rcpt. by Benjamin Lyon & Bethiah Lyon for legacy from Est. of her father DANIEL CARPENTER of Reho., paid by Obadiah Carpenter who was her guard., dtd. 7 Sept. 1724 [4:246].

Inv. of Est. of ALEXANDER MAXCEE of Attl., dtd. 2 Jan. 1722/3, pres. by Abigail Maxcee, Adm. Apprs: Ralph Freeman, John Foster & Pentecost Blackman [4:247/8].

Rcpt. by Benjamin Russell of Dart. for a legacy to his wife Abigail Russell from Est. of her father NICHOLAS HOWLAND, paid by Hannah Howland, Exec., dtd. 14 Oct. 1723. Witns: Joseph Tucker & Silviah Wood [4:248].

Rcpt. by Joseph Tucker of Dart. for a legacy to his wife Mary Tucker from Est. of her father NICHOLAS HOWLAND, paid by Hannah Howland, Exec., dtd. 30 Nov. 1723. Witns: Benjamin Russell & Silviah Wood [4:248/9].

Agrmt. abt. settl. of Est. of SAMUEL WILKINS of Brist. by his "Brethren & Sisters": Capt. Stephen Mumford & Mary his wife, Capt. Benjamin Ellery & Abiall his wife & Mr. Peter Treebe & Mehetibel his wife, all of Newport, dtd. 2 March 1720/1. Witns: Simon Peace & Peleg Sanford [4:249/50/1/2/3].

Inv. of Est. of SARAH DEANE of Taun., dtd. 6 Nov. 1723, pres. by Samuel Deane, son & Adm. Apprs: John White, John Staple & John Kinge [4:254].

Inv. of Est. of ELISEBETH PHILLIPS of Taun., dtd. 22 Oct. 1723, pres. by Benjamin Williams & Richard Williams, Adms. & sons. Apprs: Seth Williams, John Staples & John King [4:254/5].

Inv. of Est. of ELKANAH TISDELL of Taun., dtd. Nov. 1723, pres.

by Mrs. Abigall Tisdell, widow & Adm. Apprs: Seth Williams,
John Andrewes & Samuel Leonard [4:255/6].

Acct. of William Whipple, Adm. of Est. of his mother Mrs. HAN-
NAH WHIPPLE of Attl., dtd. 9 Jan. 1723. Mentions legacies by
will or codicil to: Joseph Cowell [?], Joseph Rayzee & Sarah
his wife, Benjamin Tower & Deborah his wife, William Whipple
& Jeremiah Whipple [4:256/7].

Sarah Hannover, dau. of GREENFILL HANNOVER of Taun., chose Richard Godfrey of Taun. to be her guard., dtd. 23 Jan. 1723 [4:
258].

Samuel Leonard of Taun. took Adm. of Est. of his mother Mrs.
MARY LEONARD of Taun., dtd. 23 Jan. 1723 [4:258].

Appt. of Mr. Jonathan Williams of Taun. as guard. of Mary, Abi-
gell, Elizabeth, Abiah & Mehitibell Williams, chldn. of his
wife Elizabeth Williams, dau. of Major THOMAS LEONARD of Taun.
dcd., dtd. 23 Jan. 1723 [4:258].

Acct. of Ephraim Hodges of Taun., Exec. of Est. of his father
HENNERY HODGES, dtd. 21 Jan. 1723 [4:258].

Appt. of Mr. Edward Blake of Taun. as guard. of Jane Hannover,
minor dau. of Mr. GREENFIELD HANNOVER of Taun., dtd. 26 Jan.
1723 [4:259].

Rcpt. by Jonathan Paine for legacy from Est. of his father NA-
THANIEL PAINE of Reho., paid by John Chaffe, dtd. 6 July 1722
[4:259].

Appt. of Richard Godfree of Taun. as guard. of Sarah Hannover,
minor dau. of Mr. GREENFIELD HANNOVER of Taun., dtd. 22 Jan.
1723 [4:260].

Appt. of Jonathan Williams of Taun. as guard. of Mary, Abigail,
Elizebeth, Abiall & Mehitibell Williams, minor chldn. of Elizebeth Williams, dau. of MARY LEONARD dcd., dtd. 22 Jan. 1723
[4:261].

Acct. of Sarah Wilcox, Adm. of Est. of her husb. DANIEL WILCOX
of Dart., pres. 10 Oct. 1723 [4:262/3].

Div. of Est. of ROBERT FULLER of Attl. btwn. his widow Mary Fuller & his chldn: Obediah Fuller (eldest son) [*The writing
stops in the middle of the page, the remainder being left
blank. The entry on the next page is unrelated*][4:263/4].

Appt. of Madame Dorothy Paine, widow, & Nathaniel Paine, son,
as Adms. of Est. of their husb. & father Lt. Col. NATHANIEL
PAINE, all of Brist., dtd. 17 Apr. 1723/4 [4:265].

Rcpts. for legacies from Est. of "my grandfather RICHARD BOWEN"
of Reho., paid by Richard Bowen & John Bowen of Reho., Adms.,
said rcpts signed by:
    Samuel Millard, 30 Dec. 1724; witns: Edward & Dorothy Glover.
    James Walker, 30 Dec. 1724; witns: Mary Bowen & Edward Glover
    Josiah Abell, 39 Dec. 1724; witns: Zephiniah Peck & Mary Bowen.
    Isack & Ester Averill, 30 Dec. 1724; witns: Jacob & Ruth
    Burton
    Abiah & Experience Carpenter, same date; witns: David Car-
    penter & Deborah Barbor

Phillip Walker, same date; witns: James Read & Ichabod Bowen
Daniel & Alce Chaffe, dtd. 22 Dec. 1724; witns: Joseph Cole
   & Christopher Bowen
Henery & Ester West, dtd. 30 Dec. 1724; witns: Seth & Mehit-
   ibel Garnsey
Dan Bowen, dtd. 10 Apr. 1723/4: witns: Ichabod Bowen & Rich-
   ard Bowen, Jr.
Henery & Margaret Osborn of Rhoad Island, dtd. 13 July 1723;
   witns: Edward Glover & Lewis Sweeting
Ephraim & Mary Walker, dtd. 30 Dec. 1724; witns: John French
   & Jonathan French [4:255/6/7/8/9].
Rcpt. by Martha Bowen, widow, for legacy from Est. of her husb.
  RICHARD BOWEN of Reho., paid by Richard Bowen & John Bowen of
  Reho., dtd. 10 Oct. 1723. Mentions that a covenant made btwn.
  her & the dcd. before their marriage, bearing date of 20 Dec.
  1689, is now fulfilled. Witns: Joseph Bucklen & Rachel Buck-
  len [4:268].
Petition by Silvanus Campbel, James Bolderg, Gershom Campbel,
  John Pollard & Daniel Brayman that "our brother John Finney"
  be appt. Adm. of Est. of "our Late Mother" MARY CAMBILL of
  Norton, dtd. 18 Apr. 1724 [4:269].
Appt. of John Finney of Brist. as Adm. of Est. of MARY CAMBEL
  of Norton, dtd. 22 Apr. 1724 [4:270].
Appt. of Mrs. Anne Brown, widow, to be Adm. of Est. of her husb.
  JOSIAH BROWN of Reho., dtd. 4 May 1724 [4:271].
Notice by Joseph Whipple of Providence that Mary Whipple, Adm.
  of Est. of ISRAEL WHIPPLE, still owes Joseph money from Is-
  rael's Est., dtd. 15 March 1720/1 [4:272].
Rcpt. by Joseph Whipple of Providence, Adm. of Est. of William
  Crawford, that Mary Whipple, Adm. of Est. of ISRAEL WHIPPLE
  of Attl., has paid in full the amt. said Israel owed the Est.
  of Maj. William Crawford dcd., dtd. 15 March 1720 [4:272].
Rcpt. by Hannah Whipple of Attl. for money paid by her dau.-in-
  law Mary Whipple, owed to Hannah from Est. of Mary's husb.,
  dtd. 9 June 1721 [4:272].
Acct. of Mary Whipple, Adm. of Est. of her husb. ISRAEL WHIPPLE
  of Attl. dcd. intest., dtd. 6 May 1724 [4:272/3].
Order for inv. to Mrs. Rachel Allen, widow & Exec. of Est. of
  her husb. INCREASE ALLEN of Dart., dtd. 19 May 1724 [4:274].
Will of INCREASE ALLEN of Dart., Yeoman, dtd. 31 Oct. 1722,
  prob. 19 May 1724. Wife Rachell. Sons: Benjamin, Jedediah &
  Increase Allen. Hannah Russell & Dinah Allen. Witns: John
  Tucker, William Wood & Richard Borden [4:276/7/8].
Samuel Wheaten, son of SAMUEL WHEATEN of Swan. dcd. intest.,
  chose Mr. Isack Wheaten of Swan. as his guard., dtd. 22 May
  1724 [4:278].
Appt. of Isack Wheaten of Swan., Yeoman, as guard. of Samuel
  Wheaten, minor son of SAMUEL WHEATEN of Swan., dtd. 22 May
  1724 [4:278/9].

Appt. of Daniel Smith of Reho., eldest son, to be Adm. of Est.
of his father DANIEL SMITH of Reho. dcd. intest., dtd. 19 May
1724 [4:279/80].

Inv. of Est. of Mr. DANIEL SMITH of Rehoboth, pres. 24 May 1724
by Daniel Smith, son & Adm. Apprs: Abiah Carpenter, Abiall
Smith & Joseph Bosworth [4:280/1].

Order for inv. to Samuel Tomkins, son, as Adm. of Est. of his
father NATHANIEL TOMKINS of Lit. Comp. dcd. intest., dtd. 19
May 1724 [4:281/2].

Will of NATHANIEL TOMKINS of Lit. Comp., Cordwinder, dtd. 30
May 1719, prob. 19 May 1724. No wife mentioned. Sons: Nathan-
iel & Samuel Tomkins. Daus: Elizabeth wife of William Lad,
Mary Tomkins, Marcy wife of William Roudith [or Bowdish?],
Persilla wife of Samuel Lindell, Sarah wife of Benjamin Gif-
fard, Rebeccah Tomkins & Hannah wife of Timothy Gifferd.
Witns: Warren Gibbs, William Briggs & Nathaniel Searles [4:
282/3].

Order for Inv. to Mary Staple, widow, & to Noah Staple, son,
Adms. of Est. of their husb. & father JACOB STAPLE, all of
Taun., dtd. 19 May 1724 [4:283/4].

Will of JACOB STAPLE of Taun., dtd. 24 Feb. 1723, prob. 29 May
1724. Wife Mary. 2 sons: Noah & Jacob Staple. Daus: Hannah
wife of Samuel Briggs, Mary wife of Jonathan Harvey & Abigail Staple. Witns: Samuel Danforth, John Staple & Thomas
Macomber [4:284/5].

Inv. of Est. of JACOB STAPLES of Taun., dtd. 6 Apr. 1724, pres.
by Mary Staples & Noah Staples, Execs. Apprs: Seth Williams,
Henery Andrews & John Staples [4:285/6].

Appt. of William Torrey of Brist. as Adm. of Est. of his father
ANGILL TORREY of Brist. dcd. intest., dtd. 21 May 1724 [4:287].

Appt. of Samuel Leonard of Taun. as Adm. of Est. of MARY LEON-
ARD dcd. intest., widow of Maj. Thomas Leonard dcd., dtd. 21
Jan. 1723 [4:288].

Inv. of Est. of MARY LEONARD of Taunton, widow of Major Thomas
Leonard, dtd. Jan. 1723/4, pres. by Samuel Leonard, Adm. of
his mother's Est. Apprs: Seth Williams, John Andrews & John
Kinge [4:289/90].

Rcpt. by Jonathan Bliss of Rehoboth for money due from Est. of
his brother JACOB BLISS, paid by Daniel Bliss, dtd. 16 Jan.
1723/4 [4:291].

Rcpts. by Mary Blisse of Reho., widow & guard. of Mary Blisse,
Hannah Blisse & Bethiah Blisse, for money due them from Est.
of their brother JACOB BLISS, paid by Daniel Blisse, dtd. 16
Jan. 1723/4 [4:291].

Rcpt. by Elisha Blisse of Rehoboth for money due from Est. of
his brother JACOB BLISSE, paid by Daniel Blisse, dtd. 25 Apr.
1723/4 [4:291].

Rcpt. by Miriam Blisse of Reho. for money from Est. of her brother JACOB BLISSE, paid by Daniel Blisse, dtd. 19 June 1724
[4:292].

Rcpt. by Mary Blisse as guard. of Rachel Blisse for money due
Rachel out of Est. of her bro. JACOB BLISSE, paid by Daniel
Blisse, dtd. 30 Apr. 1724 [4:292].

Rcpt. by Eparim [sic] Blisse for money due out of Est. of his
brother JACOB BLISSE, paid by Daniel Blisse, dtd. 16 Jan.
1723/4 [4:292].

Order for inv. to James Howland & George Howland, Execs. of Est.
of their father NATHANIEL HOWLAND of Dart., dtd. 16 June 1724
[4:292/3].

Will of NATHANIEL HOWLAND of Dart., dtd. 25 Feb. 1703/4, prob.
16 June 1724. Wife Rose. Sons: John, James & George Howland.
4 daus: Rebeckah Russell wife of James Russell, Sarah wife of
Timothy Akin, Mary wife of Peleg Smith & Content Howland.
Witns: Adam Mott, Timothy Shearman & William Bowdish[4:293/4/5]

Appt. of Mrs. Elesebeth Fuller of Attl., widow, to be Adm. of
Est. of her husb. JOHN FULLER of Attl. dcd. intest., dtd. 16
June 1724 [4:295/6].

Appt. of Hannah Green of Attl., widow, to be Adm. of Est. of her
husb. EPHARIM GREEN of Attl. dcd. intest., dtd. 16 June 1724
[4:296/7].

Appt. of Mr. Jethnel Peck of Reho. as guard. of Hester, Elizabeth & John Smith, minor chldn. of DANIEL SMITH late of Reho.
dtd. 16 June 1724 [4:297/8].

Appt. of Samuel Gofe of Barr. to be guard. of Mary, Anna & Nathaniel Bosworth, chldn. of JOHN BOSWORTH of Barr., dtd. 22
June 1724 [4:298/9].

Joseph Bosworth of Reho. chosen guard. by Solomon Smith & Nathaniel Smith, sons of DANIEL SMITH of Reho., dtd. 16 June
1724 [4:299].

Jethniel Peck of Reho. chosen by Hester, Elesebeth & John Smith
chldn. of DANIEL SMITH, to be their guard., dtd. 16 June 1724
[4:299].

Appt. of Thomas Macomber of Taun., brother of WILLIAM MACOMBER
of Taun. dcd. to be guard. of Abiel, William, Anna & Sarah Macomber, chldn. of William dcd., dtd. 8 Nov. 1715 [4:299].

Appt. of Joseph Bosworth of Reho. as guard. of Solomon & Nathaniel Smith, sons of DANIEL SMITH of Reho., dcd. dtd. 16 June
1724 [4:300].

Will of ARON KNAP of Taun., Husbandman, "Being very Sick & weak"
dtd. 11 Apr. 1724, prob. 16 June 1724. Wife Rachel. Sons: Benjamin, Aron, Ebenezer & Nathaniell Knap. Dau. Hannah Knap.
Witns: Samuel Cobb, Jr., Thomas Burton & Morgan Cobb [4:304/5]
[pages 301,302&303 not found].

Acct. of Samuel Leonard, Adm. to Est. of his father Major THO-
MAS LEONARD, dtd. 16 June 1724. Mentions "his son Thomas Leon-
ard." Also mentions [but does not name] the widow & 7 chldn.
Elsewhere speaks of "his five Sons," & his sons John & Samuel.
To chldn of "our Sister Elizabeth Williams." To "our Sister
Mary Tisdell"[4:305/6/7/8/9].

Rcpt. by Jonathan Williams, guard. "to my wife's children," for
legacy given to his wife Elizabeth (now dcd.) in the will of
her father THOMAS LEONARD, "my father in law," paid by "my Two
Brothers" John Leonard & Samuel Leonard, Execs. of Est. of
their father. Mentions "my honoured Mother" MARY LEONARD dcd.
dtd. 12 June 1724 [4:310].

Rcpt. by Anna Leonard for money from Est. of her father-in-law
THOMAS LEONARD due to heirs of his son George Leonard, dcd.
husb. of Anna, & for money from Est. of her mother-in-law
MARY LEONARD dcd., paid by "my two Brothers" John Leonard &
Samuel Leonard, dtd. 12 June 1724 [4:310].

Rcpt. by Mary Tisdale for money from Est. of her father Major
THOMAS LEONARD, & for money out of Est. of her mother MARY
LEONARD dcd., paid by her brothers John Leonard & Samuel Leon-
ard, Execs., dtd. 12 June 1724 [4:310].

Appt. of Jonathan Shaw of Taun. as guard. of Ebenezer Shaw, minor son of BENJAMIN SHAW of Taun., dtd. 15 July 1724 [4:311].

Ebenezer Shaw, son of BENJAMIN SHAW of Taun., chose his brother
Jonathan Shaw as his guard., dtd. 16 July 1724 [4:311].

Rcpt. by Thomas Leonard for money from Est. of his father Major
THOMAS LEONARD, & for his share of Est. of his mother MARY
LEONARD dcd., paid by his brothers John & Samuel Leonard, Ex-
ecs., dtd. 12 June 1724 [4:312].

Rcpt. by Nathaniel Paine for money from Est. of THOMAS LEONARD,
paid by John Leonard, Exec., dtd. 5 Feb. 1714 [4:312].

Rcpts. by Jonathan Williams & Elesebeth Williams for money from
Est. of her father THOMAS LEONARD, paid by her mother & brothers John & Samuel Leonard, Execs. dtd. 24 March 1713/4 [4:
312].

Rcpt. by Joseph Tisdel & Mary Tisdel for money from Est. of her
father THOMAS LEONARD, paid by her mother & brothers John &
Samuel Leonard, Execs., dtd. 24 March 1713/4 [4:312].

Rcpt. by Thomas Leonard from money from Est. of his father THO-
MAS LEONARD, paid by his mother Mary Leonard & brothers John
& Samuel Leonard, Execs., dtd. 8 Apr. 1714 [4:312].

Rcpt. by George Leonard & Elkanah Leonard for money from Est.
of their father THOMAS LEONARD, paid by their mother Mary
Leonard & brothers John & Samuel Leonard, Execs., dtd. 8 Apr.
1714 [4:312].

Rcpt. by Abigail Gibbs for money from Est. of Major LEONARD,
paid by John Leonard, Exec., dtd. Jan. 1713/4 [4:313].

Rcpt. by John King for money from Est. of THOMAS LEONARD, paid
by John Leonard, Exec., dtd. 1713 [4:313].

Rcpt. by Richard Godfree, Constable, for money paid by John
Leonard, Exec. of his father's Est., dtd. 1713 [4:313].

Rcpt. by Jonathan Williams as guard. of all the chldn. of his
wife Elizabeth dcd., for money from Est. of her father THOMAS
LEONARD of Taun., paid by his brother-in-law Samuel Leonard,
dtd. 9 Nov. 1724 [4:313].

Acct. of Elesebeth Bosworth, Adm. of Est. of her husb. JOHN BOS-
WORTH of Barr., dtd. 14 June 1724. Mentions expenses related
to a posthumous child [4:314/5].

Appt. of Mrs. Rebecca Robinson, widow, as Adm. of Est. of her
husb. BENJAMIN ROBINSON of Attl. dcd. intest., dtd. 21 July
1724 [4:315/6].

Appt. of Mrs. Rachel Freeman, widow, as Adm. of Est. of her
husb. BENJAMIN FREEMAN of Attl. dcd. intest., dtd. 21 July
1724 [4:316/7].

Order for inv. to Mrs. Mary Peckhem, Exec. of Est. of her husb.
STEPHEN PECKHEM of Dart., dtd. 21 Joly 1724 [4:317/8].

Will of STEPHEN PECKHEM of Dart., Yeoman, dtd. 1 Dec. 1722,
prob. 19 May 1724. Wife mentioned but not named. Sons: Stephen,
William, John, Joseph & Josiah. 5 daus: Aloner, Mary, Hannah,
Deborah & Jean. Witns: Samuel Willis, Phillip Cannon & Increase Allen, Jr. [4:318/9/20].

Inv. of Est. of STEPHEN PECKHEM of Dart. who died 23 Apr. 1724,
pres. by Mary Peckhem, his widow & Exec. Apprs: Joseph Russel,
Jr., Benjamin Allen & Samuel Willis [4:320/1/2/3/4].

Inv. of Est. of JOSIAH BROWN of Reho. who died 14 Apr. 1724,
dtd. 2 May 1724, pres. by Anna Brown, his widow & Adm. Apprs:
Samuel Brown, James Brown & Mathew Allen [4:324/5/6].

Inv. of Est. of EBENEZER BURT of Norton, pres. 21 July 1724 by
Mary Burt, his widow, & by Ebenezer Burt, son. Apprs: Nicholas White, Joseph Hodges & William Stone [4:326/7].

Appt. of Mary Burt, widow, & Ebenezer Burt, son. as Adms. of
Est. of their husb. & father EBENEZER BURT of Norton, dtd. 21
July 1724 [4:327/8].

Inv. of Est. of BENJAMIN FREEMAN of Attl., pres. 21 July 1724
by Rachel Freeman, his widow & Adm. Apprs: Thomas Willmouth,
Joseph Capron & Pentecost Blackman [4:328/9].

Inv. of Est. of INCREASE ALLEN of Dart., dtd. 6 July 1724, pres.
by Rachel Allen, his widow. Apprs: Benjamin Willbore, William
Wood & Nathaniel Soule [4:329/30].

Order for inv. to Joseph Wing & Benjamin Wing, sons & Execs. of
MATHEW WING of Dart., dtd. 21 July 1724 [4:332].

Will of MATHEW WING of Dart., dtd. 8 Jan. 1723, prob. 21 July
1724. Wife Elizebeth. 2 sons: Joseph & Benjamin Wing. Dau.
Abigail. Witns: Elisha Wing, Thomas Cornel & George Brownel
[4:332/3/4].

Inv. of Est. of MATHEW WING of Dart., Yeoman, dtd. 20 July 1724,
pres. by Joseph & Benjamin Wing, his sons & Execs. Apprs: Jonathan Davill, Jonathan Talman & Nathaniel Soule [4:333/4/5].

Deposition by Nathan Soule of Dart. re money he loaned to WIL-
LIAM SOULE of Dart. now dcd., & money since rcvd. from William's Est., dtd. 3 Aug. 1724 [4:335].

Rcpt. by Nathan Soule for money from Est. of WILLIAM SOULE of
Dart., paid by William & George Soule, sons & Adms., dtd. 4
Aug. 1724 [4:335].

Rcpt. by Joseph Tilling[hast?] in behalf of his father for money paid by William Soule, dtd. 3 Aug. 1724 [4:335].

Rcpt. by Samuel Willis of Dart. for money from Est. of WILLIAM
SOULE, paid by William Soule, son & Adm., dtd. 13 Jan. 1723/4
[4:336].

Rcpt. by Seth Pope of Dart. for money from Est. of WILLIAM
SOULE, paid by William Soule, son & Adm., dtd. 11 May 1724
[4:336].

Rcpt. by Phillip Taber & Joseph Russell for money from Est. of
WILLIAM SOULE, paid by William Soule, son & Adm., dtd. 14
Oct. 1724 [4:336].

Rcpt. by John Akin & Phillip Taber for money from Est. of WIL-
LIAM SOULE of Dart., dtd. 9 May 1724 [4:336].

Acct. of William Soule & George Soule of Dart., Yeomen, sons &
Adms. of Est. of their father WILLIAM SOULE of Dart., pres.
4 Aug. 1724. Mentions: "to my brother Samuel," and "To our
Unkill Nathan Soule for money which was borrowed by our father" [4:337/8/9].

Appt. of Mrs. Sarah Smith, widow, as Adm. of Est. of her husb.
ANDREW SMITH of Taun. dcd. intest., dtd. 18 Aug. 1724[4:339/
40].

Appt. of John Tisdel of Taun. to be Adm. of Est. of his sister
MARY BURT of Norton dcd. intest., dtd. 18 Aug. 1724[4:340/1].

Order for inv. to Lt. Nathaniel Peck & Zachariah Bignel, Execs.
of Est. of "there Son" EBENEZER PECK of Barr., dtd. 18 Aug.
1724 [4:341/2].

Appt. of Samuel Shorey as Adm. of Est. of his brother JOHN SHOR-
EY of Reho. dcd. intest., dtd. 9 Aug. 1724 [4:342/3].

Acct. of Abigaill Tisdel of Taun., widow & Adm. of Est. of her
husb. ELKANAH TISDEL of Taun., dtd. 30 Aug. 1724 [4:343/4/5/6].

Rcpts. by John Dillinggame, Joseph Tisdel, Epharim Hodges, William Hodges & Timothy Lindel of Salem for monies from Est. of
ELKANAH TISDEL, paid by Abigail Tisdel, his widow & Adm., dtd.
btwn. 23 Jan. 1723/4 to 25 Aug. 1724. One mentions Joseph Tisdel as being father of Elkanah [4:346/7].

Will of EBENEZER PECK of Barr., Boatman, "under great Indisposition of Body," dtd. 16 June 1724, prob. 18 Aug. 1724. Wife
Mary. Brothers: Nathaniel & Thomas Peck. "My honoured Father
Lew^t Nathaniel Peck & Zachariah Bignel both of Barrington,"
to be Execs. Mentions his 300 acres of land in Ashford, Ct.
Witns: James Bicknell, Eleazer Tiffiny & John Andrews[4:347/
8/9].

Appt. of Phillip Taber of Tiv. as guard. of Joseph King, nephew
of THOMAS KING of Providence dcd., dtd. 10 Sept. 1724[4:350].

Order for inv. to Jonathan Wilson, Exec. of Est. of FRANCIS WIL-
SON of Reho., dtd. 28 Aug. 1724 [4:351].

Order for inv. to Mercy Perry & Mary French, Execs. of Est. of
their father LEONARD NEWSUM of Reho., dtd. 25 Aug. 1724]4:
352].

Appt. of Mr. Benjamin Merchant [*sic*] as Adm. of Est. of RICHARD
SHARPE of Jamaica "but heretofore of Boston," Merchant, dtd.
8 Sept. 1724 [4:353].
Appt. of Mrs. Sarah King, widow, as Adm. of Est. of her husb.
SAMUEL KING of Norton dcd. intest., dtd. 15 Sept. 1724[4:354].
Order to Ebenezer Finney as guard. of Abigail & William Cambill,
chldn. of SILVANUS CAMBILL of Norton, and as guard. of his
own dau. Abigail, grdau. of said Silvanus, dtd. 15 Sept. 1724
[4:355].
Order for inv. to Joshua Abell, son & Exec. of Est. of his fa-
ther PRESERVED ABELL of Reho., dtd. 15 Sept. 1724 [4:355/6].
Appt. of John Weakes of Attl. as Adm. of Est. of his father RI-
CHARD WEAKES of Attl. dcd. intest., dtd. 15 Sept. 1724 [4:
356/7].
Order to John Finney of Norton as guard. of Caleb, Ruth & Jere-
miah Cambill, chldn. of SILVANUS CAMBILL of Norton, dtd. 15
Sept. 1724 [4:357/8].
Appt. of Mrs. Elesebeth Ingraham, widow, as Adm. of Est. of her
husb. OBADIAH INGRAHAM of Reho. dcd. intest., dtd. 15 Sept.
1724 [4:358/9].
Appt. of John Robinson as Adm. of Est. of his father BENJAMIN
ROBINSON of Attl. dcd. intest., dtd. 15 Sept. 1724 [4:359/60].
Appt. of John Newland as guard. of Garsham Cambel, son of SIL-
VANUS CAMBEL of Norton, dtd. 15 Sept. 1724 [4:360/1].
Appt. of John Cobb of Norton as Adm. of Est. of his father JOHN
COBB of Norton dcd. intest., dtd. 15 Sept. 1724 [4:361/2].
John Finney of Norton allowed to be guard. of Caleb, Ruth & Jer-
imiah Cambill, chldn. of SYLVANUS CAMBILL of Norton [4:362].
Ebenezer Finney of Brist. allowed to be guard. of Abigail & Wil-
liam Cambill, chldn. of SILVANUS CAMBILL, & guard. of his own
dau. Abigail, grdau. of said Silvanus [4:362].
Garsham Cambill, son of SILVANUS CAMBILL of Norton, chose John
Newland as his guard. [4:362].
Will of LEONARD NEWSUM of Reho., Tailer, "being aged and weake
in Body," dtd. 14 Sept. 1723, prob. 25 Aug. 1724. Wife Experience. Daus: Mercy Perry & Mary French. Mercy to maintain her
mother. Witns: Squire Allen, Nathan Peck & William Cole [4:
363/4].
Will of FRANCIS WILLSON of Reho., Yeoman, dtd. 25 June 1723,
prob. 28 Aug. 1724. No wife or chldn. mentioned. Cousins: Jonathan Willson son of my brother Benjamin, Margaret Whitaker,
Francis Wilson son of my brother John Willson of Billerca,
Samuel Wilson son of my brother Samuel Wilson of Woburn, John
Wilson son of my brother James Wilson of Killingly in Conet-
icut, Francis Wilson son of my brother Benjamin Willson of Reho. & Ruth the wife of John Franklin of Swan. Witns: Thomas
Shaw, James Bowen & Elazebeth Bowen [4:365/6].
Inv. of Est. of Mr. SAMUEL KING of Norton, dtd. 7 July 1724,
pres. by Sarah King, his widow & Adm. Apprs: John Hodges, John
Briggs & Samuel Hodges [4:367/8].

Inv. of Est. of MARY CAMBILL dcd. intest., widow of Silvanus
Cambill of Norton, dtd. 25 Apr. 1724, pres. by John Finney,
her son-in-law & Adm. Apprs: Samuel Hodges, Joseph Pittee &
Samuel King [4:368/9].
Inv. of Est. of BENJAMIN ROBINSON of Attl., dtd. 27 July 1724,
pres. by John Robinson, son & Adm. Apprs: Thomas Wilmouth &
Jeremiah Ingraham [4:400/1][Page-numbering error].
Inv. of Est. of ARON KNAP of Taun., dtd. 14 June 1724, pres. by
Ebenezer Knap, son & Exec. Apprs: Morgan Cobb, Jr., Samuel
Cobb, Jr. & Thomas Burtt [4:401].
Inv. of Est. of OBADIAH INGRAHAM of Reho., dtd. 10 Sept. 1724,
pres. by Elezebeth Ingraham, his widow & Adm. Apprs: John
Robinson, James Sabin & Benjamin Ingraham [4:402].
Inv. of Est. of RICHARD WEAKES of Attl., dtd. 5 Sept. 1724,
pres. by John Weakes, son & Adm. Apprs: Jeremiah Ingraham,
Thomas Wise & John Streeter [4:403/4].
Acct. of Mary Pullin, Adm. of Est. of her husb. NICHOLAS PULLIN
of Reho. dcd. intest., pres. 13 Sept. 1724. Incl. a debt "To
the Doctor in his Sickness in Marblehead" [4:404/5].
Will of PRESERVED ABELL of Reho., Yeoman, dtd. 18 Aug. 1724,
prob. 15 Sept. 1724. No wife mentioned. Son Joshua Abell.
Daus: Dorothy Walker, Experience Carpenter & Mary Walker. Grsons: Robert Abell son of my son Joshua, Ebenezer Walker son
of my eldest dau. Dorothy Walker & Abiah Carpenter son of my
2nd dau. Experience Carpenter. Witns: John Hunt, Thomas Bow-
en & Daniel Carpenter [4:406/7].
Inv. of Est. of NATHANIEL TOMKINS of Lit. Comp., dtd. 20 July
1724, pres. by Samuel Tomkins, son & Exec. Apprs: George
Pearce, [blank] Williston & Nathaniel Searles [4:408].
Order for inv. to Mrs. Sarah Dagget, widow & Exec. of her husb.
JOHN DAGGET of Attl., dtd. 20 Oct. 1724 [4:409].
Appt. of Timothy Tingley as Adm. of Est. of his father THOMAS
TINGLEY of Attl., dcd. intest., dtd. 20 Oct. 1724 [4:410/1].
Appt. of Mrs. Elezebeth Shaperd, widow, to be Adm. of Est. of
her husb. ISACCE SHAPERD of Norton, dtd. 20 Oct. 1724[4:411/2].
Appt. of Samuel Robinson & Ebenezer Robinson as Adms. of Est.
of their father SAMUEL ROBINSON of Attl. dcd. intest., dtd.
20 Oct. 1724 [4:412/3].
Appt. of Mr. Henery Smith as Adm. of Est. of his brother THOMAS
SMITH of Rehoboth dcd. intest., dtd. 20 Oct. 1724 [4:413/4].
John Dean, Hannah Dean & Ann Dean, chldn. of JOHN DEAN of Taun.
dcd. chose their mother Hannah Dean as the guard., dtd. 2
Oct. 1724 [4:414].
Hannah Dean allowed to be guard. of: Sarah Dean, David Dean,
Elizabeth Dean, Joseph Dean & Ebenezer Dean, minor chldn. of
JOHN DEAN of Taun., dtd. 20 Oct. 1724 [4:414].
Appt. of Hannah Dean as guard. of John, Hannah & Ann Dean, chldn.
of JOHN DEAN of Taun., dtd. 20 Oct. 1724 [4:415].
Appt. of Hannah Dean, widow, & Abiall Dean, son, to be Adms. of

Est. of their husb. & father JOHN DEAN of Taun., dtd. 20 Oct. 1724 [4:416].

Order for inv. to Nathaniel Robinson, son & Exec. of Est. of his father GEORGE ROBINSON of Attl., dtd. 20 Oct. 1724[4:417].

Order for inv. to John Humphrey, Exec. of Est. of his sister MARY COOPER of Reho., dtd. 20 Oct. 1724 [4:418].

Appt. of Hannah Dean as guard. of Sarah, David, Elizabeth, Joseph & Ebenezer Dean, chldn. of JOHN DEAN of Taun., dtd. 20 Oct. 1724 [4:418/9].

Appt. of Ann Smith, widow, as Adm. of Est. of her husb. ABIEL SMITH of Reho. dcd. intest., dtd. 20 Oct. 1724 [4:419/20].

Order for inv. to Mrs. Elizabeth Walker, widow & Exec. of Est. of her husb. THOMAS WALKER of Bristol, dtd. 26 Oct. 1724 [4:420/1].

Dorothy Walker, dau. of EBENEZER WALKER of Reho., chose Abiah Carpenter, Jr. as her guard., dtd. 26 Oct. 1724 [4:412].

Mrs. Dorothy Walker, widow of EBENEZER WALKER of Reho., allowed to be guard. of Elizebeth, Martha & Ebenezer Walker, chldn. of dcd. Ebenezer, dtd. 26 Oct. 1724 [4:421].

Caleb Walker chose Daniel Carpenter as his guard., dtd. 26 Oct. 1724 [4:421].

Appt. of Mrs. Dorothy Walker as guard of Elezebeth, Martha & Ebenezer Walker, chldn. of EBENEZER WALKER of Reho., dtd. 26 Oct. 1724 [4:422].

Appt. of Daniel Carpenter as guard. of Caleb Walker, son of EBENEZER WALKER of Reho., dtd. 26 Oct. 1724 [4:423].

Appt. of Abiah Carpenter as guard. of Dorothy Walker dau. of EBENEZER WALKER of Reho., dtd. 26 Oct. 1724 [4:423/4].

Appt. of Jacob Newell & Samuel Tiler as Adms. of Est. of JOYCE NEWELL of Attl. dcd. intest., dtd. 20 Oct. 1724 [4:424/5].

Order for inv. to Caleb Ormsbe & Thomas Ormsbe, Execs. of Est. of their father THOMAS ORMSBE of Reho., dtd. 20 Oct. 1724 [4:425/6].

Appt. of Mrs. Lidiah Fisher, widow, as Adm. of Est. of her husb. SAMUEL FISHER of Norton, dcd. intest., dtd. 20 Oct. 1724 [4:426/7].

Appt. of Mrs. Hannah Williams, widow, & Nathaniel Williams, son as Adms. of Est. of their husb. & father JOHN WILLIAMS of Taun., dtd. 20 Oct. 1724 [4:427/8].

Inv. of Est. of PRESERVED ABELL of Reho., dtd. 28 Sept. 1724, pres. by Joshua Abell, his son & Exec. Apprs: Josiah Carpenter, Edward Glover & Abiah Carpenter [4:428/9].

Inv. of Est. of Deacon JOHN DAGGET of Attl., dtd. 28 [?] 1724, pres. by Mrs. Sarah Dagget, his widow & Exec. Mentions his lands in Attl., on Martha's Vineyard & in Marsfield, Ct. Apprs: John Foster, Samuel Tiler & John Fuller [4:429/30].

Order for inv. to John Atwood, Exec. of Est. of his brother JOSEPH ATWOOD of Digh. dtd. 17 Nov. 1724 [4:431].

Will of FRANCIS WILLSON of Reho. [*Same as entry on pp. 365/6*].

Will of MARY COOPER of Reho., Spinster, "Being aged & weake in
Body," dtd. 19 Apr. 1714, prob. 20 Oct. 1724. Sister Sarah
Humphrey & bro.-in-law John Humphrey. "My honor^d Father Tho-
mas [Cooper] Senior [dcd.]." Brother Thomas Cooper. Sisters:
Elisebeth Ide, Deborah Peck, Judith Robinson & Marcy [no sur-
name given]. Cousin Elizabeth Read eldest dau. of my sister
Marcy. Witns: Thomas Smith, Epharim Carpenter & Daniel Carpen-
ter [4:433/4/5].

Will of THOMAS ORMSBE of Reho., Yeoman, dtd. 8 Sept. 1724, prob.
20 Oct. 1724. "To Wife Mary all the household Stufe y^t She
Brought with her." 2 sons: Caleb & Thomas Ormsbe. "To my Daughter in Law Grisel Whittaker all my first wifes wareing Clothes." Witns: Jathniel Peck, Noah Whittaker & Elizabeth Whittaker [4:435].

Will of JOHN DAGGET of Attl., Husbandman, "being aged & Infirm,"
dtd. 13 Apr. 1724, prob. 20 Oct. 1724. Wife Sarah. 3 sons: Mayhew, Ebenezer & Thomas Dagget. 5 daus: Abigal, Jane, Zilpha,
Patience & Mary [no surnames]. Witns: Thomas Stanley, Ebenezer
Guild & Thomas Buttler [4:436/7].

Appt. of Richard Harding of Swan. as guard. of Edward Thurber,
grson. of EDWARD THURBER of Swan. dcd. intest., dtd. 17 Nov.
1724 [4:437].

Inv. of Est. of SAMUEL FISHER of Norton, dtd. 18 July 1724, pres.
by Lidia Fisher, his widow & Adm. Apprs: Benjamin Williams,
William Stone & Samuel Caswell [4:438].

Inv. of Est. of ISACCE [or ISAUA?] SHAPERD of Norton, dtd. 18
July 1724, pres. by Elesebeth Shapperd, his widow. Apprs: Thomas Skinner, John Skinner & Josiah White [4:439].

Inv. of Est. of LEONARD NEWSUM of Reho., dtd. 9 Oct. 1724, pres.
by Marcy Perry & Mary French, his daus. & Execs. Apprs: Abiah
Carpenter, Edward Glover & Joseph Titus [4:440].

Will of THOMAS WALKER of Brist., Tanner, "being aged and Infirm,"
dtd. 20 Feb. 1721/2, prob. 26 Oct. 1724. Wife Elizabeth. Son
William Walker. Dau. Mary [Little? - ink blot]. Grdau. Jane
Walker now in Barbados. Witns: Dan Throope, Samuel Throop &
Samuel Howland [4:441/2].

Inv. of Est. of GEORGE ROBINSON of Attl., dtd. 16 Oct. 1724,
pres. by Nathaniel Robinson, his son & Exec. Apprs. not listed
[4:443].

Rcpt. by Simon Davis for money from Est. of NOAH FULLER, paid
by David Fuller, dtd. 10 July 1716 [4:443].

Acct. of Rachel Freeman, widow & Adm. of Est. of her husb. NOAH
FULLER, dtd. 20 Oct. 1724 [4:444/5].

Will of GEORGE ROBINSON of Attl., "Wever," "Being very Sick &
weak," dtd. 17 Sept. 1724, prob. 20 Oct. 1724. Wife Elizebeth.
Sons: Nathaniel & Noah Robinson. Daus: Elizebeth Hancock, Margaret Day, Abigail Guild & Hannah Robinson. Son-in-law Elihu
Wharefield. Daus: Mary & Elizabeth Wharefield (both under 18).

My brother William. Witns: Samuel Robinson, Jr., Ebenezer
Robinson & Noah Carpenter [4:447/8][*page numbering error*].
Acct. of Dorothy Walker, Adm. of Est. of her husb. EBENEZER
WALKER of Reho., dtd. 26 Oct. 1724 [4:449/50].
Rcpts. by Thomas Bowen, Thomas Sweete, John Read & Josiah Car-
penter for monies from Est. of EBENEZER WALKER of Reho., paid
by Dorothy Walker, his wife & Adm., dtd. Nov. 1718, May 1722
& Aug. 1724 [4:450].
Order for inv. to John Rouse, Exec. of Est. of his father SIMON
ROUSE of Dart., dtd. 17 Nov. 1724 [4:451].
Will of SIMON ROUSE of Dart., Yeoman, "being Sick of Body," dtd.
19 Dec. 1723, prob. 17 Nov. 1724. Wife Christian. Sons: James,
William & John Rouse. Dau. Marcy Stevins. Chldn. [*not named*]
of my dau.-in-law Mary (they are also called chldn. of my son
William). Son John to be Exec. with Cornelius Holmes of Ro-
chester, Plimouth County. Witns: Joseph Sampson, Joshua Morse,
Jr., Joseph Griffin & Timothy Rugles [4:451/2/3].
Inv. of Est. of SIMON ROUSE of Dart., dtd. 11 Nov. 1724, pres.
by John Rouse, Exec. Apprs. not named [4:453].
Inv. of Est. of EBENEZER PECK of Barr., dtd. 2 Oct. 1724, pres.
by Lt. Nathaniel Peck & Zachariah Bignel, Execs. Apprs: Josi-
ah Torrey, Nathaniel Peck & Joseph Allin [4:454].
Inv. of Est. of JOHN SHOREY of Reho., dtd. 8 Sept. 1724, pres.
by Samuel Shorey, Adm. Mentions land at Mansfield. Apprs: Jo-
siah Carpenter, Edward Glover & Abiah Carpenter [4:454/5].
Appt. of Joseph White as Adm. of Est. of his father JOSEPH
WHITE of Taun., dtd. 16 Dec. 1724 [4:456].
Acct. of Jonathan Taber, Exec. of Est. of his father THOMAS TA-
BER, Jr. of Dart., dtd. 17 Nov. 1724 [4:457/8/9].
Rcpts. by Jonathan Taber, John Russell, William Peckham, John
Tilton, William Allen & Joseph Taber for monies from Est. of
THOMAS TABER, paid by his son John Taber, dtd. Nov. 1722, Dec.
1722, Jan. 1723 & Nov. 1724 [4:459].
Appt. of Peter Hunt as guard. of John & Lidia Bosworth, chldn.
of JOHN BOSWORTH of Reho. dcd. intest., dtd. 15 Dec. 1724
[4:460].
Appt. of Mrs. Hannah Thomson to be guard. of Hannah, Mary & Ju-
dath, daus. of JOHN THOMPSON of Reho., dtd. 15 Dec. 1724 [4:
460/1].
Appt. of Hugh Cole & Joseph Buckling as Adms. of Est. of JOHN
ALLEN of Swan. dcd. intest., dtd. 22 Dec. 1724 [4:461/2].
Will of JOSEPH ATWOOD of Digh., Shipwright, "being very Sick
& weake," dtd. 2 Sept. 1724, prob. 17 Nov. 1724. Wife Mary.
Sons: Joseph (under 21), John & Benjamin Attwood. Dau. Ester
Attwood (unmar.). Brother John Attwood, Exec. Friend Nathan
Walker of Dighton & brother Epharim Attwood to assist my Exec.
Witns: Edward Walker, Richard Maxfield & Nathaniel Fisher [4:
462/3/4].

Petition of Mary White, widow of JOSEPH WHITE of Taun., refusing Adm. of said Est., "being an Antiant Woman and Not Cap-
iable," & requesting appt. of her eldest son Joseph White to
be Adm., dtd. 14 Dec. 1724 [4:464].

Inv. of Est. of ANGILL TORREY of Brist., dtd. 12 Aug. 1724,
pres. by William Torrey, Adm. Mentions "One Bed I Gave to
Malitiah...to Silence...to Margarit...to William..." (4 beds).
Apprs: Thomas Throope, Benjamin Cary & Edward Bosworth, Jr.
[4:465/6].

Acct. of Hannah Thomson & George Thomson on Est. of JOHN THOM-
SON of Reho., dtd. 15 Dec. 1724. Mentions land in Ashford[Ct.].
[4:466/7].

Page 468 is blank

Order for inv. to Marcy Viall, Exec. of Est. of her husb. JONA-
THAN VIALL of Barr., dtd. 4 Jan. 1724 [4:469].

Order for inv. to Catherine Markes, Exec. of Est. of her husb.
WILLIAM MARKES of Brist., dtd. 4 Jan. 1724 [4:469/70].

Order for inv. to William Paul, Exec. of Est. of his father
JAMES PAUL of Digh., dtd. 14 Jan. 1724 [4:471].

Order for inv. to Edward Walker, Exec. of Est. of ELIAZER WALKER
of Taun., dtd. 14 Jan. 1724/5 [4:471/2].

Appt. of John Austin to be Adm. of Est. of EASTER GRAY of Norton, dtd. 12 Jan. 1724/5 [4:473].

End of Volume 4

Appt. of Samuel Tiler of Attl. as guard. of Jacob Newel (over
14) & Elisha Newel (under 14), sons of JACOB NEWEL of Attl.,
dtd. 19 Jan. 1724/5 [5:1].
Appt. of Easter Joy to be Adm. of Est. of JOSEPH JOY of Attl.
dcd. intest., dtd. 19 Jan. 1724/5 [5:1].
Appt. of Capt. John Foster of Attl. as guard. of Jason Newel,
son of JACOB NEWEL of Attl., dtd. 19 Jan. 1724/5 [5:2].
Appt. of Mrs. Ruth Follet & Isaac Follet as Adms. of Est. of
ABRAHAM FOLLET of Attl. dcd. intest., dtd. 19 Jan. 1724/5,
[5:2].
Order for inv. to Samuel Fuller & Ebenezer Fuller, Execs. of
Est. of SAMUEL FULLER of Reho., dtd. 19 Jan. 1724/5 [5:3].
Appt. of Elesebeth Easterbrooke as Adm. of Est. of her husb.
THOMAS EASTERBROOKE of Swan. dcd. intest., dtd. 19 Jan. 17-
24/5 [5:3].
Order for inv. to Edward Walker, Exec. of Est. of ELEAZER WAL-
KER of Taun., dtd. 14 Jan. 1724/5 [5:4].
Order for inv. to William Paul, Exec. of Est. of JAMES PAUL of
Dight., dtd. 14 Jan. 1724/5 [5:4].
Will of WILLIAM MARKES of Brist., dtd. 15 Sept. 1724, prob. 4
Jan. 1724/5. Wife Catherine. Sons: Robert & William (both un-
der 21). Daus: Anna (eldest) & Mary (both under 21). Mentions
his land "in the parrish of Three [or Thoroe?] Coffin in the
County of Somerset...Kingdom of Grate Brittane," and land "in
New England." Witns: Timothy Ingraham, Isaac Waldron & Samuel
Howland [5:5].
Will of JONATHAN VIALL of Barr., dtd. 24 Oct. 1724, prob. 4 Jan.
1724/5. Wife Mercy. 4 sons: James, Jonathan, Constant & Joseph Viall. Dau. Elizebeth Viall (under 21). Lands in Barr. &
Reho. Witns: Ruth Stockbridge, Matthew Allen & Josiah Torrey
[5:6].
Will of ELEAZER WALKER of Taun., Yeoman, dtd. 20 Jan. 1723,
prob. 4 Jan. 1724/5. No wife or chldn. mentioned. Cousins Ed-
ward & Peter Walker sons of my brother Peter Walker dcd.;
cousin Joseph Atwood, Jr. of Digh.; cousin Joannah Nichols
wife of William Nichols of Digh. Witns: James Paul, Nathaniel
Parker & Edward Shove [5:7].
Order for inv. to Sarah Chase & Job Chase, Execs. of Est. of
JOSEPH CHASE of Shewomet, dtd. 19 Jan. 1724/5 [5:7/8].
Order for inv. to Mehetibel Blanding, Exec. of Est. of her husb.
WILLIAM BLANDING of Reho., dtd. 25 Jan. 1724/5 [5:8].
Inv. of Est. of THOMAS TINGLEY of Attl., dtd. 4 Nov. 1724, pres.
by Timothy Tingley, Adm. Apprs: Noah Carpenter, John Foster &

John Fuller [5:8/9].

Acct. of Timothy Tingley, Adm. of Est. of THOMAS TINGLEY of
Attl., dtd. 29 Jan. 1724/5. Mentions "Elizebeth Tingley Daughter of the Intestate" [5:9/10].

Agrmt. abt. div. of Est. of THOMAS TINGLEY by his chldn: Timothy, Ephraim & Elizabeth Tingley, dtd.13 Jan. 1724/5. Witns:
Jacob Stanley & John Foster [5:10/1].

Will of JAMES PAUL of Digh., Yeoman, dtd. 8 Sept. 1723, prob.
14 Jan. 1724/5. No wife mentioned. Sons: James & William
Paul. Daus: Mary Bartlett wife of Daniel Bartlett & Hannah
Pigsley wife of Robert Pigsley. Witns: Eleazer Walker, Benjamin Pool & Edward Shove [5:11].

Inv. of Est. of Mrs. JOYCE NEWEL of Attl., dtd. 3 Nov. 1724,
pres. by Samuel Tiler & Jacob Newel, Adms. Apprs: John Foster,
Noah Carpenter & John Fuller [5:12].

Acct. of Samuel Tiler & Jacob Newel, Adms. of Est. of JOYCE NEW-
EL of Attl., dtd. 31 Dec. 1724 [5:12/3].

Rcpt. by Richard Bowen for money, dtd. 7 Dec. 1724 [5:13].

Appt. of John Ide of Attl. as guard. of Joseph Newel son of JA-
COB NEWEL of Attl., dtd. 19 Jan. 1724/5 [5:13].

Appt. of Mrs. Anna Leonard of Norton as guard. of Abiel Leonard
Ephraim Leonard & Mary Leonard, minor grchldn. of "Madom"
MARY LEONARD of Taun., dtd. 14 Jan. 1724/5 [5:14].

Appt. of Noah Carpenter of Attl. as guard. of Ephraim Newel son
of JACOB NEWEL of Attl., dtd. 19 Jan. 1724/5 [5:14/5].

Appt. of Jacob Stanley as Adm. of Est. of his father SAMUEL
STANLEY of Attl. dcd. intest., dtd. 19 Jan. 1724/5 [5:15].

Appt. of Mehetibel Archer, widow, as Adm. of Est. of her husb.
JOHN ARCHER of Brist. dcd. intest., dtd. 16 Feb. 1724/5[5:16].

Appt. of John Atwood as Adm. of Est. of GREENFIELD HANNOVER of
Taun. dcd. intest., dtd. 17 Feb. 1724/5 [5:16/7].

Appt. of Mrs. Susanah Horton as Adm. of Est. of her husb. SOLO-
MON HORTON of Reho. dcd. intest., dtd. 16 Feb. 1724/5 [5:17].

Appt. of William Makepeace as Adm. of Est. of EMANUEL WILLIAMS
of Taun. dcd. intest., dtd. 17 Feb. 1724/5 [5:17/8].

Order for inv. to Mehetibel Tucker & Samuel Tucker, Execs. of
Est. of ROBERT TUCKER of Norton, dtd. 16 Feb. 1724/5 [5:18].

Will of ROBERT TUCKER of Norton, "being under Grate Sickness of
Body," dtd. 1 Jan. 1724, prob. 16 Feb. 1724/5. Wife Mehetibel.
Sons: Samuel (eldest), Robert, Benjamin, Cornelius & Daniel
Tucker. Dau. Mehetibel Tucker. Witns: George Leonard, William
Sims & William Coddington [5:19/20].

Inv. of Est. of JOSEPH JOY of Reho., dtd. 29 Dec. 1724, pres.
by Hester Joy, Adm. Apprs: Josua S[blot]h, Matthew Cushing &
John Wilmouth [5:20].

Acct. of John Ide, Exec. of Est. of NICHOLAS IDE of Attl., dtd.
19 Jan. 1724/5 [5:20/1].

Inv. of Est. of MARY COOPER of Reho., dtd. 23 Oct. 1724, pres.
by John Humphrey, Exec. Apprs: John Read, Ephraim Carpenter &
Daniel Carpenter [5:21].

Acct. of John Humphrey, Exec. of Est. of MARY COOPER of Reho.,
dtd. 19 Jan. 1724/5. Mentions paym. to var. persons, incl.
Samuel Cooper & Nathaniel Cooper [5:21/2].

Inv. of Est. of SAMUEL ROBINSON of Attl., dtd. 10 Nov. 1724,
pres. by Samuel Robinson & Ebenezer Robinson, Adms. Apprs:
Noah Carpenter, Daniel Read & Nathaniel Read [5:22/3].

Acct. of Samuel Robinson & Ebenezer Robinson, Adms. of Est. of
their father SAMUEL ROBINSON of Attl., dtd. 19 Jan. 1724/5
[5:23].

Div. & settl. of Est. of SAMUEL ROBINSON of Attl. by his sons
Ssmuel Robinson & Ebenezer Robinson of Attl., who "bought
out the whole Right of our Brother & Sister Namely John Ide
& Mehetibel Ide his wife," dtd. 15 Jan. 1724/5. Witns: Noah
Carpenter & Stephen Carpenter [5:23½].

Appt. of John Robinson as guard. of Timothy Robinson son of
BENJAMIN ROBINSON of Attl., dtd. 16 Feb. 1724/5 [5:24].

Order for inv. to Hannah Josling, Exec. of Est. of her husb.
THOMAS JOSLING of Taun., dtd. 16 Feb. 1724/5 [5:24/5].

Appt. of Nathaniel Hodges as Adm. of Est. of NATHANIEL HODGES
of Norton, dcd. intest., dtd. 16 Feb. 1724/5 [5:25].

Appt. of Noah Sabin as guard of Ruth Walker (over 14) dau. of
SAMUEL WALKER of Reho., dtd. 16 Feb. 1724/5 [5:25/6].

Appt. of Edward Bosworth of Brist. as guard. of Hanery Cary
(under 14) son of DAVID CARY of Brist., dtd. 3 March 1724/5
[5:26].

Appt. of Samuel Barrow of Middlebury, County of Plimouth, as
guard. of Joannah Smith (over 14), dau. of JOHN SMITH of Reho., dtd. 3 March 1724/5 [5:26/7].

Appt. of John Lyon as Adm. of Est. of his father JOHN LYON of
Reho. dcd. intest., dtd 16 Feb. 1724/5 [5:27].

Inv. of Est. of SAMUEL STANLEY of Attl., dtd. 10 Dec. 1724,
pres. by Jacob Stanley, Adm. Apprs: John Foster, Mayhew Dagget & Joseph Capron [5:28].

Will of WILLIAM BLANDING of Reho., Housewrite [sic], dtd. 23
Nov. 1724, prob. 25 Jan. 1724/5. Wife Mehetibel. To dau. "Elezebeth the things that were her own mothers." Son William. My
daus. (son William's sisters): Hester, Mehetibel, Bathia, Sy-
bill & Rachel. Witns: James Redaway, Mary Wilmarth & David
Turner [5:28/30].

Appt. of Jeremiah Ingraham of Reho. as guard. of Benjamin Robinson (over 14), son of BENJAMIN ROBINSON of Attl., dtd. 16
Feb. 1724/5 [5:30].

Inv. of Est. of WILLIAM BLANDING of Reho., dtd. 1 Jan. 1724/5,
pres. by Mehetibel Blanding, his wife & Exec. Apprs: Joshua
Smith, Matthew Cushing & John Wilmouth [5:31].

Inv. of HESTER GRAY of Norton, dtd. 22 Dec. 1724, pres. by
John Austin, Adm. Apprs: John Wetherill, James Leonard & John
Briggs [5:31/2].

Will of SAMUEL FULLER of Reho., Yeoman, dtd. 14 Dec. 1724, prob.
19 Jan. 1724/5. Wife Dorothy. Sons: Samuel, Ebenezer, Timothy, Moses, Aaron & Noah Fuller. Daus: Dorothy, Ruth & Mary.
Sons Samuel & Ebenezer, Execs. Witns: Benjamin Wilson, John
Wilmarth & David Turner [5:32/3].

Inv. of Est. of SAMUEL FULLER of Reho, dtd. 27 Jan. 1724/5,
pres. by Samuel & Ebenezer Fuller, his sons & Execs. Apprs:
Jonathan Ormsby, James Redaway & John Wilmouth [5:33/4].

Inv. of Est. of ROBERT TUCKER of Norton, dtd. 9 Feb. 1724/5,
pres. by Mehetibel Tucker, Exec. Apprs: Eleazer Fisher, Sr.,
Daniel Brayman & Nathan Hodges [5:34].

Inv. of Est. of JOSEPH WHITE of Taun., dtd. 4 Feb. 1724/5, pres.
by Joseph White, Adm. Apprs: Samuel Sumner, Nathaniel Thayer
& Joseph Eddy [5:35].

Appt. of John Seke [or Leke?] of North Purchase as Adm. of Est.
of CLEMENT BRIGGS of Norton East Precinct dcd. intest., dtd.
amrch 1724/5 [5:36].

Inv. of Est. of SOLOMON HORTON of Rehoboth, dtd. 23 Jan. 1724/5,
pres. by Susanah Horton, Adm. Apprs: Jonathan Ormsbee, James
Redaway & John Wilmouth [5:36].

Will of JOSEPH CHASE of Shewomet Purchase, Yeoman, dtd. 8 Nov.
1724, prob. 19 Jan. 1724/5. Wife Sarah. Sons: Job (eldest),
Stephen, Silas, George, Ebenezer & Moses (youngest, under 21)
Chase. Daus: Abigail Davis, Lidia Davis, Alse Chase, Sarah
Chase & Ruth Chase. Wife Sarah & son Job, Execs. Witns: Isaac
Chase, Samuel Chase & Francis Born [5:37/8].

Inv. of Est. of JOSEPH CHASE of Shewomet alias Swanzey, dtd. 22
Dec. 1724, pres. by Sarah Chase & Job Chase, Execs. Apprs:
John Read, Richard Bourden & Jacob Hathaway [5:38/9].

Inv. of Est. of ABRAHAM FOLLET of Attl., dtd. 7 Jan. 1724/5,
pres. by Ruth Follet & Isaac Follet, Adms. Apprs: John Foster,
Noah Carpenter & Timothy Tingley [5:39/40].

Appt. of Mary Paul of Digh. as Adm. of Est. of her husb. JAMES
PAUL of Digh. dcd. intest., dtd. 28 March 1724/5 [5:40].

Will of THOMAS JOSLING of Taun., dtd. 22 Sept. 1724, prob. 16
Feb. 1724/5. Wife Hannah. No chldn. mentioned. Mentions land
in Middleborough & in Taun. Witns: Edward Southworth, Ruth
Caswell & Elkanah Leonard [5:41].

Inv. of Est. of JOHN LYON of Reho., dtd. 12 Feb. 1724/5, pres.
by John Lyon, Adm. Mentions lands in Reho., Barr., Providence
& Roxbury. Apprs: Samuel Brown, Abiah Carpenter & David Newman [5:42].

Appt. of Jeremiah Ingraham of Brist. as guard. of Mary Archer
(minor over 14), dau. of JOHN ARCHER of Brist., dtd. 23 March
1724/5 [5:42/3].

Appt. of Mrs. Dorothy Fuller of Reho. as guard. of Mary, Moses,
Aron & Noah Fuller (all under 14) & of Dorothy, Ruth & Timo-
thy Fuller (all minors over 14), chldn. of SAMUEL FULLER of
Reho., dtd. 23 March 1724/5 [5:43].

Order for inv. to Thomas Jones, Exec. of Est. of his father THO-
MAS JONES of Digh., dtd. 16 March 1724/5 [5:44].

Appt. of Mrs. Experience Aldrich as Adm. of Est. of her husb.
PETER ALDRICH of Norton dcd. intest., dtd. 16 March 1724/5
[5:45].

Appt. of John Burt of Digh. as guard. of Ebenezer & Dorcas Jones
(both minors over 14), chldn. of THOMAS JONES of Digh., dtd.
18 March 1724/5 [5:45/6].

Appt. of Mrs. Elezebeth Brown as Adm. of Est. of her husb.
JAMES BROWN of Barr., Yeoman, dtd. 25 March 1724/5 [5:46].

Appt. of Mrs. Rachel Wilkinson & John Wilkinson as Adms. of
Est. of JOHN WILKINSON of Attl. dcd. intest., dtd. 16 March
1724/5 [5:47].

Inv. of Est. of PETER ALDRICH of Norton, dtd. 10 March 1724/5,
pres. by Experience Aldrich, Adm. Apprs: Samuel Hodges, Eliazer Fisher & Seth Richarson. Mentions land in Ashford, Ct.
[5:47/8].

Will of THOMAS JONES of Digh., dtd. 25 Jan. 1724, prob. 16
March 1724/5. No wife mentioned. Sons: Thomas, Ebenezer & Caleb Jones. Daus: Hannah Phillips, Priscilla Jones, Naomi
Jones & Dorcas Jones (last 3 unmar., last 2 under 21). Son
Caleb is blind & has "other infirmities," & is to be provided
for by his brothers. Witns: Joseph Jones, James Paul & Abraham Waldron [5:49/50].

Inv. of Est. of JONATHAN VIALL of Barr. who died 2 Dec. 1724,
dtd. 7 Jan. 1724/5, pres. by Marcy Viall, Exec. Apprs: Samuel
Viall, Mathew Allen & Benjamin Viall. Mentions lands in Reho.
& in Barr. [5:51/2].

Inv. of Est. of MARY BURT who died 6 July 1724, dtd. 12 Nov. 17-
24, pres. by John Tisdel, Adm. Apprs: John Gilbert, John Townsend & William Richmond [5:52].

Inv. of Est. of ABIEL SMITH of Reho., dtd. 20 Nov. 1724, pres.
by Anna Smith, his widow & Exec. Apprs: Daniel Carpenter, Ephraim Carpenter & John Humphrey [5:52/3].

Acct. of Bithiah Macomber of Dart., Exec. of Est. of her husb.
JOHN MACOMBER of Dart., dtd. 17 Nov. 1724 [5:53/4].

Rcpts. of Phillip Taber (Trustee of Dart.), John Cook, Elese-
beth Macomber, John Cornell & William Sole for monies from
Est. of JOHN MACOMBER, paid by Bithiah Macomber, his widow &
Exec., dtd. variously, from Nov. 1723 to 15 Oct. 1724[5:54/5].

Acct. of Rebecca Perry & Henery Smith, Adm. of Est. of DAVID
PERRY late of Reho. dcd. intest., dtd. 16 Feb. 1724/5. Incl.
item "For Bringing Up the Two Children hitherto" [5:55].

Rcpts. by Daniel Ormsbee & Jacob Ormsbee for monies from Est.
of DAVID PERRY, paid by his widow Rebecca Perry, dtd. 15 Apr.
1716 & 13 May 1719 [5:55].

Inv. of Est. of ANDREW SMITH of Taun., dtd. 14 Sept. 1724, pres.
by Sarah Smith, Adm. Apprs: Morgan Cobb, Jr., William Harvey,
Jr. & Joseph White [5:56].

Inv. of Est. of THOMAS EASTERBROOKS of Swan., dtd. 22 Jan. 1724/5
pres. by Elezebeth Easterbrooks, Adm. Apprs: William Salisbury
Benjamin Cole & Richard Harding [5:56/7].
Inv. of Est. of JOHN ARCHER of Brist., dtd. 10 Feb. 1724/5, pres.
by Mehetibel Archer, Adm. Apprs: Samuel Smith & William Walker. Only property was one house and ¼ acre [5:57/8].
Inv. of Est. of FRANCIS WILSON of Reho., pres. 16 Feb. 1724/5
by Jonathan Wilson, Exec. Incl. an Indian man servant, a Negro woman & a Negro girl. Apprs: James Frankling, James Wheel-
er & James Bowen [5:58].
Inv. of Est. of ELEAZER WALKER of Taun., dtd. 18 Feb. 1724/5,
pres. by Edward Walker, Exec. Incl. lands in Digh. & Taun.
Apprs: David Walker, Ephraim Atwood & Edward Blake [5:59].
Inv. of Est. of JAMES PAUL of Digh., dtd. 23 March 1724/5, pres.
by Mary Paul, his widow, & by William Paul, son, Adms. Apprs:
Edward Paul, Daniel Axtill & Edward Shove [5:59/60].
Acct. of Nathaniel Smith, son & Adm. of Est. of JOHN SMITH of
Reho., "Joanna Smith being Administratrix with her son but
not Intermedling Therewith," dtd. 16 March 1724/5 [5:60/1].
Rcpt. by Samuel Barrow & Joannah Barrow for "my Thirds of Said
Estate, and my Daughter Joannah Smiths Portion of said Estate,"
referring to Est. of JOHN SMITH of Reho., dtd. 9 June 1719.
Witns: Daniel Smith & Jethniel Peck [5:61].
Rcpt. by Nathaniel Smith for his portion of Est. of his father
JOHN SMITH of Reho., dtd. 9 June 1719 [5:62].
Rcpt. by Abiel Smith guard. of Jonathan Smith for money due
Jonathan out of Est. of JOHN SMITH of Reho., dtd. 6 June 1719
[5:62].
Rcpt. by Josiah Carpenter for money from Est. of JOHN SMITH,
paid by Nathaniel Smith & his mother as Adms., dtd. 8 June
1719 [5:62].
Order for inv. to Benjamin & Ebenezer Dean, Execs. of Est. of
their father BENJAMIN DEAN of Taun., dtd. 16 Apr. 1724/5 [5:62].
Appt. of Elkanah Leonard of Middleberry, Plimouth Co., as guard.
of Rebeca Leonard & Jemima Leonard, daus. of Elkanah Leonard
late of Middleberry dcd. & grdaus. of "Madom" MARY LEONARD of
Taun., dtd. 15 Apr. 1724/5 [5:63].
Appt. of Benjamin Hodges of Middleborough, Plimouth Co., as
guard. of Joseph, Simeon & Abiah Leonard, chldn. of Elkanah
Leonard of Middleborough dcd. & grchldn. of MARY LEONARD of
Taun., dtd. 20 Apr. 1724/5 [5:63].
Order for inv. to Abraham Tucker of Dartmouth, Exec. of Est. of
his father ABRAHAM TUCKER of Dart., dtd. 20 Apr. 1724/5[5:64].
Appt. of Daniel Axtill & Elkanah Bobbitt, both of Digh., as
guards. of Tabatha, Benjamin, Seth & Mary Crane, chldn. of
BENJAMIN CRANE of Digh., dtd. 20 Apr. 1724/5 [5:64/5].
Inv. of Est. of Col. NATHANIEL PAINE, Esqr., of Brist., dtd.
23 March 1723/4, pres. by Mrs. Dorothy Paine & Nathaniel

Paine, Adms. Incl. Negro men named Ben, Caseo & Dorman & an
Indian girl Fillia. Apprs: Peter Raynolds, Samuel Prall &
Benjamin Bosworth [5:65/6/7].
Order for inv. to Hester Redaway, Exec. of Est. of her husb.
PRESERVED REDAWAY of Reho., dtd. 20 Apr. 1724/5 [5:67].
Appt. of William Stone of Norton as guard. of Experiance Hodges
(over 14), dau. of SAMUEL HODGES of Nor., dtd. 29 Apr. 1724/5
[5:68].
Appt. of John Hodges of Nor. as guard. of Lidiah Hodges (over
14), dau. of SAMUEL HODGES of Nor., dtd 29 Apr. 1724/5[5:68].
Appt. of Joseph Hodges of Nor. as guard. of Silence Hodges (over
14), dau. of SAMUEL HODGES of Nor., dtd. 29 Apr. 1724/5[5:69].
Order for inv. to Mrs. Hannah Gorham, widow, & Benjamin Gorham,
son, Execs. of Est. of their husb. & father JABEZ GORHAM of
Brist., dtd. 20 Apr. 1724/5 [5:69/70].
Appt. of Samuel Leonard of Taun. as guard. of Josiah Brayman
(over 14), son of THOMAS BRAYMAN of Nor., dtd. 1 May 1725
[5:70].
Inv. of Est. of THOMAS JONES of Digh., dtd. 10 March 1724, pres.
16 March 1724/5 by Thomas Jones, his son & Exec. Apprs: Edward
Paull, Daniel Axtill & Edward Shove [5:70/1].
Will of BENJAMIN DEAN of Taun., dtd. 2 Feb. 1722/3, prob. 14
Apr. 1725. Wife Sarah. 3 sons: Israel (eldest), Benjamin & Eb-
enezer. Daus: Hannah Richmond, Mary Edson, Damaris White, Sar-
ah Danforth, Elizebeth Richmond, Mehetibel Richmond & Lidiah
Dean. Mentions "my brother Ezra Dean." 2 youngest sons Benj. &
Ebenezer to be Execs. Witns: Seth Williams, Richard Godfrey &
James Williams [5:71/2/3].
Inv. of Est. of BENJAMIN DEAN of Taun., dtd. 18 March 1724/5,
pres. by Benjamin & Ebenezer Dean, sons & Execs. Apprs: Samu-
el Williams, Benjamin Wilbore & Peter Caswell [5:73/4].
Inv. of Est. of JOHN DEAN of Taun., dtd. 26 Feb. 1724/5, pres.
by Hannah Dean & Abiel Dean, Adms. Apprs: Samuel Leonard,
John Mason & Benjamin Wilbore [5:74].
Will of JABEZ GORHAM of Brist., Yeoman, "being under much pain
and bodily illnesse," dtd. 16 March 1724/5, prob. 20 Apr. 17-
24/5. Wife Hannah. Sons: Jabez (eldest), Isaac, Joseph & Benjamin Gorham. Dau. Elezebeth wife of Shobel Baxter. Grsons.
Edward, William & Samuel Downs. Mentions a Negro named Nile.
Wife Hannah & son Benjamin, Execs. Witns: Simon Davis, Samuel Howland & Sarah Ingraham [5:75/6].
Order for inv. to Jonathan French, Exec. of Est. of JOHN FRENCH
of Reho., dtd. 20 Apr. 1724/5 [5:76/7].
Will of JOHN FRENCH of Reho., aged 68 years, dtd. 31 May 1723,
prob. 20 Apr. 1724/5. Wife Hannah. Sons: John (eldest), Jona-
than, Thomas (3rd son now living) & Ephraim (youngest) French.
4 daus: Hannah Carpenter widow, Mary Bliss widow, Elezebeth
Read & Martha Read. Son Jonathan as Exec. Friends Ens. Abiah
Carpenter & David Newman, Overseers. Witns: Jeremiah Robinson,
Ebenezer Robinson & Grace Robinson [5:77/8].

Inv. of Est. of JOHN FRENCH of Reho., dtd. 16 Apr. 1724/5, pres.
by Jonathan French, his son & Exec. Apprs: Abiah Carpenter,
Edward Glover & Noah Mason [5:78/9].

Will of ABRAHAM TUCKER of Dart., Yeoman, dtd. 20 Nov. 1724,
prob. 20 Apr. 1724/5. Wife Hannah. Sons: Henery (eldest) &
Abraham (youngest) Tucker. Daus: Mary Russell, Patience Wool-
ley, Abigail Chase wife of Joseph Chase, Martha Thomas dcd.
late wife of George Thomas of Portsmouth, Joanah Tucker, Ruth
Tucker & Hannah Tucker (last 3 under 18 & unmar.). Grchldn.
Abraham Thomas (under 21) & Mary Thomas (under 18) chldn. of
my dau. Mary Thomas dcd. "My seven Daughters Namely Mary Russel, Elezebeth Barker, Sarah Wing, Content Wing, Joanah Tucker, Ruth Tucker & Hannah Tucker." Son Abraham as Exec. Overseers to be friends & brethren John Tucker & Jacob Mott.
Witns: Richard Bourden, John Tucker & John Howland [5:79/80/1].

Acct. of Jabez Carpenter, Adm. of Est. of his father DANIEL CAR-
PENTER of Reho., dtd. 20 Apr. 1724/5. The dcd. Daniel was
guard. to Ruth Walker dau. to SAMUEL WALKER dcd. & grdau. of
Capt. SAMUEL WALKER dcd. Mentions paym. to "Noah Sabin for
Bringing up Said Ruth Walker from Three Year old," & "Money
to Timothy Walker for maintaining a old Negro Belonging to
the Estate" [5:82/3].

Acct. of Ezekiel Read, Adm. of Est. of his father Capt. MOSES
READ of Reho. who was guard. of Oliver Walker & Moses Walker,
sons of SAMUEL WALKER & grsons. of Capt. SAMUEL WALKER dcd.,
dtd. 20 Apr. 1724/5. Incl. item "for keeping or maintaining
s^d Oliver Walker from five years old To fifteen Years;" & an
item "for keeping & maintaining Said Moses Walker from a
weeke old to Eleven years old [5:83/4].

Rcpt. by Noah Sabin as guard. of Ruth Walker for money from
Est. of MOSES READ dcd., who was guard. of Oliver & Moses Wal-
ker, sons of SAMUEL WALKER dcd. & grsons. of Capt. SAMUEL WAL-
KER dcd., paid by Ezekiel Read, Adm. to Est. of his father
Moses, dtd. 20 Apr. 1724/5 [5:84].

Rcpt. by Noah Sabin as guard. of Ruth Walker for monies rcvd.
var. times since 16 Jan. 1716 from Daniel Carpenter for bringing up Ruth, dtd. 3 June 1720 [5:84].

Acct. of Daniel Brayman, Exec. of Est. of his father THOMAS
BRAYMAN of Nor., dtd. 20 Jan. 1713/4 [5:84/5].

Inv. of Est. of ABRAHAM TUCKER of Dart., Yeoman, dtd. 8 Apr.
1724/5, pres. by Abraham Tucker of Dart., son & Exec. Mentions: widow's cows, Abraham's cows, and steer belonging to
Joannah, Ruth & Hannah Tucker. Apprs: John Akin, Nathaniel
Soule & Deliverance Smith [5:86/7/8].

Order to Phillip Allen, Exec. of Est. of EBENEZER ALLEN of Dart.
to Adm. said Est. since "ye widdow & other Executor Refusing
to Administer," dtd. 18 May 1725 [5:88].

Inv. of Est. of JOSEPH ATWOOD of Digh. who died 26 Sept. 1724,

dtd. 20 Apr. 1724/5, pres. by John Atwood, Exec. Mentions
ship's carpenter tools. Apprs: David Walker, James Walker &
John Godfrey [5:89/90].

Inv. of Est. of JOHN WILLIAMS of Taun., dtd. 16 Apr. 1724, pres.
by Hannah Williams & Nathaniel Williams, Adms. Apprs: Samuel
Williams, John Mason & Benjamin Wilbore [5:90/1].

Appt. of Mrs. Abigail French as Adm. of Est. of her husb. JO-
SEPH FRENCH of Taun. dcd. intest., dtd. 19 May 1725 [5:91/2].

Appt. of [illegible] Sweeten, widow, as Adm. of Est. of her
husb. LEWIS SWEETEN of Reho. dcd. intest., dtd. 19 May 1725
[5:92].

Appt. of Mrs. Katherine Dean of Taun. as guard. of Katherine,
Silence & Mehetibel Dean (all minors over 14) & of Israel,
Susanah & Abiel Dean (all under 14), chldn. of JOHN DEAN of
Taun., dtd. 18 May 1725 [5:92/3].

Appt. of Mrs. Hannah Pool of Digh. as Adm. of Est. of her husb.
BENJAMIN POOL of Digh. dcd. intest., dtd. 19 May 1725[5:93/4].

Will of EBENEZER ALLEN of Dart., Yeoman, dtd. 18 Apr. 1725,
prob. 18 May 1725. Wife Abigail. Sons: Phillip, James, Seth &
Ebenezer Allen. Daus: Mary Briggs, Sarah Akin, Hannah Howland
& Abigail Allen. My brother Zachariah Allen. Wife Abigail &
son Phillip as Execs. Witns: Benjamin Wilbore, Samuel Wilbore
& Richard Borden [5:94/5/6].

Quit-claim by Joseph Burt of Digh. to Seth Burt of Taun. of all
rights in Est. of Joseph's father ABEL BURT of Taun., dtd. 10
June 1724 [5:96/7].

Rcpt. & release by John Dillingham of Taun. & his wife Priscilla
for legacy from Est. of her father ABEL BURT of Taun., paid
by Seth Burt, Exec., dtd. 5 June 1722 [5:97].

Acct. of Samuel Dean, Adm. of Est. of his mother Mrs. SARAH
DEAN of Taun. dcd. intest., dtd. 18 May 1725 [5:97/8].

Will of PRESERVED REDEWAY of Reho., Yeoman, dtd. 25 Dec. 1724,
prob. 20 Apr. 1724/5. Wife Hester. Sons: John, Thomas & Preserved Redeway. Dau. Hester (under 18). Mentions "untill the
Children Come of age." Wife Hester as Exec. Witns: Abraham
Carpenter, Joseph Thurber & James Redeway [5:98/9].

Acct. of Samuel Leonard, Adm. of Est. of his mother Mrs. MARY
LEONARD of Taun., dtd. 18 May 1725 [5:99/100].

Appt. of Benjamin Leonard & John King as Adms. of Est. of BEN-
JAMIN LEONARD of Taun., dtd. 18 May 1725 [5:100/2][no page
101].

Inv. of Est. of BENJAMIN POOL of Digh., Husbandman, dtd. 11 Mar.
1724, pres. by Hannah Pool, his widow & Adm. Apprs: Daniel
Axtill, Abraham Shaw & Edward Shove [5:102].

Acct. of Deborah Peck & Hezekiah Peck, Adms. of Est. of HEZEK-
IAH PECK of Attl., dtd. 19 May 1725. Mentions item "Allowed
the widdow out of the Inventory" [5:103].

Rcpts. by Abiah Carpenter & Josiah Carpenter for monies from
Est. of HEZEKIAH PECK, paid by his son Hezekiah Peck, Adm.,

dtd. 15 Jan. 1724/5 [5:104].

Rcpt. by Benjamin Crabtree, Ebenezer Tiler & John Foster, "Trustees of ye Last 50000 Loan money," for money paid by Hezekiah Peck, Adm. of Est. of his father, dtd. 21 June 1724 [5:104].

Inv. of Est. of JOSEPH FRENCH, Jr. of Taun., dtd. 6 Apr. 1725, pres. by Abigail French, his widow & Adm. Apprs: Samuel Williams, John Mason & Benjamin Wilbore [5:104].

Appt. of Joseph Hodges of Nor. as guard. of Sarah, Martha & Seth Hodges (all under 14), chldn. of SAMUEL HODGES of Nor., dtd. 25 June 1725 [5:105].

Appt. of George Leonard of Nor. as guard. of Samuel & Mereum Hodges (both under 14), chldn. of SAMUEL HODGES of Nor., dtd. 24 June 1725 [5:105/6].

Appt. of Hezekiah Peck of Attl. as guard. of Paterneile Peck (over 14) & Parthenia Peck (under 14), chldn. of HEZEKIAH PECK of Attl., dtd. 19 May 1725 [5:106].

Appt. of Edward Bosworth of Bristol as guard. of Ebenezer Torrey (minor over 14), son of ANGILL TORREY of Brist., dtd. 18 May 1725 [5:106/7].

Appt. of William Torrey of Brist. as guard. of Mary Torrey (under 14), dau. of ANGILL TORREY of Brist., dtd. 18 May 1725 [5:107].

Inv. of Est. of JAMES BROWN of Barr. who died 21 Feb. 1724/5, dtd. 8 May 1725, pres. by Elezebeth Brown, his widow & Adm. Apprs: Samuel Brown, Thomas Dexter & Mathew Allen[5:107/8/9].

Appt. of Noah Carpenter of Attl. as guard. of Mary & Martha Follet (minors over 14), daus. of ABRAHAM FOLLET of Attl [next sentence calls Abraham "of Dartmouth"], dtd. 29 May 1725 [5:109].

Acct. of John Tisdel, Adm. of Est. of MARY BURT of Nor., dtd. 16 June 1725. Mentions "A Bill or writeing under the hand of Ebenezer Burt...Bearing date July ye 26 1697 which is Twenty Eight Years Since ye Said Burt died" [5:110].

Acct. of Ruth Follet & Isaac Follet, Adms. of Est. of ABRAHAM FOLLET of Attl, dtd. 18 May 1725. Incl. an expense for "going to Ashford on ye accounte of ye Estate" [5:110/1].

Rcpts. by Thomas Bowen & Richard Bowen for monies paid by Isaac Follet & Widow Follet, Adms. of Est. of ABRAHAM FOLLET, dtd. 8 March & 17 May 1725 [5:111].

Inv. of Est. of EBENEZER ALLEN of Dart., dtd. 15 May 1725, pres. by Phillip Allen, son & Exec. [5:111/2/3].

Acct. of Mary Perry & Mercy French, Execs. of Est. of LEONARD NEWSUM of Reho., dtd. 15 June 1725 [5:114].

Rcpt. by Nathaniel Carpenter from Jonathan French & John Perry for funeral charges "for their Father" LEONARD NEWSUM, dtd. 11 Feb. 1724/5 [5:114].

Inv. of Est. of CLEMENT BRIGGS of Taun. [later called "of Norton"], dtd. 14 June 1725, pres. by John Selee [?]. Mentions

land in Middleberry. Apprs: Thomas Randel, Benjamin Drake &
John Phillips [5:114/5].

Acct. of Katherine Dean of Taun., Exec. of Est. of her husb.
ISRAEL DEAN of Taun., dtd. 15 Apr. 1725. Mentions paym. to
abt. 28 persons, incl. Ezra Dean, Thomas Dean & Elizabeth
Dean [5:116].

Rcpts. from Samuel Hayburne, Benjamin Collins, William Hoskins
& Jonathan Hayward for monies paid by Katherine Dean, Exec.
of Est. of her husb. ISRAEL DEAN, dtd. variously 1720 & 16
Nov. 1724 [5:117].

Will of WILLIAM BRIGGS of Taun., Cooper, son of Richard Briggs
of Taun., dcd., dtd. 19 Apr. 1725, prob. 15 June 1725. Wife
Elezebeth. 2 eldest sons William & Isaac Briggs. Youngest son
Noah Briggs. Dau. Elezebeth (under 18 & unmar.). Wife Eleze-
beth & son Isaac to be Execs. Witns: John Andrews, Benjamin
Collins & John Smith [5:117/8].

Inv. of Est. of WILLIAM BRIGGS of Taun., Cooper, dtd. 27 May
1725, pres. by Elezebeth Briggs & Isaac Briggs, Execs. Apprs:
John Andrews, Nathaniel Thayer & Morgan Cobb, Jr. [5:118/9].

Inv. of Est. of THOMAS SMITH of Reho., dtd. 14 Jan. 1724, pres.
by Henery Smith, Adm. Apprs: Ephraim Carpenter, John Humphrey
& Daniel Carpenter [5:119].

Acct. of Ezekiel Read, Adm. of Est. of his father MOSES READ of
Reho., dtd. 15 June 1725 [5:120/1].

Order for inv. to Elezebeth French, Exec. of Est. of her husb.
EBENEZER FRENCH of Taun., dtd. 15 July 1725 [5:121].

Appt. of Joseph Cowel of Wrentham, Suffolk Co., as guard. of
Joseph Wilkinson (minor over 14), son of JOHN WILKINSON of
Attl. dcd. intest., dtd. 13 July 1725 [5:122].

Order for inv. to Patience Greenhill, Exec. of Est. of her husb.
RICHARD GREENHILL of Lit. Comp., dtd. 20 July 1720 [5:122/3].

Inv. of Est. of SAMUEL HODGES of Nor. dcd. intest., dtd. 13 May
1725, pres. by his brothers William & Nathan Hodges, Adms.
Incl. a Negro man named Walley. Apprs: John Newland, Eliazer
Fisher, Sr. & Morgan Cobb, Jr. [5:123/4/].

Will of EBENEZER FRENCH of Taun., dtd. 22 May 1725, prob. 15
July 1725. Wife Elezebeth. Sons: Ebenezer (eldest), Jacob &
William French. 3 daus: Mehetibel, Elezebeth & Jane. Mentions
"The Child my wife is now big with," & his land in Reho. Wife
Elezebeth to be Exec. Witns: Seth Williams, John French & Sam-
uel Phillips [5:125].

Inv. of Est. of EBENEZER FRENCH of Taun., dtd. 10 July 1725,
pres. by Elezebeth French, his widow & Exec. Apprs: Samuel
Williams, John Mason & Benjamin Wilbore [5:125/6].

Inv. of Est. of PRESERVED REDEWAY of Reho., dtd. 21 Apr. 1725,
pres. by Hester Redeway, his widow & Exec. Apprs: James Redeway, Abraham Carpenter & Jacob Ormsbee [5:126/7].

Acct. of Mrs. Anna Brown, Adm. of Est. of her husb. JOSIAH BROWN of Reho., dtd. 20 July 1725. Mentions paym. to abt. 30 persons, incl. James Brown, Samuel Brown, Mary Brown, Elezebeth Brown, Daniel Brown, John Brown, Isaac Brown, Nathaniel Brown, Thomas Brown, Jabiz Brown & Sarah Brown. [5:127/8].

Rcpts. by Matthew Allen, Mary Rhoades, Abigail Harris (Providence) & Benjamin Green for monies paid by Anna Brown, Adm. of Est. of her husb. JOSIAH BROWN, dtd. btwn. 30 May 1724 & 20 Jan. 1724/5 [5:128].

Rcpt. by Nathaniel Brown for money paid by "my Daughter in Law Anna Brown," Adm. of Est. of her husb., dtd. at Reho. 19 July 1725 [5:128].

Rcpt. by John Brown for money paid by "my father Nathaniel Brown" from Est. of "my brother" JOSIAH BROWN, dtd. 16 June 1724 [5:128].

Rcpts. by Thomas Bowen, Benjamin Tillinghast & Nicholas Power (Providence) for monies paid by Anna Brown from Est. of JOSIAH BROWN, dtd. btwn. 1 June 1724 & 3 May 1725 [5:129].

Rcpt. by John Brown for money paid by "my Sister Anna Brown," dtd. Reho. 1 June 1724 [5:129].

Will of RICHARD GREENHILL of Lit. Comp., dtd. 9 Dec. 1723, prob. 20 July 1725. Wife Patience. Sons: George, William, Richard & Daniel Greenhill. Daus: Rebecca, Elezebeth, Patience, Ruth & Sarah (all under age). Mentions land that was "my Grandfathers in Law Daniel Eatons." Wife Patience & Kinsman Edward Thirston to be Execs. Witns: John Amorey, Elisha Phillips & Edward Richmond [5:129/30].

Order for inv. to Elezebeth Briggs & Isaac Briggs, Execs. of Est. of WILLIAM BRIGGS of Taun., dtd. 15 June 1724 [5:130/1].

Appt. of Elisha May of Barr. as guard. of David & Oliver Bosworth (both under 14), sons of JOHN BOSWORTH of Barr., dtd. 21 July 1725 [5:131].

Order for div. of Est. of EBENEZER WALKER of Reho. dcd. intest. to and among his widow & chldn., dtd. 25 Jan. 1724/5[5:131/2].

Div. of Est. of EBENEZER WALKER of Reho. btwn. wife Dorothy Walker & chldn: Caleb (eldest son) & Ebenezer (youngest son) Walker; Joannah Carpenter (eldest dau.), Dorothy Walker (2nd dau.) Elizabeth Walker (3rd dau.) & Martha Walker (youngest dau.), dtd. 20 July 1725. Comm: Abiah Carpenter, Edward Glover & Ephraim Carpenter [5:132/3/4/5].

Order for div. of Est. of JOHN BOSWORTH of Barr. dcd. intest., to & among his widow & chldn., dtd. 16 Feb. 1724/5 [5:135/6].

Div. of Est. of JOHN BOSWORTH of Barr. btwn. widow [not named] (now wife of James Thurber) & chldn: Nathaniel (eldest son), John (2nd son), David (3rd son), Oliver (4th son), Elesebeth (eldest dau.) the wife of John Thomas, Mary Bosworth (2nd dau.), Hannah Bosworth (3rd dau.) & Lidiah Bosworth (4th dau). Comm: James Bowen, Samuel Hill, Joseph Peck, Robert Wheaten & Peter Hunt [5:136/7/8].

Request by Abiel Macomber, aged 18, asking that his uncle Thomas Macomber continue as guard. of him & his 2 sisters [not *named*], dtd. 7 July 1725 at Taun. [5:139].

Inv. of Est. of LEWIS SWEETEN of Reho., dtd. 30 Apr. 1725, pres.
  by Zebediah [*sic*] Sweeten, his widow & Adm. Apprs: Edward
  Glover, Nathaniel Bosworth & Ens. Joseph Peck [5:139].

Appt. of John Horton of Reho. as Adm. of Est. of SOLOMON HORTON
  of Reho. dcd. intest., dtd. 20 Aug. 1725 [5:140].

Order for div. of Est. of OBEDIAH BETTYES of Reho. dcd. intest.
  btwn. his widow & chldn., dtd. 29 May 1725 [5:141].

Div. of Est. of OBEDIAH BETTYES of Reho. btwn. his widow Mary
  Bettyes "or Burt" & chldn: James (eldest son), Thomas (2nd
  son), Sarah Bettyes (eldest dau.), Hannah Bettyes, Mary Bettyes & Marcy Bettyes, dtd. 9 June 1725. Comm: Jathniel Peck,
  Jonathan Kingsley, John West, James Bowen & Samuel Bullock
  [5:141/2].

Inv. of Est. of JOHN ALLEN of Swan. dcd. intest., dtd. 24 June
  1725, pres. by Joseph Buckling & Hugh Cole, Adms. Apprs: Joseph Butterworth, William Salsbury & Richard Harding [5:143].

Inv. of Est. of THOMAS WALKER of Brist., dtd. 28 Oct. 1724,
  pres. by Elezebeth Walker, his widow & Adm. Apprs: Samuel Royall, William Throope & Thomas Lawton [5:143/3½].

Appt. of Mrs. Susannah Cooper, widow, & Nathaniel Cooper, son,
  as Adms. of Est. of THOMAS COOPER of Reho. dcd. intest., dtd.
  17 Aug. 1725 [5:143½/4].

Acct. of Rachel Freeman, Adm. of Est. of her husb. BENJAMIN
  FREEMAN of Attl., dtd. 19 May 1725 [5:144].

Rcpt. by Ralph Freeman for money paid by my dau. Rachel Freeman,
  widow of my son BENJAMIN FREEMAN, dtd. 6 June 1724 [5:145].

Rcpt. by Doctor B. Ware for money paid by Widow Freeman from
  Est. of BENJAMIN FREEMAN, dtd. 3 March 1725 [5:145].

Rcpt. by Robert Woodward for money paid by Daniel Brayman of
  Nort., Adm. of Est. of his father THOMAS BRAYMAN, dtd. 27 Dec.
  1714 [5:145].

Order for div. of Est. of EPHARIM HATHAWAY of Digh. dcd. intest.
  btwn. his widow & his chldn., dtd. 17 Oct. 1725 [5:145].

Div. of Est. of EPHARIM HATHAWAY of Digh. btwn. his widow [*not
  named*] & chldn: Epharim (eldest son), Mary, Sarah, Elizebeth
  wife of John White, Nathaniel, Josiah, Joshuah, Abigail &
  Seth, dtd. 17 Aug. 1725. Comm: Jared Talbut, Abraham Hathaway, Edward Shove & Abraham Waldron [5:146/7].

Appt. of Mrs. Rachel Wilkinson of Attl. as guard. of Hipsebeth,
  Abigail & Hannah Wilkinson (all under 14), daus. of JOHN WIL-
  KINSON of Attl., dtd. 24 Aug. 1725 [5:148].

Appt. of William Johnson of Molberry, Middlesex Co. as guard.
  of Mary Wilkinson (over 14) & Sarah Wilkinson (under 14),
  daus. of JOHN WILKINSON of Attl., dtd. 4 Aug. 1725 [5:148/9].

Inv. of Est. of WILLIAM MARKES of Brist., Merchant, dtd. 19 Jan.
  1724, pres. by Catherine Markes, Exec. Mentions his part of
  the sloop "Speedwell;" a negro woman named Elenor & lands in
  Digh. & Brist. Apprs: Simon Davis, Timothy Failes & Samuel
  Little [5:149/50/1/2/3].

Inv. of Est. of THOMAS COOPER of Reho., dtd. 10 Aug. 1725, pres.
by Susanah Cooper & Nathaniel Cooper, Adms. Apprs: Abiah Carpenter, Ephraim Carpenter & Daniel Carpenter [5:153/4].

Appt. of Samuel Day of Attl. as guard. of Ruth Follet (under
14), dau. of ABRAHAM FOLLET of Attl., dtd. 15 Sept. 1725 [5:
154/5].

Appt. of Mrs. Patience Greenhill as Adm. of Est. of her husb.
RICHARD GREENHILL of Lit. Comp. dcd. intest. [sic; but see
his will above], dtd. 1 Sept. 1725 [5:155/6].

Appt. of Mrs. Hannah Healey as Adm. of Est. of her husb. PAUL
HEALEY of Reho. dcd. intest., dtd. 1 Sept. 1725 [5:156].

Appt. of Samuel Bishop of Attl. as Adm. of Est. of his mother
SARAH BISHOP of Reho. dcd. intest., dtd. 4 Sept. 1725 [5:
157].

Acct. of Sarah Smith, Adm. of Est. of her husb. ANDREW SMITH
of Taun., dtd. 15 Sept. 1725. Mentions paym. to John Smith &
Samuel Smith [5:158/9].

Rcpts. by Samuel Briggs, Eleazer Eddee (Norton), James Leonard
& Ezra Deane for monies paid by Sarah Smith, Adm. of Est. of
her husb. ANDREW SMITH, dtd. btwn. 17 Feb. 1724/5 & 11 Sept.
1725 [5:159].

Order for inv. to Ralph Freeman, Exec. of Est. of his father
RALPH FREEMAN of Attl., dtd. 21 Sept. 1725 [5:160].

Acct. of Zibiah [?[Sweeten, Adm. of Est. of her husb. LEWIS
SWEETEN of Reho., dtd. 15 Sept. 1725. Mentions a payment "to
my father & Edward Glover my bondsmen" [5:160/1].

Acct. of Rachel Wilkinson & John Wilkinson, Adms. of Est. of
JOHN WILKINSON of Attl., dtd. 15 Sept. 1725 [5:162/3].

Rcpts. by John French, Josua Abell, Ephraim Grover & Ebenezer
Mason for monies from Est. of JOHN WILKINSON, paid by Widow
Wilkinson or by William Johnson, Trustee, dtd. btwn. 17 Sept.
1724 & 23 Aug. 1725 [5:163].

Acct. of Elisebeth Ingraham, Adm. of Est. of her husb. OBEDIAH
INGRAHAM, dtd. 15 Sept. 1725 [5:164/5].

Acct. of Elezebeth Kinnicut, Adm. of Est. of her husb. JOHN
KINNICUT of Swan., dtd. 27 Sept. 1725 [5:165/6].

Rcpt. by Richard Harding for money from Est. of JOHN KINNICUT,
paid by his widow Elesebeth Kinnicut "by the hand of her son
John Kinnicut," dtd. 15 Apr. 1724 [5:166].

Rcpts. by Nathaniel Bosworth, Ephraim Androse, Robert Joles,
Nathaniel Cole, Sr. & Hannah Carr for monies from Est. of
JOHN KINNICUT, dtd. btwn. 16 Feb. 1723 & 28 Aug. 1725[5:166/7].

Acct. of James Howland & George Howland, Execs. of Est. of their
father NATHANIEL HOWLAND of Dart., dtd. 21 Sept. 1725. Mentions legacy to Sarah Akins & money & livestock to: James Russell & his wife Rebecca, Peleg Smith & his wife Mary, Weston
Briggs & his wife Content [5:167/8].

Rcpt. by Timothy Aken & wife Sarah for money from Est. of her
father NATHANIEL HOWLAND, dtd. 1724 [5:169].

Rcpt. by James Russell & his wife Rebecca, Weston Briggs & wife
Content, & Peleg Smith & wife Mary for monies from Est. of
NATHANIEL HOWLAND, father of Rebecca, Content & Mary, paid by
James & George Howland, Execs., dtd. 17 Sept. [5:169].
Agrmt. abt. settl. of Est. of NATHANIEL HOWLAND by his chldn:
John Howland, James Russell & wife Rebecca, Peleg Smith &
wife Mary, Weston Briggs & wife Content, Timothy Aken & wife
Sarah, dtd. 17 Sept. 1725. Witns: John Russell, Timothy Shear-
man, John Briggs, Patience Briggs, James Akin & Benjamin Mosh-
er [5:170].
Will of RALPH FREEMAN of Attl., Cooper, dtd. 14 Aug. 1725, prob.
21 Sept. 1725. Wife living but not named. Sons: Jeremiah &
Ralph Freeman. Daus: Sarah & Hannah. Grchldn: Samuel & John
Freeman (both under age). Witns: Penticost Blackington, Abi-
gail Maxce & George Allen [5:170/1/2].
Acct. of Lidiah Fisher, Adm. of Est. of her husb. SAMUEL FISHER
of Nor. dcd. intest., dtd. 21 Sept. 1725 [5:172/3].
Rcpt. by Samuel Caswell for money from Est. of SAMUEL FISHER of
Nor., dtd. Norton 27 Aug. 1725 [5:173].
Agrmt. abt. settl. of Est. of JOSEPH WHITE of Taun. by his
chldn: Joseph White, Ephraim White & Edward White of Taun.;
William White & Ebenezer White both of Nor.; Lidiah Fisher
widow of Samuel Fisher dcd. late of Nor.; Nathaniel Witherill
& Mary his wife of Nor.; & Elesebeth White of Nor., dtd. 17
July 1725. Witns: Joseph Eddy & Morgan Cobb, Jr. [5:173/4].
Inv. of Est. of RICHARD GRINELL of Lit. Comp., dtd. 27 July 17-
25, pres. by Patience Greenhill, his widow & Exec. Mentions
various livestock given "to George...to William...to Richard
...to Daniel..." Apprs: John Wood, John Palmer & James Rouse
[5:175/6/7].
Appt. of [line containing name left out] as Adm. of Est. of
JOSHUA KENT of Barr. dcd. intest., dtd. 13 Oct. 1725 [5:177/8].
Order for inv. to Richard Godfrey, Exec. of Est. of his father
RICHARD GODFREY of Taun., dtd. 13 Oct. 1725 [5:178].
Order for div. of Est. of JOHN THOMSON of Reho. dcd. intest.
btwn. the widow & chldn., dtd. 17 Feb. 1724/5 [5:179].
Div. of Est. of JOHN THOMSON of Reho. btwn. his widow Hannah &
chldn: George (double share) Thomson, Elezebeth Thomson alias
Fuller, Mehetibel Thomson, Sarah Thomson, Hannah Thomson,
Mary Thomson & Judath Thomson. Mentions Hannah Thomson as
guard. of 3 of her daus: Hannah, Mary & Judath. Comm: John
West, Jathniel Peck, Jonathan Kingsley, James Bowen & Samuel
Bullock. Dtd. 21 Feb. 1724/5 [5:179/80/1].
Will of RICHARD GODFREE, Sr. of Taun., dtd. 26 Jan. 1722/3, prob.
13 Oct. 1725. Wife Mary. Sons: Richard (eldest), John & Joseph
Godfree. 5 daus: Alice Goshit, Mary Smith, Abigail Hopkins,
Joannah Burt & Sarah Walker. Sons Richard to be Exec. Witns:
Seth Williams, Samuel Pitts & James Williams [5:181/2/3].
Appt. of [line with name is omitted] as guard. of Seth Hathaway

& Joshuah Hathaway (both over 14) & Abigail Hathaway (under
14), chldn. of EPHRAIM HATHAWAY of Digh., dtd. 14 Oct. 1725
[5:183].

Order for inv. to Thomas Macomber, Exec. of Est. of his father
JOHN MACOMBER of Taun., dtd. 19 Oct. 1725 [5:184].

Will of JOHN MACOMBER "the first or Eldest of that Name in Taunton," dtd. 27 Jan. 1721, prob. 19 Oct. 1725. No wife mentioned.
Sons: Thomas (eldest), Samuel & John; son William dcd. No
daus. mentioned. Grchldn. Abiel & William Macomber and their
sisters Anna Macomber & Sarah Macomber chldn. of my son William dcd. Son Thomas to be Exec. Witns: Eliphalet Leonard,
John Crane & Thomas Danforth [5:184/5].

Inv. of Est. of JOHN MACOMBER of Taun., dtd. 1 June 1725, pres.
by Thomas Macomber, his son & Exec. Apprs: John Mason, Benjamin Wilbore & Abraham Waldron [5:186].

Order for settl. of Est. of JOHN SMITH of Reho. btwn. his chldn:
John (eldest son), Nathaniel & Joannah Smith (under 18). Joannah's guard. is Samuel Barrows, dtd. 9 Oct. 1725 [5:187].

Inv. of Real Est. of JOHN SMITH of Reho., dtd. 9 Apr. 1725. Mentions land which fell to the dcd. "by his first wife [not
named] from her Father." Apprs: Jathniel Peck, Jonathan Kingsley & James Bowen [5:187/8].

Inv. of Est. of Mrs. SARAH BISHOP, widow, of Reho., dtd. 1 Oct.
1725, pres. by Samuel Bishop, her son & Adm. Apprs: Abiah
Carpenter, John Robinson & Daniel Carpenter [5:188].

Appt. of Thomas Horton of Reho. as guard. of Anna Horton (over
14) & of Daniel & Moses Horton (both under 14), chldn. of
SOLOMON HORTON of Reho., dtd. 1 Nov. 1725 [5:189].

Appt. of John Horton of Reho. as guard. of Solomon & Simeon
Horton (both under 14), sons of SOLOMON HORTON of Reho., dtd.
1 Nov. 1725 [5:189/90].

Appt. of Joseph Garnsey of Reho. as guard. of Hannah Horton
(over 14), dau. of SOLOMON HORTON of Reho., dtd. 1 Nov. 1725
[5:190].

Appt. of John Wilmouth of Reho. as guard. of Hester Horton
(over 14) & Patience Horton (under 14), daus. of SOLOMON HOR-
TON of Reho., dtd. 1 Nov. 1725 [5:190/1].

Appt. of Mrs. Margaret Shearman as Adm. of Est. of her husb.
JOHN SHEARMAN of Dart., dtd. 8 Nov. 1725 [5:191/2].

Order for inv. to Madam Elizabeth Mcintosh, Exec. of Est. of
her husb. Col. HENERY MCINTOSH of Brist., dtd. 8 Nov. 1725
[5:192].

Will of HENERY MAKENTOSH of Brist., Esqr., "being very infirm
of Body," dtd. 1 July 1725, prob. 8 Nov. 1725. Wife Elisebeth.
Son-in-law Francis Borland. Grdaus. Elizebeth & Mary Mcintosh
(both under 21). Mentions his Est. in Surranam, in New England, in Holland & in England. Wife Elizabeth to be Exec.
Witns: Daniel Leany, Samuel Howland, Elizebeth Blagrove &
Abigail Cary [5:193/4].

Appt. of Rebecca Wilcox of Lit. Comp. as guard. of Thomas Wilcox (under 14), son of JOHN WILCOX of Lit. Comp., dtd. 16 Nov.
1725 [5:194/5].

Appt. of Jonathan Head of Lit. Comp. as guard. of Tabisha, Bar-
jonas & Rebeca Wilcox (all over 14), chldn. of JOHN WILCOX of
Lit. Comp., dtd. 16 Nov. 1725 [5:195:6].

Acct. of Samuel Bishop, Adm. of Est. of his mother SARAH BISH-
OP, dtd. 16 Nov. 1725. Mentions paym. to var. persons, incl.
John Bishop, William Bishop, Jr. & Samuel Bishop, Jr.[5:196/7].

Rcpts. by Thomas Bowen & Josiah Carpenter for monies from Est.
of SARAH BISHOP of Rehoboth, paid by Samuel Bishop, her son
& Adm., dtd. 18 Oct. 1725 [5:197].

Appt. of Nathan Basset of Medleborough, Plimouth Co., Blacksmith, as guard. of Elizebeth, Sarah & Experience Holmes (all
under 14), chldn. of EXPERIENCE HOLMES of Dart., Joiner, dtd.
23 Nov. 1725 [5:197/8].

Order for inv. to Samuel Vial, Esqr., Exec. of Est. of Capt.
THOMAS NEWTON of Brist., dtd. 21 Dec. 1725 [5:198].

Appt. of Samuel Bishop of Attl. as guard. of Rachel, John, Ebenezer & David Bishop (all over 14) & of Rebecca & Mary Bishop
(both under 14), chldn. of DAVID BISHOP late of Ashford, Co.
of Hartford, Ct., dtd. 21 Dec. 1725 [5:199].

Will of THOMAS NEWTON of Brist., Mariner, "being Aged & Infirm,"
dtd. 2 Dec. 1725, prob. 21 Dec. 1725. No wife mentioned. Son
John Newton. Daus: Abigail wife of Joseph Carpenter & Martha
now wife of Joseph Waldron and formerly wife of Stephen Toman
dcd. Grchldn. Thomas Toman, Stephen Toman & Martha Toman.
Friend Samuel Vial of Brist. to be Exec. Witns: Willima Martin, Samuel Howland & Christian Martin [5:199/200/1].

Inv. of Est. of JOSUA KENT of Barr., Yeoman, who died 14 Aug.
1725, dtd. 13 Oct. 1725, pres. by Mary Kent, his widow & Adm.
Mentions lands in Barr., Swan. & Nor. Apprs: William Salisbury, Elisha May & Edward Luther [5:201/2/3].

Acct. of Patience Wood formerly Patience Holmes, Adm. of Est.
of Deacon ABRAHAM HOLMES of Dart., dtd. 23 Nov. 1725[5:203].

Rcpt. by Thomas Blanchard of Boston for legacy to his wife Rose
from Est. of her father ABRAHAM HOLMES, paid by Patience Wood
of Middlebury, widow of Experience Holmes dcd., said Experience having been Exec. of Est. of his father Abraham., dtd.
24 Apr. 1725 [5:204].

Rcpt. by Nathan Hammond & wife Elezebeth of Rochester for legacy from Est. of her father ABRAHAM HOLMES, paid by Widow Patience Holmes of Dart., dtd. 23 Oct. 1722. Witns: Benjamin
Hammond & Pollipus Hammond [5:204].

Rcpt. by Samuel Daggett for legacy to his wife Barsheba, dau. of
ABRAHAM HOLMES of Dart., paid by Patience Holmes, widow of
Experience Holmes, now Patience Wood, dtd. 10 May 1723[5:204].

Rcpts. by Seth Pope & Samuel Prince for monies from Est. of EX-
PERIENCE HOLMES, dtd. 12 Nov. 1725 [5:204].

Order for settl. of Est. of SARAH BISHOP of Reho., dtd. 21 Dec. 1725. Sons: Edward & Samuel Bishop (elder sons), with land to be settled on their younger brother John Bishop [5:205].

Order for inv. to Seth Williams, Esqr. & Mary Hall, Execs. of Est. of SAMUEL HAGBURN of Taun., dtd. 12 Jan. 1725/6[5:205/6].

Will of SAMUEL HAGBURN of Taun., "being very aged," dtd. 24 Sept. 1723, prob. 12 Jan. 1725/6. No wife mentioned & chldn. not mentioned. To Mary Hall of Taun., widow of Joseph Hall. To Seth Williams of Taun. Said Seth & Mary to be Execs. To the Church of Christ in Oxford New England. Witns: William Robinson, Jonathan Shaw & John Hall [5:206/7].

Inv. of Est. of SAMUEL HAGBURN of Taun., dtd. 31 Dec. 1725, pres. by Seth Williams & Mary Hall, Execs. Apprs: Samuel Leonard, Jonathan Williams & Benjamin Wilbore [5:207/8].

Appt. of Joseph Cowel of Wrentham, Suffolk Co., as guard. of Rachel Wilkinson (over 14), dau. of JOHN WILKINSON of Attl., dtd. 11 Jan. 1725/6 [5:208].

Agrmt. btwn. Peter Walker, Edward Walker & James Walker, all of Taun., sons of PETER WALKER of Taun., dtd. 7 Jan. 1725/6. Robert Crossman, Overseer. Witns: Elkanah Leonard & Josiah Talbut [5:208/9/10].

Order for inv. to Sarah Bosworth, widow, & John Bosworth, Execs. of Est. of JOHN BOSWORTH of Brist., dtd. 18 Jan. 1725/6 [5: 210/1].

Will of JOHN BOSWORTH of Brist., Yeoman, "being very Sick and weake in Body," dtd. 9 Apr. 1716, prob. 18 Jan. 1725/6. Wife Sarah. Sons: John, Nathaniel, Benjamin, Edward, Jeremiah & Jacob Bosworth. Wife Sarah & son John to be Execs. Mentions his lands in Conn. Witns: Zachariah Whitman, Nathaniel Jacobs & Samuel Howland [5:211/2].

Codicil by JOHN BOSWORTH of Brist., dtd. 17 Aug. 1725. Mentions sons Edward, Benjamin, John & Jeremiah so far being without issue [5:213].

Inv. of Est. of JOHN BOSWORTH of Brist., dtd. 22 Oct. 1725, pres. by Sarah Bosworth & John Bosworth, Execs. Apprs: Thomas Throop, Samuel Howland & Benjamin Bosworth [5:213/4].

Acct. of John Lyon, Adm. of Est. of his father JOHN LYON of Reho. dtd. 18 Jan. 1725/6. Mentions paym. to Joshuah Lyon, Caleb Lyon & Benjamin Lyon [5:215/6].

Rcpt. by Benjamin Lyon for money from Est. of his father JOHN LYON, paid by his brother John Lyon, Adm., dtd. 3 Jan. 1725/6 [5:217].

Rcpts. by William Jenckes, Nathaniel Cooper, Ephraim Carpenter, Thomas Cumstock (Providence), George Dunbar (Newport), Job Carr, Josiah Carpenter & Joseph Tillinghast (Newport), for monies from Est. of JOHN LYON of Reho., paid by his son John Lyon, dtd. btwn. 11 Feb. 1724/5 to 29 March 1725/6[5:217/8].

Acct. of William Torrey, Adm. of Est. of ANGILL TORREY of Brist. dtd. 18 Jan. 1725/6 [5:218/9].

Rcpts. by Sarah Holbrook, Dorothy Paine, Elizabeth Walker, Hanery Bragg & Joseph Waldron for monies from Est. of ANGILL TORREY of Brist., dtd. btwn. 26 Sept. 1724 to 2 Nov. 1725[5:219].

Appt. of Daniel Carpenter of Reho. as guard. of Caleb Lyon (over 14), son of JOHN LYON of Reho., dtd. 18 Jan. 1725/6 [5:219].

Appt of John Lyon of Reho. as guard. of Joshua Lyon (over 14), son of JOHN LYON of Reho., dtd. 18 Jan. 1725/6 [5:219/21].

Acct. of Edward Hall, Adm. of Est. of his father JOHN HALL of Reho., dtd. 18 Jan. 1725/6 [5:221].

Quit-claim & release to their brother Edward Hall of Reho., Husbandman, by Mary Hall, Easther Hall & Hannah Hall, "Spinster daughters" of JOHN HALL of Reho. Edward has been "taking care of our mother & Sister Martha Hall." Dtd. 30 Oct. 1721. Witns: Abiah Carpenter, Joseph Fisher, Samuel Mason & Ephraim Hall [5:222/3].

Quit-claim & release by Ephraim Hall to his brother Edward Hall both of Reho., both Husbandmen & sons of JOHN HALL, dtd. 3 Jan. 1725/6. Witns: Joseph Brown & Anna Brown [5:223].

Quit-claim & release by John Hall to his brother Edward Hall, sons of JOHN HALL of Reho., dtd. 3 Oct. 1721. Witns: Daniel Smith & Freelove Smith [5:224].

Div. of Est. of Mrs. SARAH BISHOP of Reho. btwn. her chldn: Edward Bishop (eldest son), Samuel Bishop (2nd son), Jonathan Bishop (3rd son), William Bishop (4th son), David Bishop dcd., John Bishop (5th living son) & Ebenezer Bishop (6th son), Priscilla Day wife of Samuel Day & Sarah Jorden (youngest dau.), dtd. 15 Feb. 1725/6. Comm: Abiah Carpenter, John Robinson & Daniel Carpenter [5:224/5].

Appt. of Jonathan Peck of Brist. as Adm. of Est. of his brother NICHOLAS PECK of Brist., dtd. 24 Feb. 1725/6 [5:226].

Rcpt. by Josiah Fisk & wife Sarah, "as we are David Bishops Children," for money paid by "our Unkele Samuel Bishop," Adm. to "our honor[d] Grandmother" SARAH BISHOP of Reho., dtd. 12 Feb. 1725/6 [5:226].

Rcpt. by John Bishop, Samuel Day & Priscilla his wife, William Bishop, Sarah Jorden, Jonathan Bishop & Ebenezer Bishop for monies paid by their brother Samuel Bishop of Attl., Adm. of Est. of their mother SARAH BISHOP of Reho., dtd. 30 Dec. 1725 [5:227].

Acct. of Rachel Wilkinson & John Wilkinson, Adms. of Est. of JOHN WILKINSON of Attl. dcd. intest., dtd. 26 Feb. 1725/6 [5:227/8].

Order for inv. to Elezebeth Willis, Exec. of Est. of her husb. THOMAS WILLIS of Taun., dtd. 15 March 1725/6 [5:228].

Appt. of Seth Babbit of Easton as Adm. of Est. of TIMOTHY COOPER of Easton dcd. intest., dtd. 15 March 1725/6 [5:229].

Order for inv. to John Thomas, Exec. of Est. of his father JOHN THOMAS of Swan., dtd. 14 March 1725/6 [5:230].

Appt. of Lidiah Britton as Adm. of Est. of her husb. WILLIAM
BRITTON of Taun. dcd. intest., dtd. 16 Feb. 1725/6 [5:230/1].

Will of JOHN THOMAS of Swan., Cordwinder, dtd. 14 Nov. 1724,
prob. 14 March 1725/6. No wife mentioned. Sons: John (eldest),
James, Nicholas, Lewis, Abial & Amos Thomas. 3 daus: Elizebeth Thomas, Prudence Thomas & Ruth Thomas. Refers to "my uncle Nicholas Tanner." Mentions lands in Swan, Barr. & Reho.
Son John to be Exec. Witns: John West, Job Carpenter & Samuel
Twogood [5:231/2/3].

Will of THOMAS WILLIS of Taun., Yeoman, "being very Sick and
weak," dtd. 27 March 1724/5, prob. 15 March 1725/6. Wife Elezebeth. Sons: Thomas (eldest), Abraham (2nd) & Silas (3rd) Willis (all under 14). Daus: Tabitha Willis (eldest), Elizebeth
Willis (2nd), Charity Willis (3rd), Abigail Willis (4th) &
Katherine Willis (5th). Wife Elezebeth to be Exec. Witns: Daniel Owen, John Willis & Samuel Sumner [5:233/4/5].

Inv. of Est. of THOMAS WILLIS of Taun., dtd. 19 Apr. 1724/5,
pres. by Elezebeth Willis, his widow & Exec. Apprs: Nathaniel
Thayer, Morgan Cobb, Jr. & Samuel Sumner [5:235/6].

Appt. of Samuel Bullock of Reho. as guard. of Robert Carr & Hannah Carr (both under 14), chldn. of ROBERT CARR of Swan., dtd.
18 March 1725/6 [5:236/7].

Appt. of James Bowen of Reho. as guard. of Mary Carr (over 14)
& Caleb Carr (under 14), chldn. of ROBERT CARR of Swan., dtd.
18 March 1725/6 [5:237].

Appt. of John Fuller of Attl. as guard. of Samuel Follet (over
14), son of JOHN FOLLET of Attl., dtd. 15 March 1725/6 [5:
237/8].

Appt. of John Fuller & Sarah Fuller of Attl. as guards. of Jonathan & Elizabeth Follet (both over 14) & of Robert & Susannah
Follet (both under 14), chldn. of JOHN FOLLET of Attl., dtd.
15 March 1725/6 [5:238].

Acct. of Sarah Fuller formerly Follet, who was widow of JOHN
FOLLET, & of John Follet his son, Adms., dtd. 15 March 1725/6.
Mentions a trip to Ashford (Ct.) to sell lands [5:239/40].

Acct. of Mehetibel Cole, widow, & Benjamin Cole, Adms. of Est.
of her husb. EBENEZER COLE of Swan., dtd. 15 March 1725/6
[5:240/1].

Inv. of Est. of Capt. THOMAS NEWTON of Brist., dtd. 10 Jan. 17-
25/6, pres. by Samuel Viall, Exec. Mentions debts to the Est.
"from Capt John Newton to his father." Apprs: Peter Raynolds,
William Throope & Samuel Howland [5:241/2/3].

Acct. of John Martin, Adm. of Est. of JOHN MARTIN of Reho. dcd.
intest., dtd. 22 March 1725/6 [5:243].

Acct. of Hannah Wilson, Adm. of Est. of her former husb. ROBERT
CARR of Swan. dcd. intest., dtd. 18 March 1725/6. Mentions
paym. to Job Carr, Jonathan Wilson & "to Rates & Charges at
Ashford" [5:244/5].

Acct. of Joseph Atwood, Adm. of Est. of GRENFIELD HANNOVER of
Taun., dtd. 25 March 1725/6. Mentions: Anna the eldest dau.
& wife of Edward Blake, Mary French grandmother to dcd.'s
chldn., John Dean guard. of Mary Duglas 2nd dau., Richard
Godfree guard. of Sarah Hannover the 3rd dau. & Edward Blake
guard. of Jane Hannover the 4th dau. [5:246/7/8].

Acct. of Alce Thomas, Adm. of Est. of her husb. EPHARIM THOMAS
of Tiv., dtd. 15 March 1725/6 [5:248/9].

Acct. of Samuel Shorey, Adm. of Est. of his brother JOHN SHOREY
of Reho., dtd. 11 Apr. 1725/6 [5:249/50].

Appt. of Capt. John Andreas of Taun. as guard. of Moses Knap
(minor over 14), son of JOHN KNAP of Taun., dtd. 12 Apr. 17-
25/6 [5:251].

Appt. of Peter Walker of Taun. as guard. of Jonathan Knap (minor over 14), son of JOHN KNAP of Taun., dtd. 12 Apr. 1725/6
[5:251].

Inv. of Est. of RICHARD GODFREE of Taun., dtd. 30 March 1725/6,
pres. by Richard Godfree, his son & Exec. Apprs: Seth Williams, Esqr., Morgan Cobb & Samuel Pitts [5:252].

Appt. of Jacob Hall as Adm. of Est. of HANNAH HOSKINS of Taun.
dtd. 12 Apr. 1725/6 [5:252/3].

Acct. of John Weeks of Attl., Adm. of Est. of RICHARD WEEKS of
Attl. dcd. intest., dtd. 19 Apr. 1725/6 [5:253/4].

Acct. of Anna Smith, Adm. of Est. of her husb. ABIEL SMITH of
Reho. dcd. intest., dtd. 19 Apr. 1725/6. Mentions paym. to
Hanery Smith, Joshuah Smith & Edward Smith [5:254/5].

Rcpt. by Jonathan Smith of money "divided unto me in my nonage"
from Est. of his father ABIEL SMITH, paid by Anna Smith, widow. Also for a bond from "my Brother N: Smith," dtd. 23
March 1725/6. Witns: Jathniel Peck & Thomas Ormsbe [5:255].

Order for inv. to John Hathaway, Exec. of Est. of his father
ABRAHAM HATHAWAY of Digh., dtd. 19 July 1726 [5:256].

Will of ABRAHAM HATHAWAY, Sr. of Digh., "being arrived to a
Considerable Age," dtd. 18 Aug. 1725, prob. 19 Apr. 1725/6.
Wife Rebecca. Sons: Abraham, Thomas, Ebenezer, Samuel, John,
Benjamin & Eleazer Hathaway. Dau. Rebeccah Hathaway (under 21
& unmar.). Friends Jared Talbut, Deacon Joseph Dean & Lt. Eb-
enezer Pitts to make a div. of the lands. Son John to be Exec.
Witns: Jared Talbut, Nathaniel Fisher & Elisebeth Cary[5:256/
7/8].

Acct. of Phillip Allen, Exec. of Est. of his father EBENEZER
ALLEN of Dart., dtd. Apr. 1726. Mentions selling & delivering
the Negro. Legacies to: Mother Allen (her thirds), Seth Allen,
Abigail Allen, David Akin, Thomas Briggs, James Allen, Ebenezer Allen, Isaac Howland & Phillip Allen [5:258/9].

Agrmt. btwn. Capt. Thomas Briggs & Seth Allen, both of Dart.,
abt. said Briggs selling all rights to Est. of his father-in-
law EBENEZER ALLEN to Seth Allen, dtd. 30 May 1725. Witns:
James Howland & John Akin [5:260].

Rcpts. by David Akin, Thomas Briggs & Isaac Howland for monies
from Est. of their father-in-law EBENEZER ALLEN, dtd. btwn.
10 March 1725 & 19 Apr. 1726 [5:260].

Rcpts. by Ebenezer Allen & Abigail Allen for monies from Est.
of their father EBENEZER ALLEN, paid by their brother Phillip
Allen, dtd. 10 March 1725 & 14 Apr. 1726 [5:260].

Appt. of Comfort Briggs of Digh. as Adm. of Est. of her husb.
EBENEZER BRIGGS of Digh., dtd. 17 May 1726 [5:261].

Appt. of Mrs. Anna Smith as guard. of Ruth Smith (minor over 14)
dau. of ABIEL SMITH of Reho., dtd. 25 Apr. 1726 [5:261].

Inv. of Est. of WILLIAM BRITTAIN of Taun. dcd. intest., dtd. 6
Aug. 1725, pres. by Lidiah Britten, Adm. Apprs: John King,
Benjamin Leach & Samuel Leonard [5:262/3].

Order for inv. to Mary & Richard Salsbury, Execs. of Est. of
WILLIAM SALSBURY of Swan., dtd. 16 May 1726 [5:263/4].

Order for inv. to Matthew Gooding, Exec. of Est. of his mother
DEBORAH GOODING of Digh., dtd. 17 May 1726 [5:264].

Will of WILLIAM SALSBURY of Swan., Farmer, dtd. 9 March 1726,
prob. 16 May 1726. Wife Mary. Sons: William (eldest), John,
Richard, Benjamin (unmar.), Ephraim & Daniel Salsbury (last
2 under age). Daus: Anna Bullock, Mary Bullock dcd., Susannah Wheaten, Martha Wheeler, Experience Bullock, Patience
Easterbrooks, Rachel Salsbury (unmar.) & Rebecca Salsbury (unmar.). Son Ephraim is to take full care of his mother. Grchldn: John, Israel, Elkanah, Daniel & Mary Bullock chldn. of
dau. Mary Bullock dcd. Wife Mary & son Richard to be Execs.
Witns: John Bastow, Aron Kingsley & Joseph Mason [5:265/6].

Acct. of Jonathan French, Exec. of Est. of JOHN FRENCH of Reho.
dtd. 16 May 1726. Legacies to: John French, Thomas French,
Ephraim French & Mary Bliss. Also mentions "David Thurston
ye Husband of Hannah Carpenter" [5:266].

Acct. of Deborah Whipple, Exec. of Est. of her husb. JEREMIAH
WHIPPLE of Attl., dtd. 15 May 1726. Mentions paym. to "my
mother Hannah Whipple," "to William Whipple," & "to my father Joseph Bucklin" [5:267].

Appt. of Nathaniel Peck of Barr. as guard. of Elesebeth Paine
(over 14), dau. of NATHANIEL PAINE of Reho. dcd. intest.,
dtd. 17 May 1726[:267/8].

Acct. of Samuel Tomkins, Exec. of Est. of his father NATHANIEL
TOMKINS of Lit. Comp., dtd. 20 May 1726. Mentions one cow
each at same value to: Timothy Gifford, Benjamin Gifford,
Samuel Linden, William Lad & Mary Tomkins. Also paym. to Nathaniel Tomkins [5:268].

Inv. of Est. of PAUL HEALY of Reho., dtd. 14 Aug. 1725, pres.
by Hannah Healy, his widow & Adm. Apprs: Abiah Carpenter,
Noah Mason & Noah Butterworth [5:268/9].

Inv. of Est. of EBENEZER BRIGGS of Digh., dtd. 30 March 1726,
pres. by Comfort Briggs, his widow & Adm. Apprs: Isaack Pool,

Matthew Briggs & Epharim Attwood, [5:269/70].

Acct. of Mary Williams, former wife & Adm. of Est. of NICHOLAS PULLIN of Reho. dcd. intest., dtd. 17 May 1726 [5:270].

Will of DEBORAH GOODING, widow of George Gooding of Digh. dcd. "being Very Sick," dtd. 29 Oct. 1720, prob. 16 May 1726. Son Matthew Gooding. Daus: Joannah Godfrey [or Gooding?], Mary Walker & Sarah Gooding. Son Matthew to be Exec. Witns: Joseph Attwood, Joseph Dean, Jr. & Epharim Attwood [5:271].

Order for inv. to Phillip & Thomas Gray, Execs. of Est. of their father EDWARD GRAY of Tiv., dtd 21 June 1726 [5:272].

Appt. of Epharim Wheaten of Reho. as guard. of Samuel Whittaker (over 14), son of SAMUEL WHITTAKER of Reho., dtd. 21 June 1726 [5:272/3].

Order for inv. to Mary Cook & Chaplin Cook, Execs. of Est. of THOMAS COOK of Tiv., dtd. 21 June 1726 [5:273].

Appt. of Capt. John Andrews of Taun. as guard. of Ruth Knap (minor over 14), dau. of JOHN KNAP of Taun., dtd. 30 June 1726 [5:274].

Will of EDWARD GRAY of Tiv., Yeoman, dtd. 10 Dec. 1722, prob. 21 June 1726. Wife Mary. Sons: Edward dcd., Phillip, Thomas, John, William & Samuel Gray (last 2 under 14). Daus: Sarah wife of Samuel Bradford, Mary wife of John Bennet, Elizabeth, Pheebe, Hannah & Lidiah. Dau.-in-law [Reeb?] Gray widow of son Edward dcd. Mentions that if "Either of my Two sons which I had by my first wife Dye before he be Twenty one Years," without issue, that then that land be "inherited by ye Surviveing Son of my first wife;" & "if either of my sons by this wife Dye before he be Twenty one," without issue, then that land be div. btwn. "the Surviveing sons of my Present wife." "My Eight Youngest Children Viz. Phillip, Thomas, John, William, Samuel, Pheebe, Hannah & Lidiah." Mentions negro woman Zippa & negro boy Sambo. Sons Phillip & Thomas to be Execs. Witns: John Palmer, Jonas Lend & Richard Billings[5:274/5/6/7].

Appt. of Thomas Manley of Easton as guard. of Zachariah Briggs, brother of CLEMENT BRIGGS of Easton dcd. intest., dtd. 14 July 1726 [5:277].

Appt. of Epharim Randel of Easton as guard. of John Briggs (over 14) & of Lidiah Briggs (under 14), bro. & sis. of CLEMENT BRIGGS of Easton, dtd. 14 July 1726 [5:278].

Will of THOMAS COOK of Tiv., Cordwinder, dtd. 25 Apr. 1726, prob. 21 June 1726. Wife Mary. Sons: Stephen, Joseph & Chaplin (youngest) Cook. Daus: Deborah Cook, Mary Cook & Amy (under 18) Cook. Wife Mary referred to as mother of son Chaplin. Mentions that "my Said Wife Shall have Sufficient house Rooms to live in my now Dwelling house with one of her daughters if She See cause." Wife Mary & son Chaplin to be Execs. Witns: Richard Borden, Samuel Hicks & John Talman [5:279/80].

Inv. of Est. of THOMAS COOK of Tiv., dtd. 31 May 1726, pres. by

Mary Cook & Chaplin Cook, Execs. Apprs: Richard Bourden, Joseph Anthoney, Jr. & William Cory [5:280/1].

Acct. of Zebiah Sweeten, Adm. of Est. of her husb. LEWIS SWEETEN, dtd. 21 June 1726 [5:282].

Acct. of Mary Paul, Adm. of Est. of JAMES PAUL, Jr. of Digh., dtd. 19 July 1726 [5:282/3].

Acct. of Anne Hail of Swan., Adm. of Est. of her husb. RICHARD HAILE of Swan., dtd. 21 June 1726. Mentions paym. to Mary Haile & to Hannah Hale and "allowance for her widdows Laying in as a Posthumus Child after the death of the father and for Nursing Charges" [5:283/4].

Acct. of John Selee, Adm. of Est. of CLEMENT BRIGGS, dtd. 21 June 1726. Mentions expense of going to Bridgewater to get a deed acknowledged & to Plimouth to have it recorded [5:284/5].

Inv. of Est. of JOHN THOMAS of Swan., dtd. 27 June 1726, pres. by John Thomas, his son & Exec. Apprs: John West, James Bowen & Samuel Bullock [5:285/6].

Order for Inv. to William Hodges, Exec. of Est. of THOMAS GILBERT of Taun., dtd. 14 July 1726 [5:287].

Will of THOMAS GILBERT of Taun., "Labouring under the Infirmities of old age," dtd. 19 Jan. 1723, prob. 14 July 1726. No wife mentioned. Son Nathaniel Gilbert. Daus: Hannah Phillips dcd., Sarah Willis, Susanah Hodges & Experience Townsend. "Legal Representatives of my Daughter Hannah Phillips Dece[d] Viz Hannah Leonard Mehetibel Leonard & Lidiah [*Phillips of Willis?*]." Son-in-law William Hodges as Exec. [*Two notations in margin stating "Lines left out."*]. Witns: Samuel Williams, Seth Williams & Samuel Williams, Jr. [5:287/8].

Inv. of Est. of THOMAS GILBERT of Taun., dtd. 12 July 1726, pres. by William Hodges, Exec. Apprs: John Andrews, John Mason & Morgan Cobb the 2nd [5:288].

Appt. of Mrs. Elezebeth Willis of Taun. as guard. of Abigail & Catherine Willis, daus. of THOMAS WILLIS of Taun., dtd. 14 July 1726 [5:289].

Order for appraisal of real est. of THOMAS BRAYMAN of Nort., as requested by his sons John & Josiah Brayman. Mentions sons Daniel Brayman & James Brayman dcd. and "their sisters," dtd. 22 July 1726 [5:289/90].

Order for div. of Est. of GILBERT BROOKS of Reho. Mentions his will devising to his 9 daus. an equal share in his Est., except the share for his dau. Rachel was given to his grson. Benoni Wiggings, & said Benoni "hath been out of this Province in Some Remote Part for more than Twenty Years Past," dtd. 17 May 1726 [5:290].

Inv. of Est. of EDWARD GRAY of Tiv., dtd. 23 July 1726, pres. by Phillip & Thomas Gray, Execs. Mentions 5 negro slaves. Apprs: Phillip Taber, John Sisson & Thomas Corey [5:291/2].

Div. of Est. of THOMAS BRAYMAN of Nort. btwn. his chldn: Daniel (eldest son), John, James dcd., Nathaniel & Josiah (youngest son), dtd. 23 March 1726. Comm: John Skinner, Eleazer Fisher, Jeremiah Ingraham, William Stone & Benjamin Williams. Mentions that the sons will pay money to the 4 daus., not named [5:292/3/4].

Appraisal of real est. in Reho. & Attl. of GILBERT BROOKS of Reho., dtd. 14 June 1726. Sets off land for grson. Benoni Wiggins, neither he nor his respres. being heard from. Mentions "Land Laid out To Francis Stevens Children." Comm: John Foster, Noah Carpenter, Joseph Bucklin, Daniel Carpenter & John Bishup [5:294/5].

Will of JOHN PETERS, dtd. 24 Nov. 1724, prob. 20 June 1726. "Translated and Interpreted from the Indian Writting into English Writting with Diligent Comparation by Hammond Coginhew." My Brother Solomon Briand. My father Peter Trip. Land in Dart. Witns: Josuah Momech, Sarah Silas & Abraham Briand [5:296].

Appt. of Caleb Eddy of Swan. as guard. of Ebenezer Eddy (over 14) & of Mary & Benjamin Eddy (under 14), chldn. of EBENEZER EDDY of Swan., dtd. 8 Aug. 1726. [5:297].

Acct. of Mary Burt & Ebenezer Burt, Adms. of Est. of EBENEZER BURT of Nor., dtd. 24 July 1726. Mentions paym. to the widow of an "allowance for her Charge of Lying in with a Posthumus Child after ye death of ye father" [5:298].

Order for inv. to Samuel Bishop, Exec. of Est. of SAMUEL BISHOP 0f Attl., dtd. 16 Aug. 1726 [5:299].

Appt. of Mrs. Anna Smith of Reho. as guard. of Ruth Thomas (under 14), dau. of JOHN THOMAS of Swan., dtd. 16 Aug. 1726 [5: 299/300].

Will of SAMUEL BISHOP of Attl., Yeoman, "being Very Sick and Weak in Body," dtd. 6 June 1726, prob. 16 Aug. 1726. Wife Mary. Sons: Samuel, Daniel, Joseph (under 21), Benjamin (under age), "three youngest sons Edward Gideon and Thomas (under 16) Bishop. Daus: Mehetibel Carpenter, Mary Follet, Hannah Bishop & Sarah Bishop. San Samuel to be Exec. Directs his Exec. to "bind out my three sons namely: Benjn Edward & Gideon to good trades." Witns: Isaac Bucklin, Ebenezer Robinson & Noah Carpenter [5:300/1/2].

Order for inv. to Elezebeth & Samuel Titus, Execs. of Est. of SAMUEL TITUS of Attl., dtd. 16 Aug. 1726 [5:302].

Will of SAMUEL TITUS of Attl., Husbandman, dtd. 29 May 1726, prob. 16 Aug. 1726. Wife Elizebeth. Sons: Samuel & John Titus. Dau. Elezebeth. Wife Elizebeth & son Samuel to be Execs. Witns: Benjamin Day, Caleb Hall & Ebenezer White[5:303/4].

Will of JAMES BARNABE of Free., Cordwinder, dtd. 22 June 1726, prob. 16 Aug. 1726. No wife mentioned. Son Ambrose Barnabe. Dau. Lidiah Perry. Son Ambrose to be Exec. Witns: Haviland Torrey, Thomas Spooner & Francis Adams [5:304/5].

Div. of Est. of GREENFIELD HANNOVER of Taun., into 4 shares, dtd. 8 July 1726. Comm: Samuel Williams, John Mason & Abraham Waldron [5:306/7].

Order for distrib. of Est. of GREENFIELD HANNOVER of Taun., dtd.
16 Aug. 1726, to his chldn: Edward Blake in the right of his
wife Anna eldest dau., Mary Duglas dau. of Mary Duglas the
2nd dau., Sarah Hannover the 3rd dau. & Jane Hannover the 4th
dau. [5:307].

Order for div. of Est. of JOHN FOLLET of Attl. dcd. intest.,
dtd. 13 May 1726 [5:307/8].

Div. of Est. of JOHN FOLLET of Attl. btwn. his widow Sarah Follet (now Fuller) and chldn: John Follet (eldest son), Ruth
Freeman, Abigail Follet, Samuel Follet, Persis Follet, Elizabeth Follet, Susanah Follet, Jonathan Follet & Robert Follet,
dtdd. 16 Aug. 1726. Comm: John Foster, Joseph Bucklin, Noah
Carpenter & Samuel Day [5:308/9/10].

Order for div. of Est. of ABIEL SMITH of Rehob., dtd. 25 Apr.
1726 [5:311].

Div. of Est. of ABIEL SMITH of Reho. btwn. his widow Anna Smith
& his chldn: Abiel Smith (only son) & Ruth Smith (only dau.).
Mentions land in Barr. held in partnership with Henery Smith
& the heirs of Ebenezer Smith, dtd. 6 June 1726. Comm: Joseph
Bucklin, Noah Carpenter & John Bishop. Mentions Anna Smith as
guard. of dau. Ruth Smith (under 18 & unmar)[5:311/2/3/4/5].

Div. of widow's thirds of Est. of JOHN WILKINSON of Attl. to
his widow Rachel Wilkinson, dtd. 21 May 1726. Comm: George
Leonard, John Skinner, William Richardson, James Tiffiny &
Seth Richardson [5:316].

Order to confer remaining 2/3 of Est. of JOHN WILKINSON of Attl.
upon his son John Wilkinson, he to make paym. to the other
chldn: Joseph (under 21), Hipzebeth, Abigail, Hannah, Mary,
Sarah & Rachel Wilkinson (all under 18 & unmar.). Consent
given by Rachel Wilkinson guard. of Hipzebeth, Abigail & Hannah; by William Johnson guard. of Mary & Sarah & by Joseph
Cowel guard. of Joseph & Rachel, dtd. 16 Aug. 1726. Comm:
George Leonard & William Richardson [5:316/7/8].

Inv. of TIMOTHY COOPER of Easton dcd. intest., dtd. 23 June
1726, pres. by Seth Babbit, Adm. Apprs: John Phillips, Edward Hayward & Morgan Cobb [5:318].

Appt. of Mary Walker of Taun. as Adm. of Est. of her husb.
JAMES WALKER of Taun., Brewer, dtd. 20 Sept. 1726 [5:319].

Appt. of George Bairsto as Adm. of Est. of his father GEORGE
BAIRSTO of Reho. dcd. intest., dtd. 20 Sept. 1726 [5:319/20].

Acct. of John Robinson, Adm. De bonis non of Est. of JOHN ROB-
INSON [sic; but later notation calls it Est. of Benjamin Robinson. Previous entries show that John Robinson was appt.
Adm. of Est. of Benjamin Robinson in 1724.] of Attl., dtd.
14 Sept. 1726 [5:320/1].

Inv. of Est. of JABEZ GORHAM of Brist., dtd. 2 May 1725, pres.
by Hannah Gorham & Benjamin Gorham, Execs. Speaks of items at
the tanyard. Mentions the value of "half of the Negro." Apprs:
John Birdge, William Throope & Samuel Howland [5:321/2].

Appt. of Mrs. Mary Devil as Adm. of Est. of her husb. JOSEPH
DEVIL of Dart. dcd. intest., dtd. 14 Nov. 1726 [5:323].

Appt. of Katherine Mortimore as Adm. of Est. of her husb. WAL-
TER MORTIMORE of Taun., dtd. 14 Nov. 1726 [5:323/4].

Appt. of Joseph Jones as Adm. of Est. of his father JOSEPH
JONES of Taun. dcd. intest., dtd. 14 Nov. 1726 [5:324/5].

Appt. of Mrs. Hannah Simmons as Adm. of Est. of her husb. RE-
MEMBRANCE SIMMONS of Swan. dcd. intest., dtd. 14 Nov. 1726
[5:325/6].

Inv. of Est. of JOSEPH DEVIL of Dart., dtd. 14 Nov. 1726, pres.
by Mary Devil, Adm. Apprs: Jeremiah Devil, William Soule &
George Brownel [5:326/7].

Appt. of Patience Greenhil of Lit. Comp. as guard. of William
& Rebeccah Greenhil (both over 14) & of Elezebeth, Patience,
Richard, Ruth, Daniel & Sarah Greenhil [age group not men-
tioned], chldn. of RICHARD GREENHIL of Lit. Comp., dtd. 18
Oct. 1726 [5:327/8].

Inv. of Est. of REMEMBRANCE SIMMONS of Swan., dtd. 19 Sept. 1726
pres. by his widow Hannah Simmons, Adm. Apprs: Joseph Mason,
Jon [sic] Peirce & William Anthony [5:328/9].

Acct. of Susanah Cooper & Nathaniel Cooper, Adms. of Est. of
their husb. & father THOMAS COOPER of Reho., dtd. 15 Nov. 1726
[5:329/30].

Inv. of Est. of SAMUEL BISHOP of Attl., dtd. 28 Sept. 1726,
pres. by Samuel Bishop, his son & Exec. Apprs: Benjamin Day,
Isaac Bucklin & Ebenezer Robinson [5:330/1].

Acct. of Samuel Bishop, Exec. of Est. of his father SAMUEL BI-
SHOP of Attl., dtd. 20 Dec. 1726. Mentions paym. to "my hon-
oured Mother Mary Bishop," & to Hannah Bishop, Sarah Bishop &
"Jon Brother to ye Testator" [5:331/2].

Appt. of Jonathan Kingsley of Reho. as Adm. of Est. of EBENEZER
EDDY of Swan. dcd. intest., dtd. 27 Dec. 1726 [5:332].

Order for inv. to Mehetibel Slocum [sic; but a few sentences
further down she is called "Meribah"], widow, & Ebenezer Slocum, brother, Execs. of Est. of BENJAMIN SLOCUM of Dart., dtd.
27 Dec. 1726 [5:333].

Rcpt. by Hannah Bishop for money from Est. of her father SAMUEL
BISHOP, paid by her brother Samuel Bishop., dtd. Attl. 14 Dec.
1726 [5:333].

Rcpt. by Mary Bishop for money from Est. of her husb. SAMUEL
BISHOP, paid by her son Samuel Bishop, dtd. 14 Dec. 1726 [5:333].

Rcpt. by Jon [sic] Bishop for money paid by "Samuel Bisshop Executor to his fathers Last Will & Testament," dtd. 14 Dec. 1726
[5:333].

Rcpt. by Sarah Bishop for money from Est. of her father, paid
by her brother Samuel Bishop, dtd. 14 Dec. 1726 [5:334].

Appt. of Joseph Waldron of Brist. as guard. of Stephen Toman &
Martha Toman (both over 14), grchldn. of Capt. THOMAS NEWTON
of Brist., dtd. 29 Dec. 1726 [5:334].

Appt. of Abigail [*"Abigail" is superimposed upon "Elizebeth,"
written first*] White, Adm of Est. of her husb. the Rev. EB-
ENEZER WHITE of Attl., dtd. 23 Dec. 1726 [5:334/5].

Appt. of George Hall of Easton as guard. of Lidiah, Deborah,
George & Thomas Hall (all over 14) & Isaac, Kathiah, Abel,
Nathan & Abigail Hall (all under 14), grchldn. of KATHERINE
DEAN of Taun., dtd. 12 Jan. 1726/7 [5:335].

Order for inv. to Benjamin Williams, Exec. of Est. of his mother
KATHERINE DEAN of Taun., dtd. 12 Jan. 1726/7 [5:336].

Appt. of James Redaway of Reho. as guard. of John & Preserved
Redaway (both under 14), chldn. of PRESERVED REDAWAY of Reho.
dtd. 12 Jan. 1726/7 [5:336].

Appt. of Jacob Ormsbee of Reho. as guard. of Thomas Redaway (under 14), son of PRESERVED REDAWAY of Reho., dtd. 12 Jan. 1726/7
[5:337].

Inv. of Est. of NICHOLAS PECK of Brist., dtd. Dec. 1726, pres.
by Jonathan Peck, Adm. Apprs: Charles Church, Timothy Failes
& Samuel Royall [5:337/8].

Acct. of John Horton, Adm. de bonis non of Est. of SOLOMON HOR-
TON of Reho. dcd. intest., dtd. 27 Dec. 1726. Incl. money received from David Horton & money paid to Hannah Horton[5:338].

Will of BENJAMIN SLOCUM of Dart., "Marchant being very Sick and
Weak," dtd. 25 Nov. 1726, prob. 27 Dec. 1726. Wife Meribah.
Son Benjamin Slocum (under age). Has some reason to believe
his wife is now with child. Witns: Adam Hunt, Ebenezer Slocum
& William Hartt [5:339/40].

Codicil of BENJAMIN SLOCUM of Dart., Marchant, dtd. 27 Nov. 1726.
Nominates, as guards. of his sons, "my loving frind Holder Slocum and my well beloved brother Ebenezer Slocum." Witns: William Richetson, Adam Huntt & William Hartt [5:340/1].

Rcpt. by Richard Church for money "left by my Father," paid by
"my Brother Nath[ll] Church," dtd. 14 Jan. 1726 [5:341].

Rcpt. by Jonathan Glading & Joseph Glading for legacies from Est.
of DAVID CARY of Brist. to their wives, "Sarah and Priscilla
two of the Daughters of the said Cary," paid by Elizabeth Kid-
der, widow, and her son David Cary, Execs., dtd. 18 Jan. 1726/7
Witns: Samuel Howland & Nathaniel Bosworth [5:341].

Inv. of Est. of BENJAMIN SLOCUM of Dart., dtd. 6 Dec. 1726, presented by Meribah Slocum, widow, & Ebenezer Slocum, brother &
Exec. Lists many items of cloth, clothing as if for clothier
or tailor. Apprs: not named [5:341/2/3/4].

Acct. of Samuel Vial, Esq., Exec. of Est. of Capt. THOMAS NEW-
TON of Brist., dtd. 27 Dec. 1726. Mentions paym. "to John Newton upon the Agreement between him & his Sisters and to be a
ballance on all accts between him and his father" [5:344/5].

Will of KATHERINE DEAN of Taun., widow of Thomas Dean of Taun.,
dtd. 14 March 1725/6, prob. 12 Jan 1726/7. Son Thomas Dean.
Daus: Hannah Dean, Katherine wife of Samuel Leonard, Lidiah
wife of George Hall, Mercy wife of Daniel Williams & Eliza-

beth wife of Benjamin Williams. Grson. John Tisdel, Jr. Son-
in-law Benjamin Williams to be Exec. Witns: James Leonard,
John Williams & Ebenezer Campbil [5:346].
Appt. of Sarah Skelton, widow, as Adm. of Est. of her husb.THO-
MAS SKELTON of Reho. dcd. intest., dtd. 21 Feb. 1726/7[5:347].
Appt. of Jacob Ormsbeee of Reho. as guard. of Hannah, Mary & Ju-
dath [*no surname*](all under 14), daus. of HANNAH THOMSON of
Reho. dcd. intest., dtd. 21 Feb. 1726/7 [5:347/8].
Order for inv. to Lidiah Williams, widow & Exec. of Est. of her
husb. N: Williams of Taun., dtd. 21 Feb. 1726/7 [5:348/9].
Appt. of Jacob Ormsbe of Reho. as Adm. of Est. of HANNAH THOM-
SON of Reho., dtd. 21 Feb. 1726/7 [5:349].
Appt. of Hannah Shaw, widow, as Adm. of Est. of her husb. JOHN
SHAW of Reho., dtd. 21 Feb. 1726/7 [5:350].
Will of NATHANIEL WILLIAMS of Taun., "being Very Sick," dtd. 23
Aug. 1726, prob. 21 Feb. 17267. Wife Lydia. 2 sons Edmund &
Nathaniel Williams. Daus: Lydiah, Bethiah, Judith & Elizabeth
[*no surnames given*]. Witns: Ebenezer Campbil, Ebenezer Wil-
liams & Hannah Williams [5:350/1].
Inv. of Est. of SAMUEL TITUS of Attl., dtd. 21 Aug. 1726, pres.
by his son Samuel Titus, Exec. Apprs: Noah Carpenter, John
Foster & Samuel Day [5:351].
Acct. of Ebenezer Carpenter, Adm. of Est. of his father WILLIAM
CARPENTER of Attl., dtd. 21 Feb. 1726/7. Legacies to: my moth-
er Elezebeth Carpenter, my sister Mehetibel Carpenter, my bro-
ther Seth Carpenter, my sister Meriam Carpenter, my sister
Priscilla Carpenter, my brother Mical Carpenter & my brother
John Carpenter [5:352].
Rcpt. by Elezebeth Carpenter for money from Est. of her husb.,
paid by her son. Ebenezer Carpenter, dtd. Attl. 17 Apr. 1725
[5:352].
Rcpt. by Michal Carpenter for money from Est. of his father,
paid by his brother Ebenezer Carpenter, dtd. 4 March 1723 [5:
352].
Rcpts. by Priscilla Carpenter, John Carpenter, Seth Carpenter,
Mehetibel Carpenter & Miriam Carpenter for monies rcvd. from
Est. of their father, paid by their brother Ebenezer Carpenter
dtd. btwen. 20 Sept. 1721 to 1 Nov. 1726 [5:353].
Inv. of Est. of EBENEZER EDDY of Swan. dcd. intest., dtd. 2 Jan.
1726/7, pres. by Jonathan Kingsley, Adm. Apprs: John West,
James Bowen & Samuel Bullock [5:353/4].
Inv. of Est. of THOMAS SKELTON, Weaver, of Reho., dtd. 4 Feb.
1726/7, pres. by Sarah Skelton, his widow & Adm. Apprs: Abiah
Carpenter, Timothy Walker & Thomas Reade [5:354].
Appt. of Mrs. Dorothy Paine of Brist. as guard. of Sarah Paine
(over 14), dau. of Col. NATHANIEL PAINE, Exq. of Brist., dtd.
24 Feb. 1726/7 [5:355].
Appt. of John Williams of Boston, County of Suffolk, as guard.
of Dorothy Williams (over 14), dau. of Col. NATHANIEL PAINE

of Brist., dtd. 24 Feb. 1726/7 [5:355/6].

Appt. of Samuel Royal of Brist. as guard. of Alathea Drown (over 14) & [Trenah?] Drown (under 14), grchldn. of Col. NATHANIEL PAINE of Brist., dtd. 24 Feb. 1726/7 [5:356].

Appt. of Samuel Gofe of Reho. as guard. of Hezekiah & James Gofe (both over 14), sons of ANTHONY GOFE of Barr., dtd. 10 March 1726/7 [5:356/7].

Appt. of Joseph Willis of Reho. as guard. of John Bliss (over 14), son of SAMUEL BLISS of Reho., dtd. 16 March 1726/7 [5: 357].

Acct. of Katharine Markes, Exec. of Est. of her husb. WILLIAM MARKES of Brist., dtd. 20 March 1726/7. Mentions: land sold in Digh., one negro woman sold & 161 Pounds for a debt in Surranam [5:358.9/60].

Order for inv. to Rebeca Allen, widow & Exec. of Est. of her husb. SQUIRE ALLEN of Reho., dtd. 24 March 1726/7 [5:360/1].

Order for inv. to Mrs. Priscilla Waldo, widow & Exec. of Est. of the Rev. JOHN SPARHAWK of Brist., dtd. 25 March 1726/7 [5: 361].

Rcpt. & release by Joseph Carpenter of Brist., House Carpenter, for money rcvd. by his wife Abigail from Est. of her father Capt. THOMAS NEWTON of Brist., paid by Samuel Vial, Exec., dtd. 9 March 1726/7. Witns: N. Blagrove & Joseph Waldron [5: 361/2].

Bond by Joseph Carpenter of Brist., House Carpenter, & Thomas Lawton of Brist., Gent., to return legacy paid to Joseph's wife Abigail from Est. of her father THOMAS NEWTON if unknown debts become known, dtd. 8 March 1726/7. Witns: Edward Ingraham & Samuel Smith, Jr. [5:362/3].

Rcpt. by Joseph Waldron of Brist., Glassier, for money rcvd. by his wife Martha from Est. of her father THOMAS NEWTON paid by Samuel Vial, Exec., dtd. 13 March 1726/7. Witns: Nathaniel Blagrove & Gideon Smith [5:363].

Bond by Joseph Waldron of Brist., Glassier, to return legacy paid to his wife Martha from Est. of her father THOMAS NEWTON if unknown debts come to light, dtd. 13 March 1726/7[5:363/4],

Rcpt. by Joseph Waldron of Brist., Glassier, as guard. of Martha & Stephen Toman, minor chldn. of Stephen Toman of Brist. dcd., for monies rcvd. from Est. of Capt. THOMAS NEWTON of Brist., paid by Samuel Vial, Exec., dtd. 13 March 1726/7 [5: 364].

Bond by Joseph Waldron of Brist., Glassier, as guard. of Martha & Stephen Toman, minor chldn. of Stephen Toman of Brist. dcd., to pay back Samuel Vial, Exec. of Est. of THOMAS NEWTON if unknown debts come to light, dtd. 13 March 1726/7[5:365].

Order for inv. to Capt. Joseph Brown, Exec. of Est. of his son JEREMIAH BROWN of Attl., dtd. 1 Apr. 1726/7 [5:365/6].

Order for inv. to Barnabas Howland, Exec. of Est. of BENJAMIN HOWLAND of Dart., dtd. 21 March 1726/7 [5:366/7].

Order for inv. to Mary Dagget, Exec. of Est. of her husb. JO-
SEPH DAGGET of Attl. [*next sentence calls him "of Rehoboth"*],
dtd. 21 March 1726/7 [5:367].
Will of JOSEPH DAGGET, Sr. of Reho., Wheel Right, dtd, 23 Dec.
1726, prob. 21 March 1726/7. Wife Mary. Sons: John (eldest),
Joseph (2nd) & Israel (youngest) Dagget. Daus: Mary, Hepzibeth & Martha [*no surnames*]. Wife Mary as Exec. Witns: Epharim Carpenter, Epharim French & Jonathan Robinson [5:367/8].
Inv. of Est. of JOSEPH DAGGET of Reho., dtd. 13 March 1726/7,
pres. by his widow Mary Dagget, Exec. Apprs: Epharim Carpenter, Daniel Parrin & Daniel Carpenter [5:369].
Rcpt. by Nehemiah Allen for money from Est. of his uncle JOHN
ALLEN, paid by Joseph Bucklin, Exec., dtd. 24 Feb. 1725/6
[5:369].
Apts. of Mrs. Patience Church, widow, as Adm. of Est. of her
husb. Capt. CONSTANT CHURCH of Free. dcd. intest., dtd 5 Apr.
1726/7 [5:370].
Acct. of Sarah King, widow & Adm. of Est. of her husb. SAMUEL
KING of Nor., dtd. 21 March 1726/7 [5:370/1].
Inv. of Est. of JOSEPH JONES of Taun., dtd. 2 Nov. 1726, pres.
by Joseph Jones, son & Adm. Apprs: Samuel Richmond, Benjamin
Shaw & Israel Dean [5:371/2].
Will of BENJAMIN HOWLAND of Dart., Yeoman, dtd. 5 March 1721/2,
prob. 21 March 1726/7. Wife. Judath. Sons: Barnabas & Isaac
Howland. Daus: Abigail Howland now wife of Jonathan Richet-
son, Desire Howland and Lidiah Howland now wife of George
Soule. Son Barnabas as Exec. Brother Nicholas Howland & friend
John Russel as Overseers. Witns: George Howland, Timothy
Shearman & Timothy Aken [5:373/4].
Rcpt. by Joseph Allen, James Addoms, Nathaniel Peck & Thomas
Peck for monies from Est. of JOHN ALLEN of Swan., paid by
Hugh Cole & Joseph Bucklin, Execs., dtd. 11 Jan. 1724. Witns:
Squire Allen & Joseph Hunt [5:374].
Rcpt. by [Barach?] Bucklin & [*illegible*] for money from Est. of
their uncle JOHN ALLEN of Swan., paid by Joseph Bucklin, Ex-
ec., dtd. 26 Nov. 1725 [5:374].
Rcpt. by Benaiah Barcas for legacy to his wife Lidiah Barcas
from Est. of her uncle JOHN ALLEN, paid by Joseph Bucklin,
Exec., dtd. 10 Dec. 1725 [5:375].
Rcpts. by Ebenezer Allen, Samuel Allen & Daniel Allen for monies from Est. of their uncle JOHN ALLEN of Barr., then Brist.
paid by Hugh Cole of Swan. & Joseph Bucklin of Reho., Execs.,
dtd. 1 July 1724 & 11 Jan. 1724/5. Witns: Squire Allen & Joseph Hunt [5:375].
Will of SQUIRE ALLEN of Reho., Phisition, dtd. 25 Feb. 1725/6,
prob. 24 March 1726/7. Wife Rebecca. Eldest son William Allen
& youngest son Stephen Allen (both under 21). Land quit-
claimed by my brother Jeremiah Allen. Wife Rebecca as Exec.
Witns: Rachel Allen, Jerusha Norton & Samuel Allen[5:376].

Inv. of Est. of JAMES WALKER of Taun., dtd. 20 Sept. 1726, pres. by his widow & Adm. Mary Walker. Apprs: Edward Shove, Thomas Briggs & John Attwood [5:376/7].

Inv. of Est. of NATHANIEL WILLIAMS of Taun., dtd. 16 Dec. 1726, pres. by Lidiah Williams, Exec. Apprs: John King, Jacob Hall & Ebenezer Williams [5:377/8].

Appt. of Bethiah Lane, widow, as Adm. of Est. of her husb. SAMUEL LANE of Attl. dcd. intest., dtd. 21 March 1726/7[5:378/9].

Inv. of Est. of SAMUEL LANE of Attl. who died 17 Dec. 1726, dtd. 10 Jan. 1726/7, pres. by his widow & Adm. Bethiah Lane. Apprs: Samuel Brintnel, Thomas Skinner & Andrew Starkey [5:379].

Order for div. of Est. of JOHN WILCOX of Lit. Comp. btwn. the widow & chldn., dtd. 16 Nov. 1725 [5:379/80].

Div. of Est. of JOHN WILCOX of Lit. Comp. btwn. the widow [not named] & chldn: Jacob (eldest son), Daniel (2nd son), John (3rd son), Jabish (4th son), Berjonas (5th son), Thomas (6th son), Elezebeth wife of Joseph Tripp & Rebecca Wilcox (2nd dau)., dtd. 21 March 1726/7. Comm: Thomas Church, John Palmer, John Wood & Jonathan Head [5:380/1/2].

Inv. of Est. of BENJAMIN HOWLAND of Dart., Yeoman, dtd. 1 March 1726/7, pres. by Barnabas Howland, Exec. Apprs: Deliverance Smith, Hanery Howland & John Russel [5:382/3].

Will of JEREMIAH BROWN of Attl., Husbandman, "Being Very Sick," dtd. 3 March 1726/7, prob. 1 Apr. 1726/7. No wife mentioned. My father Joseph Brown. My brother Beniah Brown. Hannah Freeman of Attl., dau. of Ralph Freeman dcd. Father Joseph Brown to be Exec. Witns: John Slack, Penticost Blackinton & William Ware [5:383/4].

Inv. of Est. of CONSTANT CHURCH of Free., Gent., dtd. 3 Apr. 1726/7, pres. by his widow & Adm. Patience Church. Apprs: Thomas Gage, Joseph Read & Silvanus Soule [5:384/5/6].

Acct. of Mrs. Dorothy Paine & N. Paine, Adms. of Est. of Col. NATHANIEL PAINE of Brist., dtd. 6 March 1726/7. Incl. 5 pages of rcpts. & debts from & to a multitude of persons [5:386/7/8 90/1].

Will of JOHN SPARHAWK, Minister of the Gospell in Bristol, "being Sick & very Weak," dtd. 28 Apr. 1718, prob. 15 March 1726/7. Wife Priscilla. 2 sons John & Nathaniel Sparhawk (both under 21). Wife Priscilla as Exec. Witns: N. Blagrove, Augustus Lucas & Deliverance Fry [5:392/3].

Will of SETH POPE of Dart., "being now Grown into Years," dtd. 1 Apr. 1720, prob. 7 Apr. 1726/7. Wife Rebecca. Sons: John Pope of Sandwich, Seth Pope of Sandwich & Hannah his wife, Elnathan Pope o& Samuel Pope (youngest). Daus: Susanah Hathaway wife of Jonathan Hathaway, Sarah Peabody, Mary Church & Hannah Hunt. Elesebeth Chipman "my former Daughter in Law now Wife of Lew^t John Chipman of Sandwich" and her son Handy Chipman (under 21). My brother Isaac Pope. My negro boy named Robin Grson. Seth Pope son of my son John Pope. Son-in-law Sam-

uel Hunt & sons John Pope & Samuel Pope as Execs. Witns: Row-
land Cotton, William Basset, Sr., William Basset, Jr. & Benjamin Bourne [5:393/4/5/6].
Codicil of SETH POPE of Dart., Trader, dtd. 18 Feb. 1725. Son
John Pope of Sandwich is now dcd. Experience Pope widow of
son John dcd. Sons of son John Pope dcd: Seth (eldest), Thomas (2nd), Ezra & Charles Pope. Daus. of son John Pope dcd:
Deborah, Toby, Sarah, Elizabeth, Mary & Joannah Pope. Mentions his same wife & other chldn. as given in above will.
Witns: Benjamin Clifton, John Handy & Mary Green [5:396/7/8].
Order for inv. to James Leonard & Seth Leonard, Execs. of Est.
of their father JAMES LEONARD of Taun., dtd. 13 Apr. 1726/7
[5:398].
Will of JAMES LEONARD of Taun., "being aged & under bodily Weak-
ness," dtd. 4 March 1725/6, prob. 13 Apr. 1726/7. Wife Rebecca. Sons: James (eldest), Stephen & Seth Leonard. 3 daus. by
my 1st wife: Unis, Prudence & Hannah Crane who married John
Crane of Digh. dcd. Other daus: Lydia Brettin, Sarah Hodges,
Elesebeth Hall, Abigail Dean dcd. & Darkis Leonard. "My Late
Father in Law Mr Anthoney Culiver" and my late wife Lydia
dcd. Grson. Zephaniah Leonard. Grdau. Abigail Dean & other
chldn. [not named] of my dau. Abigail Dean dcd. My brothers
Thomas Leonard & Uriah Leonard. My indentured servant Patri-
arch Robinson & Abigail Robinson. Sons James & Seth Leonard
as Execs. Witns: Seth Williams, Timothy Jones & Samuel Leon-
ard, Jr. [5:399/400/1/2/3].
Codicil of JAMES LEONARD of Taun., dtd. 26 Aug. 1726. Mentions
daus. Lidia, Sarah, Elesebeth & chldn. of dau. Abigail Dean
dcd. (Same witns.)[5:403].
Inv. of Est. of CHARLES CHURCH of Free., Dent., dtd. 27 March
1726/7, pres. by his widow & Adm. Mary Church. Apprs: John
Read, William Winslow & Samuel Forman [5:403/4].
Appt. of Nathaniel Brayman as Adm. of Est. of JAMES BRAYMAN of
Nor. dcd. intest., dtd. 12 Apr. 1726/7 [5:405].
Inv. of Est. of JAMES BRAYMAN of Nor., dtd. 12 Feb. 1724/5,
pres. by Nathaniel Brayman, Adm. Apprs: Samuel Hodges, Jo-
seph Hodges & John Andrews [5:405/6].
Appt. of Josiah Linkhorn of Taun. as Adm. of Est. of THOMAS
LINKHORN of Taun. dcd. intest., dtd. 11 Apr. 1726/7[5:406].
Acct. of Damaris Manchester, Exec. of Est. of her husb. STEPHEN
MANCHESTER of Tiv., dtd. 18 Apr. 1726/7 [5:407].
Acct. of Cumfort Chub previously Comfort Briggs, Adm. of Est.
of her previous husb. EBENEZER BRIGGS of Digh., dtd. 7 May
1727. Mentions paym. to John Briggs, Mathew Briggs, Benjamin
Briggs & "to my Brother Thomas Briggs" [5:407/8].
Acct. of Elezebeth Kinnicut, widow & Adm. of Est. of her husb.
JOHN KINNICUT of Swan., dtd. 6 May 1727 [5:408/9].
Inv. of Est. of Dr. SQUIRE ALLEN of Reho., dtd. 31 March 1726/7
pres. by Rebecca Allen, Exec. Apprs: Samuel Allen, Joseph

Peck & Joseph Bosworth [5:409].

Order for inv. to Eseck Carr & Mary Briggs, Execs. of Est. of JOB BRIGGS of Lit. Comp., dtd. 18 Apr. 1726/7 [5:409/10].

Will of JOB BRIGGS of Lit. Comp., Yeoman, "being Weak & low," dtd. 25 Feb. 1726/7, prob. 18 Apr. 1726/7. Wife Mary. Sons: Eldest [*not named*], William (2nd), Oliver, Joseph & Jeremiah (all under age). Dau. Deborah (under age). Mentions "the Child my wife is now bigg with." My brother William. Friends Capt. John Palmer & Thomas Church, Esq. to be Overseers. Wife Mary Briggs & my brother-in-law Eseck Carr, Jr. as Execs. Witns: George Wood, William Wilbour & Jonathan Grinhill [5: 410/1/2].

Inv. of Est. of JOB BRIGGS, Yeoman, of Lit. Comp., dtd. 10 Apr. 1726/7, pres. by Eseck Carr & Mary Briggs, Execs. Apprs: John Wood, Thomas Brownel & Joseph Southworth [5:412/3].

Acct. of Epharim Randel, guard. of John Briggs dcd., minor son of CLEMENT BRIGGS late of Easton, dtd. 19 Apr. 1726/7[5:413/4].

Order for inv. to Samuel Hunt & John Jenne, Execs. of Est. of JOHN JENNE of Dart., dtd. 26 Apr. 1726/7 [5:414/5].

Will of JOHN JENNE of Dart., Husbandman, "being Very Sick and Weak," dtd. 21 March 1726/7, prob. 26 Apr. 1726/7. No wife mentioned. Sons: John Jenne & Samuel Jenne dcd. Grsons. Job Jenne & Hix Jenne. Daus: Sarah Shearman, Mehetibel Gifford & Lidiah Benson. Dau. Lidiah Benson's son John Allen. Dau-in-law Mary Shearman. Grdaus. Lidiah Badcock, Hannah Jenne & Mary Jenne. "My Rev[d] Pastor Sam[ll] Hunt" to be Exec. Witns: Seth Spooner, Stephen West & Wing Spooner [5:416/7].

Inv. of Est. of JOHN JENNE of Dart., Yeoman, dtd. 19 March 17-26/7, pres. by Samuel Hunt & John Jenne, Execs. Apprs: William Spooner, Samuel Spooner & Stephen West, Jr. [5:416/7].

Order for inv. to Joseph Read of Free., Exec. of Est. of his mother HANNAH READ of Free., dtd. 6 May 1727 [5:417].

Will of HANNAH READ of Free., widow of John Read, dtd. 1 June 1722, prob. 6 May 1727. Sons: John & Joseph Read. Daus-in-law Mary Read & Sarah Read. Grsons: John Shearman, Benjamin Shearman, Joseph Shearman, Oliver Shearman & Thomas Shearman. Son Joseph as Exec. Witns: Joseph Brittman, Silvanus Soule & Richard Pearce [5:417/8].

Inv. of Est. of JOHN SHAW of Reho., dtd. 3 Apr. 1726/7, pres. by Hannah Shaw, his widow & Adm. Apprs: James Kingsley, James Bowen & Samuel Bullock [5:418/9].

Acct. of Hannah Shaw, widow & Adm. of Est. of her husb. JOHN SHAW of Reho., dtd. 8 May 1727 [5:419/20].

Order for inv. to Mrs. Mary Smith, widow, & Benjamin Smith, son Execs. of Est. of HEZEKIAH SMITH of Dart., dtd. 16 May 1727 [5:421].

Will of HEZEKIAH SMITH of Dart., dtd. 11 July 1723, prob. 21 March 1726/7. Wife Mary. Son Benjamin Smith. Married daus: Mary Trafford, Elezebeth [*no surname*] & Mehetibel [*no surname*]. Unmar. daus: Deborah, Hannah & Sarah. Grson. Samuel

Trafford. Friends John Tucker & Nathaniel Howland as Over-
seers. Wife Mary & son Benjamin to be Execs. Witns: Timothy
Shearman, George Howland & William Bowdish [5:421/2].
Inv. of Est. of HEZEKIAH SMITH of Dart., Yeoman, dtd. 6 March
1726/7, pres. by Mary & Benjamin Smith, Execs. Apprs: Henry
Howland, John Russel & Deliverance Smith [5:423/5].
Appt. of Mrs. Bethiah Lyon, widow, as Adm. of Est. of her husb.
BENJAMIN LYON of Reho. dcd. intest., dtd. 16 May 1727[5:425].
Inv. of Est. of BENJAMIN LYON of Reho., dtd. 10 May 1727, pres.
by Bethiah Lyon, his widow & Adm. Apprs: Abiah Carpenter, No-
ah Mason & Timothy Walker [5:425/6].
Acct. of Patience Greenhil, Adm. of Est. of her husb. RICHARD
GREENHIL of Lit. Comp., recorded 25 June 1727[5:426/7/8/9].
Order for settl. remainder of Est. of RICHARD GREENHIL of Lit.
Comp. upon his 5 daus: Rebecca, Elizabeth, Patience, Ruth &
Sarah Greenhil, as requested by their mother & guard. Pa-
tience Greenhil [5:429/30].
Order for inv. to Samuel & Joseph Durfey, Execs. of Est. of
their father WILLIAM DURFEY of Tiv., dtd. 24 June 1727 [5:
430].
Will of WILLIAM DURFEY of Tiv., Yeoman, dtd. 16 Feb. 1726/7,
prob. 24 June 1727. Wife Mary. Sons: Samuel, Joseph & David
Durfey. Dau. Abigail Durfey. Sons Samuel & Joseph as Execs.
Witns: Thomas Gray, John Howland & Richard Bourden [5:431/
2/3].
Acct. of Margaret Terry, formerly widow of the Rev. JOHN WESTON
of Swan. now Barr., dtd. 10 June 1727. Mentions a charge "for"
the Posthumus Child" [5:434].
Appt. of Nathaniel Smith as Adm. of Est. of JONATHAN SMITH of
Reho. dcd. intest., dtd. 18 May 1727 [5:435].
Order for inv. to Eleazer Slocum & Ebenezer Slocum, Execs. of
Est. of their father ELEAZER SLOCUM of Dart., dtd. 20 June
1727 [5:435/6].
Will of ELEAZER SLOCUM of Dart., Yeoman, dtd. 11 March 1726/7,
prob. 20 June 1727. Wife Eliphel. Sons: Eleazer, Ebenezer &
Benjamin dcd. Slocum. Daus: Meribah Richetson wife of William
Richetson & Joanna Wheedon wife of Daniel Wheedon. Grson.
Benjamin Slocum son of son Benjamin dcd. Meribah Slocum the
widow of my son Benjamin dcd., she now being with child. Sons
Eleazer & Ebenezer to be Execs. Witns: Phillip Allen, James
Allen & William Hart [5:436/7/8/9].
Inv. of Est. of ELEAZER SLOCUM of Dart., dtd. 5 June 1727, pres.
by sons Eleazer & Ebenezer Slocum, Execs. Apprs: Nathaniel
Soule, Daniel Wood & John Russel [5:439/40/1].
Appt. of Benjamin & Hezekiah Carpenter as Adms. of Est. of their
father BENJAMIN CARPENTER of Swan., dtd. 20 July 1727[5:441/2].
Appt. of Eleazer Slocum as Adm. of Est. of his brother JOHN SLO-
CUM of Dart., since Eleazer Slocum, father & Exec. of his son

JOHN SLOCUM is now dcd., dtd. 21 June 1727[5:442/3].

Will of JOHN SLOCUM of Dart., Yeoman, "being very Sick & Weak," dtd. 3 Nov. 1726, prob. 28 Dec. 1726. No wife mentioned. Brothers Eleazer & Benjamin Slocum. Sisters Maribah Richetson & Hannah Wedon. Kinsmen John Slocum son of my brother Eleazer Slocum, William Richetson, Jr. & Gideon Slocum. My father Eleazer Slocum to be Exec. Witns: Holder Slocum, James Allen & William Hart [5:443/4].

Inv. of Est. of JOHN SLOCUM of Dart., dtd. 24 Nov. 1726, pres. by Eleazer Slocum, his brother & Adm. Apprs: Deliverance Smith, James Allen & Holder Slocum [5:444/5].

Acct. of Experience Aldrich, widow & Adm. of Est. of her husb. PETER ALDRICH of Nor. dcd. intest., dtd. 24 June 1727[5:445/6].

Appt. of Experiance Aldrich of Nor. as guard. of Sarah Aldrich, dau. of PETER ALDRICH of Nor., dtd. 20 June 1727 [5:446].

Order for inv. to Elezebeth Brown, widow & Exec. of Est. of her husb. JOHN BROWN of Attl., dtd. 20 June 1727 [5:447].

Will of JOHN BROWN of Attl., Cooper, "being Very Sick & Weak," dtd. 2 May 1727, prob. 20 June 1727. Wife Elezebeth. Leaves all his est. to wife to "bring up my Small Children...for her and Either of theire Support." Overseers to be brethren & Friends Benjamin Brown, Christopher Bowen, Ebenezer Carpenter Timothy Tingley & Edward Capron. Wife Elezebeth as Exec. Witns: Jabez Brown, Edward Capron & John Foster [5:447/8].

Inv. of Est. of JOHN BROWN of Attl., dtd. 13 June 1727, pres. by Elezebeth Brown, his widow & Exec. Apprs: John Foster, Christopher Bowen & Epharim Carpenter [5:448/9].

Acct. of Sarah Chase & Job Chase, Execs. of Est. of JOSEPH CHASE of Swan., dtd. 20 June 1727. Mentions legacies paid to: Abigail Chase, Lidiah Davis, Alec [Alice] Baker, Isabel Chase, Ruth Chase & Job Chase. Also mentions monies paid to Sarah Chase as guard. of Sarah, Stephen, Silas, George & Moses Chase [5:449/50].

Acct. of Sarah Dagget, Adm. of Est. of her husb. JOHN DAGGET of Attl., dtd. 20 June 1727. Mentions legacies paid to: Mahew Dagget, Ebenezer Dagget & Thomas Dagget. Also mentions money paid to her daus: Abigail Guild, Jane Hall, Zilpher Robinson, Patience Robinson & Mary Dagget [5:450/1].

Inv. of Est. of EBENEZER WHITE of Attl., dtd. 2 Dec. 1726, pres. by Abigail White, his widow & Adm. Apprs: Noah Carpenter, John Foster & Timothy Tingley [5:451/2].

Acct. of Elezebeth Easterbrooks, widow & Adm. of Est. of her husb. THOMAS EASTERBROOKS of Swan., dtd. 8 May 1727[5:452/3].

Acct. of John Thomas, Exec. of Est. of his father JOHN THOMAS of Swan., dtd. 17 July 1727. Mentions legacies paid to: Hezekiah Kingsley, Prudance Thomas & Ruth Thomas "by her Guardian Anna Smith [5:453/4].

Rcpt. by Hezekiah Kingsley & Elesebeth Kingsley for money from Est. of "our Father" JOHN THOMAS of Swan, paid by "our brother John Thomas," Exec. dtd. 6 June 1727 [5:454].

Rcpt. by Anna Smith as guard. of Ruth Thomas for money from Est.
of Ruth's father JOHN THOMAS, paid by John Thomas, Exec., dtd.
26 June 1727 [5:454].

Rcpt. by Prudence Thomas for money from Est. of her father JOHN
THOMAS of Swan., paid by her brother John Thomas, Exec. dtd.
26 June 1727 [5:455].

Appt. of Mrs. Mary Washburn, widow, as Adm of Est. of her husb.
JONATHAN WASHBURN of Taun. dcd. intest., dtd. 20 June 1727
[5:455].

Order for inv. to William Torrey, Exec. of Est. of his brother
JOSEPH TORREY of Brist., dtd. 18 July 1727 [5:456].

Will of JOSEPH TORREY of Brist., Yeoman, "being Sick & Weak,"
dtd. 7 Apr. 1727, prob. 18 July 1727. Brothers William Torrey
& Ebenezer Torrey. Sisters: Silence Torrey, Margaret Torrey
& Mary Torrey. Cousin Benjamin Bosworth. Mentions his lands
in Mendon, County of Suffolk. Witns: Jeremiah Phiney, Jonathan Peck & Josiah Torrey [5:456/7].

End of Volume 5

Appt. of Deliverance Halloway, widow, & N. Halloway, son, as
Adms. of the Est. of NATHANIEL HALLOWAY of Taun. dcd. intest.
dtd. 18 July 1727 [6:1].

Appt. of Mercy Davis, widow, as Adm. of Est. of her husb. JO-
SEPH DAVIS of Attl. dcd. intest., dtd. 18 July 1727 [6:2].

Inv. of Est. of NATHANIEL HALLOWAY of Taun., Yeoman, dtd. 3
July 1727, pres. by Deliverance & Nathaniel Halloway, his widow & son, Adms. Incl. "a quarter of his Fathers homestead
lying in Dighton." Apprs: Daniel Axtell, Henry Hoskins & Ephraim Allen [6:2/3].

Inv. of Est. of BENJAMIN CARPENTER of Swan., pres. 22 July 1727
by Benjamin & Hezekiah Carpenter, Adms. Mentions monies "drawn
out by the widow Martha Carpenter in Lieu of her Dowry."
Apprs: Jonathan Kingsley, James Bowen & Samuel Bullock[6:3/4].

Order to John Glading, Exec. of Est. of his father JOHN GLADING
of Brist., dtd. 18 July 1727 [6:5].

Will of JOHN GLADING of Brist., Tayler, "in yᵉ Seventy Seventh
year of My age," dtd. 31 Jan. 1718, prob. 12 July 1727. Wife
Sarah. Sons: John (eldest), William & Joshua Glading. Daus: Su-
sanah Millard, Elezebeth Willis dcd., Mary Williams & Hannah
Briggs. Mentions chldn. of dau. Elezebeth Willis dcd. Son
John as sole Exec. Witns: John Cary, Eliazer Cary & Samuel
Southworth [6:5/6].

Inv. of Est. of JOHN GLADING of Brist., dtd. 18 July 1727, pres.
by John Glading, his son, Exec. Apprs: William Throope, Samuel Royall & Joseph Wardwel [6:6/7].

Order to Capt. John Foster of Attl., Exec. of Est. of MARY GUILE
of Attl., dtd. 15 Aug. 1727 [6:7/8].

Will of MARY GILE of Attl., Widow, dtd. 12 July 1727, prob. 15
Aug. 1727. Sons Calip Hall & Joshuah Hall. 2 daus: "Mary Bur-
rows & Hannah Homan that is now Mary Tiffiney & Hannah Bennett." Witns: Joseph Capron, Hezekiah Peck & Thomas Willmouth
[6:8/9].

Order to Deborah Barbar, widow & Exec. of Est. of JOSEPH BARBAR
of Reho., dtd. 28 July 1727 [6:9].

Will of JOSEPH BARBAR of Reho., Husbandman, dtd. 30 June 1727,
prob. 28 July 1727. Wife Deborah. Sons Joseph & Thomas (both
under age). Dau. Susanah (under age). "Yᵉ Child which my Wife
is now bigg with." Wife Deborah as Exec. Witns: James Redaway,
Abiah Carpenter & John Wilmouth [6:10].

Inv. of Est. of JONATHAN SMITH of Reho., dtd. 15 Aug. 1727,
pres. by Nathaniel Smith, Adm. Apprs: James Bowen, Jethniel

Peck & Samuell Bullock [6:10/1].

Acct. of Nathaniel Smith, Adm. of Est. of JONATHAN [*sic; named twice in this entry, but it was JOHN SMITH in Vol. 5 for whom Nathaniel was Adm., in 3 diff. entries*] SMITH of Reho., dtd. 16 Aug. 1727. Legacy to Samuel Barrow, guard. of Joanna Smith, "in full for what was due out of her fathers estate" [6:11].

Acct. of Mary Kent, widow, Adm. of Est. of her husb. JOSUAH KENT of Barr. dcd. intest., dtd. 15 Aug. 1727 [6:12].

Acct. of Benjamin & Hezekiah Carpenter, Adms. of Est. of BENJA-MIN CARPENTER of Swan., dtd. 15 Aug. 1727. Incl. item for grave stones "one for ye Deceased and one for his former wife Mentions paym. to Martha Carpenter, widow of the dcd.[6:12/3].

Inv. of Est. of WILLIAM DURFEY of Tiv., Yeoman, dtd. 17 July 1727, pres. by William & Joseph Durfey, Execs. Mentions lands in Tiv. & Dart. Incl. one negro woman & 2 negro boys. Apprs: Joseph Wanton, Richard Bourden & Joseph Anthoney [6:13/4].

Appt. of John Child of Swan. as guard. of John & Nathaniel Easterbrooks (over 14) & Mary, Benjamin & Sarah Easterbrooks (under 14), chldn. of THOMAS EASTERBROOKS of Swan., dtd. 9 Aug. 1727 [6:14].

Appt. of Richard Harding of Swan. as guard. of Rachel Easter-brooks (over 14), dau. of THOMAS EASTERBROOKS of Swan., dtd. 6 Aug. 1727 [6:14/5].

Appt. of John West of Reho. as guard. of Mehetibel West, grdau. of BENJAMIN CARPENTER of Swan., dtd. 28 Aug. 1727 [6:15].

Appt. of Job Carpenter of Swan. as guard. of Renew West, grdau. of BENJAMIN CARPENTER of Swan., dtd. 28 Aug. 1727 [6:16].

Appt. of Hannah Winslow, widow, as Adm. of Est. of her husb. JOSEPH WINSLOW of Swan. dcd. intest., dtd. 4 Sept. 1727[6:16/7].

Appt. of William Winslow of Free. as Adm. of Est. of JOSEPH WINS-LOW of Swan., his widow & Adm. Hannah Winslow having since dcd., dtd. 6 Oct. 1727 [6:17].

Order to Jonathan Eddy, Exec. of Est. of DELIVERANCE SMITH of Taun., dtd. 10 Oct. 1727 [6:18].

Will of DELIVERANCE SMITH of Taun., widow, dtd. 24 Aug. 1727, prob. 13 Sept. 1727. Sons: Ebenezer Edde (eldest), Eleazer Edde (2nd), Joseph Edde, Jonathan Edde (4th). Daus: Mercy Fisher dcd. (eldest), Hannah Fisher (2nd), Susanah Durfey (3rd) & Patience White (4th). Elezebeth my son Ebenezer's wife. Abigail Edde my son Joseph's dau. Charity Edde my son Eleazer's dau. Experiance Fisher dau. of my dau. Mercy Fisher dcd. Son Jonathan Edde as Exec. Witns: Ephraim White, Nathan White & Samuel Sumner [6:18/9].

Acct. of Samuel Titus, Exec. of Est. of his father SAMUEL TITUS of Attl., dtd. 19 Sept. 1727 [6:19/20].

Inv. of Est. of GEORGE BAISTO of Reho., dtd. 9 May 1726, pres. by George Baisto, Adm. Mrs. Mercy Baisto late wife of George dcd. Apprs: Joseph Titus, Saml Perry & Tho. Read[6:20/1].

Acct. of George Baisto, Adm. of his father GEORGE BAISTO of Re-

ho., dtd. 19 Sept. 1727. Incl. items for 2 coffins & 2 pairs
of gravestones. Mentions Samuel Baisto as a bondsman [6:21].

Appt. of Mrs. Mary Kent of Barr. as guard. of Mary, Susanah,
Hannah & Lidia (all under 14), chldn. of JOSUAH KENT of Barr.
dtd. 17 Oct. 1727 [6:22].

Appt. of Benjamin Cary of Brist. as guard. of Sarah Kent (over
14), dau. of JOSUAH KENT of Barr., dtd. 17 Oct. 1727 [6:22].

Appt. of Hanery Josling of Attl. as guard. of Hannah, Ruth, Nathaniel & Abigail Whiple, chldn. of ISRAEL WHIPLE of Attl.,
dtd. 17 Oct. 1727 [6:23].

Acct. of Hannah Simmons, widow & Adm. of Est. of her husb. RE-
MEMBRANCE SIMMONS of Swan., dtd. 15 Sept. 1727. Mentions "to
my Daughter Hannah," & "to my Son Joseph" [6:23/4].

Order to Rebecca Kerby, Exec. of Est. of her husb. JOHN KERBY
of Dart., dtd. 7 Oct. 1727 [6:24].

Will of JOHN KIRBY of Dart., Husbandman, dtd. 2 July 1724, prob.
17 Oct. 1727. Wife Rebecca. 5 sons: Richard, John, James, Thomas & William Kirby. Daus: Sarah Winslow, Rebecca, Elezebeth,
Mary & Abigail Kirby. Wife Rebecca as Exec. Witns: Josiah Mor-
rchson, Eliashib Smith & Benjamin Hammond [6:25/6].

Inv. of Est. of JOHN KIRBEY of Dart., Gentleman, dtd. 1 Sept.
1727, pres. by Rebeca Kirbey, his widow & Exec. Apprs: Eli-
shib Smith, Hanery Howland & Theophelus Ellys [6:27].

Order to James Wheler & Edward Luther, Execs. of the Est. of
EBENEZER MARTIN of Barr., dtd. 11 Oct. 1727 [6:28].

Will of EBENEZER MARTIN of Barr., Husbandman, "being very Sick
& Weake in body," dtd. 9 Sept. 1727, prob. 17 Oct. 1727. Wife
Abigail. Mentions "my sons" & "my daughters" (all under age)
without naming any of them. My father James Wheler & Edward
Luther as Execs. Witns: Ezra Ormsbee, Mary Kent & Richard
Round [6:28/9].

Order to Thomas Slack, Exec. of Est. of his father WILLIAM SLACK
of Attl., dtd. 17 Oct. 1727 [6:29].

Will of WILLIAM SLACK of Attl., Ship Carpenter, "being Aged,"
dtd. 3 Feb. 1726/7, prob. 17 Oct. 1727. Wife Mary. Sons: Thomas, John, Samuel & Joseph Slack. Dau. Elezebeth Ide. Son-in-
law Jonathan Jencks. Grdaus: Jerusha, Elezebeth, Hannah & Rebecca Jencks. Grson. William Slack son of Samuel. Indian servant Cesar. Witns: Samuel Day, Jonathan Fuller & Noah Carpenter [6:30/1].

Order to Mary Cook, widow & Exec. of Est. of her husb. JOHN
COOK of Tiv., dtd. 17 Oct. 1727 [6:31/2].

Will of Capt. JOHN COOK of Tiv., Yeoman, dtd. 15 Sept. 1727,
prob. 17 Oct. 1727. Wife Mary. Sons: Thomas (eldest), John,
Peleg, George & Joseph (youngest) Cook. Daus: Sarah Witman,
Pheby Allen, Mary Peirce dcd., Deborah Talman, Martha Sharman
& Patience Church. Wife Mary as Exec. Witns: Benjamin Durfey,
Jacob Hathaway, Joseph Borden & Richard Bourden [6:32/3].

Appt. of Anna Corey, widow, as Adm. of Est. of her husb. THOMAS
COREY of Dart., dcd. intest., dtd. 17 Oct. 1727 [6:33].

Inv. of Est. of THOMAS COREY, Jr. of Dart., dtd. 1 July 1727,
pres. by Anna Corey, widow & Adm. Apprs: Philip Taber, Jon:
Taber & Icabod Taber [6:34].

Acct. of Mary Walker, widow & Adm. of Est. of JAMES WALKER of
Taun. dcd. intest., dtd. 17 Oct. 1727. Mentions debts paid to
Elezebeth Walker, Peter Walker, Nathan Walker & Nehemiah Wal-
ker [6:35].

Inv. of Est. of JOSEPH DAVISE of Attl. who died 4 May 1727, dtd.
27 June 1727, pres. by Marcy Davise his widow & Adm. Apprs:
Joseph Razie, Hanery Joslin & Anthoney Sprage [6:35/6].

Order for div. of real est. of NATHANIEL PAINE of Brist., dtd.
9 Aug. 1727. Mentions that Nathaniel's widow Dorothey Paine
has quitted-claim 8/9ths of her husb. real est. [6:36/7].

Div. of real est. of NATHANIEL PAINE of Brist. into 9 shares
btwn. his widow Dorothey Paine & his chldn: Nathaniel (eldest son), Stephen (2nd son), Samuel Varnun in the right of
his wife Elezebeth, heirs of Mrs. Mary Drown (dau.) dcd., Lt.
Col. Church in the right of his wife Hannah, Timothy Failes
in the right of his wife Alathea, John Williams in the right
of his wife Dorothey & to "M^S Sarah Paine [sic] one share,
dtd. 17 Oct. 1727. Comm: William Throope, Benjamin Cary, Robert Joles, Thomas Throope & William Walker [6:37/8].

Order to Susanah Taber, widow & Exec. of Est. of her husb. JOHN
TABER of Dart., dtd. 21 Nov. 1727 [6:39].

Will of JOHN TABER of Dart., Husbandman, "being Sorely Wounded
& Weake," dtd. 18 June 1718, prob. 21 Nov. 1727. Wife Susanah.
2 eldest sons Phillip & William Taber. Youngest son Thomas
Taber (under 21). 2 daus. Mary & Sarah (both under 18 & unmar.).
My brother Phillip Taber & my brother-in-law Robert Bennit as
Overseers. Wife Susanah as Exec. Witns: Philip Taber, Thomas
Britman & William Potter [6:39/40].

Inv. of Est. of JOHN TABER of Dart., dtd. 28 Aug. 1727, pres.
by Susanah Taber, Exec. Mentions "his Daughter Mary Heart."
Apprs: Philip Taber, Robert Bennit & Thomas Corey [6:40/1].

Acct. of Thomas Smith, Adm. of Est. of his brother JAMES SMITH
of Nantucket, dtd. 20 Nov. 1727 [6:42].

Order to Samuel Danforth, Exec. of Est. of SAMUEL DANFORTH of
Taun., dtd. 25 Nov. 1727 [6:42/3].

Appt. of Hanery Howland & John Russel, both of Dart., as guards.
of Hannah Briggs of Dart. "non Compus mentis," widow of JOHN
BRIGGS of Tiv., dtd. 28 Nov. 1727 [6:43].

Appt. of John Wilmouth of Reho. as guard. of Joseph Barbar (over
14), son of JOSEPH BARBAR of Reho., dtd. 25 Nov. 1727 [6:43/4].

Inv. of Est. of JOSEPH BARBAR of Reho., dtd. 12 Oct. 1727, pres.
by Deborah Barbar, his widow & Exec. Apprs: N. Wilmarth, James
Redaway & Thomas Allen [6:44].

Will of SAMUEL DANFORTH of Taun., Clerke, dtd. 5 May 1725, prob.
21 Nov. 1727. Wife mentioned often but not named. Sons: Samuel, James & Thomas Danforth. Daus: Elezebeth dcd. former
wife of John Walley, Sarah wife of William Downs of Boston,

Mary wife of Jacob Barney, Hannah Danforth, Bethiah Danforth, Rachel Danforth & Katherine Danforth (last 4 under 21 & unmar.) My father-in-law Rev. Mr. James Allen dcd. Dcd. dau. Elezebeth's husb. John Walley to get "land at the North End of Boston." Mentions his lands near Worcester, at Taun., at Woodstock & at Norton. Son Samuel as Exec. Witns: Ephraim Hodges, Jonathan Harvey & Benjamin Harvey [6:45/6/7].

Order to div. Est, of BENJAMIN CARPENTER of Swan. btwn. his chldn., dtd. 4 Sept. 1727 [6:47].

Div. of Est. of BENJAMIN CARPENTER of Swan. btwn. his chldn: Benjamin (eldest son), Jotham, John, Job, Hezekiah & Edward Carpenter, to Prences(?) West survivors, Elizebeth Winslow, Hannah Martin, Submit Perce & Keziah Horton, dtd. 20 Nov. 17-27. Comm: Hezekiah Luther, Samuel Gardner, William Anthoney, William Wood & Barnard Haile [6:47/8/9].

Appt. of Jacob Barney of Taun. as guard. of Rachel & Bethiah Danforth (over 14), & Katherine Danforth (under 14), daus. of SAMUEL DANFORTH of Taun., dtd. 10 Jan. 1727/8 [6:49/50].

Appt. of Anna Haile of Swan. as guard. of Amos Haile (over 14), son of RICHARD HAILE of Swan., dtd. 10 Jan. 1727/8 [6:50].

Appt. of Simon Burr of Reho. as Adm. of Est. of his brother ISAAC BURR of Reho. dcd. intest., dtd. 2 Jan. 1727/8 [6:50/1].

Appt. of Elisha May of Barr. as Adm. of Est. of EPHRAIM MAY of Reho., since his widow & Exec. Deliverance May is now dcd., dtd. 9 Jan. 1727/8 [6:51/2].

Appt. of Elisha May of Barr. as Adm. of Est. of DELIVERANCE MAY of Reho. dcd. intest., dtd. 9 Jan. 1727/8 [6:52].

Appt. of Joseph Carpenter of Brist. as Adm. of Est. of CALEB CARPENTER of Swan. dcd. intest., dtd. 10 Jan. 1727/8 [6:52/3].

Inv. of Est. of KATHERINE DEAN of Taun., dtd. 1 Dec. 1726, pres. by Benjamin Wiliams, Exec. Apprs: Richard Godfree, Samuel Pitts & Samuel Sumner [6:53].

Inv. of DELIVERANCE SMITH of Taun., dtd. 14 Nov. 1727. pres. by Jonathan Eddy, Exec. Apprs: John Briggs, 2nd, John Newland, Sr. & James Leonard [6:54].

Appt. of Samuel Forman of Free. as guard. of Elezebeth & Hannah Rothbotham (over 14), daus. of JOSEPH ROTHBOTHAM of Brist., dtd. 16 Jan. 1727/8 [6:54/5].

Order to John & Samuel White, Execs. of Est. of their father JOHN WHITE of Taun., dtd. 16 Jan. 1727/8 [6:55].

Will of JOHN WHITE of Taun., "being aged and under Sickness of body," dtd. 2 Sept. 1726, prob. 16 Jan. 1727/8. Sons: John, Samuel & Josiah White. 6 daus: Hannah, Abigail, Susanah, Mehetibel, Margaret & Esther [no surnames]. Wife not named but says "my Wife must be maintained." Sons John & Samuel as Execs. Witns: Samuel Danforth, Hannah Hall & Hannah Campbil [6:56].

Inv. of Est. of JOHN WHITE of Taun., dtd. 7 June 1727, pres. by John & Samuel White, his sons & Execs. Apprs: Samuel Leonard, Abraham Jones & Benjamin Wilbour [6:56/7].

Order to Elezebeth Mias, widow, & Joseph Southworth, Execs. of
Est. of NICHOLAS MIAS of Lit. Comp., dtd. 16 Jan. 1727/8
[6:58].
Will of NICHOLAS MIAS of Lit. Comp., dtd. 4 Sept. 1727, prob.
16 Jan. 1727/8. Wife Elezebeth. Sons Gitto & Oliver (under
21). Daus: Phebe & Alce (both under 18). Friend Joseph
Southworth & my wife Elezebeth as Execs. Witns: William
Briggs, John Horswel & William Davis [6:58/9].
Inv. of Est. of NICHOLAS MIAS of Lit. Comp., dtd. 12 Jan. 1727/8
pres. by Elezebeth Mias, widow, & John Southworth, Execs.
Apprs: John Wood, John Church & William Richmond [6:59/60].
Acct. of William Hodges & Nathan Hodges, Adms. of Est. of their
brother SAMUEL HODGES of Norton, dtd. 25 Jan. 1727/8. Mentions item "to William Hodges for Keeping of Seth Hodges after
the Death of his father Samuel," one "to Keeping of Martha
hodges aboute two months," & one "to Necessarys for ye Childreen to fit them to be put out" [6:60/1].
Acct. of Joseph Tisdal "Surviving Executor" of Est. of his father JOSEPH TISDAL of Taun., dtd. 24 Jan. 1727/8. Mentions
"To M^s Mary Tisdal widdow towards her thirds," and legacies
per will to Elezebeth Leonard, Sarah Read, Abigail Howard,
legal repres. of Hannah Hodges & legal repres. of Mary Winslow. Also mentions John Tisdal, Jr. [6:62/3/4].
Agrmt. abt. div. of real est. of THOMAS COOPER, Sr. of Reho.
dcd. intest., signed by his sons Nathaniel (eldest) & Noah
Cooper of Reho. & Josiah & Thomas (youngest) Cooper of Attl.,
dtd. 18 Dec. 1727. Mentions the 1/3rd part that "belonged to
our Honoured mother during her life," and their sister Susanah Carpenter widow. Witns: Thomas Read, Jr., Ezekiel Read &
Jedeiah Carpenter [6:64/5/6].
Will of JOHN TISDAL of Taun., Yeoman, "being Very Sick," dtd.
26 Jan. 1727/8, prob. 5 Feb. 1727/8. Wife Abigail. Sons John
(eldest), Abraham (2nd, under 21), Israel (3rd, under 21),
Ephraim & Jedediah Tisdal. Daus: Deborah Tisdal, Abigail Tisdal & Anna Tisdal. Wife Abigail as Exec. Witns: John French,
2nd, Eleazer French & Samuel Sumner [6:66/7/8].
Order to Joseph Read & John Read, Jr. of Free. as comm. to re-
ceive claims against insolvent Est. of Capt. CHARLES CHURCH
of Free., dtd. 20 Feb. 1727/8 [6:68].
Appt. of David & Hannah Thurston of Reho. as guards. of Abisha
& Zerviah Carpenter (both over 14), chldn. of JONATHAN CARPEN-
TER of Reho., dtd. 20 Feb. 1727/8 [6:68/9].
Appt. of Thomas Throope of Brist. as guard. of Thomas Peck (over
14), son of JONATHAN PECK of Brist., dtd. 20 Feb. 1727/8 [6:69].
Order to Jonathan Russel, Exec. of Est. of his father JONATHAN
RUSSEL of Dart., dtd. 20 Feb. 1727/8 [6:70].
Will of JONATHAN RUSSEL of Dart., Yeoman, dtd. 9 June 1725, prob.
20 Feb. 1727/8. Wife not mentioned. 3 sons: Jonathan, James
& William Russel. 2 daus: Deborah Allen & Dorothey Sharman.
Grson. George Russel. Son Jonathan as Exec. Witns: Deliver-

ance Smith, Beriah Goddard & Peleg Smith [6:70/1].

Inv. of Est. of JONATHAN RUSSEL of Dart., dtd. 13 Dec. 1727, pres. by Jonathan Russel, his son & Exec. Apprs: Deliverance Smith, John Russel & Isaac Shearman [6:71/2].

Acct. of Ephraim Carpenter & wife Martha, guards. of Martha Carpenter, dau. of ZACHARIAH CARPENTER of Reho., dtd. 20 Feb. 1727/8. Said minor is now dcd. [6:72].

Order to John Paine, Exec. of Est. of his father RALPH PAINE of Free., dtd. 20 Feb. 1727/8 [6:73].

Will of RALPH PAINE of Free., Husbandman, dtd. 23 Apr. 1722, prob. 20 Feb. 1727/8. Wife Dorothey. Sons: John, Thomas & Joseph Paine. 2 daus. Mary Slocum & Sarah Briggs. Son John as Exec. Witns: Abraham Simmons, Benjamin Terry & Seth Smith [6:73/4].

Inv. of Est. of RALPH PAINE of Free., dtd. 20 Jan. 1727/8, pres. by John Paine, his son & Exec. Apprs: William Winslow, Jacob Hathaway & Benjamin Terry [6:74/5].

Acct. of Ephraim Carpenter & wife Martha, guards. of Patience Carpenter, dau. of ZACHARIAH CARPENTER, said minor now being dcd., dtd. 20 Feb. 1727/8. Mentions that guards. maintained Patience "from one year old to Nine year old" [6:75/6].

Inv. of Est. of HANNAH THOMSON of Reho., dtd. 3 Apr. 1727, pres. by Jacob Ormsbee, Adm. Mentions Est. of "her three children for whome She was Guardian." Apprs: Jonathan Kingsley, James Bowen & Samuel Bullock [6:77/8].

Acct. of Jacob Ormsbee, Adm. of Est. of HANNAH THOMSON of Reho., dtd. 20 Feb. 1727/8 [6:78].

Inv. of Est. of JOSEPH WINSLOW & his wife HANNAH of Swan. both dcd., dtd. 6 Jan. 1727/8, pres. by William Winslow, brother of Joseph & Adm. Apprs: William Anthoney, Hezekiah Luther & Samuel Gardner [6:78].

Appt. of Susanah Hathaway as Adm. of Est. of her husb. JONATHAN HATHAWAY of Dart. dcd. intest., dtd. 6 March 1727/8 [6:79].

Inv. of Est. of JONATHAN HATHAWAY of Dart., Yeoman, dtd. 2 Dec. 1727, pres. by Susanah Hathaway, his widow & Adm. Apprs: Nathaniel Blackwell, Elnathan Pope & Stephen West, Jr. [6:79/80].

Appt. of Nathaniel Millard of Reho. as Adm. of Est. of his brother SOLOMON MILLARD of Reho., dtd. 1 March 1727/8 [6:80/1].

Order to Mary Eirle, widow & Exec. of Est. of her husb. JOHN EIRLE of Tiv., dtd. 19 March 1727 [6:81].

Will of JOHN EIRLE of Tiv., Yeoman, dtd. 12 Feb. 1727/8, prob. 19 March 1727/8. Wife Mary. Sons: John, Daniel & Benjamin. Daus: Mary, Rebecca & Elizebeth [no surnames]. Wife Mary as Exec. Friends Edward Richmond, Capt. John Palmer & Thomas Manchester as Overseers. Witns: Stephen Manchester, Edward Richmond & Benjamin Richmond [6:81/2].

Inv. of Est. of JOHN EIRLE of Tiv., dtd. 2 Feb. 1727/8, pres. by Mary Eirle, his widow & Exec. Apprs: Joseph Anthoney, Jr. Stephen Manchester & Thomas Manchester [6:82/3].

Inv. of Est. of ISAAC BURR of Reho., dtd. 19 March 1727/8, pres. by Simon Burr, his bro. & Adm. Apprs: James Bowen, Jonathan Kinglsey & Samuel Bullock [6:83/4].

Rcpt. & release by Thomas Toman of Newport, Mariner, for legacy from Est. of his grfather. Capt. THOMAS NEWTON of Brist., paid by Samuel Vial of Brist., Exec. dtd. 3 Oct. 1727. Witns: N. Blagrove & Timothy Ingraham [6:84/5].

Rcpt. by John Newton of a cane from Est. of his father, paid by Samuel Vial [6:85].

Inv. of Est. of DELIVERANCE MAY of Reho., dtd. 19 March 1727/8, pres. by Elisha May, Adm. Apprs: Jabiz Bosworth, Daniel Hunt & Jathniel Peck [6:85].

Appt. of Joseph Southworth of Lit. Comp. as guard. of Constant Southworth, minor grson. of WILLIAM SOUTHWORTH of Lit. Comp., dtd. 19 March 1727/8 [6:86].

Appt. of Elezebeth Carpenter as Adm. of Est. of JOSIAH CARPENTER of Reho. dcd. intest., dtd. 8 Apr. 1728 [6:86/7].

Appt. of Elezebeth Carpenter as guard. of Comfort Carpenter (over 14), son of JOSIAH CARPENTER of Reho., dtd. 8 Apr. 1728 [6:87].

Order to William & James Drake, Execs. of Est. of their father WILLIAM DRAKE of Taun., dtd. 20 Apr. 1728 [6:88].

Will of WILLIAM DRAKE of Taun., Husbandman, dtd. 15 Sept. 1727, prob. 20 Feb. 1727/8. Wife Sary [sic]. Sons: William (eldest), Joseph, James, Daniel & Benjamin (youngest). Daus: Abigail, Rebeckah, Lydia & Sarah (last under 18)[no surnames]. Witns: James Burtt, John Richmond & John Tisdal, Jr. [6:88/9].

Inv. of Est. of WILLIAM DRAKE, Sr., dtd. 10 Apr. 1728, pres. by William & James Drake, his sons & Execs. Apprs: John Richmond, Elnathan Thrasher & Micah Prat [6:89/90].

Acct. of Susanah Hathway, widow & Adm. of Est. of her husb. JONATHAN HATHWAY of Dart., dtd. 9 Apr. 1728 [6:91].

Order to William & Jeduthan Spooner, Execs. of Est. of JOHN SPOONER of Dart., dtd. 9 Apr. 1728 [6:91/2].

Will of JOHN SPOONER, Jr. of Dart., "being at this present Sick & Weak," dtd. 4 March 1728, prob. 9 Apr. 1728. No wife mentioned. Sons: Jeduthan, Benjamin, John, Thomas & Peter (under) 21) Spooner. 4 daus: Pheby Spooner, Mary Spooner, Elezebeth Spooner & Rosamond Spooner (all under 21). William Spooner & Stephen West, Jr., both of Dart., to be Trustees to take the care & oversight of children I leave under age. William Spooner & Jeduthan Spooner as Execs. Witns: Stephen West, Jr., David Clark & Christopher Turner [6:92/3].

Inv. of Est. of JOHN SPOONER, Jr. of Dart., dtd. 22 March 1727/8 pres. by William Spooner & Jeduthan Spooner, Execs. Apprs: Benjamin Hammond, Nathaniel Delano & Stephen West [6:93].

Will of JAMES EDMASTER of Free., Husbandman, "being weak in body & my Wife ANN EDMASTER being Very Sick & Weake...our Last Will

& Testament," dtd. 13 May 1723, prob. 11 Apr. 1728.   Our sons
James (eldest), Joseph & William Edmaster.   Out 7 daus: Ann
Smith, Marcy Freelove, Hannah Edmaster, Susanah Edmaster, Re-
becca Edmaster, Deliverance Edmaster & Thankful Edmaster. Son
James as Exec. Witns: Thomas Terrey, William Davis & William
Davis, Jr. [6:94].
Inv. of Est. of MARY GUILE of Attl., dtd. 28 July 1727, pres.
by John Foster, Exec. Apprs: Hezekiah Peck, Joseph Capron &
Thomas Wilmouth [6:95].
Order to Judith Williams, Exec. of Est. of EBENEZER WILLIAMS of
Taun., dtd. 12 Apr. 1728 [6:95].
Will of EBENEZER WILLIAMS of Taun., "being Seized with Sickness,"
dtd. 8 Sept. 1727, prob. 11 Apr. 1728. Wife Judith. "To my
Brother Richard Williams his youngest son [not named]." Wife
Judith & cousin Seth Williams to be Execs. Witns: Seth Wil-
liams, James Hall & Ebenezer Andrews. On 11 Apr. 1728 Seth
Williams relinquished Exec. [6:96].
Appt. of Seth Burt of Taun. as guard. of Ephraim Tisdal (over
14), son of JOHN TISDAL of Taun., dtd. 11 Apr. 1728 [6:96/7].
Appt. of Ann Williams as Adm. of Est. of RICHARD WILLIAMS of
Taun. dcd. intest., dtd. 11 Apr. 1728 [6:97].
Inv. of Est. of RICHARD WILLIAMS of Taun., dtd. 28 Oct. 1727,
pres. by Ann Williams, Adm. Apprs: Benjamin Wilbour, Samuel
Pitts & John Godfrey [6:97].
Inv. of Est. of ELEXANDER BALCUM of Attl. dcd. intest., dtd. 21
Feb. 1727/8, pres. by Sarah Bolcom, Adm. Mentions part of
the stock was challenged by Baruch & Joseph Bolcom. Apprs:
John Foster, Thomas Skinner & John Skinner [6:98/9].
Order to Hannah Winslow, widow & Exec. of Est. of her husb. RI-
CHARD WINSLOW of Free., dtd. 16 May 1728 [6:99].
Appt. of Mrs. Lidia Perrey, widow, as Adm. of Est. of her husb.
WILLIAM PERREY of Free. dcd. intest., dtd. 16 Apr. 1728[6:100].
Order to William Robinson, Exec. of Est. of THOMAS ROBARTS of
Swan., dtd. 16 Apr. 1728 [6:100].
Order to Joseph Anthoney, Exec. of Est. of his father JOSEPH AN-
THONEY of Tiv., dtd. 16 Apr. 1728 [6:101].
Will of JOSEPH ANTHONEY of Tiv., dtd. 8 March 1712/3, prob. 19
March 1727/8. Wife Mary. Sons: John & Joseph Anthoney. Dau.
Susanna Anthoney. Mentions lands in Tiv. & in Portsmouth.
Son Joseph as Exec. Witns: Samuel Shearman, Martha Shearman,
Francis Brayton, Jr. & John Anthony [6:101/2].
Inv. of Est. of JOSEPH ANTHONEY of Tiv., dtd. 15 Apr. 1728, pres.
by Joseph Anthoney, Exec. Apprs: John Howland, John Tollman
& Thomas Jeffries [6:102/3].
Will of RICHARD WINSLOW of Free., "Practishioner of Physick &
Chirugion being very sick," dtd. 7 Aug. 1727, prob. 16 Apr.
1728. Wife Hannah. 4 sons: Richard (eldest), Hezekiah, Wil-
liam & Edward Winslow. Daus: Sarah Winslow (eldest, under 20),
& Hannah Winslow (youngest). My brothers William Winslow &

John Winslow & my wife Hannah as Execs. Mentions lands in
Free. & in Lisester [*sic*]. Witns: Elnathan Shearman, Jonathan Winslow & John Read [6:103/4].

Inv. of Est. of RICHARD WINSLOW of Free., Practitioner, dtd. 9
Jan. 1728, pres. by Hannah Winslow, his widow & Exec. Apprs:
Jonathan Dodson, John Read & Jacob Hathway [6:104/5].

Acct. of Mary Dagget, Exec. of Est. of her husb. JOSEPH DAGGET
of Reho., dtd. 16 Apr. 1728. Incl. legacies per will paid to:
Timothy Ide, Nathaniel Cooper & Noah Chaffee [6:105].

Will of THOMAS ROBERTS of Swan., Schoolmaster, "being not well,"
dtd. 22 March 1727, prob. 16 Apr. 1728. No wife or chldn.
mentioned. To Abraham Baker & his wife [*not named*] and their
daus. Dinah & Rebeccah. "To Francis Baker my muskit." To Jeremiah Werill. To Joseph Baker. Friend William Robinson as Exec. Witns: Benjamin Norten, Joseph Traffern & John Smith
[6:105/6].

Inv. of Est. of THOMAS ROBERTS, Schoolmaster, dtd. 5 Apr. 1728,
pres. by William Robinson, Exec. Apprs: William Anthoney, Jacob Hathway & Preserved Brayton [6:106/7].

Inv. if Est. of WILLIAM PERRY of Free., Shipwright, dtd. 8 March
1727/8, pres. by Lidia Perry, his widow & Adm. Apprs: William
Winslow, Benjamin Terry & Isaac Hathway [6:107].

Appt. of Jethniel Peck of Reho. as guard. of Abigail Smith, widow of DANIEL SMITH, who is non Compus mentis, dtd. 13 May
1728 [6:108].

Order to John Sweeting, Exec. of Est. of HENERY SWEETING of Reho.
dtd. 13 May 1728 [6:108/9].

Will of HANERY SWEETING of Reho., Clothworker, dtd. 8 June 1723,
prob. 13 May 1728. No wife mentioned. Dau. Mary Mason wife of
Noah Mason, dau. Joanah Samson wife of James Samson, son Henery Sweeting, dau. Susanah Hunt wife of John Hunt, dau. Experience Cary wife of John Cary, son Lewis Sweeting, dau. Elezebeth Sweeting, dau. Annah Sweeting (last 2 unmar.) & son John
Sweeting. Sons Henery Sweeting & Noah Mason to assist son John
who is Exec. Witns: Leonard Newsum, Jonathan French & John
West [6:109/10].

Will of JOHN EASTERBROOKS of Swan., Surgion, dtd. 10 Sept. 1718,
prob. 13 May 1728. Wife Mehetible. Sons: William, Charles &
John (youngest) Easterbrooks. Daus: Sarah Easterbrooks, Hannah
Easterbrooks, Judith Easterbrooks, Lidia Easterbrooks & Deb-
orah Easterbrooks (all under 22). Mentions lands in Swan.,
Reho. & Ashford, Ct. Wife Mehetibel & son William as Execs.
Brother Thomas Easterbrooks, Joseph Butterworth, Benjamin Cole
& Robart Carr as Overseers. Witns: Ebenezer Cole, Joseph
Butterworth, Jr. & John Devotion [6:110/1].

Order to Mehetibel Easterbrooks, widow, & William Easterbrooks,
son, Execs. of Est. of JOHN EASTERBROOKS of Swan., dtd. 13
May 1728 [6:112].

Order to William, Thomas & Joseph Brightman, Execs. of Est. of
HENERY BRIGHTMAN of Free., dtd. 25 May 1728 [6:112].

Order to Benjamin Wise, Exec. of Est. of THOMAS WISE of Attl.,
  dtd. 21 May 1728 [6:113].
Appt. of Mrs. Bethiah Slack, widow, as Adm. of Est. of her husb.
  JOHN SLACK of Attl., dtd. 21 May 1728 [6:113].
Will of THOMAS WISE of Attl., Husbandman, dtd. 26 Apt. 1728,
  prob. 21 May 1728. Wife Elizabeth. Son Joseph Wise, chldn. of
  my son John Wise, dau. Elizabeth Fuller, dau. Dorcas Follet
  & son Benjamin Wise. Son Benjamin as Exec. Witns: John
  [Shoter?], Noah Carpenter & John Wedge [6:114].
Will of JOHN BARNEY of Taun., dtd. 22 Feb. 1727/8, prob. 21 May
  1728. Wife Mary. 5 sons: John, Jonathan, Joseph, Jacob & William Barney. 4 daus: Mary wife of Benjamin Carpenter, Elizabeth wife of Peter Caswell, Annah wife of William Leonard &
  Sarah wife of James Williams. Mentions that 5 sons are to
  "take Care and maintain my ... Wife Mary Barney their aged
  Mother." Sons John & Jonathan as Execs. Witns: Larrence Hart,
  Samuel Danforth & Joseph Willis [6:115].
Inv. of Est. of JOHN EASTABROOKE of Swan., Chirurgion, who died
  26 Apr. 1728, dtd. 17 May 1728. pres. by Mehhetibel Easta-
  brooks & William Easterbrooks, Execs. Mentions lands in Swan.
  & in Ashford, Ct. Apprs: Joseph Mason, Barnard Haile & Jo-
  seph Butterworth, Jr. [6:115/6].
Inv. of Est. of JOSEPH PALMER of Lit. Comp., dtd. 14 May 1728,
  pres. by William & John Palmer, Adms. Apprs: Nathaniel Searls
  Jo: Bhriggs [sic] & Daniel Wilcocks [6:116].
Acct. of Sarah Earll, Adm. of Est. of her former husb. JOHN BOR-
  DEN of Swan. dcd. intest., dtd. 21 May 1728. Incl. paym. to:
  Mary Borden for rent, Mary Borden, Jr., Hope Borden & "To ye
  Widdow for her Charges in Lying of a Child after ye Death of
  ye father" [6:117].
Inv. of Est. of HENRY SWEETING of Reho., dtd. 15 May 1728, pres.
  by John Sweeting, Exec. Incl. bonds due from Henry Sweeting &
  from Elizabeth Sweeting. Apprs: John West & Jathnill Peck
  [6:117/8].
Inv. of Est. of JOSEPH STAPLES of Taun., dtd. 11 Jan. 1727/8,
  pres. by Ann Staples, Adm. Apprs: Richard Godfree & Henry
  Hoskins [6:118].
Appt. of William & John Palmer as Adms. of Est. of JOSEPH PALMER
  of Lit. Comp., dtd. 21 May 1728 [6:118/9].
Appt. of Mrs. Bethiah Slack, widow, as Adm. of Est. of her husb.
  JOHN SLACK of Attl., dtd. 21 May 1728 [6:119].
Inv. of Est. of JOHN TISDALE of Taun., dtd. 20 Feb. 1727/8, pres.
  by Abigail Tisdale, Exec. Apprs: Samuel Williams, John Burt &
  Samuel Sumner [6:120].
Will of HENERY BRIGHTMAN of Newport, Yeoman, dtd. 3 Oct. 1716,
  prob. in Portsmouth 9 Apr. 1728, recorded in Portsmouth in
  Register of Will pages 88 & 89, prob. in Brist. 21 May 1728,
  calling him "Henery Brightman late of Freetown." No wife men-
  tioned. Sons: William (eldest), Thomas (2nd) & Joseph (young-

est) Brightman. Daus: Hester Chandler & Sarah Hoar. 3 grsons:
Henery Brightman the son of William, Henery Brightman the son
of Thomas & Henery the son of Joseph Brightman. Grson. Henery
Hoar. Mentions lands in Newport, Portsmouth & Dart. Witns:
Benedick Arnold, Capt. Richard Dunn & Capt. William Weeden
[6:121/2/3].

Codicil to his will by HENERY BRIGHTMAN of Free., formerly of
Rhode Island, Yeoman, dtd. 15 Feb. 1727/8. Son Joseph Brightman & his wife Susanah. Son-in-law John Chandler. Witns: John
Weaver, Susannah Flagger & Joseph Read. Presented to Council
[of Portsmouth?] 8 Apr. 1728, pres. at Brist. 21 May 1728[6:
123/4].

Will of NICHOLAS WHITE of Taun., "being aged & Labouring under
Sickness & Pain," dtd. 15 Sept. 1724, prob. 21 May 1728. Wife
not mentioned. Eldest sons Nicholas & Matthew White, son Tho-
mas White (all living) & son Benjamin White dcd. Dau. Dorcas
Leonard wife of Seth Leonard. Chldn. [not named] of son Tho-
mas White. Mentions lands in Taun. & Norton. Sons Nicholas &
Matthew as Execs. Witns: Eleazer Comer, Shadrick Wilbour &
Jonathan Williams [6:124/5].

Order to Mrs. Mary Raynolds, widow & Exec. of Est. of her husb.
Capt. PETER RAYNOLDS of Brist., dtd. 28 June 1728 [6:125/6].

Will of PETER RAYNOLDS of Brist., dtd. 8 Dec. 1726, prob. 28
June 1728. Wife Mary. Sons: Peter (eldest), Eleazer & Nathaniel (under 21) Raynolds. Dau. Mary Raynolds (under 18). Wife
Mary as Exec. Witns: Samuel Howland, Abigail Howland & Samuel Howland, Jr. [6:126/7].

Acct. of Benjamin & Hezekiah Carpenter, Adms. of Est. of BENJA-
MIN CARPENTER of Swan., dtd. 18 June 1728. Mentions Job Carpenter & Jotham Carpenter [6:128].

Appt. of William Easterbrooks of Swan. as guard. of Charles
Easterbrooks (over 14), son of JOHN EASTERBROOKS of Swan., dtd.
18 June 1728 [6:129].

Appt. of Thomas Kinney as Adm. of Est. of his father JOHN KINNEY
of Dart., dtd. 10 July 1728 [6:130/1].

Inv. of Est. of JOHN KINNEY of Dart., dtd. 6 July 1728, pres.
by Thomas Kinney, Adm. Apprs: William Sponer, John West &
Stephen West [6:131].

Appt. of Stephen West of Dart. as guard. of Abigail & Hannah
Kinney, daus. of JOHN KINNEY of Dart., dtd. 11 July 1728[6:132].

Appt. of Lemuel Pope of Dart. as guard. of Seth, Hannah & Deborah Hathaway (all over 14), chldn. of JONATHAN HATHAWAY of
Dart., dtd. 10 July 1728 [6:132/3].

Appt. of Samuel Vial, Esq., of Brist. as guard. of Joseph Vial
(over 14), son of JONATHAN VIAL of Barr., dtd. 20 July 1728
[6:133].

Appt. of Martha Taber, widow, as Adm. of Est. of THOMAS TABER
of Brist. dcd. intest., dtd. 26 July 1728 [6:134].

Inv. of Est. of JOHN SLACK of Attl., dtd. 10 June 1728, pres.

by Bethiah Slack, his widow & Adm. Apprs: Samuel Day, Noah
Carpenter & Anthony Sprauge [*sic*][6:134/5].
Inv. of Est. of WILLIAM SLACK of Attl., dtd. 18 Nov. 1727, pres.
by Thomas Slack, his son & Exec. Apprs: Noah Carpenter, Sam-
uel Day & Jonathan Fuller [6:135/6].
Order to Jonathan Phiney, Exec. of Est. of his father JONATHAN
PHINEY of Swan., dtd. 20 Aug. 1728 [6:136].
Will of JONATHAN PHINEY of Swan., Yeoman, dtd. 27 Aug. 1724,
prob. 20 Aug. 1728. Wife Joannah. Son Jonathan Phiney. Daus:
Joannah Clerk, Elizabeth Bradford, Mary Clerk, Lidia Potter &
Hannah Phiney. Son Jonathan to be Exec. Witns: Daniel Luther,
John Phiney & John Kinnicut [6:137/8].
Inv. of Est. of JOSIAH CARPENTER of Reho., dtd. 19 Apr. 1728,
pres. by Elizabeth Carpenter, his widow & Adm. Apprs: Benja-
min Hunt, Abiah Carpenter & Daniel Carpenter [6:138/9].
Acct. of Edward Gray, "only Surviving Executor" of Est. of his
father THOMAS GRAY of Lit. Comp., dtd. 20 Aug. 1728. Incl.
legacies per will to: Phebe Gray, William Richmond, John Pea-
body & Edward Gray. Mentions "my brother Thomas" [6:140/1].
Order to Mary Brownel, widow & Exec. of Est. of her husb. ROB-
ERT BROWNEL of Lit. Comp., dtd. 20 Aug. 1728 [6:14].
Will of ROBERT BROWNEL of Lit. Comp., dtd. 29 Jan. 1717/8, prob.
20 Aug. 1728. Wife Mary. Sons: Thomas & Benjamin Brownel.
Daus: Patience, Margaret & Ann [*no surname*]. Dau. Mary's 3
chldn. [*not named*]. Grson. Wilbour. Wife Mary as Exec. & Thom-
as Brownel, Jr. & Joseph Wilbour, Jr. to be overseers. Witns:
John Wilbour, Jr., Charles Brownel & Edward Richmond[6:142/3].
Inv. of Est. of ROBERT BROWNEL of Lit. Comp., dtd. 17 [*no month*]
1728, pres. by Mary Brownel, his widow & Exec. Apprs: John
Palmer, William West & Joseph Southworth [6:143/4].
Rcpt. by Caleb Walker for money from Est. of his father EBENE-
ZER WALKER of Reho., having been paid to David Carpenter,
guard. of Caleb, rcvd. from Daniel Carpenter of Reho., dtd.
2 Nov. 1727. Witns: Timothy Read & Eleazer Carpenter[6:144].
Appt. of Elesebeth Davis of Brist. as guard. of Elezebeth & Mary
Makentosh, daus. of LANTHLAND MAKENTOSH of Brist. dcd. & grdaus
of HENERY MAKENTOSH of Brist., dtd. 23 Aug. 1728 [6:144].
Inv. of Est. of THOMAS TABER of Brist., dtd. 12 Aug. 1728, pres.
by Martha Taber, his widow & Adm. Apprs: John Glading, Jr.,
N: Woodbury & Jeremiah Phiney, Jr. [6:145].
Acct. of Anna Williams, widow & Adm. of Est. of her husb. RICH-
ARD WILLIAMS of Taun., dtd. 26 Aug. 1728 [6:146].
Acct. of Patience Church, widow & Adm of Est. of her husb. Capt.
CONSTANT CHURCH of Free., dtd. 6 Sept. 1728 [6:147/8].
Inv. of Est. of MARY LINKON of Taun., pres. 11 Sept. 1728 by
Nathaniel Linkon, Adm. Apprs: Morgan Cobb, John Mason & Mor-
gan Cobb, 2nd [6:149].
Acct. of Nathaniel Linkon, Adm. of Est. of MARY LINKON of Taun.
dtd. 11 Sept. 1728 [6:149/50].

Inv. of Est. of SOLOMON MILLARD of Reho., dtd. 2 March 1727/8,
pres. by N. Millard, his brother & Adm. Apprs: James Bowen,
Samuel Bullock & Jacob Ormsby [6:150].

Acct. of Seth Babit, Adm. of Est. of TIMOTHY COOPER of Easton,
dtd. 12 Sept. 1728. Incl. paym: "To morning Apparill for the
widdow & Children," to Deborah Cooper, to Tabitha Cooper & to
Lidiah Cooper [6:151/2].

Acct. of Bethiah Lyon, Adm. of Est. of her husb. BENJAMIN LYON
of Reho., dtd. 17 Sept. 1728. Incl. paym. to Elizabeth Lyon,
to John Lyon & to Caleb Lyon [6:152/3].

Acct. of Samuel Hunt & John Jenne, Execs. of Est. of JOHN JENNE
of Dart., dtd. 17 Sept. 1728. Incl. paym. of legacies per will
to: Susanah Saverey,Lidiah Benson wife of Joseph Benson, Gideon Gifferd & Sarah Sharman [6:153].

Appt. of Mrs. Hannah Russel, widow, as Adm. of Est. of her husb.
SETH RUSSEL of Dart., dcd. intest., dtd. 17 Sept. 1728[6:154].

Inv. of Est. of SETH RUSSEL of Dart., dtd. 20 Aug. 1728, pres.
by Hannah Russel, his widow & Adm. Apprs: Joseph Russel, Deliverance Smith & William Bowdish [6:155/6].

Order to Patience Pratt, widow, & Samuel Pratt, son, Execs. of
Est. of SAMUEL PRATT of Taun., dtd. 17 Sept. 1728 [6:156].

Will of SAMUEL PRATT, Sr. of Taun., dtd. 31 May 1728, prob. 17
Sept. 1728. Wife Patience. Sons: Josiah, Jonathan, Benjamin,
Samuel, Peter & Paul Pratt. Daus: Hannah Pratt (under 20) &
Patience Pratt (under 18)(both unmar.). Grson. Samuel Caswell.
Wife Patience & son Samuel as Execs. Witns: Morgan Cobb, 2nd,
Nathaniel Knap, Jr. & David Pollard [6:156/7/8/9].

Appt. of Susanah Hathaway of Dart. as guard. of Jonathan, Silas
& Elnathan Hathaway (all under 14), sons of JONATHAN HATHAWAY
of Dart., dtd. 17 Sept. 1728 [6:159/60].

Acct. of Rachel Allen, widow & Exec. of Est. of her husb. IN-
CREASE ALLEN of Dart., dtd. 17 Sept. 1728. Incl. paym. of legacies per will to Elesebeth Allen & Dinah Allen [6:160].

Acct. of Marcy Davis of Attl., widow & Adm. of Est. of her husb.
JOSEPH DAVIS of Attl., dtd. 15 Oct. 1728 [6:160/70][*page numbering error*].

Order to Esther Trasher, widow & Exec. of Est. of her husb.
CHRISTOPHER TRASHER of Taun., dtd. 8 Oct. 1728 [6:171].

Will of CHRISTOPHER THRESHER of Taun., dtd. 17 Apr. 1728, prob.
8 Oct. 1728. Wife Esther. 3 sons: Daniel, Christopher & Azariah (all under 21). 3 daus: Marcy, Esther & Abiah (all under
18 and unmar.). Land from my father John Thrasher. Wife Esther as Exec. Witns: William Canady, Elkanah Leonard & Israel Thrasher [6:171/2].

Div. of Est. of Capt. SAMUEL LOW of Barr., btwn. his widow [*not
named*] & his chldn: son Samuel Low, dau. Rachel Dehane & dau.
Ann Malein, dtd. 29 March 1727/8. Comm: Samuel Humphrey, Nathaniel Peck, Samuel Kent, Elisha May & Joseph Mason, Jr. [6:
172/3].

Inv. of Est. of the Rev. Mr. SAMUEL DANFORTH of Taun., dtd. 31
Jan. 1727/8, pres. by Samuel Danforth, his son & Exec. Apprs:
N. Fisher, Joseph Avery & Othniel Campbell [6:173/4].
Acct. of Hannah Pool, Adm. of Est. of BENJAMIN POOL of Digh.,
dtd. 19 Nov. 1728. Incl. paym. "To the widdow for her Charge
in Lying in With Two Imposthumus Childreen" [6:174].
Acct. of Daniel Smith, Adm. of Est. of DANIEL SMITH of Reho.,
dtd. 19 Nov. 1728 [6:175].
Acct. of Hannah Haile, Adm. of Est. of JOHN HAILE of Swan., dtd.
19 Nov. 1728. Incl. paym. of debts to: Anne Haile, Barnard
Haile & "mother Haile" [6:175/6].
Appt. of Jacob Ormsbe of Reho. as Adm. of Est. of his sister
ESTHER REDAWAY of Reho., dtd. 19 Nov. 1728 [6:176/7].
Order for div. of real est. of JONATHAN CARPENTER of Reho. dcd.
intest., btwn. his widow & chldn., dtd. 21 Feb. 1728[6:177].
Div. of Est. of JONATHAN CARPENTER of Reho. btwn. his widow Han-
nah & chldn: eldest son [not named] who has dcd. since his
father, 2nd son Abisha, eldest dau. Hannah [no surname], 2nd
dau. Martha Carpenter, 3rd dau. Zerviah Carpenter, 4th dau.
Hepzebeth Carpenter & youngest dau. Sarah Carpenter, dtd. 19
Nov. 1728. Comm: Abiah Carpenter, Daniel Perrin & Daniel Car-
penter [6:178/9/80].
Appt. of Mrs. Deborah Carr, widow, as Adm. of Est. of her husb.
ESEK CARR of Lit. Comp. dcd. intest., dtd. 22 Nov. 1728[6:181].
Order to Isaac Mason & John Wood, Jr., both of Swan., & James
Lewis of Reho., Execs. of Est. of JOHN MILLARD of Reho., dtd.
5 Dec. 1728 [6:181/2].
Will of JOHN MILLARD of Reho., Yeoman, dtd. 23 Nov. 1728, prob.
5 Dec. 1728. Wife Deborah. 5 sons: Robert, Barnard, John, Job
& James Millard. 2 daus: Keziah Millard & Experiance Millard.
Gives to his wife "all the Goods and Whatsoever She brought
with her to me When I married her." Mentions he supposes his
wife is now "with Child." 3 trusty friends Isaac Mason, John
Wood, Jr. & James Lewis as Execs. Witns: James Bowen, Elisha
Bowen & Seth Eddy [6:182/3].
Order to Daniel Luther, Exec. of Est. of his father THEOPHILUS
LUTHER of Swan., dtd. 17 Dec. 1728 [6:184].
Will of THEOPHELUS LUTHER of Swan., dtd. 18 Aug. 1721, prob. 17
Dec. 1728. No wife mentioned. Sons: Theophelus (eldest), Mar-
tin, Nathan, John, Oliver & Daniel Luther. 2 daus: Joanah &
Mary [no surnames]. Mentions my brother Joshua. Witns: Thom-
as Easterbrooks, Ebenezer Luther & Joseph Mason [6:184/5].
Appt. of Mrs. Anne Allen, widow, as Adm. of Est. of her husb.
NEHEMIAH ALLEN of Attl. dcd. intest., dtd. 17 Dec. 1728 [6:
185/6].
Inv. of Est. of NEHEMIAH ALLEN of Attl., dtd. 9 Dec. 1728, pres.
by Anne Allen, his widow & Adm. Apprs. not named [6:186].
Inv. of Est. of JOHN MILLARD of Reho., pres. 27 Dec. 1728 by
[left blank space], Exec. Apprs: Jonathan Kingsley, James

Bowen & Elisha Bowen. Mentions that part which was given to his wife per will [6:187/8].

Appt. of John Wood, Jr. of Swan. as guard. of Robert Millard (over 14) & Keziah Millard (under 14), chldn. of JOHN MILLARD of Reho., dtd. 27 Dec. 1728 [6:188].

Quit-claim & release by Isaac Gorham of New Haven, Ct., Cooper, of any right to land in Brist. owned by his dcd. father JABEZ GORHAM of Brist., in return for legacy from his brother Benjamin Gorham of Brist., Tanner, dtd. 18 May 1725, recorded 10 Jan. 1728/9 Witns: Samuel Howland & Abigail Howland [6:189].

Quit-claim & release by Joseph Gorham of Fairfield, Ct., Cordwinder, of all right to land in Brist. owned by his dcd. father JABEZ GORHAM of Brist. [remainder identical to above quit-claim by his brother Isaac], dtd. 17 June 1725. Witns: Jabiz Gorham & Joseph Howland [6:190].

Appt. of Samuel Millard of Swan. as guard. of Job Millard (under 14), son of JOHN MILLARD of Reho., dtd. 1 Jan. 1728/9 [6:191].

Appt. of John Horton of Reho. as guard. of John Millar (under 14), son of JOHN MILLAR of Reho., dtd. 1 Jan. 1728/9[6:191/2].

Appt. of Isaac Mason of Swan. as guard. of Experiance & Barnard Millar (both under 14), chldn. of JOHN MILLAR of Reho., dtd. 1 Jan. 1728/9 [6:192].

Quit-claim by James Danforth of Taun., Husbandman, & his wife Sarah, to his brother Samuel Danforth of Taun., Clothier, of any rights to Est. of his father SAMUEL DANFORTH of Taun., James already having rcvd. his portion, dtd. 2 Feb. 1727/8. Witns: Jacob Barney & Ephraim Hodges [6:192/3].

Release by John Walley "now living in Roxbury," Co. of Suffolk, in consideration of a tract of land near Wocester, releases Samuel Danforth of Taun., Clark, of any claims by said Walley "for the Entertaynment given at my house unto Sarah Danforth Hannah Danforth Thomas Danforth & Bethiah Danforth severall years in their minority while I lived at Boston or on account of sd Thomas Danforth leaving my Service in the time of the Small pox at Boston." Sarah Danforth is now wife of William Downs of Boston, Upholder, dtd. 31 July 1723 [sic]. Witns: Larance Hart & Ebenezer Campbel [6:193].

Quit-claim by Thomas Danforth of Taun., Brasier, "one of the children of yᵉ Revᵈ Samuel Danforth lately deceased," to his brother Samuel Danforth of Taun., Clothier, all further rights in the Est. of their father SAMUEL DANFORTH, dtd. 18 March 17-17/8. Witns: James Varney & Othiel Campbel [6:194].

Quit-claim by William Downs of Boston, Upholder, & Sarah his wife, she being one of the daus. of the Rev. SAMUEL DANFORTH of Taun., to her brother Samuel Danforth of Taun. as Exec. of their father's Est., dtd. at Boston 22 Feb. 1727/8. Witns: James Varney & Hannah Danforth [6:194/5].

Order to Samuel & Joseph Coe, Execs. of Est. of their father

JOHN COE of Lit. Comp., dtd. 21 Jan. 1728/9 [6:195].
Rcpt. & release by Jacob Barney of Taun., Blacksmith, as guard.
of Bethiah, Rachel & Katherine Danforth, chldn. of the Rev.
SAMUEL DANFORTH of Taun., for paym. of their legacies from
Est. of their father, as paid by their brother Samuel Danforth
of Taun., Fuller, Exec. of said Est., dtd. 22 Feb. 1727/8 [6:
196].
Quit-claim by Jacob Barney of Taun., Blacksmith, & Mary his wife
dau. of the Rev. SAMUEL DANFORTH of Taun., to her brother Samuel Danforth of Taun., Clothier, Exec. of their father's Est.,
quitting claim to any further rights in said Est., dtd. 22 Feb.
1727/8 [6:196/7].
Quit-claim by Hannah Danforth of Taun., dau. of the Rev. SAMUEL
DANFORTH of Taun., to her brother Samuel Danforth of Taun.,
Clothier, Exec. of their father's Est., quitting claim to any
further rights in said Est., dtd. 22 Feb. 1727/8 [6:197].
Will of JOHN COE of Lit. Comp., Husbandman, dtd. 4 Dec. 1728,
prob. 21 Jan. 1728/9. Wife Sarah. Sons: Samuel (eldest), John
(2nd) & Joseph (3rd) Coe. Daus: Lidia (eldest) wife of John
Bailey, Jr., Sarah (2nd) wife of Samuel Tomkins, Elezebeth
(3rd) wife of Edward Burgess & Hannah (youngest) [no surname].
Sons Samuel & Joseph as Execs. Mentions lands in Casco Bay.
Witns: Thomas Church, John Peabody & William Richmond[6:198/9].
Inv. of Est. of JOHN COE of Lit. Comp., dtd. 9 Jan. 1728, pres.
by Samuel & Joseph Coe, his sons & Execs. Apprs: Joseph South-
worth, William Richmond & Edward Gray [6:199/200].
Appt. of Jethniel Peck of Reho. as Adm. of Est. of his son SOL-
OMON PECK of Reho. dcd. intest., dtd. 21 Jan. 1728/9[6:200/1].
Appt. of Mrs. Elezebeth Linzey, widow, as Adm. of Est. of her
husb. JOHN LINZEY of Brist., dtd. 21 Jan. 1728/9 [6:201].
Order to Joseph & James Dean, Execs. of Est. of JOSEPH DEAN of
Digh., dtd. 11 Feb. 1728/9 [6:202].
Will of JOSEPH DEAN of Digh., Yeoman, dtd. 23 Dec. 1728, prob.
11 Feb. 1728/9. Wife Mary. Sons: Joseph (eldest), Samuel &
James Dean. Grson. Joseph Read. Dau. Sarah Read. To wife Mary
20 pounds money, "which I have Covenanted with her before
Marriage." Witns: Benjamin Jones, John Tew & George Bliss
[6:202/3].
Appt. of Samuel Gallop of New London, Ct. as Adm. of Est. of
his brother NATHANIEL GALLOP of Brist. dcd. intest., dtd. 18
Feb. 1728/9 [6:204].
Appt. of Marcy Knap, widow, as Adm. of Est. of her husb. JOHN
KNAP of Taun. dcd. intest., dtd. 18 Feb. 1728/9 [6:204/5].
Inv. of Est. of SAMUELL PRATT of Taun., dtd. 23 Oct. 1728,
pres. by Patience Pratt, his widow, & Samuel Pratt, his son,
Execs. Apprs: John Andrews, John Mason & Morgan Cobb, 2nd
[6:205].
Inv. of Est. of ESEK CARR, Jr. of Lit. Comp., dtd. 10 Feb. 17-
28/9, pres. by Deborah Carr, his widow & Adm. Note in margin

says that the Inv. of part of the Est. of Benjamin Head be-
longed by will to his widow, who is now the widow of said ES-
EK CARR, and it was not divided out when this present Inv. of
Esek Carr was taken. Said Inv. is on page 233. Apprs: John
Wood, Thomas Brownel & Joseph Southworth [6:206].

Inv. of Est. of NATHANIEL GALLOP of Brist., dtd. 18 Feb. 1728/9
pres. by Samuel Gallop, his brother & Adm. Apprs: William
Throope, Samuel Royal & Samuel Howland [6:206/7].

Acct. of John Paine, Exec. of Est. of RALPH PAINE of Free., dtd.
19 Feb. 1728/9. Mentions paym. "To a Coffin for his Wife."
[6:207].

Inv. of Est. of THOMAS LINKON of Taun. dcd. intest., dtd. 17 Apr.
1728, pres. by Josiah Linkon, brother & Adm. Mentions paym.
"for John Linkon father to the Intestate." Apprs: Samuel
Pratt, John Mason & Morgan Cobb, 2nd [6:208].

Acct. of Nathaniel Millard of Reho., Adm. of Est. of his brother SOLOMON MILLARD of Reho. dcd. intest., dtd. 19 Feb. 17-
28/9. Mentions paym. "for funeral Charges of ye Entestate &
his Wife" [6:208/9].

Appt. of Thomas Church, Esq. of Lit. Comp. as guard. of William
Dye of Lit. Comp. "who is non Compus mentis," dtd. 3 March
1728/9 [6:210].

Appt. of Abigail Carpenter, widow, as Adm. of Est. of her husb.
JOSEPH CARPENTER of Brist., dtd. 3 March 1728/9 [6:210/1].

Order to William Gallop of Brist., Exec. of Est. of SARAH SMITH
of Brist., dtd. 6 March 1728/9. Mentions that Elisha Calendar
one of the Execs. to Est. of Sarah Smith relinquished his Exec.,
the "other Executor Living in York Administration is granted to
Willm Gallop alone" [6:211].

Will of SARAH SMITH of Brist., widow & formerly Exec. & widow of
Est. of Edward Antill of the City of New York, Gentleman.,
dtd. 26 Dec. 1725, prob. 6 March 1728/9. Sons William & Edward
Antill. Daus: Elezebeth Callender & Mary Gallop. Grdau. Elezebeth Gallop dau. of my dau. Mary. Mentions lands on "north
or hudsons River" and in Minevaird East Jersey. Incl. a negro
woman called Issabell. Son Edward Antill, & sons-in-law Elisha
Callender & William Gallop as Execs. Witns: William Munroe,
Capt. Thomas Lawton, Ebbinton [sic] and John Sampson[6:212/3].

Codicil by SARAH SMITH of Brist., widow, dtd. 10 Feb. 1726/7.
Negro woman Isabel. Witns: Samuel Howland, Elizabeth McIn-
toshe & Samuel Howland, Jr. [6:213].

Rcpt. & discharge by Marcy Slocum of Newport, widow, for land
from Est. of her father RALPH PAINE of Free., as rcvd. from
John Paine of Free., Exec., dtd. 13 March 1728/9. Witns: Jacob Hathway & Anthoney Dodson [6:213/4].

Rcpt. & discharge by Amos Briggs of Free. & Sarah his wife, for
land from Est. of her father RALPH PAINE of Free., as rcvd.
from John Paine of Free., Exec., dtd. 30 March 1728. Witns:
Jacob Hathway & Anthoney Dodson [6:214].

Appt. of Hannah Hail of Swan. as guard. of Barnard, Freelove &
Liles Hail (all over 14) & of Hannah Hail (under 14), chldn.
of JOHN HAIL of Swan., dtd. 12 March 1728/9 [6:215].
Rcpt. & discharge by Adam Jones of Digh., Cordwinder, & Mary
his wife, for a legacy from the Est. of her father STEPHEN
PECKHAM of Dart., paid by William Peckham of Dart., Currier &
Exec., dtd. 16 Dec. 1725. Witns: Bartholomew West & Timothy
Ruggles [6:215].
Appt. of James Redaway of Reho. as guard. of Easter Redaway (un-
der 14), dau. of PRESERVED REDAWAY of Reho., dtd. 18 March
1728/9 [6:216].
Appt. of Benjamin Wilbour of Taun. as guard. of James Danforth
"who is non Compus Mentis," dtd. 18 March 1728/9 [6:216].
Appt. of David Turner of Reho. as guard. of Marcy, Ruth & Jere-
miah Millard (all over 14), chldn. of SOLOMON MILLARD of Re-
ho., dtd. 18 March 1728/9 [6:217].
Appt. of John Manchester as Adm. of Est. of his mother MARY GRAY
(widow of Edward Gray) of Tiv., dtd. 18 March 1728/9[6:217/8].
Quit-claim by Jabez Delino of Dart., Carpenter, & his wife Han-
nah, to any further rights in Est. of her father STEPHEN PECK-
HAM, having rcvd. a legacy paid by William Peckham of Dart.,
Currier & Exec., dtd. 16 Dec. 1725. Witns: Bartholomew West
& Timothy Ruggles [6:218].
Inv. of Est. of widow ESTHER REDAWAY of Reho., dtd. 7 Dec. 1728,
pres. by Jacob Ormsbe, Adm. Apprs: Jethniel Peck, Jr., Dan-
iel Smith & James Redaway [6:218/9].
Acct. of Jacob Ormsbe, Adm. of Est. of his sister ESTHER REDA-
WAY, dtd. 18 March 1728/9. Mentions paym. for 12 weeks of care
& nursing [6:219].
Acct. of Simon Burr, Adm. of Est. of his brother ISAAC BURR of
Reho., dtd. 18 March 1728/9. Incl. a paym. "to mother Mary
Burr" [6:219/20].
Inv. of Est. of William Dye of Lit. Comp. "who is demed non
Compus mentis," dtd. 15 March 1728, pres. by Thomas Church,
his guard. Apprs: Jonathan Thurston, Joseph Southworth & Wil-
liam Richmond [6:220].
Acct. of Mary Peckham, Exec. of Est. of her husb. STEPHEN PECK-
HAM of Dart., dtd. 18 March 1728/9 [6:221].
Acct. of Susanah Taber, widow & Exec. of Est. of her husb. JOHN
TABER of Dart., dtd. 18 March 1728/9 [6:221/2].
Order for div. of Est. of NATHANIEL GALLOP of Brist., btwn. his
brothers & sisters, dtd. 19 Feb. 1728/9 [6:222].
Div. of real est. of NATHANIEL GALLOP of Brist. dcd. intest.,
btwn. his brothers & sisters: Samuel Gallop, William Gallop,
Elezebeth Bowerman & Mary Bailey, dtd. 19 Feb. 1728/9. Comm:
William Throope, Samuel Royal, Samuel Little, Samuel Smith &
William Walker [6:222/3].
Acct. of Yetmarcy Howland, widow, & Samuel Howland, brother, Adms.
of Est. of JOSIAH HOWLAND of Brist., dtd. 25 Feb. 1728/9. Men-

tions: property "sold to Brother Jabiz Howland;" paym. to "Samuel Howland for his Quarter part of the house;" paym. "to Joseph Howland which was due on the Last Division" & paym. "to Mother Howland for her Yearly Allowance" [6:223/4].

Order to Jonathan Slead, Exec. of Est. of his father WILLIAM SLEAD of Swan., dtd. 15 Apr. 1729 [6:225].

Will of WILLIAM SLEAD of Shewamet in Swan., Yeoman, dtd. 16 March 1729, prob. 15 Apr. 1729. Wife Sarah. Sons: William, Jonathan & Edward. 7 daus: Sarah wife of Silvanus Sole, Mary wife of John Winslow, Elezabeth wife of Barnard Haile, Hannah wife of James Wheaten, Martha wife of James Luther, Phebe wife of Stephen Bowen & Lidia wife of Ebenezer Baker. Incl. a negro girl Mareah & "my Two Slaves Viz my Negro Man Sampson & my Spanish Indian man Roger." Son Jonathan as Exec. Witns: John Read, Samuel Lee & Samuel Gardner [6:225/6].

Inv. of Est. of MARY GRAY of Tiv., widow, dtd. 19 March 1728/9, pres. by John Manchester, her brother & Adm. Apprs: Samuel Sanford, John Sisson & Thomas Gray [6:227].

Inv. of Est. of THOMAS WISE of Attl., dtd. 10 June 1728, pres. by Benjamin Wise, his son & Exec. Apprs: Samuel Day, Noah Carpenter & Anthony Sprauge [6:227/8].

Inv. of Est. of NICHOLAS WHITE of Norton, dtd. 4 Dec. 1728, pres. by Nicholas White, his son & Exec. Mentions "his son Matthew" & "his son Nicholas." Apprs: Joseph Hodges, William Stone & Benjamin Williams [6:228/9].

Inv. of Est. of JOHN LINZEY of Brist., dtd. 15 Feb. 1728/9, pres. by Elezebeth Linzey, his widow & Adm. Apprs: William Throope, Samuel Royal & Samuel Smith [6:229/30].

Inv. of Est. of JOSEPH CARPENTER of Brist., dtd. 27 March 1729, pres. by Abigail Carpenter, his widow & Adm. Apprs: William Munroe, Thomas Lawton & William Walker [6:230/1].

Acct. of Hezekiah Luther, Exec. of Est. of his father HEZEKIAH LUTHER of Swan., dtd. 23 Apr. 1729. Incl. paym. for "Grave Stones for ye deceaseds Wife" [6:231].

Appt. of Mrs. Judath Streeter, widow, & John Streeter, son, as Adms. of Est. of JOHN STREETER of Attl. dcd. intest., dtd. 5 May 1729 [6:232].

Appt. of Ebenezer Dean of Taun. as guard. of Seth, Mary, Benjamin & Damaris White (all under 14), chldn. of NICHOLAS WHITE of Norton [Farther down a partially erased "Nicholas" has been written over to read "theire Father Mathew White."], dtd. 8 May 1729 [6:232/3].

Inv. of remainder of Est. of EZEK CARR of Lit. Comp., dtd. 24 Feb. 1728/9, pres. by Deborah Carr, his widow & Exec. Mentions this is "Part of y^e Estate of $Benj^n$ Head Which by his Will belonged to his widdow y^e Now Widdow of Eseck Carr," reference being made to page 206. Apprs: John Palmer, Thomas Brownel & Joseph Southworth [6:233].

Order to Thomas Wood of Lit. Comp., Exec. of Est. of his father THOMAS WOOD of Lit. Comp., dtd. 20 May 1729 [6:233/4].

Appt. of Anthoney Sprauge, Adm. of Est. of his father ANTHONEY
    SPRAUGE of Attl., dtd. 20 May 1729 [6:234/5].
Acct. of Jonathan Russel, Exec. of Est. of his father JONATHAN
    RUSSEL of Dart., dtd. 20 May 1729. Mentions residuary legatees
    Deborah Allen & Dorothey Shearman, & legacies to George Rus-
    sel & Jonathan Russel [6:235].
Will of THOMAS WOOD of Lit. Comp., dtd. 22 Aug. 1728, prob. 20
    May 1729. No wife mentioned. Sons Thomas & John Wood. Daus:
    Elezebeth Phiney, Content Shaw, Rebecca Shaw, Mary Sisson, De-
    sire Wood & Deliverance Wood. Grdau. Content Sisson (under 14).
    Son Thomas as Exec. Witns: William Wilbour, Jonathan Sisson
    & Isaac Wilbour [6:235/6].
Inv. of Est. of THOMAS WOOD of Lit. Comp., dtd. 15 May 1729,
    pres. by Thomas Wood, son & Exec. Apprs. not listed[6:236/7].
Acct. of William Briggs, Exec. of Est. of BENJAMIN HEAD of Lit.
    Comp., dtd. 20 May 1729. Incl. paym. of 1/3rd of pers. est.
    "to his Widdow" [6:238].
Acct. of Jonathan Russel, Exec. of Est. of his father JONATHAN
    RUSSEL of Dart. No date given [6:238].
Inv. of Est. of JONATHAN PHINEY of Swan., dtd. 18 Nov. 1728,
    pres. by Jonathan Phiney, son & Exec. Apprs: Samuel Mason,
    Ebenezer Luther & Barnard Haile [6:239].
Inv. of Est. of ANTHONEY SPRAUGE of Attl., dtd. 14 May 1729,
    pres. by Anthoney Sprauge, son & Adm. Apprs: Noah Carpenter,
    Elisha Peck & Israel Whiple [6:239/40].
Order to Joseph Wilbour, Exec. of Est. of his father JOSEPH WIL-
    BOUR of Lit. Comp., dtd. 5 June 1729 [6:240].
Will of JOSEPH WILBOUR of Lit. Comp., Yeoman, dtd. 11 Jan. 17-
    27/8, prob. 5 June 1729. Wife Anna. Sons: William, Joseph,
    John, Thomas, Benjamin & Stephen Wilbour. Daus: Anna Wood,
    Mary Eldridge & Abigail Wilbour. Grsons. Josiah Closson & Tim-
    othy Closson. Son-in-law Thomas Burgg. Son Joseph as Exec.
    Witns: John Price, Joseph Simmons & Richard Billings, 2nd.
    [6:240/1/2].
Codicil by JOSEPH WILBOUR of Lit. Comp., dtd. 23 Apr. 1729. Sons
    Joseph, William & Thomas Wilbour. Grchldn: Joseph Burrg, John
    Burgg, Jacob Burgg & Mary Burrg. Witns: Joseph Simmons, Rich-
    ard Billings & Gideon Southworth [6:242].
Inv. of JOSEPH WILBOUR of Lit. Comp., dtd. 2 June 1729, pres.
    by Joseph Wilbour, son & Exec. Apprs: John Wood, Thomas
    Brownel & Joseph Southworth [6:243].
Appt. of James Tripp of Dart. as guard. of Stephen Wilcox of
    Lit. Comp. "who is non Compus mentis," dtd. 17 June 1729 [6:
    244].
Appt. of William Briggs of Lit. Comp. as guard. of William
    Head (over 14), son of BENJAMIN HEAD of Lit. Comp., dtd. 17
    June 1729 [6:244].
Order to Patience West & Samuel Lee, Execs. of Est. of RICHARD
    WEST of Tiv. [sic], dtd. 17 June 1729 [6:245].

Will of RICHARD WEST of Free., Shipwrite, "being very Sick,"
dtd. 26 May 1729, prob. 17 June 1729. Wife Patience. Son Thomas (under age). Mentions his lands in Free. as well as "all
my Estate Rights & previlidges ... coming to me in Portsmouth
in the County of Hampshire in Grait Brittain ... for Service
done on bord his majesties Shipp Capt Norris Commandor." Wife
Patience & "my Brother Samuel Lee" as Execs. Witns: Richard
Harding, Hezekiah Luther & Thomas Cornall [6:245/6].
Inv. of Est. of RICHARD WEST of Free., dtd. 11 June 1729, pres.
by Patience West & Samuel Lee, Execs. Apprs: John Read, Sam-
uel Forman & Stephen Southworth [6:246].
Order to Joseph Davenport, Exec. of Est. of his father JONATHAN
DAVENPORT of Lit. Comp. dtd. 17 June 1729 [6:246/7].
Will of JONATHAN DAVENPORT of Lit. Comp., Carpenter, dtd. 28
March 1729, prob. 17 June 1729. Wife Hannah. Sons: Thomas,
Jonathan, Simon (unmar.), Ebenezer, John, Joseph & Benjamin
Davenport. Daus: Hannah House & Sarah Davenport (unmar.). Son
Joseph as Exec. Witns: Samuel Crandel, James Fisher & Nathan-
iel Searels [6:247/8].
Appt. of Mrs. Hannah King of Tiv. as Adm. of Est. of her son
JOSEPH KING of Lit. Comp. dcd. intest., dtd. 17 June 1729
[6:248/9].
Acct. of Mary Devil, widow & Adm. of Est. of her husb. JOSEPH
DEVIL of Dart., dtd. 17 June 1729. Incl. diff. paym. to Jer-
emiah Devil [6:249/50].
Order for div. of Est. of SOLOMON MILLARD of Reho., dtd. 18
March 1728/9 [6:250].
Div. of Est. of SOLOMON MILLARD of Reho. btwn. his chldn: Da-
vid Millard (eldest son), Elizebeth Millard (eldest dau.),
Jeremiah Millard (2nd son), Rebecca Millard (2nd dau.), Mercy
Millard & Ruth Millard, dtd. 14 Apr. 1729. Comm: James Bowen,
Samuel Bullock, Jacob Ormsbee, Nathaniel Smith & Jathniel Peck
Jr. [6:250/1/2].
Appt. of Martha Reed, widow, as Adm. of Est. of her husb. THOMAS
REED of Reho., "with ye Codicill annexed," dtd. 24 June 1729
[6:252].
Codicil by THOMAS READ, Jr. of Reho., "being Very Sick & not
Capable fully to Settle my Estate Yet onto my Beloved wife
Martha," dtd. 29 Apr. 1729. Incl. money "which Was part of her
father George Barstos Estate." Witns: Abiah Carpenter, John
Read & Daniel Carpenter [6:252/3].
Inv. of Est. of JOHN TOOGOOD of Swan., dtd. 17 March 1729, pres.
by John Toogood, his son & Adm. de bonis non. Apprs: Joseph
Peck, Peter Hunt & Jabiz Bosworth [6:253].
Inv. of Est. of JOHN KNAP of Taun. dcd. intest., dtd. 6 Feb.
1728/9, pres. by Marcy Knap, his widow & Adm. Apprs: James
Leonard, John Mason & Morgan Cobb, 2nd [6:253/4].
Inv. of Est. of JONATHAN DAVENPORT of Lit. Comp., dtd. 21 June
1729, pres. by Joseph Davenport, his son & Exec. Apprs: Jo-

seph Southworth, Elisha Woodworth & Edward Gray [6:254/5].
Acct. of Nicholas White of Norton, Exec. of Est. of his father
  NICHOLAS WHITE of Norton, dtd. 11 July 1729 [6:255/6].
Inv. of Est. of THOMAS READ, Jr. of Reho., dtd. 13 June 1729,
  pres. by Martha Read, his widow & Adm. Apprs: Abiah Carpenter, John Read & Daniel Carpenter [6:257].
Order to Rebecca Bowen, widow & Exec. of Est. of her husb.
  CHRISTOPHER BOWEN of Attl., Husbandman, dtd. 15 July 1729
  [6:258].
Will of CHRISTOPHER BOWEN of Attl., Yeoman, "being Very Sick,"
  dtd. 4 Apr. 1729, prob. 15 July 1729. Wife Rebeca. Sons: Amos
  (eldest, under age), Christopher, Caleb & Nathaniel Bowen.
  Wife to be Exec. & guard. of 2 youngest sons Caleb & Nathaniel. My 2 brothers Icabod Bowen & Dan Bowen to be guards. of
  my 2 eldest sons Amos & Christopher. Witns: Benjamin Crabtree, Dan Bowen & Noah Carpenter, Jr. [6:258/9].
Inv. of Est. of CHRISTOPHER BOWEN of Attl., dtd. 7 July 1729,
  pres. by Rebecca Bowen, his widow & Exec. Apprs: Noah Carpenter, Elisha Peck & Ebenezer Carpenter [6:259/60].
Acct. of Sarah Shelton, widow & Adm. of Est. of her husb. THO-
  MAS SHELTON of Reho., dtd. 15 July 1729 [6:260/1].
Agrmt. btwn. widow & chldn. of DANIEL FISHER, Sr. of Taun., dtd.
  29 July 1707 [sic]. Widow Hannah Fisher called "our aged mo-
  ther." Chldn: Daniel (eldest son), Samuel, Eliazer, Israel,
  Nathaniel, Hannah Brayman wife of Thomas Brayman, Mary Edy
  wife of Ebenezer Edy & Marcy Fisher. Witns: George Leonard,
  John Briggs & Jeremiah Newland. On 19 July 1729 these signers
  appeared in court: Ebenezer Edy, Mary Edy, Daniel Fisher, Eli-
  azer Fisher, Israel Fisher & Nathaniel Fisher [6:261/2].
Order to John Beverly, Exec. of Est. of his father LEONEX BEV-
  ERLY of Reho., Yeoman, dtd. 28 July 1729 [6:263].
Will of LEONEX BEVERLY of Reho., dtd. 29 Oct. 1729 [sic], prob.
  25 July 1729. Wife Sarah. Sons: David, George & John Beverly.
  Daus: Leah Bulluck, Rachel Beverly & Elezebeth Hoskins. Grson.
  Leonex (under 21) eldest son of dau. Leah Bulluck. Wife Sarah
  to get "all the househoold Stuf that She brought to me." Son
  John to be Exec. Mentions lands in Reho., Swan. & Barr. Witns:
  Edward Carpenter, Elizebeth Carpenter & David Turner[6:263/4].
Order to Thomas Terry, Esq., Exec. of Est. of SILAS TERRY of
  Free. [one place mistakenly says "of Tiverton"], dtd. 12 Aug.
  1729 [6:264/5].
Will of SILAS TERRY of Free., "Being Sick & Weeke," dtd. 2 June
  1729, prob. 12 Aug. 1729. Wife Sarah. My child Remember Terry
  (under 18). Wife Sarah to get "all the moveables which She
  brought with her to me." Brother John Terry. Uncle Thomas
  Terry to be Exec. My uncle Benjamin Terry. Mentions my "Lands
  in this Goverment & in Rhode Island Goverment." Also mentions
  "that Part of my fathers moveable Which is in my father Gages
  [?] hands." Witns: Abel Burtt, John Cole & John Tisdale [6:
  265/6].

Inv. of Est. of SILAS TERRY of Free., dtd. 11 Aug. 1729, pres.
by Thomas Terry, Esq., Exec. Apprs: Jonathan Dodson, William
Winslow & Jacob Hathway [6:266/7].

Acct. of Thomas Kinney, Adm. of Est. of his father JOHN KINNEY
of Dart., dtd. 12 Aug. 1729 [6:267].

Inv. of Est. of JOSEPH KING of Lit. Comp., dtd. 26 June 1729,
pres. by Hannah King, Adm. Apprs: William Briggs, John Manchester & Ebenezer Taber [6:267/8].

Order to Stephen West & Nathaniel Spooner, Execs. of Est. of
WILLIAM SPOONER of Dart., dtd. 19 Aug. 1729 [6:268].

Will of WILLIAM SPOONER of Dart., Yeoman, dtd. 11 July 1729,
prob. 12 Aug. 1729. No wife mentioned. Sons: Nathaniel, Isaac
(under 21), William (under age) & Ebenezer (under 12). Daus:
Sarah Spooner, Mary Spooner & Alce Spooner. Grsons: John Badcock & Benjamin Badcock (both under age). Son Nathaniel Spooner & Stephen West, Jr. to be Execs. Witns: John Taber, Samuel Spooner & Samuel Willis [6:268/9/70].

Inv. of Est. of Leiut. WILLIAM SPOONER of Dart., dtd. 15 Aug.
1729, pres. by Stephen West, Exec. Apprs: Seth Spooner, Nathaniel Sapperd & Nathaniel Delano [6:270/1].

Inv. of Est. of Stephen Wilcox of Dart. "who is non Compus mentis," dtd. 11 July 1729, pres. by James Tripp, guard. Apprs:
Samuel Cornell, John Tripp & Beriah Goddard [6:271].

Acct. of Mehetibel Titus formerly widow & Adm of Est. of JOSHUA
ORMSBEE of Reho., dtd. 20 Aug. 1729 [6:271].

Order to Mehetibel Bucklin, widow & Exec. of Est. of her husb.
JOSEPH BUCKLIN of Reho., dtd. 19 Aug. 1729 [6:272].

Will of JOSEPH BUCKLEN of Reho., Yeoman, dtd. 13 Feb. 1727/8,
prob. 19 Aug. 1729. Wife Mehetibel. Sons: Joseph (eldest),
Benjamin, John, Nehemiah, Jonathan & William (youngest, under
21) Bucklin. Daus: Deborah Whiple, Martha Bucklen, Rachel Bucklen & Esther Bucklen. Mentions his lands in Reho., Attl. &
Petucket Falls. Wife Mehetibel as Exec. Witns: Henery Smith,
Samuel Bishop & Noah Carpenter [6:272/3/4].

Codicil by JOSEPH BUCKLEN of Reho., dtd. 19 Aug. 1729. Sons Benjamin, Jonathan, Nehemiah & William Bucklen. Same witns. [6:
275].

Agrmt. btwn. Anna Williams of Taun., widow of THOMAS TERRY of
Free. & her 3 sons: Thomas Terry (eldest), John Terry & Benjamin Terry (youngest, under 21), dtd. 8 June 1704. Partition
made with help of "John Rogers (of Roxbury) the Uncle of the
Said Parties Concerned" & Leut. James Leonard of Taun., Leut.
Job Winslow & Leut. Josiah Winslow of Free. Approved 4 Feb.
1716 [6:275/6/7].

Will of SAMUEL WALDRON of Digh., Yeoman, dtd. 8 Aug. 1727, prob.
19 Aug. 1729. Wife Hannah. Sons: Abraham (eldest), Samuel
(2nd) & Benjamin (3rd) Waldron. Daus: Mary Waldron (eldest)
& Abigail Waldron (2nd). Brother George Waldron of Brist.
Wife Hannah & son Benjamin as Execs. Witns: Samuel Sumner,

Richard Stevens & Nicholas Stevens [6:278/9].

Appt. of Thomas Kinney of Dart. as guard. of Nathaniel Kinney (under 14), son of JOHN KINNEY of Dart., dtd. 19 Aug. 1729 [6:279/80].

Appt. of Silas & Mehetibel Titus of Reho. as guards. of Mary & Ann Ormsbee (both under 14), daus. of JOSHUA ORMSBEE of Reho., dtd. 30 Aug. 1729 [6:280].

Order to David & James Cudworth, Execs. of Est. of their father JAMES CUDWORTH of Free., dtd. 11 Sept. 1729 [6:281].

Will of JAMES CUDWORTH of Free., Yeoman, dtd. March 1729 [*no day given*], prob. 11 Sept. 1729. No wife mentioned. Sons: David & James Cudworth. Daus: Kathiah Davis, Lidia Cudworth, Abigail [*no surname*], Mary Cudworth & Zerviah Cudworth. Sons David & James as Execs. Witns: Edward Shove, John Paul & John Harvey [6:281/2/3].

Inv. of Est. of Capt. JAMES LEONARD of Taun., pres. 11 Sept. 1729 by James & Seth Leonard, Execs. Apprs: John Andrews, John Mason & Samuel Sumner [6:283].

Inv. of Est. of JAMES FOBES, "A free Negro man" of Lit. Comp., dtd. 9 Sept. 1729. pres. by Thomas Church, Adm. Apprs: Aron Davis, William White & John Price [6:284].

Inv. of Est. of James Danforth of Taun., "non Compus mentis," dtd. 10 Sept. 1729, pres. by [*blank space*] Wilbour, guard. Apprs: John Mason, John Godfree & Abiel Dean [6:284/5].

Acct. of Marcy Knap, widow & Adm. of Est. of JOHN KNAP of Taun., dtd. 11 Sept. 1729 [6:285/6].

Acct. of Ann Staples, widow & Adm. of Est. of JOSEPH STAPLES of Taun., dtd. 11 Sept. 1729 [6:286].

Acct. of Patience Church, Adm. of Est. of Capt. CONSTANT CHURCH of Free., dtd. 11 Sept. 1729 [6:287].

Acct. of Abigail Carpenter, widow & Adm. of Est. of JOSEPH CAR-PENTER of Brist., dtd. 11 Sept. 1729 [6:288].

Inv. of Est. of LENOX BEAVERLY of Reho., dtd. 4 Sept. 1729, pres. by John Beaverly, son & Exec. Mentions land adjoining George Beaverly's. Apprs: Jonathan Kingsley, James Bowen & Samuel Bullock [6:288/9].

Acct. of Elizabeth Healy, late widow & Adm. of Est. of OBEDIAH INGRAHAM of Reho., dtd. 17 Sept. 1729 [6:289].

Inv. of Est. of JOHN STREETER of Attl., dtd. 3 July 1729, pres. by Judith Streeter & John Streeter, Adms. Apprs: Samuel Day, Benjamin Wise & John Foster [6:290].

Inv. of Est. of THOMAS REMINGTON of Barr., dtd. 23 July 1729, pres. by Mary Remington, widow & Adm. Apprs: James Addams, John Read & Mathew Allen [6:290/1].

Order to John Wood of Lit. Comp., Exec. of Est. of THOMAS WOOD of Lit. Comp., dtd. 16 Sept. 1729 [6:291].

Will of THOMAS WOOD of Lit. Comp., Yeoman, dtd. 20 Aug. 1729, prob. 16 Sept. 1729. Brother Anthony Shaw & my sister [*not named*] his wife. Sister Desire Wood & sister Deliverance Wood.

Brother John Wood to be Exec. Witns: John Wood, Thomas Bailey & Richard Billings [6:291/2].

Inv. of THOMAS WOOD of Lit. Comp., dtd. 12 Sept. 1729, pres. by John Wood, Adm. Apprs: John Palmer, John Church & Edward Southworth [6:292/3].

Order to Henery Howland, Exec. of Est. of his father HENERY HOWLAND of Dart., dtd. 16 Sept. 1729 [6:293/4].

Will of HENERY HOWLAND of Dart., House Carpenter, dtd. 20 Aug. 1729, prob. 16 Sept. 1729. Wife Elizabeth "haith Unjustly Departed from me & Clandestinely Taken with her Great Part of my househoold Goods." Sons: Zoeth, Henery, Thomas, Stephen & William Howland. 4 daus: Mary, Hannah, Deborah (under 18) & Meribah [no surnames]. Son Henery to be Exec. Witns: Holder Slocum, Thomas Briggs & Beriah Goddard [6:294/5].

Inv. of HENERY HOWLAND of Dart., dtd. 11 Sept. 1729, pres. by Henery Howland, Exec. Apprs: James Howland, William Bowdish & David Akin [6:295/6].

Appt. of Hannah Russel of Dart. as guard. of Elezebeth, Constant & Ruth Russel (all under 14), chldn. of SETH RUSSEL of Dart., dtd. 16 Sept. 1729 [6:296/7].

Inv. of THEOPHILUS LUTHER of Swan., who died 3 Oct. 1725 [sic], dtd. 3 Feb. 1728/9, pres. by Daniel Luther, Exec. Apprs: Joseph Mason, Ebenezer Luther & Benjamin Munroe [6:297].

Acct. of Daniel Luther, Exec. of Est. of THEOPHILUS LUTHER of Swan., dtd. 16 Sept. 1729. Legacies to: Ephraim Hix, Nathan Luther, John Pearce, Oliver Luther & Martin Luther [6:298].

Order to Humphrey Smith, Exec. of Est. of DELIVERANCE SMITH of Dart., Yeoman, the other Exec. having renounced his Exec., dtd. 23 Sept. 1729 [6:298/9].

Will of DELIVERANCE SMITH of Dart., Yeoman, dtd. 23 June 1729, prob. 20 Sept. 1729. Wife Mary. 3 sons: Peleg, Humphrey & George Smith. 6 daus: Deborah, Anne, Alec, Hope, Mary & Abigail [no surnames](last 4 unmar.). Cousin Benjamin Smith. Brother Hezekiah Smith. Sons Peleg & Humphrey as Execs. Witns: James Tripp, Jr., Isaac Smith & William Sanford [6:299/300].

Inv. of Est. of DELIVERANCE SMITH of Dart., dtd. 9 Aug. 1729, pres. by Humphrey Smith, Exec. Apprs: Henery Howland, James Howland & Nathaniel Soule [6:301/2/3].

Order to set off 1/3rd of Est. of NATHANIEL WHITTIKER of Reho. to Abigail Murra wife of David Murra but late widow of said Whittiker, dtd. 29 March 1729 [6:303].

Setting off 1/3rd of Est. of NATHANIEL WHITTIKER of Reho. to his former widow, Abigail Murra wife of David Murra, dtd. 4 Apr. 1729. Comm: Samuel Bullock, Jonathan Chaffe, Jacob Ormsbe, Peter Hunt & Joseph Peck [6:303/4].

Acct. of Hannah Russel, widow & Adm. of Est. of SETH RUSSEL of Dart., dtd. 16 Sept. 1729 [6:304].

Appt. of Martha Baker, widow, as Adm. of Est. of JOSEPH BAKER of Reho. dcd. intest., Yeoman, dtd. 16 Sept. 1729 [6:305].

Appt. of Mrs. Content Briggs of Dart., widow, as Adm. of Est. of WESTON BRIGGS of Dart., dtd. 16 Sept. 1729 [6:305/6].

Order to John Cotton of Newton, Co. of Middlesex, & Grizel Cotton of Brist., 2 of the Execs. of Est. of the Rev. NATHANIEL COTTON of Brist., Jacob Wendal the 3rd Exec. having renounced Exec., dtd. 23 Sept. 1729 [6:306].

Will of NATHANIEL COTTON of Brist., Clerk, dtd. 17 July 1728, prob. 20 Sept. 1729. Wife Grizel. Son Roland Cotton. Mentions without naming them, "my other Children." My eldest brother John Cotton of Newton, my friend Jacob Wendall of Boston, Merchant, & my wife Grizel to be Execs. Witns: John White, Henery Bragg & Samuel Howland [6:307].

Inv. of Est. of WESTON BRIGGS of Dart., dtd. 24 June 1729, pres. by Content Briggs, widow & Adm. Apprs: Benjamin Allen, Thomas Smith & William Bowdish [6:307/8].

Will of WILLIAM FULTON of Brist., Shop Keeper, dtd. 25 Aug. 1729 prob. 29 Sept. 1729. Wife Mary. Sons: John & Andrew (dcd.) Fulton. Dau. Margaret Fulton, "in or near the City of Glasgow in Scotland." Children [not named] of son Andrew. Wife Mary as Exec. Witns: Charles Church, Samuel Howland & Abigail Woodbury [6:309/10].

Acct. of Elisha May, Adm. of Est. of DELIVERANCE MAY of Reho., dtd. 21 Oct. 1729 [6:310].

Acct. of Elisha May, Adm. de bonis non of Est. of EPHRAIM MAY of Reho., dtd. 21 Oct. 1729. Incl. legacy per will to Hannah May [6:311].

Appt. of Abraham Baker of Swan. as guard. of Joseph Baker (under 14), son of JOSEPH BAKER of Swan., dtd. 21 Oct. 1729 [6:311/2].

Order for settl. Est. of JOSHUA ORMSBE of Reho., dtd. 13 Aug. 1729 [6:312].

Settl. of Est. of JOSHUA ORMSBE of Reho. btwn. his former widow Mehetibel Titus now wife of Silas Titus, & his chldn: Joshua Ormsbe (only son) & daus: Mehetibel wife of Joshua Fuller, Mary Ormsbe & Ann Ormsbe, dtd. 21 Oct. 1729. Comm: Abiah Carpenter, Noah Mason & Noah Butterworth [6:312/3].

Order to Elezebeth Ladd, widow & Exec. of Est. of WILLIAM LADD of Lit. Comp., dtd. 21 Oct. 1729 [6:313.4].

Will of WILLIAM LADD, dtd. 13 Aug. 172[9 or 0?], prob. 21 Oct. 1729. Wife Elezebeth. Sons Joseph & Samuel Ladd. Daus: Sarah Ladd, Mary Seabery, Priscilla Manchester, Elezebeth Thurril [sic], Katherine Ladd, Lidia Ladd, Hannah Ladd & Ruth Ladd. Grson. Nathaniel Ladd son of my son William. Wife Elezebeth to be Exec. Witns: Josiah Sawer, Samuel Seaberry & Benjamin Seaberry [6:314/5].

Inv. of Est. of WILLIAM LADD of Lit. Comp. dtd. 20 Oct. 1729, pres. by Elezebeth Ladd, his widow & Exec. Apprs: George Paciss[?], Samuel Tomkins & William Hunt [6:315].

Appt. of Daniel Baker of Swan. as guard. of Daniel Baker (under

14), son of JOSEPH BAKER of Swan., dtd. 20 Oct. 1729 [6:316].
Appt. of Mrs. Martha Baker of Swan. as guard. of Job, Isabel &
George Baker (all under 14), chldn. of JOSEPH BAKER of Swan.,
dtd. 21 Oct. 1729 [6:316/7].
Inv. of Est. of JAMES CUDWORTH of Free., dtd. 20 Oct. [no year]
pres. 21 Oct. 1729 by David & James Cudworth, his sons & Ex-
ecs. Apprs: William Winslow, Walter Chace & Samuel Tisdal
[6:317].
Inv. of Est. of JOSEPH BAKER of Swan., dtd. 25 Aug. 1729, pres.
by Martha Baker, widow & Exec. Apprs: William Anthoney, John
Blevin & Edward Simmons [6:317/8].
Acct. of Ann Allen, widow & Adm. of Est. of NEHEMIAH ALLEN of
Attl., dtd. 21 Oct. 1729 [6:318/9].
Acct. of Seth Babit, Adm. of Est. of TIMOTHY COOPER of Easton,
dtd. 22 Oct. 1729. Mentions Elezebeth Cooper his widow [6:
319/20].
Order to Rebecca Carpenter, widow & Exec. of Est. of MICHAIL
CARPENTER of Attl, dtd. 27 Oct. 1729 [6:320].
Will of MICHAIL CARPENTER of Attl., Husbandman, "being Very
Sich and Weak," dtd. 14 Aug. 1729, prob. 27 Oct. 1729. Wife
Rebeca. Son Oliver Carpenter (only child, under 21). Wife Re-
beca to be Exec. Witns: Benjamin Brown, William Whiple, Jr.
& Noah Carpenter [6:320/1].
Inv. of Est. of MICHAIL CARPENTER of Attl., dtd. 15 Sept. 1729,
pres. by Rebecca Carpenter, his widow & Exec. Apprs: Elisha
Peck, Israel Whiple & Ebenezer Carpenter [6:321/2].
Order to Oliver Earl of Swan., Exec. in 2nd degree of Est. of
his father THOMAS EARL of Warwick, R.I. Mary Earl, widow of
Thomas & sole Exec. in the will, is now dcd., dtd. 3 Nov. 17-
29 [6:322/3].
Will of THOMAS EARL of Warwick, R.I., dtd. 27 Apr. 1727, prob.
in Warwick 19 May 1727, prob. in Brist. 20 Oct. 1729. Wife
Mary. Sons: Oliver, Thomas & William Earl. Daus: Mary Baker,
Sarah Earl, Lydia Earl & Rebeca Earl. Grdaus: Sarah Baker (un-
der 18), Lydia Baker & Mary Baker (last 2 under age). Wife
Mary as Exec. Friends John Potter (son of John Potter dcd.)
& Roger Burllinggame, Jr. of Providence to be Overseers.
Witns: Daniel Everit, William Brenton & Peter Roberts [6:
323/3½].
Inv. of Est. of THOMAS EARL of Swan. "& Left by Mary Earl Relict
& widow...deceased," dtd. 11 Oct. 1729, pres. by Oliver Earl,
his son & Exec. in 2nd degree. Apprs: Samuel Lee, William
Anthoney & James Luther [6:323½/4].
Appt. of Daniel Baker of Swan. as guard. of Francis & Jemima
Baker (both over 14), chldn. of JOSEPH BAKER of Swan., dtd.
3 Nov. 1729 [6:324].
Order to Hannah Willson of Newport, widow & Exec. of Est. of
JONATHAN WILLSON of Newport, dtd. 4 Nov. 1729 [6:325].
Will of JONATHAN WILLSON of Newport, Yeoman, dtd. 9 Dec. 1726,

prob. at Newport 18 Sept. 1729, prob. at Brist. 10 Oct. 1729.
Wife Hannah. Dau. Sarah Willson (under 18). Dau.-in-law Mary
Carr, son-in-law Robert Carr, dau-in-law Hannah Carr & son-
in-law Caleb Carr [*stepchildren?*]. My brother Benjamin Will-
son. Wife Hannah to be Exec. Witns: James Cary, Elezebeth
Collins & Bridget Cary [6:325/6].
Inv. of Est. of JONATHAN WILLSON of Newport "as is found in the
Limits of the County of Bristol...Massachusets Bay," pres. at
Bristol 11 Nov. 1729 by Hannah Willson, widow & Exec. Apprs:
Jonathan Kingsly, James Bowen & Samuel Bullock [6:326/7].
Will of THOMAS BUFFINGTON of Swan., Husbandman, "Being Aged,"
dtd. 16 Feb. 1726, prob. 11 Nov. 1729. Wife mentioned but not
named. Sons: Thomas dcd. & Benjamin Buffington. Dau. Abigail
King. Grson. Thomas Buffington son of my son Thomas dcd. Son
Benjamin to be Exec. Witns: John Blethen, John Southwick &
Daniel Southwick[6:327/38][*page numbering error*].
Order to Benjamin Buffington of Swan., Exec. of Est. of THOMAS
BUFFINGTON of Swan., dtd. 11 Nov. 1729 [6:338/9].
Appt. of Robert Watson of Barr., Brickmaker, as guard. of John
& Sarah Watson (both over 14), chldn. of [*blank*] WATSON of
Mendon, Co. of Suffolk, dtd. 16 Dec. 1729 [6:339].
Order to Elezebeth Wilbour, widow & Exec. of Est. of BENJAMIN
WILBOUR, the other Exec. Henery Wilbour being under 18, dtd.
1 Dec. 1729 [6:339/40].
Will of BENJAMIN WILBOUR of Dart., Yeoman, dtd. 21 Apr. 1729,
prob. 1 Dec. 1729. Wife Elezebeth. Sons: Daniel, William, Ben-
jamin, Samuel, Henery, George & Joseph Wilbour. Daus: Abigail
Wilbour, Bersheba Wilbour, Elezebeth Wilbour & Mary Wilbour
(all under age). "My wife being now with Child." Wife & son
Henery to be Execs. Mentions land in Tiv. Witns: Seth Allen,
Thomas Akin & William Hart [6:340/1/2].
Inv. of Est. of BENJAMIN WILBOUR of Dart., dtd. 19 June 1729,
pres. by Elezebeth Wilbour, his widow. Apprs: John Akins,
Phillip Allen & William Hart [6:343/4].
Inv. of Est. of JOSEPH BUCKLEN of Reho., dtd. 1 Dec. 1729, pres.
by Mehetibel Bucklen, his widow & Exec. Apprs: Noah Carpen-
ter, Henry Smith & Samuel Bishop [6:344].
Acct. of Mary Church, widow & Adm. of Est. of Capt. CHARLES
CHURCH of Free., dtd. 18 Nov. 1729. Mentions "claims of y^e
Insolvent Estate" [6:344/5].
Appt. of Ebenezer Linkon of Taun., Adm. of Est. of ELEZEBETH
WITHERIL of Taun., dtd. 14 Jan. 1729/30 [6:345/6].
Inv. of Est. of ELEZEBETH WITHERIL of Taun., dtd. 12 Jan. 17-
29/30, pres. by Ebenezer Linkon of Taun., Adm. Apprs: Benjamin Wilbour, Joseph Willis & Joseph Wilbour [6:346].
Appt. of Ebenezer Linkon of Taun. & Samuel Linkon of Norton,
both yeomen, as guards. of Rebecca Wetheril (under 14), dau.
of EPHRAIM WETHERIL of Taun. dcd., dtd. 14 Jan. 1729/30 [6:
341].

Acct. of Hannah Willson, formerly Hannah Carr, widow & Adm. of
Est. of her former husb. ROBERT CARR, dates not noted[6:347/8].
Appt. of Martha Robinson, widow & Adm. of Est. of WILLIAM ROBIN-
SON of Swan., House Carpenter, dtd. 3 Feb. 1729/30 [6:348].
Inv. of Est. of WILLIAM ROBINSON of Swan., dtd. 12 Jan. 1729/30,
pres. by Martha Robinson, widow & Adm. Apprs: William Antho-
ney, Benjamin Buffington & Edward Simmons [6:349].
Order to Mrs. Sarah Paine, widow, as Adm. of Est. of Col. NATH-
ANIEL PAINE of Brist. dcd. intest., dtd. 2 Feb. 1729/30[6:350].
Report of claims against Est. of CHARLES CHURCH of Free., Gent-
leman, pres. by Mary Church, Adm. Amounts to nearly 1,000
Pounds owed to dozens of persons, leaving it badly insolvent,
dtd. Nov. 1729. Mentions land in Plimouth. Comms: Joseph Read
& John Read. [6:350/1/2].
Order to Benjamin Cary & Samuel Howland both of Brist., Execs.
of Est. of ABIGAIL CARY of Brist., dtd. 12 Feb. 1729/30[6:353].
Will of ABIGAIL CARY of Brist., widow, "being aged," dtd. 7 May
1722, prob. 12 Feb. 1729/30. Only dau. Abigail wife of Samuel
Howland of Brist. Grdaus: Abigail Cary dau. of son John dcd.,
Abigail Cary dau. of my son Eleazer, Abigail Cary dau. of my
son James, Abigail Cary dau. of my son Benjamin, Abigail Howland dau. of my son-in-law Samuel Howland & Jemima Cary dau.
of my son Josiah. My husb. Deacon John Cary dcd. Our eldest
son John Cary dcd. Grson. John Cary son of my son John Cary.
Witns: Charles Church, Samuel Smith & Henery Bragg [6:353/4].
Inv. of Est. of ABIGAIL CARY of Brist., dtd. 12 Feb. 1729/30,
pres. by Benjamin Cary & Samuel Howland, Execs. Mentions Abigail dau. of John Cary, Abigail dau. of Eleazer Cary & Abigail
dau. of Samuel Howland [6:354/5].
Will of MARY TISDAL of Taun., widow of Joseph Tisdal, dtd. 9
July 1726, prob. at Marshfield, Co. of Plimouth 8 May 1728,
the dcd. having been "Late of Taunton ... But Last Resident
in Bridgewater." Recorded 18 Feb. 1729/30 at Brist. Chldn. (under 18 but not named) of dau. Mary dcd. who was wife of Joseph
Winslow of Swan., chldn. (son under 21, daus. under 18, none
named) of my dau. Hannah dcd. who was wife of William Hodges
of Norton now of Taun., my dau. Sarah Reed wife of Thomas Reed
of Digh., my dau. Abigail Hayward wife of Ephraim Hayward, Jr.
of Bridgewater, my dau. Elizebeth Leonard wife of Elkanah
Leonard of Middleborough, chldn. (unnamed) of my son Elkanah
dcd. & my son Joseph Tisdal. Son Joseph to be Exec. Witns:
Benjamin Allen, Samuel Lathroop & Joseph Cary [6:355/6/7].
Order to Susanah Dennis, widow & Exec. of Est. of Capt. ROBERT
DENNIS of Tiv., dtd. 17 Feb. 1729/30 [6:355].
Will of ROBERT DENNIS of Tiv., Yeoman, "Sick and painfull of
body," dtd. 29 Dec. 1729, prob. 17 Feb. 1729/30. Wife Susana.
Sons: John, Thomas & Humphrey (dcd.) Dennis. Daus: Comfort
wife of Phillip Taylor (son of John Taylor), Ann Dennis, Tab-
atha Dennis, Sarah Dennis, Elizabeth Dennis, Deborah Dennis

& Lidia Dennis (last 4 under 18). To wife Susanah is given
"all the Land & housing whereon we now Live in Tiverton....
it being the Same which was given to her by her father."
Calls Susana the mother of his chldn. Negro man Newport, negro man Quazquo & negro girl Dinah. Witns: John Dennis, Thomas Cook & Richard Bourden [6:357/8/9].

Appt. of Benjamin Cary of Brist. as guard. of Mary Kent (over
14), dau. of JOSHUA KENT of Barr., dtd. 17 Feb. 1729/30 [6:
356/60].

Order to William Torrey of Mendon, Co. of Suffolk, Adm. of Est.
of his brother EBENEZER TORREY of Brist., dtd. 28 Feb. 1729/
30 [6:360].

Appt. of Benjamin Cary of Brist. as guard. of Susanah, Hannah &
Lidiah Kent (all under 14), daus. of JOSHUA KENT of Barr.,
td. 17 Feb. 1729/30 [6:361].

Appt. of Nicholas White, Jr. of Norton as guard. of his wife
Sarah White (over 14), dau. of SAMUEL KING of Norton, dtd. 17
Feb. 1729/30 [6:361].

Appt. of Sarah King of Norton as guard. of Hezekiah King (over
14), son of SAMUEL KING of Norton, dtd. 17 Feb. 1729/30[6:362].

Appt. of Jedediah Caswell of Norton as guard. of his wife Mary
Caswell (over 14), dau. of SAMUEL KING of Norton, dtd. 17 Feb.
1729/30 [6:362].

Appt. of Eseck Brown of Swan. as guard. of Patience Cranston
(over 14), dau. of THOMAS CRANSTON of Newport, R.I., dtd. 12
March 1729/30 [6:363].

Appt. of Samuel Lee of Swan. as Adm. of Est. of JEREMIAH WIL-
LIAMS "a molato man" of Swan. dcd. intest., dtd. 12 March
1729/30 [6:363/4].

Appt. of Anna Smith of Reho. as Adm. of Est. of her son ABIAL
SMITH of Reho. dcd. intest., dtd. 17 March 1729/30 [6:364].

Appts. of Mrs. Rebecca Wood of Swan. as guard. of Hannah, Thankfull, Susanah & Rebecca Wood (all under 14), daus. of GEORGE
WOOD of Swan., all dtd. 17 March 1729/30 [6:364/5/6].

Order to William Wood & John Baker, brothers & Execs. of Est.
of GEORGE WOOD of Swan., dtd. 17 March 1729/30 [6:366].

Will of GEORGE WOOD of Swan., Weaver, "being Very Sick," dtd.
22 Feb. 1729/30, prob. 17 March 1729/30. Wife Rebecca. Sons:
Thomas, Gersham & James Wood (all under 21). 6 daus: Rebecah
Wood, Susanah Wood, Thankful Wood, Abigail Wood, Lydia Wood
& Hannah Wood (all under 18 & unmar.). Brothers William Wood
of Swan. & John Baker of Reho., yeomen, to be Execs. Witns:
John Simmons, Thomas Wood, Jr. & Susanah Baker [6:367/8].

Order to Hannah Millar, widow & Exec. of Est. of SAMUEL MILLAR
of Reho., dtd. 17 March 1729/30 [6:368].

Will of SAMUEL MILLAR of Reho., Yeoman, "being Very Sick," dtd.
9 Feb. 1729/30, prob. 17 March 1729/30. Wife Hannah. Dau. Hannah Millar. My 3 sisters: Hester West, Elce Chaffe & Margaret
Orsben. Wife Hannah to be Exec. Witns: Thomas Bowen, Henery

West & Daniel Bullock [6:368/9].

Order to John & Joseph Chaffee, Execs. of Est. of their mother
ANNIS CHAFFEE of Swan., dtd. 17 March 1729/30 [6:369].

Will of ANNIS CHAFFEE, widow of Joseph Chaffee late of Swan.
now Barr., "being aged," dtd. 25 Apr. 1729, prob. 17 March
1729/30. 2 sons: John & Joseph Chaffee. Daus: Mary Whittiker,
Ann Chaffee (unmar.), Elizebeth Paine, Abigail Chaffee (unmar) & Sarah Luther. Sons John & Joseph to be Execs. Witns:
Nathaniel Carpenter, Daniel Smith & Abiel Smith. At time of
prob., Nathaniel Carpenter was called "the only Surviveing
Wittness" [6:370].

Order to Mary Hix, Exec. of Est. of SAMUEL HIX of Reho., dtd.
17 March 1729/30 [6:370/1].

Will of SAMUEL HIX of Reho., Yeoman, "being Very Sick," dtd. 20
Jan. 1729/30, prob. 17 March 1729/30. Wife Mary. Son Nathaniel
Hix (under age). Daus: Lidia Hix, Ja[ne?][partially unread-
able] Hix, Mary Hix & Experance Hix (all under 18). Wife to
be Exec. Witns: Daniel Bullock, Seth Garnsey & Jotham Carpenter [6:371/2].

Order to Judith Gatchel, widow & Exec. of Est. of JOHN GATCHEL
of Dart., dtd. 17 March 1729/30 [6:372].

Will of JOHN GATCHEL of Dart., Yeoman, dtd. 11 Oct. 1729, prob.
17 March 1729/30. Wife Judith. Daus: Mary & Susanah (under
18). Mentions wife to take care of "my father & mother" [not
named]. Wife to be Exec. Brother-in-law David Aken & friend
Isaac Howland to be Overseers. Witns: Isaac Howland, Henery
Howland & Thomas Briggs [6:372/3].

Order to Mrs. Dorothey Bailey, widow & Exec. of Est. of WILLIAM
BAILEY of Lit. Comp., dtd. 17 March 1729/30 [6:373].

Will of WILLIAM BAILEY of Lit. Comp., Yeoman, dtd. 9 Feb. 1729,
prob. 17 March 1729/30. Wife Dorothey. Sons: William, Samuel,
John & George Bailey (last 3 under 21). Daus: Sarah, Abigail
& Ruth (last 2 under 21)[no surnames]. Mentions "my five Daughters," but only names these 3. Wife to be Exec. Witns: Joseph Southworth, William Hall & Abraham Brown [6:374].

Commission by George the Second to Nathaniel Blagrove, Esq.,
appointing him Judge of Probate, signed by Lt. Governor William Dummer, Esq., dtd. 26 Sept. 1729 [6:375].

Inv. of Est. of WILLIAM BAILEY of Lit. Comp., dtd. 14 March 17-
29/30, pres. by Dorothey Bailey his widow & Exec. Apprs: Lt.
John Wood, Capt. John Palmer & Joseph Southworth [6:375/6].

Inv. of Est. of ABIEL SMITH of Reho., dtd. 23 Feb. 1729/30, pres.
by his mother & Adm. Anna Smith. Mentions his lands in Reho.,
Barr. & Attl. Apprs: Noah Carpenter, John Read & Ephraim Carpenter [6:376/7].

Acct. of Elezebeth Shappard, widow & Adm. of Est. of ISAAC
SHAPPERD of Norton dcd. intest., dtd. 17 March 1729/30. Men-
tions payms. to: Isaac Shappard, the widow Marcy Shappard &
Joshua Shappard [6:377/8].

Inv. of Est. of JOHN GATCHEL of Dart., dtd. 6 Dec. 1729, pres.
   by Judith Gatchel, his widow & Exec. Apprs: James Howland,
   James Barker & Nathaniel Searle [6:378/9].
Acct. of Simon Burr "the Surviveing Executor" of Est. of SIMON
   BURR of Reho., dtd. 17 March 1729/30 [6:379/80].
Acct. of Anthoney Sprauge, Adm. of Est. of his father ANTHONEY
   SPRAUGE of Attl., dtd. 17 March 1729/30. Incl. paym. to "Me-
   hetibel Sprauge for Nursing" [6:380/1].
Acct. of Jethniel Peck, Adm. of Est. of SOLOMON PECK of Reho.,
   dtd. 21 March 1729/30 [6:381/2].
Inv. of Est. of SOLOMON PECK of Reho., dtd. 28 Jan. 1728/9,
   pres. by Jethniel Peck, Adm. Apprs: James Bowen, Samuel Bul-
   lock & Jacob Ormsbee [6:382].
Inv. of Est. of THOMAS BUFFINGTON of Swan., dtd. 12 Jan. 1729/30
   pres. by Benjamin Buffington, Exec. Apprs: William Anthoney,
   John Blethen & Edward Simmons [6:382].
Inv. of Est. of ANNIS CHAFFE, widow, of Barr., dtd. 18 March
   1720, pres. by John & Joseph Chaffe, her sons & Execs. Apprs:
   Samuel Mason, Samuel Barns & Jabiz Bosworth [6:383].
Will of JOHN PECK of Attl, "Being Very Sick," dtd. 14 March 17-
   29/30, prob. 25 March 1729/30. Wife Rebecca. Son John Peck.
   "Child which is yet unborn." Wife to be Exec. Witns: Abraham
   Cummins, Hezekiah Peck & Thomas Wilmouth [6:383/4].
Acct. of Sarah Balcum, widow & Adm. of Est. of ALEXANDER BALCUM
   of Attl., dtd. 29 March 1730 [6:384].
Appt. of Ephraim Lane of Norton as Adm. of Est. of his brother
   JOHN LANE of Attl., the widow having relinquished her rights
   of Adm., dtd. 30 March 1730 [6:385].
Appt. of Mrs. Hannah Pidge, widow, as Adm. of Est. of JOSIAH
   PIDGE of Attl., dtd. 30 March 1730 [6:385/6].
Appt. of William Ware of Norton, Practioner [sic], as guard. of
   Noah Fuller (over 14), son of NOAH FULLER of Attl, dtd. 30
   March 1730 [6:386].
Appt. of [name not given] as guard. of Mary Ware (under 14),
   grdau. of ALEXANDER MAXEE of Attl., dtd. 30 March 1730[6:386].
Appt. of Jeremiah Freeman, Husbandman, & Rachel Freeman, both
   of Attl. as guards. of Stephen Fuller (over 14), son of NOAH
   FULLER of Attl, dtd. 30 March 1730 [6:387].
Appt. of William Barney of Taun. as guard. of Lidia Williams
   (over 14), dau. of EMANUEL WILLIAMS of Taun., dtd. 30 March
   1730 [6:387].
Appts. of John William of Taun. as guard. of Simion Williams
   (under 14) & Phebe Williams (over 14), chldn. of EMANUEL WIL-
   LIAMS of Taun., both dtd. 30 March 1730 [6:388].
Inv. of Est. of JOSIAH PIDGE of Attl., dtd. 27 March 1730,
   pres. 30 March 1730 by Hannah Pidge, his widow & Adm. Apprs:
   John Foster, Thomas Stanley & Benjamin Day [6:388/90][page
   numbering error].
Inv. of Est. of JOHN LANE of Attl., dtd. 7 Oct. 1729, pres. by

Ephraim Lane, Adm. Mentions bond of Ebenezer Lane of Attl.
Apprs: Ebenezer Fisher, William Stone & Josiah White [6:390].

End of Volume 6

Agrmt. abt. settl. of Est. of their father SAMUEL STANDLEY of
Attl., signed by his sons: Jacob, Joseph, Nathaniel & John
Standley, all of Att., dtd. 1 Jan. 1725/6. Mentions that said
John Standley will support our mother as long as she lives.
Also mentions the uncle of the signers, John Handley. Witns:
Thomas Standley & Mahew Dagget [7:1/2].

Order for div. of Est. of JOSHUA KENT of Barr. dcd. intest.,
dtd 23 Feb. 1730 [7:2/3].

Div. of Est. of JOSHUA KENT of Barr. btwn. his widow Mary Kent
& his chldn: Sarah Kent (dau.), Mary Kent (dau.), Susanah
Kent (dau.), Hannah Kent (dau.) & Lidiah Kent (dau.), dtd. 17
March 1729/30. Mentions lands in Norton, Swan. & Barr. Comm:
Elisha May, John Child, Jabez Bosworth, Robert Joles & Edward
Luther [7:3/4/5].

Acct. of William Makepeace of Taun., Adm. de bonis non of Est.
of EMANUEL WILLIAMS of Taun., dtd. 30 March 1730 [7:6/7].

Inv. of Est. of EMANUEL WILLIAMS of Taun., dtd. 8 & 9 Feb. 17-
24/5, pres. by William Makepeace, Adm. de bonis non. Apprs:
Samuel Williams, John Staple & Benjamin Wilbore [7:8/9].

Inv. of pers. est. of JEREMIAH WILLIAMS of Swan., "a Molato
Man." dtd. 13 March 1729/30, pres. by Samuel Lee, Adm. Apprs:
William Anthony, Ezeck Brown & John Lewther [7:9/10].

Inv. of Est. of ROBERT DENNIS of Tiv., dtd. 2 March 1729/30,
pres. by Susanah Dennis, his widow & Exec. Apprs: Richard
Borden, Thomas Cook & Thomas Manchester [7:10/1].

Will of THOMAS THURSTON of Free., Yeoman, "Being very Sick &
Weak," dtd. 20 March 1729/30, prob. 21 Apr. 1730. Wife Mehitabel. 6 sons: Edward, Thomas, Peleg, Jonathan, Samuel & John.
5 daus: Ruth Eddy, Elizabeth Thurston, Ann Sprage, Mehetable
Joslin & Mary Thurston (youngest dau., under 18). My brother-
in-law Peleg Trip of Road Island & my wife to be Execs. Witns:
John Read, Thomas Paine, John Read, Jr. & Mary Gaige. Notation on 21 Apr. 1730 that Peleg Tripp of Newport refused to
be Exec. [7:12/3/4].

Inv. of Est. of THOMAS THURSTON of Free., dtd. 20 Apr. 1730,
pres. by Mehetibel Thurston, Exec. Apprs: John Read, John
Farrow & Thomas Gaige [7:14/5].

Order to Mehetable Thurston, widow, & to Peleg Tripp of Newport
(who hath relinquished Exec.) to proceed with exec. of Est.
of THOMAS THURSTON of Free., dtd. 28 Apr. 1730 [7:15/6].

Appt. of Thomas Gray of Tiv. as guard. of Samuel [or Lemuel?]
Gray (under 14), son of EDWARD GRAY, dtd. 21 Apr. 1730 [7:16/7].

Appt. of Jeremiah Bennet of Tiv. as guard. of his wife Lidia
Bennet (minor over 14), dau. of EDWARD GRAY of Tiv., dtd. 21
Apr. 1730 [7:17/8].

Appt. of Mrs. Hannah Millar of Reho. as guard of Hannah Millar
(under 14), dau. of SAMUEL MILLAR of Reho., dtd. 21 Apr. 1730
[7:18/9].

Inv. of Est. of GEORGE WOOD of Swan., dtd. 15 Apr. 1730, pres.
by William Wood & John Baker, Execs. Apprs: James Bowen, Barnard Haile & Palitiah Mason [7:19/20].

Will of WILLIAM DYE of Lit. Comp., Yeoman, dtd. 24 July 1725,
prob. at Town Council of So. Kingston, R.I. 9 March 1729,
pres. at Bristol 21 Apr. 1730. No wife mentioned. Son William
Dye of Stonington, Ct. & son John Dye dcd. Daus. Elizabeth
Harris wife of Michael Harris of So. Kingston, R.I. & Elinor
How of Lit. Comp. My 2 grsons: Richard Dye & Daniel Dye sons
of my son John Dye dcd. Grdau. Temperance Dye dau. of my son
John Dye dcd. Grdau. Hete [*Mehitabel*]. Son-in-law Michael
Harris of So. Kingston & Samuel Coe of Lit. Comp. to be Execs.
Witns: John Buckmaster, Ebenezer Shearman & Lt. Col. Christo-
pher Allen. The latter two both saw "William Dye Late of Lit-
tle Compton Deceased in South Kingston Signe Seal and Declare
the Within" [7:20/1/2][*See his other will on 7:345, below.*]

Inv. of Est. of SAMUEL MILLAR of Reho., dtd. 21 Apr. 1730, pres.
by Hannah Millar, his widow & Exec. Apprs: James Bowen, Daniel Bullock & John Kelton [7:22/3].

Inv. of Est. of JAMES HIX of Reho., dtd. 31 March 1730, pres.
by Mary Hix, his widow & Adm. Apprs: James Bowen, Daniel Bullock & John Kelton [7:23/4].

Will of JAMES BENNET of Lit. Comp., Cordwinder, "being Very
Sick," dtd. 1 Feb. 1729/30, prob. 21 Apr. 1730. Wife Marcy.
Sons James & John Bennet (both under 21). Daus. Marcy Bennet
& Ruth Bennet. Mentions his lands in Lit. Comp. & in Wood-
stock, Suffolk Co. Witns: Nathaniel Newel, Nathaniel Searls
& Sarah Newel [7:24/5].

Will of ARON DAVIS of Lit. Comp., dtd. 11 Jan. 1714/5, prob. 21
Apr. 1730. Wife Mary. Son William Davis (under 21). Dau.
Sarah [Sheifeld - *unclear*]. Grson. Aron Sheifeld [*overwritten
by, or written over, "Davis;" unclear as to which is meant*].
Wife Mary & friend Joseph Wanton of Tiv. to be Execs. Witns:
John Wood, Edward Richmond & Jonathan Wood [7:28/9].

Will of PHILLIP SISON of Dart., Cordwinder, dtd. 8 March 1728/9,
prob. 21 Apr. 1730. Brother Thomas Sisson of Dart. Witns:
Silvanus Soule, Benjamin Davil & John Mosher [7:28/9][*page
numbering repetition*].

Will of ROBERT GIFFORD of Dart., Yeoman, dtd. 5 March 1724, prob.
30 Apr. 1730. Wife Elezebeth. Sons: Jeremiah, Benjamin, Stephen, Timothy & Simeon. Grdau. Experence dau. of Benjamin.
Son Simion to be Exec. Witns: Elisha Wing, Icabod Nye, Jabez
Hillar & Timothy Ruggles [7:28/9/30].

Inv. of ROBART GIFFORD of Dart., dtd. 4 Apr. 1730, pres. by Simeon Gifford, Exec. Apprs: John Akin, Phillip Allen & James Allen [7:30/1].

Appt. of Nathaniel Dagget of Attl. as guard. of Gershom Wood (over 14), son of GEORGE WOOD of Swan., dtd. 26 Apr. 1730 [7:31/2].

Order to Simeon Gifford, son & Exec. of Est. of ROBERT GIFFORD of Dart., dtd. 21 Apr. 1730 [7:32].

Appt. of William Davis of Lit. Comp. as Adm. of Est. of his father, ARON DAVIS, since Mary Davis & Joseph Wanton, named as Execs. in the will, have relinquished their Exec., dtd. 19 May 1730 [7:33].

Inv. of Est. of ARON DAVIS of Lit. Comp., dtd. 10 Apr. 1730, pres. by William Davis, Adm. Mentions his share of land in West Quemaug in R.I. Apprs: John Wood, John Sisson & William Richmond [7:34/5].

Inv. of Est. of JAMES BENNIT of Lit. Comp., dtd. 9 March 1729, pres. by Mary Bennit, his widow & Exec. Apprs: John Wood, John Palmer & Joseph Southworth [7:35/6].

Appt. of Martha Hammon of Reho., widow, as guard. of Elezebeth, Mary, Eleazer & Elkanah Hammon (all under 14), chldn. of WILLIAM HAMMON of Reho., dtd. 26 May 1730 [7:36/7].

Order to John Hoskins, Exec. of Est. of his father WILLIAM HOSKINS of Taun., dtd. 26 May 1730 [7:37/8].

Will of WILLIAM HOSKINS of Taun., "being Grown into old age," dtd. 6 March 1730, prob. 27 May 1730. Wife Sarah. Sons: William, Henery, Josiah, Stephen dcd. & John Hoskins. Daus: Ann Smith "widow and Relict of Nathaniel Smith," Sarah Smith wife of Nathaniel Smith [sic], Hannah Macomber wife of William Macomber. Chldn. of my son Stephen, named Stephen, Mary & Abiah Hoskins. Of son Josiah's legacy he said "I Paid Fifty Pounds to his father Beverly for the Land were he now lives," presumably meaning Josiah's father-in-law. Mentions his rights in the land which the Gen. Court shall give "to those that went in the Expedition to Narraganset fight," and to his rights of title "in New Roxbury or Woodstock." Son John to be Exec. Witns: Samuel Hoskins, Henery Hodges & John Godfree [7:38/9/40].

Appt. of Mary Hoskins, widow, as Adm. of Est. of her husb. STEPHEN HOSKINS of Taun., dtd. 26 May 1730 [7:40/1].

Appt. of Mary Hoskins of Taun. as guard. of Mary, Stephen & Abiah Hoskins (all under 14), chldn. of STEPHEN HOSKINS of Taun., dtd. 26 May 1730 [7:41].

Acct. of John Manchester, Adm. of Est. of MARY GRAY of Tiv. dcd. intest., dtd. 19 May 1730 [7:42/3].

Order to Thomas Hathaway, Exec. of Est. of his father JOHN HATHAWAY of Digh., dtd. 11 June 1730 [7:43/4].

Will of JOHN HATHAWAY of Free., Yeoman, "being aged," dtd. 23 May 1724, prob. 11 June 1730. Wife Christian. Sons: Jacob,

Isaac, John dcd., Ephraim & Thomas Hathaway. 5 daus: Hannah, Sarah, Martha, Abigail & Experience [*no surnames*]. Grdau. Hannah dau. of my dcd. son John. Witns: William Hoskins, Ephraim Pray & Edward Shove [7:44/5/6].

Will of ELEZEBETH DAVIS wife of Simon Davis of Brist., "being very sick," dtd. 29 May 1730, prob. 16 June 1730. 2 grdaus. Elezebeth Mackentosh & Mary Mackentosh (both under 14), friend Nathaniel Kay of Newport to be their guard. 2 kinswomen Elesebeth Gallop & Mary Gallop (both under 21 & unmar.), daus. of my kinswoman Mary Gallop. Friends Nathaniel Kay & William Munroe to be Execs. Witns: Nathaniel Hubbard, John Usher & Richard Pearce. Notation signed 13 June 1730 by husb. Simon Davis that he approves of this will, witn. by Stephen Paine & Stephen Talman [7:46/7/8].

Acct. of Sarah Bosworth & John Bosworth, Execs. of Est. of JOHN BOSWORTH of Brist., dtd. 16 June 1730 [7:48/9].

Acct. of Benjamin Cary & Samuel Howland, Execs. of Est. of ABIGAIL CARY of Brist., dtd. 16 June 1730 [7:49/50].

Acct. of Anna Smith, Adm. of Est. of her son ABIEL SMITH of Reho., dtd. 16 June 1730 [7:50/1].

Acct. of Martha Read, widow & Adm. of Est. of her husb. THOMAS READ, Jr. of Reho., dtd. 16 June 1730 [7:51/2].

Acct. of Nicholas White of Nort., Exec. of Est. of his father NICHOLAS WHITE of Nort., dtd. 17 June 1730 [7:52/3].

Inv. of Est. of STEPHEN HOSKINS of Taun., dtd. 5 June 1730, pres. by Marcy [*or Mary - illegible*] Hoskins, his widow & Adm. Apprs: James Leonard, Morgan Cobb & Henry Hodges[7: 53/4].

Appt. of Mrs. Elesebeth Machoon, widow, as Adm. of Est. of her husb. THOMAS MACHOON of Swan., dtd. 16 June 1730 [7:54/5].

Appt. of Mrs. Patience Luther, widow, as Adm. of Est. of her husb. HEZEKIAH LUTHER of Swan, Yeoman, dcd. intest., dtd. 16 June 1730 [7:55/6].

Acct. of Joseph Wilbour of Lit. Comp., Exec. of Est. of his father JOSEPH WILBOUR of Lit. Comp., dtd. 31 June 1730. Mentions legacies per will payed to: Josiah Closson, Timothy Closson, Benjamin Wilbour, Stephen Wilbour, Thomas Burges, Joseph Burges, John Burges, Thomas Burges, Jacob Burges, Mary Burges, Joseph Wilbour, Samuel Wilbour & Daniel Wilbour. Various paym. "to my mother" [7:57/8].

Inv. of Est. of WILLIAM HAMMON of Reho. dcd. insolvent, dtd. 3 July 1730, pres. by James Redaway of Rehob., Adm. Apprs: Jathniel Peck & James Wheeler[7:59].

Inv. of Est. of SAMUEL HIX of Reho., dtd. 27 March 1730, pres. by Mary Hix, his widow & Exec. Apprs: James Bowen, Daniel Bullock & John Kelton [7:59/60].

Acct. of Mehetibel Bucklen, Exec. of Est. of her husb. JOSEPH BUCKLEN of Reho., dtd. 21 July 1730. Mentions pays. "To my three Sons Joseph Benjamin & John Their fathers Cloathing

Given to them by Will." Incl. paym. of legacy to Rachel Bucklen [7:60].

Will of JAMES TRIPP of Dart., Yeoman, dtd. 10 May 1729, prob.
21 July 1730. Wife Elizabeth. Sons: John (eldest), Robert,
James, Francis, Stephen & Israel Tripp. Dau. Elizabeth Michel.
4 daus: Mary Goddard, Lydia Tripp, Thankfull Taylor & Isabel
(under 18) Tripp. Negro boy Tobey. Son John to be Exec. Witns:
Solomon Drowne, Abiall Tripp & William Anthony [7:62/3/4/5].

Appt. of John Tripp of Dart. as Adm. of Est. of JOHN QUONONA
of Dart., dtd. 18 Aug. 1730 [7:65/6].

Appt. of Mehetibel Davis as Adm. of GIAS DAVIS of Brist. dcd.
intest., dtd. 18 Aug. 1730 [7:67].

Acct. of Ephraim Randal of Easton, Guard. of Lidia Briggs, minor dau. of CLEMENT BRIGGS of Easton dcd., dtd. 18 Aug. 1730
[7:68].

Inv. of Est. of JOHN HATHAWAY of Digh., Husbandman, dtd. 27
July 1730, pres. by John Hathaway, his son & Exec. Apprs:
Benjamin Leonard, Richard Wood & John Paul [7:69].

Acct. of Ephraim Lane of Nort., Adm. of Est. of JOHN LANE of
Attle., dtd. 18 Aug. 1730. Frequent reference to items for
"the widow and children" [7:69/70/1].

Inv. of Est. of JAMES TRIPP of Dart., dtd. June 1730, pres. by
John Tripp, his son & Exec. Mentions "the farm where his Son
Francis Lives." Apprs: James Tripp, Beriah Goddard & Samuel
Cornell [7:71/2/3].

Order for div. of Est. of JOHN HAILE of Swan. btwn. his widow &
chldn. [7:73/4].

Div. of Est. of JOHN HAILE of Swan. btwn. his widow [not named]
and chldn: John Haile (eldest son), Barnard Haile, Freelove
Hales (dau.), Lillis Haile (dau.) & Hannah Hail (dau.). Comm:
Joseph Mason, Benjamin Cole, Hezekiah Luther, John Wood, Jr.
& Hezekiah Bowen [7:74/5/6/7/8].

Inv. of Est. of the Rev. NATHANIEL COTTON of Brist., pres. 2
Sept. 1730 by Grizel Cotton, Exec. Incl. very long list of
books. Apprs: Nathaniel Hubbard, Jonathan Woodbury & Samuel
Royall [7:78/9/80/1/2].

Record of a Council held at Harvard College in Cambridge con-
cerning an appeal to a decree by Nathaniel Blagrove, Judge of
Probate, dtd. 23 Sept. 1730. Ordered that Nathaniel Kay Esq.
& William Munroe be granted adm. of Est. of Mrs. ELESEBETH
DAVIS of Brist. [7:82].

Order to Nathaniel Kay of Newport & William Munroe of Brist.,
Execs. of Est. of ELESEBETH DAVIS of Brist., dtd. 21 Oct.
1730 [7:83].

Appt. of Ebenezer Tiler of Attl., Yeoman, as guard. of Hannah
Fuller (over 14), dau. of JOHN FULLER of Attl., dtd. 20 Oct.
1730 [7:84].

Appt. of Nathan Hodges of Nort. as guard. of Timothy Williams
(over 14), son of JOHN WILLIAMS of Taun., dtd. 21 Oct. 1730
[7:85].

Appt. of Hannah Williams of Taun., widow, as guard. of Simeon
Williams (under 14), son of JOHN WILLIAMS of Taun., dtd. 24
Oct. 1730 [7:85/6].

Appts. of Samuel Tiler of Attl. as guard. of Elesebeth Fuller
(under 14) & Samuel Fuller (over 14), chldn. of JOHN FULLER
of Attl., dtd. 20 Oct. 1730 [7:86/7/8].

Inv. of Est. of Madam ELIZABETH DAVIS of Brist., dtd. 10 July
1730, pres. by Nathaniel Kay & William Munroe, Execs. Very
lengthy, incl. 23 negroes, men, women & chldn. Apprs: Ebenezer Brinton, Thomas Lawton & William Walker [7:88/9/90/1/2-
/3/4].

Acct. of Hannah Williams & Nathaniel Williams, Adms. of Est. of
JOHN WILLIAMS of Taun., dtd. 20 Oct. 1730. Mentions land in
Easton [7:95].

Inv. of GAIUS DAVIS of Brist., dtd. 20 Oct. 1730, pres. by Mehetibel Davis, his widow & Adm. Incl. one negro woman.
Apprs: Jonathan Woodbury, Samuel Royall & Joshua Bailey [7:
96/7].

Appt. of Susanah Crossman, widow, as Adm. of Est. of her husb.
SETH CROSSMAN of Taun. dcd. intest., dtd. 20 Oct. 1730 [7:
97/8].

Acct. of Humphrey Smith, Exec. of Est. of DELIVERANCE SMITH of
Dart., dtd. Nov. 1730. Mentions legacies to: Widow Mary Smith,
Alce Smith, Abigail Smith dcd., Mary Smith, "Thomas Briggs
husband to the Late Hope Smith"[sic], Beriah Goddard husb. of
the late Ann Goddard dcd., Eleazer Slocum husb. to the late
Deborah, George Smith, Peleg Smith & Humphrey Smith[7:99/100].

Rcpt. by Mary Smith for legacy from Est. of her husb. DELIVER-
ANCE SMITH of Dart., paid by her son Humphrey Smith, Exec.
dtd. 12 Nov. 1730 [7:101].

Rcpt. by Alce Smith for legacy from Est. of her father DELIVER-
ANCE SMITH of Dart., paid by her brother Humphrey Smith, Exec.
incl. her portion of her dcd. sister Abigail Smith's share,
dtd. 14 Nov. 1730 [7:101].

Rcpt. by Mary Smith for legacy from Est. of her father DELIVER-
ANCE SMITH of Dart., paid by her brother Humphrey Smith, Exec.
dtd. 14 Nov. 1730 [7:101].

Rcpt. by George Smith for legacy from Est. of his father DELIV-
ERANCE SMITH of Dart., paid by his brother Humphrey Smith,
dtd. 12 Nov. 1730 [7:101].

Rcpt. by Peleg Smith for legacy from Est. of his father DELIV-
ERANCE SMITH of Dart., paid by Humphrey Smith, dtd. 12 Nov.
1730 [7:102].

Rcpt. by Thomas Briggs for legacy to his wife [unnamed], dau.
of DELIVERANCE SMITH of Dart., paid by Humphrey Smith, Exec.
dtd. 14 Nov. 1730 [7:102].

Rcpt. by Beriah Goddard for legacy to his wife [unnamed], dau.
of DELIVERANCE SMITH of Dart., paid by Humphrey Smith, dtd.
23 Oct. 1730 [7:102].

Rcpt. by Samuel Wheten of Newport, Cooper, for legacy from Est.
of SAMUEL WHETEEN of Swan., Cordwinder, paid by his uncle &
guard. Isaac Wheteen of Swan., Husbandman, dtd. 20 March 1729/
30 [7:103].

Rcpt. by Eleazer Slocum for legacy to his wife [unnamed] from
Est. of her father DELIVERANCE SMITH, paid by Humphrey Smith,
dtd. 11 Nov. 1730 [7:103].

Order for div. of Est. of NICHOLAS WHITE of Nort. btwn his
chldn., dtd. 9 Sept. 1730 [7:104].

Div. of Est. of NICHOLAS WHITE of Nort. dcd. intest., btwn. his
chldn: Nicholas White (eldest son), Mathew White dcd. (son),
Thomas White (son) & Dorcas Leonard wife of Seth Leonard (dau.)
dtd. 15 Dec. 1730. Comm: George Leonard, Joseph Hodges, William Stone, Josiah Keith & Benjamin Williams [7:104/5/6].

Acct. of Elesebeth Linzey, widow & Adm. of Est. of JOHN LINZEY
of Brist., dtd. 15 Dec. 1730 [7:106/7].

Rcpt. by Caleb Lyon for legacy from Est. of his father JOHN
LYON of Reho., as paid by his guard. Daniel Carpenter of Reho.
dtd. 29 June 1730 [7:108].

Appt. of Arthur [unclear]ning of Reho. as guard. of Nathaniel
Hunt (over 14), son of NATHANIEL HUNT of Reho., dtd. 18 Jan.
1730/1 [7:108/9].

Appt. of Nathaniel Peck of Barr., Yeoman, as guard. of Naomi
May & Bethia May (both over 14), daus. of EPHRAIM MAY of
Reho., dtd. 22 Jan. 1730/1 [7:109/10].

Appt. of Thomas Peck of Reho. as guard. of his wife Deliverance Peck (a minor over 14), dau. of EPHRAIM MAY of Reho.,
dtd. 22 Jan. 1730/1 [7:111].

Appt. of John Read of Barr., Yeoman, as guard. of Rebeca Hunt
(under 14), dau. of NATHANIEL HUNT of Reho., dtd. 22 Jan.
1730/1 [7:112].

Appts. of Elizabeth Linzey of Brist., widow, as guard. of Benjamin & William Linzey (both over 14) & of Gemima Linzey (under 14), chldn. of JOHN LINZEY of Brist., dtd. 2 Feb. 1730/1
[7:112/3/4/5].

Appt. of Ruth Cary of Brist., widow, as guard. of Nathaniel
Cary (over 14), son of JOSIAH CARY of Brist., dtd. 16 Feb.
1730/1 [7:115/6].

Appt. of Benjamin Raynolds of Brist., Cordwainer, as guard. of
Thomas Rawson (over 14), son of WILSON RAWSON of Uxbridge
County of Suffolk, dtd. 16 Feb. 1730/1 [7:116/7].

Appt. of Mrs. Hannah Simmons of Swan., widow, as guard. of Jo-
seph Simmons & Bathsheba Simmons (both minors over 14) & of
Benjamin & Elizabeth Simmons (both under 14), chldn. of RE-
MEMBERANCE SIMMONS of Swan., dtd. 16 Feb. 1730/1 [7:117/8].

Acct. of Thomas Church, guard. of WILLIAM DYE dcd. of Lit. Comp.
who was "non Compus mentis," dtd. March 1729. Incl. item "To
Ellenor How for her Labour time & Trouble in Tending on her
father Since the first of March Last" [7:119/20].

Acct. of Martha Baker of Swan., widow & Adm. of Est. of JOSEPH
BAKER of Swan., dtd. 16 Feb. 1730/1 [7:120/1].
Inv. of Est. of WILLIAM HOSKINS of Taun., dtd. 12 June 1730,
pres. by John Hoskins, Exec. Apprs: James Leonard, Henry
Hodges, Jr. & Morgan Cobb 2nd [7:122/3].
Order to Daniel, Joseph & John Barney, Execs. of Est. of their
father JOSEPH BARNEY of Reho., dtd. 16 Feb. 1730/1[7:123/4].
Will of JOSEPH BARNEY of Reho., Yeoman, dtd. 29 Aug. 1728, prob.
16 Feb. 1730/1. No wife mentioned. Sons: Daniel, Joseph &
John Barney. Daus: Elizabeth the wife of Joseph Mason, Esther
Barney, Sarah Barney & Anne Barney (all under 18 & unmar.).
Sons Daniel, Joseph & John to be Execs. Witns: Seth Bullock,
Squier Bullock & James Bowen [7:124/5/6/7].
Inv. of Est. of Col. NATHANIEL PAIN of Brist., dtd. Feb. 1729/
30, pres. by Sarah Paine, widow & Exec. Incl. 2 negro men, a
negro woman, a negro boy & a negro girl. Apprs: Nathaniel
Hubbard, Jonathan Woodbury & Samuel Royall [7:128/9/30/1].
Inv. of Est. of SETH CROSSMAN of Taun., Husbandman, dtd. 24
Dec. 1730, pres. by Susanah Crossman, widow & Adm. Apprs:
Morgan Cobb 2nd & Samuel Sumner [7:131/2].
Appt. of Mary Cole of Swan., widow, as Adm. of Est. of JOSEPH
COLE of Swan., Yeoman, dtd. 9 March 1730/1 [7:132].
Acct. of Mrs. Elesebeth Carpenter, widow & Adm. of Est. of her
husb. JOSIAH CARPENTER of Reho. dcd. intest., dtd. 16 March
1730/1 [7:133/4].
Inv. of Est. of JOSEPH BARNEY of Reho., dtd. 20 Feb. 1730/1,
pres. by Daniel, Joseph & John Barney, Execs. Incl. one negro
man, one negro woman & 2 negro chldn. Apprs: Jonathan Kings-
ley, James Bowen & Samuel Bullock [7:134/5].
Appt. of Daniel Carpenter of Reho., Yeoman, as guard. of Ebenezer Walker (minor over 14), son of EBENEZER WALKER of Reho.,
dtd. 15 March 1730/1 [7:135].
Appt. of Nathaniel Briggs of Taun. as Adm. of Est. of his father WILLIAM BRIGGS of Taun., dtd. 16 March 1730/1 [7:136].
Rcpt. & quit-claim by Daniel Whitaker & Mary his wife, Samuel
Luther & Sarah his wife, all of Reho., & by Anne Chaffe &
Abigail Chaffe, releasing "our Brothers John Chaffe and Jo-
seph Chaffe," Execs. of the the Est. of their mother ANNIS
CHAFFE, having received all due them, dtd. 20 Nov. 1730/1.
John Chaffe was "of Woodstock" & Joseph Chaffe was of Barr.
[7:137].
Appts. of Joseph Raze of Attl. as guard. of Shubal & Joseph Da-
vis (both under 14), sons of JOSEPH DAVIS of Attl., dtd. 16
March 1730/1 [7:137/8].
Order for div. of Est. of JOHN.LINZEY of Brist. btwn. his wi-
dow & childn., dtd. 9 Feb. 1730/1 [7:139].
Div. of Est. of JOHN LINZEY of Brist. btwn. his widow Eliza-
beth & his chldn: Samuel Linzey, John Linzey, Benjamin Linzey, William Linzey, Jemima Linzey, Mary Oxx & Elesebeth

Ingraham, dtd. 16 March 1730/1. Comm: Jonathan Woodbury, Sam-
uel Royal, John Bozworth, Benjamin Bozworth & William Walker
[7:139/40/1].
Inv. of Est. of HEZEKIAH LUTHER, Jr. of Swan., House Carpenter,
dtd. 17 July 1730, pres. by Patience Luther, his widow & Adm.
Apprs: William Anthony, Samuel Lee & Hezekiah Kingsley [7:
141/2].
Quit-claim & recpt. by Stephen Paine, Taylor, & Edward Paine,
Weaver, both of Preston, New London Co., Ct., discharging
John Butterworth & Moses Read, both of Reho., as Execs. of
Est. of "our Honoured father" STEPHEN PAINE of Reho., dtd. 19
March 1730 [7:142/3].
Appt. of Abial Macomber of Taun. as guard. of Sarah Macomber
(minor over 14), dau. of WILLIAM MACOMBER of Taun., dtd. 26
March 1731 [7:143/4].
Appt. of Marcy [or Marey] Morey, widow, as Adm. of Est. of NI-
CHOLAS MOREY of Digh., dtd. 27 March 1731 [7:144/5].
Acct. of John & Joseph Chaffe, Execs. of Est. of their mother
ANNIS CHAFFE of Barr., dtd. 1 Apr. 1731. Incl. legacies per
will to: Mary Whitaker wife of Daniel Whitaker, Ann Chaffe,
Elesebeth Paine wife of Josiah Paine, Sarah Luther wife of
Samuel Luther & Abigail Chaffe [7:145/6].
Order to Noah Butterworth, Exec. of Est. of his father JOHN
BUTTERWORTH of Reho., dtd. 20 Apr. 1731 [7:146].
Will of Capt. JOHN BUTTERWORTH of Reho., Yeoman, dtd. 3 Nov.
1724, prob. 20 Apr. 1731. No wife mentioned. Sons: John (el-
dest), Samuel & Noah Butterworth. Daus: Sarah Read, Mary
Jencks & Patience Perry. Grson. Seth Titus (under 21). Niece
Experiance Cook dau. of my brother Benjamin Butterworth. Gr-
dau. Patience Titus. Grdau. Bethiah Lyon. Son Noah to be Exec.
Witns: John Greenwood, David Turner & Timothy Walker [7:147
/8/9].
Appt. of Deborah Whipple of Attl., widow, as guard. of David &
Jeremiah Whipple (both minors over 14) & of Sarah Whipple
(under 14), chldn. of JEREMIAH WHIPPLE of Attl., dtd. 4 May
1731 [7:149/50/1].
Appt. of Eliphalet Leonard of Easton as Adm. of Est. of JAMES
HODGE of Easton, "their is not Kindred in this Province Cap-
able of Taking Administration," dtd. 18 May 1731 [7:151/2].
Order to Mary Vial, widow & Exec. of Est. of JAMES VIAL of
Barr., dtd. 18 May 1731 [7:153].
Appt. of Unis Ingoles, widow, as Adm. of Est. of EDMUN INGOLS
of Reho., dtd. May 1731 [7:153/4].
Appt. of Elesebeth Shaw, widow, as Adm. of Est. of SAMUEL SHAW
of Taun., Yeoman, dtd. 18 May 1731 [7:155].
Will of JAMES VIAL of Barr., dtd. 26 Jan. 1730/1, prob. 18 May
1731. Wife Mary. Son John Vial (under 21). Daus: Mercy Vial
(eldest), Mary Vial & Sarah Vial. Wife Mary to be Exec. Witns:
Daniel Allen, Thomas Vial & Peleg Heath [7:156/7].

Inv. of Est. of SAMUEL SHAW of Taun., dtd. 23 Nov. 1730, pres.
by Elesebeth Shaw, widow & Adm. Apprs: John King, John Mason
& Ebenezer Robinson [7:158/9].

Order to div. Est. of JOSIAH CARPENTER of Reho. btwn. his widow
& chldn., dtd. 23 March 1730/1 [7:159/60].

Div. of Est. of JOSIAH CARPENTER of Reho. btwn. his widow Elesebeth Carpenter & his chldn: Comfort Carpenter (son) & Elesebeth Peck, (dau.), dtd. 18 May 1731. Comm: Benjamin Hunt,
David Newman, Noah Mason, Edward Glover & Daniel Parin [7:
160/1/2].

Acct. of William Robinson, Exec. of Est. of THOMAS ROBARTS, dtd.
18 May 1731, pres. by Martha Robinson, widow & Adm. of Est. of
William Robinson dcd. of Swan., said William having been residuary legatee in the will of said Robarts. Incl. legacies
to Abraham Barker & his wife & to Joseph Barker [7:162/2¼].

Acct. of Martha Robinson, widow & Adm. of Est. of WILLIAM ROB-
INSON of Swan., dtd. 18 May 1731. Incl. an item which "Said
Accomptant Prays for allowance for woll and Clothing for her
Children not here Charged and also for Defraying ye Charge of
her Laying in" [7:162¼/2½].

Appt. of Hanery Tew of Newport as guard. of Sarah Tew (minor
over 14), dau. of WILLIAM TEW of Tiv., dtd. 15 June 1731 [7:
162½/3].

Order to William Wilbour of Lit. Comp., Exec. of Est. of JO-
SEPH CRANDAL of Lit. Comp., Yeoman, dtd. 15 June 1731 [7:163].

Order to Hannah Brown, widow & Exec. of Est. of Capt. JOSEPH
BROWN of Attl., dtd. 15 June 1731 [7:164].

Will of JOSEPH CRANDAL of Lit. Comp., Yeoman, dtd. 10 March 17-
29/30, prob. 15 June 1731. Wife Elesebeth. "My Three Children
Rebecca Isaac & Ezra." Brother-in-law William Wilbour to be
Exec. Witns: Daniel Hillard, Warren Gibbs & Josiah Closson
[7:165/6].

Will of Capt. JOSEPH BROWN of Attl., "being Aged," dtd. 13 March
1727/8, prob. 15 June 1731. Wife Hannah. Sons: Jabiz Brown,
John Brown dcd., Joseph Brown (to Joseph or his heires) & Benjamin Brown. 3 daus: Hannah Ledoight, Lidia Ledoight & Mary
French. Wife Hannah to be Exec. Witns: William Whipple, Israel Whipple & John Foster [7:166/7].

Inv. of Est. of Capt. JOSEPH BROWN of Attl., dtd. 4 June 1731,
pres. by Hannah Brown, his widow & Exec. Apprs: Elisha Peck,
Ebenezer Carpenter & Israel Whiple [7:168].

Inv. of Est. of Capt. JOHN BUTTERWORTH of Reho., dtd. 28 Apr.
1731, pres. by Noah Butterworth, his son & Exec. Apprs: Abiah
Carpenter, Benjamin Hunt & Edward Glover [7:169]

Inv. of Est. of WILLIAM BRIGGS of Taun. dcd. intest., dtd. 2
March 1731, pres. by Nathaniel Briggs, Adm. Apprs: Joseph
Hodges, Thomas Burt & Morgan Cobb 2nd [7:170/1].

Acct. of Content Briggs, widow & Adm. of Est. of WESTON BRIGGS
of Dart., dtd. 15 June 1731 [7:171].

Acct. of John Sweeting, Exec. of Est. of his father HENERY
SWEETING of Reho., dtd. 15 June 1731. Inc. legacies per will
to: Mary Mason, Henery Sweeten, Joanah Sampson, Susanah Hunt
wife of John Hunt, Experiance Cary wife of John Cary, Elesebeth Sweeten now Elesebeth Martin, John Sweeting, Anna Sweeting now Anna Walker [7:172/3].

Rcpts. by Henery Sweeting of Providence, R.I., Hat Maker, for
legacies from Est. of his father HENERY SWEETING of Reho.,
paid by his brother John Sweeting of Reho., Exec., dtd. 11
June 1728 & 16 June 1729. Witns: John West & Joseph Mason,
Jr. [7:173/4].

Rcpt. by John Hunt of Reho. for legacy from Est. of HENERY SWEET-
ING of Reho., paid by John Sweeting, Exec., dtd. 12 March
1730 [7:174]

Rcpt. dtd. 18 June 1729 by Noah Mason of Reho., Cordwaner, &
Mary his wife for a legacy from Est. of HENERY SWEETING
willed to testator's son-in-law James Sampson living in Tiverton in England, said Mason being empowered by a letter under Sampson's hand of 10 March 1729. Witns: Jonathan Perry &
John West [7:174].

Rcpt. by John Cary & Experience Cary of Bridgewater, Co. of Plimouth, for legacy from Est. of her father HENERY SWEETING,
paid by John Sweeting, dtd. 18 Dec. 1728 [7:175].

Rcpt. by William Martin & Elesebeth Martin of Barr. for legacy
from Est. of her father HENERY SWEETING of Reho., paid by
John Sweeting of Reho., dtd. 17 May 1728 [7:175].

Rcpt. by "Anna Sweeting alias Walker" & her husb. Nathaniel
Walker of Reho., Husbandman, for a legacy from the Est. of
her father HENERY SWEETING of Reho., paid by John Sweeting of
Reho., Exec., dtd. 17 May 1728. Witns: William Martin & John
West [7:175/6].

Inv. of Est. of NICHOLAS MOREY of Digh., dtd. 30 March 1731,
pres. by Marcy [or Marey?] Morey, his widow & Adm. Incl. 2
negro men: Hector & Pomp; & one "mallato boy Named Jeminy."
Apprs: John Cummins, Silvester Richmond & Morgan Cobb 2nd
[7:176/7/8/9].

Inv. of Est. of JAMES HODGE of Easton, dtd. 27 May 1731, pres.
by Eliphalet Leonard, Adm. Incl. lands in Bridgewater. Apprs:
Ephraim Randal, John Phillips & Benjamin Drake [7:179].

Acct. of Hannah Simmons, widow & Adm. of Est. of REMEMBRANCE
SIMMONS of Swan. dcd. intest., dtd. 16 Feb. 1730/1. Mentions
that "the Land was Sold by order of the Superior Court 1727"
[7:180/1].

Inv. of Est. of JOSEPH COLE of Swan., dtd. 16 March 1730/1, pres.
by Mary Cole, widow & Adm. Apprs: William Anthoney, Hezekiah
Luther & Hezekiah Kingsley [7:181½/182].

Will of FRANCIS STEVENS of Reho., dtd. 17 June 1731, prob. 29
June 1731. No wife mentioned. Sister Elesebeth Linkhorn dcd.,
heirs of my sister Esther Tingley, my sister Mary Fuller. My

cousen Francis Fuller. The son of John Sweetland. My cousin
John Sweetland to be Exec. Witns: John Bowen, Zerviah Bowen
& Ezekiah Reed [7:182/3].

Order to John Sweetland of Attl., Exec. of Est. of FRANCIS STE-
VENS of Reho., dtd. 29 June 1731 [7:183/4].

Acct. of Patience Luther, Adm. of Est. of her husb. HEZEKIAH
LUTHER of Swan., dtd. 20 July 1731 [7:184/5].

Appt. of Mary Shearman, widow, as Adm. of Est. of JOSEPH SHEAR-
MAN of Free., dtd. 27 July 1731 [7:185/6].

Inv. of Est. of JOSEPH SHEARMAN of Free., dtd. 13 May 1731,
pres. by Mary Shearman, widow & Adm. Apprs: Aron Bowen, Anti-
pas Hathaway & Silvanus Sole [7:186].

Order to Walter Chase of Free., Exec. of Est. of BENJAMIN CHASE
of Free., dtd. 20 July 1731 [7:187].

Will of BENJAMIN CHASE of Free., Cooper, dtd. 6 Sept. in the
3rd year of the reign of George the 2nd [1730], prob. 20 July
1731. No wife mentioned. Sons Benjamin & Walter Chase. Grsons:
Benjamin Grinhil & Daniel Grenhill. Daus: Bethiah Dunham,
Philip [sic] Hathaway (called dau. 3 times) and son-in-law
Jacob Hathaway, Mary dcd. & dau. Sarah dcd. Grdau. Sarah
Hathaway wife of Isaac Hathaway. Son Walter to be Exec. Mentions lands in Free. & in Middleborough. Witns: Isaac Hathaway, Jr., William Hart & Benjamin Darnell [7:187/8/9].

Order for div. of Est. of ANTHONY SPRAGUE of Attl., dtd. 13
Jan. 1731 [7:189/90].

Div. of Est. of ANTHONY SPRAGUE of Attl. dcd. intest. btwn. his
chldn: Anthony Sprague (eldest son), Sarah Whitman, Elesebeth
Whiple, Mary Whiple, Pheba Sprague, Lydiah Harris & Mercy
Jenckes, dtd. 24 May 1731. Comm: John Foster, Noah Carpenter,
Henery Tolman & Daniel Perrin [7:190/1/2].

Order for div. of Est. of REMEMBRANCE SIMMONS of Swan. dcd. intest., dtd. 25 Feb. 1730/1 [7:192].

Div. of Est. of REMEMBRANCE SIMMONS of Swan. btwn. his widow
[not named] & his chldn: Remembrance Simmons (eldest son),
Hannah (eldest dau.) wife of Oliver Simmons, Abial (2nd son),
Bathsheba (2nd dau.), Joseph (3rd son), Benjamin (4th son),
Elesebeth (3rd dau.). Comm: William Anthoney, Hezekiah Lu-
ther, Eseck Brown, Jonathan Hill & Abraham Waldron[7:192/3/4].

Inv. of Est. of JOSEPH CRANDAL of Lit. Comp., dtd. 11 June 1731,
pres. by William Wilbour, Exec. Apprs: William Hall, Elihu
Woodworth & William Richmond [7:195/6].

Inv. of Est. of SAMUEL HUNT of Dart., dtd. 30 Apr. 1730/1, pres.
by [blank] Hunt, widow & Adm. Apprs: Nathaniel Shappard,
Stephen West & Nathaniel Blackwel [7:196/7].

Petition by Richard Tew, George Sisson & William Sanford, Execs.
of Est. of WILLIAM TEW of Tiv., requesting 1 mo. before pres.
an acct., dtd. 20 July 1731. Agreed to by the guard. [un-
named] who had been chosen by Sarah Tew, dau. of the dcd.
[7:197].

Appts. of Elesebeth Crandal of Lit. Comp., widow, as guard. of
Rebecca Crandal, Isaac Crandal & Ezra Crandal (all under 14),
chldn. of JOSEPH CRANDAL of Lit. Comp., dtd. 17 Aug. 1731
[7:198/9].

Acct. of Patiance Haddaway [*later called "Hathaway"*], late widow & Adm. of Capt. CONSTANT CHURCH of Free., dtd. 16 Sept.
1731. Incl. paym. to: "Mr White for My Children" & "To Widdow
Mary Church" [7:200/1].

Acct. of Benjamin Wilbour of Taun., guard. of James Danforth
"who is non Compus mentis," dtd. 17 Sept. 1731. Mentions a
dwelling house & land "Left in the hands of Sarah Danforth
wife of James Danforth...for the Support of the Family" [7:
201/2/3].

Inv. of Est. of BENJAMIN CHASE of Free., dtd. 29 July 1731,
pres. by Walter Chase, Exec. Apprs: William Winslow, James
Dodson & Samuel Tisdale [7:203/4].

Order to Sarah Gibbs, widow & Exec. of Est. of JAMES GIBBS of
Brist., dtd. 24 Sept. 1731 [7:204].

Will of JAMES GIBBS of Bris., "Malster...being weak and in Pain
in body," dtd. 19 Dec. 1729, prob. 24 Sept. 1731. Wife Sarah.
Sons: George, John & James Gibbs. Daus: Ann Tyley & Jane Fowl-
er. Wife Sarah to be Exec. Witns: William Martin, William
Bragg & Samuel Howland [7:205/6].

Acct. of Patience Pratt & Samuel Pratt, Execs. of Est. of SAM-
UEL PRATT of Taun., dtd. 21 Sept. 1731 [7:206/7].

Appts. of Abigail White of Taun., widow, as guard of Thomas,
Sarah & John White (all minors over 14) & of Abraham, Mary,
Nathaniel, Joanah, Uslah (female) & Abigail White (all under
14), chldn. of THOMAS WHITE of Taun., dtd. 21 Sept. 1731 [7:
207/8/9/10/1/2/3/4/5].

Appt. of Samuel Hacket of Raynham, Yeoman, as Adm. of Est. of
JACOB HOSKINS of Raynham, dtd. 16 Sept. 1731 [7:215/6].

Will of SAMUEL DEAN of Taun., dtd. 28 June 1728, prob. 12 Oct.
1731. Wife Sarah. 4 sons: Isaac, Samuel, William & Nathan
Dean. Dau. Bethiah Clap. Wife Sarah & son Samuel to be Execs.
Mentions lands in Taun. & in Norton. Witns: Seth Williams,
James Williams & David Williams [7:216/7/8].

Appt. of Mary Barney, widow, as Adm. of Est. of JACOB BARNEY of
Taun. dtd. 19 Oct. 1731 [7:219].

Appt. of Eliphalet Leonard of Easton, Yeoman, as guard. of James
Hodge (under 14), son of JAMES HODGE of Easton, dtd. 19 Oct.
1731 [7:220].

Appt. of Benjamin Drake of Easton as guard. of Seth Hodge (under 14), son of JAMES HODGE of Easton, dtd. 19 Oct. 1731 [7:
221].

Order to Benjamin Drake of Easton, Exec. of Est. of THOMAS
DRAKE of Easton, dtd. 19 Oct. 1731 [7:221/2].

Will of THOMAS DRAKE of the East End of Taun. North Purchase or
East Precinct of Norton,   dtd. 15 June 1719 [*sic*], prob.

19 Oct. 1731. Wife Hannah. Sister Elizebeth Phillips & brother Benjamin Drake. Brother Benjamin to be Exec. & neighbors Thomas Randal & Ephraim Randal to be Overseers. Witns: Susanah Randal, Israel Randal & Ephraim Randal [7:222/3/4].

Appt. of William Hayward of Easton, Weaver, as guard. of Mary Hodge (minor over 14), dau. of JAMES HODGE of Easton, dtd. 19 Oct. 1731 [7:223/4].

Appt. of Barnard Haile, Jr. of Swan. as Adm. of Est. of his mother HANNAH HAILE of Swan., widow dcd. intest., dtd. 19 Oct. 1731 [7:225/6].

Appt. of Experiance Mason of Swan., widow, as Adm. of Est. of SAMPSON MASON of Swan., dtd. 25 Oct. 1731 [7:226/7].

Appt. of Jonathan Hill of Swan., Yeoman, as guard. of Stephen Eddy (under 14), son of EBENEZER EDDY of Swan., dtd. 1 Nov. 1731 [7:227/8].

Appt. of Elesebeth Haile, widow, as Exec. of Est. of JOHN HAILE of Swan. dcd. intest., dtd. 1 Nov. 1731 [7:228/9].

Acct. of Jonathan Kingsley, Adm. of Est. of EBENEZER EDDY of Swan., dtd. 25 Oct. 1731 [7:229/30].

Acct. of James Redaway, Adm. of Est. of WILLIAM HAMMON of Reho. dcd. insolvent, dtd. 22 Oct. 1731. Mentions an allowance to "the Widdow for Necessarys for house Keeping" [7:231].

Report of debts owed by Est. of SETH CROSSMAN of Taun., dtd. 9 Nov. 1731. Comm: Samuel Sumner & Benjamin Wilbour [7:232].

Order abt. insolvent Est. of SETH CROSSMAN of Taun., dtd. 9 Nov. 1731. Mentions "The Inventory and Account presented by Susanah Crossman Deceased," but then directs the "said Administratrix" to pay creditors [7:232/3].

Report on debts of Est. of WILLIAM HAMMON of Reho., Husbandman, dtd. 9 Nov. 1731. Comm: Jethniel Peck & Nathaniel Wilmouth [7:233/4].

Appt. of John French of Attl. as Adm. "De bonis non" of Est. of EBENEZER WHITE of Attl., since the Adm., Abigail White, is since dcd., dtd. 16 Nov. 1731 [7:234/5].

Appt. of Jonathan Hill of Swan., Yeoman, as guard. of Phebe Eddy (minor over 14), dau. of EBENEZER EDDY of Swan., dtd. 16 Nov. 1731 [7:235/6].

Appt. of Mary Chaffe, widow, as Adm. of Est. of HEZEKIAH CHAFFE of Reho., "Phicitian," dtd. 16 Nov. 1731 [7:236/6].

Appts. of Mayhew Dagget of Attl., Yeoman, as guard. of Martha White & Hannah White (minors over 14), daus. of EBENEZER WHITE of Attl., dtd. 16 Nov. 1731 [7:237/8/9].

Appt. of Jonathan Hill of Swan. to be guard. of Sarah Eddy (minor over 14), dau. of EBENEZER EDDY of Swan., dtd. 16 Nov. 1731 [7:239/40].

Appt. of Benjamin Slack of Attl., Yeoman, as guard. of Ebenezer White (minor over 14), son of EBENEZER WHITE of Attl., dtd. 16 Nov. 1731 [7:240].

Appt. of Deborah Nutting, widow, as Adm. of Est. of JONATHAN

NUTTING of Attl., "Ginsmith" [*sic*], dtd. 16 Nov. 1731 [7:241].

Order to Isaac Howland of Dart., Exec. in 2nd degree of Est. of JOHN GATCHEL of Dart., Adm. having been committed to Judith Gatchill as Exec., but she has since married, dtd. 17 Nov. 1731 [7:242].

Appt. of Benjamin Slack of Attl. as guard. of Abigail White (minor over 14), dau. of EBENEZER WHITE of Attl., dtd. 16 Nov. 1731 [7:243].

Order to Sarah Dean, widow, & Samuel Dean, son, Execs. of Est. of SAMUEL DEAN of Taun., dtd. 12 Oct. 1731 [7:244].

Acct. of "Judith Hix Late Judith Gatchel," widow & Exec. of Est. of JOHN GATCHEL of Dart., dtd. 17 Nov. 1731 [7:244/5].

Acct. of Elezebeth Walker, Exec. of Est. of THOMAS WALKER of Brist., dtd. 16 Nov. 1731. Incl. item "To Edward Little half of his Legacy" [7:246].

Inv. of Est. of HANNAH HAIL of Swan., dtd. 27 Oct. 1731, pres. by Barnard Haile, her son & Adm. Apprs: George Sisson, Benjamin Munroe & Jonathan Kingsley [7:247].

Inv. of Est. of JONATHAN NUTTING of Attl., dtd. 12 Nov. 1731, pres. by Deborah Nutting, his widow & Adm. Apprs: Silvanus Scott, Elisha Peck & Israel Whipple [7:248].

Order for div. of Est. of JOHN FULLER of Attl. dcd. intest., dtd. 12 Jan. 1731 [7:249].

Div. of Est. of JOHN FULLER, Jr. of Attl. btwn. "his Late Widdow Elizebeth Martin" & his chldn: Samuel Fuller (eldest son), Mary Fuller (dau.), John Fuller (son), Hannah Healey (dau.), & Elizebeth Fuller (dau.), dtd. 15 Jan. 1730/1. Comm: Noah Carpenter, John French, Henery Tolman & Daniel Perrin [7:249/50/1/2].

Petition by David Akin refusing to be Overseer of Est. of JOHN GATCHEL of Dart., dtd. 25 Nov. 1731. Witns: Benjamin Smith & Barnabas Howland [7:252].

Acceptance by Elezebeth Crandall, widow of JOSEPH CRANDALL of Lit. Comp., of terms of will of her late husb. "in Leue of her Thirds," dtd. 16 Nov. 1731 [7:252].

Acct. of Richard Tew, George Sisson & William Sanford, Execs. of Est. of WILLIAM TEW of Tiv., "who Dyed 5th 2 m^o," dtd. 12 Nov. 1731. Very lengthy. Mentions paym. to "Henery Tew Guardian to Sarah and Dorcas Tew," & "To the widdow Abigail Tew." Incl. item "To the funeral Expenses of Two Children (viz) Abigail & Edward Tew who Dyed ye 11th & 22^d of August 1718." Paym. for "Time and Trouble Expended in Removing ye familey of Said Tew from Tiverton to Portsmouth." Paym. "To Scholing Sarah Tew and William Tew 10 weeks." Item "then R̄eceived under my Care Dorcas & Sarah Tew by the Request of their mother who Departed This Life the 30 of the Sixth month 1723." Various items for tending for Abigail Tew in her sickness and paying for her funeral. An item to "Richard Tew in money to pay his Sister Peckom." An item to "Anna the wife of Henery

Tew for the Grave Stones for William Tew his Wife and Three
Children." Mentions "Sarah Tew Left my house to Live with her
aunt [*Abigail*] Wrightington." Item "To the abode of Dorcas
Tew from the thirteenth of September 1723 until the thirteenth
of September 1731" [7:253/4/5/6/7/8/9/60/1/2/3/4].
Appt. of Mary Ide of Reho., widow, as Adm. of Est. of JOSIAH
IDE of Reho. dcd. intest., dtd. 13 Dec. 1731 [7:264/5].
Appt. of George Beverly of Reho. as Adm. of Est. of his brother
JOHN BEVERLEY of Reho., dtd. 21 Dec. 1731 [7:265/6].
Order to James Lewis of Reho., Exec. of Est. of his mother ELEZ-
EBETH LEWIS of Swan., dtd. 29 Nov. 1731 [7:266/7].
Will of ELEZEBETH LEWIS of Swan., "widdow and Lately wife of
Thomas Lewis" of Swan., "being at Present Sick," dtd. 8 Nov.
1731, prob. 29 Nov. 1731. Daus: Mary wife of Isaac Carter,
Deborah wife of Samuel Eddy, Experiance Mason widow, Tabitha
wife of Daniel Martin & Lidia Lewis. Son Samuel Lewis to be
Exec. Grchldn: Elezebeth & Sarah Carter daus. of dau. Mary
Carter; Abigail Eddy dau. of dau. Deborah Eddy; Nathan & Ben-
jamin Mason sons of dau. Experiance Mason & Hannah & Lidia
Martin daus. of dau. Tabitha Martin. Witns: Daniel Bowen,
Elisha Mason & Ephraim Lambard [7:267/8/9].
Inv. of Est. of SAMPSON MASON of Swan., Yeoman, dtd. 5 Nov. 17-
31, pres. by Experiance Mason, his widow & Adm. Apprs: Heze-
kiah Bowen, John Wood, Jr. & Daniel Luther [7:269/70].
Inv. of Est. of JOHN HAIL of Swan., Yeoman, dtd. 12 Nov. 1731,
pres. by Elezebeth Hail, his widow & Adm. Apprs: Hezekiah
Bowen, John Wood, Jr. & Daniel Luther [7:270/1].
Appt. of George Beverley of Swan. as Adm. "De bonis non" of Est.
of LEONEX BEVERLEY of Reho., Adm. having been granted to John
Beverley son of dcd. "Who is Since Deceased Intestate," dtd.
21 Dec. 1731 [7:271/2].
Will of JOHN CROSSMAN, Sr. of Taun., "being Very Sick," dtd. 18
May 1727, prob. 21 Dec. 1731. Wife included but not named. 4
sons: John, Jonathan, Benjamin & Henery Crossman. Daus: Abi-
gail White, chldn. of my dcd. dau. Sarah Babit, Johannah Rogers, Mercy Linkon & Deborah Crossman. Grdau. Abigail White.
Witns: Morgan Cobb, 2nd, John Harvey & Nathaniel Burt [7:272/
3/4].
Appt. of Meribah Shearman, widow, as Adm. of Est. of MOSES
SHEARMAN of Dart. dcd. intst., dtd. 18 Jan. 1731/2 [7:275].
Inv. of Est. of JOSIAH IDE of Reho., dtd. 16 Dec. 1731, pres.
by Mary Ide, widow & Adm. Apprs: Abiah Carpenter, John Robinson & Edward Glover [7:276/7].
Inv. of Est. of MOSES SHEARMAN of Dart., dtd. 25 Dec. 1731,
pres. by Meribah Shearman, widow & Adm. Apprs: Joseph Rus-
sel, Benjamin Allen & Stephen West [7:278/9].
Div. of Est. of SAMUEL KING of Norton btwn. his widow Sarah
King & his chldn: heirs of eldest son Samuel King dcd., dau.
Ruth King, dau. Mary Caswell, dau. Sarah White, dau. Ann King,

son Hezekiah King & son Nehemiah King, dtd. 10 July 1731.
Comm: Joseph Hodges, Benjamin Hodges & William Stone [7:279/
80/1/2/3].
Inv. of Est. of EBENEZER TORREY of Brist., pres. 26 Jan. 1731/2
by William Torrey, Adm. Apprs: Nathaniel Bosworth, Nathaniel
Woodbury & William Peck [7:283/4].
Acct. of William Torrey, Adm. of Est. of EBENEZER TORREY of
Brist., dtd. 26 Jan. 1731.2 [7:284/5].
Order to Ezra Dean & Ephraim Dean, Execs. of Est. of their fa-
ther EZRA DEAN of Taun., dtd. 15 Feb. 1731/2 [7:285/6].
Will of EZRA DEAN of Taun., dtd. 28 Sept. 1727, prob. 15 Feb.
1731/2. No wife mentioned. Sons: Ezra Dean (eldest), Ephraim
Dean & chldn. of my son Seth Dean dcd. Dau. Margaret Shaw.
My father Walter Dean. Grson. Silas son of Seth Dean dcd. Gr-
dau. Bethiah Shaw dau. of dau. Margaret Shaw. Grson: Stephen
son of son Ezra Dean. Witns: Abiell Dean, Stephen Wilbour &
John Dean [7:286/7/8].
Appt. of Hannah Wheeten, widow, as Adm. of Est. of JAMES WHEET-
EN of Swan., dtd. 1 Feb. 1731/2 [7:289].
Appt. of Benjamin Cole of Swan., Yeoman, as guard. of Edward,
Mary, Benjamin & Ebenezer Cole (all minors over 14), chldn.
of EBENEZER COLE of Swan., dtd. 25 Feb. 1731/2 [7:290/1/2].
Order to Mary Mason, widow & Exec. of Est. of her husb. ISAAC
MASON of Swan., dtd. 21 March 1731/2 [7:292/3].
Will of ISAAC MASON, Jr. of Swan., yeoman, "being Very Weak &
Low in Body," dtd. 24 Feb. 1731/2, prob. 21 March 1731/2.
Wife Mary. Sons: Caleb (eldest), Noah & Isaac Mason. Dau.
Phebe Mason (under age & unmar.). Wife Mary to be Exec. Witns:
Samuel Wheteen, Barnard Hail & Joseph Mason [7:293/4/5].
Inv. of Est. of HEZEKIAH CHAFFE of Reho., dtd. 18 Nov. 1731,
pres. by Mary Chaffe, widow & Adm. Apprs: Samuel Vial, Jo-
seph Allen & Joseph Chaffe [7:295/6].
Inv. of Est. of JACOB BARNEY of Taun., Gentleman, dtd. 7 Nov.
1731, pres. by Mary Barney, widow & Adm. Apprs: John Mason,
Benjamin Wilbour & John Sumner [7:296/7].
Appt. of Rebeca Abel of Reho., widow, as Adm. of Est. of JOSHUA
ABELL of Reho. dcd. intest., dtd. 12 Apr. 1732 [7:297/8].
Appt. of Rachel Perrin, widow, as Adm. of Est. of JOHN PERRIN
of Reho., dtd. 18 Apr. 1732 [7:298/9].
Appt. of Martha Read, widow, as Adm. of Est. of ZACHARIAH READ
of Reho., dtd. 18 Apr. 1732 [7:299/300].
Appt. of Marcy Carpenter, widow, as Adm. of Est. of JEDEDIAH
CARPENTER of Reho. dcd. intest., dtd. 18 Apr. 1732 [7:300/1].
Appt. of Sarah Titus, widow, as Adm. of Est. of ROBART TITUS of
Attl., dtd. 18 Apr. 1732 [7:301/2].
Appts. of Caleb Hall of Attl., Yeoman, as guard. of Experiance
& Edward White (both under 14), chldn. of EBENEZER WHITE of
Attl., dtd. 18 Apr. 1732 [7:302/3/4].
Appt. of Hannah Peidge of Attl., widow, as guard. of Hannah

Peidge (minor over 14), dau. of JOSIAH PEIDGE of Attl., dtd. 18 Apr. 1732 [7:304/5].

Appt. of Amos Shephardson of Attl., Yeoman, as guard. of his wife Margaret Shepherdson (minor over 14), dau. of JOSIAH PEIDGE of Attl., dtd. 18 Apr. 1732 [7:305].

Appt. of Timothy Tingley of Attl., Yeoman, as guard. of Thankful White (under 14), dau. of EBENEZER WHITE of Attl., dtd. 18 Apr. 1732 [7:306].

Appt. of Yetmarcy Palmer, widow, as Adm. of Est. of ISAAC PALMER of Lit. Comp., Mariner, dtd. 26 Apr. 1732 [7:306/7].

Appt. of Timothy Tingley of Attl., Yeoman, as guard. of Elezebeth Peidge (minor over 14), dau. of JOSIAH PEIDGE of Attl., dtd. 18 Apr. 1732 [7:307/8].

Appt. of Hannah Peidge of Attl., widow, as guard. of Jonathan Peidge (under 14), son of JOSIAH PEIDGE of Attl., dtd. 18 Apr. 1732 [7:308/9].

Appt. of Mary Walker, widow, as Adm. of Est. of EPHRAIM WALKER of Reho. dcd. intest., dtd. 18 Apr. 1732 [7:309/10].

Acct. of Nathaniel Sponer & Stephen West, Jr., Execs. of Est. of WILLIAM SPONER of Dart., dtd. 18 Apr. 1732. Incl. legacies per will to: Sarah Sponer, Mary Haskall & her husb. Mark Haskall, Elice Sponer & Nathaniel Sponer [7:310/1].

Inv. of Est. of JOHN PERRIN of Reho., dtd. 22 March 1731/2, pres. by Rachel Perrin, widow & Adm. Incl. items for dyeing cloth. Apprs: Samuel Hill, Daniel Paine & Daniel Carpenter [7:311/2].

Inv. of Est. of ROBART TITUS of Attl., pres. 18 Apr. 1732 by Sarah Titus, widow & Adm. Apprs: Daniel Perrin, Daniel Carpenter & Daniel Chaffe [7:312/3].

Inv. of Est. of JEDEDIAH CARPENTER of Reho., dtd. 24 Dec. 1731, pres. by Mercy Carpenter, widow & Adm. Incl. blacksmith shop & tools. Apprs: Daniel Carpenter, Daniel Perrin & Luke Thurston [7:313/4].

Acct. of Capt. John Foster, Exec. of Est. of MARY GUILE of Attl., dtd. 18 Apr. 1732. Incl. money paid to Joseph Guile. Also incl. legacies per will to: Caleb Hall, Joshua Hall, Joseph Tifiney husb. of Mary Tifiney & Hannah Bennet & her husb. John Bennet [7:314/5].

Acct. of Hannah Peidge, Adm. of Est. of JOSIAH PEIDGE of Att., dtd. 18 Apr. 1732. Incl. paym. "to my father Freeman for Board." Item "to Lying in and funerall Charges for my Child" [7:316/7].

Inv. of Est. of ZACHARIAH READ of Reho., dtd. 1 Apr. 1732, pres. by Martha Read, widow & Adm. Apprs: Daniel Carpenter, Noah Sabin & Daniel Perrin [7:318].

Div. of Est. of PETER ALDRICH of Norton btwn. his widow Experiance Aldrich & his chldn: Peter Aldrich, Experiance the wife of William Mackpeice & Sarah Aldrich, dtd. 18 Apr. 1732. Comm: John Austin, Benjamin Hodges, Ebenezer Dagget & Josiah White [7:318/9/20/1].

Order for div. of Est. of ELEXANDER MAXCEE of Attl. dcd. intest.
dtd. 23 [*blank*][7:322].

Div. of Est. of ALEXANDER MAXEY of Attl. btwn. his widow [*not
named*] & his chldn: Joseph Maxey, Josiah Maxey, Abigail Has-
call, Mary Ware's heirs, Easter Ward & Benjamin Maxey. Comm:
John Foster, Mahew Dagget, Thomas Stanley, Penticost Blackenton & Ebenezer Dagget [7:322/3/4/5].

Inv. of Est. of JAMES READ of Reho., dtd. 21 March 1732, pres.
by Aron Reade, his son & Adm. Apprs: Abiah Carpenter, Daniel
Perrin & Daniel Carpenter [7:325/6].

Acct. of John French, Adm. de bonis non to Est. of the Rev. EB-
ENEZER WHITE of Attl., dtd. 2 May 1732. Incl. paym. "For Nursing & boarding of Thankful White May 28 to May 1729." Items
"Victuals and Cloths for Experiance White 3 years" & "Boarding Edward White 2 years" [7:326/7/8].

Acct. of Mary Salisbury & Richard Salsbury, Execs. of Est. of
WILLIAM SALSBURY of Swan. dtd. 10 May 1732. Incl. item rcvd.
from Ephraim Salsbury for sale of land per will. Incl. legacies per will to: Benjamin Salsbury, Rachel Cole wife of Samuel Cole & Rebecca Bushee wife of John Bushee [7:329/30].

Appt. of Rebecca Brown, widow & Adm. of Est. of WILLIAM BROWN
of Reho. dcd. intest., dtd. 16 May 1732 [7:330/1].

Order to Abiah Carpenter & Thomas Carpenter, sons & Execs. of
Est. of ABIAH CARPENTER of Reho., dtd. 16 May 1732 [7:331/2].

Will of ABIAH CARPENTER of Reho., Yeoman, dtd. 4 Apr. 1732, prob.
16 May 1732. Wife Mary. Sons: Abiah (eldest), Thomas & Cornelius (youngest) Carpenter. Daus: Rachel Bliss & Mary Carpenter.
Grdau. Sarah Chaffee (under 18 & unmar.). 2 eldest sons Abiah
& Thomas to be Execs. Mentions a covenant he had made with
wife Mary before their marriage. Witns: Samuel Barrsto, Paul
Titus & John Greenwood [7:332/3/4/5].

Appt. of Thomas Wilmouth of Attl., Whelewright, as guard. of
Samuel Freeman (under 14), son of BENJAMIN FREEMAN of Attl.,
dtd. 16 May 1732. [*One place in this entry he is alternately
called "son of Abiah Carpenter," an apparent copyist's error*]
[7:335/6].

Inv. of Est. of EPHRAIM WALKER of Reho., dtd. 25 Apr. 1732,
pres. by Mary Walker, widow & Adm. Apprs: Edward Glover, Ezekiel Read & Timothy Ide [7:336/7].

Inv. of Est. of ABIAH CARPENTER of Reho., dtd. 9 May 1732, pres.
by Abiah Carpenter & Thomas Carpenter, Execs. Apprs: Daniel
Carpenter, Edward Glover & Timothy Ide, Jr. [7:337/8].

Inv. of Est. of WILLIAM BROWN of Reho., dtd. 16 March 1731/2,
pres. by Rebecca Brown, widow & Adm. Apprs: Daniel Carpenter,
Daniel Perrin & Samuel Hill [7:338/9].

Inv. of Est. of JOSHUA ABELL of Reho., dtd. 12 May 1732, pres.
by Rebecca Abell, widow & Adm. Apprs: Daniel Carpenter, Timothy Ide, Jr. & Edward Glover [7:339/40].

Inv. of Est. of EBENEZER MARTIN late of Reho., Yeoman, dtd. at

Barr. 25 Oct. 1727, pres. 16 May 1732 by James Wheler & Edward
Luther, Execs. Apprs: Elisha May, Samuel Kent & Ezra Ormsbee
[7:340/1].

Acct. of James Wheler & Edward Luther, Execs. of Est. of EBEN-
EZER MARTIN late of Barr., dtd. 16 May 1732. Incl. legacies
of household goods & money per will "to the widdow" [7:341/2/3]

Acct. of "Hannah Morey Late Hannah Millar," widow & Exec. of Est.
of SAMUEL MILLAR of Reho., dtd. 16 May 1732 [7:343/4].

Acct. of Henery Smith, Adm. of Est. of his brother THOMAS SMITH
of Reho., dtd. 16 May 1732. Mentions paym. "to Twelve Days
Tending on the Said Deceased in ye time of his Last Sickness."
Incl. paym. of debts to: Mary Smith, Jonathan Smith, Anna
Smith & Daniel Smith [7:344/5].

Will of WILLIAM DYE of Lit. Comp., Yeoman, "being aged," dtd.
17 May 1720, prob. 16 May 1732. No wife mentioned. Son William
Dye. Daus: Elezebeth Lewis [sic] & Elinor How. Grdau. Mehetibel
Dye. Heirs of my son John Dye dcd. The Rev. Richard Billings
to be Exec. Witns: John Palmer, William Hall & Job Palmer.
[No mention is made here of the will by the same William Dye,
dated in South Kingston, R.I. 5 years later, in 1725, and probated in Bristol in 1730, as noted above in 7:20/1/2][7:345/6].

Order to Thomas Brownel of Lit. Comp., one of the Execs. of the
Est. of his father THOMAS BROWNEL of Lit. Comp., Mary Brownel
the widow having renounced her executorship, dtd. 20 June 17-
32 [7:347].

Will of THOMAS BROWNEL of Lit. Comp., Yeoman, dtd. 1730 [no day
or month], prob. 20 June 1732. Wife Mary. Sons: Thomas, John,
George, Jeremiah & Charles Brownel. Grdau. Mary Carr. Wife
Mary & son Thomas to be Execs. Witns: John Wilbour, Jr., Nathaniel Searle & Elizebeth Wilbour [7:348/9].

Inv. of Est. of SAMUEL DEAN of Taun., dtd. 20 Jan. 1731/2, pres.
by Samuel Dean his son & Exec. Apprs: John Mason, Benjamin
Wilbour & William Hodges [7:349/50].

Appt. of Margaret Short of Easton, widow, as Adm. of Est. of
MATHEW SHORT of Easton, dtd. 13 July 1732 [7:350/1].

Order to Ebenezer Shearman, "Son and the only Surviveing Executor" of Est. of DANIEL SHEARMAN of Dart., dtd. 20 June 1732
[7:351/2]

Appt. of David Harvey, Adm. of Est. of his father WILLIAM HAR-
VEY of Taun., dtd. 20 June 1732 [7:352/3].

Inv. of Est. of ISAAC MASON, Jr., Yeoman, dtd. at Swan. 22
March 1732, pres. by Mary Mason, widow & Adm. Apprs: Samuel
Wheteen, Daniel Luther & Barnard Hail [7:353/4].

Order to Phebe Porter, widow, & to Benjamin Porter, son, Execs.
of Est. of WILLIAM PORTER of Nort., dtd. 18 July 1732 [7:354
/5].

Will of WILLIAM PORTER of Nort., "being in the fifty Eaight
year of my age and being at this Time Sick," dtd. 29 July 17-
31, prob. 20 June 1732. Wife Phebe. 4 sons: Benjamin (eldest),

Seth, Jonathan & Jabiz Porter. 2 daus: Judith Hersin (eldest)
& Anna Porter. Mentions his land in Norton, in Salem & Tops-
field in the Co. of Essex. Wife Phebe & son Benjamin to be
Execs. Witns: Samuel Caswel, William Dean & George Leonard
[7:355/6/7].
Will of DANIEL SHEARMAN of Dart., Yeoman, "being weak and under
decay of body," dtd. 8 Sept. 1729, prob. 20 June 1732. Wife
Sarah. 5 sons: Moses, Ebenezer, Seth, Israel & James Shearman, "when they shall arrive at the age of Twenty one years."
3 daus: Isabel Shearman, Rachel Shearman & Ruth Shearman.
Sons Moses & Ebenezer to be Execs. Witns: Barnabas Chace,
Jonathan Shearman & William Bowdish [7:358/9/60/1].
Appt. of Thomas Danforth of Taun. as guard. of James Danforth
of Taun. "who is non Compus mentis," dtd. 20 June 1732 [7:361
/2].
Inv. of Est. of THOMAS BROWNEL of Lit. Comp., dtd. 1 June 1732,
pres. by Thomas Brownel, his son & an Exec. Apprs: John Pal-
mer, Joseph Southworth & William Richmond [7:362/3/4].
Acct. of Oliver Earl of Swan., Exec. in 2nd degree of Est. of
his father THOMAS EARL, dtd. 20 June 1732. Incl. paym. "To
Doctors and funerall Charges for mother." Items for "Keeping
and boarding Brother Thomas 1 year" & "To Keeping and boarding
Brother Thomas one year more to ye first of November last"
[7:364/5].
Appt. of Martha Glading, widow, as Adm. of Est. of her husb.
JOHN GLADING of Brist., dtd. 20 June 1732 [7:365/6].
Acct. of Benjamin Wilbour, guard. of James Danforth non Compus
mentis, dtd. 20 June 1732. Incl. "things provided for the
Support of ye familey of s^d Danforth" [7:366/7/8].
Inv. of Est. of the Rev. MATHEW SHORT of Easton, dtd. 10 Nov.
1731, pres. by Margaret Short, widow & Adm. Apprs: Benjamin
Drake, Ephraim Randall & John Phillips [7:368/9].
Acct. of Hannah King of Tiv., Adm. of Est. of JOSEPH KING of
Lit. Comp., dtd. 25 July 1732. Incl. equal payms. to: Benja-
min King, Samuel Cook, Hannah Berley, "ye mother," "Ebenezers
part in his mothers hands" [7:369/70].
Appt. of Jonathan Woodbury of Brist. as Adm. of Est. of his mo-
ther MARY FULTON of Brist., dtd. 25 July 1732 [7:370/1].
Order to Samuel Humphrey of Barr. & to John Humphrey of Reho.,
Execs. of Est. of their father SAMUEL HUMPHREY of Barr. [*date
not noted; entry discontinued in middle of page*][7:371].
Will of SAMUEL HUMPHREY of Barr., "being in the Eighty Third
year of my age," dtd. 30 May 1732, prob. 10 July 1732. No
wife mentioned. Sons: Samuel, Jonas, John, Josiah & James
Humphrey. Daus: Mary Humphrey (unmar.), Martha Cooper & chldn.
of my dau. Sarah Peirce dcd. Sons Samuel & John to be Execs.
Witns: Zachariah Buknel, Nathaniel Peck & Peleg Heath [7:372
/3/4].
Order to Thomas, Joseph & Samuel Borden, Execs. of Est. of their

father RICHARD BORDEN of Tiv., dtd. July 1732 [7:374].
Will of RICHARD BORDEN of Tiv., Yeoman, dtd. 10 Feb. 1730/1,
  prob. 18 July 1732. Wife Innocent. Sons: John (eldest), Thomas (2nd), Joseph (3rd) & Samuel (youngest) Borden. 3 daus:
  Sarah Hazard, Mary Gifford & Rebecca Borden (youngest). Grson. Richard Borden son of my son Thomas. Negros: Juno (woman), Kato (boy) & Judeth (girl). Indian boy Job. Mentions
  his smith shop & tools & his grist mill. Witns: John Read,
  Jo[n] Blanchet & George Borden [7:374/5/6/7/8/9/80].
Inv. of Est. of DANIEL SHEARMAN of Dart., Yeoman, "Who deceased
  y[e] 13 Day of May annoque Domi 1732," dtd. 26 May 1732, pres.
  by Ebenezer Shearman, Exec. Mentions lands in Dart. & in Ro-
  chester. Apprs: John Akin, Thomas Smith & Joseph Russel
  [7:380/1/2].
Appt. of Mrs. Meribah Shearman of Dart. as guard. of Sarah
  Shearman (under 14), dau. of MOSES SHEARMAN of Dart., dtd. 18
  July 1732 [7:382/3].
Appt. of Sarah Shearman of Dart., widow, as chosen to be guard.
  by Israel Shearman (minor over 14), son of DANIEL SHEARMAN of
  Dart., dtd. 18 July 1732 [7:383/4].
Order to Elezebeth Tiffeny, widow, & John Tiffeny, Execs. of
  Est. of JAMES TIFFENY of Attl., dtd. 18 July 1732 [7:384].
Will of JAMES TIFFENY of Attl., "being Very Sick," dtd. 20 June
  1732, prob. 18 July 1732. Wife Elezebeth. Sons: James, Samuel,
  Benjamin, John & Noah Tiffeny. Daus: Elezebeth's children,
  Anna, Rebecca, Sarah, Martha, Lidia, Bathsheba, Keziah & Ali-
  thea [no surnames given]. Wife Elezebeth & son John to be Ex-
  ecs. Witns: Ephraim Lane, Ebenezer Lane & John Fuller [7:
  385/6].
Appt. of Henery Bragg, Merchant, as Adm. of Est. of his brother
  NICHOLAS BRAGG of Brist., "y[e] widdow having Refused To administer," dtd. 2 Aug. 1732 [7:386/7].
Acct. of Henery Bragg, Adm. of Est. of his father HENERY BRAGG
  of Attl., dtd. 2 Aug. 1732. Incl. item "Paid mother Bragg her
  part of the Estate." Paym. to William Bragg, who was living
  on the farm which was sold [7:387/8].
Appt. of William Munroe of Brist., Yeoman, as Adm. of Est. of
  his brother BENJAMIN MUNROE of Swan., "The Widdow having Refused to Administer," dtd. 7 Aug. 1732 [7:389].
Appts. of Mary Irish of Lit. Comp., widow, to be guard. of Samuel Irish (minor over 14), Hannah Irish & Anna Mercy Irish
  (both under 14), chldn. of JONATHAN IRISH of Lit. Comp., dtd.
  15 Aug. 1732 [7:390/1/2].
Appt. of Anna Hill, widow, as Adm. of Est. of SAMUEL HILL of
  Reho. dcd. intest., dtd. 15 Aug. 1732 [7:391/2/2][page number duplication].
Appt. of Mary Irish of Lit. Comp., widow, as guard. of Jesse
  Irish (minor over 14), son of JONATHAN IRISH of Lit. Comp.,
  dtd. 15 Aug. 1732 [7:392/3].

Appt. of Mary Irish, widow, as Adm. of Est. of JONATHAN IRISH
of Lit. Comp., dtd. 15 Aug. 1732 [7:393/4].
Order to Patiance Hathaway, widow, & Jonathan Hathaway, son,
Execs. of Est. of JOHN HATHAWAY of Dart., dtd. 15 Aug. 1732
[7:394/5].
Will of JOHN HATHAWAY of Dart., Yeoman, dtd. 11 July 1732, prob.
15 Aug. 1732. Wife Patiance. Sons: John, Jonathan, Richard,
Honiwill, Abiah, Benjamin, James, Ebenezer & Arthur Hathaway.
Daus: Sarah Cannon, Joannah Blackwell, Mary Duglas, Hannah
Bomer, Patiance Peckham & Elesebeth Hathaway. Wife Patiance
& son Jonathan to be Execs. Witns: Richard Pearce, Samuel
Peckham & Stephen West [7:395/6/7/8/9].
Inv. of Est. of SAMUEL HILL of Reho., dtd. 9 Aug. 1732, pres.
by Anna Hill, widow & Adm. Apprs: Joseph Bosworth, Edward
Glover & Samuel Mason [7:400].
Inv. of Est. of BENJAMIN MUNROE of Swan., dtd. 9 Aug. 1732,
pres. by William Munroe, Adm. Apprs: James Bowen, Barnard
Hail & Robert Joles [7:401].
Appt. of Richard Dye of Tiv. as Adm. "Cum Testimento Annexo" of
Est. of his grandfather WILLIAM DYE of Lit. Comp., since the
Exec. named in the will, Richard Billings, refuses to serve,
dtd. 15 Aug. 1732 [7:402].
Inv. of Est. of JAMES WHEETEEN of Swan., dtd. 23 March 1731/2,
pres. by Hannah Wheeteen, widow & Adm. Apprs: William Antho-
ney, Hezekiah Luther & Esek Brown [7:403/4].
Appt. of Peres Bradford of Milton, County of Suffolk, Gentleman,
& William Richmond & Nathaniel Searle, both of Lit. Comp.,
Yeomen, as Adms. of Est. of their grandfather JOHN ROGERS of
Barr., "The Widow and Two Daughters Refusing to Administer,"
dtd. 5 Sept. 1732 [7:404/5].
Acct. of Hannah Wheteen, widow & Adm. of Est. of JAMES WHETEEN
of Swan., dtd. 15 Aug. 1732 [7:405/6].
Acct. of "Mehetibel Mason Late Mehetibel Davis Late Widdow" &
Adm. of Est. of her husb. GUIAS DAVIS of Brist., dtd. 15 Aug.
1732 [7:406/7].
Inv. of Est. of RICHARD BORDEN of Tiv., Yeoman, dtd. 9 Aug. 17-
32, pres. by Thomas, Samuel & Joseph Borden, his sons & Execs.
Incl. value of a negro boy & a negro girl. Incl. items: "To
half Samuel Homestead," "To half Thomas Homestead" & "To half
Joseph Homestead." Apprs: John Read, Joseph Anthoney & Sam-
uel Talman [7:408/9/10].
Appts. of Silvester Richmond of Lit. Comp. as guard. chosen by
Mary Richmond & Roger Richmond (both minors over 14), grchldn.
of JOHN ROGERS of Barr., dtd. 5 Sept. 1732 [7:410/1/2].
Appt. of Comm. to examine debts of insolvent Est. of NICHOLAS
BRAGG of Brist., dtd. 25 Sept. 1732 [7:412].
Inv. of Est. of JACOB HOSKINS of Taun., dtd. 5 Sept. 1732, pres.
by Samuel Hacket, Adm. Apprs: John Staple, Joseph Jones &
John White "who are now of Raynham" [7:412].

Acct. of Samuel Hacket of Raynham, Adm. of Est. of JACOB HOS-
KINS of Taun., dtd. 12 Sept. 1732 [7:413].

Appts. of Lidia Williams of Taun., widow, as guard. of Nathaniel
& Lidia Williams (both minors over 14) & of Judith Williams,
Elezebeth Williams & Bithia Williams (all under 14), chldn. of
NATHANIEL WILLIAMS of Taun., dtd. 12 Sept. 1732 [7:413/4/5/6].

Acct. of Mary Chaffe, widow & Adm. of Est. of HEZEKIAH CHAFFE
of Reho., dtd. 12 Sept. 1732. Incl. paym. "for Charges of
Lying with a Post humus Child" [7:416/7/8].

Acct. of Margaret Short, widow & Adm. of Est. of MATHEW SHORT
of Easton, dtd. 14 Sept. 1732. Incl. items: "Provisions Spent
in the family To Support ye widdow and Ten Children"[7:418/9].

Inv. of Est. of JOHN BEVERLY of Reho., dtd. 28 Jan. 1731/2,
pres. by George Beverly, his brother & Adm. Apprs: James Bow-
en, Samuel Bullock & John Horton [7:419].

Acct. of William Munroe, Adm. of Est. of his brother BENJAMIN
MUNROE of Swan., dtd. 14 Sept. 1732 [7:420].

Acct. of Lydia Williams of Raynham, widow & Adm. of Est. of NA-
THANIEL WILLIAMS of Taun., dtd. 12 Sept. 1732 [7:421].

Inv. of Est. of NICHOLAS BRAGG of Brist., dtd. 25 Apr. 1732,
pres. by Henery Bragg, Adm. Incl. value of an indian woman.
Apprs: Samuel Royal, Samuel Smith & Paul Unis [7:421/2/3].

Acct. of Henery Bragg, Adm. of Est. of his brother NICHOLAS
BRAGG of Brist., dtd. 11 Sept. 1732. Incl. "A Debt Due at
Sanchristopher as we Judge" of 100 pounds [7:423/4].

Order to Mary Hunt, widow & Exec. of Est. of BENJAMIN HUNT of
Reho., dtd. 19 Sept. 1732 [7:424/5].

Will of BENJAMIN HUNT of Reho., Gentleman, dtd. 4 Jan. 1732,
prob. 19 Sept. 1732. Wife Mary. 3 daus: Tabatha Wheeteen,
Sibyl Mason & Hulda Bowen. Incl. negros: Tobey (man), Nanc
(woman) & Mingo (boy). Wife Mary to be Exec. Witns: Joshua
Abell, Noah Newman & Edward Glover [7:425/6/7/8].

Inv. of Est. of BENJAMIN HUNT of Reho., dtd. 30 Aug. 1732, pres.
by Mary Hunt, widow & Exec. Apprs: Daniel Perrin, Edward
Glover & Samuel Mason [7:428/9].

Inv. of Est. of WILLIAM PORTER of Norton, dtd. at Stoughton,
Suffolk, 3 Sept. 1732, pres. by Phebe Porter & Benjamin Por-
ter, Execs. Incl. that part of Est. in Stoughton. Apprs:
Benjamin Estre, Joseph Hewins, Jr. & John Hixson [7:429/30].

Inv. of Est. in Norton of WILLIAM PORTER of Norton, dtd. 4 Sept.
1732, pres. by Phebe Porter & Benjamin Porter, Execs. Apprs:
Ephraim Leonard, Benjamin Williams & William Dean [7:430].

Appts. of Stephen Wilbour of Dart., Yeoman, as guard. of Job,
Ann and Abner Wilbour (all under 14), grchldn. of JONATHAN
IRISH of Lit. Comp'., dtd. 17 Oct. 1732 [7:431/2].

Appts. of Thomas Wilbour of Lit. Comp., Yeoman, as guard. of
George, Jonathan & Joseph Wilbour (all under 14), grsons. of
JONATHAN IRISH of Lit. Comp., dtd. 17 Oct. 1732 [7:432/3/4].

Inv. of Est. of JOHN ROGERS of Barr., dtd. 12 Sept. 1732, pres.

by his grsons. Peres Bradford, William Richmond & Nathaniel
Searles, Adms. Apprs: Benjamin Viall, Samuel Allen & James
Addams [7:434/5].
Order to Nehemiah Hoskins, Exec. of Est. of his father SAMUEL
HOSKINS of Taun., dtd. 17 Oct. 1732 [7:435/6].
Will of SAMUEL HOSKINS of Taun., dtd. 17 March 1731/2, prob.
17 Oct. 1732. Wife Mercy. Sons: Samuel, Joshua & Nehemiah
Hoskins. Daus: Lydia, Mercy & Hannah [no surnames]. Son Ne-
hemiah to be Exec. Witns: Seth Williams, William Richmond
& George Townsend [7:437/8].
Inv. of Est. of THOMAS DRAKE of Easton, dtd. 7 Oct. 1732, pres.
by Benjamin Drake, Exec. Apprs: Ephraim Randal, William
Leonard & Israel Randal [7:438/9].
Acct. of Benjamin Drake, Exec. of Est. of THOMAS DRAKE of Easton
dtd. 17 Oct. 1732. Incl. paym. to "Tending and Nursing in his
wifes Last Sickness." Item "to Sarah Drake for tending in
former Sickness" [7:439/40].
Acct. of Epharim Lane, Adm. of Est. of JOHN LANE of Att., dtd.
17 Oct. 1732 [7:440/1].
Inv. of Est. of JAMES TIFFENEY, Yeoman, dtd. at Attl. 18 Dec.
1732, pres. by Elezebeth Tiffeney, widow, & by John Tiffeney,
Execs. Incl. 100 acres in Ashford, Conn. Apprs: William Richardson, Hezekiah Peck & Obediah Fuller [7:441/2].
Inv. of Est. of JONATHAN IRISH of Lit. Comp., dtd. 31 Aug. 1732,
pres. by Mary Irish, widow & Adm. Mentions lands in Lit. Comp.
& in Tiv. Apprs: Robert Woodman, James Rouse & John Price.
[7:442/3].
Order to Hannah Vial, widow & Exec. of Est. of JONATHAN VIAL of
Barr., dtd. 6 Nov. 1732 [7:443/4].
Will of JONATHAN VIALL of Barr., Yeoman, dtd. 24 March 1732,
prob. 6 Nov. 1732. Mother Mercy Vial. Wife Hannah. Wife to be
Exec. Witns: Samuel Vial, Terrance Dunnelly & Samuel Howland
[7:445/6].
Appt. of Mercy Hathaway, widow, as Adm. of Est. of JOHN HATHAWAY
of Digh., dtd. 7 Nov. 1732 [7:446/7].
Appt. of Ann Bowen, widow, as Adm. of Est. of EBENEZER BOWEN of
Reho., dtd. 9 Nov. 1732 [7:447/8].
Appt. of Hepzebeth Chaffe, widow, as Adm. of Est. of NOAH CHAFFE
of Reho., dtd. 9 Nov. 1732 [7:448/9].
Inv. of Est. of EBENEZER BOWEN of Reho., dtd. 19 Oct. 1732, pres.
by Ann Bowen, widow & Adm. Apprs: John Hunt, Daniel Carpenter
& Nathaniel P[illegible][7:449/50].
Inv. of Est. of NOAH CHAFFE of Reho., dtd. 1 Nov. 1732, pres.
by Hipzabeth Chaffe, widow & Adm. Apprs: Edward Glover, Ezek-
iel Read & Timothey Ide [7:450/1].
Order to Nathan Cobb, "son and only Surviveing Executor" of
Est. of SAMUEL COBB of Taun., "Lidia Cobb Executrix in Said
Will is also deceased before the Will was proved," dtd. 21
Nov. 1732 [7:451/2].

Appt. of Nathan Cobb of Taun. as Adm. of Est. of his brother
NICHOLAS COBB of Attl., dtd. 21 Nov. 1732 [7:452/3].
Appt. of Nathan Cobb as Adm. of Est. of his mother LIDIA COBB
of Taun., dtd. 21 Nov. 1732 [7:453/4].
Will of SAMUEL COBB of Taun., Husbandman, "being Sick and Weak,"
dtd. 14 June 1732, prob. 21 Nov. 1732. Wife Lidia. Sons: Nathan, Nathaniel, Nicholas & Ebenezer Cobb. Daus: Rebecca,
Mercy, Bethia & Lidia [no surnames]. Wife Lidia & son Nathan
to be Execs. Mentions lands in Taun. & Attl. Witns: John Wil-
lis, Morgan Cobb, 2nd & Morgan Cobb, 3rd [7:454/5/6].
Inv. of Est. of NICHOLAS COBB of Attl., dtd. 22 Sept. 1732, pres.
by Nathan Cobb, brother & Adm. Apprs: William Hodges, John
Harvey & Morgan Cobb, 2nd [7:456/7].
Inv. of Est. of Deacon SAMUEL HUMPHREY of Barr., dtd. 9 Aug.
1732, pres. by Samuel & John Humphrey, Adms. Apprs: James
Adams, Zachariah Bicknel & Nathaniel Peck [7:457/8/9].
Appt. of Daniel Smith of Reho. as Adm. of Est. of his mother
ABIGAIL SMITH of Reho., late widow of Daniel Smith, Esq. of
Reho. dcd., dtd. 1 Nov. 1732 [7:459/60].
Order to John Read, Exec. of Est. of ISRAEL READ of Reho., dtd.
28 Nov. 1732 [7:460/1].
Inv. of Est. of SAMUEL COBB of Taun., dtd. 22 Sept. 1732, pres.
by Nathan Cobb, son & Exec. Mentions "his Deceased Wifes Ap-
paril." Apprs: William Hodges, John Harvey & Morgan Cobb,
2nd [7:461/2].
Will of ISRAEL READ of Reho., Husbandman, "being aged and weak
of body," dtd. 2 Nov. 1732, prob. 28 Nov. 1732. Wife Rebecca.
Sons: John, Israel dcd., Joseph & Jeremiah Read. Daus: Rebec-
ca, Elezebeth, Anna & Ruth [no surnames]. Friend John Read of
Reho. to be Exec. Witns: Ephraim Carpenter, Ezekiel Read &
Daniel Carpenter [7:462/3/4].
Inv. of Est. of EDMUND INGOLS of Reho., pres. 28 Nov. 1732 by
Unis Ingols, widow & Adm. Apprs: Jonathan Kingsley, James
Bowen & Samuel Bullock [7:464/5].
Appt. of Bethia Bragg, widow, & Elezebeth Howland, spinster,
both of Brist., as Adms. of Est. of their father JABEZ HOW-
LAND of Brist., dtd. 27 Nov. 1732 [7:466].
Appt. of Bethia Shaw, widow, & Thomas Shaw, son, as Adms. of
Est. of THOMAS SHAW of Reho., dtd. 1 Dec. 1732 [7:467].
Order to Grace Wardwel, widow, & Joseph Wardwel, son, Execs. of
Est. of UZAL WARDWEL of Brist., dtd. 7 Dec. 1732 [7:468].
Will of UZAL WARDWEL of Brist., Yeoman, "being aged and weak,"
dtd. 10 Jan. 1728, prob. 7 Dec. 1732. Wife Grace. 5 sons:
Joseph, Uzal, James, William & Benjamin Wardwel. 6 daus: Mary
Barker, Grace Giddeons, Sarah Bosworth, Alec Glading, Abigail
Green & Hannah Crompton. Wife Grace & son Joseph to be Execs.
Witns: Samuel Smith, Edward Ingraham & Samuel Howland [7:468
/9/70].
Order to set off 1/3 of the real est. of NICHOLAS BRAGG of Brist
to his widow, Bethiah Bragg, dtd. 15 Nov. 1732 [7:471].

Setting off of 1/3 of real est. of NICHOLAS BRAGG of Brist. to
his widow, Bethiah Bragg, dtd. 23 Nov. 1732. Comm: Samuel
Royal, William Munroe, Benjamin Bosworth, Samuel Smith & Paul
Unis [7:471/2].
Appt. of Samuel Little of Brist., Gentleman, to be guard. as
chosen by Jabiz Howland (minor over 14), son of JABIZ HOWLAND
of Brist., dtd. 19 Dec. 1732 [7:472/3].
Appt. of "John Briggs the Second" of Nort., Yeoman, to be guard.
of James Briggs (under 14), son of RICHARD BRIGGS of Nort.,
dtd. 9 Jan. 1732/3 [7:473/4].
Appt. of Ephraim Leonard of Nort., Gentleman, to be guard. as
chosen by George Briggs (minor over 14), son of RICHARD BRIGGS
of Nort., dtd. 9 Jan. 1732 [7:474/5].
Appt. of "John Briggs ye Second" of Nort., Yeoman, to be guard.
as chosen by Timothy Briggs (minor over 14), son of RICHARD
BRIGGS of Nort., dtd. 9 Jan. 1732/3 [7:475/6].
Order to John Briggs & Timothey Briggs, both of Nort., Execs.
of Est. of RICHARD BRIGGS of Nort., dtd. 10 Jan. 1732/3 [7:
476/7].
Order to James Brittun of Digh., Yeoman, Exec. of Est. of his
grmother. MARCY MOREY of Digh., dtd. 10 Jan. 1732/3 [7:477
/8].
Will of RICHARD BRIGGS of Nort., "being sick," dtd. 25 Oct. 17-
32, prob. 10 Jan. 1732/3. Wife Marcy. Sons: Richard (eldest),
Timothey (2nd), George (3rd) & James (4th) Briggs (last two
under 21). No daus. mentioned. My 2nd son Timothey & "my
Loving Brother John Briggs" to be Execs. Witns: George Leonard, John Briggs, 3rd, Azriah Briggs & Hannah Briggs [7:478
/9/80].
Will of MARCY MOREY of Digh., widow, "being Sick and weak," dtd.
25 Oct. 1732, prob. 10 Jan. 1732/3. Grson. James Brittun the
son of my son William Brittun of Taun. dcd. My grfather. Briant Pendleton. My father James Pendleton. My former husb. Jo-
seph Cross. My last husb. Nicholas Morey dcd. Grchldn. William
Brittun, Abiel Brittun, Ebenezer Brittun, Pendleton Brittun,
Mary Hall, Lidia Brittun, Sarah Brittun, Elezebeth Brittun &
Abigail Brittun, chldn. of my son William Brittun dcd. Grson.
James Brittun to be Exec. Witns: Nathaniel Fisher, Oliver
Simmons & Elkanah Leonard. Mentions her rights in lands in
"the Province of Newhamshire," of the est. of her grfather.
Briant Pendleton [7:480/1/2].
Inv. of Est. of BENJAMIN LEONARD of Taun., dtd. 13 May 1725,
pres. by Capt. John King & Benjamin Leonard, Adms. Apprs:
John Andrews, John Mason & Benjamin Wilbour [7:482/3].
Inv. of Est. of JONATHAN VIAL of Barr., dtd. 20 Nov. 173[?],
pres. 17 Jan. 1732/3 by Hannah Vial, Exec. Apprs: Samuel Al-
len, Joseph Allen & Nathaniel Paine [7:484].
Order to James & Nathaniel Phillips, Execs. of Est. of JAMES
PHILLIPS of Taun., dtd. 23 Jan. 1732/3 [7:485].

Will of JAMES PHILLIPS of Taun., dtd. 23 March 1731/2, prob. 23
Jan. 1732/3. Wife Elezebeth. Sons: James, Nathaniel & Samuel
Phillips. 7 daus: Sarah [no surname], Elezebeth Phillips, Mary
Paul, Abigail French, Experiance Phillips, Rebecca Phillips &
Kethiah Phillips. Wife Elezebeth & sons James & Nathaniel to
be Execs. Witns: Seth Williams, Richard Godfrey, Jr. & Abiel
Smith. Notation that "the Widdow Elezebeth Phillips hath Re-
linquished her right of Executorship" [7:485/6/7].

Appts. of William Munroe of Brist., Yeoman, to be guard. of
Charles & Henery Munroe (both minors over 14) & of Mercy Mun-
roe (under 14), chldn. of BENJAMIN MUNROE of Swan., dtd. 16
Feb. 1732/3 [7:488/9].

Rcpt. & release by Mary Slocum, widow of PELEG SLOCUM of Dart.,
for a negro woman Hannah and for money "Paid by my son Holder"
and "Paid by my Daughter in Law Rebecca Slocum Relict of my
Son Peleg Slocum Deceased," dtd. 30 Jan. 1732/3. Witns: Samuel
Hull & Henery Hadly [7:490].

Appt. of William Munroe of Brist., Yeoman, to be guard of Mary &
Shub[ael] Munroe (both under 14), chldn. of BENJAMIN MUNROE
of Swan., dtd. 16 Jan. 1732/3 [7:490/1].

Order to Holder Slocum of Dart., Yeoman, Exec. of Est. of his
father PELEG SLOCUM of Dart., Joseph Slocum of Newport, also
son of the dcd. Peleg having relinquished his right of Exec.,
dtd. 21 Feb. 1732/3 [7:491/2].

Will of PELEG SLOCUM of Dart., Yeoman, dtd. 13 Jan. 1731, prob.
7 Feb. 1732/3. Wife Mary. Sons: Holder, Peleg (dcd.), Joseph
& Giles (dcd.) Slocum. Daus: Content Easton & Elezebeth Barker. Grsons: Peleg, Giles & Jonathan Slocum (all under 21),
sons of my son Peleg dcd. Grdau. Katherine Slocum (under 18
& unmar.), dau. of my son Peleg dcd. Grsons: John Hedley,
Henery Hedley & John Chapman. Dau-in-law Rebecca Slocum widow
of my son Peleg dcd. Dau-in-law [unnamed] widow of my son
Giles dcd. My brother Eleazer Slocum. Sons Holder & Joseph
Slocum to be Execs. Mentions his lands: in Dart.; in Elizabeth
Islands, Town of Chilmark, Dukes County; in Newport, R.I. &
on Patience Island "in Narrowganset bay." Mentions legacy to
"the monthly meeting of frinds Commonly Called Quackers to
which I belong." Witns: Thomas Hammon, Jonathan Gifford &
William Sanford [7:492/3/4/5/6/7].

Inv. of Est. of Mrs. MARY FULTON of Brist., dtd. 27 July 1732,
pres. by Jonathan Woodbury, her son & Adm. Apprs: Samuel
Royall, Samuel Smith & Nathaniel Woodbury [7:497/8/9].

Order to Sarah Merehow, widow, & to Samuel Merehow, both of
Dart., Execs. of Est. of SAMUEL MEREHOW of Dart., dtd. 20
Feb. 1732/3 [7:499/500].

Will of SAMUEL MEREHOW of Dart., Yeoman, dtd. 11 Jan. 1731/2,
prob. 20 Feb. 1732/3. Wife Sarah. Cousin Samuel Merehow of
Dart. Wife Sarah & cousin Samuel to be Execs. Witns: John
Russel, Samuel Shearman & George Soul [7:500/1].

Inv. of Est. of SAMUEL MEREHOW of Dart., pres. 20 Feb. 1732/3
by Sarah Merehow & Samuel Merehow, Execs. Apprs: John Akin,
Isaac Howland & John Russel [7:502/3].
Inv. of Est. of JAMES PHILLIPS of Taun., dtd. 5 Feb. 1732/3,
pres. by James & Nathaniel Phillips, Execs. Apprs: Seth Burt,
Elkanah Babit & John Crane [7:503/4].
Inv. of Est. of ISRAEL READ of Reho., dtd. 6 Dec. 1732, pres.
by John Read, Exec. Apprs: Ephraim Carpenter, Daniel Carpen-
ter & Noah Sabin [7:504/5].
Inv. of Est. of THOMAS SHAW of Reho., dtd. 5 Dec. 1732, pres.
by Bethiah Shaw & Thomas Shaw, Adms. Apprs: James Bowen,
John Horton & Samuel Bullock [7:505].
Appts. of William Munroe of Brist., Yeoman, to be guard. of
Thomas Howland (under 14) & Patiance Howland (minor over 14),
chldn. of JABIZ HOWLAND of Brist., dtd. 23 Feb. 1732/3 [7:
506/7].
Appt. of John Smith of London, Great Britain, now residing in
Boston, Co. of Suffolk, "Next of Kin Administrator de bonis
non of the Estate of his Grait Uncle" NICHOLAS MOREY of Digh.,
it not having been administered by the Exec. Mary Morey dcd.,
widow of Nicholas, dtd. 17 March 1732/3 [7:507/8].
Appt. of Isaac Brown of Barr., Yeoman, to be guard. as chosen
by Amos Brown (minor over 14), son of WILLIAM BROWN of Reho.,
dtd. 22 Feb. 1732/3 [7:508/9].
Appt. of Benjamin Brown of Reho., Yeoman, to be guard. as chosen by James Brown (minor over 14), son of JAMES BROWN of
Barr., dtd. 22 Feb. 1732/3 [7:509].
Appt. of Samuel Read of Reho., Husbandman, as Adm. of Est. of
his father NATHANIEL READ of Reho., "ye widow refusing,"
dtd. 20 Feb. 1732/3 [7:509/10].
Appt. of Samuel Mason of Reho., Yeoman, to be guard. of Nathaniel Hunt (minor over 14), son of NATHANIEL HUNT of Reho., his
former guard. Arthur Pruning "is absconded and gone out of
the Cuntrey," dtd. 20 March 1732/3 [7:510/1].
Order to Benjah Babit, Exec. of Est. of his father EDWARD BABIT
of Digh., the widow Elezebeth Babit having relinquished her
right of Exec., dtd. 20 March 1732/3 [7:511].
Order to Phebe Sponer, widow, & James Cushman, Cordwainer, Execs.
of Est. of NATHANIEL SPONER of Dart., dtd. 20 March 1732/3
[7:512].
Order to Jacob Taber, one of the Execs. of the Est. of his father THOMAS TABER of Dart., Joseph Taber, John Taber & Phillip
Taber having refused Exec., dtd. 20 March 1732/3 [7:512/3].
Appt. of Phillip Wheeler of Reho. to be guard. as chosen by Edmund Ingols, Joseph Ingols & Unis Ingols (all minors over 14),
chldn. of EDMUND INGOLS of Reho., dtd. 20 March 1732/3 [7:
513].
Appt. of Mrs. Unis Ingols of Reho. as guard. of Samuel & Lois
Ingols (both under 14), chldn. of EDMUND INGOLS of Reho., dtd.
20 March 1732/3 [7:514].

Will of THOMAS TABER of Dart., Yeoman, dtd. 15 June 1723, prob.
20 March 1732/3. Wife Mary., Sons: Thomas, Joseph, John, Jacob
& Phillip Taber. 6 daus: Easther Perry & her husb. [unnamed],
Lidia Kinney, Sarah Hart & her husb [unnamed], Mary Morton &
her husb. [unnamed], Bethiah Blackwel & her husb. Caleb Black-
wel, blacksmith & Abigail Taber & her husb. [sic; unnamed].
My former man servant Simson Sponer. "My Four [sic] Sons Above
Named" to be Execs. Witns: Stephen West, Christopher Turner
& Catherine Turner [7:514/5/6/7/].
Will of NATHANIEL SPONER of Dart., Yeoman, dtd. 5 July 1732,
prob. 20 March 1732/3. Wife Phebe, who is to "have all Such
moveables that She brought with her to me." 2 daus: Alls
[Alice] & [hidden]ea (both under 18 & unmar.). Directs his
wife to take care of "my brother Ebenezer" (under 12). Wife
Phebe & James Cushman of Dart., Cordwainer, to be Execs.
Witns: William Badcock, Cornelius Cannon & William Palmer [7:
518/9].
Will of EDWARD BABIT of Digh., Yeoman, dtd. 5 Feb. 1727, prob.
20 March 1732/3. Wife Elezebeth. Sons: Erasmos, Seth, Nathan,
Benjah, Edward, Nathaniel & George. Daus: Sarah wife of Wil-
liam Thayer, Abigail Burt, [Waitstill?], Ruth & Hannah.
Wife Elezebeth & son Benjah to be Execs. Mentions lands in
Digh. & in Nort. Witns: Edward Shove, Isaac Hathaway & Abra-
ham Waldron [7:519/20/1].
Inv. of Est. of EDWARD BABIT of Digh., dtd. 16 March 1732, pres.
by Benjah Babit, Exec. Apprs: Edward Shove, Benjamin Leonard
& Isaac Hathaway [7:521/2].
Inv. of Est. of JOHN TITUS, Jr. of Reho., dtd. 18 Dec. 1732,
pres. by [blank] Titus, Adm. Apprs: Stephen Wilmouth, William
Dryer & Jasiel Peck [7:522].
Inv. of Est. of THOMAS MACKONE of Swan., dtd. 17 July 1730, pres.
by Elezebeth Mackoon, widow & Adm. Apprs: William Anthoney,
Samuel Lee & Hezekiah Kingsley [7:522/3].
Inv. of Est. of NATHANIEL SPONER of Dart., dtd. 16 Jan. 1732/3
pres, by Phebe Sponer & James Cushman. Apprs: Nathaniel
Blackwell, Stephen West, Jr. & William Badcock [7:523/4].
Inv. of Est. of ISAAC PALMER of Brist., dtd. 26 Aug. 1732, pres.
by Yetmercy Palmer, widow & Adm. Apprs: Samuel Royall, Sam-
uel Smith & Paul Unis [7:524].
Inv. of Est. of JOHN GLADING, Jr. of Brist., dtd. 14 July 1732,
pres. by Martha Glading, widow & Exec. Apprs: Samuel Royall,
Samuel Smith & Nathaniel Woodbury [7:524/5/6].
Inv. of Est. of JABIZ HOWLAND of Brist., dtd. 6 Dec. 1732, pres.
by Bethia Bragg & Elezebeth Howland, his daus. & Adms. Incl.
negro man Newport, negro man Titero & unnamed negro woman.
Apprs: Simon Davis, Jonathan Woodbury & Samuel Royall [7:526
/7/8].
Inv. of Est. of Mrs. LIDIA COBB of Taun. dcd. intest., widow of
Samuel Cobb, dtd. 30 March 1733, pres. by Richard Cobb, her

son & Adm.   Apprs: John Willis, Samuel Darbey & Morgan Cobb
[7:529].
Appts. of Mary Ide of Reho., widow, to be guard. of Mary, Elez-
ebeth, Josiah & Daniel Ide (all under 14), chldn. of JOSIAH
IDE of Reho., dtd. 17 Apr. 1733 [7:529/30].
Order to Elinor Briggs, widow & Exec. of Est. of JOB BRIGGS of
Lit. Comp., dtd. 17 Apr. 1733 [7:531].
Will of JOB BRIGGS of Lit. Comp., dtd. 7 Jan. 1732/3, prob. 17
Apr. 1733. Wife Elinor. Chldn: eldest son Jeremiah Briggs,
dau. Mary Bourden.wife of Thomas Bourden, dau. Sarah Durphey
wife of Thomas Durphey, dau. Elezebeth Malum wife of Mark Mal-
um, dau. Almey Briggs, dau. Wait Briggs, son Job Briggs, son
John Briggs & Son Enoch Briggs. Negro woman Rose. Mentions
lands in Lit. Comp. & Tiv. Wife Elinor to be Exec. Witns:
Abial Tripp, John Briggs & Phillip Taber [7:531/2].
Inv. of Est. of JOB BRIGGS of Lit. Comp., dtd. 16 Apr. 1733,
pres. by Elinor Briggs, widow & Exec. Apprs: Phillip Taber,
Jonathan Wood & William Wood [7:533/4].
Appts. of Elinor Briggs of Lit. Comp., widow, to be guard. of
Wait, John & Enoch Briggs (all under 14), chldn. of JOB BRIGGS
of Lit. Comp., dtd. 17 Apr. 1733 [7:534/5].
Appt. of Rebeca Slocum of Dart., widow, to be guard. of Peleg,
Jonathan & Katherine Slocum (all under 14), chldn. of PELEG
SLOCUM, Jr. of Dart., dtd. 15 May 1733 [7:535/6/7].
Appt. of Hannah Read, widow, as Adm. of Est. of BENJAMIN READ
of Swan., dtd. 15 May 1733 [7:537/8].
Appt. of Samuel Chace of Swan, Yeoman, as Adm. of Est. of his
wife SARAH CHACE, dtd. 15 May 1733 [7:538/9].
Order to Silvester Woodman of Lit. Compt., Yeoman, Exec. of
Est. of his father JOHN WOODMAN of Lit. Comp., dtd. 15 May
1733 [7:539].
Will of JOHN WOODMAN of Lit. Comp., Yeoman, dtd. 3 May 1733,
prob. 15 May 1733. Wife Elezebeth. Sons: Silvester (eldest),
Enoch (under 21) & William (under 21) Woodman. Daus: [Sarah?]
Woodman, Elezebeth Woodman, Edith Woodman (under 18 & unmar.).
My brother Robert. Mentions lands in Lit. Comp. & Tiv. Son
Silvester to be Exec. Witns: James Rouse, Robart Woodman &
John Hoswel [7:539/40/1/2].
Div. of Est. of JAMES WHETEEN of Swan., setting off 1/3 to his
widow Hannah Wheteen, dtd. 15 May 1733. Comm: William Antho-
ney, Hezekiah Luther, Daniel Wilbour, Eseck Brown & Hezekiah
Kingsley [7:543].
Acct. of Mary Hix, widow, & Ephraim Hix, Adms. of Est. of her
husb. JAMES HIX of Reho., dtd. 15 May 1733 [7:543/4].
Acct. of Phebe Porter, widow, & Benjamin Porter, son, Execs.
of Est. of WILLIAM PORTER of Nort., dtd. 7 June 1733. Incl.
legacies per will to: "Anna Porter now Thayer" & "Judith Hewins." Paym. to Phebe Porter, Exec., for the charges for moving
her goods "from Norton to brantrey." Item for cost of "one Jor-

ney to Topsfield To Lett out ye Estate y^t was their." Refers
to var. trips to Stoughton [7:545/6].

Appt. of John Smith of Taun.; Yeoman, as Adm. of Est. of his son
JOHN SMITH, Jr. of Taun. dcd. intest., dtd. 19 June 1733 [7:
546/7].

Order to Martha Shearman, widow & Exec. of Est. of her husb.
SAMUEL SHEARMAN of Swan., the other Exec., Eber Chace, having
relinquished his Exec., dtd. 19 June 1733 [7:547/8].

Order to Ebenezer Freeman, Exec. of Est. of his father DAVID
FREEMAN of Attl., dtd. 19 June 1733 [7:548/9].

Order to Martha Barsto, widow & Exec. of Est. of her husb.
GEORGE BARSTO of Reho., dtd. 19 June 1733 [7:549/50].

Will of SAMUEL SHEARMAN of Swan., Yeoman, "being Sick and Weak,"
dtd. 9 June 1733, prob. 19 June 1733. Wife Martha. 2 sons:
William & Samuel (both under age). Daus: Abigail & Alec (both
under age). Wife Martha to be Exec. Witns: Preserved Brayton
Jonathan Slead & William Hart [7:551/2].

Will of DAVID FREEMAN of Attl., Yeoman, "being very weak of
body," dtd. 8 June 1730, prob. 19 June 1733. Wife Elezebeth.
Son Ebenezer. 2 daus: Hannah Peidge & Margaret Short. Grson.
Jonathan Peidge. As preface to leaving to his wife livestock
& the right to live in his house, he said "altho by Covenant
I am free yet I do give and bequeath unto Elezebeth..." Son
Ebenezer to be Exec. Witns: Samuel Tingley, Ebenezer Foster,
Jonathan Freeman & Noah Carpenter [7:552/3/4].

Will of GEORGE BEARSTO of Reho., Husbandman, "being Sick of
Body," dtd. 10 M[hidden] 1733, prob. 19 June 1733. Wife Mar-
tha. Sons: John & George (both under 21). Daus: Martha, Hannah
& Sarah [no surnames]. Mentions "uncle Sampson Mason." Wife
Martha to be Exec. Witns: Noah Mason, Samuel Barsto & Edward
Glover [7:554/5/6].

Inv. of Est. of GEORGE BARSTO of Reho., dtd. 24 March 1733, pres.
by Martha Barsto, widow & Exec. Apprs: Samuel Mason, Ezekiel
Read & Edward Glover [7:557].

Inv. of Est. of JOHN WOODMAN of Lit. Comp., dtd. 22 May 1733,
pres. by Silvester Woodman, Exec. Apprs: James Rouse, Robart
Woodman & James Horswel [7:558/9].

Acct. of Elezebeth Haile, Adm. of Est. of JOHN HAILE of Swan.,
dtd. 19 June 1733. Paym. for "Clothing ye Children" [7:559/60].

Appt. of Mrs. Abia Maccomber of Taun., widow, as Adm. of Est.
of ABIAL MACCOMBER of Taun. dcd. intest., dtd. 20 June 1733
[7:561].

Acct. of Aron Read, Adm. of Est. of his father JAMES READ of
Reho., dtd. 19 June 1733. Incl. Payms. "to M^s Dorothy Read"
& "to Samuel Read" [7:562/3].

Acct. of Mary Mason, widow & Adm. of Est. of her husb. ISAAC
MASON of Swan., dtd. 19 June 1733. Incl. paym. "for Clothing
for the Children." Items paid to: Isaac Mason, Oliver Mason,
Experiance Mason, Hezekiah Mason, Joseph Mason & Job Mason
[7:563/4].

Acct. of Sarah Titus, widow & Adm. of Est. of her husb. ROBART
TITUS of Attl., dtd. 19 June 1733 [7:565].

Inv. of Est. of THOMAS WAITE of Dart., dtd. 16 June 1733, pres.
by Sarah Waite, widow & Adm. Apprs: Nathaniel Soule, Gabrial
Hix & Benjamin Chace [7:566/7/8].

Appt. of Elezebeth Fisher of Nort., widow, as Adm. of Est. of
EDMUND FISHER of Nort. dcd. intest., dtd. 10 July 1733 [7:
568/9].

Appt. of "John Briggs the Eldest of Norton," Yeoman, as Adm. of
Est. of his wife MARY BRIGGS of Nort., dtd. 10 July 1733 [7:
570].

Order to Israel Thrasher of Taun., Exec. of Est. of his father
JOHN THRESHER of Taun., dtd. 12 July 1733 [7:571].

Will of JOHN THRESHER of Taun., dtd. 20 May 1727, prob. 11 June
1733. No wife mentioned. Sons: Christopher, John & Israel
(youngest) Thresher. Daus: Damaris wife of Moses Sechel [un-
clear], Sarah Richmond, Mercy Thrasher, Hannah Thrasher &
Katherine Thrasher (last 3 unmar.). Son Israel to be Exec.
Witns: Nathaniel Smith, Henery Hoskins & Elkanah Leonard [7:
572/3/4].

Codicil by JOHN THRESHER, dtd. 8 Sept. 1732. Mentions his son
Christopher who died since John's will was written. Son Christopher's portion will go to his children & heirs. Witns: Henery Hoskins, Mathew Briggs & Elkanah Leonard [7:574/5].

Inv. of Est. of JOHN THRESHER of Taun., dtd. 19 March 1732/3,
pres. by Israel Thresher, Exec. Mentions land given to John
Thresher, land given to Damaris Sehin [?] & land to Israel
Thresher. Apprs: William Hoskins, Israel Dean & Henery Hoskins [7:575/6].

Inv. of Est. of RICHARD BRIGGS of Nort., dtd. 14 March 1732/3,
pres. by John Briggs & Richard [sic] Briggs, Execs. Mentions
bed & furniture "that was Set off To ye Widdow." Apprs: John
Hodges, John Briggs & Daniel Brayman [7:576/7/8].

Inv. of Est. of BENJAMIN READ of Swan., dtd. 17 July 1733, pres.
by Hannah Read, widow & Adm. Apprs: Hugh Cole, George Sisson
& James Mason [7:578].

Order to Ruth Smith, widow & Exec. of Est. of ELEAZER SMITH of
Dart., the other Exec., son John Smith, now being in the "Province of Pensilvana," dtd. 17 July 1733 [7:579].

Will of ELEAZER SMITH of Dart., Yeoman, "Being Grown into years
and under Decay of Body," dtd. 15 Apr. 1729, prob. 17 July
1733. Wife Ruth. Sons: John (eldest), Thomas & Joseph Smith.
Only dau. Eliphal Harper. Grson. David Smith. Kinswoman Hopestill Sa[hidden]. Witns: Henery Howland, John Shapperd & Samuel Sprauge [sic][7:579/80/1].

Inv. of Est. of ELEAZER SMITH of Dart., dtd. 4 July 1733, pres.
by Ruth Smith, widow & Exec. Apprs: John Akin, James Howland
& [hidden][7:581/2/3].

Citation for John Peirce of Reho., Yeoman, & John Hulet of Swan.,

Husbandman, to appear before the probate court at Widow Howland's to answer to the charge of embezzling and conveying
away some of the Est. of JOHN ROGERS of Barr., whom they were
with "in his Sickness and Darkness," said complaint being
made by Silvester Richmond, Ichabod Richmond & Ephraim Atwood, heirs of said Rogers, dtd. 11 July 1733. They were later acquitted [7:583/4].

Appt. of Kethiah Horton of Reho., widow, as Adm. of Est. of
THOMAS HORTON of Reho., dtd. 17 July 1733 [7:584/5].

Acct. of Meribah Shearman, widow & Adm. of Est. of MOSES SHEAR-
MAN of Dart., dtd. 17 July 1733 [7:585/6].

Acct. of Mary Irish, widow & Adm of Est. of JONATHAN IRISH of
Lit. Comp., dtd. 17 July 1733 [7:586/7].

Inv. of Est. of EDMOND FISHER of Nort., dtd. 21 Nov. 1732, pres.
by Elezebeth Fisher, widow & Adm. Apprs: John Wetherill, Jonathan Lawrance & John Briggs [7:587/8].

Acct. of Eliphalet Leonard, Adm. of Est. of JAMES HODGE of East.
dtd. 18 July 1733]7:588/9].

Inv. of Est. of Capt. THOMAS TABER of Dart., dtd. 28 May 1733,
pres. by Jacob Taber, his son & Exec. Apprs: Christopher Turner, Isaac Pope & Thomas Nye [7:589/90].

Rcpt. by Caleb Arnold of Newport and Sarah Arnold Lately Named
Sarah Tew," for legacy from Est. of her father WILLIAM TEW of
Tiv., as paid by Richard Tew, George Sisson & William Sandford, Execs., dtd. at Newport 7 March 1732/3. Also incl. "all
Satisfaction for the personal Estate of Abigail Tew widdow of
the said Willm Tew," excepting for that portion reserved to
support Dorcas Tew, dau. of said William Tew and an idiot [7:
591].

Inv. of Est. of SAMUEL SHEARMAN of Swan., dtd. 26 June 1733,
pres. by Martha Shearman, widow & Exec. Apprs: William Anthoney, Hezekiah Luther & Preserved Brayton [7:591/2/3].

Appt. of John Taylor, Jr. of Lit. Comp., Yeoman, to be guard.
as chosen by Elezebeth Taylor (minor over 14), grdau. of PETER
HOSWEL of Lit. Comp. [next sentence calls him "of Dart."] dcd.
intest., dtd. 1 Aug. 1733 [7:593].

Appt. of Benjamin Jones of Digh., Gentlewoman, to be guard. of
Hannah, Pricilla & Susanna Winslow (all under 14), daus. of
JOSEPH WINSLOW of Swan., dtd. 21 Aug. 1733 [7:594].

Rcpt. by George Leonard of Nort. for legacy from Est. of his
father, Major GEORGE LEONARD of Nort., as paid by his mother
Anna Leonard, widow & Exec., dtd. 3 Nov. 1730. Mentions "My
sister Anna Leonard Deceased." Witns: Samuel Hollet & Sarah
Randel [7:595].

Rcpt. by Ephraim Leonard of Nort., Bloomer, for legacy from Est.
of his father Major GEORGE LEONARD of Nort., as paid by his
mother Anna Leonard, widow & Exec., dtd. 17 July 1730. Also
mentions Abial [child of said George?] and "my Sister Anna

Leonard Who Dyed after She Came to the Age of Twenty one
years." Mentions "my Grandmother Mary Leonards Estate Who
Dyed Intestate." Witns: Joseph Raynolds & Phebe Raynolds
[7:595/6].

Rcpt. by Joseph Raynolds & Phebe Raynolds of Brist. for legacy
from Est. of her father GEORGE LEONARD of Nort., as paid by
her mother Anna Leonard of Nort., Exec., dtd. 9 Oct. 1728.
Mentions "our Sister Anna Leonard Late Deceased." Also mentions "the Estate of our Grandmother Mary Leonard of Taunton."
Witns: William Throope & Joshua Smith [7:596/7].

Rcpt. by Warham Williams & Abigail Williams of Watertown for
legacy from Est. of her father GEORGE LEONARD of Nort., as
paid by her mother Anna Leonard of Nort., dtd. at Watertown
20 Aug. 1730. Also mentions "our Sister Anna Leonard of Norton Late Deceased," "our Sister Marcy Leonard Late Deceased"
& "our Honoured Grandmother Mary Leonard of Taunton Deceased."
Witns: Thomas Livermore & Allen Teley [7:597/8].

Rcpts. by Nathaniel Leonard, Ephraim Leonard & George Leonard
for legacies from the Est. of their sister ANNA LEONARD, as
paid by their mother Anna Leonard, dtd. 6 & 8 Apr. 1728 [7:
598].

End of Volume 7

Appt. of Jonathan Linkolen of Nort., Husbandman, to be guard.
as chosen by Ruth Cambel (minor over 14), dau. of SILVANUS
CAMBEL of Nort., dtd. 18 Sept. 1733 [8:1].

Appt. of Peleg Huddleston of Dart., Yeoman, as guard. of William Huddleston of Dart. "who is Non Compus mentis," dtd. 21
1733 [8:1/2].

Acct. of Patiance Hathway & Jonathan Hathway, Execs. of Est. of
JOHN HATHWAY of Dart., dtd. 21 Aug. 1733. Incl. legacies per
will to: Mary Dugles, Elezebeth Hathway, Arthur Hathway, Joannah Blackwell, Ruben Peckcom, Sarah Cannon & Hannah Bommer.
Incl. payms. of debts to: Richard Hathway & Hunnewel Hathway
[8:3].

Rcpt. by Mary Dugles & George Dugles of North Kingston, R.I. for
legacy from Est. of her father, JOHN HATHWAY, paid by Patiance
Hathway & Jonathan Hathway, Execs., dtd. 28 July 1733 [8:3/4].

Rcpt. by Elezebeth Hathway for legacy from Est. of her father
JOHN HATHWAY of Dart., paid by Patiance Hathway & Jonathan
Hathway, Execs., dtd. 9 July 1733 [8:4].

Rcpt. by Arthur Hathway for legacy from Est. of his father JOHN
HATHWAY of Dart., paid by Patiance Hathway & Jonathan Hathway,
Execs., dtd. 28 May 1732 [8:4].

Rcpt. by Joannah Blackwell & Nathaniel Blackwell of Dart. for
legacy from Est. of her father, JOHN HATHWAY, paid by Patiance
Hathway & Jonathan Hathway, Execs. dtd. 28 March 1733 [8:4].

Rcpt. from Hannah Boomer of Free. for legacy from Est. of her
father, JOHN HATHWAY, paid by Patiance Hathway & Jonathan Hathway, Execs., dtd. 18 Aug. 1733 [8:5].

Rcpt. by Sarah Cannon & John Cannon of Dart. for legacy from
Est. of her father, JOHN HATHWAY, paid by Patiance Hathway &
Jonathan Hathway, Execs., dtd. 28 March 1733 [8:5].

Rcpt. by Patiance Peckcom & Reuben Peckcom of Dart. for legacy
from Est. of her father, JOHN HATHWAY, paid by Patiance Hathway & Jonathan Hathway, Execs., dtd. 9 July 1733 [8:5].

Acct. of Unis Ingols, widow & Adm. of Est. of EDMUND INGOLS of
Reho., dtd. 13 Sept. 1733 [8:5/6].

Appts. of Joseph Winslow of Swan., Yeoman, to be guard. as chosen by Mary Winslow & Job Winslow (minors over 14), chldn. of
JOSEPH WINSLOW of Swan., dtd. 13 Sept. 1733 [8:6/7/8].

Acct. of Ebenezer Shearman, Exec. of Est. of DANIEL SHEARMAN of
Dart., dtd. 18 Sept. 1733. Incl. legacies per will to: the wi-
dow [not named], Isabel Shearman, Ruth Shearman, Seth Shearman,
Sarah Shearman as guard. of Israel Shearman & Marabah Shearman

as guard. of Sarah Shearman [8:8/9].
Acct. of Joseph Titus of Reho., Adm. of Est. of JOHN TITUS, Jr.
of Reho. dcd. intest., dtd. 13 Sept. 1733. Incl. paym. "for
the widdow for her Charge of Lying with a Posthumus Child"
[8:9].
Order to Samuel Royal & Samuel Smith, Execs. of Est. of JOHN
BIRGE of Brist., dtd. 18 Sept. 1733 [8:10].
Will of JOHN BIRGE of Brist., Taylor, dtd. 4 Oct. 1729, prob.
18 Sept. 1733. No wife mentioned. Dau. Elzibeth Lewis & son-
in-law Joseph Lewis; dau. Mary Dolliver & son-in-law John Dolliver; grson. John Dolliver (under 21); dau-in-law Hannah
Birge & grdau. Patience [no surname, but apparently dau. of
said Hannah Birge]. To Ann Liscomb, widow. Samuel Royal & Samuel Smith, both of Brist., to be Execs. Witns: Stephen
Paine, Joseph Wardwel & Isaac Ingraham [8:10/1/2].
Order to James, Ebenezer & John Adams, Execs. of Est. of their
father, JAMES ADAMS of Barr., dtd. 18 Sept. 1733 [8:12/3].
Will of JAMES ADAMS of Barr., Yeoman, dtd. 19 March 1732/3,
prob. 18 Sept. 1733. Wife included but not named. 3 sons:
James, Ebenezer & John Adams. Daus: Mary [no surname] & Sar-
ah Tiffeney. Sons James, Ebenezer & John to be Execs. Witns:
Samuel Curtis, Samuel Humphrey & Mary Humphrey [8:13/4].
Inv. of Est. of William Huddleston of Dart., "who is non Compus
mentis," dtd. 17 Sept 1733, pres. by Peleg Huddleston, guard.
Apprs: Philip Allen, John Tripp & Beriah Goddard [8:14].
Appt. of Samuel Cooper of Reho. to be guard. as chosen by Nathan
Read (minor over 14), son of JAMES READ of Reho., dtd. 18 Sept.
1733 [8:15].
Appt. of John Hoswell of Lit. Comp., Adm. of Est. of his father
PETER HOSWEL of Lit. Comp., "ye widow Refusing," dtd. 18
Sept. 1733 [8:15/6].
Appt. of Patiance Simmons of Digh., widow, as Adm. of Est. of
JOHN SIMMONS of Digh., Husbandman, dtd. 18 Sept. 1733 [8:16].
Appt. of Jonathan Linkolen of Nort., Husbandman, to be guard. of
Jeremiah Cambel (minor over 14), son of SILVANUS CAMBEL of
Nort., dtd. 18 Sept. 1733 [8:17].
Inv. of Est. of JOHN SIMMONS Of Digh., Yeoman, dtd. 17 Sept.
1733, pres. by Patiance Simmons, widow & Adm. Apprs; Abraham
Shaw, Josiah Talbut & William Paul [8:17/8].
Appt. of Benjamin Cole of Swan., Yeoman, as Adm. of Est.of SAM-
UEL COLE of Swan., "at the Request of mehetibel Cole his mo-
ther," dtd. 9 Oct. 1733 [8:18/9].
Order to Jonathan Merithew of Dart., Exec. of Est. of his son
SAMUEL MERITHEW of Dart., dtd. 11 Oct. 1733 [8:19].
Will of SAMUEL MERITHEW of Dart., Yeoman, "being very weak in
body," dtd. 20 Sept. 1733, prob. 4 Oct. 1733. No wife men-
tioned. My father Jonathan Merithew. Sisters Mary Merithew,
Grace Burlingham, Desire, Susannah & Dinah [no surnames].
Brothers Roger Merithew & Jeremiah Merithew. Father to be

Exec. Witns: Isaac Howland, Barnabas Howland & Ebenezer
Briggs [8:19/20].
Agrmnt. on settl. of Est. in Taun. of JOSEPH WILLIAMS of Taun.
dcd. intest., signed by "Elezebeth Williams and Anne Williams
of Bridgewater...County of Plimouth...being all the Children
now Living of the Deceased being Legally Capable to act," dtd.
16 Feb. 1732. Witns: Seth Williams & Benjamin Williams [8:
20/1/2].
Inv. of Est. of JOHN BIRGE of Brist., dtd. 15 Oct. 1733, pres.
by Samuel Royal & Samuel Smith, Execs. Mentions "The House
and Land Willed to John Dollever." Apprs: Jonathan Woodbury,
Joseph Wardwel & Eleazer Raynolds [8:22/3].
Appt. of Ephraim Hix of Reho., Yeoman, to be guard. as chosen
by James Hix (minor over 14), son of JAMES HIX of Reho., dtd.
22 Oct. 1733 [8:23/4].
Appt. of Jonathan Kingsley of Reho. to be guard. as chosen by
Hezekiah Hix (minor over 14), son of JAMES HIX of Reho., dtd.
22 Oct. 1733 [8:24].
Appt. of Elezebeth Read of Reho., widow, to be guard. of Ephraim
Read (under 14), son of NATHANIEL READ of Reho., dtd. 20 Nov.
1733 [8:24/5].
Appt. of Daniel Perrin of Reho., Husbandman, to be guard. as
chosen by Moses Read (minor over 14), son of NATHANIEL READ of
Reho., dtd. 20 Nov. 1733 [8:25].
Appt. of Elizabeth Read of Reho. to be guard. of Ezra Read (un-
der 14), son of NATHANIEL READ of Reho., dtd. 20 Nov. 1733
[8:26].
Order to Martha Sawyer, widow, & to John Sawyer, son, Execs. of
Est. of JOSIAH SAWYER of Tiv., dtd. 20 Nov. 1733 [8:27].
Order to Hannah Shearman & Henery Gidley, Execs. of Est. of SAM-
UEL SHEARMAN of Dart., dtd. 20 Nov. 1733 [8:28].
Acct. of Jethniel Peck of Reho., guard. of ABIGAIL SMITH, widow
& relict of Daniel Smith, Esq. of Reho., "who was non Compus
mentis," dtd. 17 Nov. 1733. Mentions: "A Legacy given to the
Said Abigail Smith by her father [sic; father-in-law?] Daniel
Smith Late of Dorchester Deceased." Mentions "her son Daniel
Smith," who was paid for keeping his mother yearly from June
1727 to June 1731, then "to Keeping her Eaight months in the
year 1732" [8:29/30].
Will of SAMUEL SHEARMAN of Dart., "Growing into years," dtd. 2
March 1732/3, prob. 20 Nov. 1733. Wife Hannah. No sons men-
tioned. 5 daus: Elizabeth Gidley, Joannah Cran, Abigail Shear-
man, Hannah Merithew & Alce Shearman. "My Loving Son Henery
Gidley" to be Exec. Witns: Timothey Richetson, Darius Talman
& William Bowdish [8:29].
Will of JOSIAH SAWYER of Tiv., "being Sick and Weak," dtd. 15
Sept. 1733, prob. 20 Nov. 1733. Wife Martha. Sons: John Sawyer
& Josiah (under 21) Sawyer. Daus: Hannah Williston, Mercy,
Mary, Abigail & Priscilla [no surnames]. Wife Martha & son

John to be Execs. Mentions lands in Tiv. & in Lit. Comp. Witns:
Samuel Crandal, Isaac Case & Joseph Tompkins [8:30/1].

Inv. of Est. of SAMUEL SHEARMAN of Dart., dtd. 16 Nov. 1733,
pres. by Hannah Shearman & Henery Gidley, Execs. Apprs: John
Russel, Eliashib Smith & Jabiz Barker [8:31/2/3].

Inv. of Est. of JOHN HATHWAY of Digh., Yeoman, dtd. 17 Nov. 17-
33, pres. by Marcy Hathway, widow & Adm. Apprs: Mathew Briggs,
Abraham Waldroon & Silvester Richmond [8:33/4].

Inv. of Est. of JOSIAH SAWYER of Tiv., Yeoman, dtd. 15 Nov. 17-
33, pres. by Martha Sawyer & John Sawyer, Execs. Apprs: Nathaniel Searle, George Peirce & Samuel Tompkins [8:34/5].

Acct. of Mercy Hathway, widow & Adm. of Est. of JOHN HATHWAY of
Digh., dtd. 20 Nov. 1733 [8:35/6].

Acct. of Samuel Read, Adm. of Est. of his father NATHANIEL READ
of Reho., dtd. 23 Nov. 1733. Incl. money from: "Ebenezer
Read of Uxbridge" [8:36].

Acct. of James Tripp of Dart., guard. of Stephen Wilcox "who was
non Compus mentis and is now Restored to his Right mind again,"
dtd. 20 Nov. 1733. Mentions land sold by order of the court on
the 2nd Tue. of Sept. 1729. Incl. paym. "To an Indian for Taking up his Son Daniel y^t was Drowned" [8:37].

Will of JOSEPH DURPHEY of Tiv., Yeoman, son of William Durphey
of Tiv. dcd., "being about to go a voige To Sea," dtd. 14 Nov.
1731, prob. 20 Nov. 1733. Brother Samuel Durphey. Lands in Tiv.
& rights to lands in Lit. Comp. Brother Samuel to be Exec.
Witns: Jonathan Read, William Durphey & Edward Wanton [8:37/8].

Inv. of Est. of ABIGAIL SMITH of Reho., widow & relict of Daniel
Smith, Esq. of Reho., dtd. 26 Dec. 1732, pres. by Daniel Smith
son & Adm. Apprs: Jethniel Peck, Joseph Bosworth & Daniel Peck.
[8:38/9].

Acct. of Daniel Smith, Adm. of Est. of his mother ABIGAIL SMITH
of Reho., widow, dtd. 20 Nov. 1733 [8:39].

Acct. of John Read, Exec. of Est. of ISRAEL READ of Reho., dtd.
18 Dec. 1733. Incl. legacies per will to: John Read, heirs of
Israel Read, Josiah Read, Jeremiah Read, Rebecca Read, Elezebeth Read & Ruth Read. Incl. payms. of debts to "Widdow Hannah
Read" & "Widdow Martha Read." Item paid "to Ezekiel Read for
clothing and other Necessarys for ye widdow" [8:39/40].

Inv. of Est. of MARY MOREY of Digh., dtd. 29 Nov. 1733, pres.
by James Brittain, Exec. Apprs: Ebenezer Pitts, Benjamin
Jones & Oliver Simmons [8:41].

Appt. of Morgan Cobb, 2nd, of Taun. to be guard as chosen by
Richard Cobb (minor over 14), son of SAMUEL COBB of Taun., dtd.
26 Dec. 1733 [8:41/2].

Acct. of Henery Bragg, Adm. of Est. of his brother NICHOLAS
BRAGG of Brist. dcd. insolvent, dtd. 29 Dec. 1733. Mentions,
but does not name, the widow [8:42/3].

Appt. of Ephraim Huet of East. as Adm. of Est. of his father
EPHRAIM HUET of East., dtd. 9 Jan. 1733 [8:43].

Order to Sarah Brown of Barr., widow & Exec. of Est. of OLIVER
BROWN of Barr., dtd. 15 Jan. 1733 [8:44].
Will of OLIVER BROWN of Barr., Carpenter, "being Sick and weak
in body," dtd. 19 Dec. 1733, prob. 15 Jan. 1733. Wife Sarah.
Daus: Rebecca Brown (under 18) & Anna Brown. "My father and
mother Joyntly to Educate and Bring up my afors[d] Daughter
[*Rebecca*]. Bequeaths to wife Sarah all of that "which She
Stood possesed of before She became my wife." Witns: John
Aplin, Benjamin Brown & Hezekiah Brown [8:44/5].
Inv. of Est. of EPHRAIM HUET of East., dtd. 19 Nov. 1733, pres.
by Ephraim Huet, his son & Adm. Apprs: Thomas Manley, Mark
Lathroop & Josiah Keith [8:45/6].
Inv. of Est. of JAMES ADAMS of Barr., dtd. 29 Oct. 1733, pres.
by James, Ebenezer & John Adams, sons & Execs. Apprs: Sam-
uel Low, James Smith & Edward Bosworth [8:47].
Order for div. of Est. of JOSEPH WINSLOW of Swan. dcd. intest.,
dtd. 22 Sept. 1733 [8:47/8].
Div. of Est. of JOSEPH WINSLOW of Swan. btwn. his chldn: Oliver
(eldest son), Joseph (2nd son), Job (3rd son), Ruth (eldest
dau.), Mary (2nd dau.), Hannah (3rd dau.), Susannah (4th dau.)
& Pricilla (5th dau.) [*no surnames*], dtd. 25 Oct. 1733. Comm:
William Anthoney, Preserved Brayton, Hezekiah Luther, Heze-
kiah Kingsley & Abraham Waldroon [8:48/9/50].
Affidavit by Marah Rogers, widow of JOHN ROGERS of Barr., dtd.
25 Sept. 1733 [8:50].
Rcpt. by Thomas Martin of Brist., Blockmaker, for money rcvd.
from his guard., Robert Joles of Brist., Yeoman, dtd. 1 Feb.
1733/4 Witns: Abraham Crane & Thomas Jolls [8:50/1].
Report of Comm. to examine claims of creditors against Est. of
NICHOLAS BRAGG of Brist., dtd. 14 May 1733. Comm: Jonathan
Woodbury & Samuel Royal [8:51].
Order to Henery Bragg, Adm., to proportion debts owed against
balance remaining in Est. of his brother NICHOLAS BRAGG, dtd.
25 Jan. 1733/4. Mentions the 1/3 set out to the widow [8:
51/2].
Acct. of Unis Ingols, widow & Adm. of Est. of EDMUND INGOLS of
Reho., dtd. 16 Jan. 1733/4 [8:52].
Order to Josiah Talbut of Digh., Exec. of Est. of JARED TALBUT,
Esq., of Digh., dtd. 19 Feb. 1733/4 [8:52/3].
Will of JARED TALBUT of Digh., Yeoman, "being very Sick and weak
of body," dtd. 16 Jan. 1733/4, prob. 19 Feb. 1733/4. Wife Re-
beca. Sons: Jared, Josiah, Jacob & Seth Talbut. Dau. Eleze-
beth Richmond. My pastor Nathaniel Fisher. To Oliver Darbey.
Son Josiah to be Exec. Witns: Mathew Briggs, Ebenezer Jones
& Ichabod Richmond [8:53/4/5].
Inv. of Est. of SAMUEL COLE of Swan., dtd. 29 Oct. 1733, pres.
by Benjamin Cole, Adm. [8:55].
Acct. of Alce Cornel, late widow & Adm. of Est. of EPHRAIM THOMAS
of Tiv., dtd. 8 Feb. 1733/4 [8:56].

Inv. of Est. of OLIVER BROWN of Barr., dtd. 24 Jan. 1733/4, pres.
by Sarah Brown, widow & Exec. Apprs: Samuel Allen, Josiah
Humphrey & Benjamin Vial [8:56/7].

Appt. of Michail Smith to be Adm. of Est. of his father JUDATH
SMITH of Dart. dcd. intest., the eldest son, Richard Smith,
having refused Adm., dtd. 19 Feb. 1733/4 [8:57/8].

Inv. of Est. of JUDATH SMITH of Dart., dtd. 25 Dec. 1733, pres.
by Michail Smith, son & Adm. Apprs: Philip Shearman, James
Shearman & Isaac Smith [8:58/9].

Order for div. of Est. of NATHANIEL READ of Reho. dcd. intest.,
dtd. 26 Nov. 1733 [8:59].

Div. of Est. of NATHANIEL READ of Reho. btwn. his widow [not
named] and chldn: Samuel (eldest son), Moses (2nd son), Ephraim (3rd son) & Ezra (youngest son) Read. No daus. given.
Comm: Daniel Carpenter, Ephraim Carpenter & Ezekiel Read
[8:60/1/2].

Acct. of Isaac Mason, John Wood & James Lewis, Execs. of Est.
of JOHN MILLARD of Reho., dtd. 19 Feb. 1733/4. Incl. payms.
to: "the Guardians of John Millars two Daughters," "Deborah
Millard Widdow of the Deceased...to her Support at her Lying
in" & "Spent on the two young Children the fourth & 5 year."
[8:62/3].

Appt. of Patiance Wingg, widow, as Adm. of Est. of her husb. ED-
WARD WING of Dart. dcd. intest., dtd. 26 Feb. 1733/4 [8:64].

Appts. of Hezekiah Kinsley of Swan., Blacksmith, to be guard.
of Phebe, Mary & [blank; called a son] Cole, chldn. of SAM-
UEL COLE of Swan., dtd. 26 Feb. 1733/4 [8:64/5/6].

Appts. of Capt. Edward Hayward of East. to be guard. as chosen
by Ruth Huet & Solomon Huet (both minors over 14), chldn. of
EPHRAIM HUET of East., dtd. 26 Feb. 1733/4 [8:66/7].

Appts. of Ephraim Hix, Jr. of Reho., Yeoman, to be guard. as
chosen by Mary Hix (over 14) & by Lois & Freelove Hix (both
under 14), chldn. of JAMES HIX of Reho., dtd. 26 Feb. 1733/4
[8:67/8].

Appt. of Samuel Kingsley of East., Yeoman, to be guard. as chosen by Mercy Huet (minor over 14), dau. of EPHRAIM HUET of
East., dtd. 26 Feb. 1733/4 [8:68/9].

Acct. of Ephraim Huet of East., Adm. of Est. of his father EPH-
RAIM HUET of East., dtd. 19 March 1733/4. Incl. item for "Going to Bridgewater to acknolidge 2 Deeds" [8:69].

Order to Mehetibel Carpenter, widow & Exec. of Est. of her husb.
CORNELIUS CARPENTER of Reho., dtd. 12 March 1733/4 [8:70].

Will of CORNELIUS CARPENTER of Reho., Husbandman, "being very
weak of body," dtd. 4 Aug. 1733, prob. 12 March 1733/4. Wife
Mehetibel. Dau. Mehetibel Carpenter (under 18 & unmar.). The
2 eldest sons of my brothers Abiah Carpenter & Thomas Carpenter. To the Rev. John Greenwood of the First Church of Christ
in Rehoboth. Wife to be Exec. Witns: Samuel Bairsto, William
Mathews & John Greenwood [8:70/1].

Appt. of Elezebeth Huddleston of Dart., widow, to be guard. of
William & Elezebeth Huddleton (both under 14), chldn. of WIL-
LIAM HUDDLESTON of Dart., dtd. 20 March 1733/4 [8:72].

Appt. of Elezebeth Huddleston of Dart., widow, as Adm. of Est.
of WILLIAM HUDDLESTON of Dart., dtd. 20 March 1733/4 [8:72/3].

Appt. of Peter Walker of Reho., Yeoman, to be guard. as chosen
by Martha Read & Noah Read (minors over 14), chldn. of THOMAS
READ of Reho., dtd. 19 March 1733/4 [8:73].

Appt. of Peter Walker of Reho., Yeoman, and "his wife Martha Walker Late widdow of Thomas Read," to be guards. of Hannah Read
& Sarah Read (both under 14), daus. of THOMAS READ of Reho.,
dtd. 19 March 1733/4 [8:73/4].

Appts. of Morgan Cobb, 2nd, of Taun., Yeoman, to be guard as
chosen by Joseph Harvey & Benjamin Harvey (minors over 14) &
of Abigail Harvey (under 14), chldn. of WILLIAM HARVEY of
Taun., dtd. 19 March 1733/4 [8:74/5].

Appt. of Noah Wood of Swan., Husbandman, & "his wife Elezebeth
Wood Late widdow of John Haile Junr" to be guards. of Elisha,
Job & Hannah Haile (all under 14), chldn. of JOHN HAILE, Jr.
of Swan., dtd. 22 March 1733/4 [8:75/6].

Appt. of Nathan Mason of Swan., Husbandman, to be guard. as
chosen by his wife Lilis Mason (minor over 14), dau. of JOHN
HAILE of Swan., dtd. 22 March 1733/4 [8:76].

Inv. of Est. of WILLIAM HUDDLESTON of Dart., dtd. 14 Feb. 1733,
pres. by Elizabeth Huddleston, widow & Adm. Apprs: John Russel, Phillip Allen & Beriah Goddard [8:76/7].

Inv. of Est. of ABIAL MACOMBER of Taun., dtd. 23 July 1734[sic],
pres. by Abia Macomber, widow & Adm. Apprs: Richard Godfrey,
Samuel Pitts & Seth Staples [8:77/8].

Inv. of Est. of SAMUEL MERITHEW of Dart., dtd. 28 Nov. 1733,
pres. by Jonathan Merithew, his father & Exec. Apprs: James
Tripp, Jr., Jonathan Smith & Peleg Smith [8:78].

Acct. of Barnard Hail of Swan., Adm. of Est. of his mother HAN-
NAH HAIL of Swan., dtd. 19 March 1733/4 [8:78/78¼].

Inv. of Est. of MARY BRIGGS of Nort., dtd. 18 Dec. 1733, pres.
by John Briggs, her husb. & Adm. Apprs: Nathaniel Hodges,
Simeon Wetherill & Ebenezer Burt [8:78¼/78½].

Acct. of Experiance Mason, widow & Adm. of Est. of SAMPSON MASON
of Swan., dtd. 19 March 1733/4. Incl. paym. "To my father
Mason"[father-in-law?][8:78½].

Div. of Est. (ordered 20 Feb. 1733/4) of JOSEPH BAKER of Swan.
dcd. intest., btwn his widow [not named] & his chldn: Francis
Baker (eldest son), Daniel Baker (son), Jemima Sole (dau.),
Job Baker (son), Isabel Baker (dau.), Samuel Baker (son) &
George Baker (son.), dtd. 2 March 1733/4. Comm: William Anthoney, Preserved Brayton, Hezekiah Luther, Eseck Brown & Edward Simmons [8:78/80/1].

Acct. of Peleg Huddleston, guard. of his brother WILLIAM HUDDLE-
STON of Dart., "who was non Compus mentis and is since Deceased," dtd. 20 March 1733/4. William's wife [unnamed][8:
81/2].

Appt. of Noah Wood of Swan., Husbandman, & "his wife Elezebeth
Wood Late Widdow of John Haile," to be guard. of John Hail
(under 14), son of JOHN HAIL of Swan., dtd. 22 March 1733/4
[8:82/3].
Appt. of Peletiah Mason, Jr. of Swan., Husbandman, to be guard.
as chosen by his wife Hannah Mason (minor over 14), dau. of
JOHN HAIL of Swan., dtd. 22 March 1733/4 [8:83].
Appt. of Seth Witherill of Nort., Husbandman, eldest brother of
GEORGE WITHERILL of Nort., to be Adm. of his brother's Est.,
their mother, Hannah Witherill, refusing, dtd. 10 Apr. 1734
[8:84].
Appt. of Samuel Caswell of Nort., "Practioner of Phisick," to
be guard. as chosen by his son Samuel Caswell, Jr. (minor
over 14), grson. of SAMUEL PRATT of Taun., dtd. 10 Apr. 1734
[8:84/5].
Appt. of Cornelius Jenne, eldest son of LETTIS JENNE of Dart.,
to be Adm. cum testimento annexo of his father's Est., since
Desire Jenne, widow of Lettis Jenne, has relinquished Exec.,
dtd. 19 March 1733/4 [8:85].
Will of LETTIS JENNE of Dart., Yeoman, "being under Infirmity
of body," dtd. 24 Jan. 1731/2, prob. 19 March 1734. Wife Desire. Sons: Cornelius (eldest), Ignatius, Caleb, Samuel & Nathaniel. Son-in-law Jeduthan Sponner; dau. Sarah wife of Sampson Sponner; dau. Reliance [?] wife of Thomas Pope; dau. Mary
wife of Thomas West; grdau. Ruth Sponner (under 10); dau. Elezebeth (under 21) [no surname] & dau. Pernel (under 21)[no
surname]. Witns: Samuel Hammond, Abraham Russel (a Quaker)
& Benjamin Hammond [8:85/6/7].
Appts. of Mary Jones of Digh., wife of Adam Jones, to be guard.
as chosen by her chldn. Seth, Benjamin & Mary Crane (minors
over 14), chldn. of BENJAMIN CRANE of Digh., dtd. 11 Apr. 17-
34 [8:88].
Appts. of John Akin of Dart., Gentleman, to be guard. of Mary
Gatchel & Susanna Gatchel (both under 14), daus. of JOHN GAT-
CHEL of Dart., dtd. 11 Apr. 1734 [8:90].
Order to Elezebeth Pitts, widow, & to George Pitts, son, Execs.
of Est. of Capt. EBENEZER PITTS of Digh., dtd. 16 Apr. 1734
[8:91].
Will of EBENEZER PITTS of Digh., Yeoman, "being arrived To a
Considerable age and much Indisposed of body," dtd. 29 Jan.
1733/4, prob. 17 Apt. 1734. Wife Elezebeth. Son George Pitts.
Daus: Elezebeth Paul wife of John Paul, Mary Andrews wife of
Samuel Andrews, Hopestill Talbut wife of Nathaniel Talbut &
Mercy Pitts. Div. to be made by my friends Deacon Abraham
Shaw, Henery Pitts & Abraham Waldroon. Mentions "my Hono^d fa-
ther John Hoskins Late of Dighton Deceased" [father-in-law?].
Wife Elezebeth & son George to be Execs. Witns: Ebenezer
Jones, John Wetherill & Nathaniel Fisher [8:91/2/3/4].
Appt. of Thomas Morey of Nort., Yeoman, to be guard. as chosen

by Benjamin Healey (minor over 14), son of PAUL HEALEY of
Reho., dtd. 16 Apr. 1734 [8:94].

Order to Isaac Chase of Swan., Exec. of Est. of his father JA-
COB CHASE of Swan., dtd. 16 Apr. 1734 [8:94/5].

Will of JACOB CHASE of Swan., Yeoman, "being very Sick in body,"
dtd. 25 Jan. 1733/4, prob. 16 Apr. 1734. Wife mentioned but
not named. Sons: Isaac, Jacob, Samuel, Ephraim, Joseph, Joshua & Oliver Chase. Daus: Hannah Read & Mary Woodmansee. Son
Isaac to be Exec. Friend George Sisson to be Overseer. Witns:
George Sisson, Benjamin Barton & John Earl [8:95].

Appt. of Mary Paul, widow, to be Adm. of Est. of WILLIAM PAUL
of Digh., dtd. 16 Apr. 1734 [8:96].

Inv. of Est. of WILLIAM PAUL of Digh., dtd. 18 March 1733/4,
pres. by Mary Paul, widow & Adm. Apprs: Abraham Shaw, Josiah
Talbut & Abraham Waldroon [8:96/7].

Inv. of Est. of EDWARD WINGG of Dart., dtd. 7 March 1733/4,
pres. by Patiance Wingg, widow & Adm. Apprs: Daniel Wood,
Eliashib Smith & William Bowdish [8:97/8].

Acct. of Daniel Axtel & Elkanah Babit, guards. of Benjamin
Crane, Seth Crane, Tabitha Briggs late Tabatha Crane & Mary
Crane, chldn. of BENJAMIN CRANE of Digh., dtd. 11 Apr. 1734.
Incl. items for "time in binding out Seth & Mary" & "for bind-
ing out Benja^n twice." Incl. rent for 7 years from Adam Jones
for the house and upland [8:99/100].

Appt. of Samuel Little of Brist., Gentleman, to be guard. as
chosen by Thomas Howland (minor over 14), son of JABEZ HOWLAND
of Brist., dtd. 16 Apr. 1734 [8:100].

Div. of Est. of EPHRAIM HEWET of East. btwn. his chldn: Ephraim
(eldest son), Hannah the wife of Edward White, Susanah wife of
John Linkon, Henry, Solomon, Mercy Hewet, Elezebeth Drake &
Ruth Hewet (youngest dau.), dtd. 16 Apr. 1734. Mentions Capt.
Howard as guard. of Solomon Hewet. Comm: Morgan Cobb, 2nd,
Ephraim Randall, Eliphalet Leonard & Daniel Owen [8:101/2/3].

Inv. of Est. of WILLIAM HARVEY of Taun. dcd. intest., dtd. 13
Jan. 1732/3, pres. by David Harvey, son & Adm. Mentions land
in Taun. & East. Apprs: William Thayer, Benjamin Willis &
Morgan Cobb, 2nd [8:103/4].

Order to Robart Wheteen & Daniel Wheeten, Execs. of Est. of
their father EPHRAIM WHETEEN of Reho., dtd. 10 May 1734[8.104].

Will of EPHRAIM WHETEEN of Reho., Yeoman, dtd. 20 May 1729, prob.
10 May 1734. Wife Hannah. Sons: James, Ephraim, Robart & Daniel Wheteen. Daus: Abigail (to have a room in the house), Mary
wife of Richard Bullock, Hannah wife of Isaac Bowen, Alce wife
of Daniel Barney & Freelove wife of Josiah Barney. Sons Robart
& Daniel to be Execs. Witns: James Bowen, William West & Obe-
dian Bowen [8:104/5/6].

Acct. of Bethia Davis late Bethia Bragg, and of Elezebeth Little
late Elezebeth Howland, Adms. of Est. of their father JABIZ
HOWLAND of Brist., dtd. 2 Apr. 1734. Incl. paym. "advanced

To four the Daughters in ye fathers Life time." Balance is "to be devided into Eight parts" [8:106/7/8/9].

Acct. of Yetmercy Howland late Yetmercy Palmer, widow & Adm. of Est. of ISAAC PALMER of Lit. Comp., dtd. 10 May 1734[8:109/10].

Order to Philip Shearman, Exec. of Est. of his father JOHN SHEAR-MAN of Dart., since Timothey Shearman son of the dcd. John refused Exec., dtd. 21 May 1734 [8:110].

Will of JOHN SHEARMAN of Dart., 19 June 1720, prob. 21 May 1734. Wife Sarah. Sons: Phillip, Isaac, Ephraim & Timothey Shearman. Daus: Abigail Chase & Hannah Akin. Grson. John Shearman. Grchldn: Jonathan Shearman & Phebe Shearman. My brother Peleg Shearman dcd. Sons Phillip & Timothey to be Execs. Witns: John Russel, Jr., George Howland & William Bowdish [8:111/2]

Order for div. of Est. of EDMUND INGOLS of Reho., dtd. 21 Jan. 1733/4 [8:113].

Div. of Est. of EDMUND INGOLS of Reho. btwn. his widow Unis Ingols & his chldn: Benjamin Ingols (double share), Ebenezer Ingols, Edmund Ingols, Joseph Ingols, Samuel Ingols, Elezebeth wife of Ephraim Martin, Lois Ingols & Unis Ingols, dtd. 30 Jan. 1733/4. Comm: Samuel Wheler, Samuel Bullock, Thomas Dimone & Stephen Moulten [8:113/4].

Order to div. real est. of JABIZ HOWLAND of Brist., dtd. 15 Apr. 1734 [8:115].

Div. of real est. of JABIZ HOWLAND btwn. his chldn: Jabiz Howland (eldest son), Thomas Howland, Bethiah Davis, Mercy Martindal, Elezebeth Little, Sarah Lawton & Patiance Howland, dtd. 21 May 1734. Comm: Thomas Throope, Samuel Royal, John Bosworth & Jonathan Peck [8:115/6].

Order to Mary Briggs, widow, & Thomas Briggs, son, Execs. of Est. of Capt. THOMAS BRIGGS of Lit. Comp. [next sentence has "of Dartmouth"], dtd. 21 May 1734 [8:116/7].

Will of THOMAS BRIGGS of Dart., Yeoman, dtd. 28 March 1734, prob. 21 May 1734. Wife Mary. Sons: Ebenezer, Daniel, Thomas, Paul, Benjamin, Edward & Job Briggs. Daus: Thankful Briggs (unmar.) & Mary Briggs (youngest, under 18, unmar.). Wife Mary & son Thomas to be Execs. Witns: Jonathan Merethew (Quaker), Barnabas Howland & Henry Howland [8:117/8/9/20/1].

Inv. of Est. of JOHN SHEARMAN of Dart., dtd. 27 Apr. 1734, pres. by Phillip Shearman, son & Exec. Apprs: Richard Sanford, Daniel Wood & William Bowdish [8:121/2].

Inv. of Est. of Capt. THOMAS BRIGGS of Dart., dtd. 17 May 1734, pres. by Mary Briggs, widow, & Thomas Briggs, son, Execs. Apprs: Nathaniel Soule, Jeremiah Wilcox & James Allen [8:122/3/4].

Appt. of John Russel of Dart., Blacksmith, to be guard. as chosen by Alce Shearman (minor over 14), dau. of SAMUEL SHEARMAN of Dart., dtd. 21 May 1734 [8:124].

Appt. of Zerviah Potter, widow, to be Adm. of Est. of NATHANIEL POTTER of Tiv. dcd. intest., dtd. 21 May 1734 [8:124/5].

Inv. of Est. of NATHANIEL POTTER of Tiv., dtd. 25 Oct. 1733,
pres. by Zerviah Potter, widow & Adm. Apprs: Daniel Lawton,
Aron Bowen & Benjamin Brayton [8:125/6].

Inv. of Est. of CORNELIUS CARPENTER of Reho., dtd. 8 Apr. 1734,
pres. by Mehetibel Carpenter, widow & Exec. Apprs: Noah Mason, Jonathan French & Edward Glover [8:126].

Inv. of Est. of JACOB CHASE of Swan., pres. 18 June 1734 by
Isaac Chase, Exec. Apprs: George Sisson, James Mason & Benjamin Barton [8:127].

Inv. of Est. of Elder EPHRAIM WHETON of Reho., dtd. 24 May 1734
pres. by Robert & Daniel Wheaton, sons & Execs. Mentions real
est. given to Ephraim Wheaten & to Daniel Wheaten. Apprs. not
listed [8:127/8].

Appt. of Patiance Peck, widow, to be Adm. of Est. of NATHAN PECK
of Reho. dcd. intest., dtd. 18 June 1734 [8:128].

Inv. of Est. of NATHAN PECK of Reho., dtd. 27 May 1734, pres. by
Patiance Peck, widow & Adm. Mentions lands in Reho. & Attl.
Apprs: Jonathan Chaffe, David Thurston & Edward Glover [8:129].

Will of BARNABAS SPONER of Dart., Yeoman, dtd. 7 Feb. 1733, prob.
18 June 1734. Wife Zerviah. Son Moses (eldest & only son, under 21). Dau. Jane (under 21, unmar.). "The Child my Wife now
goes with." Directs support of "my aged and Honoured father."
Wife Zerviah & Samuel Willis, Esq., of Dart. to be Execs.
Witns: George Jenne, Jonathan Hathway, Allis Jenne & Timothey
Rugles [8:130/1/2].

Inv. of Est. of BARNABAS SPOONER of Dart., dtd. 14 June 1734,
pres. by Zerviah Spooner, widow & Exec. Apprs: Christopher
Turner, William Badcock & Job Jenne [8:132/3].

Order to Nathan Dean of Taun., Exec. of Est. of his brother ISAAC
DEAN of Taun., dtd. 10 July 1734 [8:133/4].

Will of ISAAC DEAN of Taun., "being Sick and Weak," dtd. 28 Nov.
1733, prob. 10 July 1734. Mother Sarah Dean. Brothers: Samuel,
William & Nathan Dean. Brother Nathan to be Exec. Witns: Seth
Williams, Benjamin Williams & Mary Robinson [8:134/5].

Inv. of Est. of Capt. JARED TALBUT of Digh., dtd. 15 March 1733/4
pres. by Samuel Talbut, son & Exec. Incl. negros John, Jeffrey
& Hette (woman). Apprs: Abraham Shaw, Henery Pitts & Morgan
Cobb, 2nd [8:135/6].

Inv. of Est. of Capt. EBENEZER PITTS of Digh., dtd. 3 July 1734,
pres. by Elezebeth Pitts & George Pitts, Execs. Apprs: Abraham Shaw, Henery Pitts & Abraham Waldroon [8:136/7/8].

Order to Mary Read of Taun., widow & Exec. of Est. of WILLIAM
READ of Taun., dtd. 16 July 1734 [8:138/9].

Will of WILLIAM READ of Taun., Husbandman, "being very Sick and
Weak in body," dtd. 31 March 1726, prob. 16 July 1734. Wife
Marah [Mary]. Sons: William & John Read (both under 21). Dau.
Mary Read (under 18). Permits wife to use or dispose of "move-
ables as She had when I married with her." Wife to be Exec.
Joseph Tisdal & Morgan Cobb, 2nd, to be Overseers. Witns: Sam-

uel Pratt, Morgan Cobb, 2nd & Josiah Richmond [8:139/40].

Inv. of Est. of WILLIAM READ of Taun., dtd. 15 July 1734, pres. by Mary Read, widow & Exec. Apprs: Samuel Richmond, Joseph Tisdal & Joseph Richmond [8:140/1].

Acct. of Hugh Cole of Swan., surviving Exec. of Est. of JOHN ALLEN of Swan., dtd. 16 July 1734. Mentions Joseph Bucklen "the other Executor Who is Deceased." Legacies: "To my Self a Legacie to my wife," to Nehemiah Allen, to Baruch & Isaac Bucklen, to Benjah Barcas, to Ebenezer Allen, to Samuel Allen, to Daniel Allen, to Joseph Allen James Adams Jr. Thomas Peck & to Joseph Bucklen & his wife. Item to the accountant "for Boarding his Uncle John Allen one year" [8:141/2].

Order to Ephraim Martin of Reho., Exec. of Est. of his father EPHRAIM MARTIN of Reho., dtd. 16 July 1734 [8:142/3].

Will of EPHRAIM MARTIN of Reho., Yeoman, "being ill and Weak in body," dtd. 10 May 1734, prob. 16 July 1734. Wife Thankfull. Sons: Ephraim, Edward, Seth & Benjamin Martin. Daus: Thankfull Martin, Experiance Jenks, Judith Martin, Lidia Martin & Elezebeth Martin. Son Ephraim to be Exec. Witns: James Thurber, Ebenezer Bullock & Samuel Thurber [8:143/4/5].

Appt. of George Sisson of Swan., Yeoman, to be guard. as chosen by Benjamin Borden (minor over 14), son of JOHN BORDEN of Swan., dtd. 20 Aug. 1734 [8:145].

Order to John Stacey of Taun., Exec. of Est. of his father JOHN STACEY of Taun., dtd. 20 Aug. 1734 [8:145/6].

Will of JOHN STACEY of Taun., Husbandman, dtd. 20 March 1732/3, prob. 20 Aug. 1734. No wife mentioned. Sons: John (eldest) & James Stacey. Daus: Mehetibel, Mary, Abigail & Easther [no surnames]. Son John to be Exec. Witns: Morgan Cobb, 2nd, Morgan Cobb, 3rd & David Darbey [8:146/7].

Inv. of Est. of STEPHEN CHURCH of Swan., Indian Man, dtd. 22 Oct. 1733, pres. by Caleb Luther, Adm. Mentions value of "his wifes wearing Cloths." Apprs: John Cole, Benjamin Cole & Samuel Atherton [8:147].

Order to George & Thomas Manchester, Execs. of Est. of their father GEORGE MANCHESTER of Tiv., dtd. 20 Aug. 1734 [8:147/8].

Will of GEORGE MANCHESTER of Tiv., Yeoman, dtd. 27 Dec. 1729, prob. 20 Aug. 1734. No wife mentioned. Sons: George, Thomas & William Manchester. Daus: Margaret Brownel, Mary Manchester, Sarah Hix, Ann Manchester (unmar.) & Content Crandall. Sons George & Thomas to be Execs. Witns: Samuel Sandford, Rescome Sandford & Mathew Maccomber [8:148/9].

Order for div. of Est. of ABIGAIL SMITH of Reho., former wife of Daniel Smith, Esq., dcd., dtd. 26 Nov. 1733 [8:150].

Div. of Est. of ABIGAIL SMITH of Reho. btwn. her chldn: Daniel Smith (eldest son), Solomon Smith (2nd son), Nathaniel Smith (3rd son), John Smith (youngest son), Freelove (eldest dau.) wife of John Bucklen, Abigail (2nd dau.) wife of Jacob Perry, Esther (3rd dau.) & Elezebeth Smith (youngest dau.), dtd. 20

Aug. 1734. Lands in Reho. & Attl.   Comm: Daniel Carpenter,
Ezekiel Read & John Bisshop [8:150/1/2].

Appt. of John Austin of Nort., Yeoman, to be Adm. of Est. of
EDMUND FISHER of Nort. dcd. intest., Edmund's widow & Adm.
Elezebeth Fisher now being dcd., dtd. 20 Aug. 1734 [8:153].

Appt. of William Shearly of Boston, Co. of Suffolk, Esq., principal creditor, to be Adm. of Est. of THOMAS SMITH "Late of
London in Grait Brittain Poultier," dtd. 12 Sept. 1734 [8:
153/4].

Order to Alce Brown, widow & Exec. of Est. of TOBIAS BROWN of
Tiv., dtd. 12 Sept. 1734 [8:154].

Will of TOBIAS BROWN of Tiv., Yeoman, "being weak of body,"
dtd. 1 Apr. 1734, prob. 12 Sept. 1734. Wife Alce. Sons: John,
Abraham, William, Nicholas & Robart (last 2 under 21) Brown.
Daus: Sarah Shaw & Alce Brown (unmar.). Wife to be Exec. Mentions negro woman Mol & negro girl Pegge. Lands in Tiv. &
Lit. Comp. Witns: William Simmons, Jr., Thomas Gray & Phillip Taber [8:155/6/7].

Appt. of William Easterbrooks of Swan. to be guard. of John
Easterbrooks "a minor who is non Compus mentis," dtd. 9 Sept.
1734 [8:158].

Appt. of Capt. Ephraim Leonard of Nort. to be guard. as chosen
by Ephraim Andreas (minor over 14), son of EPHRAIM ANDREAS of
Swan., dtd. 10 Sept. 1734 [8:158/9].

Acct. of Mercy Vial, only surviving Exec. of Est. of JONATHAN
VIAL of Barr., dtd. 20 Aug. 1734 [8:159].

Rcpt. for legacies from Est. of ABIGAIL SMITH, widow of Daniel
Smith dcd. of Reho., signed by the heirs: Solomon Smith, Nathaniel Smith, John Bucklen & Freelove Bucklen, Jacob Perry &
Abigail Perry, Esther [illegible], Jath[illegible] & [illeg-
ible], as paid by Daniel Smith, Adm. & son of dcd. Abigail,
dtd. 20 March 1733/4 [8:159].

Inv. of Est. of EPHRAIM MARTIN of Reho., dtd. 15 Aug. 1734, pres.
by [blank] Martin, son & Exec. Apprs: Jonathan Kingsley,
James Bowen & Samuel Bullock [8:160].

Appt. of Robert Wheeten & Daniel Wheeten, Yeomen of Reho., to
be Adms. of Est. of their father EPHRAIM WHEETEN of Reho. dcd.
intest., dtd. 19 Nov. 1734 [8:161].

Inv. of Est. of Elder EPHRAIM WHEETEN of Reho., dtd. 24 May 1734
pres. by Robert & Daniel Wheeten, sons & Execs. Apprs: Jonathan Kingsley, Samuel Bullock & Jabiz Bosworth [8:161].

Inv. of "Remaining Part of the Estate" of SAMUEL SHEARMAN of
Dart., dtd. 8 May 1734, pres. by Hannah Shearman & Henery Gidley, Execs. Apprs: John Russel, Eliashib Smith & Jabiz Barker [8:162].

Acct. of Hannah Shearman, widow, & Henery Gidley, Execs. of Est.
of SAMUEL SHEARMAN of Dart., dtd. 15 Oct. 1734 [8:162/3].

Acct. of David Harvey of Taun., Adm. of Est. of his father WIL-
LIAM HARVEY of Taun., dtd. 19 Nov. 1734 [8:163/4].

Acct. of William Wilbour, Exec. of Est. of JOSEPH CRANDALL of
Lit. Comp., dtd. 19 Nov. 1734. Mentions sale of "The Sloope"
in Newport. Item abt. setting off the widow's thirds [8:164/5].
Appt. of Elizebeth Linzey of Brist., widow, to be Adm. of Est.
of her husb. JOHN LINZEY of Brist. dcd. intest., dtd. 20 Nov.
1734 [8:166].
Appt. of Rebecca Willis of Reho., widow, to be Adm. of Est. of
her husb. JOSEPH WILLIS of Reho. dcd. intest., dtd. 17 Dec.
1734 [8:166/7].
Order to Jonathan Sisson of Dart., Exec. of Est. of his father
JAMES SISSON of Dart., dtd. 17 Dec. 1734 [8:167].
Will of JAMES SISSON of Dart., Yeoman, dtd. 15 June 1734, prob.
17 Dec. 1734. No wife mentioned. Sons: Richard, James, Jonathan & Thomas Sisson. 5 daus: Sarah Davil, Rebecca West, Content (dcd.), Mary & Hannah [no surnames]. Grdau. Susanah Sisson. Chldn. [not named] of my dau. Content dcd. Son Jonathan
to be Exec. Witns: David Irish, William Davil, Jr. & Beriah
Goddard [8:168/9].
13 rcpts. for legacies from Est. of "my uncle" (in all cases)
FRANCIS STEVENS of Reho., paid by John Swetland of Attl., Exec., signed by: James Arnold & Elizebeth Arnold, Josiah Linkon, Jonah Linkon, Francis Fuller, Mary Fuller, Elezebeth Tingley, Ephraim Tingley, Timothey Tingley, Elezebeth Barrows, John
Linkon, Daniel Linkon, Stephen Remington & Lidia Remington, &
[name left off], dtd. variously btwn. 20 Jan. 1731/2 & 21 Apr.
1732 [8:169/70].
Appt. of Alce Brown of Tiv., widow, to be guard. as chosen by
Nicholas Brown (minor over 14), son of TOBIAS BROWN of Tiv.,
dtd. 30 Dec. 1734 [8:171].
Appt. of Susanah Dennis of Tiv., widow, to be Adm. of Est. of
her son THOMAS DENNIS of Tiv. dcd. intest., dtd. 30 Dec. 1734
[8:171/2].
Inv. of Est. of TOBIAS BROWN of Tiv., dtd. 23 Sept. 1734, pres.
by Alce Brown, widow & Exec. Apprs: Ebenezer Taber, Phillip
Gray & Thomas Manchester [8:172].
Acct. of Samuel Royal & Samuel Smith, Execs. of Est. of JOHN
BIRDGE of Brist., dtd. 26 Dec. 1734. Incl. legacies: to Elez-
ebeth Lewis "the bond her husband owed by will given her," to
Joseph Lewis "as attorney for four of his Childreen," to Jo-
seph Lewis "Guardian to Two of his Childreen," to Patiance
Cutbirth [sic], to Widow Ann Liscomb, to Nathaniel Blagrove
Esq., to Samuel Royal, to Samuel Smith, to Elezebeth Lewis &
Mary Dolliver as residuary legatees [8:173/4].
Rcpt. for legacies from Est. of JOHN BIRGE of Brist., paid by
Samuel Royal & Samuel Smith, Execs., said rcpt. signed by Jo-
seph Lewis of Haddam, Co. of Hartford, Ct., attorney for his
chldn. (who are grchldn. of the dcd. John Birge): Elezebeth
Shailer [sic] wife of Hezekiah Sharley [or Shailey] of Haddam;
Rebekah Lee wife of Joseph Lee of Gilford, Co. of New Haven,

Ct.; Sarah Beckwith wife of Thomas Beckwith of Lime, Co. of
New London, Ct. & Hannah Lewis of Haddam, dtd. 26 Oct. 1734
[8:174].

Rcpt. by Hannah Birge of Brist., widow, for legacy from Est. of
her father-in-law JOHN BIRGE of Brist., paid by Samuel Royal
& Samuel Smith, Execs., dtd. 26 Jan. 1733/4. Witns: William
Bragg & Alce Unis [8:174].

Rcpt. by Patiance Cuthbert of Brist., Spinster, for legacy from
Est. of her grfath. JOHN BIRGE of Brist., paid by Samuel Royal & Samuel Smith, dtd. 26 Jan. 1733/4. Witns: Isaac Ingraham & Elezebeth Ingraham [8:174].

Rcpts. by Joseph Lewis of Haddam, Co. of Hartford, Ct. as guard.
of his minor chldn. Deborah Lewis & John Lewis for legacies
from Est. of the chldn's. grfath. JOHN BIRGE of Brist., paid
by Samuel Royal & Samuel Smith, dtd. 26 Oct. 1734 [8:175].

Rcpt. by Joseph Lewis & wife Elezebeth of Haddam, Co. of Hart-
ford, Ct., & by John Doliver & wife Mary of Grenwich, Co. of
Kingston, R.I., for legacies from Est. of the wives' father,
JOHN BIRGE, of Brist., paid by Samuel Royal & Samuel Smith,
Execs., dtd. 11 May 1734. Witns: Stephen Paine & Joseph How-
land [8:175].

Appt. of Benjamin Hodges of Nort. to be guard. as chosen by Bartholomew Burt (minor over 14), son of EBENEZER BURT of Nort.,
dtd. 16 Jan. 1734 [8:175/6].

Order to Elezebeth Sampson, widow & Exec. of Est. of JOHN SAMP-
SON of Brist., dtd. 17 Jan. 1734. [8:176].

Will of JOHN SAMPSON of Brist., Mariner, "being very much indisposed by Sickness and Pain," dtd. 9 Dec. 1728, prob. 17 Jan.
1734. Wife Elezebeth. Son John Sampson (under 21). Dau. Mary
Sampson (under 21). Wife to be Exec. Witns: Timothey Ingraham, Samuel Howland & Hannah Linzey [8:177/8].

Order for div. of Est. of HANNAH HAIL of Swan., former widow
of John Hail of Swan., dtd. 26 March 1734 [8:178].

Div. of Est. of HANNAH HAIL of Swan. btwn. the chldn. of Hannah
& her husb. John Hail dcd.: John Hail dcd. (eldest son), Barnard Hail (surviving son), Freelove (dau.) wife of Oliver Kingsley, Lillis (dau.) wife of Nathan Mason & Hannah (dau.) wife
of Pelitiah Mason, dtd. 9 March 1734. Comm: James Bowen, Jonathan Kingsley, Esek Brown, Hezekiah Luther & Samuel Bullock
[8:178/9/80].

Inv. of Est. of JAMES SISSON of Dart., dtd. 2 Dec. 1734, pres.
by Jonathan Sisson, son & Exec. Apprs: George White, William
Devil, Jr. & Beriah Goddard [8:180/1].

Order for div. of Est. of JAMES HIX of Reho. dcd. intest., dtd.
March 1733/4 [8:181].

Div. of real est. of JAMES HIX of Reho. btwn. his widow Mary Hix
alias Mary Eddy & his chldn: Mary Hix (eldest dau.), Hezekiah
Hix (eldest son), Freelove (2nd dau.), James Hix (2nd son), &
Lois Hix (youngest dau.), dtd. 28 March 1734. Comm: James Bow-

en, Samuel Bullock, Nathaniel Peck, Jr. & Ebenezer Peck [8:
182].
Inv. of Est. of JOSEPH WILLIS of Reho., dtd. 19 Dec. 1734, pres.
by Rebecca Willis, widow & Adm. Apprs: Samuel Gofe, James
Redaway & John Wilmarth [8:183].
Appt. of Silvanus Soule of Tiv., Yeoman, to be guard. as chosen
by Joseph Thomas (minor over 14), son of EPHRAIM THOMAS of Tiv.
dtd. 28 Jan. 1734 [8:183/4].
Appt. of Joseph Mason of Swan., Yeoman, to be guard. as chosen
by Barnice Hail (minor over 14), dau. of RICHARD HAIL of Swan.
dtd. 10 Feb. 1734 [8:184].
Order to Susanah Cary & Allen Cary, Execs. of Est. of BENJAMIN
CARY of Brist., dtd. 10 Feb. 1734 [8:184/5].
Will of BENJAMIN CARY of Brist., Yeoman, "being very Sick & Weak
in body," dtd. 18 Jan. 1734/5, prob. 10 Feb. 1734/5. Wife Susanah. Sons: Allen (eldest), Benjamin, Nathaniel, John, Joseph
& Seth Cary (last 3 under 21). Daus: Susanah Cary (eldest),
Abigail, Mehetibel, Elezebeth, Lidia & Bethiah (last 5 under
18 & unmar.). Wife & sons to care & provide for John Penniman
during his life. Wife & son Allen to be Execs. Friend Thomas
Throope & bro-in-law Samuel Howland to be Overseers. Witns:
Thomas Bowen, John Dyer & Jonathan Peck [8:185/6/7].
Codicil to will of BENJAMIN CARY of Brist., directing some land
to be sold, dtd. 18 Jan. 1734/5. Same witns. as will [8:187/8].
Order to Ann Devil, widow & Exec. of Est. of her husb. BENJAMIN
DEVIL of Dart., dtd. 18 Feb. 1734 [8:188].
Order to Elihu Woodworth of Lit. Comp., Exec. of Est. of his
mother MARY WOODWORTH of Dart. [*sic; but next sentence calls
her "your mother Hannah Woodworth"*], dtd. 18 Feb. 1734 [8:
189/90].
Will of HANNAH WOODWORTH of Lit. Comp., Widow, dtd. 17 June 17-
34, prob. 18 Feb. 1734. Sons: Elisha & Elihu Woodworth. Daus:
Naomi wife of William Hall & Hannah Jackson. Grsons: Thomas,
William, Ebenezer & Nathaniel Church (all under 21). Grdaus:
Mary & Pricilla Church (both under 18). Son Elihu to be Exec.
Witns: Joseph Southworth, Robert Taylor & Constant Southworth
[8:190/1]
Inv. of Est. of HANNAH WOODWORTH of Lit. Comp., Widow, dtd. 7
Jan. 1734, pres. by Elihu Woodworth, son & Exec. Apprs: Jon-
athan Davenport, Robert Taylor & Joseph Davenport [8:191].
Accts. of John Phiney, guard. of CALEB CAMBIL, JEREMIAH CAMBIL,
MARY CAMBIL & RUTH CAMBIL, minor chldn. of SILVANUS CAMBIL of
Nort. dcd., dtd. 19 & 20 Feb. 1734. Incl. items for the 14th
part of the "Income of the Real Estate for the Space of Nine
Years." Also incl. item for keeping Ruth for abt. a year "in
victuals Drinking Washing & Lodging" [8:192/3/4].
Will of BENJAMIN DEVIL of Dart., Yeoman, "being Very Sick and
weak of body," dtd. 16 Dec. 1734, prob. 10 Feb. 1734. Wife
Ann. Sons: Peter & John (under 21) Devil. Daus: Sarah Mosher,

Elezebeth Devil, Rebeca Brownel, Freelove Devil, Anne Devil &
Mary Devil. Wife Ann to be Exec. Witns: Samuel Wilbour, Ru-
ben Devil & Restcome Sanford [8:194/5/6].
Inv. of Est. of BENJAMIN DEVIL of Dart., dtd. 10 Feb. 1734, pres.
by Ann Devil, widow & Adm. Apprs: George Lawton, Icabod Pot-
ter & Jeremiah Devil [8:196].
Appts. of Job Lewis, Esq., of Boston, Co. of Suffolk, to be
guard. of Miss Elezebeth Mackentosh & Miss Mary Mackentosh
(both under 14), grdaus. of Col. HENERY MACKENTOSH, Esq., of
Brist., dtd. 2 Apr. 1734 [8:197/8].
Appt. of Rebecca Brown of Reho., widow, to be guard. of Noah
Brown, Isaac Brown & Ann Brown (all under 14), chldn. of WIL-
LIAM BROWN of Reho., dtd. 18 March 1734 [8:198].
Appt. of John Kent of Reho. to be guard. as chosen by Jerusha
Brown & Bethiah Brown (minors over 14), daus. of WILLIAM BROWN
of Reho. [8:198/9].
Appt. of Thomas Carpenter of Reho., Yeoman, to be guard. of his
son Peter Carpenter (under 14), nephew of CORNELIUS CARPENTER
of Reho., dtd. 18 March 1734 [8:199].
Appt. of Abiah Carpenter of Reho., Yeoman, to be guard. of his
son Abiah Carpenter (under 14), nephew of CORNELIUS CARPEN-
TER of Reho., dtd. 18 March 1734 [8:200].
Appt. of Daniel Bisshop of Attl., Yeoman, to be guard of Ezra
Brown (under 14), son of WILLIAM BROWN of Reho., dtd. 18 March
1734 [8:200].
Appt. of Daniel Bisshop of Attl. to be guard. as chosen by his
wife Elezebeth Bisshop formerly Elezebeth Brown (minor over
14), dau. of WILLIAM BROWN of Reho., dtd. 18 March 1734 [8:
201].
Order to David Day, Exec. of Est. of his father NATHANIEL DAY
of Attl., dtd. 17 March 1734 [8:201/2].
Will of NATHANIEL DAY of Attl., Husbandman, dtd. 14 Apr. 1733,
prob. 17 March 1734. Wife Ruth. Sons: Benjamin, Nathaniel &
David Day. Daus: Ruth Ingraham, Mary Hoping, Meriam Day, Deborah Day & Dorcas Day. Son David to be Exec. Witns: John Alverson, John Peidge & George Allen [8:202/3].
Order to John Read & Ann Read, Execs. of Est. of their brother
JAMES READ of Taun., dtd. 18 March 1734 [8:203/4].
Will of JAMES READ of Middleborough, Co. of Plimouth, Yeoman,
"being Sick and Weak & in Low condition," dtd. 21 Jan. 1734,
prob. 18 March 1734. Prob. data calls him "Late of Taunton."
Brothers: John, William & Thomas Read. Sisters: Ann Read, Susanah Read & Martha Ingle. My father James Read dcd. The Rev.
Mr. Benjamin Rugles. Sister Ann & brother John to be Execs.
Witns: Peter Thacker, Edward Richmond, Jr. & Elkanah Leonard
[8:204/5].
Appt. of Martha Durphey of Brist., widow, to be Adm. of Est. of
her husb. THOMAS DURPHEY of Brist. dcd. intest., dtd. 12 Apr.
1735 [8:205/6].

Acct. of Rebecca Brown, widow & Adm. of Est. of WILLIAM BROWN
of Reho. dcd. intest., dtd. 18 March 1734. Incl. item for
"three Coffins" [8:206].

Acct. of Mehetibel Carpenter, Exec. of Est. of CORNELIUS CAR-
PENTER of Reho., dtd. 18 March 1734. Incl. paym. "to Sarah
Bowers Nursing my husband half a year in his Sickness" [8:
207].

Acct. of Elezebeth Wilbour, Exec. of Est. of BENJAMIN WILBOUR
of Dart., dtd. 19 March 1734. Incl. paym. of legacies: to Daniel Wilbour, to Abigail Wilbour now Abigail Lapham & to Barsheba Wilbour now Barsheba Richetson [8:208].

Appt. of Hannah Delano of Dart., widow, to be Adm. of Est. of
JABIZ DELANO of Dart. dcd. intest., dtd. 8 Apr. 1735[8:208/9].

Inv. of Est. of JABIZ DELANO of Dart., dtd. 14 Feb. 1734, pres.
by Hannah Delano, widow & Adm. Apprs: Stephen West, Jr., Lemuel Pope & Cornelius Jenne [8:209/10].

Order to Nathan Owen & Seth Owen of Taun., Execs. of Est. of
their father DANIEL OWEN of Taun., dtd. 11 Apr. 1735 [8:211].

Will of DANIEL OWEN of Taun., Husbandman, dtd. 13 Feb. 1732,
prob. 11 Apr. 1735. Wife Sarah. Sons: Daniel, William, Ephraim,
Joseph, Nathan & Seth. Daus: Elezebeth White & Mehetibel [no
surname]. Sons Nathan & Seth to be Execs. Witns: Joseph Eddy,
Elezebeth Woodward, Joseph Eddy, Jr. & Azariah Eddy [8:212].

Appt. of William Gallop of Brist., House Carpenter, to be guard.
of his dau. Elezebeth Gallop (under 14), grdau. of SARAH SMITH
of Brist., dtd. 15 Apr. 1735 [8:213].

Order to Timothey Jones & Hatherly Jones of Raynham, sons & Execs. of Est. of their father ABRAHAM JONES of Rayn., dtd. 15
Apr. 1735 [8:213/4].

Will of ABRAHAM JONES of Raynham, "being in competent health,"
dtd. 20 March 1732, prob. 15 Apr. 1735. Wife included but not
named. Sons: Timothey (of Rayn.), Isaac, Jacob, Israel & Hatherly Jones. Daus: Ruth Dean & Sarah Pratt dcd. The chldn. of
Sarah Pratt dcd. Grants household items to wife "that She
brough at marrage with me." Sons Timothey & Hatherly to be
Execs. Witns: John Wales, Zephiniah Leonard & Hannah Leonard
[8:214/5/6].

Codicil to will of ABRAHAM JONES of Rayn., dtd. 27 Nov. 1734,
same witns. as will [8:216].

Order to Joseph Kent & Hezekiah Kent, Execs. of Est. of their
father JOSEPH KENT of Reho., dtd. 15 Apr. 1735 [8:217].

Will of JOSEPH KENT of Reho., Yeoman, dtd. 12 March 1734/5, prob.
15 Apr. 1735. Wife Mary. Sons: Joseph, John, Hezekiah & James
Kent. Daus: Lydia Bosworth, Dorothey Newman, Susanah Bowen &
Mary Kent. Wife to rcv. 10 pounds "Due by Contract," as well
as other items. Sons Joseph & Hezekiah to be Execs. Witns:
Jonathan Chaffe, John Lindley & David Turner [8:217/8/9].

Order to John Seamans & his wife Pricilla, Execs. of Est. of
her father Dr. WILLIAM WOOD of Swan., dtd. 15 Apr. 1735 [8:
219].

Will of WILLIAM WOOD of Swan., "Docter of Phisick," "being Weak
& Low in body," dtd. 26 Dec. 1734, prob. 15 Apr. 1735. No wife
mentioned. Daus: Pricilla Seamans (eldest) wife of John Seamans of Swan. "that Dwelleth with me," Penelope Carr wife of
Caleb Carr of Warwick, R.I., Freelove wife of John Howland of
Swan. & Tabitha Seamans wife of James Seamans of Swan. Son-in-
law John Seamans & my dau. Pricilla to be Execs. Witns: James
Lewis, Daniel Martin, Elisha Bowen, Job Mason & Joseph Mason
[8:220/1].

Order to Joseph Allen, Exec. of Est. of his father JOSEPH ALLEN
of Dart., dtd. 18 March 1734 [8:221].

Will of JOSEPH ALLEN of Dart., Yeoman, dtd. 24 Dec. 1734, prob.
18 March 1734. Wife Gennet. Son Joseph Allen. Daus: Lidia
Allen, Phillis Gifford, Rachel Kirbey & Elezebeth Gifford. Son
Joseph to be Exec. Witns: Ebenezer Fish, George Cornell &
James Allen [8:222/3].

Inv. of Est. of JOSEPH KENT of Reho, dtd. 7 Apr. 1735, pres. by
Joseph & Hezekiah Kent, sons & Execs. Apprs: Edward Glover,
Jonathan Chaffe & Ezekiel Read [8:224].

Acct. of Bethiah Lane, widow & Adm. of Est. of SAMUEL LANE of
Attl., dtd. 15 Apr. 1735 [8:225].

Agrmt. abt. div. of real est. of SAMUEL LANE of Attl., btwn. his
widow Bethiah Lane of Attl. & his sons: John Lane & Ebenezer
Lane, dtd. 15 Apr. 1735. Witns: Stephen Paine & Zephiniah
Leonard [8:225/6/7].

Bond of Rebecca Slocum of Dart., widow of PELEG SLOCUM, Jr. as
guard. of their chldn: Peleg, Giles, Jonathan & Katherine Slocum, with Edward Winng of Sandwich, Co. of Barnstable, also
serving as guard. with her, dtd. 18 June 1733. Said Rebecca &
Wingg made bond to Holder Slocum, Exec. of Est. of his father
PELEG SLOCUM [Sr.], who is grfath. of said 4 chldn. "Said Rebecca Slocum now being in Election to be married." Witns: Edward Wanton & William Sanford [8:227/8/9].

Inv. of Est. of ABRAHAM JONES of Rayn., dtd. 2 Apr. 1735, pres.
by Timothey & Heatherley Jones, Execs. Apprs: Ebenezer Robinson, Josiah Dean & Samuel Leonard, Jr. [8:229/30].

Order of the Council held in the Council Chamber in Boston on
21 Nov. 1734, granting the appeal of Francis Borland & Jane
his wife & James Varney & Jane his wife, reversing Judge of Probate for Bristol Co., Nathaniel Blagrove, & directing him to
grant Adm. to the appellants in the Est. of JOHN FARWEL late
of London [8:231].

Appt. of Francis Borland & Jane his wife and James Varney & Jane
[sic] his wife, all of Boston, Co. of Suffolk, to be Adms. of
Est. of JOHN FARWEL late of London dcd. intest., dtd. 21 May
1735 [8:231/2].

Inv. of Est. of JOSEPH ALLEN of Dart., dtd. 11 Feb. 1734/5, pres.
by Joseph Allen, Exec. Apprs: John Allen, James Allen & Timothey Gifford [8:232/3].

Order to Samuel Toogood of Swan., Exec. of Est. of his mother
MARTHA CARPENTER of Swan., dtd. 21 Apr. 1735 [8:233][*dupli-
cate page numbering*].
Will of MARTHA CARPENTER of Swan., Widow of Benjamin Carpenter,
dtd. 2 Sept. 1734, prob. 21 Apr. 1735. Son Samuel Toogood.
Daus: Ann Finney, Rachel Goff, Dorothey Miller & Martha Goff.
John son of my dau. Ann Finney. Rachel & Martha daus. of my
dau. Dorothey Miller. Bethiah dau. of my dau. Martha Goff.
Son Samuel to be Exec. Witns: Samuel Maxwell, Hannah Maxwell
& John Cole [8:233/4].
Order to Samuel Howland of Brist., Exec. of Est. of MARY BOS-
WORTH of Brist., dtd. 23 Apr. 1735 [8:234/5].
Will of MARY BOSWORTH of Brist., Schoolmistress, "being Aged
and Infirm of body," dtd. 22 March 1734/5, prob. 23 Apr. 1735.
Kinswoman Mercy Heart wife of Richard Heart, kinswoman Susan-
ah Phillips wife of Joseph Phillips, kinswoman Mercy Twing
wife of John Twing, kinsman Edward Bosworth of Barr., kinsman
Joseph Phillips of Brist., kinsmen Nathaniel Jacobs & Nathan-
iel Phillips. Friend Samuel Howland to be Exec. Witns: Ben-
jamin Cary, William Linzey & Keziah Linzey [8:235/6].
Order to Timothey & Daniel Ide, Execs. of Est. of their father
TIMOTHEY IDE of Reho., dtd. 20 May 1735 [8:236/7].
Acct. of Mary Hix, widow & Exec. of Est. of SAMUEL HIX of Reho.,
dtd. 21 Apr. 1735 [8:237/8].
Acct. of Patiance West & Samuel Lee, Execs. of Est. of RICHARD
WEST of Free., dtd. 21 Apr. 1735 [8:238].
Will of TIMOTHEY IDE of Reho., Yeoman, dtd. 8 Apr. 1732, prob.
20 May 1735. Wife Elezebeth. Sons: Timothey (eldest), Josiah
(dcd.) & Daniel Ide. Daus: Elezebeth Read wife of Daniel Read,
Mary Read wife of Ezekiel Read, Sarah Carpenter wife of Ezek-
iel Carpenter, Rachel Perrin, Experiance Lindley wife of Tho-
mas Lindley who "Proves Such a bad husband." Mentions land
laid out to his father Nicholas Ide. Mentions son Timothey's
grfath. Thomas Cooper. Grchldn: Daniel, Josiah, Elezebeth &
Mary Ide chldn. of son Josiah dcd. Incl. land & rights in Reho,
Barr., Attl. & Wrentham. Sons Timothey & Daniel to be Execs.
Witns: John Robinson, Nathaniel Walker & Daniel Carpenter [8:
239/40/1].
Codicil to will of TIMOTHEY IDE of Reho., dtd. 8 Feb. 1734/5.
Permits dau. Experiance Lindley "Liberty to Come freely to a
Roome and fire in my Present Dwelling house as also to Set and
place a bed in said house...So Long as She Shall need them."
Witns: Josiah Cotton, Edward Glover & Timothey Mason [8:241/2].
Appt. of Martha Cooper of Reho., widow, to be Adm. of Est. of
her husb. NATHANIEL COOPER of Reho., Shopkeeper, dcd. intest.
dtd. 20 May 1735 [8:242].
Appt. of Margaret Dagget of Attl., widow, to be Adm. of Est. of
her husb. JOSEPH DAGGET of Attl. dcd. intest., dtd. 20 May
1735 [8:242/3].

Acct. of Samuel Lee, Adm. of Est. of JEREMIAH WILLIAMS of Swan.
"Mollato Man," dtd. 21 Apr. 1735 [8:243/4].
Inv. of Est. of MARY BOSWORTH of Brist., dtd. 24 Apr. 1735,pres.
by Samuel Howland, Exec. Apprs: Samuel Royal, Samuel Smith &
Paul Unis [8:244/5].
Acct. of Phebe Spooner, widow, & James Cushman, Execs. of Est.
of NATHANIEL SPOONER of Dart., dtd. 20 May 1735 [8:245].
Inv. of Est. of Capt. TIMOTHEY IDE of Reho., dtd. 24 Apr. 1735,
pres. by Timothey & Daniel Ide, sons & Execs. Apprs: Joseph
Wheeten, Daniel Carpenter & Edward Glover [8:245/6].
Order to Benjamin Earl, Exec. of Est. of his mother MARY EARL
of Tiv., dtd. 28 May 1735 [8:246/7].
Will of MARY EARL of Tiv., Widow, "being Sick and Weak in body,"
dtd. 26 Apr. 1735, prob. 28 May 1735. Daus: Mary Earl & Rebecca Earl. My father Daniel Wilcox dcd. Son Benjamin Earl
to be Exec. Cousin Phillip Taber to be Overseer. Witns: Rob-
ert Bennit, William Manchester & David Durphey. She mentions
"All my Childreen both maile and femaile" [8:247/8].
Appts. of Edward Luther of Barr., Yeoman, to be guard. as chosen
by Hannah Kent, Susanah Kent & Lidiah Kent (minors over 14),
daus. of JOSHUA KENT of Barr., dtd. 17 June 1735 [8:248/9/50].
Inv. of Est. of JAMES READ of Taun., dtd. 18 June 1735, pres. by
John Read & Ann Read, Execs. Apprs: Edward Richmond, Richard
Godfrey & James Williams [8:250/1].
Inv. of Est. of NATHANIEL COOPER of Reho., dtd. 18 Apr. 1735,
pres. by Martha Cooper, widow & Adm. Apprs: Edward Glover,
Timothey Ide & Ezekiel Read [8:251/2].
Inv. of Est. of JOSEPH DAGGET of Attl., dtd. 10 March 1734/5,
pres. by Margaret Dagget, widow & Adm. Apprs: John Foster,
Mayhew Dagget & Samuel Tiler [8:252/3].
Acct. of John Austin, Adm. de bonis non to Est. of EDMUND FISHER
of Nort., dtd. 17 June 1735. Mentions Elezebeth Fisher the
former Adm. who is since dcd. Incl. items: "Charges Expended
on the widdow in her Lying in with A Posthumus Child" & "Funeral Charge on the said widdow" [8:253].
Acct. of Joseph Allen, Exec. of Est. of his father JOSEPH ALLEN
of Dart., dtd. 17 June 1735. Incl. legacies: "to my Honoured
mother Jenney Allen," to Lidia Allen wife of Increase Allen,
to Phillis Gifford wife of Enos Gifford, to Rachel Kerbey wife
of Icabod Kerbey & to Elezebeth Gifford wife of Gideon Gifford
[8:254].
Inv. of Est. of MARY EARL of Tiv., Widow, dtd. 28 May 1735,pres.
by Benjamin Earl, son & Exec. Apprs: Thomas Manchester, Robert Bennit & William Manchester [8:255].
Agrmt. abt. widow's portion of Est. of JOSEPH ALLEN of Dart.
btwn. his son Joseph Allen (as Exec.) and his "mother in Law"
[*stepmother?*] Jannet Allen, widow of Joseph dcd., dtd. 1 Apr.
1735. Witns: Jabiz Barker & James Allen [8:256/7].
Rcpts. by Increase Allen & his wife Lidia, Enos Gifford & his

wife Phillis, Ichabod Kirbey & his wife Rachel & Gideon Gifford & his wife Elezebeth, all of Dart., for legacies from
Est. of JOSEPH ALLEN of Dart., father of Lidia, Phillis, Rachel & Elezebeth, paid by their brother Joseph Allen of Dart.
Exec., dtd. 1 Apr. 1735. Witns. for all: Jabiz Barker &
James Allen [8:257/8].
Appt. of Josiah Pratt of Nort., Yeoman, to be guard. of his
sons Josiah Pratt, Nehemiah Pratt & his dau. Naomi Pratt (all
under 14), grchldn. of ABRAHAM JONES of Rayn., dtd. 12 July
1735 [8:258/8½][*page numbering error*].
Order for div. of Est. of THOMAS READ of Reho., dtd. 12 March
1734 [8:258½].
Div. of Est. of THOMAS READ of Reho. btwn. his widow Martha &
his chldn: Thomas (eldest son), Noah (2nd son), Peter (youn-
est son), Martha Read (eldest dau.), Hannah Read (2nd dau.) &
Sarah Read (youngest dau.), dtd. 15 July 1735. Mentions land
in Reho. & Attl. Comm: Daniel Perrin, Edward Glover & Daniel
Carpenter [8:258½/9/60/1].
Order for div. of Est. of WILLIAM BROWN of Reho. dcd. intest.,
dtd. 14 Apr. 1735 [8:261].
Div. of Est. of WILLIAM BROWN of Reho. btwn. his unnamed widow
& his chldn. His eldest son [*not named*] was alive at time of
his father's death but is now himself dcd., so his two shares
were div. among surviving chldn: Amos (eldest surviving son),
Ezra (2nd surv. son), Noah (3rd surv. son), Elezebeth (eldest
dau.), Bethiah (2nd dau.), Jerusha (3rd dau.), Isaac (4th
surv. son), Ann (4th & youngest dau.), dtd. 15 July 1735.
Comm: Daniel Carpenter, Edward Glover & Daniel Perrin [8:261/
2/3].
Rcpt. by Ichabod Shaw & Sarah Shaw of Nort. for legacy from Est.
of her father PETER ALDRICH of Nort., as paid by her mother
Experiance Aldrich of Nort., widow & Adm., dtd. 12 March 17-
34/5. Witns: George Leonard & John Cobb [8:264].
Rcpt. by William Makepeice & Experiance Makepeice of Nort. for
legacy from Est. of her father PETER ALDRICH of Nort., paid
by her mother Experiance Aldrich, Adm. Mentions "our part of
the Land Lying in Conneticut," dtd. 18 June 1731. Witns: John
Briggs & Jonathan Blake [8:264].
Rcpt. by Peter Aldrich of Nort. for legacy from Est. of his fa-
ther PETER ALDRICH of Nort., paid by his mother Experiance Al-
drich, widow & Adm., dtd. 8 Apr. 1732. Witns: John Cobb &
Ichabod Shaw [8:264/5].
Appt. of Obediah Read of Reho. as Adm. of Est. of ANNA SMITH of
Reho. dcd. intest., dtd. 15 July 1735 [8:265].
Order to Hannah Walker, widow, & to John Walker, son, Execs. of
Est. of WILLIAM WALKER of Brist., dtd. 23 July 1735 [8:266].
Will of WILLIAM WALKER of Brist., Gentleman, "being Indisposed
as to my bodyly health," dtd. 4 June 1735, prob. 13 July 1735.
Wife Hannah. Son John Walker. Daus: Rachel, Elezebeth & Mary

[*no surnames*]. Mentions paym. to "my mother," but does not
name her. My negro men Peleg & Ceaser. Mentions his tanyard.
Wife & son to be Execs. Witns: Benjamin Cary, Nathaniel Cary
& Joseph Howland [8:266/7].

Inv. of Est. of ANNA SMITH of Reho., widow, dtd. 4 July 1735,
pres. by Obediah Read, Adm. Apprs: Daniel Carpenter, Edward
Glover & Ezekiel Read [8:268].

Order to Luke Hart, one of the Execs. of the Est. of WILLIAM
HART of Dart., the other Execs., Sarah Hart, widow, & William
Hart, son, refusing to serve, dtd. 19 Aug. 1735 [8:268/9].

Will of WILLIAM HART of Dart., "being Grown into years & being
under Decay of body," dtd. 1 Feb. 1733/4, prob. 19 Aug. 1735.
Wife Sarah. Sons: Luke, William & Archippus. Daus: Hannah Hart
& Mary Hart. Wife Sarah & sons Luke & William to be Execs.
Witns: Timothy Maxfield, Joseph Mosher & Phillip Mosher [8:
269/70].

Inv. of Est. of WILLIAM HART of Dart., House Carpenter, dtd. 30
July 1735, pres. by Luke Hart, son & Exec. Apprs: Jabiz Barker, Eliashib Smith & Timothey Maxfield [8:271/2].

Inv. of Est. of MARTHA CARPENTER, widow & relict of Benjamin
Carpenter late of Swan., dtd. 8 Apr. 1735, pres. by Samuel Toogood, her son & Exec. Apprs: Barnard Hail, Caleb Luther & Hezekiah Kingsley [8:272/3].

Acct. of Thomas Horton of Reho., Yeoman, guard. of Daniel Horton
a minor son of SOLOMON HORTON of Reho., dtd. 27 Aug. 1735.
Incl. payms. for: "Keeping said minor who was Lame and Troubled
with fitts Sixteen weeks"[8:272].

Order for div. of Est. of JOHN BOURDEN of Swan., dtd. 15 Aug.
1735 [8:274].

Div. of Est. of JOHN BOURDEN of Swan. btwn. his widow (now named
Sarah Earl wife of John Earl) & his chldn: John Bourden (eldest son), Joseph Bourden, Benjamin Bourden (youngest son),
Elizebeth Woodwel & an unnamed deceased dau., dtd. 16 Sept. 17-
35. Comm: Richard Harden, Robert Joles, Thomas Throope, Benjamin Bosworth & Jonathan Peck [8:274/5].

Acct. of Elezebeth Linzey, widow & Edm. of Est. of JOHN LINZEY
of Brist., dtd. 16 Sept. 1735 [8:276/7].

Acct. of George Beverley of Reho., Adm. of Est. of his brother
JOHN BEVERLEY of Reho., dtd. 1 Sept. 1735. Incl. paym. "To Ezekiel Carpenter for mourning the widdow" [8:277/8].

Acct. of Zerviah Spooner, widow & Exec. of Est. of BARNABAS
SPOONER of Dart., dtd. 12 Sept. 1735 [8:278/9].

Acct. of Patiance Simmons, widow & Adm. of Est. of JOHN SIMMONS,
Jr. of Digh., dtd. 16 Sept. 1735. Incl. payms. to: Hannah Simmons, Edward Simmons, John Simmons, Noble Simmons, Constant
Simmons & Remembrance Simmons. Item to the widow "for her Lying in With a Posthumus Child" [8:279/80].

Acct. of Benjamin Cole, Adm. of Est. of SAMUEL COLE of Swan., dtd.
16 Sept. 1735 [8:280/1].

Appt. of Abigail Church of Brist., widow, to be Adm. of Est. of
ISRAEL CHURCH of Brist., dtd. 16 Sept. 1735 [8:282].

Order to Mercy Williams, widow, & Isaac Williams, son, Execs.
of Est. of DANIEL WILLIAMS of Taun., dtd. 16 Oct. 1735 [8:
282/3].

Order to Sarah French, widow & Exec. of Est. of her husb. JOSEPH
FRENCH of Taun., dtd. 16 Oct. 1735 [8:283].

Will of DANIEL WILLIAMS of Taun., dtd. 22 Aug. 1735, prob. 16
Oct. 1735. Wife Mercy. Sons: Isaac & Daniel (under 21) Williams. Daus: Bethiah Hall, Phebe & Mercy (under 21) [no sur-
names]. Wife Mercy & son Isaac to be Execs. Witns: John Richmond, Elnathan Thresher & Seth Williams [8:284/5].

Will of JOSEPH FRENCH of Taun., dtd. 2 July 1725, prob. 16 Oct.
1735. Wife Sarah. Sons: John, Joseph (dcd.) & Seth French. 2
daus: Sarah French & Mary French. Wife to be Exec. Witns:
Seth Williams, Samuel Philips & Silas Terrey [8:285/6].

Order to Sarah Lake, widow & Exec. of Est. of her husb. JOEL
LAKE of Tiv., dtd. 16 Oct. 1735 [8:286].

Order to Rebecca Smith, widow & Exec. of Est. of her husb. HEN-
ERY SMITH of Reho., dtd. 21 Oct. 1735 [8:287].

Will of JOEL LAKE of Tiv., Mason, "being very weak in body,"
dtd. 18 Feb. 1729/30, prob. 21 Oct. 1735. Wife Sarah. Sons:
Edward, Joel, Caleb, Joseph, David, Jonathan, Giles & Jeremiah Lake (last 2 under 21). Daus: Hannah Lake & Sarah (under
18) Lake. Wife Sarah to be Exec. Witns: Hannah Baly, Restcome
Sanford & Benjamin Chace [8:287/8].

Inv. of Est. in Tiv. of EDWARD CHACE, Blomer [sic], dtd. 6 Oct.
1735, pres. by Walter Chace, his father & Adm. Incl. "one
halfe of an open sloope." Apprs: George Winslow, Samuel Tisdale & Ambrose Barnaby [8:288/9].

Acct. of Deborah Carr, widow & Adm. of Est. of ESEK CARR of Lit.
Comp., dtd. 21 Oct. 1735. Incl. paym. "to his father Esek Carr"
[8:289].

Will of HENERY SMITH of Reho., Yeoman, "being very Sick and weak
in body," dtd. 14 Oct. 1729, prob. 21 Oct. 1735. Wife Rebeca.
Sons: Henery (eldest), Samuel & John Smith (all under 21).
Daus: Rebeca (under 21), Elezebeth (under 18) & Judith (under
18) [no surnames]. My brother Thomas Smith. Mentions lands in
Reho. & in Barr. Wife Rebeca to be Exec. Witns: Isaac Bucklen
Daniel Carpenter & Abiel Smith [later this witness called "Abi-
gail Smith"][8:290/1/2].

Inv. of Est. of Deacon HENERY SMITH of Reho., dtd. 13 Oct. 1735,
pres. by Rebecca Smith, widow & Exec. Apprs: Daniel Carpenter
John Humphrey & Ezekiel Read [8:292].

Appt. of Jemima Glading, widow, to be Adm. of Est. of her husb.
NATHANIEL GLADING of Brist., dtd. 21 Oct. 1735 [8:292/2].

Order to Easther Gladding, widow & Exec. of Est. of her husb.
WILLIAM GLADING of Brist., dtd. 18 Nov. 1735 [8:293].

Order to George Pearce, Exec. of Est. of MARY BROWNEL of Lit.

Comp., dtd. 18 Nov. 1735 [8:294].

Will of WILLIAM GLADING of Brist., Joyner, "being Very Weak,"
dtd. 14 Oct. 1735, prob. 18 Oct. 1735. Wife Esther. Sons: William & Solomon (both under 21). Wife Esther to be guard. of
2 sons & to be Exec. My brother Jonathan Gladding. Witns:
Samuel Howland, Jonathan Glading, Edward Brownel & Charles
Glading [8:294/5].

Will of MARY BROWNEL of Lit. Comp., widow, dtd. 9 June 1735,
prob. 18 Nov. 1735. Sons: Thomas Brownel, George Brownel, Jeremiah Brownel, Charles Brownel & John Brownel. Grson. Samuel
Brownel son of son Charles Brownel. My brother George Pearce
to be Exec. My grdau. Mary Carr. Witns: John Dennis, Thomas
Brownel & Nathaniel Searl [8:296/7].

Inv. of Est. of MARY BROWNEL of Lit. Comp., widow, dtd. 11 Nov.
1735, pres. by George Pearce, Exec. Apprs: Jonathan Records,
Jonathan Wilbour & Nathaniel Searl [8:297].

Inv. of Est. of WILLIAM SOLE of Tiv., dtd. 29 Oct. 1734, pres.
by Rachel Sole, widow & Adm. Mentions land at Tiv. & Dart.
Apprs: Thomas Manchester, John Manchester & Philip Gray [8:
297/8].

Acct. of Rachel Sole, widow & Adm. of Est. of WILLIAM SOLE of
Tiv., dtd. 18 Nov. 1735 [8:298/9].

Inv. of Est. of Capt. WILLIAM WALKER of Brist., dtd. 18 July 17-
35, pres. by Hannah Walker & John Walker, Execs. Mentions negro men Cesar & Peleg. Apprs: Samuel Royal, Samuel Smith &
George Munroe [8:299/300/1].

Order to Elezebeth French, widow & Adm. of Est. of JOHN FRENCH
of Attl., he having deceased while the chosen Exec., John
French, was still minor, dtd. 16 Dec. 1735 [8:301].

Will of JOHN FRENCH of Attl., Inholder, dtd. 4 Dec. 1732, prob.
16 Dec. 1735. Chldn. of my 2nd wife Mary, viz: Lidia, Rachel
& Elezebeth [no surnames]. My son-in-law Edward White. My
dau-in-law [sic] Experiance White. My dau. Hannah French. My
son John French. To my wife Elezebeth. Son John to be Exec.
Witns: Thomas Wilmouth, Stephen Wilmouth & Noah Blanding [8:
302/3].

Rcpt. by Joseph Jacobs of Newp., R.I., Mariner, by letter of
attorney for legacy from Est. of THOMAS WALKER of Brist., Tanner, given to his grdau. "Jane Walker of Bridgetown in the Island of Barbados in America Spinster," paid by Elizebeth Walker of Brist., widow & Exec., dtd. [blank] Oct. 1735. Charles
Bolton of Barbados acted on behalf of said Jane. Witns: John
Cook & Samuel Howland [8:303].

Inv. of Est. of JOHN FRENCH of Attl., dtd. 3 Dec. 1735, pres. by
Elizebeth French, widow & Adm. Also has an inv. of "those
things which Elezebeth the Late Wife of the Said John French
Late deceased brought with her To his house which he gave her
in his Last will." Apprs: Daniel Perrin, Mahew Dagget & Daniel Carpenter [8:303/4/5].

Inv. of Est. of DANIEL OWEN of Taun., dtd. 2 June 1735, pres.

by Nathan Owen & Seth Owen, Execs. Apprs: Nathaniel Thayer, Joseph Eddy & Joseph Willis [8:305].

Acct. of Elezebeth Brown, widow & Adm. of Est. of JAMES BROWN of Barr., dtd. 16 Dec. 1735 [8:305/6].

Appt. of Benjamin Brown of Reho., Yeoman, to be guard. as chosen by Abijah Brown (minor over 14), dau. of JAMES BROWN of Barr., dtd. 16 Dec. 1735 [8:306/7].

Appt. of Elezebeth Brown of Barr., widow, to be guard. of Lidia Brown (under 14), dau. of JAMES BROWN of Barr., dtd. 16 Dec. 1735 [8:308].

Appt. of Esther Brown of Barr., widow, to be Adm. of Est. of ISAAC BROWN of Barr. dcd. intest., dtd. 16 Dec. 1735 [8:308/9].

Order to Ebenezer Brintnel, Exec. of Est. of his father SAMUEL BRINTNEL of Nort., dtd. 14 Jan. 1735 [8:309].

Will of SAMUEL BRINTNAL of Nort., "being now in the Seventieth year of my age and being at this time Weak of body," dtd. 19 Nov. 1735, prob. 14 Jan. 1735/6. Wife Elizabeth. Sons: Samuel, Ebenezer (2nd son) & Nathaniel (youngest son) Brintnal. Daus: Hannah Wetheril wife of John Wetheril, 2nd, of Taun., Abigail Dean wife of Ezra Dean of Taun. & Penelipy Brintnal (unmar.). Grdau. Easter Brintnal dau. of my son Ebenezer. To Sarah Green (under 18) dau. of the widow Hannah Green of Attl. Grants permis. to wife & dau. Penelipy to live in part of his dwelling house, with his wife to be maintained "according to the agreement which I made with her when I married her." Mentions his lands at Nort. & Stoughton (bought from Commiss. of Dorchester). Son Ebenezer to be Exec. Witns: Benjamin Ware, Andrew Grover, Ebenezer Skinner & George Leonard [8:309/10/1/2].

Inv. of Est. of SAMUEL BRINTNAL of Nort., Gentleman, dtd. 16 Dec. 735, pres. by Ebenezer Brintnal, Exec. Apprs: John Briggs, 2nd, William Stone & Benjamin Williams [8:312/3].

Appt. of Mary Craw of Tiv., widow, to be Adm. of Est. of her husb. RICHARD CRAW of Tiv. dcd. intest., dtd. 16 Jan. 1735/6 [8:313/4].

Inv. of Est. of ISRAEL CHURCH of Brist., dtd. 23 Sept. 1739, pres. by Abigail Church, widow & Adm. Apprs: Samuel Royal, Samuel Smith & William Peck [8:314/5].

Order to Elkanah Babbit & Josiah Babbit, Execs. of Est. of their father ELKANAH BABIT of Berk., dtd. 20 Jan. 1735/6 [8: 315/6].

Will of ELKANAH BABIT of Berk., dtd. 22 Dec. 1735, prob. 20 Jan. 1735/6. Wife Elezebeth. Sons: Elkanah, Josiah, Benjamin & Joseph (youngest) Babit. Daus: Damaris Hathway wife of Isaac Hathway, Dorcas Harvey wife of Ebenezer Harvey, Hopestill Phillips wife of James Phillips, Elezebeth Holloway wife of Malachy Holloway & Sarah Briggs wife of David Briggs, Jr. Gershom Crane & James Phillips to be Overseers to guide my son Joseph. Sons Elkanah & Josiah to be Execs. Witns: Abial Atwood, Israel Briggs & John Crane [8:316/7/8].

Inv. of ELKANAH BABIT of Berk., dtd. 16 Jan. 1735/6, pres. by
Elkanah & Josiah Babit, Execs. Apprs: Abel Burt, Abial Atwood & John Crane [8:318].

Inv. of Est. of NATHANIEL DAY of Attl., "Husbandman Who Deceased
february the fifth 1734/5," dtd. 5 May 1735, pres. by David
Day, son & Exec. Apprs: Samuel Titus, John Alverson & John
Foster, Jr. [8:319].

Acct. of Joseph Kent & Hezekiah Kent, Execs. of Est. of JOSEPH
KENT of Reho., dtd. 16 March 1735/6. Incl. legacies per will
to: Lidia Bosworth, Dorothey Newman, Susanah Bowen & Mary Kent
[8:319/20].

Rcpt. from Mary Kent of Reho., Spinster, for legacy from Est.
of her father JOSEPH KENT of Reho., paid by her bros. Joseph
& Hezekiah Kent, Execs., dtd. 12 March 1735/6. Witns: Samuel
Hills & John Lindley [8:320].

Rcpt. from Joseph Bosworth & his wife Lidia, Noah Newman & his
wife Dorothey and Peter Bowen & his wife Susanah Bowen, all
of Reho., for legacies from Est. of "our Honoured Father" JO-
SEPH KENT of Reho., paid by "Our Brother Joseph Kent," Exec.,
dtd. 19 June 1735. Witns: Samuel Howland, [blank] Thurston,
John Lindley & Edward Glover [8:320].

Rcpt. & quit-claim by Mary Kent of Reho., widow of JOSEPH KENT
of Reho. for monies rcvd. "in fulfillment of ye Promise by Contract by me made with my Said Late husband before marrage,"
paid by James Kent of Reho., dtd. 5 June 1735. Said Joseph's
will was dtd. 12 March 1734/5. She also rcvd. household stuff
& moveables "which I brought with me to the house of my Said
husband after our marrage." Witns: Daniel Carpenter & John
Lindley [8:321].

Appt. of Ephraim Carpenter of Reho., Yeoman, to be guard. as
chosen by Noah Titus (minor over 14), son of ROBERT TITUS of
Attl., dtd. 16 March 1735/6 [8:322].

Appt. of Daniel Perrin of Reho., Yeoman, to be guard. as chosen
by Robert Titus & Sarah Titus (minors over 14), chldn. of RO-
BERT TITUS of Attl., dtd. 16 March 1735/6 [8:322/3].

Appt. of John Stephens of Attl., Yeoman, & Sarah his wife, to
be guards. of Jonathan & Hannah Titus (both under 14), chldn.
of ROBERT TITUS of Attl., dtd. 16 March 1735/6 [8:323].

Appt. of Abigail Read of Reho., widow, to be Adm. of Est. of her
husb. GEORGE READ of Reho. dcd. intest., dtd. 16 March 1735/6
[8:323/4].

Discharge & quit-claim by Mary Slocum of Dart., widow of PELEG
SLOCUM of Dart. to "my well beloved son Isaac Barker of Pem-
brook in the County of Plimouth," dtd. 14 July 1734. Witns:
Silvester Barker & Elizabeth Barker, Jr. [8:324].

Inv. of Est. of GEORGE READ of Reho., dtd. 8 March 1735/6, pres.
by Abigail Read, widow & Adm. Apprs: Ezekiel Read, Edward Glover & Noah Mason [8:325].

Acct. by John Read, Exec. of Est. of his uncle ISRAEL READ of

Reho., dtd. 16 March 1735/6. Incl. items for care of Rebecca
Read, widow of Israel, "She being bed Red and unable to help
her Self" from 3 March to 13 March 1735/6 [8:325/6].

Acct. of John Baker, only surviving Exec. of Est. of his bro-
in-law GEORGE WOOD of Swan., the other Exec. William Wood be-
ing now dcd., dtd. 17 March 1735/6. Incl. legacies to: Rebecca
Wood widow of said George, and Thomas Wood son of said George.
Mentions John & Pricilla Seamans who are Execs. of Est. of said
William Wood dcd. [8:326/7].

Acct. of Caleb Luther, Adm. of Est. of STEPHEN CHURCH, "Indian
man Late of Swanzey," dtd. 16 March 1735/6. Incl. items: for
expenses of Sarah the wife of the dcd.; "to Nursing when She
was Sick" & "to a winding Sheet to bury her" [8:327/8].

Appt. of Joseph Richmond & William Maccomber, Yeomen of Taun.,
to be Adms. of "your Brother" WILLIAM RICHMOND of Taun. dcd.
intest., dtd. 16 March 1735/6 [8:328/9].

Inv. of Est. of NATHANIEL GLADING of Brist., dtd. 21 Oct. 1735,
pres. by Jemima Gladding, widow & Adm. Apprs: Samuel Royal,
Samuel Smith & Joseph Wardwel [8:329/30].

Acct. of Patiance Wingg, Adm. of Est. of EDWARD WINGG of Dart.,
dtd. 16 March 1735 [8:330/1].

Order for div. of Est. of JAMES BROWN of Barr. dcd. intest.,
dtd. 20 Dec. 1735 [8:331/2].

Div. of Est. of JAMES BROWN of Barr. btwn. his unnamed widow &
his chldn: James Brown (eldest son), Elezebeth Adams (eldest
dau.), Abijah Brown (2nd dau.), Lidia Brown (3rd dau.) & Michal Brown (youngest son), dtd. 15 Jan. 1735/6. Comm: Richard Harden, Robert Joles, Thomas Throope, Benjamin Bosworth
& Jonathan Peck [8:332/3/4].

Inv. of Est. of ISAAC BROWN of Barr., dtd. 8 March 1735/6, pres.
by Easther Brown, widow & Adm. Apprs: Benjamin Vial, Samuel
Mason & Joseph Allen [8:334/5].

Order to Sarah Hall, widow, & James Hall, son, Execs. of Est.
of JOHN [sic; but written above it in a later hand is "James"]
HALL of Rayn., dtd. 15 Apr. 1736 [8:335].

Will of JAMES HALL of Rayn., "being under bodily Indisposition,"
dtd. 3 Dec. 1735, prob. 15 Apr. 1736. Wife Sarah. Sons: James,
Nathan, Macy [sic], Edmund & David Hall. Daus: Mary Hall & Sarah Hall (both under 18). Mentions my wife's father Thomas Williams. Wife Sarah & son James to be Execs. Witns: Zephiniah
Leonard, John Hall & Philip King [8:336/7].

Inv. of Est. of WILLIAM RICHMOND of Taun., Husbandman, dtd. 26
Feb. 1735, pres. by Joseph Richmond & William Maccomber [8:
337/8].

Inv. of Est. of RICHARD CRAW of Tiv., dtd. 23 Jan. 1735/6, pres.
by Marcy Craw, widow & Adm. Apprs: Thomas Manchester, John
Borden & John Hoswel [8:338].

Order to Thankfull Axtil, widow, & Daniel Axtil, son, Execs. of
Est. of DANIEL AXTIL of Berk., srs. 20 Apr. 1736 [8:338/9].

Will of DANIEL AXTIL of Digh., Yeoman, "being under Grait bodily
  Indisposition," dtd. 4 Apr. 1735, prob. 20 Apr. 1736. Wife
  Thankfull. Sons: Daniel, William, Henry, Samuel, Ebenezer &
  Thomas Axtil (last 2 under 21). Daus: Elezebeth Burt wife of
  Thomas Burt, Rebeca Axtil, Hannah Axtil & Thankful Axtil (last
  3 under 21 & unmar.). Wife & son Daniel to be Execs. Witns:
  Abraham Hathway, Ephraim Allen & Nathaniel Fisher [8:339/40/1].
Inv. of Est. of DANIEL AXTEL of Berk., dtd. 9 Feb. 1735, pres.
  by Thankfull Axtil & Daniel Axtil, Execs. Apprs: Edward Shove,
  John Paul & John Crane [8:341/2].
Acct. of Philip Shearman, Exec. of Est. of JOHN SHEARMAN of Dart.
  dtd. 20 Apr. 1736. Incl. legacies per will to: Philip Shear-
  man, Sarah Shearman the widow, Isaac Shearman, Abigail Chace,
  Ephraim Shearman, Timothey Shearman, Hannah Akin, Jonathan
  Shearman, John Shearman & Phebe Shearman [8:342/3].
Order to Tabitha Bishop, widow & Exec. of Est. of WILLIAM BISHOP
  of Attl., dtd. 20 Apr. 1736 [8:343/4].
Will of WILLIAM BISHOP of Attl., Yeoman, "being very Sick and
  Weak," dtd. 11 Dec. 1735, prob. 20 Apr. 1736. Wife Tabatha.
  sons: John, Edward, William & Peleg Bishop. Daus: Elezebeth
  Bishop, Martha Philips, Rebecca Man & Dorothey Bishop. Grson.
  Robert Man. Wife to be Exec. Witns: Gideon Bishop, Benjamin
  Bishop & Noah Carpenter [8:344/5].
Inv. of Est. of WILLIAM BISHOP of Attl., dtd. 9 Jan. 1735, pres.
  by Tabitha Bishop, widow & Exec. Apprs: Samuel Day, Noah Car-
  penter & Ebenezer Carpenter [8:345/6].
Acct. of Tabitha Bishop of Attl, widow & Exec. of Est. of her
  husb. WILLIAM BISHOP of Attl., dtd. 20 Apr. 1736 [8:346/7].
Appt. of James Cushman of Dart., Yeoman, to be guard. of Rebecca
  Spooner & Alce Spooner (both under 14), daus. of NATHANIEL
  SPOONER of Dart., dtd. 18 May 1736 [8:347/8].
Appt. of Penelope Butterworth of Reho., widow, to be Adm. of Est.
  of NOAH BUTTERWORTH of Reho. dcd. intest., dtd. 18 May 1736
  [8:348].
Appt. of Margaret Pope, widow, to be Adm. of Est. of her husb.
  ELNATHAN POPE of Dart. dcd. intest., dtd. 18 May 1736[8:348/9].
Inv. of Est. of ELNATHAN POPE of Dart., dtd. 29 March 1736, pres.
  by Margaret Pope, widow & Adm. Apprs: Christopher Turner,
  Isaac Pope & Samuel Sponer [8:349/50].
Action by Madam Elizebeth Davis, directing Nathaniel Kay & Wil-
  liam Monroe, Gentlemen, out of "my Real and Personal Estate
  Entrusted in your hands," to buy a tract of land for her from
  Capt. George Wanton of Newport, dtd. 27 May 1736. Witns: Na-
  thaniel Hubbard, Esq. & Hannah Walker [8:351].
Accts. of Susanah Cary & Allen Cary, Execs. of Est. of Deacon
  BENJAMIN CARY of Brist., who was guard. of Hannah Kent, Susan-
  ah Kent & Lidia Kent, daus. of JOSHUA KENT of Barr., dtd. 18
  May 1736. Incl. paym. for comm. to div. an Est. btwn. Samuel
  Kent & the 3 chldn. [8:351/2/3].

Inv. of Est. of Lewt. NOAH BUTTERWORTH of Reho., dtd. 14 May
1736, pres. by Penelope Butterworth, widow & Adm. Apprs: Timothey Walker, Noah Mason & Luke Thurston [8:354].

Rcpts. from Mary Brownel of Lit. Comp. for her annual payms.
from Est. of her husb. THOMAS BROWNEL of Lit. Comp., dtd. 17-
32, 1734 & 1735, paid by her son Thomas Brownel, Exec. [8:
355].

Rcpt. by George Pearce of Lit. Comp. for legacy to Mary Brownel
from Est. of her husb. THOMAS BROWNEL of Lit. Comp., paid by
Thomas Brownel, Exec., said Pearce being Exec. for est. of
MARY BROWNEL who is now dcd., dtd. 3 May 1736 [8:355].

Inv. of Est. of Deacon BENJAMIN CARY of Brist., dtd. 19 Feb.
1734/5, pres. by Susanah Cary & Allen Cary, Execs. Apprs:
Robert Joles, Benjamin Bosworth & Jonathan Peck [8:355/6/7].

Rcpt. by Richard Church for legacy from Est. of his father JO-
SEPH CHURCH of Lit. Comp., paid by his bro. Nathaniel Church,
Exec., dtd. 10 Sept. 1735. Witns: Nathaniel Searl, Jr. & Al-
len Cary [8:358].

Rcpt. & discharge from Mary Slocum of Dart., widow, for legacy
from Est. of her husb. PELEG SLOCUM of Dart., paid by her son
Holder Slocum of Dart., Exec., dtd. 16 July 1735. Incl. a negro woman Hannah. Witns: John Barker & David Akin [8:358].

Rcpt. & discharge by John Brownel, George Brownel, Jeremiah
Brownel & Charles Brownel, all of Lit. Comp., for legacies
from Est. of their father THOMAS BROWNEL, paid by their bro.
Thomas Brownel, Exec., dtd. 13 Dec. 1735. Witns: Mary Carr &
Grace Church [8:359].

Rcpt. by Mary Carr of Lit. Comp., Spinster, for legacy from Est.
of her grfath. THOMAS BROWNEL of Lit. Comp., paid by her uncle
Thomas Brownel, Exec., dtd. 13 Dec. 1735. Witns: Jeremiah
Brownel & Charles Brownel [8:359].

Petition to the General Court at Boston by Charles Church of
Brist. for a div. of real est. of his father BENJAMIN CHURCH,
Esq., dtd. 19 Nov. 1735. Mentions his bro. Thomas Church. Mentions that his bro. Constant Church has died, leaving "Severall Childreen which are all minors" [8:360].

Order for div. of real est. of BENJAMIN CHURCH, Esq., dtd. 5 Apr.
1736 [8:361].

Div. of real est. of BENJAMIN CHURCH, Esq., btwn. his heirs: Thomas Church (son); Charles Church (son); Benjamin Church George
Wanton & his wife Abigail Wanton heirs of Edward Church dcd.
(son); Elizebeth Sampson (dau.) & heirs of Constant Church dcd.
(son), dtd. 18 May 1736. Comm: John Wilmouth, Daniel Carpenter, Jethniel Peck & James Redaway [8:361/2].

Acct. of George Pearce of Lit. Comp., Exec. of Est. of MARY
BROWNEL of Lit. Comp., not dated. Incl. legacies to: Thomas
Brownel, John Brownel, Jeremiah Brownel, Charles Brownel, Mary
Carr (grdau.) & George Brownel [8:363].

Acct. of John Church & Leah Blackman, Execs. of Est. of JONATHAN
BLACKMAN of Lit. Comp., dtd. 15 June 1736. Incl. negro James
Tobey. Incl. item "Paid the Widdow of the Deceased Toward the
Charge of her Lying in" [8:363/4].
Appt. of Rebeca Whitmarsh of Digh., widow, to be Adm. of Est.
of JONATHAN WHITMARSH of Digh. dcd. intest., dtd. 15 June 1736
[8:364/5].
Appts. of Bethiah Slack of Attl., widow, to be guard. as chosen
by her daus. Dorcas & Elezebeth Slack (minors over 14) & of
William & John Slack (both under 14), chldn. of JOHN SLACK of
Attl., dtd. 20 July 1736 [8:365/6].
Order to Samuel Peck of Reho., Exec. of Est. of his father SAM-
UEL PECK of Reho., dtd. 20 July 1736 [8:366/7].
Will of SAMUEL PECK of Reho., "being aged and weak of body," dtd.
1 May 1736, prob. 20 July 1736. Wife Rachel. Sons: Abiezer &
Samuel Peck. Daus: Rachel wife of Simon Dillis & Hannah (dcd.)
[no surname]. Chldn. of my dau. Hannah dcd: Elezebeth, Hannah,
Margaret & "to her son Comfort...lands...where his father Nich-
olas Peck now lives." Chldn. [unnamed] of my dau. Rachel. Son
Samuel to be Exec. Witns: John Jacob, Ebenezer Fuller & Ra-
chel Fuller [8:367/8].
Order to Marcy Linkon, widow & Exec. of Est. of her husb. JON-
AH LINKON of Taun., dtd. 16 July 1736 [8:368/9].
Will of JONAH LINKON of Taun., "having been under Longe Confine-
ment by Sickness," dtd. 4 June 1735, prob. 16 July 1736. Wife
Mercy. 6 daus: Elezebeth, Phebe, Jemima, Mercy, Darcas & Si-
lence (all under 18 & unmar.). Wife to be Exec. John Godfrey
of Taun. to aid my wife. Witns: Samuel Williams, Nathaniel
Crossman & Nehemiah Linkon [8:369/70].
Order by the Grait and General Court of the Province to div. real
est. in Counties of Bristol, Dukes, York & Middlesex of WIL-
LIAM SANDFORD of R.I., Gentleman, dtd. 19 Apr. 1735/6[8:370/1].
Div. of above real est. of WILLIAM SANDFORD of R.I., dcd. intest.
btwn: his 3 daus: Mary Oliver (eldest) wife of Andrew Oliver
of Boston, Merchant; Margaret Hutchenson wife of Thomas Hutchenson, Jr. of Boston, Merchant; & Grizel Sandford (youngest),
dtd. 23 June 1736. Comm: Col. Charles Church & Richard Harden, Esq. (Brist. Co.); John Allen, Esq. (Dukes Co.); Joseph
Hill, Esq. (York Co.) & Capt. Joseph Blanchard (Middlesex Co.)
[8:371/2/3/4].
Order to Thomas Richmond, Exec. of Est. of his father SAMUEL
RICHMOND of Taun., dtd. 20 July 1736 [8:375].
Will of SAMUEL RICHMOND of Taun., "Being under much Infirmity
of Body," dtd. 11 June 1736, prob. 20 July 1736. Wife Elezebeth. Sons: Samuel, Oliver, Thomas & Silas Richmond. Daus: Hannah Booth, Lidia Thomas & Mehetibel Horton. Legacy to wife
incls. "What moveables my Said Wife brought with her unto me."
Incl. lands in Taun. & Middleboro. Son Thomas to be Exec.
Witns: Henry Caswell, Nathaniel Caswel & John Godfrey[8:375/6].

Acct. of Benjamin Earl, Exec. of Est. of his mother MARY EARL
of Tiv., dtd. 20 July 1736. Incl. item for cost of "one Jor-
ney from Warwick to prove the Will" [8:376/7].
Acct. of Bethiah Slack of Attl., widow & Adm. of Est. of JOHN
SLACK of Attl., dtd. 20 July 1736 [8:377/8].
Order to Samuel Tiler, Yeoman, & Katherine Tiler, widow, Execs.
of Est. of EBENEZER TILER of Attl., dtd. 9 Aug. 1736 [8:378/9].
Will of EBENEZER TILER of Attl., Husbandman, "being very Sick,"
dtd. 29 May 1736, prob. 9 Aug. 1736. Wife Katherine. Chldn:
son Ebenezer, dau. Elizebeth wife of Ebenezer White, dau. Phebe,
son Job. dau. Katherine, son William, son John (under 21) &
dau. Hannah (under 18). Mentions lands in Ashford, Ct. & in
Attl. Brother Samuel Tiler & wife Katherine to be Execs. Witns:
Alexander Bragg, Joseph Welman & William Carpenter [8:379/80].
Inv. of Est. of JAMES HALL of Rayn., dtd. 25 May 1736, pres. by
Sarah Hall & James Hall, Execs. Apprs: Zephiniah Leonard, Sam-
uel Leonard, Jr. & Philip Kingg [8:381/2].
Appt. of Elezebeth Woodman of Lit. Comp., widow, to be Adm. of
Est. of her son ENOCH WOODMAN of Lit. Comp., dtd. 10 Aug. 1736
[8:382/3].
Inv. of Est. of ENOCH WOODMAN of Lit. Comp., son of John Wood-
man of Lit. Comp., dtd. 4 Aug. 1736, pres. by Elezebeth Wood-
man, his mother & Adm. Apprs: James Rouse, Robert Woodman &
John Hunt [8:383].
Appt. of Stephen Wilcox, Jr. of Dart. to be guard. of his father
Stephen Wilcox of Dart. "Who is non Compus mentis," dtd. 20
July 1736 [8:384].
Appt. of Freelove Chaffe of Reho. to be Adm. of Est. of AMOS
CHAFFEY of Reho. dcd. intest., dtd. 17 Aug. 1736 [8:384/5].
Appt. of Jonathan Chaffey of Reho., Yeoman, to be guard. of
Christopher Chaffey (under 14), son of NOAH CHAFFEY of Reho.,
dtd. 19 Aug. 1736 [8:385].
Appt. of Edward Glover of Reho., Yeoman, to be guard. of Shubal
Chaffey (under 14), son of NOAH CHAFFEY of Reho., dtd. 19 Aug.
1736 [8:385/6].
Appt. of Jonathan Chaffey of Reho., Yeoman, to be Adm. of Est.
of his brother NOAH CHAFFEE of Reho., since Noah's widow Hipzebeth Chaffey, having been appt. Adm., is now dcd., dtd. 19
Aug. 1736 [8:386/].
Petition to General Court at Boston signed by Mrs. Grizel Cotton,
widow of WILLIAM SANDFORD of R.I. & guard. of their dau. Grizel Sandford & Adm. of said William's Est.; Mary Oliver & her
husb. Andrew Oliver; & Margaret Hutchenson & her husb. Thomas
Hutchenson, Jr. (Mary & Margaret also daus. of William Sandford dcd.), dtd. 19 Apr. 1735. Petition requests 1/3 of the
rcpts. from the div. of said dcd's. lands in Counties of Bristol, Dukes, York & Middlesex btwn. the 3 daus. of the dcd. Comm.
was appt. [8:387].
Appt. of Ann Bowen of Reho., widow, to be guard. of Elijah Bowen,

Caleb Bowen & Amey Bowen, chldn. of EBENEZER BOWEN of Reho., dtd. 17 Aug. 1736 [8:387/8].

Appt. of Freelove Chaffey of Reho., widow, to be Adm. of Est. of AMOS CHAFFEY of Reho., dtd. 17 Aug. 1736 [same as entry on 8:384/5][8:388].

Appt. of Jonathan Chaffey to be guard. of Christopher [same as entry on 8:385][8:389].

Appt. of Deborah Nutting of Attl., widow, to be guard. of Jonathan Nutting (under 14), son of JONATHAN NUTTING of Attl., dtd. 26 Aug. 1736 [8:389/90].

Appt. of Israel Dagget of Reho., Yeoman, to be Adm. of Est. of his sister HIPZEBETH CHAFFEY of Reho. dcd. intest., the elder brother John Dagget refusing Adm., dtd. 26 Aug. 1736 [8:390].

Acct. of Deborah Nutting, widow & Adm. of Est. of JONATHAN NUTTING of Attl., dtd. 17 Aug. 1736 [8:381].

Acct. of Ann Bowen, widow & Adm. of Est. of EBENEZER BOWEN of Reho., dtd. 17 Aug. 1736 [8:391/2].

Inv. of Est. of JONATHAN WHITMARSH of Digh., dtd. 17 Aug. 1736. Apprs: Mathew Briggs, Josiah Talbut & Henry Pitts [8:392/3].

Acct. of Samuel Howland, Exec. of Est. of MARY BOSWORTH, School Dame, of Brist., dtd. 17 Aug. 1736. Incl. legacies per will to: Richard Heart & Mary his wife, Joseph Phillips & Susanah his wife, & John Twing in behalf of his wife [8:393/4].

Inv. of Est. of AMOS CHAFFEY of Reho., dtd. 16 Aug. 1736, pres. by Freelove Chaffey, his widow & Adm. Apprs: Joseph Bosworth, Samuel Mason & Edward Glover [8:394/5].

Order to Elnathan Pope of Dart., Exec. of Est. of his father ISAAC POPE of Dart., dtd. 21 Sept. 1736 [8:395].

Will of ISAAC POPE of Dart., Yeoman, "being Weak in Body," dtd. 19 Nov. 1734, prob. 21 Sept. 1736. Wife Alce. Sons: Thomas, Isaac & Elnathan Pope. Daus: Abigail Jenne, Margaret Pope & Deborah Spooner. Incl. land in North Yarmouth. Son Elnathan to be Exec. Witns: Jonathan Taber, Susanah Hathway & John Sogg [8:395/6/7].

Inv. of Est. of ISAAC POPE of Dart., dtd. 15 Sept. 1736, pres. by Elnathan Pope, son & Exec. Apprs: Stephen West, Jr., James Cushman & Jonathan Taber [8:397/8].

Appt. of Job Lewis of Boston, Co. of Suffolk, to be guard. as chosen by Miss Elizebeth Mackentosh (minor over 14), grdau. of HENRY MACKENTOSH of Brist., dtd. 5 Oct. 1736 [8:398/9].

Order to Peter Taylor of Lit. Comp., Yeoman, Exec. of Est. of his father PETER TAYLOR of Lit. Comp., dtd. 13 Oct. 1736 [8. 399].

Appt. of Ann Munroe of Swan., widow, to be Adm. of Est. of her son AMOS HAIL of Swan. dcd. intest., dtd. 21 Sept. 1736 [8: 400].

Appt. of Hannah Pool of Digh., widow, to be guard. of Benjamin Pool (under 14), son of BENJAMIN POOL of Digh., dtd. 21 Sept. 1736 [8:400/1].

Appt. of Joseph Stevens of Digh., Yeoman, to be guard. as chosen by his wife Sarah Stevens (minor over 14), dau. of BENJA-
MIN POOL of Digh., dtd. 21 Sept. 1736 [8:401].

Acct. of Hannah Dilano, widow & Adm. of Est. of JABIZ DILANO of
Dart., dtd. 11 Sept. 1736 [8:401/2/3].

Acct. of Patiance Hathway, late widow & Adm. of Est. of Capt.
CONSTANT CHURCH of Tiv., recorded 14 Oct. 1736. Incl. paym.
"To Marcy Church widdow and Administratrix of Capt. Charles
Church" [8:403].

Appt. of Hannah Pool of Digh., widow, to be guard. of Mary &
Hannah Pool (both under 14), daus. of BENJAMIN POOL of Digh.,
dtd. 21 Sept. 1736 [8:403/4].

Order for div. of Est. of JOSIAH TURNER of Reho., dtd. 23 Aug.
1736 [8:404].

Div. of real est. of JOSIAH TURNER of Reho. btwn. his widow Han-
nah Turner & his chldn: Josiah Turner (eldest son), Abiezer
Turner dcd. & Nathaniel Turner dcd. (youngest son), dtd. 8
Sept. 1736. Comm: Richard Harding, Thomas Throope, Benjamin
Bosworth, Richard Pearce & Jonathan Peck [8:404/5/6].

Appt. of Nathan Hodges of Nort., Yeoman, to be Adm. of Est. of
JOHN WILLIAMS of Taun. dcd. intest., as requested by mother &
brothers of dcd. John, dtd. 21 Sept. 1736 [8:406].

Appt. of Samuel Willis, Esq., of Dart. to be Adm. of Est. of his
bro-in-law SAMUEL HALL of Taun. dcd. intest., his widow having
renounced Adm. & the creditors requesting said Willis, dtd. 14
Oct. 1736 [8:406/7].

Will of PETER TAYLOR of Lit. Comp., Yeoman, dtd. 13 May 1730,
prob. 13 Oct. 1736. Wife Hannah. Sons: Peter & William (under
15) Taylor. Daus: Elizebeth wife of John Davenport, Mary, Mercy,
Hannah & Anne (last 4 under 18). Incl: "my five youngest Chil-
dreeen viz these which I had by my Present wife." Son Peter
to be Exec. Witns: Benjamin Southworth, George Thurston &
James Fisher [8:407/8/9].

Inv. of Est. of PETER TAYLOR of Lit. Comp., dtd. 6 Oct. 1736,
pres. by Peter Taylor, son & Exec. Apprs: John Wood, William
Richmond & William Wilbour [8:409/10].

Appt. of Hannah Britton of Digh., widow, to be Adm. of Est. of
her husb. JAMES BRITTON of Digh. dcd. intest., dtd. 19 Oct.
1736 [8:410/1].

Appt. of Abigail Bourden of Tiv., widow, to be Adm. of Est. of
her husb. JOSEPH BOURDEN of Tiv., Clothier, dcd. intest., dtd.
19 Oct. 1736 [8:411].

Inv. of Est. of JOSEPH BOURDEN of Tiv., dtd. 12 Oct. 1736, pres.
by Abigail Bourden, widow & Adm. Apprs: John Read, Samuel Forman & Richard Bowen [8:411/2].

Acct. of Mercy Carpenter, widow & Adm. of Est. of JEDEDIAH CAR-
PENTER of Reho., dtd. 20 Oct. 1736. Incl. item "Charges in My
Lying in" [8:413].

Appt. of Jonathan Woodbury, Esq., of Brist. to be Adm. of Est.

of Capt. SIMON DAVIS of Brist., since Bethia Davis, widow, &
Samuel Howland, Cooper, Execs., have renounced Exec., dtd. 20
Oct. 1736. The chldn. of said Simon requested said Woodbury
to be Adm. [8:413/4].
Will of SIMON DAVIS of Brist., Gentleman, "being Aged and In-
firm of Body," dtd. 4 July 1734, prob. 20 Oct. 1736. Wife
Bethiah. "My Childreen Nicholas & Simon Davis Sarah Norton Ann
Newton Elezebeth Bragg and Francis Throop." Gives to "wife
Bethiah all the Estate She Brought with her at the time of our
marrag." Also mentions his wife's son Nicholas Bragg. My gr-
son. George Bradley of Newport. Wife Bethiah & friend Samuel
Howland, Cooper, to be Execs. Witns: William Martin, Nathaniel Bosworth & William Hoar [8:414/5].
Order to John Soul, Exec. of Est. of his father NATHAN SOUL of
Dart., dtd. 20 Oct. 1736 [8:415/6].
Will of NATHAN SOUL of Dart., Yeoman, dtd. 20 Nov. 1735, prob.
19 Oct. 1736. Wife Mary. Sons: John (eldest), Cornelius & Timothey (youngest) Soule. Daus: Content Soule & Mary (under lawful age) Soul. Mentions "my Honoured father George Soul." Wife
to be guard. of dau. Mary. Son John to be Exec. Witns: Gabriel Hix, Stephen Wilbour & Icabod Brownel [Marginal notation
says there is an "Omission." Original will incl. son George.]
[8:416/7/8].
Inv. of Est. of NATHAN SOUL of Dart., dtd. 15 Oct. 1736, pres.
by John Soul, son & Exec. Apprs: Philip Taber, Nathaniel
Sole & Gabriel Hix [8:418/9/20].
Appt. of Dorothey Wiliston of Lit. Comp. to be Adm. of Est. of
her husb. ICABOD WILISTON of Lit. Comp. dcd. intest., dtd. 16
Nov. 1736 [8:421][same entry is repeated on 8:422].
Order to Joan Potter, widow, & William Potter, son, Execs. of
Est. of NATHANIEL POTTER of Dart., dtd. 16 Nov. 1736 [8:421/2].
Acct. of Mary Goodspeed formerly Mary Howland, widow, & Daniel
Howland, eldest son, Execs. of Est. of DANIEL HOWLAND of Tiv.,
dtd. 21 March 1714 [sic], recorded 17 Nov. 1736. Incl. payms.
by rcpt. to Thomas Corey, John Howland, Isaac Lawton & William
Wanton [8:422/3].
Will of NATHANIEL POTTER of Dart., Yeoman, dtd. 15 Nov. 1732,
prob. 16 Nov. 1736. Wife Joan. Son William Potter. Dau. Mary
Wood wife of Isaac Wood. Grsons. Nathaniel Potter & David Pot-
ter sons of son William. My negro Ceaser. Wife Joan & son Wil-
liam to be Execs. Witns: George Wood, Nathaniel Potter, Jr.
& Beriah Goddard [8:423/4/5].
Inv. of Est. of NATHANIEL POTTER of Dart., dtd. 1 Nov. 1736,
pres. by Joan Potter & William Potter, Execs. Apprs: Ichabod
Potter, Icabod Sole & Jonathan Wood [8:425].
Inv. of Est. of ICABOD WILLISTON of Lit. Comp., Gentleman, dtd.
16 Nov. 1736, pres. by Dorothey Williston, widow & Adm. Apprs:
John Palmer, David Hillard & Samuel Bullock [8:425/6].
Inv. of Est. of HIPZEBETH CHAFFEY of Reho., dtd. 30 Aug. 1736,
pres. by Israel Dagget, brother & Adm. Apprs: Edward Glover

Ezekiel Read & John Hunt [8:426/7].

Inv. of Est. of Capt. SIMON DAVIS of Brist., dtd. 28 Oct. 1736, pres. by Jonathan Woodbury, Adm. Apprs: Samuel Royal, Samuel Smith & Joseph Russell [8:427/8/9].

Appt. of Katherine Tiler of Attl. to be guard. of John Tiler, William Tiler, Job Tiler & Hannah Tiler (all under 14), chldn. of EBENEZER TILER of Attl., dtd. 21 Dec. 1736 [8:429/30].

Appt. of Samuel Tiler of Attle., Yeoman, to be guard. as chosen by Catherine Tiler (minor over 14), dau. of EBENEZER TILER of Attl., dtd. 21 Dec. 1736 [8:430].

Appts. of Hezekiah Peck of Attl., Yeoman, to be guard. as chosen by John Fuller & Phebe Fuller (minors over 14), chldn. of JOHN FULLER of Attl., dtd. 21 Dec. 1736 [8:430/1].

Rcpts. by chldn. of JOHN GARNZEY for legacies from his Est., as paid by Seth Garnzey, dtd. variously btwn. Apr. 1723 & May 1734. Rcpts. from chldn: Ebenezer Garnzey, (Jacob Ormsbe guard. of) Beriah Garnzey, Mary Hix wife of Samuel Hix, Mehetibel Horton wife of John Horton, Henry Garnzey, Mehetibel [*sic; but probably means "Waitstill"*] Titus wife of Timothey Titus, Hannah Horton wife of Thomas Horton, Joseph Garnzey, Elezebeth Bowen wife of James Bowen & Sarah Titus widow [8:432/3/4].

Rcpts. by Sarah Garnzey, widow of JOHN GARNZEY, for legacies from his Est., paid by Seth Garnzey, dtd. 4 Apr. 1726 & 28 June 17-27 [8:432/3].

Order to Elezebeth Crabtree of Attl., widow, Exec. of Est. of BENJAMIN CRABTREE of Attl., dtd. 21 Dec. 1736 [8:434].

Will of BENJAMIN CRABTREE of Attl., Yeoman, "Being Sick and Weak in body," dtd. 23 Nov. 1736, prob. 21 Dec. 1736. Wife Elezebeth. Son Benjamin Crabtree. Grsons: John Crabtree & Benjamin Crabtree. Wife to be Exec. Witns: Noah Carpenter, John Foster & Jonathan Foster [8:434/5/6].

Inv. of Est. of EBENEZER TILER of Attl., dtd. 23 Aug. 1736, pres. by Samuel Tiler & Katherine Tiler, Execs. Apprs: Henry Talman, Hezekiah Peck & Richard Atwel [8:436/7].

Acct. of Katherine Tiler & Samuel Tiler, Execs. of Est. of EBENEZER TILER of Attl., dtd. 21 Dec. 1736 [8:437].

Inv. of Est. of JONATHAN PHINNEY of Swan., dtd. 16 Dec. 1736, pres. by Mercy Phinney, widow & Adm. Apprs: Robert Joles, Thomas Throope & Jonathan Peck [8:438].

Appt. of Daniel Shaperdson of Attl., Yeoman, to be guard. as chosen by Mary Coy (minor over 14), dau. of CALEB COY of Beverly, Co. of Essex, dtd. 13 Jan. 1736 [8:439].

Acct. of Hezekiah Luther of Swan., Exec. of Est. of his father HEZEKIAH LUTHER of Swan., dtd. 18 Jan. 1736. Incl. item: "For Keeping my Brother Joseph Luther Who was a Dum man from the Time of my fathers Decease to ye Time of my Brothers Decease being Twelve Years Seven months and Two weeks" [8:439/40].

Appt. of Mary Darbey wife of Samuel Darbey of Taun., and only sister of JOHN BRIANT of Berk., to be Adm. of John's Est., his widow Abigail Briant refusing Adm., dtd. 18 Jan. 1736 [8:440/1].

Agrmt. abt. settl. of Est. of SIMON DAVIS of Brist. btwn. his
widow Bethiah Davis & his chldn: Nicholas Davis of Boston,
Co. of Suffolk, Merchant; Simon Davis of Brist., Mariner; Shu-
bael Norton of Brist., Mariner, & his wife Sarah; Jonathan
Woodbury, Esq., of Brist.; Henry Bragg of Brist., Merchant,
& wife Elezebeth; & Francis Throope of Woodstock widow of the
Rev. Amos Throope, dtd. 22 Sept. 1736. Incl. item abt. "what
was mine at Time of marrage." Witns: Isaac Martindal & Samuel Howland [8:441/2].
Order to Thomas Davis of Free., Yeoman, Exec. of Est. of his fa-
ther WILLIAM DAVIS of Free., Yeoman, dtd. 15 Feb. 1736 [8:442
/3].
Will of WILLIAM DAVIS of Free., Husbandman, "being Very Sick and
Weak," dtd. 6 Aug. 1732, prob. 15 Feb. 1736. Wife Mary. Sons:
William (eldest), Thomas (2nd), John (3rd), Jonathan, Remembrance & Joseph Davis. Daus: Rebecca Pain, Elezebeth Cole, Abigail Hathway, [blank] Evins, Hannah Gaige & Ruth Davis. Son
Thomas to be Exec. Witns: Thomas Terry, George Winslow & John
Terry [8:443/4].
Order to Charles Carpenter of Reho., Yeoman, Exec. of Est. of
his father SAMUEL CARPENTER of Reho., dtd. 15 Feb. 1736 [8:
444/5].
Rcpts. & discharges to George Pearce, Adm. for their legacies
from Est. of their mother MARY BROWNEL of Lit. Comp. by: Thom-
as Brownel, John Brownel, George Brownel, Jeremiah Brownel,
Charles Brownel & Mary Carr (grdau.), dtd. 31 Dec. 1735 & 21
May 1736 [8:445].
Will of SAMUEL CARPENTER of Reho., Husbandman, dtd. 16 Dec. 17-
36, prob. 15 Feb. 1736. No wife mentioned. Sons: Samuel, Tim-
othey, Andrew, Edmund, Jedediah (dcd.), Nathan, Uriah & Charles.
Daus: Patiance Peck & Freelove Chaffey. Grchldn: Anne, Rebecah,
Caleb & Patiance chldn. of my son Jedediah Carpenter dcd. Son
Charles to be Exec. Witns: John Bowen, Ebenezer Titus & Ed-
ward Glover [8:446/7/8].
Inv. of Est. of SAMUEL CARPENTER of Reho., dtd. 9 Feb. 1736, pres.
by Charles Carpenter, Exec. Apprs: Noah Mason, Timothey Ide &
Edward Glover [8:448/9].
Rcpts. by Benjamin Crabtree of Attl. for legacies from Est. of
his father BENJAMIN CRABTREE of Attl., paid by his mother Elez-
ebeth Crabtree, widow & Exec., dtd. 30 Dec. 1736 [8:449].
Inv. of Est. of Dr. WILLIAM WOOD of Swan., dtd. 18 March 1734/5,
pres. by John Seamans & his wife Pricilla Seamans, Execs.
Apprs: Job Mason, James Lewis & Daniel Martin [8:449/50].
Inv. of Est. of Capt. SAMUEL PECK of Reho., dtd. 15 Feb. 1736/7,
pres. by Samuel Peck, son & Exec. Apprs: Thomas Allen, John
Jacobs & Ebenezer Fuller [8:450/1].
Acct. of Benjamin Cole, Adm. of Est. of SAMUEL COLE of Swan.,
dtd. 21 Feb. 1736/7 [8:451].
Appt. of Thomas Bowen, Esq., of Reho. to be Adm. of Est. of his
father RICHARD BOWEN of Reho. dcd. intest., the widow Marcy

Bowen refusing Adm., dtd. 10 March 1736 [8:452/3].

Rcpts. by Patiance Grinhill & Elezebeth Grinhill for legacies from Est. of RICHARD GRINHILL of Lit. Comp., paid by their mother Patiance Grinhill, Exec., dtd. 18 July 1733 [8:453].

Appt. of Patiance Grenhill of Lit. Comp., widow, to be guard. as chosen by her son Daniel Greenhill (minor over 14), son of RICHARD GREENHILL of Lit. Comp., dtd. 9 March 1736[8:453/4].

Order to [blank], Exec. of Est. of his father DANIEL JENCKS of Attl., dtd. 15 March 1736 [8:454].

Will of DANIEL JENCKS OF Attl., Yeoman, dtd. 5 May 1729, prob. 15 March 1736/7. Wife Catherine. Son Daniel Jencks. Daus: Mary Wetherhead, Elezebeth Hopkins, Martha Aldrich, Susanah Hopkins, Hannah Rutenburge & Ruth Whipple. Son Daniel to be Exec. Witns: John Lovet, Israel Whipple, Daniel Peck & Noah Carpenter [8:454/5].

Inv. of Est. of DANIEL JENCKS of Attl., Yeoman, dtd. 2 March 17-36/7, pres. by Daniel Jencks, son & Exec. Apprs: Noah Carpenter, Benjamin Williams & David Whiple [8:456].

Inv. of Est. of BENJAMIN CRABTREE of Attl., Yeoman, dtd. 27 Dec. 1736, pres. by Elizebeth Crabtree, widow & Exec. Apprs: Noah Carpenter, Beriah Baccus & Benjamin Day [8:456/7].

Appts. of William Hall of Lit. Comp., Gentleman, to be guard. as chosen by William Woodman & Edith Woodman (minors over 14), chldn. of JOHN WOODMAN of Lit. Comp., dtd. 23 March 1736 [8:457/8].

Appt. of Stephen Wilcox of Dart., Taylor, to be Adm. of Est. of his father STEPHEN WILCOX dcd. of Dart., the widow Judith Wilcox refusing, dtd. 6 Apr. 1737 [8:459].

Appt. of Edward Cornel of Dart., Cordwainer, to be guard. of John Wilcox (under 14), son of STEPHEN WILCOX of Dart., dtd. 6 Apr. 1737 [8:460].

Inv. of Est. of STEPHEN WILCOX of Dart., dtd. 11 Dec. 1736, pres. by Steven Wilcox, son & Adm. Only real est., "the Intested Leaving no Estate at the Time of his Death." Apprs: Philip Taber, Benjamin Tripp & James Tripp [8:460].

Acct. of Stephen Wilcox of Dart., guard. to his father STEPHEN WILCOX "Who was non Compus mentis," now dcd., dtd. 6 Apr. 17-37 [8:460/1].

Inv. of Est. of JOHN COBB of Nort., presently insolvent, dtd. 28 March 1737, pres. by George Leonard, Esq., Adm. Apprs: John Briggs, 2nd & John Andrews [8:461/2].

Appt. of Samuel Little of Brist., Gentleman, to be Adm. of Est. of his mother SARAH LITTLE of Brist., widow, dcd. intest., dtd. 19 Apr. 1737 [8:462/3].

Order to Sarah Church of Lit. Comp., Spinster, Exec. of Est. of her mother GRACE CHURCH of Lit. Comp., dtd. 19 Apr. 1737 [8:463/4].

Will of GRACE CHURCH of Lit. Comp., widow of Joseph Church, dtd. 19 May 1732, prob. 19 Apr. 1737. Sons: Nathaniel, Caleb, Richard,

Israel Church. Daus: Sarah Church, Deborah Briggs & Elezebeth
Palmer. Grson. Joseph Church & grdau. Grace Church. Dau. Sarah
to be Exec. Witns: Thomas Church, Samuel Howland & Sarah
Church [8:464/5].

Inv. of Est. of GRACE CHURCH of Lit. Comp., pres. 19 Apr. 1737
by Sarah Church, dau. & Exec. Apprs: John Wood, William Hall
& William Richmond [6:465/6].

Inv. of Est. of WILLIAM DAVIS of Free., Yeoman, dtd. 3 Feb. 17-
36/7, pres. by Thomas Davis, son & Exec. Apprs: Isaac Hathway,
Jonathan Winslow & John Terry [8:467].

Inv. of Est. of THOMAS DURPHEY of Brist., dtd. 30 May 1735, pres.
by Martha Durphey, widow & Adm. Apprs: Samuel Royal, Samuel
Smith & Paul Unis [8:467/8/9].

Acct. of Mary Mitchel late Mary Paul of Digh., widow & Adm. of
Est. of WILLIAM PAUL of Digh., dtd. 19 Apr. 1737 [8:469/70].

Appt. of William Gallop of Brist., Joyner, to be guard. of his
dau. Mary Gallop (under 14), niece of ELEZEBETH DAVIS of Brist.
dtd. 17 May 1737 [8:471].

Rcpt. & disch. by SOLOMON HEWET of East. (now 21) for goods &
money formerly held by his guard. Capt. Edward Hayward of East.
dtd. 5 June 1736. Witns: Ephraim Lane & Rachel Leonard [8:
471].

Appt. of Josiah Kent of Barr., Yeoman, to be Adm. of Est. of his
father SAMUEL KENT of Barr. dcd. intest., the widow having refused Adm., dtd. 17 May 1737 [8:471/2].

Appt. of Thomas Manchester of Tiv., Yeoman, to be guard. as chosen by Ann Craw (minor over 14), dau. of RICHARD CRAW of Tiv.,
dtd. 17 May 1737 [8:472/3].

Appt. of Pricilla Bowen of Swan., widow, to be Adm. of Est. of
DANIEL BOWEN of Swan. dcd. intest., dtd. 17 May 1737 [8:473/4].

Inv. of Est. of DANIEL BOWEN of Swan., pres. 17 May 1737 by Pricilla Bowen, widow & Adm. No Apprs. shown [8:474].

Appt. of Alce Unis of Brist., widow, to be Adm. of Est. of PAUL
UNIS of Brist., Mariner, dcd. intest., dtd. 19 May 1737 [8:
475].

Inv. of Est. of JAMES BRITTAIN of Digh., dtd. 26 Oct. 1736, pres.
by Hannah Brittain, widow & Adm. Incl. land in Digh. & Rayn.
Apprs: Mathew Briggs, Thomas Read & Ephraim Hathway [8:475/6].

Acct. of Edward Howard, guard. of RUTH HEWETT dcd., minor dau.
of EPHRAIM HEWIT dcd. of East. [8:476].

Inv. of Est. of Dr. SAMUEL HALL of Taun., dtd. 10 June 1737, pres.
by Samuel Willis, Adm. Incl. land in Rayn. Apprs: John Godfrey, Timothey Jones & Jonathan Shaw [8:477].

Inv. of Est. of Dr. RICHARD BOWEN of Reho., dtd. 6 Apr. 1737,
pres. by Thomas Bowen, Esq., son & Adm. Incl. land & rights
in Reho., Attl. & Barr. Apprs: Joseph Wheaten, Daniel Carpenter & Edward Glover [8:477/8].

Appt. of William Woodcock of W[alpole? - unclear], Co. of Suffolk
to be Adm. of Est. of JONATHAN WOODCOCK of Attl., Yeoman, dcd.

intest., the widow refusing Adm., dtd. 20 June 1737 [8:478/9].
Order to Lidia & Susanah "wifes of Simieon Witheril and Joseph
   Godfrey of Norton," daus. & Execs. of Est. of their father WIL-
   LIAM MACKPEICE of Taun., dtd. 21 June 1737 [8:479].
Will of WILLIAM MACKPEICE of Taun., "under grait Indisposition
   of Body," dtd. 16 Nov. 1736, prob. 21 June 1737. No wife men-
   tioned. Sons: Seth, William & Thomas Mackpeice. Daus: Abigail
   (dcd.), Annah, Mary, Susanah, Lidia, Deborah, Remember & Pri-
   cilla [no surnames]. 6 chldn. [not named] of my dau. Abigail
   dcd. Daus. Lidia & Susanah to be Execs. Witns: Seth Williams,
   Mercy Mason & Stephen Maccomber [8:480/1].
Inv. of Est. of WILLIAM MACKPEICE of Taun., dtd. 5 Jan. 1736,
   pres. by Lidia Witheril & Susanah Godfrey, daus. & Execs.
   Apprs: Samuel Pitts, John Briggs & John Godfrey [8:481].
Order to Marcy Mason, widow, & Jonathan Shaw, Yeoman, both of
   Taun., Execs. of Est. of JOHN MASON of Taun., dtd. 21 June
   1737 [8:481/2].
Will of JOHN MASON of Taun., dtd. 24 Feb. 1735, prob. 21 June
   1737. Wife Mercy. Daus: Mary Cobb wife of Benjamin Cobb of
   Nort., Rebecah Sumner wife of Samuel Sumner of Taun. & Mercy
   Shaw wife of Jonathan Shaw of Rayn. Grsons. John Cobb & Jona-
   than Shaw. Wife Mercy & son-in-law Jonathan Shaw to be Execs.
   Witns: Samuel Williams, Ezra Dean & Thomas Clapp [8:482/3].
Appt. of Joshua Atherton & Uriah Atherton, Yeomen of Nort., to
   be Adms.of Est. of their father JOSHUA ATHERTON of Nort., Yeo-
   man, dcd. intest., dtd. 21 June 1737 [8:483/4].
Inv. of Est. of JOSHUA ATHERTON of Nort., dtd. 17 Apr. 1737,
   pres. by Joshua & Uriah Atherton, sons & Adms. Apprs: Samuel
   Caswel, Benjamin Cobb & William Dean [8:484/5].
Inv. of Est. in Taun. & Nort. of HANNAH HOSKINS of Taun. dcd.
   intest., dtd. Nov., Dec. & Jan. 1726 [sic], pres. 21 June 17-
   37 by Jacob Hall, Adm. Apprs: Seth Williams, Richard Godfrey
   & John Godfrey [8:485/6].
Inv. of Est. of PAUL UNIS of Brist., dtd. 27 May 1737, pres. by
   Alce Unis, widow & Adm. Apprs: Samuel Royal, Samuel Smith &
   Joshua Bailey [8:486/7/8].
Inv. of Est. of SAMUEL RICHMOND of Taun., pres. 21 June 1737 by
   Thomas Richmond, son & Exec. Apprs: John Mason, Joseph Rich-
   mond & John Godfrey [8:488/9].
Appt. of Hannah Sweaten of Attl., widow, to be Adm. of Est. of
   her husb. HENRY SWEATEN, Mariner, of Attl. dcd. intest., dtd.
   19 July 1737 [8:489].
Appt. of Dan Carpenter of Attl., Clothier, to be Adm. of Est.
   of his cousin EBENEZER CARPENTER of Attl. dcd. intest., "Seth
   Carpenter his Brother and his Uncles Refusing to Administer,"
   dtd. 19 July 1737 [8:489/90].
Appts. of David Whitmarsh of Digh., Yeoman, to be guard. as chosen by William Paul (minor over 14) & of John Paul & Hannah
   Paul (both under 14), chldn. of WILLIAM PAUL of Digh., dtd.

19 July 1737 [8:490/1].
Appt. of Abigail Dean of Taun., widow, to be Adm. of Est. of her
husb. EZRA DEAN of Taun., "Practioner of Phisick," dcd. intest.
dtd. 19 July 1737 [8:491/2].
Inv. of Est. of EZRA DEAN of Taun., dtd. 13, 14 & 16 July 1737,
pres. by Abigail Dean, widow & Adm. Incl. a negro woman Dinah.
Apprs: Benjamin Wilbour, Jonathan Williams & Abiel Dean [8:
492/3].
Order to Elizabeth Brown of Reho., widow, & Stephen Arnold of
Providence, R.I., Shipwright, Execs. of Est. of NATHAN BROWN
of Reho., dtd. 19 July 1737 [8:493/4].
Will of NATHAN BROWN of Reho., Shipwright, "being Sick and Weak
of body," dtd. 14 Sept. 1736, prob. 19 July 1737. Wife Elize-
beth. Bro-in-law Stephen Arnold of Prov., Shipwright. Sister
Lidia Chapman of Seabrook. Cousin Allen Brown. Cousin Peleg
Brown of Barr. Wife & bro-in-law Stephen Arnold to be Execs.
Witns: Stephen Walker, Rebecah Paine & Thomas Bowen[8:494/5].
Order to George Westgeat, Yeoman, & Mary Earl, Spinster, both
of Tiv., Execs. of Est. of REBECCA EARL of Tiv., Spinster, dtd.
19 July 1737 [8:495].
Will of REBECAH EARL of Tiv., dau. of John Earl & Mary Earl dcd.,
"being very Sick and Weak of Body," dtd. 27 Apr. 1737, prob.
19 July 1737. Sisters Mary Earl & Elezebeth Westgeat. Bro-in-
law George Westgeat & sister Mary to be Execs. Witns: Robert
Bennet, David Durfee & Samuel Durfee [8:496].
Inv. of Est. of REBECAH EARL of Tiv., dtd. 18 July 1737, pres.
by George Westgate & Mary Earl, Execs. Apprs: Robert Bennit,
Thomas Manchester & Samuel Durfey [8:497].
Inv. of Est. of HENRY SWEATEN of Attl., Mariner, dtd. 18 May
1737, pres. by Hannah Sweaten, widow & Adm. Apprs: Noah Carpenter, Benaiah Baccas & Benjamin Day [8:497/8].
Appt. of Stephen Smith of digh., Yeoman, to be guard. as chosen
by Mary Paul (minor over 14) & of Susanah Paul (under 14),
daus. of WILLIAM PAUL of Digh., dtd. 19 July 1737 [8:498/9/
500].
Appt. of John Paul of Berk., Yeoman, to be guard. of James Paul
(under 14), son of WILLIAM PAUL of Digh., dtd. 19 July 1737
[8:499].
Order to Robert Joles of Brist. & Joseph Mason of Swan., Yeomen,
Execs. of Est. of JOHN WHEATEN of Swan., dtd. 1 Aug. 1737 [8:
500].
Will of JOHN WHEATEN of Swan., Blacksmith, "being Grown into
old age," dtd. 25 May 1736, prob. 1 Aug. 1737. Wife Elezebeth.
Sons: Joseph Wheaton of Reho., James Wheaten (dcd.), Samuel
Wheaten (dcd.), John Wheaten (dcd.) & Isaac Wheaten. Daus:
Mary Ingraham, Charity Bourn, Pricilla Hix & Patiance Hix.
Grson. William Hix. Grdau. Elezebeth Chace dau. of my son John
dcd. Friends Robert Joles & Joseph Mason to be Execs. Incl.
lands in Swan & Barr. Witns: John Throope, Ebenezer Luther &

John Butterworth [8:500/1/2].

Order to Preserved Fish of Portsmouth, R.I., Yeoman, John Howland, James Howland & James Tripp, Yeomen of Dart., Execs. of Est. of JOHN COOK of Tiv., dtd. 1 Aug. 1737 [8:502].

Will of JOHN COOK of Tiv., Yeoman, dtd. 23 Jan. 1736/7, prob. 1 Aug. 1737. Wife Ruth. Sons: John & Thomas Cook. Daus: Ruth Fish, Mary Howland, Deborah Howland & Ann Tripp. Sons-in-law Preserved Fish, John Howland, James Howland & James Tripp to be Execs. Incl. negro woman Phillis. Witns: Peleg Shearman, Richard Sisson & Giles Slocum [8:503/4].

Inv. of Est. of JOHN COOK of Tiv., dtd. 25 July 1737, pres. by Preserved Fish, John Howland, James Howland & John Tripp, Execs. Apprs: Thomas Manchester, John Sisson & Samuel Crandal [8:504].

Inv. of Est. of NATHAN BROWN of Reho., dtd. 1 Aug. 1737, pres. by Elizebeth Brown & Stephen Arnold, Execs. Apprs: Edward Glover, Timothey Ide & Noah Mason [8:505].

Inv. of Est. of SARAH LITTLE of Brist., dtd. 22 Aug. 1737, pres. by Samuel Little, son & Adm. Part of the Inv. was "Taken att Mr Edward Littles." Apprs: Samuel Royal, Samuel Smith & Cornelius Waldroon [8:505/6].

Acct. of Judath Streter & John Streter, Adms. of Est. of JOHN STRETER of Attl., dtd. 16 Aug. 1737 [8:507].

Order to Pricilla Chace of Swan., widow & Exec. of Est. of her husb. WILLIAM CHACE of Swan., dtd. 16 Aug. 1737 [8:507/8].

Will of WILLIAM CHACE of Swan., Yeoman, dtd. 25 Jan. 1733, prob. 16 Aug. 1737. Wife Pricilla. Sons: William, Eber, Hezekiah & Joseph Chace. Grdau. Hannah Brayton dau. of my son Eber Chace. After Joseph's name it says "(his Son Abraham)." Witns: Preserved Brayton, John Brayton & William Hart [8:508].

Will of ABRAHAM TISDAL of Taun., Yeoman, "being Sick and Weak of Body," dtd. 30 June 1737, prob. 20 Sept. 1737. No wife or children mentioned. Mother Abigail Tisdal. Brothers Israel, Ephraim & John Tisdal. My 3 sisters [not named]. To Mr. Thomas Clapp Minister of our town. Bros. Israel & Ephraim to be Execs. Witns: James Cooper, Micah Pratt & Abel Burt [8:509/10].

Inv. of Est. of ABRAHAM TISDAL of Taun., Yeoman, dtd. 16 Aug. 1737, pres. by Israel & Ephraim Tisdal, Execs. Apprs: Samuel Pitts, Abel Burt & Samuel White [8:510/1].

Order to Israel Tisdal & Ephraim Tisdal, Yeomen of Taun., Execs. of Est. of their brother ABRAHAM TISDAL of Taun., dtd. 20 Sept. 1737 [8:511].

Order to Jonathan Kingsley of Reho., Yeoman, Exec. of Est. of EASTHER FOX of Swan., widow, dtd. 20 Sept. 1737 [8:511/2].

Will of EASTHER FOX of Swan., widow, "being very aged," dtd. 12 Jan. 1733/4, prob. 20 Sept. 1737. Sons: Benjamin Andreas (dcd.) John Andreas, Ephraim Andreas (dcd.). Daus: Easther Russel (dcd.), Joannah Hillard (dcd.), Hannah Goler of Long Island &

Lidiah Clerk of Stoning Town. Mentions,without naming, chldn.
of son Ephraim by his 1st wife & chldn. by his 2nd wife. Dau.
Joannah Hillard's chldn. mentioned but not named. Ann Russell
dau. of my dau. Easther Russel dcd. Jonathan Kingsley of Reho.
to be Exec. Witns: Joseph Mason, Jonathan Kingsley & Rebec-
cah Wood [8:512/3].
Inv. of Est. of EASTHER FOX of Swan., dtd. 27 Sept. 1737, pres.
by Jonathan Kingsley, Exec. Apprs: Peres Bradford, Richard
Harding & Barnard Haile [8:513/4].
Acct. of Samuel Willis, Esq., Adm. of Est. of SAMUEL HALL of
Taun. dcd. intest., dtd. 28 Oct. 1737. Incl. item for the wi-
dow for keeping the family [8:514/5].
Acct. of Hannah Hunt, widow & Adm. of Est. of the Rev. Mr. SAM-
UEL HUNT of Dart., dtd. 26 Oct. 1737. Incl. paym. "To John
Hunt of Boston" [8:515/6].
Acct. of Penelope Butterworth, widow & Adm. of Est. of NOAH BUT-
TERWORTH of Reho., dtd. 26 Oct. 1737 [8:516/7].
Acct. of Elinor Stoddar late Elinor Briggs, widow & Exec. of Est.
of JOB BRIGGS of Lit. Comp., dtd. Oct. 1737. Incl. legacies to:
Mary Bourden wife of Thomas Bourden, Sarah Durphey wife of Tho-
mas Durphey, Elezebeth Malem, Almey Briggs, Wait Briggs (her
mother Elinor Stoddard being her guard.) [8:517/8].
Inv. of st. of SAMUEL KENT of Barr., dtd. 21 May 1737, pres. by
Josiah Kent, son & Adm. Incl. a negro man Peter. Lands in Swan.
& Barr. No Apprs. listed [8:518/9/20].
Acct. of George Leonard, Adm. of Est. of JOHN COBB of Nort. dcd.
intest., dtd. 2 Nov. 1737. Incl. pay. for provisions for the
widow & chldn. [8:520/1].
Acct. of Joan Potter, widow, & William Potter, son, Execs. of
Est. of NATHANIEL POTTER of Dart., dtd. 21 Oct. 1737 [8:521].
Order to Gemima Gladding of Brist., widow, Exec. of Est. of her
mother RUTH CARY of Brist., dtd. 20 Sept. 1737 [8:522].
Will of RUTH CARY of Brist., widow, "being Sick in Body," dtd.
24 June 1737, prob. 19 Sept. 1737. Son Nathaniel Cary. Dau.
Jemima Glading widow of Nathaniel Glading of Brist. Dau. Jemima to be Exec. Witns: Elisha May, Hannah Royal & Joseph Howland [8:522/3].
Appt. of Francis Ball, Corker, & Joshua Bailey, Cooper, to be
Adms. of Est. of JONATHAN BALL of Brist., Mariner, dcd. intest.
"one of the [sons?] of said Francis Ball," dtd. 20 Sept. 1737
[8:523].
Appt. of Benjamin Buffington, Jr. of Swan., Yeoman, to be guard.
as chosen by Moses Chace (minor over 14), son of JOSEPH CHACE
of Swan., dtd. 26 Sept. 1737 [8:524].
Appt. of Hannah Hunt of Dart., widow, to be guard. as chosen by
her daus. Rebeccah & Sarah Hunt (minors over 14), daus. of SAM-
UEL HUNT of Dart., dtd. 27 Sept. 1737 [8:524/5].
Appt. of Israel Dagget of Reho., Yeoman, to be guard. as chosen
by Simeon Dagget (minor over 14), son of JOSEPH DAGGET of Attl.

dtd. 15 Nov. 1737 [8:525].

Acct. of Martha Shearman, widow & Exec. of Est. of SAMUEL SHEAR-
MAN of Swan., Eber Chase one of the Execs. having refused,
dtd. 15 Nov. 1737. Incl. item for repairing "the house in the
woods for her Self and family to Dwell in by Reason She Lett
out the Homestead farm for Rent money to Save the Farm for
her Son." Legacies to: herself & Abigail wife of Joseph Buffington [8:525/6/7].

Order to Daniel Shreiff of Lit. Comp., Shipwright, Exec. of Est.
of his father DANIEL SHREIFF of Lit. Comp., dtd. 20 Dec. 1737
[8:527/8].

Will of DANIEL SHRIEFF of Lit. Comp., Husbandman, "being Aged
and Weak of Body," dtd. 8 June 1737, prob. 20 Dec. 1737. Wife
Jane. Sons: Thomas, William & Caleb Shrieff. Daus: Martha Lin-
iken & Elezebeth Dyer. Grson. Benjamin Shrieff. Son Daniel to
be Exec. Witns: Joseph Head, Edward Manchester & Jonathan
Head [8:528/9].

Inv. of Est. of DANIEL SHRIEFF of Lit. Comp., dtd. 23 Nov. 1737,
pres. by Daniel Shrieff, son & Exec. Apprs: Edward Manchester
John Sandford & Jonathan Head [8:529].

Acct. of Seth Wetheril of Wrentham, Co. of Suffolk, Adm. of Est.
of his brother GEORGE WETHERIL of Nort., insolvent, dtd. 20
Dec. 1737. Incl. paym. to "Benjamin Newland for horse Roome
and tendance when Said George Wetheril was Sick att his house"
[8:529/30].

Acct. of Ebenezer Brintnel, Exec. of Est. of SAMUEL BRINTNAL of
Nort., dtd. 20 Dec. 1737. Incl. legacies: to Hannah Wetheril,
to Easther Brintnal, to Sarah Green, to Abigail Dean, to Samuel Brintnal & to Penelope Brintnal [8:530/1].

Inv. of Est. of JOHN WHEATEN of Swan., dtd. 1 Sept. 1737, pres.
by Robert Joles & Joseph Mason, Execs. Apprs: Barnard Hail,
Ebenezer Luther & John Child [8:531/30A][*page numbering error*].

Order to Sarah Paddock of Swan., widow & Exec. of Est. of her
husb. JAMES PADDOCK of Swan., dtd. 20 Dec. 1737 [8:530A/31A].

Will of JAMES PADDOCK of Swan., Yeoman, "being weak of body," dtd.
16 Aug. 1736, prob. 20 Dec. 1737. Wife Sarah. Dau. Mary Paddock (under age & unmar.). Witns: Joseph Butterworth, Benjamin Butterworth & John Kinnicut [8:531A/32].

Order to Henry West of Reho., Yeoman, Exec. of Est. of JOHN WEST
of Reho., dtd. 26 Dec. 1737 [8:532].

Will of JOHN WEST of Reho., Cordwainer, "being Sick and Weak of
Body," dtd. 7 Apr. 1737. prob. 26 Sept. 1737. Wife Mehetibel.
Sons: John, William & Henry West. Daus: Mehetibel Garnzey
(dcd.; eldest), Elezebeth Wheeler & Ann Nash. Grdaus: Meheti-
bel Garnzey & Elinor ("who Now lives with me") Garnzey (both
under 18) daus. of my dau. Mehetibel Garnzey dcd. Grdaus: Pa-
tiance, Rosamond, Jemimah & Ann Garnzey, other daus. of my dau.
Mehetibel dcd. Son Henry to be Exec. Friends James Bowen &
Samuel Bullock to be Overseers & Trustees for my wife. Witns:
Peres Bradford, John Millard & Ephraim Martin [8:532/3].

VOLUME 9

1737-1740

Appt. of John Robbins of Attl., Yeoman, to be guard. as chosen
by Abigail, Sarah & Rachel Streeter (minors over 14), chldn.
of JOHN STREETER of Attl., dtd. 16 Aug. 1737 [9:½].
Appt. of Benjamin Wise of Attl., Yeoman, to be guard. of Isaac,
Hannah & Amey Streeter of Attl. (all under 14), chldn. of
JOHN STREETER of Attl., dtd. 16 Aug. 1737 [9:½+][page number-
ing error].
Inv. of Est. of JOHN WEST OF Reho., Cordwainer, dtd. 3 Oct. 1737
pres. by Henery West, son & Exec. Apprs: Peres Bradford, John
Millard & Ephraim Martin [9:1].
Appt. of Katherine Hodges of Taun., widow, to be Adm. of Est. of
THOMAS HODGES of Taun., dtd. 20 Dec. 1737 [9:2].
Inv. of Est. of JOSEPH HOWLAND of Brist., dtd. 22 Sept. 1737,
pres. by Samuel Howland, brother & Adm. Apprs: Samuel Royal,
Samuel Smith & Cornelius Waldroon [9:3].
Appt. of Sarah Norton of Brist. to be Adm. of Est. of her husb.
SHUBAL NORTON of Brist., Mariner, dtd. 13 Dec. 1737 [9:3/4].
Appt. of Patiance Eddy of Swan., widow, as Adm. of Est. of her
husb. SETH EDDY of Swan., Shipwright, dcd. intest., dtd. 13
Jan. 1737 [94/5].
Appts. of David Whiple of Attl., Yeoman, to be guard. of Eleze-
beth Carpenter (minor over 14) & Keziah Carpenter, daus. of
EBENEZER CARPENTER of Attl., dtd. 17 Jan. 1737 [9:5/6].
Appt. of James Lewis of Reho, Weaver, to be guard. of James
Millard, son of JOHN MILLARD of Reho., dtd. 17 Jan. 1737/8
[9:7].
Appt. of James Cole of Swan., Clothier, to be guard. of Joseph
Cole, son of JOSEPH COLE of Swan., dtd. 17 Jan. 1737/8 [9:7/8].
Acct. of Mary Cole, widow & Adm. of Est. of JOSEPH COLE of Swan.,
dtd. 17 Jan. 1737/8. Incl. payms. for "his funerall Charges and
his Childs" & "Grave Stones for him and his Child." Item by the
widow "for her Charge of Lying in with A Posthumus Child" [9:
8/9].
Acct. of Martha Durphey, widow & Adm. of Est. of THOMAS DURPHEY
of Brist., dtd. 21 Sept. 1737. Incl. allowance "for one Note
that was appraised in the Inventory from John Hubbards Pas-
sage from the Westindies in the Sloop Said Durphey was master
of which was given by Capt. Almey" [9:10/1].
Acct. of Marcy Craw, widow & Adm. of Est. of RICHARD CRAW of
Tiv., dtd. 20 Sept. 1737 [9:11].
Petition by Hannah Wilson of Reho., late of Newport, to "The
House of Representatives" [General Court] abt. selling real
est. and making div. of Est. of JONATHAN WILSON of Newport,
R.I., dtd. 26 Sept. 1730 [9:12].

265

Acct. of Hannah Little late Hannah Wilson, widow & Exec. of Est.
of her husb. JONATHAN WILSON of Newport, R.I., dtd. 24 Sept.
1737. Incl. payms. to heirs: Jonathan Wilson (only son), Sarah
Wilson (dau.), the widow "now wife of Capt Samuel Little" &
"The Deceaseds Childreen in Law" [9:12/3].
Appt. of James Lewis of Reho., Weaver, to be guard. of James
Millard, son of JOHN MILLARD of Reho., dtd. 17 Jan. 1737/8
[9:13/4].
Acct. of Mary Cole, Adm. of Est. of JOSEPH COLE of Swan., dtd.
17 Jan. 1737/8 [*same as acct. previously given, on 9:8/9,
above*][9:14/5].
Rcpt. by Anna Tillinghast, formerly wife of Josiah Brown for
legacy from Est. of her father THOMAS ALLEN of Barr., paid
by her mother Anna Allen, widow, of Reho. on 18 Apr. 1723,
dtd. at Kings County 27 Dec. 1731 [9:16].
Appt. of Job Lewis of Boston, Co. of Suffolk, to be guard. of
Mary Mackentosh (minor over 14), grdau. of Col. HENERY MACKEN-
TOSH, Esq. of Brist., dtd. 1 Dec. 1737 [9:16].
Inv. of Est. of EBENEZER CARPENTER of Attl., Cooper, dcd. intest.
dtd. 28 July 1737, pres. by Dan Carpenter, Adm. Apprs: Beniah
Ba[*illegible*], Benjamin Day & David Whiple [9:17/8].
Order to Elezibeth Hill, widow, & Barnard Hill, Execs. of Est. of
JONATHAN HILL of Swan., dtd. 21 Feb. 1737/8 [9:18].
Will of JONATHAN HILL of Swan., Farmer, "being in good health,"
dtd. 18 March 1729/30, prob. 21 Feb. 1737/8. Wife Elizebeth.
Sons: Barnard (eldest), Jonathan (under 21), Caleb (under 21),
Thomas & Nathaniel Hill. 5 daus: Martha, Mary, Elizebeth, Re-
beccah & Sarah (all under 18 & unmar.). My brother Thomas Hill.
My negro man. Mentions lands in Swan. & in Warwick, R.I. (cal-
led Cowesit Purchase). Witns: Samuel Lee, Caleb Eddy & Joseph
Mason [9:18/9/20/1].
Inv. of Est. of JONATHAN PAUL of Brist., dtd. 21 Feb. 1737/8,
pres. by Francis Paul & Joshua Bailey, Adms. Apprs: Samuel
Royal, Samuel Smith & Cornelius Waldroon [9:21].
Will of MARTHA SOUTHWORTH of Lit. Comp., "Late of Ceabrook in
the County of New London," Conn., widow, dtd. 13 June 1729,
prob. 8 Apr. 1738. Sons: Joseph Blague, Samuel Blague, Gideon
Southworth & Andrew Southworth. Dau. Mary Southworth. Grson.
William Southworth. Grdau. Mary Blague. Son-in-law Joseph
Southworth to be Exec. Negro girl Kate. Witns: Elihu Woodworth, Benjamin Church & Timothey Clason [9:22/3].
Rcpt. from Thomas Hill for legacy to his wife Elizebeth Hill
from Est. of her father THOMAS ALLEN of Swan. alias Barr.,
paid by her brother Mathew Allen & by her mother Anne Allen,
Execs., dtd. 28 Sept. 1721 [*sic*]. Witns: Jonathan Vial & Rebeccah Allen. Acknowledged by subscriber in Kings County on
2 Dec. 1731 [9:23].
Rcpt. by Joseph Cole & his wife Rebeccah for legacy from Est.
of her father THOMAS ALLEN of Swan. alias Barr., paid by her

brother Mathew Allen & her mother Anne Allen, widow, Execs.,
dtd. Reho. 16 Dec. 1723. Witns: Thomas Hill & Thomas Medberry.
"Rebeccah Hill [sic] The Above Subscriber formerly the wife of
Joseph Cole Deceased Personally Came on ye 27th day of Decem-
ber 1731" to court in Kings County [9:24].
Appt. of Dan Carpenter of Attl., Clothier, to be guard. of Pri-
cilla Carpenter (under 14), dau. of EBENEZER CARPENTER of
Attl., dtd. 31 Jan. 1737 [9:24/5].
Appt. of Samuel Bishop of Attl., Yeoman, to be guard. of William
Carpenter (under 14), son of EBENEZER CARPENTER of Attl., dtd.
31 Jan. 1737 [9:25].
Acct. of Dan Carpenter, Adm. of Est. of EBENEZER CARPENTER of
Attl., dtd. 31 Jan. 1737/8. Incl. payms. for: "Docter Ebenezer
Laine for what he did for William & Pricilla in their Sick-
ness" [9:25/6/7].
Appt. of Sarah Child of Swan., widow, to be Adm. of Est. of her
husb. JAMES CHILD of Swan., dtd. 21 Feb. 1737/8 [9:27/8].
Acct. of "Elezebeth Boid Late Elezebeth French," widow & Adm.
of Est. of JOHN FRENCH of Attl., who "Deceased During the minority of John French Who is appointed Executor to the Last
Will and testament," dtd. 21 Feb. 1737/8. Incl. paym. of legacies per will: to Rachel, Elezebeth & Lidia [no surnames]
"his Second Wifes Daughters;" to Edward White, to Experiance
White & to Hannah French. Said Elezebeth Boid also asks allowance "for what was given her by her husband John Frenches will
which She had before marriage," but was included in the inv.
[9:28/9/30].
Inv. of Est. of JAMES PADDOCK of Swan., dtd. 5 Jan. 1737/8, pres.
by Sarah Paddock, widow & Exec. Apprs: Richard Harding, Robert Joles & Peres Bradford [9:30/1].
Inv. of Est. of SETH EDDY of Swan., Ship Carpenter, dtd. 19 Feb.
1737/8, pres. by Patiance Eddy, widow & Adm. Apprs: John Cum-
mings, Edward Palmer & Martin Luther [9:31/2].
Order for div. of Est. of JOSHUA FINNEY of Swan. dcd. intest.,
dtd. 19 Dec. 1737 [9:32/3].
Rcpt. from Josias Lyndon, guard. of Sarah & Jonathan Wilson,
chldn. of JONATHAN WILSON, for legacy to them from their father's Est., paid by Capt. Samuel Little & Hannah Little his
wife, Exec., dtd. 1 May 1738 [9:33].
Div. of 1/3 of the Est. of JOSHUA FINNEY of Swan., which was
laid out previously to his widow Mercy Finney, now dcd., dtd.
11 Jan. 1737/8, to be div. btwn. his chldn: Joshua (eldest
son), John (2nd son), Samuel (3rd son), Josiah (youngest son),
Mercy wife of John Man (youngest dau.), Elezebeth Luther wife
of Nathan Luther (2nd dau.) & Mary Finney (eldest dau.). Comm:
Richard Harding, Peres Bradford, Robert Joles, Barnard Hail &
Samuel Miller [9:33/4/5].
Order to Mary Tripp of Dart., widow & Exec. of Est. of her husb.

JAMES TRIPP of Dart., dtd. 21 March 1737 [9:36].

Will of JAMES TRIPP of Dart., dtd. 28 May 1737, prob. 21 March 1737/8. Wife Mary. Sons: Timothey & Isaac Tripp. Dau. Mary Tripp (under 18 & unmar.). Grdaus: Mehetibel Tripp (under 20 & unmar.) & Mary Tripp. Wife Mary to be Exec. Witns: Mary Hathway, Josiah Taber & Philip Taber [9:36/7/8].

Order to William Corey of Newport, R.I. & Philip Corey of Tiv., Yeomen, Execs. of Est. of their father THOMAS COREY of Tiv., dtd. 21 March 1737/8 [9:38/9].

Will of THOMAS COREY of Tiv., Yeoman, dtd. 23 Sept. 1734, prob. 21 March 1737/8. Wife Susanah. Sons: William (eldest), Thomas (dcd.) Corey of Dart. & Phillip Corey. Daus: Patiance Corey, Mary Durfey wife of Thomas Durfey & Sarah Brown wife of Abraham Brown. Grson. Thomas Corey (under 21) son of my dcd. son Thomas. My son Philip to take oversight of said grson. John [sic]. My Indian boy Sam alias Zachariah & my Indian girl Dinah. My brother-in-law Philip Taber. Sons William & Phillip to be Execs. Witns: Philip Taber, Josiah Taber & Philip Taber [sic][9:39/40/1/2].

Inv. of Est. of JAMES TRIPP of Dart., dtd. 3 March 1738, pres. by Mary Tripp, widow & Exec. Apprs: Philip Taber, Edward Cornel & Beriah Goddard [9:42/3/4].

Appt. of Caleb Cole of Swan., Yeoman, to be guard. as chosen by Mercy Cole (minor over 14), dau. of JOSEPH COLE of Swan., dtd. 21 March 1737/8 [9:44/5].

Appt. of Mary Peck of Reho., widow, to be Adm. of Est. of her husb. JOSEPH PECK of Reho., dtd. 21 March 1737/8 [9:45/6].

Appt. of Joshua Bailey of Brist., Cooper, to be Adm. "Cum Testimento annexo" of Est. of THOMAS CHURCH of Taun., Indian man, since James Williams of Taun., who was named Exec. in the will has refused this trust. 21 Feb. 1737/8 [9:46/7].

Will of THOMAS CHURCH of Taun., Indian man, dtd. 28 Aug. 1735, prob. 14 Jan. 1735. Wife Eve Church. James Williams to be Exec. Witns: Seth Williams, Israel Sumner & Bethiah Abel[9:47].

Power of attorney given by Isaac Royal of Charlestown, Co. of Middlesex, father & guard. of Isaac Royal, Jr. of Charlestown, appointing Robert Oliver of Dorchester, Co. of Suffolk, to be his attorney, dtd. 13 May 1738. Elezebeth wife of Isaac Royal, Jr. is "Late Elezebeth Mackentosh Daughter of LAUGHLAND MACKENTOSH Late of Bristol." Witns: John Fayerweather & Thomas Palmer, Jr. [9:48].

Order to Nathaniel Crossman, Exec. of Est. of his father ROBERT CROSSMAN of Taun., dtd. 18 Apr. 1738 [9:48/9].

Will of ROBERT CROSSMAN aged 78 years, dtd. 20 Aug. 1736, prob. 18 Apr. 1738. No wife mentioned. Sons: Nathaniel & Seth Crossman. Daus: Hannah Packerd Late of Bridgewater & Elizebeth Liscomb. Grchldn: Seth, Jeremiah, Robert, Sarah, Susanna & Hannah Crossman all chldn. of my son Seth Crossman. Dau-in-law Susanah Crossman & her chldn. [not named]. Grchldn: Israel & Robert

Packerd, chldn. of my dau. Hannah Packerd. Son-in-law Robert
Liscomb. Grchldn: Robert Liscomb, Richard Liscomb, Elezebeth
Codding & Mary Wilmarth (dcd.), chldn. of my dau. Elezebeth
Liscomb. Son Nathaniel to be Exec. Witns: Thomas Clapp, Sam-
uel Sumner & Edward Shove [9:49/50/1/2/3].
Appt. of John Williams of East., Yeoman, to be Adm. of Est. of
his mother REBECCA LEONARD of Rayn., at the request of Josiah
& Benjamin Williams, the elder brothers, dtd. 18 Apr. 1738
[9:53/53½][page numbering error].
Inv. of Est. of SAMUEL BUTTERWORTH of Reho., dtd. 14 Apr. 1738,
pres. by Patiance Butterworth, widow & Adm. Apprs: Joseph
Wheaten, Edward Glover & Timothy Ide [9:53¼/53][page numbering
error].
Inv. of Est. of REBECCA LEONARD of Rayn., widow, dtd. 8 Apr.
1738, pres. by John Williams, her son & Adm. Apprs: James
Williams, Samuel White & Samuel Leonard, Jr. [9:53/4].
Inv. of Est. of JAMES CHILD of Swan., Yeoman, dtd. 23 Feb. 17-
37/8, pres. by Sarah Child, widow & Adm. Apprs: Peres Brad-
ford, Richard Harding & Robert Joles [9:54/5].
Inv. of Est. of JONATHAN HILL of Swan. "who Deceased february
the Ninth 1737/8," dtd. 14 Apr. 1738, pres. by Elezebeth Hill
& Barnard Hill, Execs. Apprs: Eseck Brown, Jonathan Slade &
Job Mason [9:55/6].
Appt. of Seth Hach of Taun., Yeoman, as Adm. of Est. of his fa-
ther WILLIAM HACH of Taun., the widow [not named] and eldest
son William Hach refusing Adm., dtd. 24 Apr. 1738 [9:56/7].
Appt. of Patiance Butterworth of Reho., widow, to be Adm. of
Est. of her husb. SAMUEL BUTTERWORTH of Reho., dtd. 18 Apr.
1738 [9:57/8].
Appt. of Patiance Butterworth of Reho., widow, to be guard. of
Hannah & Samuel Butterworth (both under 14), chldn. of SAMUEL
BUTTERWORTH of Reho., dtd. 18 Apr. 1738 [9:58].
Appt. of Daniel Goshett of Taun., Cordwainer, to be Adm. of Est.
of his father HENRY GOSHETT of Taun., Shipwright, dtd. 18 Apr.
1738 [9:58/9].
Will of HENRY GOSHET of Taun., Yeoman, "Being Sixty Two years
old," dtd. 8 March 1737. prob. 18 Apr. 1738. Wife Sarah. Son
Daniel Goshet. Daus: Sarah Pitts, Abigail Jones, Mercy Perrey,
Hannah Smith, Martha Crossman, Elezebeth Perrey & Susannah
Goshet (youngest). Grson. Henry Goshet. Son Daniel to be Exec.
Witns: Samuel Sumner, Samuel Sumner, Jr. & Seth White [9:59
/60/1].
Inv. of Est. of BARNARD LITTLE, late of Jamica [sic], dtd. Brist.
23 Feb. 1737/8, pres. by John Usher, Adm. Consists only of
"One Negro Boy named Primas." Apprs: Jonathan Woodbury, Sam-
uel Royal & Joseph Russel [9:62].
Appt. of James Cole of Swan. to be Adm. of Est. of MARY COLE of
Swan., widow dcd. intest., dtd. 16 March 1738 [9:62/3].

Appt. of Abigail Paine of Reho., widow, to be Adm. of Est. of
her husb. NATHANIEL PAINE of Reho. dcd. intest., dtd. 16 May
1738 [9:63].

Inv. of Est. of Capt. SHUBAL NORTON of Brist., dtd. 11 Feb. 17-
37/8, pres. by Sarah Norton, widow & Adm. Incl. var. items related to mariner's trade & var. notes, incl. "Saint Christo-
phers Notes 65-0-0." Apprs: Samuel Royal, Samuel Smith & Joseph Russel [9:64/64¼/64½][page numbering error].

Inv. of Est. of THOMAS COREY of Tiv., dtd. 28 Feb. 1737/8, pres.
by William & Philip Corey, sons & Execs. Apprs: Thomas Manchester, William Briggs & John Sisson [9:64-3/4].

Appt. of Thomas Stoddar of Lit. Comp., Yeoman, to be Adm. of Est.
of MEHETIBEL DYE of Lit. Comp. dcd. intest., said Stoddar being
"one of the Principal Creditors," dtd. 16 May 1738 [9:65].

Appt. of Ebenezer Burt of Nort., Yeoman, to be guard. of Submit
Burt (under 14), dau. of EBENEZER BURT of Nort., dtd. 15 June
1738 [9:65½].

Order to div. Est. of JOHN STREETER of Attl. in response to petition from John Foster, Jr. & Francis Fuller, Freeholders,
dtd. 21 Feb. 1738 [9:65½/66].

Inv. of real est. of JOHN STREETER of Attl., dtd. 8 March 1737/8
pres. by Apprs: Noah Carpenter, Samuel Tiler & Jeremiah Ingraham [9:66].

Div. of real est. of JOHN STREETER, settling it on the eldest
son, John Streeter, he having bought the widow's [not named]
& is obligated to "Pay the other Ten Children of Said John
Streeter," dtd. 16 May 1738. Other 10 chldn. of JOHN STREETER,
James, Josiah, Jeremiah, Mary Ward, Abigail, Rachel, Sarah,
Amey, Isaiah & Hannah (last 4 are under 18 & the 3 girls also
noted as unmar.)[9:66/7/8/9].

Inv. of Est. of NATHANIEL PAINE of Reho., dtd. 27 Apr. 1738,
pres. by Abigail Paine, widow & Adm. Apprs: Edward Glover,
Joseph Wheaten & Joseph Allen [9:69/70].

Order to Ebenezer Carpenter of Reho., Yeoman, Exec. of Est. of
his father JAMES CARPENTER of Reho., Yeoman, dtd. 16 May 17-
38 [9:70/1].

Will of JAMES CARPENTER of Reho., Yeoman, "being weak of body,"
dtd. 2 March 1737/8, prob. 16 May 1738. Wife Grace. Sons: Ebenezer & Steven Carpenter. Daus: Dorothy Mansfield, Lidia Wilmouth & Joanah Carpenter. Grdau. Susanah Carpenter. Son Ebenezer to be Exec. Witns: Aron Read, John Sweeting & Edward
Glover [9:71/2]3].

Inv. of Est. of JAMES CARPENTER of Reho., dtd. 9 May 1738, pres.
by Ebenezer Carpenter, son & Exec. Apprs: Edward Glover, Joseph Wheaten & Timothey Ide [9:74].

Order to James Tripp of Dart., Yeoman, Exec. of Est. of MARY
GATCHEL of Dart., dtd. 16 May 1738 [9:74/5].

Will of MARY GETCHEL of Dart., widow, dtd. 4 July 1734, prob.

16 May 1738. Daus-in-law: Mary Ellis, Sarah Russel & Persilla
Burgis. Grdaus: Mary Getchel & Susanah Getchel (sisters).
Friend James Tripp to be Exec. Witns: Obediah Butler, Philip
Allen & James Allen [9:75/6/7].

Inv. of Est. of MARY GETCHEL of Dart., dtd. 8 Apr. 1734, pres.
by James Tripp of Dart., Exec. Apprs: James Howland, John
Shepard & Peleg Smith [9:77].

Acct. of Timothey Ide & Daniel Ide, Execs. of Est. of Capt. TIM-
OTHEY IDE of Reho., dtd. 16 May 1738. Inc. equal payms. to:
Elezebeth Read wife of Daniel Read, Mary Read wife of Ezekiel
Read, Sarah Carpenter wife of Ezekiel Carpenter, Rachel Perrin
& Experiance Lyndle wife of Timothey Lyndle [9:77/8].

Appt. of James Gibs of Brist., Mariner, to be Adm. of Est. of
PETER PROVOST of Brist., Mariner, dcd. intest., said Gibs being
"one of the Principal Creditors," dtd. 18 Apr. 1738 [9:78/9].

Inv. of Est. of PETER PROVOST of Brist., dtd. 24 Apr. 1738, pres.
by James Gibbs, Adm. Mentions "Goods Sold att the mast att Sea
on board the Sloop Dolphin James Gibbs Commander." Apprs: Samuel Royal, Samuel Little & Joshua Bailey [9:79/80].

Inv. of Est. of MARY COLE of Swan., dtd. 23 May 1738, pres. by
James Cole, Adm. Apprs: Peres Bradford, Richard Harding &
William Turner [9:80].

Appt. of Hannah Hail of Swan., widow, to be Adm. of Est. of her
husb. BARNARD HAIL of Swan. dcd. intest., dtd. 16 May 1738
[9:81].

Order to Isabel Shearman of Dart., Exec. of Est. of her mother
SARAH SHEARMAN of Dart., dtd. 20 June 1738 [9:82].

Will of SARAH SHEARMAN of Dart., widow, dtd. 15 June 1733, prob.
20 June 1738. Sons: James, Ebenezer, Seth, Israel & Moses
(dcd.) Shearman. Daus: Isabel Shearman, Rachel Shearman &
Ruth Shearman. Grdau. Sarah Shearman dau. of my dcd. son
Moses. Son Seth & dau. Isabel to be Execs. Witns: Thomas
Smith, Stephen Wilcox, Jr., Thomas Mughlton & David Smith [9:
82/3/4].

Inv. of Est. of SARAH SHEARMAN of Dart., dtd. 26 May 1738, pres.
by Isabel Shearman, Exec. Apprs: James Howland, John Akin &
Thomas Smith [9:84/84½].

Order to Joseph Wilbour of Lit. Comp., Exec. of Est. of [not
stated, but meant for WILLIAM WILBOUR], dtd. 20 June 1738
[9:84½].

Will of WILLIAM WILBOUR of Lit. Comp., Yeoman, dtd. 30 Dec. 17-
32, prob. 20 June 1738. Wife not mentioned. Sons: William, Jo-
seph, Jeremiah & Samuel (dcd.) Wilbour. Daus: Hannah Liponcut,
Abigail Hillard, Jane Dennis, Sarah Talman & Phebe Shaw. Son
Joseph to be Exec. Witns: Israel Shaw, Peter Shaw & Nathaniel
Searl [9:84½/5/6].

Acct. of Hannah Wheaten, widow & Adm. of Est. of JAMES WHEATEN
of Swan., dtd. 20 June 1738. Incl. item for "Two Powers of

Attorney Sent Over to Carolina" [9:86/7].

Inv. of Est. of JOSEPH PECK of Reho., dtd. 28 March 1728, pres. by Mary Peck, widow & Adm. Apprs: Daniel Carpenter, Joshua Smith & John Perrin [9:88/9].

Appt. of Benjamin Hodges of Nort., Yeoman, to be guard. as chosen by Lewis Sweeten (minor over 14), son of LEWIS SWEETEN of Reho., dtd. 20 June 1738 [9:89].

Appt. of Thomas Smith of Dart., Yeoman, to be guard. as chosen by Deborah Wing (minor over 14), dau. of EDWARD WING of Dart., dtd. 20 June 1738 [9:90].

Order to Jale Chace of Swan., widow, Exec. of Est. of [name not stated, but meant for HEZEKIAH CHACE], dtd. 19 June 1738[9:91].

Inv. of Est. of WILLIAM WILBOUR of Lit. Comp., dtd. 19 June 1738, pres. by Joseph Wilbour, son & Exec. Apprs: Thomas Brownel, Jonathan Head & Henry Head [9:91/2].

Appt. of Nathaniel Gammage of Attl., Yeoman, to be Adm. of Est. of his father JOSHUA GAMMAGE of Attl. dcd. intest., dtd. 20 June 1738 [9:92/3].

Will of HEZEKIAH CHACE of Swan., Yeoman, dtd. 1 Apr. 1738, prob. 19 June 1738. Wife Jale. Sons: Barnabas (eldest), Hezekiah (2nd) & Enoch (youngest) Chace. Daus: Barshaby Chace, Jale Chace, Phebe Chace, Christian Chace & Sibbel Chace (all under 18). Brother Eber Chace & friend Edward Slade to be Overseers, Wife Jale to be Exec. Witns: Benjamin Norten, Samuel Eddy & Benjamin Buffington, Jr. [9:93/4/5].

Inv. of Est. of BERNARD HAIL of Swan., Yeoman, dtd. 26 May 1738, pres. by Hannah Hail, widow & Adm. Apprs: Peres Bradford, Richard Harding & William Turner [9:95/6].

Inv. of Est. of HEZEKIAH CHACE of Swan., Yeoman, dtd. 9 June 1738, pres. by Jale Chace, widow & Exec. Apprs: Stephen Cornel, Benjamin Norten & Samuel Eddy [9:96/7].

Inv. of Est. of THOMAS HODGES of Taun. dcd. intest., dtd. 26 Jan. 1737/8, pres. by Katherine Hodges, widow & Adm. Apprs: Morgan Cobb, Nathaniel Briggs & Philip Mason [9:98].

Inv. of Est. of WILLIAM HACH of Taun., dtd. 17 May 1738, pres. by Seth Hach, son & Adm. Apprs: Mathew Briggs, Thomas Eliot & Nicholas Stephens, Jr. [9:99].

Inv. of Est. of MEHETIBEL DYE of Lit. Comp., dtd. 24 May 1738, pres. by Thomas Stoddar, Adm. Apprs: William Palmer, George Brownel & Thomas Brownel [9:99/100].

Order to Restcome, Peleg & Samuel Sandford, Yeomen, Execs. of Est. of their father SAMUEL SANDFORD of Tiv., dtd. 19 Sept. 1738 [9:100/1].

Will of SAMUEL SANFORD of Tiv., Weaver, "being aling and Weak of Body," dtd. 27 Dec. 1737, prob. 19 Sept. 1738. Wife Deborah. Sons: Restcome (eldest), Peleg & Samuel Sanford. 2 daus: Mary Tabor & Eliphal Hart. 3 sons to be Execs. Witns: Samuel Hart, Jonathan Hart & Nathaniel Soul [later oath calls him "Searl"][9:101/2/3/4].

Appt. of Penelope Bourden of Free., widow, to be Adm. of Est.
of her husb. STEPHEN BOURDEN of Free., dtd. 19 Sept. 1738
[9:104].
Appt. of Hope Dagget of Reho., widow, to be Adm. of Est. of
her husb. JOHN DAGGETT of Reho. dcd. intest., dtd. 19 Sept.
1738 [9:105].
Inv. of Est. of JOHN DAGGETT of Reho., dtd. 14 July 1738, pres.
by Hope Daggett, widow & Adm. Pers. est. 507-00-11; real est.
894-0-0. Apprs: Edward Glover, Timothy Walker & Noah Mason
[9:105/6].
Inv. of Est. of STEPHEN BOURDEN of Free., dtd. 10 Aug. 1738,
pres. by Penelope Bourden, widow & Adm. Pers. est. 484-14-0;
real est. 2000-0-0. Apprs: Benjamin Durphey, Aron Bowen &
Richard Bowen [9:107/8].
Appt. of Damaris Peck of Reho., widow, to be Adm. of Est. of her
husb. JATHNIEL PECK, Jr. of Reho. dcd. intest., dtd. 28 Oct.
1738 [9:108/9].
Appt. of Joshua Bailey of Brist., Cooper, to be guard. of Mercy
Ingraham of Brist., widow, "Who is non Compus Mentis," dtd.
19 Sept. 1738 [9:109].
Inv. of Est. of JOSHUA GRUMMAGE of Attl., dtd. 25 Sept. 1738,
pres. by Nathaniel Grummage, son & Adm. Pers. est. 227-10-0;
real est. 1160-0-0. Apprs: Samuel Day, John Robbins & Benja-
min Wise [9:109/10].
Inv. of Est. of JOHN BRYANT of Berk., dtd. 17 Oct. 1738, pres.
by Mary Darbey, Adm. Pers. est. 95-15-8; real est. 446-0-0.
Apprs: Nathaniel Crossman, Samuel Pitts & Stephen Hodges [9:
110/1].
Acct. of Hannah Sweeten of Attl., Adm. of Est. of her husb.
HENRY SWEETEN of Attl., dtd. 17 Oct. 1738 [9:111/2].
Order to Henry Chace of Tiv., Yeoman, Exec. of Est. of his fa-
ther ABRAHAM CHACE of Tiv., dtd. 17 Oct. 1738 [9:113].
Will of ABRAHAM CHACE of Tiv., Yeoman, dtd. 10 May 1737, prob.
17 Oct. 1738. Wife Elezebeth. Sons: Josiah (dcd.), Abraham
(unmar.), Phinias & Henry Chace. Daus: Elizebeth Chisson,
Mary Chace, (unmar.), Tabitha Petty, Johannah Otis, Experiance
Chace, Mary Chace & Mallisent Crandall. Grdau. Elizebeth Petty
(unmar.). Grson. Daniel Chace son of my son Phinias Chace.
Mentions lands in Tiv. & in Dart. Witns: John Read, Stephen
Gifford & Samuel Forman [9:113/4/5/6].
Acct. of Hannah Hunt of Dart., widow, Adm. of Est. of the Rev.
Mr. SAMUEL HUNT of Dart., dtd. 17 Oct. 1738 [9:116/7].
Acct. of Thomas Stoddar of Lit. Comp., Yeoman, Adm. of Est. of
MEHETIBEL DYE "mollato woman Late of Little Compton," dtd. 17
Oct. 1738 [9:117/8].
Acct. of Zerviah Potter, widow & Adm. of Est. of NATHANIEL POT-
TER of Tiv., dtd. 17 Oct. 1738. Incl. item: "the Charge of
Lying in With a Child after the Death of the father" [9:118/].
Acct. of Nathaniel Gammage of Attl., Adm. of Est. of his father
JOSHUA GAMMAGE of Attl., dtd. 27 Oct. 1738 [9:119].

Acct. of Mary Peck, widow & Adm. of Est. of her husb. JOSEPH
PECK of Reho., dtd. 17 Oct. 1738 [9:120/1].

Acct. of Priscilla Bowen of Swan., widow & Adm. of Est. of DAN-
IEL BOWEN of Swan., dtd. 27 Oct. 1738 [9:121/2].

Acct. of Mary Darbey, Adm. of Est. of JOHN BRYANT of Barkley,
dtd. 27 Oct. 1738 [9:122/3].

Order to Mary Talbut, widow, & to Benjamin Talbut, Yeoman, both
of Digh., Execs. of Est. of SAMUEL TALBUT of Digh., dtd. 21
Nov. 1738 [9:123/4].

Will of SAMUEL TALBUT, Sr. of Digh , Yeoman, "being Bound Abroad
and not Knowing wether Death may not Prevent my Return home
again," dtd. 21 Aug. 1738, prob. 21 Nov. 1738. Wife Mary. Sons:
Samuel, Nathaniel & Benjamin Talbut. Daus: Mary Hoar [omitted]
Whitmarsh & Sarah Kiles (widow). Wife Mary & son Benjamin to
be Execs. Witns: Silvester Richmond, Samuel White & Nathaniel
Fisher [9:124/5/6].

Order to Hannah Hathaway of Barkley, widow & Exec. of Est. of
her husb. THOMAS HATHWAY of Barkley, dtd. 21 Nov. 1738 [9:
126/7].

Will of THOMAS HATHWAY of Digh. [sic], Yeoman, "Labouring under
Such Bodily Deceases as Confine me to my house and being Dailey
in Expectation of Death," dtd. 20 Aug. 1734, prob. 21 Nov. 17-
38. Wife Hannah. Sons: Benjamin & Thomas Hathway. Daus. Hannah
& Jemima (both unmar.). Wife Hannah to be Exec. Witns: Nathaniel Fisher, Daniel Axtel & Daniel Axtel, Jr. [9:127/8].

Inv. of Est. of THOMAS HATHWAY of Barkley, dtd. 4 Oct. 1738,
pres. by Hannah Hathway, widow & Exec. Pers. est. 136-07-6;
real est. 700-0-0. Apprs: John Paul, Benajah Babit & John
Crane [9:128/9].

Order to James Tripp of Dart., appt. Adm. of Est. of THOMAS GAT-
CHEL of Dart., because Mary Gatchel, widow & Exec. named in
the will, has dcd. before the will was proved, & Sarah Russel,
one of the daus., refused Adm., dtd. 21 Nov. 1738 [9:130/1].

Will of THOMAS GATCHEL of Dart., "Tayler," "in good health," 16
Feb. [year not given, but was called "the fifth year of the
Reigne of our Sovereigne Lord the King George," which would
be 1732], prob. 21 Nov. 1738. Wife Mary. Son John. Daus: Mary
Ellis, Sarah [sic] Gatchel & Pricilla Burges. Witns: Oliver
Allen, Philip Shearman & Ephraim Shearman [9:131/2].

Inv. of Est. of HENRY GOSSHET of Taun., dtd. 20 Nov. 1738, pres.
by Daniel Gosshet, son & Adm. Pers. est. 155-17-7; real est.
700-0-0. Apprs: Nicholas Stephens, Benjamin Wilbour & Samuel
White [9:132/3].

Inv. of Est. of THOMAS GITCHEL of Dart., dtd. 17 Nov. 1738, pres.
by James Tripp, Exec. Pers. est. 80-16-6; no real est. Apprs:
Peleg Smith, John Sheperd & James Howland [9:133/4].

Inv. of Est. of Lewt. JATHNIEL PECK of Reho., dtd. 4 Nov. 1738,
pres. by Damaris Peck, widow & Adm. Pers. est. 362-9-6; real
est. 460-0-0. Apprs: Daniel Carpenter, Samuel Bullock & Philip
Wheeler [9:134/5].

Inv. of Est. of WILLIAM SLADE of Swan., dtd. 18 Nov. 1738, pres.
by Hannah Slade, widow & Adm. Pers. est. 1054-01-7; real est.
5580-0-0. Apprs: William Anthoney, Preserved Brayton & Daniel Wilbour [9:135/6].

Appt. of Benjamin Selle of Nort., Yeoman, to be Adm. of Est. of
JOHN HILL of Attl., "the widdow and his father [*sentence not
continued on next line*]," dtd. 19 Dec. 1738 [9:137].

Inv. of Est. of ABRAHAM CHACE of Tiv., Yeoman, who "Deceased
the 18th Day of September in the year 1738," dtd. 30 Nov. 17-
38, pres. by Henry Chace, son & Exec. Mentions lands in Tiv.
& Dart. Pers. est. 641-16-6; real est. 1837-0-0. Apprs:
John Jennings, Stephen Gifford & Samuel Forman [9:137/8/9].

Inv. of Est. of JOHN HILL of Attl, dtd. 19 Dec. 1738, pres. by
Benjamin Selle of Nort. Pers. est. 167-14-11; real est. 275-
0-0. Apprs: Joseph Hodges, Nathaniel Hodges & Daniel Brayman
[9:139/40].

Appt. of Benjamin Wardwel of Brist., Cooper, to be Adm. of Est.
of his son BENJAMIN WARDWEL of Brist., Cooper, dcd. intest.,
dtd. 19 Dec. 1738 [9:140].

Inv. of Est. of SAMUEL TALBUT of Digh., dtd. 8 Dec. 1738, pres.
by Mary Talbut, widow & Exec. Pers. est. 211-11-0; real est.
1000-0-0. Apprs: Mathew Briggs, Ephraim Atwood & Abraham
Shaw [9:141].

Will of JOHN FRANKLEN of Swan., Cordwainer, "being very Weak and
Infirm of Body," dtd. 11 Sept. 1738, prob. 19 Jan. 1738/9.
Wife Hannah. Only chldn. named are daus. Hopestill wife of
John Jones & Ruth wife of Richard Round. Mentions div. of his
Est. "amongst my Childreen," granting his wife use of "all my
Real Estate until my youngest surviveing Child arrives att the
age of Seven years." Mentions a paym. to his wife "in Dis-
charge of A Certain Bond Given by me unto her Said Wife before
my Intermarrage with her." Wife to be Exec. Witns: Peres
Bradford, John Carpenter & Philip Cooye [9:142/3].

Inv. of Est. of SAMUEL TALBUT of Digh., dtd. 8 Dec. 1738 [*entry
terminates abruptly with the words "This Inventory was entered
before"*][9:143].

Order to Mary Bliss of Reho., widow & Exec. of Est. of her dau.
BETHIAH BLISS of Reho., dtd. 15 Aug. 1738 [9:144].

Order to Hannah Franklen of Swan., widow & Exec. of Est. of her
husb. JOHN FRANKLEN of Swan., dtd. 19 Jan. 1738/9 [9:144/5].

Appt. of Priscilla Bowen of Swan., widow, to be guard. as chosen
by Obediah Bowen (minor over 14), son of DANIEL BOWEN of Swan.,
dtd. 15 Aug. 1738 [9:145].

Appt. of Hannah Franklen of Swan., widow of JOHN FRANKLEN of
Swan., to be guard. of Ebenezer, Lemuel & Record Franklen,
chldn. of JOHN FRANKLEN, dtd. 16 Jan. 1738/9 [9:146].

Will of BETHIAH BLISS of Reho., Spinster, "Being very Sick and
weak," dtd. 25 May 1738, prob. 15 Aug. 1738. Brother Jonathan
Bliss. Mother Mary Bliss to be Exec. Witns: Jathniel Peck,

Jr., Daniel Ormsbee & Ruth Ormsbee [9:146/7].

Appts. of Daniel Smith of Reho., Yeoman, to be guard. as chosen by Elezebeth Butterworth (minor over 14) & of Sibel & Huldah Butterworth (both under 14), daus. of NOAH BUTTERWORTH of Reho., dtd. 26 Jan. 1738/9 [9:148/9].

Appt. of Penelope Butterworth of Reho., widow, to be guard. of her son Nathaniel Butterworth (under 14), son of NOAH BUTTER-WORTH of Reho., dtd. 26 Feb. 1738/9 [9:149/50].

Appts. of Joseph Bosworth of Reho., Yeoman, to be guard. as chosen by Lidiah Butterworth (minor over 14) & of Noah Butterworth, chldn. of NOAH BUTTERWORTH of Reho., dtd. 26 Feb. 1738/9 [9:150/1].

Appt. of Jonathan Kingsley of Reho., Yeoman, to be guard. of Abel Franklen & Elezebeth Franklen (minors over 14), chldn. of JOHN FRANKLEN of Reho., dtd. 20 March 1738/9 [9:152].

Inv. of Est. of JOHN WILLIAMS of Taun., Single Man, dcd. intest., dtd. 12 May 1738, pres. by Nathan Hodges, Adm. Mentions lands in Rayn. & in East. Incl. notes for: "Nathaniel Williams of Taun., Silas Williams of East. & Simeon Williams of Taun.. Total est. 254-13-0. Apprs: John Williams, Joseph Godfree & Eleazer Keith [9:152/3].

Order to John Child of Swan., Housewright, Exec. of Est. of his father JOHN CHILD of Swan., dtd. 20 Feb. 1738/9 [9:153/4].

Will of JOHN CHILD of Swan., Husbandman, "being very Sick and weak," dtd. 10 Jan. 1738/9, prob. 20 Feb. 1738/9. Wife Elezebeth. Sons: John & Oliver Child. Daus: Margaret, Sarah, Susanah, Martha, Bethiah & Mary [no surnames]. Grdau. Elezebeth Easterbrooks. Indian girl Esther Boots (under 18 & unmar.). Dau-in-law Sarah Child, widow. Son John to be Exec. Witns: William Knowles, John Lewin & Edward Luther [9:154/5/6].

Acct. of Thomas Bowen, Esq., Adm. of Est. of his father Docter RICHARD BOWEN of Reho., dtd. 25 July 1738. Mentions Richard Bowen & John Bowen, Execs. of their dcd. father Richard [9:156/7].

Order to Deborah Slocum, widow, & to Humphrey Smith, Yeoman, both of Dart., Execs. of Est. of ELEAZER SLOCUM of Dart., dtd. 20 March 1738/9 [9:157/8].

Will of ELEAZER SLOCUM of Dart., Yeoman, dtd. 18 Jan. 1738, prob. 20 March 1738/9. Wife Deborah. Sons: John, Eleazer, Humphrey & David Slocum (last 3 under 21). Daus: Mary Slocum, Eliphal Slocum, Ann Slocum & Deborah Slocum (last 3 under 18). "My beloved Wife and Brother [-in-law?] Humphrey Smith" to be Execs. Witns: James Allen, Holder Slocum & Cornelius Bennit [9:158/9/60/1].

Appt. of Sarah Sampson of Dart., widow, to be Adm. of Est. of her husb. JOSEPH SAMPSON of Dart., dtd. 20 March 1738/9[9:162].

Inv. of Est. of JOSEPH SAMPSON of Dart., dtd. 2 March 1738/9, pres. by Sarah Slocum, widow & Adm. Real. est. 2500-0-0; pers. est. not totalled. Apprs: Zacheus Tobey, Judath Paddock &

James Cushman [9:162/3/4].
Inv. of Est.of ELEAZER SLOCUM, Yeoman, dtd. 13 March 1738/9,
pres. by Deborah Slocum & Humphrey Smith, Execs. Mentions
"The farm Given John Slocum." Pers. est. 940-06-8; real est.
4780-0-0. Apprs: James Allen, Holder Slocum & Cornelius Bennit [9:164/5/6].
Appt. of Nicholas Thomas of Swan., Yeoman, to be Adm. of Est.
of his brother LEWIS THOMAS of Swan., "your Two Elder Brothers
Refusing," dtd. 20 March 1738/9 [9:166/7].
Order to Elezebeth Bowen of Reho., widow & Exec. of Est. of her
husb. JAMES BOWEN of Reho., dtd. 20 March 1738/9 [9:167/8].
Will of JAMES BOWEN of Reho., Wheelwright, "being att this Time
Somewhat Indisposed and Weak of body," dtd. 8 Oct. 1738, prob.
20 March 1738/9. Wife Elezebeth. Son Obediah Bowen. 5 eldest
daus: Lydiah, Elezebeth, Tabitha, Mary & Patience; 2 youngest
daus: Experience & Abigail [no surnames]. Grson. James Bowen
(under 21). Wife to be Exec. Witns: Jonathan Kingsley, Samuel
Bullock & Samuel Bullock, Jr. [9:168/9].
Order to James Bucklen of Reho., Yeoman, Exec. of Est. of JAMES
BUCKLEN of Reho., Yeoman, dtd. 20 March 1738/9 [9:169/70].
Will of JAMES BUCKLEN of Reho., Yeoman, "being Sick and Weak of
body," dtd. 5 Sept. 1738, prob. 20 March 1738/9. Wife Mary.
Sons: James, Timothey & Nehemiah Bucklen. Daus: Naomy & Mary
Bucklen. Witns: Daniel Perrin, Israel Peck & Samuel Smith
[9:170/1/2].
Order by the Town Council of Newport, R.I. to Thomas Bailey,
Exec. of Est. of JOHN BAILEY of Newport, dtd. 2 Feb. 1735 [9:
172].
Will of JOHN BAILEY of Newport, R.I., Yeoman, "aged 80 years,"
dtd. in Newport 8 May 1734, prob. Newport 2 Feb. 1738/9, pres.
in Brist. 15 May 1739. No wife mentioned. Sons: William (dcd.),
Thomas, John & Samuel Bailey. Daus: Mary Raynolds, Abigail
Weeden & Ruth (dcd.). Grsons: William, George, Samuel & John
Bailey, sons of my dcd. son William Bailey. Dau.-in-law Doro-
thy Bailey, widow of dcd. son William. Grdau. Sarah Walsworth
[perhaps dau. of dcd. dau. Ruth?]. Grson. Benjamin Bailey (un-
der 21) son of my son John. Grchldn. Mary Weeden & William
Weeden, chldn. of my dau. Abigail Weeden. Daus-in-law [sic]
Martha Simmons & Jane Rogers. Sons-in-law: Daniel Sabeer, Ja-
biz Raynolds & William Weeden. Mentions lands in Lit. Comp. &
Portsmouth. Dau-in-law Alec Bailey. Son Thomas to be Exec.
Witns: James Clark, William Sandford & Mary Sandford [9:173/
4/5/6].
Inv. of Est. of JOHN BAILEY of Newport, R.I., "Who Deceased the
thirteenth Day of the Month Called January AD: 1735," dtd. at
Newport 2 Feb. 1735. Apprs: James Clerk & William Sandford
[9:176/7].
Rcpt. by Seth Shearman for a legacy from Est. of his mother SARAH
SHEARMAN of Dart., paid by his sister Isabel Shearman, Exec.,

dtd. at Dart. 14 May 1739 [9:177].

Rcpt. by Israel Shearman for legacy paid from Est. of his mother
SARAH SHEARMAN of Dart. (the will bearing the date 12 June
1733), paid by his sister Isabel Shearman, Exec., dtd. at Dart.
14 May 1739 [9:177].

Rcpt. by Barnabas Chace & his wife Ruth Chace of Dart. for legacy from the Est. of her mother SARAH SHEARMAN of Dart., paid
by her sister Isabel Shearman, Exec., dtd. 12 May 1739 [9:
178].

Rcpt. by John Roon & his wife Meribah Roon of Dart. for a legacy from the Est. of her mother SARAH SHEARMAN of Dart., paid
by "our Sister Isabel Shearman," Exec. Witns: Timothey Maxfield & Seth Sharman [9:178].

Rcpts. by James Shearman & Ebenezer Shearman of Dart. for legacies from the Est. of their mother SARAH SHEARMAN of Dart.,
paid by their sister Isabel Shearman, Exec., dtd. 14 May 1739
[9:179].

Rcpt. by Henry Hedley of Dart. for legacy from Est. of his mother-in-law SARAH SHEARMAN, mother of his wife Rachel, paid by
her sister Isabel Shearman, Exec., dtd. 15 May 1739. Witns:
Daniel Howland & Samuel Howland [9:179].

Rcpt. by Israel Shearman for legacy from Est. of his mother SAR-
AH SHEARMAN of Dart., who had held it in trust after the decease of Israel's father Daniel Shearman, now paid by his sister Isabel Shearman, Exec., dtd. 16 May 1739. Witns: Seth
Shearman & Ruth Shearman [9:180].

Appt. of Dorothy Hunt of Reho., widow, to be Adm. of Est. of
her husb. DANIEL HUNT of Reho., Weaver, dcd. intest., dtd.
20 March 1738/9 [9:180/1].

Appt. of William Robinson of Taun., Yeoman, to be Adm. of Est.
of his father INCREASE ROBINSON of Taun. dcd. intest., dtd.
20 March 1738/9 [9:181/1].

Inv. of Est. of JOHN FRANKLEN of Swan., Cordwainer, dtd. 5 Feb.
1738/9, pres. by Hannah Franklen, widow & Exec. Pers. est.
276-01-10; real est. 280-0-0. Apprs: Peres Bradford, William
Turner & Jonathan Kingsley [9:182].

Inv. of Est. of JAMES BUCKLEN of Reho., dtd. 19 March 1738, pres.
by James Bucklen, son & Exec. Real est. 1200-0-0; pers. est.
not totalled [9:183/4].

Acct. of William Ware of Nort. abt. acct. of his late wife ZEB-
IAH WARE, who before her decease had been Adm. of Est. of her
husb. LEWIS SWEETEN of Reho., dtd. 21 March 1738/9. Mentions
that said William Ware was lately guard. of Lewis Sweeten,
minor son of LEWIS SWEETEN of Reho. Incl. item that land of
LEWIS SWEETEN had been sold in 1725 by permission of the
court [9:184/5/6].

Appt. of Mary Cobb of Nort., widow, to be guard. of John, Sarah,
Anna & Sybel Cobb (all under 14), chldn. of JOHN COBB of Nort.
dtd. 14 May 1739 [9:186/7].

Order to Hopestill Ormsbe, widow & Exec. of Est. of JACOB ORMSBE
of Reho., dtd. 17 Apr. 1739 [9:187/8].
Will of JACOB ORMSBE of Reho., Yeoman, "Being very Sick and
weak," dtd. 1 March 1738/9, prob. 15 May 1739. Wife Hopestill.
Sons: Samuel & Jacob Ormsbe. Dau. Dorothey Wilmouth wife of
John Wilmouth. Grchldn. Waitstill Fuller & Jacob Fuller (both
under 21). Grdau. Ruth Fuller. Wife to be Exec. Witns: Edward
Martin, Daniel Ormsbe & Samuel Thurber [9:188/9/90].
Order to Nehemiah Walker of Taun., Yeoman, Exec. of Est. of BAR-
SHEBA WALKER of Taun., dtd. 17 Apr. 1739 [9:190].
Will of BATHSHEBA WALKER, widow & relict of James Walker of
Taun., dtd. 25 March 1738/9, prob. 17 Apr. 1739. Daus: Eleze-
beth May (eldest), Bathsheba wife of Richard Godfrey, Meheti-
bel wife of Cornelius White, Mercy wife of Thomas Eliot, Re-
beccah wife of William Linkorn & Mary wife of John Gilbert.
Grdau. Elezebeth, wife of Samuel Andrews & dau. of my dau.
Elezebeth May. Son Nehemiah to be Exec. Other sons mentioned
but not named. Witns: Nathaniel Crossman, Hannah Woodward &
Robert Crossman [9:191/2].
Acct. of Abigail Church, widow & Adm. of Est. of ISRAEL CHURCH
of Brist., dtd. 17 Apr. 1739. Incl. money received: "of my
father Samuel Howland" & "of the Executors to the will of M^s
Grace Church decesed" [9:192/3].
Appt. of Abigail Church of Brist., widow, to be guard. of Sarah
Church (under 14), dau. of ISRAEL CHURCH of Brist., dtd. 17
Apr. 1739 [9:194].
Appt. of Benjamin Hodges of Nort., Yeoman, to be guard. as cho-
sen by Mary Cobb (minor over 14), dau. of JOHN COBB of Nort.,
dtd. 14 May 1739 [9:194/5].
Order for Nicholas Howland of Dart., Yeoman, Exec. of Est. of
his mother HANNAH HOWLAND of Dart., widow, dtd. 21 May 1739
[9:195/6].
Will of HANNAH HOWLAND of Dart., widow, dtd. 29 March 1734, prob.
21 May 1739. Sons: Samuel, Nicholas, Daniel, Job & Benjamin
Howland. Daus: Abigail Russel, Mary Tucker, Rebeccah Sandford,
Hannah Wood & Edith Howland (first 3 called "eldest" & last
2 called "youngest"). Son Nicholas to be Exec. Sons-in-law
Benjamin Russel & Joseph Tucker to have oversight of my dau.
Edith while she is a minor. Witns: Isaac Chace, James Peck-
com & William Bowdish [9:196/7/8].
Inv. of Est. of HANNAH HOWLAND of Dart., dtd. 14 May 173[?],
pres. 21 May 1739 by Nicholas Howland, son & Exec. Pers. est.
1701-13-1; no real est. Apprs: Jabiz Barker, Henry Howland
& James Howland [9:198/9].
Acct. of George Leonard, Esq., Adm. of Est. of JOHN COBB of
Nort. dcd. intest., dtd. 14 May 1739. Incl. paym. to the wi-
dow [not named] for provisions for the family [9:200/1].
Acct. of John Baker, only surviving Exec. of his brother-in-law
GEORGE WOOD of Swan., Weaver, dtd. 15 May 1739. Incl. legacies

to: Rebeccah Wood, widow of George; to Rebeccah Wood, dau. &
to Gershom Wood, son [9:201/2/3].
Order to Martha Maxey of Attl., widow, Exec. of Est. of her husb.
BENJAMIN MAXEY of Attl., dtd. 15 May 1739 [9:203/4].
Will of BENJAMIN MAXEY of Attl., Yeoman, "being Very Sick," dtd.
19 March 1738, prob. 15 May 1739. Wife Martha. No chldn. mentioned. Brothers Joseph Maxey, Henry Maxey & Josiah Maxey. Elexander Maxey son of my bro. Joseph Maxey. Wife Martha to be
Exec. Witns: John Follet, Benjamin Wise & John Foster [9:
204/5].
Order to Sarah Thurston, widow, & Samuel Gray, Yeoman, both of
Lit. Comp., Execs. of Est. of EDWARD THURSTON of Lit. Comp.,
dtd. 15 May 1739 [9:205/6].
Will of EDWARD THURSTON of Lit. Comp., Yeoman, dtd. 20 March
1738/9, prob. 15 May 1739. Wife Sarah. Only son George Thurston. Daus: Mary Brownel, Elezebeth White, Ruth Thurston, Sarah Thurston & Hope (youngest, under 21) Thurston. Wife Sarah
& friend Samuel Gray to be Execs. Indian boy Isaac & unnamed
negro man. Witns: Benjamin Southworth, William Richmond &
Thomas Brownel [9:206/7/8].
Inv. of Est. of EDWARD THURSTON of Lit. Comp., dtd. 18 Apr. 1739,
pres. by Sarah Thurston & Samuel Gray, Execs. Pers. est. 716-
9-6; real est. 3000-0-0. Apprs: John Palmer, James Rouse &
William Richmond [9:208/9].
Appt. of Jonathan Kingsley of Reho., Yeoman, to be guard. as
chosen by Joseph Franklen (minor over 14), son of JOHN FRANK-
LEN, dtd. 15 May 1739 [9:209/10].
Inv. of Est. of JAMES BOWEN of Reho., dtd. 12 Apr. 1739, pres.
by Elezebeth Bowen, widow & Exec. Pers. est. 729-13-1; real
est. 850-0-0. Apprs: Jonathan Kingsley, Samuel Bullock & Samuel Bullock, Jr. [9:210].
Acct. of Sarah Paddock, widow & Exec. of Est. of JAMES PADDOCK
of Swan., dtd. 15 May 1739 [9:211].
Acct. of Dorothey Wiliston, Adm. of Est. of ICABOD WILISTON of
Lit. Comp., dtd. 15 May 1739. Incl. item for an indian man
John [9:212/3].
Appt. of Mary Southworth, widow, & Constant Southworth, eldest
son, to be Adms. of Est. of JOSEPH SOUTHWORTH of Lit. Comp.
dcd. intest., dtd. 15 May 1739 [9:213/4].
Inv. of Est. of DANIEL HUNT of Reho., "Inholder," dtd. 22 March
1738/9, pres. by Dorothey Hunt, widow & Adm. Incl. a negro woman & her 2 chldn. [not named]. Pers. est. 1409-17-8; real
est. 1764-10-0. Apprs: Peres Bradford, Timothy Ide & Samuel
Mason [9:214/5].
Appt. of Baruch Bucklen of Reho., Yeoman, to be Adm. of Est. of
his father BARUCH BUCKLEN of Reho., Yeoman, dcd. intest., dtd.
19 June 1739 [9:215/6].
Appt. of Nathaniel Perry of East., Husbandman, to be Adm. of Est.
of JOSEPH SMITH of East., at the request of the widow, Dorothy

Smith, who refused Adm., dtd. 19 June 1739 [9:216/7].

Order to Freelove Kingsley of Swan., widow & Exec. of Est. of
her husb. OLIVER KINGSLEY of Swan., dtd. 19 June 1739[9:217/8].

Will of OLIVER KINGSLEY of Swan., Farmer, "Being Weak of body,"
dtd. 7 June 1739, prob. 19 June 1739. Wife Freelove. Sons: Pardon & Peleg Kingsley. Daus: Lidiah, Ann & Freelove. My wife's
father John Hail dcd. Wife to be Exec. Witns: John Turner,
Joseph Kingsley, Thomas Wood & Hezekiah Kingsley [9:218/9].

Acct. of Margaret Tree, late widow & Adm. of Est. of JOSEPH DAG-
GET of Attl. dcd. intest., dtd. 19 June 1739 [9:219/20].

Inv. of Est. of Capt. JOSEPH SOUTHWORTH of Lit. Comp., dtd. 18
May 1739, pres. by Martha Southworth & Constant Southworth,
Adms. Pers. est. 974-12-0; real est. 4800-0-0. Apprs: David
Hillard, Thomas Bailey & Nathaniel Searls, Jr. [9:220/1/2].

Rcpt. by William Earl of Portsmouth, R.I., Tanner, son of THO-
MAS EARL, for legacy from Est. of "our Honoured father and
mother" and also the Est. that was left "after the Decease of
my Brother Thomas Earl," as paid by my brother Oliver Earl,
dtd. 9 Nov. 1734. Witns: George Thomas & Mary Thomas[9:222].

Rcpt. by Israel Gibbs & Rebeckah Gibbs for legacy from Est. of
"our Honoured father and mother" THOMAS and MARY EARL, paid
by Oliver Earl, Exec., dtd. Swan. 11 Nov. 1734. Witns: William Manchester & James Alger [9:222].

Rcpt. by Sarah Earl for legacy from Est. of her father & mother
THOMAS & MARY EARL, paid by Oliver Earl, Exec., dtd. Swan. 11
Nov. 1734. Witns: James Luther & Elisha Baker [9:222].

Rcpt. by Lydia Tucker & Thomas Tucker for legacy from Est. of
"our Honoured father and mother" THOMAS & MARY EARL, paid by
Oliver Earl, Exec., dtd. Swan. 11 Nov. 1734. Witns: Sarah
Earl & Sarah Baker [9:222/3].

Rcpt. by Elisha Baker & his wife Mary Baker for legacy from Est.
of her parents, THOMAS & MARY EARL of Warwick, R.I., paid by
her brother Oliver Earl, Exec., dtd. 11 Nov. 1734. Mentions her
brother Thomas Earl dcd. & her brother William Earl. Her brother Oliver became Exec. after the death of their mother, the
said MARY. Witns: Silas Carpenter & Philip Arnold [9:223].

Inv. of Est. of BARUCH BUCKLEN of Reho. dcd. intest., dtd. 6
June 1734, pres. 19 June 1739 by Baruch Bucklen, son & Adm.
Pers. est. 101-6-0; no real est. Apprs: Joseph Wheaten, Dan-
iel Carpenter & Timothey Ide [9:223/4].

Appt. of Ruth Joy of Reho., widow, to be Adm. of Est. of her
husb. DAVID JOY of Reho., Weaver, dcd. intest., dtd. 7 May.
1739 [9:224/5].

Inv. of Est. of DAVID JOY of Reho., Weaver, dtd. 1 May 1739,
pres. by Ruth Joy, widow & Adm. Pers. est. 407-13-5; real est.
1000-0-0. Apprs: Peres Bradford, Thomas Allen & Mathew Cushing [9:225/6].

Appt. of Amos Snel, Jr. of Bridgewater, Co. of Plimouth, Yeoman,
to be Adm. of Est. of THOMAS FREELOVE of Free., "at the request

of the widdow and Childreen," dtd. 19 June 1739 [9:226/7].
Appt. of Easther Maxfield of Brist., Spinster, to be Adm. of
Est. of THOMAS SWAN of Brist., Husbandman, dcd. intest., dtd.
28 May 1739 [9:227/8].
Appt. of Hannah Cook of Tiv., widow, to be Adm. of Est. of her
husb. CHAPLIN COOK of Tiv. dcd. intest., dtd. 17 July 1739
[9:228/9].
Acct. of Elnathan Pope, Exec. of Est. of his father ISAAC POPE
Dart., dtd. 17 July 1739. Mentions a legacy paid "to Alce Pope
Widdow of Isaac Pope" [9:229/30].
Rcpt. from Alec [sic] Pope of Dart., widow, for legacy from Est.
of her husb. ISAAC POPE of Dart., paid by her son Elnathan
Pope, Exec., dtd. 29 Nov. 1736. Witns: Samuel Spooner & Ste-
phen West, Jr. [9:230].
Rcpt. & discharge by Deborah Spooner, wife of Samuel Spooner of
Dart., for legacy from Est. of her father ISAAC POPE of Dart.,
paid by Elnathan Pope, Exec., dtd. 20 March 1738/9. Witns:
Ephraim Jenne & Stephen West, Jr. [9:230].
Rcpt. by Abigail Jenney, wife of John Jenney of Dart., for legacy from Est. of her father ISAAC POPE of Dart., paid by Elnathan Pope, Exec. Witns: James Elles & Stephen West, Jr.
[9:231].
Order to Elezebeth Bullock, widow, & to Israel Bullock, John
Bullock & Richard Bullock, all Yeomen of Barr., Execs. of Est.
of their husb. & father JOHN BULLOCK of Barr., dtd. 17 July
1739 [9:231/2].
Will of JOHN BULLOCK of Barr., Weaver, "being weak in Body,"
dtd. 10 March 1735/6, prob. 17 July 1739. Wife Elezebeth. 3
sons: Israel, John & Richard Bullock. 3 daus: Elezebeth Bullock, Prudence Bullock & Mary Bullock (all unmar.). Grdau.
Anne Brown. Wife & 3 sons to be Execs. Witns: Peleg Richmond,
Nathaniel Vial & Thomas Vial [9:232/3/4].
Order for div. of Est. of Dr. RICHARD BOWEN of Reho. dcd. intest.
dtd. 2 Oct. 1738 [9:234].
Div. of Est. of RICHARD BOWEN of Reho., Phisician, btwn. his
chldn: Thomas Bowen, Esq. (eldest son), Jabez Bowen (2nd son)
chldn. of Ebenezer Bowen dcd. (youngest son), Elezebeth Brown
(eldest dau.), Damaris Peck (2nd dau.) & Urania Bush wife of
John Bush (youngest dau.). Mentions lands in Reho., Attl. &
Barr. Comm: Richard Harding, Peres Bradford, Noah Carpenter,
John Sweetland & Jonathan Chaffey [9:235/6/7/8].
Appt. of George Brownel of Dart., Yeoman, to be guard. as cho-
sen by Seth Tabor (minor over 14), son of THOMAS TABOR of
Dart., dtd. 20 Aug. 1739 [9:238/9].
Appt. of Hannah Leadoyt of Attl., widow, to be guard. as chosen
by Joseph, Benjamin & James Leadoyt (minors over 14), sons of
BRYANT LEADOYT of Attl., dtd. 1 Aug. 1739 [9:239/40].
Appt. of Alce Brown of Portsmouth, R.I., widow, to be guard. as
chosen by Robert Brown (minor over 14), son of TOBIAS BROWN

of Tiv., dtd. 1 Aug. 1739 [9:240].

Order to Ruth Tisdal of Taun., widow & Exec. of Est. of her husb. JOSEPH TISDAL of Taun., dtd. 21 Aug. 1739 [9:240/1].

Will of JOSEPH TISDAL of Taun., dtd. 27 May 1739, prob. 21 Aug. 1739. Wife Ruth. Sons: Joseph, Loved, Seth, Job, Ebenezer & Simion Tisdal (last 2 under 21). Daus: Bathsheba Walker, Mary Tisdal wife of Israel Tisdal & Hannah Terry. Mentions his rights to lands "in ye New Township number one on the West Side of Conneticut River near Fort Dummer." Witns: Nathaniel Knapp, Stephen Wood & Benjamin Wilbour [9:241/2/3/4].

Inv. of Est. of JOSEPH SMITH of East., dtd. 29 June 1739, pres. by Nathaniel Perry, Adm. Pers. est. 177-17-0; real est. 280-0-0. Apprs: John Phillips, Eliphal Leonard & Benjamin Williams [9:245/6].

Appts. of Ann Hill of Reho., widow, to be guard. as chosen by Benjamin, William & Phebe Hill (minors over 14), chldn. of SAMUEL HILL of Reho., dtd. 18 Sept. 1739 [9:246/7].

Inv. of Est. of OLIVER KINGSLEY of Swan., dtd. 4 July 1739, pres. by Freelove Kingsley, widow & Exec. Pers. est. 301-11-6; real est. 650-0-0. Apprs: Hezekiah Luther, Hezekiah Bowen & John Wood, Jr. [9:247/8].

Acct. of Nathaniel Crossman, Exec. of Est. of his father ROBERT CROSSMAN of Taun., dtd. 21 Aug. 1739 [9:248/9].

Inv. of Est. of CHAPLIN COOK of Tiv., Yeoman, dtd. 20 July 1739, pres. by Hannah Cook, widow & Adm. Pers. est. 429-12-3; real est. 900-0-0. Apprs: Robert Bennit, Stephen Cook & Samuel Durphey [9:249/50].

Acct. of Ann Hill, Adm. of Est. of SAMUEL HILL of Reho., dtd. 18 Sept. 1739 [9:250/50½][*page numbering error*].

Memo. that Bonne, an Indian slave belonging to Est. of Capt. SHUBAL NORTON, was gone to sea when we took the inv., but is here valued, dtd. 17 Aug. 1739, pres. by Sarah Norton, widow & Adm. Value 133-5-0. Apprs: Samuel Royal, Samuel Smith & Joseph Russel [9:250½].

Acct. of Sarah Norton, widow & Adm. of Est. of SHUBAL NORTON of Brist., dtd. 7 Aug. 1739. Mentions a power of attorney "to Send to Munserat" [9:251].

Rcpt. by Thomas Durfey & Mary Durfey for legacy from Est. of her father THOMAS COREY OF Tiv., paid by William Corey of Newport & Philip Corey of Tiv., Execs., dtd. 31 Aug. 1739. Witns: John Willbour & Restcome Sandford [9:252].

Rcpt. by Susanah Corey, widow, for legacy from Est. of her husb. THOMAS COREY of Tiv., paid by William & Philip Corey, Execs., dtd. 13 Jan. 1738/9. Witns: Philip Tabor & Benjamin Wait [9:252].

Rcpt. by Samuel Cook & Patiance Cook for legacy from Est. of her father THOMAS COREY of Tiv., paid by Wm. Corey of Newp. & Philip Corey of Tiv., Execs., dtd. 31 Aug. 1739. Witns: John Willbour & Restcome Sandford [9:252].

Rcpt. from Abraham Brown & Sary Brown for legacy from Est. of her father THOMAS COREY of Tiv., paid by Wm. Corey of Newp. & Philip Corey of Tiv., Execs., dtd. 31 Aug. 1739. Witns: John Willbour & Restcome Sandford [9:252/3].

Appt. of comm. to rcv. & examine claims against Est. of SHUBAL NORTON of Brist., Mariner, it having been represented insolvent by Sarah Norton, widow & Adm., dtd. 5 Feb. 1737/8 [9:253].

Report of Comm. to examine claims against Est. of SHUBAL NORTON of Brist., dtd. 20 Sept. 1739. Comm: Jonathan Woodbury, Robert Joles & Samuel Royal [9:253/4/5].

Order to set off 1/3 of real est. of SHUBAL NORTON of Brist., Mariner, to his widow, Sarah Norton, dtd. 9 Aug. 1739 [9:255/6].

Setting off of 1/3 of real est. of Capt. SHUBAL NORTON of Brist. to his widow, Sarah Norton, dtd. 18 Sept. 1739 Comm: Samuel Royal, Joseph Raynolds, Samuel Smith, Benjamin Bosworth & Joseph Russel [9:256/7].

Acct. of James Tripp of Dart., Exec. of Est. of MARY GATCHEL of Dart., dtd. 16 Oct. 1739. Mentions payms. for: "Going to Rochester to Pay a Legacy to Mary Ellis," "a Legacy to Sarah Russel," "a Legacy to Pricilla Burgg" & "a Legacy to John Akin Guardian To Mary Gatchel and Susanah Gatchel"[9:257/8].

Acct. of James Tripp of Dart., Adm. of Est. of THOMAS GATCHEL of Dart., dtd. 16 Oct. 1739. Incl. legacies: to Mary Ellis in Rochester, to Pricilla Burge, to Sarah Russel, to John Gatchel dcd. & to "Captin Akin Guardian to the Childreen of said John Gatchel" [9:258/9].

Rcpts. by Sarah Russel of Dart. & Priscilla Burgg of Dart. for legacies from Est. of MARY GATCHEL, rcvd. from James Tripp, Exec. Witns: Henry Headley & Rachel Headley, dtd. 12 Oct. 1739 [9:259].

Rcpt. by John Akin for legacy from Est. of MARY GATCHEL of Dart. to her grchldn. Mary & Susanah Gatchel, said Akin being their guard., paid by James Tripp, Exec., dtd. March 1738/9. Witns: David Akin & John Akin [9:260].

Rcpt. from Sarah Russel for legacy from Est. of THOMAS GATCHEL, paid by James Tripp, Exec., dtd. 12 Oct. 1739. Witns: Henry Hedley & Rachel Hedley [9:260].

Order to Nathaniel Bosworth of Brist., Blockmaker, Exec. of Est. of BENJAMIN WARDWEL of Brist., dtd. 16 Oct. 1739 [9:260/1].

Will of BENJAMIN WARDWEL of Brist., "being in a very Weak and Low Condition," dtd. 29 Aug. 1739, prob. 16 Oct. 1739. No wife named. Sons: Usual, William, Jonathan, David & Isaac Wardwel. Daus: Mary & Olive [no surnames]. "To my Son in Law [stepson] Samuel Holmes Eldest Son of My Last Wife." My brother Joseph Wardwel. "My Beloved Brother in Law Nathaniel Bosworth of Bristol Blockmaker" to be Exec. Witns: Samuel Oxx, James Wardwel & Samuel Howland [9:261/2].

Appt. of John Tabor of Dart., Blacksmith, to be Adm. of Est. of
his son THOMAS TABOR of Dart., "Trayder," dtd. 16 Oct. 1739
[9:262/3].

Order to Icabod Bowen & Peter Bowen, Yeomen of Reho., Execs. of
Est. of their father RICHARD BOWEN of Reho., dtd. 18 Sept. 17-
39 [9:263].

Will of RICHARD BOWEN of Rehob., Husbandman, "being Very Sick
and Weak of body," dtd. 29 Aug. 1739, prob. 18 Sept. 1739.
Wife Patiance. Sons: Ichabod, Dan, Peter, Richard, Uriah, David & Christopher (dcd.) Bowen. Daus: Mary Cole & Zerviah
Jones [a widow? - she was given liberty of dwelling in his
house as long as she lives]. Grchldn. [not named](all under
21), chldn. of my son Christopher dcd. Sons Ichabod & Peter
to be Execs. Witns: Edward Glover, Ezekiel Carpenter & Rebecah Abel [9:264/5].

Acct. of Israel Dagget, Adm. of Est. of his sister HEPHZIBETH
CHAFFEY of Reho., dtd. 18 Sept. 1739. Incl. item to Jonathan
Chaffey, who was Adm. to Est. of his brother Noah [9:265/6/7].

Appt. of Ann Hill of Reho., widow, to be guard. of James Hill
(under 14), son of SAMUEL HILL of Reho., dtd. 18 Sept. 1739
[9:267].

Appt. of Israel Dagget of Reho., Yeoman, to be guard. of Hannah
Dagget (under 14), dau. of JOSEPH DAGGET of Attl., Yeoman, dtd.
18 Sept. 1739 [9:268].

Appt. of Thomas Lawton & Samuel Little to be Adms. of Est. of
"there Son [sic]" THOMAS LITTLE of Brist., Mariner, at request of his widow, dtd. 1 Sept. 1739 [9:268/9].

Appt. of Huldah Carpenter of Reho., widow, to be Adm. of Est.
of her husb. COMFORT CARPENTER of Reho., Gentleman, dcd. intest., dtd. 15 Oct. 1739 [9:269/70].

Acct. of James Tripp of Dart., Exec. of Est. of MARY GATCHEL of
Dart., dtd. 16 Oct. 1739. Incl. legacies paid: to Mary Ellis
in Rochester, to Sarah Russel, To Pricilla Burgg & to John
Akin as guard. of Mary Gatchel & Susanah Gatchel [9:270/1].

Appt. of Nathaniel Bosworth of Brist., Blockmaker, to be Adm.
of Est. of BENJAMIN WARDWEL, Jr. of Brist., since his father,
Benjamin Wardwel has since deceased, dtd. 27 Oct. 1739 [9:
271/2].

Appt. of James Leonard of Taun., Gentleman, to be guard. as chosen by Mary Paddock (minor over 14), dau. of JAMES PADDOCK of
Swan., dtd. 27 Oct. 1739 [9:272/3].

Appt. of Samuel Leonard, Jr. of Rayn., Yeoman, to be guard. as
chosen by David Hall & Edmund Hall (minors over 14), sons of
JAMES HALL of Rayn., dtd. 27 Oct. 1739 [9:273].

Acct. of Mary Southworth & Constant Southworth, Adms. of Est.
of JOSEPH SOUTHWORTH of Lit. Comp., dtd. 16 Oct. 1739. Incl.
paym. for "mourning Apparril for two of the Daughters." [9:
274/5].

Inv. of Est. of THOMAS TABOR of Dart., dtd. 12 Oct. 1739, pres.
by John Tabor, father & Adm. Pers. est. 207-18-9; real est.
140-0-0. Apprs: James Cushman, Samuel Spooner & Cornelius
Lewis [9:275/6].

Acct. of Mercy Finney, widow & Adm. of Est. of JONATHAN FINNEY
of Swan. dcd. intest., dtd. 16 Oct. 1739. Incl. payms. for:
"Clothing made up for the Childreen" & "Charge of Lying in
with a Posthumus Child" [9:276/8][*page numbering error*].

Acct. of Damaris Peck, Adm. of Est. of her husb. JATHNIEL PECK,
Jr. of Reho. dcd. intest., dtc. Oct. 1739 [9:279/80].

Acct. of "Elizebeth Powers Late Elizebeth Mackoon," Adm. of Est.
of her husb. THOMAS MACKOON of Swan., dtd. 24 Oct. 1739 [9:
280/1].

Appt. of Capt. Daniel Carpenter of Reho. to be guard. of Oliver
Carpenter (under 14), son of EDMUND CARPENTER of Reho., dtd.
20 Nov. 1739 [9:281/2].

Order to Josiah Hathaway of Dart., Exec. of Est. of his father
JOHN HATHAWAY of Dart., dtd. 20 Nov. 1739 [9:282].

Will of JOHN HATHAWAY of Dart., Yeoman, "Being Weak & A Declin-
ing Condition of Body," dtd. 20 Dec. 1738, prob. 20 Nov. 1739.
Wife Alce. 3 sons: Josiah, Zephaniah & John Hathaway. 3 daus:
Joannah, Rachel & Alce Hathaway. Son Josiah to be Exec. Witns:
Benjamin Russel, Nathaniel Spooner & Stephen West, Jr. [9:283
/4/5].

Acct. of Jonathan Chaffe, Adm. De Bonis non to Est. of NOAH
CHAFFE of Reho., dtd. 20 Nov. 1739. Incl. item. "for Laying
out Land for the Childreen" [9:285/6].

Appt. of Thomas Bowen of Reho., Esq., to be guard. as chosen by
Dorothey Hunt (minor over 14), dau. of DANIEL HUNT of Reho.,
dtd. 20 Nov. 1739 [9:286/7].

Order to Comfort Taylor of Lit. Comp. widow & Exec. of Est. of
her husb. PHILIP TAYLOR of Lit. Comp., dtd. 20 Nov. 1739 [9:
287/8].

Will of PHILIP TAYLOR of Lit. Comp., Cordwainer, "Being Sick
& Weak," dtd. 20 March 1739, prob. 20 Nov. 1739. Wife Comfort.
Sons: Joseph (eldest) & Philip (2nd son) Taylor (both under
21). 4 daus: Susanah Taylor, Abigail Taylor, Deborah Taylor &
Comfort Taylor (all under 18). Witns: Joseph Wood, William
Wilbour & Job Taylor [9:288/9/90].

Inv. of Est. of JOHN HATHAWAY of Dart., dtd. 5 Oct. 1739, pres.
by Josiah Hathaway, son & Exec. Pers. est. 270-9-1; real est.
965-0-0. Apprs: Jonathan Hathway, James Cushman & Jerah [*unclear*] Swift [9:290/1].

Inv. of Est. of COMFORT CARPENTER of Reho., dtd. 30 Oct. 1739,
pres. by Huldah Carpenter, widow & Adm. Incl. item for "Quarter Part of A Sloop Called the Joly venter." Pers. est. 841-
2-5; sloop share 140-0-0; real est. 1000-0-0. Apprs: Joseph
Wheaten, Edward Glover & Daniel Carpenter [9:291/2/3].

Order to Rachel Allen of Barr., widow & Exec. of Est. of her
husb. SAMUEL ALLEN of Barr., dtd. 13 Nov. 1739 [9:293].
Will of SAMUEL ALLEN of Barr., "Being Sick and Weak of Body,"
dtd. 23 Feb. 1731/2, prob. 13 Nov. 1739. Wife Rachel. Brothers
Daniel Allen, Ebenezer Allen & Joseph Allen. Sister Mary Adams.
Nephews Nathaniel Peck & Thomas Peck. Nephew Samuel Allen, son
of my brother Joseph Allen. To the Rev. Peleg Heath, my be-
loved friend. Wife to be Exec. Witns: Joshua Bicknel, John
Brailey & Sarah Thrasher [9:294/5/6].
Appt. of John Hunt of Reho., Yeoman, to be guard. as chosen by
Oliver Hunt (minor over 14), son of DANIEL HUNT of Reho., dtd.
26 Nov. 1739 [9:296/7].
Appt. of John Shapperd of Dart., Yeoman, to be guard. of Edward
Wingg (under 14), son of EDWARD WINGG of Dart., dtd. 20 Nov.
1739 [9:297].
Appt. of Abraham Tucker of Dart., Yeoman, to be Adm. of Est. of
his mother HANNAH TUCKER of Dart., widow, dcd. intest., dtd.
20 Nov. 1739 [9:298].
Inv. of Est. of PHILIP TAYLOR of Lit. Comp., dtd. 2 Nov. 1739,
pres. by Comfort Taylor, widow & Exec. Pers. est. 487-10-0;
real est. 1236-0-0. Apprs: James Rouse, William Richmond &
William Wilbour [9:299/300].
Order to John Brown of Newp., R.I., Mariner, Exec. of Est. of
his father NATHANIEL BROWN of Reho., dtd. 13 Dec. 1739 [9:
300/1].
Will of NATHANIEL BROWN of Reho., "Shipwright now Residing in
Providence...Now Aged and Well Stricken in years," dtd. 20
May 1738, prob. 5 Dec. 1739. No wife mentioned. Sons: Nathan-
iel (of Providence) & John Brown. Daus: Esther Sweeting, Sarah
Bullock, Penelope Butterworth, Lidia Chapman, Keziah Brown,
Elezebeth Thurston & Mary Brown (dcd.). Grson. Allen Brown.
"Grandson Peleg Brown the Son of my Daughter Mary Brown De-
ceased." Land in Reho. & in Providence. Son John to be Exec.
Witns: George Brown, Robert Nixon & Richard Waterman, Jr. [9:
301/2/3/4].
Order to Rebecah Carpenter of Reho., widow & Exec. of Est. of
her husb. EDMUND CARPENTER of Reho., dtd. 20 Nov. 1739 [9:
304].
Will of EDMUND CARPENTER of Reho., Cordwiner, "Being Weak of
Body," dtd. 29 June 1739, prob. 20 Nov. 1739. Wife Rebecah.
Son Oliver (under 16). Mentions lands in Reho. & Barr. Wife
to be Exec. Witns: Ezekiel Read, Thomas Read, Jr. & Daniel
Carpenter [9:305/6].
Inv. of Est. of EDMUND CARPENTER of Reho., dtd. 16 Aug. 1739,
pres. by Rebeccah Carpenter, widow & Exec. Pers. est. 381-2-6;
real est. 268-0-0. Apprs: John Humphrey, Edward Glover & Ezekiel Read [9:306/7].
Order to John Jones of Boston, Co. of Suffolk, Merchant, Exec.
of Est. of his father WILLIAM JONES of Reho., dtd. 30 Nov.

1739 [9:308].
Order to Jonathan Paddleford, Jr. of Taun., Yeoman, Exec. of
Est. of his wife SARAH PADDLEFORD of Taun., dtd. 18 Dec. 1739
[9:308/9].
Appt. of Noah Clafflen of Attl., Yeoman, to be guard. of his son
Noah Clafflen, grson. of JOHN FRENCH of Attl., dtd. 18 Dec.
1739 [9:309/10].
Appt. of Joseph Allen of Barr., Gentleman, to be guard. as cho-
sen by his son Samuel Allen (minor over 14), nephew of SAMUEL
ALLEN of Barr., dtd. 18 Dec. 1739 [9:310/1].
Agrmt. signed by heirs of JOSHUA SHERMAN of Dart., Yeoman, dtd.
11 Dec. 1739. Signers: Alce Sherman (his widow); Jonathan Sher-
man (son); Phebe Wood (dau.) & her husb. Daniel Wood. Witns:
Abraham Sherman & Samuel Willis [9:311/2].
Appt. of John Easterbrooks of Swan., Shipwright, to be guard. as
chosen by Joannah Franklen (minor over 14), dau. of JOHN FRANK-
LEN of Swan., dtd. 18 Dec. 1739 [9:312/3].
Appt. of Jabiz Bosworth of Reho., Gentleman, to be guard. as chosen by James Franklen (minor over 14), son of JOHN FRANKLEN of
Swan., dtd. 18 Dec. 1739 [9:313/4].
Appt. of John Tinkcom of Dart., Yeoman, to be Adm. of Est. of
his father JOHN TINKCOM of Dart. dcd. intest., dtd. 15 Jan.
1739 [9:314/5].
Order to Jonathan Linkon & John Andrews, Yeomen of Nort., Execs.
of Est. of ELEAZER EDDY of Nort., dtd. 15 Jan. 1739 [9:315/6].
Will of ELEAZER EDDY of Nort., "Being Near aboute the fifty
ninth year of my age and being but weak of Body," dtd. 7 Nov.
1739, prob. 15 Jan. 1739. No wife mentioned. Sons: John (eldest; living in Colchester, Conn.), Caleb (2nd), Eleazer (3rd),
Joshua (4th), Obediah, Jonathan & Oliver Eddy (last 3 under
21). Daus: Elizebeth Penney, Hannah Miller & Charity Baker.
Grson. John Penney, son of my dau. Elizebeth. Mentions his
homestead farm "which I have Improved this 40 years." 2 neighbors Jonathan Linkon & John Andrews to be guards. of my youngest sons Obediah, Jonathan & Oliver, said Linkon & Andrews to
be Execs. Witns: William Thayer, John Briggs, 2nd, George
Leonard & Hannah Thayer [9:316/7/8/9/20].
Will of WILLIAM JONES of Reho., Merchant, "Being very Sick and
Weak," dtd. 17 Sept. 1739, prob. 30 Nov. 1739. Wife Elizebeth.
Sons: John Jones of Boston in New Engl., Thomas Jones of Wil-
lington, Co. of Somerset in Great Brittain & William Jones
late of Newport dcd. Dau. Elizebeth Shorlan wife of Peter Shor-
lan "in Willington Aforesaid." My brothers & sister: Amos
Jones, John Jones & Margaret Ven wife of William Ven. The Rev.
Docter Timothey Culler of Boston. Persons of unstated relation-
ship: Joseph Marion of Boston; Israel Peck of Reho. & his wife
Elizebeth & Jonathan Bucklen of Reho. & his wife Margaret &
Peggy their dau. Son John to be Exec. Witns: John Humphrey,
John Bucklen & John Greenwood [9:320/1/2].

Will of SARAH PADDLEFORD, wife of Jonathan Paddleford, Jr. of
Taun., "Labouring under Illness and Indisposition of Body,"
dtd. 4 Dec. 1738, prob. 18 Dec. 1739. Husb. Jonathan Paddleford, Jr. Son Richard Wilson (under 21), who is given into
care of my husb. Jonathan. My father-in-law Jonathan Paddleford of Taun. My sister Abigail Paddleford of Taun. Mentions
monies due her on the island of Barbados from the family of
Hagburns, due me at the time of my intermarriage with said
Jonathan, from John Pickrin, John Waterman & one Gibbens all
of said island. Negro man Valeon. Negro woman Partheno. 2 negro men in Barbados named Catto & Grinnage. Negro boy Ulises
in Taun. Husb. Jonathan to be Exec. Witns: Peter Presho, Judath Chase & James Williams [9:322/3/4].
Acct. of Hannah Franklen, widow & Exec. of Est. of JOHN FRANK-
LEN of Swan., Cordwainer, dtd. 18 Dec. 1739. Mentions a bond
to the widow given to her by the dcd. John before marriage
[9:324/4/5][page numbering error].
Inv. of Est. of JOHN CHILD of Swan., Yeoman, dtd. 18 Dec. 1739,
pres. by John Child, son & Exec. Pers. est. 298-7-5; real est.
21-0-0. Apprs: Samuel Miller, Bernard Hail & Edward Luther
[9:325/6].
Will of JOSEPH RUSSEL of Dart., Yeoman, dtd. 11 March 1735/6,
prob. 18 Dec. 1739. Wife Elizebeth. Sons: Joseph, John, Benjamin & Seth (dcd.) Russel. Daus: Mary Lapham wife of John
Lapham, Rebeckah Barker wife of Jabiz Barker. Grson. William
Russel, son of my son Joseph. Grdaus: Elizebeth Russel, Constant Russel & Ruth Russel, daus. of my son Seth dcd. Grsons:
Joshua Smith & Caleb Smith, sons of Thomas Smith of Providence,
R.I. Grsons: Joseph Lapham & Joseph Barker. My cousin John
Russel. Mentions his grist mill. Sons John & Benjamin Russel
& son-in-law Jabiz Barker to be Execs. Witns: Isaac Shearman,
Thomas Kimpton, Zephaniah Tabor & Samuel Willis [9:327/8/9/-
30/1].
Appt. of Mary Fuller of Reho. to be guard. of Joseph, Aron &
Pricilla Peck, chldn. of JOSEPH PECK of Reho., dtd. 19 Feb.
1739 [9:332].
Appt. of Hannah Little of Brist., widow, to be guard. of her
dau. Haile Little, dau. of SAMUEL LITTLE of Brist., Gentleman,
dtd. 19 Feb. 1739 [9:332/3].
Appt. of Samuel Little of Brist., Mariner, to be Adm. of Est.
of his father SAMUEL LITTLE of Brist., Gentleman, dcd. intest.
dtd. 19 Feb. 1739 [9:333/4].
Order to William Read of Barr., Yeoman, Exec. of Est. of his father JOHN READ of Barr., dtd. 19 Feb. 1739 [9:334/5].
Will of JOHN READ of Barr., Yeoman, "being Weak of Body," dtd.
6 June 1739, prob. 19 Feb. 1739. Wife included but not named;
she to rcv. "that which I Engaged her before Marrage." Sons:
John, William & George (dcd.) Read. Daus: Mercy Tiffeny & Bethiah Watson. Grson. George Read, son of my son George Read dcd.

Dau-in-law Abigail Read, widow of my son George dcd. "Charles
Peck Whom I Brought up" (under 21). Mentions lands in Barr. &
in Willington [*location not stated*]. Land rights in Narraganset to go to son John. Son William to be Exec. Witns: David
Turner, Timothey Lefavour & Elizebeth Lefavour [9:335/6/7].

Order to Thomas Joles of Brist., Yeoman, Exec. of Est. of his
father ROBERT JOLES of Brist., dtd. 19 Feb. 1739 [9:337/7½]
[*page numbering error*].

Will of ROBERT JOLES of Brist., Yeoman, "Being Weak of Body,"
dtd. 14 Jan. 1739/40, prob. 19 Feb. 1739. Wife Experiance.
Son Thomas Joles. Dau. Mary Munroe. Negros: Barsh & Dimme (women), Kate (girl) & Gad & Cesar (lads). Son Thomas to be Exec.
Witns: James Smith, Samuel Miller & David Turner [9:337½/8/9].

Order to Seth Spooner of Dart., Yeoman, Exec. of Est. of his
father SAMUEL SPOONER of Dart., dtd. 19 Feb. 1739 [9:339/40].

Will of SAMUEL SPOONER of Dart., Yeoman, dtd. 21 Sept. 1731,
prob. 19 Feb. 1739. Wife Experiance. Sons: William, Samuel,
Seth, Daniel, Wing & Joshib Spooner. 5 daus: Mary, Hannah,
Annah, Experiance & Bulah [*no surnames*]. Son Seth to be Exec.
Witns: William Badcock, Thomas Waist, Thomas Pope & Timothey
Ruggles [9:340/1/2].

Order to Jonathan Buffington of Swan., Yeoman, Exec. of Est. of
his father BENJAMIN BUFFINGTON of Swan., Yeoman, dtd. 4 Feb.
1739 [9:342/3].

Will of BENJAMIN BUFFINGTON of Swan., Husbandman, dtd. 7 July
1733, prob. 4 Feb. 1739. Wife included but not named. Sons:
Benjamin, William, Joseph & Jonathan Buffington. 3 daus: Elez-
ebeth Baker, Easther Chace & Hannah Buffington. Directs son
Jonathan to "maintain his Grandmother So Long as She Liveth."
Son Jonathan to be Exec. Witns: Jonathan Blethen, Peleg Chace
& John Blethn, Jr. [9:343/4].

Order to Hezekiah Cole of Swan., Yeoman, Exec. of Est. of his
father JOHN COLE, 2nd, of Swan., Yeoman, dtd. 19 Feb. 1739
[9:344/5].

Will of JOHN COLE "ye Second of Swanzey," Yeoman, "Being Sick
and Weak of Body," dtd. 4 Jan. 1739/40, prob. 19 Feb. 1739.
Wife Deborah; part of what she is to receive is "Whatsoever
that She Brought to me att and Since our marrage." Sons: John,
Hezekiah & Seth Cole. Daus: Joanna wife of Timothey Smith &
Mary wife of William Case. Indian girl Deliverance. Son Hezekiah to be Exec. Witns: Andrew Cole, Joseph Cole & Peres Bradford [9:345/6/7/8].

Appt. of Mercy Finney of Swan., widow, to be guard. of Hannah
Finney, dau. of JONATHAN FINNEY of Swan., dtd. 19 Feb. 1739
[9:348/9].

Appt. of Joseph Wardwel of Brist., Cordwainer, to be guard. as
chosen by William Wardwel (minor over 14), son of BENJAMIN
WARDWEL of Brist., dtd. 19 Feb. 1739 [9:349/50].

Appt. of Elizebeth Finch of Reho., widow, to be Adm. of Est. of
her husb. HENRY FINCH of Reho. dcd. intest., dtd. 19 Feb. 1739
[9:350/1].
Appt. of William Hix of Dart., Yeoman, to be guard. as chosen
by Thomas Corey (minor over 14), son of THOMAS COREY of Dart.
dtd. 19 Feb. 1739 [9:351/2].
Inv. of Est. of BENJAMIN BUFFINGTON of Swan., dtd. 14 Jan. 1739/
40, pres. by Jonathan Buffington, son & Exec. Pers. est. 434-
7-1; real est. 1980-0-0. Apprs: Edward Simmons, Miel Pearce &
William Hart [9:352/3].
Appt. of Caleb Luther of Swan., Yeoman, to be guard. as chosen
by William Easterbrooks (minor over 14), son of THOMAS EASTER-
BROOKS of Swan., dtd. 19 Feb. 1739 [9:353/4].
Acct. of Penelope Butterworth, widow & Adm. of Est. of NOAH BUT-
TERWORTH of Reho., dtd. 7 March 1739 [9:354/5].
Order to Elezebeth Marick of Taun., widow & Exec. of Est. of her
husb. STEPHEN MARICK of Taun., dtd. 13 March 1739 [9:356].
Will of STEPHEN MARICK of Taun., "much Indisposed and Weak of
Body," dtd. 25 May 1739. prob. 13 March 1739. Wife Elezebeth.
No chldn. mentioned. Wife to be Exec. Witns: Seth Williams,
Richard Godfrey & Rebecah Pitts [9:356/7].
Appt. of Benjamin Bosworth of Brist., Yeoman, to be Adm. of Est.
of MARY RAYNOLDS of Brist., "by the Request of all the Childreen of the Said MS Mary Raynolds," dtd. 18 Feb. 1739 [9:357
/8].
Inv. of Est. of MARY RAYNOLDS of Brist., dtd. 19 Feb. 1739/40,
pres. by Benjamin Bosworth, Adm. Pers. est. 286-2-6; real est.
450-0-0. Apprs: Samuel Royal, Samuel Smith & Joseph Russel
[9:358/9].
Agrmt. abt. div. of Est. btwn. chldn. of MARY RAYNOLDS of Brist.,
dcd. intest., dtd. 22 Feb. 1739, signed by chldn: Peter Raynolds of Infield, Co. of Hampshire, Mass., Clerk; Eleazer Raynolds & Nathaniel Raynolds, Cordwainer; and Mary Church & her
husb. Constant Church of Brist., Gentleman. Mentions her real
est. "in the Coloney of Conneticut," & in Brist. Witns: Stephen Paine & Benjamin Bosworth [9:359/60/1/2].
Appt. of Jonathn Bucklen of Reho. to be Adm. of Est. of his brother BENJAMIN BUCKLEN of Reho., "att the Request of the Brothers," dtd. 19 Feb. 1739 [9:362/3].
Appt. of John Newel & Moses Newel, both of Brookline, Co. of Suffolk, Mass., to be Adms. of Est. of MARAH ROGERS of Reho. dcd.
intest., dtd. 19 Feb. 1739. Said John & Moses are sons of Mary
Newel of said Brookline, "Who is Nearest akin" to MARAH ROGERS,
but is advanced in years & under bodily infirmity & cannot
take Adm. [9:363/4].
Appt. of Henry Sampson of Dart., Yeoman, to be guard. as chosen
by Hezekiah Tinkcom & Martha Tinkcom (minors over 14), chldn.
of JOHN TINKCOM of Dart., dtd. 18 March 1739 [9:364/5].

Appt. of Joseph Tabor of Dart., Yeoman, to be guard. as chosen
by Peter Tinkcom (minor over 14), son of JOHN TINKCOM of Dart.
dtd. 18 March 1739 [9:365/6].

Appt. of Amos Bosworth of Reho., Yeoman, to be guard. as chosen
by Samuel Ingols (minor over 14), son of EDMUND INGOLS of Reho., dtd. 18 March 1739 [9:367].

Order to James Walker & Nathaniel Walker, Yeomen of Reho., Execs.
of Est. of their father PHILIP WALKER of Reho., Yeoman, dtd.
18 March 1739 [9:367/8].

Will of PHILIP WALKER of Reho., Yeoman, dtd. 15 March 1739, prob.
18 March 1739. No wife mentioned. Sons: Nathaniel, James, Philip, Daniel & Stephen Walker. Daus: Esther Avery, Sarah Holdrige
Mary Robinson & Jane Newman. Grsons: Oliver, Philip & Elijah
Walker, sons of my son Philip. Mentions lands in Reho. & Attl.
Sons James & Nathaniel to be Execs. Witns: Timothey Ide, Daniel Ide & Edward Glover [9:368/9/70/1].

Inv. of Est. of BARUCH BUCKLEN of Reho. dcd. intest., dtd. 25
Feb. 1739/40, pres. by Hannah Bucklen, widow & Adm. Pers. est.
368-14-0; real est. 1273-6-8. Apprs: Daniel Perrin, Daniel
Carpenter & Obediah Read [9:371/2].

Inv. of Est. of PHILIP WALKER of Reho., dtd. 10 March 1739/40,
pres. by James Walker & Nathaniel Walker, Execs. Pers. est.
170-0-0; real est. 1580-0-0. Apprs: Nathaniel Mason, Daniel
Ide & Edward Glover [9:372/3].

Appt. of Hannah Bucklen of Reho., widow, to be Adm. of Est. of
her husb. BARUCH BUCKLEN of Reho. dcd. intest., dtd. 18 March
1739 [9:373/4].

Inv. of Est. of BENJAMIN BUCKLEN of Reho., dtd. 18 March 1739,
pres. by Jonathan Bucklen, Adm. Pers. est. 99-9-6; no real
est. Apprs: Ezekiel Read, David Whiple & Ezekiel Carpenter
[9:374/5].

Inv. of Est. of ROBERT JOLES of Brist., dtd. 14 March 1739/40,
pres. by Thomas Joles, son & Exec. Pers. est. 1603-2-8; real
est. 2266-0-0. Incl. negros: Bash, Demme, Ceaser, Gad, Dianna,
Mino, Rose & Cate. Apprs: John Throop, Thoms Kinnicut & Thomas Throop, Jr. [9:375/6].

Inv. of Est. of NATHANIEL BROWN of Reho., dtd. 7 Dec. 1739,
pres. by John Brown, son & Exec. Pers. est. 51-8-0; no real
est. Apprs: Samuel Mason, Noah Mason & Samuel Bairsto[9:377].

Inv. of Est. of Capt. SAMUEL LITTLE of Brist., dtd. 27 Feb. 1739,
pres. by Samuel Little, son & Adm. Incl. ferry boat & "farm
with ye ferry." Pers. est. 1355-4-0; real est. 6500-0-0.
Apprs: Samuel Royal, Benjamin Bosworth & Samuel Woodbury [9:
377/8/9].

Order to Joseph Wood of Lit. Comp., Yeoman, Exec. of Est. of
his father JOHN WOOD of Lit. Comp., dtd. 18 March 1739[9:380].

Will of JOHN WOOD of Lit. Comp., Yeoman, dtd. 23 Jan. 1733, prob.
18 March 1739. Wife Mary. Son Joseph Wood. Daus: Mary wife of
John Bailey, Dorothey wife of Joseph Rogers & Hannah Peck.

Sons & daus. [*not named*](all under 21) of my dau. Hannah Peck.
My negro Rose. Son Joseph to be Exec. Witns: John Wood, Jr.,
Constant Southworth & Joseph Southworth [9:380/1/2].
Inv. of Est. of JOHN WOOD of Lit. Comp., dtd. 8 March 1739/40,
pres. by Joseph Wood, son & Exec. Pers. est. 656-4-4; real
est. 3500-0-0. Apprs: William Richmond, Samuel Gray & Nathan-
iel Searl, Jr. [9:382/3/4].
Inv. of Est. of RICHARD BOWEN of Reho., dtd. 1 Oct. 1739, pres.
by Ichabod & Peter Bowen, Execs. Pers. est. 318-7-6; real est.
13910?[*unclear*]. Apprs: Edward Glover, Ezekiel Carpenter &
Noah Newman [9:384].
Inv. of Est. of JOHN READ of Barr., dtd. 28 Feb. 1739, pres. by
William Read, Exec. Pers. est. [?]; real est. 650-0-0. Apprs:
Mathew Allen, Josiah Humphrey & James Smith [9:385/6].
Inv. of Est. of JOHN TINKCOM of Dart., dtd. 26 Feb. 1739/40,
pres. by [*blank*] Tinkcom, son & Adm. Incl. numerous lots.
Pers. est. 214-8-16; real est. 4627-0-0. Apprs: Cornelius
Jenney, Henry Sampson & Jonathan Delino [9:386/7].
Rcpt. by Nathaniel Munroe of Brist. & his wife Mary for legacy
from Est. of her father ROBERT JOLES of Brist., paid by Thomas
Joles, Exec., dtd. 22 Apr. 1740. Witns: Stephen Paine & Wil-
liam Munroe [9:388].
Appt. of Thomas Smith of Dart., Yeoman, to be guard. as chosen
by Abraham Wingg (minor over 14), son of EDWARD WINGG of Dart.
dtd. 15 Apr. 1740 [9:389/90].
Order to Jonathan Thurston of Newport, R.I., Merchant, Exec. of
Est. of his father JONATHAN THURSTON of Dart., dtd. 15 Apr.
1740 [9:390].
Will of JONATHAN THURSTON of Lit. Comp., Yeoman, "but now Resident and Living in Dartmouth...Being weak of Body," dtd. 22
Apr. 1735, prob. 15 Apr. 1740. No wife mentioned. Sons: Edward, Jonathan, Joseph & Job Thurston. Daus: Mary Brownel, Content Wood, Abigail White, Susanah Carr, Elenor Peters, Patiance
Southworth & Sarah Sawday [*last 3 apparently dcd.*]. Grson.
Lovet Peters son of my dau. Elenor. Grdau. Rebeccah Southworth
dau. of my dau. Patiance. Chldn. [*not named*] of my dau. Sarah
Sawday. Witns: Nathaniel Soul, Francis Tripp & William Hix
[9:390/1/2].
Appts. of Benjamin Allen of Dart., Yeoman, to be guard. as chosen by Constant Russel & Elezebeth Russel (minors over 14) &
of Ruth Russel (under 14), chldn. of SETH RUSSEL of Dart.,
dtd. 15 Apr. 1740 [9:393/4].
Order to Stephen Shearman of Dart., Yeoman, Exec. of Est. of his
father PHILIP SHEARMAN of Dart., dtd. 15 Apr. 1740 [9:394/5].
Will of PHILIP SHEARMAN of Dart., Yeoman, dtd. 16 May 1737, prob.
15 Apr. 1740. Wife Hannah. Sons: Jabiz, Stephen, John (dcd.),
Ichabod & Abraham Shearman. Grson. John Shearman (under 21)
son of my son John dcd. Dau-in-law Margaret Shearman [*widow
of son John dcd.?*]. My brother Timothey Shearman. Son Stephen

to be Exec. Witns: William Sandford, Jonathan Shearman & Barnabas Russel [9:395/6/7/8/9].

Appt. of Isaac Bucklen of Reho., Yeoman, to be Adm. of Est. of BARUCH BUCKLEN of Reho., because the previous Adm., Baruch Bucklen, son of BARUCH dcd., is also now dcd., dtd. 15 Apr. 1740 [9:399/400].

Appt. of Benjamin Davice of Attl., Yeoman, to be guard. as chosen by Sarah Davice (minor over 14), dau. of JOSEPH DAVICE of Attl., dtd. 15 Apr. 1740 [9:400].

Inv. of Est. of NATHANIEL BROWN of Reho., dtd. 7 Dec. 1739, pres. by John Brown, son & Exec. Pers. est. 151-8-0; no real est. Apprs: Noah Mason, Samuel Mason & Samuel Bairsto [9:400¾] [page numbering error].

Order to Samuel Bourden of Tiv., Yeoman, Adm. of Est. of his brother THOMAS BOURDEN of Tiv., who dcd. during the minority of his son Richard Bourden, said Richard having been appointed Exec. in the will, dtd. 15 Apr. 1740 [9:400½].

Will of THOMAS BOURDEN of Tiv., Yeoman, dtd. 27 Feb. 1740, prob. 15 Apr. 1740. Wife Mary. Sons: Richard (eldest) & Christopher (2nd, under 21) Bourden. Daus: Deborah Bourden (eldest), Mary Bourden & Rebeccah Bourden (last 2 under 18). Mentions lands in Tiv. & Dart. Witns: Thomas Shearman, Benjamin Jenks & John Bowen [9:400½/400-3/4/401/401½].

Inv. of Est. of JONATHAN THURSTON of Dart., dtd. 8 Apr. 1740, pres. by Jonathan Thurston, son & Exec. Incl. only clothes & bonds due him. Total value 357-11-0. Apprs: Nathaniel Soul, Ichabod Potter & William Hix [9:401½/2].

Inv. of Est. of THOMAS FREELOVE of Free., Yeoman, dtd. 22 June 1739, pres. by Amos Snel, Adm. Pers. est. 179-18-6; real est. 70-0-0. Apprs: Aron Bowen, Caleb Bowen & Joseph Read, Jr. [9:402/3].

Inv. of Est. of ELEAZER EDDY of Nort., dtd. 22 Jan. 1739/40, pres. by Jonathan Linkon & John Andreas, Execs. Pers. est. 417-8-11; no real est. Apprs: George Leonard, William Thayer & John Briggs, 2nd [9:403/4/5].

Agrmt. abt. div. of Est. of MARY COLE, first wife of John Cole, 2nd (dcd.) of Swan. btwn. her only chldn: Seth Cole, Blacksmith & Mary wife of William Case, Husbandman, all of Swan.; Joannah wife of Timothey Smith of Berkley, Husbandman; John Cole & Hezekiah Cole. Mentions their grandfather Nathaniel Lewis, dtd. 18 Apr. 1740. Witns: Peres Bradford, John Throope, Jr. & Stephen Paine [9:405/6/7].

Order to Mrs. Margaret Watts of Brist., widow & sole legatee, Exec. of Est. of her husb. RICHARD WATTS of Brist., Clerk, dtd. 1 May 1740 [9:408].

Will of RICHARD WATTS of Brist., Clerk, "Being very weak and Ill," dtd. 15 March 1739, prob. 1 May 1740. Wife Margaret, who is also Exec. Witns: John Usher, William Cox & Samuel Howland [9:408/9].

Acct. of "Sarah Chandler formerly Sarah Paine," Adm. of Est. of
her former husb. NATHANIEL PAINE of Brist., dtd. 2 May 1740.
Incl. paym. for "Charges of Lying with A Posthumus Child."
Item "To the Supporting my Childreen with Clothing and Pro-
vision in Sickness and health and for the Scholing & c Near
Ten year" [9:410/1].

Appt. of Huldah Carpenter of Reho., widow, to be guard. of Cyr-
ril, Cloe, Cynthia, Orinda & Comfort Carpenter (all under 14),
chldn. of COMFORT CARPENTER of Reho., dtd. 20 May 1740[9:412].

Appt. of Philip Wheler of Reho., Yeoman, to be Adm. of Est. of
his brother JAMES WHELER of Reho., dcd. intest., dtd. 20 May
1740, the widow having refused Adm. [9:412/3].

Appt. of Mary Church of Brist., widow, to be Adm. of Est. of
CONSTANT CHURCH of Brist., dtd. 20 May 1740 [9:413/4].

Appt. of Samuel Bullock, Jr. of Reho., Yeoman, to be guard. as
chosen by James Wheler (minor over 14), son of JAMES WHELER
of Reho., dtd. 20 May 1740 [9:414/5].

Appt. of Huldah Carpenter of Reho., widow of Comfort Carpenter
dcd., to be Adm. of Est. of her mother-in-law ELEZEBETH CARPEN-
TER of Reho., mother of said Comfort, dtd. 20 May 1740[9:415].

Order to Hannah Waldroon of Brist., widow & Exec. of Est. of her
husb. ISAAC WALDROON of Brist., dtd. 15 July 1740 [9:416].

Will of ISAAC WALDROON of Brist., "Being under Considerable Ill-
ness of Body," dtd. 26 June 1740, prob. 15 July 1740. Wife
Hannah. My brother Cornelius Waldroon. My sister Martha Nibbs.
Chldn. [not named] of my brother Cornelius. Witns: Samuel
Smith, John Bragg & Samuel Howland [9:416/7/8].

Inv. of Est. of JOHN COLE, 2nd, of Swan., Yeoman, dtd. 21 Feb.
1739/40, pres. by Hezekiah Cole, son & Exec. Pers. est. 221-
0-0; real est. 1800-0-0. Apprs: Peres Bradford, Caleb Luther
& Andrew Cole [9:418/9].

Appt. of Mary Welman of Nort., widow, to be Adm. of Est. of her
husb. ISAAC WELMAN of Nort. dcd. intest., dtd. 17 June 1740
[9:419/20].

Appt. of John Kinnicut of Swan., Cordwainer, to be Adm. of Est.
of JOANNAH FINNEY of Swan., dtd. 17 June 1740 [9:420/1].

Order to William Wilbour of Lit. Compt., Yeoman, Exec. of Est.
of his father SAMUEL WILBOUR of Lit. Comp., dtd. 17 June 1740
[9:421].

Order to John & William Maccomber, both of Dart., Execs. of Est.
of their father ABIAL MACCOMBER of Dart., dtd. 17 June 1740
[9:422].

Will of ABIAL MACCOMBER of Dart., Yeoman, dtd. 22 May 1740, prob.
17 June 1740. My mother Bethyah Maccomber. Brothers: Philip,
John, William & Job Maccomber (last 3 are youngest). Sisters
Mary Closson & Mary [sic] Maccomber. Uncle Ephraim Maccomber.
Brothers John & William to be Execs. Witns: Daniel Tripp, Oth-
niel Tripp & Philip Tabor [9:423/4].

Inv. of Est. of ISAAC WELMAN of Nort., Husbandman, dtd. 7 March

1739/40, pres. by Mary Welman, Adm. Pers. est. 166-5-5; real
est. 740-0-0. Apprs: Ephraim Grover, Sr., Benjamin Williams
& William Dean [9:424/5].

Acct. of James Cole of Swan., Adm. of Est. of MARY COLE of Swan.
dcd. intest., dtd. 17 June 1740 [9:425/6].

Inv. of Est. of JOSEPH RUSSEL of Dart., Yeoman, dtd. 24 Dec. 17-
39, pres. by John Russel, Benjamin Russel & Joseph Barker, Execs. Pers. est. 1360-8-0; no real est. Apprs: Isaac Smith,
James Howland & Isaac Shearman [9:426/7].

Declaration by Hannah Vial of Barr., widow of JONATHAN VIAL of
Barr., that she sets free her negro slave servant named Henry
Bridge, dtd. 2 May 1733. Witns: Elizebeth Vial & Peleg Heath
[9:427/8].

Will of SAMUEL WILBOUR of Lit. Comp., Yeoman, dtd. 14 Jan. 1729/
30, prob. 17 June 1740. No wife mentioned. Sons: Samuel, William & Isaac (under 21) Wilbour. Daus: Martha Pearce, Mary
Brownel, Johanah Taylor, Thankful Irish, Elizebeth Peckcom,
Abial [sic] Wilbour & Hannah Wilbour. Son William to be Exec.
Witns: Samuel Coe, William Peabody, Jr. & Joseph Peabody [9:
428/9/30].

Inv. of Est. of SAMUEL WILBOUR of Lit. Comp., dtd. 11 June 1740,
pres. by Samuel [sic] Wilbour, son & Exec. Pers. est. 2534- ·
13-3; real est. 2810-0-0. Apprs: William Richmond, Joseph
Wood & William Peabody, Jr. [9:430/1/2].

Inv. of Est. of THOMAS LITTLE of Brist., dtd. 14 Apr. 1740, pres.
by Thomas Lawton, the only surviving Adm. Pers. est. 283-10-
6; no real est. Apprs: Samuel Royal, Joshua Bailey & Samuel
Smith [9:432].

Acct. of Joshua Bailey & Francis Ball, Adms. of Est. of JONATHAN
BALL of Brist., dtd. 17 June 1740 [9:433].

Order to Elizebeth Bishop of Attl, widow & Exec. of Est. of her
husb. SAMUEL BISHOP of Attl, dtd. 17 June 1740 [9:434].

Will of SAMUEL BISHOP of Attl., "Being Sick and Weak," dtd. 19
Oct. 1739, prob. 17 June 1740. Wife Elizebeth. Sons Samuel Bishop (under 21), dau. Mehetibel & "the Child unborn Which my
Wife Now Goes with." Wife to be Exec. Witns: Timothey Tingley, Benjamin Day & Noah Carpenter [9:434/5/6].

Div. of Est. of EBENEZER PITTS of Dighton, Yeoman, btwn. his
daus: Elizebeth wife of John Paul, Mary wife of Samuel Andrews,
Hopestill wife of Nathaniel Talbut & Mercy Pitts (youngest),
dtd. 4 May 1734. Comm: Abraham Shaw, Henry Pitts & Abraham
Waldroon [9:436/7].

Order to Nathaniel Bosworth of Brist., Gentleman, Exec. of Est.
of his mother MARY BOSWORTH of Brist., dtd. 17 June 1740 [9:
438].

Will of MARY BOSWORTH of Brist., widow, dtd. 2 Apr. 1735, prob.
17 June 1740. Sons: Nathaniel & Benjamin Bosworth. Daus: Bridget, Mary [no surnames] & Esther (dcd.) wife of Obediah Papillion. Grsons: John Papillion, Samuel Papillion & Peter Papillion

sons of my dau. Esther dcd. Grdau. Bridget Bosworth dau. of
my son Nathaniel. Son Nathaniel to be Exec. Witns: William
Gladding, Jr., Jonathan Gladding & Samuel Howland [9:438/9].
Rcpt. from Abraham Samson & Penelope Samson of Duxbury for legacy from Est. of "my Hono[d] Father" JAMES SAMSON of Dart., paid
by "Brother Henry Samson," Exec., dtd. Duxbury 23 Nov. 1727
[9:440].
Quit-claim by "James Samson of Wells in the County of York...
Massachusets Bay," Yeoman, to his brother Henry Samson of Dart.
Husbandman, of all his rights to the thirds their mother, Hannah Samson, rcvd. from Est. of his father JAMES SAMSON, dtd.
24 July 1726. Witns: Mary Adams & William Palmer [9:440].
Rcpt. by Benjamin Hilmon & Susanah Hilmon of Dart. for legacy
from Est. of her father JAMES SAMSON of Dart., paid by brother
Henry Samson, Exec., dtd. 11 Dec. 1727. Witns: Rebeccah Samson & John Clark [9:440].
Rcpt. by Joseph Samson of Dart. for legacy from Est. of his father JAMES SAMSON of Dart., paid by his brother Henry Samson,
dtd. 8 Dec. 1727. Witns: Rebeccah Samson & John Rouse[9:440/1].
Rcpt. by Solomon [sic] Hammond & Pricilla Hammond of Dart. for
legacy from Est. of her father JAMES SAMSON of Dart., paid by
her brother Henry Samson, Exec., dtd. 6 Dec. 1727. Witns: Joseph Turner & William Honar [9:441].
Quit-claim by Shubal Smith & his wife Anna Smith of Chilmark,
Dukes County, Yeoman, to her brother Henry Samson of Dart., of
any rights to the thirds her mother, Hannah Samson, rcvd. from
Est. of her father JAMES SAMSON of Dart., dtd. 7 July 1726.
Witns: John Hammond & William Palmer [9:441].
Appt. of Obediah Fuller & Jacob Newel, Yeomen of Attl., to be
guards. of Joseph Newel of Attl. "Who is non Compos mentis,"
dtd. 7 Aug. 1740 [9:442].
Appt. of Experiance Mackpeice of Nort., widow, to be Adm. of
Est. of her husb. WILLIAM MACKPEICE of Nort. dcd. intest., dtd.
19 Aug. 1740 [9:442/3].
Appt. of Sarah Perrin of Reho., widow, to be Adm. of Est. of
her husb. DANIEL PERRIN, Jr. of Reho., Yeoman, dcd. intest.,
dtd. 19 Aug. 1740 [9:443/4].
Order to Aron Jenney of Dart., Yeoman, Exec. of Est. of his father MARK JENNEY of Dart., dtd. 19 Aug. 1740 [9:444/5].
Acct. of William Munroe, only surviving Exec. of Est. of Madam
ELIZEBETH DAVIS of Brist., dtd. 23 July 1740. Mentions that
the former Exec., Nathaniel Kay, Esq., is now dcd. & acct. was
made with his widow & Exec., Mrs. Ann Kay. Incl. item for "A
Lawyer att Surianam." Incl. legacies: "to Mr. Gallops Childreen," "to Simon Davis, Esq." & "A Legacy to my Self." Item
for "Cash att Sundry times to the Guardian Job Lewis and Robert Oliver Attorney to Isaac Royal Esq[r] father of Isaac Royal
Jun[r] Who married Elizebeth one of the minors." Incl.: "Molatto
man Harry," "Five Negro men viz Mingo Hector Anthoney Cesar &

Fortune," "Three Negro Women Named Betty Dianna and Nanny," & "Negro Woman Philice" [9:445/6/7/8/9/8/9/50][*page numbering error*].

Will of EBER CHACE of Swan., Yeoman, "Being very Sick of Body," dtd. 12 June 1740, prob. 15 July 1740. Wife Mary [*also called "Marah"*]. Sons: Daniel, William & Eber Chace. Daus: Patiance Luther wife of Esek Luther, Hannah Brayton wife of Stephen Brayton, Alce Anthoney wife of James Anthoney & Mary Anthoney ("lately married") wife of Abraham Anthoney. Incl. negro boy Will, negro girl Betty & old negro Ora. Sons Daniel & William to be Execs. Witns: Jonathan Slade, Obediah Baker & William Hart [9:450/1/2/3].

Appt. of Martha Hunt of Reho. widow, to be Adml of Est. of her husb. WILLIAM HUNT of Reho., Yeoman, dcd. intest., dtd. 15 July 1740 [9:453/4].

Appt. of Capt. Daniel Carpenter of Reho. to be guard. as chosen by Elizebeth Lyon (minor over 14), dau. of BENJAMIN LYON of Reho., dtd. 16 Sept. 1740 [9:454/5].

Appt. of Henry Hodges of Taun., Gentleman, to be guard. as chosen by Seth Crossman (minor over 14), son of SETH CROSSMAN of Taun. dtd. 16 Sept. 1740 [9:455/6].

Order to Christopher Mason & Charles Mason, Yeomen of Swan., Execs. of Est. of their father BENJAMIN MASON of Swan., dtd. 16 Sept. 1740 [9:456].

Will of BENJAMIN MASON of Swan., Yeoman, "Being Sick and Weak of Body," dtd. 22 Aug. 1740, prob. 16 Sept. 1740. Wife Ruth. Sons: Christopher (eldest son) & Charles Mason. Dau. Hannah Slade. 100 acres of land in Ashford, Conn. to Hannah. Sons to be Execs. Witns: John Seamans, John Mason & Job Mason [9:457/8].

Order to Joseph Maccomber of Dart., Yeoman, Exec. of Est. of his sister SARAH MACCOMBER of Dart., dtd. 15 July 1740 [9:459].

Will of SARAH MACCOMBER of Dart., Spinster, "being very sick and weak of Body," dtd. 3 June 1740, prob. 15 July 1740. Father William Maccomber. Brothers: Mathew, William, Samuel, Timothey & Joseph Maccomber. Sisters: Elizebeth Maccomber, Ruth Maccomber, Margaret Maccomber & Hannah Soul. Bro. Joseph to be Exec. Witns: Ichabod Brownel, Restcome Sanford & John Soul [9:459/60/1].

Inv. of Est. of WILLIAM MACKPEICE of Nort., dtd. 1 July 1740, pres. by Experiance Mackpeice, widow & Adm. Pers. est. 400-4-10; real est. 1400-0-0. Apprs: John Briggs, 2nd, Simeon Witherel & Benjamin Cobb [9:461].

Inv. of Est. of EBER CHACE of Swan., Yeoman, dtd. 9 July 1740, pres. by William Chace, Exec. Pers. est. 1749-18-6; real est. 4730-0-0. Apprs: Edward Slade, Job Chace & William Hart [9:461/2/3].

Inv. of Est. of DANIEL PERRIN, Jr. of Reho., dtd. 10 July 1740, pres. by Sarah Perrin, widow & Adm. Pers. est. 422-14-0; real

est. 365-0-0. Apprs: Daniel Carpenter, Ephraim Carpenter &
Edward Glover [9:463/4].
Appr. of Hester Hammond of Reho., widow, to be Adm. of Est. of
JOHN HAMMOND of Reho. dcd. intest., dtd. 15 July 1740[9:464/5].
Inv. of Est. of JOHN HAMMOND of Reho., dtd. 12 July 1740, pres.
by Hester Hammon, widow & Adm. Pers. est. 277-17-0; no real
est. Apprs: Joseph Wheaten, Edward Glover & Noah Newman [9:
465].
Will of MARK JENNEY of Dart., Yeoman, dtd. 29 Jan. 1734, prob.
19 Aug. 1740. Wife Elizebeth. Sons: Nathan, Samuel, Lettice
[sic] & Aron Jenney. Daus: Anne [no surname], Bulah & Elizebeth (last 2 unmar.). Son Aron to be Exec. Mentions an est.
assured to Nathan "by his Grandfather Barstow." Witns: Richard Peirce, William Badcock, Jeremiah Griffiths & Timothey
Rugles [9:466/7/8/9].
Inv. of Est. of MARK JENNEY of Dart., dtd. 1 Aug. 1740, pres.
by Aron Jenney, Exec. Pers. est. 286-4-1; real est. 2086-0-
0. Apprs: Christopher Turner, Nathaniel Blackwel & Cornelius
Jenney [9:469].
Order to Sarah Spooner of Dart., widow & Exec. of Est. of her
husb. JEDUTHAN SPOONER of Dart., dtd. 15 Aug. 1740 [9:470].
Will Of JEDUTHAN SPOONER of Dart., Cordwainer, "Being Under Grait
Weekness," dtd. 15 Apr. 1740, prob. 19 Aug. 1740. Wife Sarah.
Chldn: Ruth Spooner, Charity Spooner & "Child which my beloved
Wife Sarah Spooner now Goes with." Wife to be Exec. Witns:
Samuel Willis, James Cushman & Jereth Swift [9:470/1].
Inv. of pers. est. of JEDUTHAN SPOONER of Dart., dtd. 13 [blank]
1740, pres. by Sarah Spooner, widow & Exec. Value: 186-4-6.
Apprs: James Cushman, Jereth Swift & Benjamin Burgis[9:471/2].
Acct. of James Cole of Swan., Adm. of Est. of MARY COLE of Swan.
dtd. 17 June 1740 [9:472].
Order to div. Est. of JOSEPH DAVICE of Attl. dcd. intest., dtd.
15 Apr. 1740 [9:473].
Div. of Est. of JOSEPH DAVICE of Attl. btwn. his widow [no first
name] Rose (now wife of Joseph Rose) & his chldn: Benjamin Davice (eldest son), Shubal Davice, Joseph Davice, Mercy Onely,
Mary Davice & Sarah Davice, dtd. 26 May 1740. Comm: Daniel
Peck, Noah Carpenter, Ichabod Peck & William Weleval [9:473/
4/5].
Inv. of Est. of JOANAH FINNEY of Brist., widow, dtd. 23 June
1740, pres. by John Kinicut, Adm. Pers. est. 202-9-6; no real
est. Apprs: Peres Bradford, Richard Harding & Barnard Haile
[9:476].
Order to div. Est. of JOSEPH COLE & MARY COLE his wife of Swan.,
dtd. 18 June 1740 [9:476/7].
Div. of Est. of JOSEPH COLE of Swan. & MARY COLE his wife btwn.
the chldn: Joseph Cole (only son) & Mercy Cole (only dau.),
dtd. 12 July 1740. Comm: Peres Bradford, Richard Harding,
Hezekiah Bowen, William Turner & Barnard Haile[9:477/8/9].

Inv. of Est. of JAMES WHEELER, Jr. of Reho., Yeoman, dtd. 4 June
1740, pres. by Philip Wheeler, Adm. Pers. est. 540-19-6; real
est. 2625-0-0. Apprs: Peres Bradford, Samuel Bullock & Daniel
Ormsbe [9:479/80].

Rcpt. by Joana White & Martha White for legacy from Est. of their
father [not named] of Attl., as paid by Capt. Mahew Dagget,
their guard., dtd. 23 Oct. 1738. Witns: Ebenezer White & Abigail Carpenter [9:480].

Acct. of John Tinkcom of Dart., Adm. of Est. of his father JOHN
TINKCOM of Dart., dtd. 16 Sept. 1740 [9:481].

Inv. of Est. of WILLIAM HUNT of Reho., dtd. 14 July 1740, pres.
by Martha Hunt, widow & Adm. Pers. est. 205-4-6; real est.
170-0-0. Apprs: Edward Glover, Joseph Wheaten & Ezekiel Carpenter [9:481/2].

Inv. of Est. of JOHN SAMSON of Brist., dtd. 6 Feb. 1734/5, pres.
by Elezebeth Woodbury, his late widow & Exec. Pers. est. 1009
-7-0; no real est. Incl. a negro man, Peleg, and a wooden
boat & gear. Apprs: Samuel Royal, Obediah Papillion & Edward
Ingraham [9:482/3].

Acct. of Daniel Carpenter, guard. of Elizebeth Lyon, minor dau.
of BENJAMIN LYON of Reho., dtd. 16 Sept. 1740. Mentions 1/3
of Est. going to the Adm., Bethiah Lyon. Money rcvd. from
"Obediah Carpenter of Attleborough Husband to the Said Bethiah." Mentions land of dcd. Benjamin in Smithfield, Co. of
Providence, R.I., that was leased by the said Obediah & Bethiah, beginning 28 Spr. 1730. "Obediah Carpenter father in law
[step-father] to the Above said Elizebeth Lyon" supported her
for 12 years [9:483/4].

Inv. of moveable Est. of PHILIP SHEARMAN of Dart., dtd. 15 March
1739/40, pres. by Stephen Shearman, Exec. Value: 241-19-0.
Incl. note to Philip Shearman from his son Abraham Shearman.
Apprs: James Howland, Jonathan Shearman & William Bowdish
[9:484/5].

Appt. of Katherine Starkey, widow, & Nathaniel Starkey, Yeoman,
to be Adms. of Est. of JOHN STARKEY of Attl. dcd. intest., dtd.
21 Oct. 1740 [9:485].

Appt. of Caleb Russel of Dart., Yeoman, to be guard. of Samuel,
Abraham, Patiance & Pearce Bourden (all under 14), chldn. of
JOSEPH BOURDEN of Tiv., dtd. 21 Oct. 1740 [9:486].

Appt. of George Bourden of Tiv., Yeoman, to be guard. of George,
Stephen, Lucena, Mary & Meribe Bourden (all under 14), chldn.
of STEPHEN BOURDEN of Free., dtd. 21 Oct. 1740 [9:486/7].

Appt. of Samuel Bourden of Tiv., Yeoman, to be guard. as chosen
by Richard Bourden (minor over 14), son of THOMAS BOURDEN of
Tiv., dtd. 21 Oct. 1740 [9:487/8].

Order to John Bosworth of Brist., Yeoman, Exec. of Est. of TIM-
OTHEY LEFAVOUR of Brist., Mariner, dtd. 21 Oct. 1740[9:488/9].

Will of TIMOTHEY LEFAVOUR of Brist., Mariner, "Being Very Ill,"

dtd. 4 Sept. 1740, prob. 21 Oct. 1740. Wife Elizebeth to be
guard. of "all my Childreen" [not named]. Father-in-law John
Bosworth to be Exec. Witns: Samuel Howland, Sarah Norton &
Mary Oxx [9:489/90].
Order to Elezebeth Read, widow, & to Daniel Read, son, Execs.
of Est. of DANIEL READ of Attl., dtd. 21 Oct. 1740[9:490/1].
Will of DANIEL READ of Attl., Yeoman, "Being Sick and Weak of
body," dtd. 25 Apr. 1740, prob. 21 Oct. 1740. Wife [not named]
to be guard. of daus. Sons: Daniel, Ichabod, Samuel, Benjamin,
& Samuel Read. Daus: Elizebeth, Abigail, Rachel & Thankful
[no surnames]. Son Daniel to be guard. of all my sons until
they are 21. Wife & son Daniel to be Execs. Directs son Ichabod to "Pay to his three own Sisters," but does not name them.
Witns: John Fuller, John Robinson, Jr. & Noah Carpenter [9:
491/2/3].
Appt. of Sarah Blanding of Reho., widow, to be Adm. of Est. of
her husb. JOHN BLANDING of Reho., dtd. 21 Oct. 1740 [9:493/4].
Inv. of Est. of Capt. DANIEL READ of Attl., dtd. 10 Oct. 1740,
pres. by Elizebeth Read, widow, & Daniel Read, son, Execs.
Pers. est. 953-7-7; real est. 2471-0-0. Incl. lands in Reho.
& in Uxbridge. Apprs: Noah Carpenter, John Ide & Ebenezer
Robinson [9:494/5].
Appt. of John Bliss of Reho., Yeoman, to be guard. as chosen by
Samuel Holmes (minor over 14), son of JOHN HOLMES of Nort.,
dtd. 21 Oct. 1740 [9:495/6].
Appt. of Richard Round, Jr. of Reho., Husbandman, to be guard.
of Hezekiah Luther (under 14), son of HEZEKIAH LUTHER of Swan.
dtd. 1 Nov. 1740 [9:496/7].
Appt. of John Paul of Barkley, Yeoman, to be Adm. of Est. of his
father EDWARD PAUL of Barkley, Yeoman, the widow Easther Paul
having refused Adm., dtd. 14 Oct. 1740 [9:497/7].
Appt. of Samuel Mason of Reho., Yeoman, to be guard. as chosen
by Noah Paine (minor over 14), son of JONATHAN PAINE of Reho.
dtd. 21 Oct. 1740 [9:498].
Inv. of Est. of JONATHAN PAINE of Reho., dtd. Oct. 1740, pres.
by [blank] Paine, widow & Adm. Pers. est. 467-10-2; real est.
360-0-0. Apprs: Samuel Mason, Benjamin Brown & Joseph Kent
[9:499].
Inv. of Est. of ELIZEBETH CARPENTER of Reho., widow, dtd. 12
July 1740, pres. by Huldah Carpenter, Adm. Pers. est. 112-2-
6; no real est. Apprs: Ezekiel Carpenter, Joseph Wheaten &
Daniel Carpenter [9:499/500].
Agrmt. abt. div. of Est. of SAMUEL WILBOUR of Lit. Comp. by his
chldn: Samuel Wilbour, William Wilbour, Isaac Wilbour, Martha
wife of James Peirce, Mary wife of Charles Brownel, Joanna
wife of John Taylor, Thankful wife of John Irish, Elizebeth
wife of Joseph Peckcom, Abial (dau.) Wilbour & Hannah wife of
John Dennis., dtd. 13 Aug. 1740 [9:500/1/2/2¼/2½][page numbering error].

Acct. of Penelope Bowen, late Penelope Borden, Adm. of Est. of
STEPHEN BORDEN of Free., dtd. 19 Aug. 1740 [9:502½/3].

Appt. of Martha [sic; probably means "Mathew"] Short of East.,
Yeoman, to be guard. as chosen by Ebenezer & Elizebeth Short
(minors over 14), chldn. of MATHEW SHORT of East., dtd. 18
Sept. 1740 [9:503/4].

Appt. of Mathew Short of East. to be guard. of Glover Short (under 14), son of MATHEW SHORT of East., dtd. 18 Sept. 1740 [9:
504].

Appt. of Thomas Hunt of Weymouth, Co. of Suffolk, Yeoman, to be
guard. as chosen by Sarah Short (minor over 14) & Lidiah Short
(under 14), daus. of MATHEW SHORT of East., dtd. 18 Sept. 1740
[9:504/5].

Appt. of Ebenezer White of Weymouth, Co. of Suffolk, Yeoman, to
be guard. of Mary Short (under 14), dau. of MATHEW SHORT of
East., dtd. 18 Sept. 1740 [(;505/6].

Inv. of Est. of EDWARD PAUL of Barkley, dtd. 20 Oct. 1740, pres.
by Jonathan Paul, Adm. Pers. est. 329-3-0; real est. 232-0-0.
Apprs: John Crane, Daniel Axtell & Benajah Babbit [9:506/7].

Acct. of Sarah Child, widow & Adm. of Est. of JAMES CHILD of
Swan., dtd. 21 Oct. 1740. Incl. payms. for: "Clothing used in
the familey among ye Childreen" & "Charge of Lying in with A
Posthumus Child after the Death of ye father" [9:507/8].

Appt. of Ruth Bosworth of Brist., widow, to be Adm. of Est. of
her husb. BENJAMIN BOSWORTH of Brist. dcd. intest., dtd. 16
Dec. 1740 [9:508/8¼][page numbering error].

Appt. of Lidiah Brintnal of Nort., widow, to be Adm. of Est. of
her husb. SAMUEL BRINTNAL of Nort. dcd. intest., dtd. 16 Dec.
1740 [9:508¼/8½].

Appt. of Mary Dagget of Attl. to be Adm. of Est. of her husb.
EBENEZER DAGGET of Attl. dcd. intest., dtd. 16 Dec. 1740 [9:
508½/9].

Inv. of Est. of JOHN BLANDING of Reho., dtd. 29 Sept. 1740, pres.
by Sarah Blanding, widow & Adm. Pers. est. 141-18-0; real
est. 166-0-0. Apprs: Abraham Carpenter, David Carpenter & Thomas Carpenter [9:509/10].

Appt. of Oliver Mason of Swan., Yeoman, to be guard. as chosen
by Nathan Mason (minor over 14), son of SAMPSON MASON of Swan.
dtd. 20 Jan. 1740 [9:510/1].

Inv. of Est. of THOMAS PICKENS of Free., dtd. 8 March 1740, pres.
by Andrew Pickens, Adm. Mentions: "the widdows Bed" & "Two
Colts Given to his two Youngest Sons." Pers. est. 328-0-0;
real est. 600-0-0. Apprs: Samuel Tisdal, Lott Strangg & David
Cudworth [9:511].

Acct. of Nathaniel Perry of East., Yeoman & Adm. of Est. of JO-
SEPH SMITH of East., dtd. 21 Oct. 1740. Incl. paym. "for what
the widdow had for her Necessary Support & Childreen" [9:512/3]

Appts. of Nathaniel Perry of East., Yeoman, to be guard. as chosen by Hannah Smith & Gemima Smith (minors over 14), daus. of

JOSEPH SMITH of East., & of Susanah & Thankful Smith (both under 14), daus. of JOSEPH, dtd. 21 Jan. 1740 [9:513/4/5].
Inv. of Est. of HENRY FINCH of Reho., dtd. 10 March 1740, pres.
by Elizebeth Finch, widow & Adm. Pers. est. 214-19-10; real
est. 469-0-0. Apprs: Samuel Bullock, Philip Wheler & Richard
Whitiker [9:515/6].
Appt. of Sarah Read, widow, & Thomas Read, Husbandman, both of
Digh., to be Adms. of Est. of THOMAS READ of Digh. dcd. intest.
dtd. 17 Feb. 1740 [9:516].
Inv. of 2/3 of real est. of the Rev. Mr. SAMUEL HUNT of Dart.,
dtd. 14 May 1739. Apprs: Zacheus Tobey, James Cushman & Nathaniel Blackwell [9:517].
Order that 2/3 of real est. of the Rev. Mr. SAMUEL HUNT of Dart.
dcd. intest. be given to his only son, Ephraim Hunt, who must
then pay his sisters: Deborah Belcher wife of Joseph Belcher,
Joannah Hunt, Rebecca Hunt & Sarah Hunt, dtd. 16 Dec. 1740
[9:517/8].

End of Volume 9

Inv. of Est. of ANDREW STARKEY of Attl., Yeoman, dtd. 14 Nov. 1740, pres. by Katherine Starkey & John Starkey, Adms. Pers. est. 457-7-2; real est. 1450-0-0. Incl. lands in Attl. & Nort. Apprs. not named [10:2].

Acct. of Katherine Starkey & John Starkey, Adms. of Est. of AN-DREW STARKEY of Attl., dtd. 18 March 1740. Incl. payms. for provisions "spent in the family" [10:3].

Appt. of Joseph Caproon of Attl., Yeoman, to be guard. as cho-sen by Benjamin Caproon (minor over 14), son of JOHN CAPROON of Attl., dtd. 18 March 1740 [10:4].

Order to Sarah Torrey of Barr., widow & Exec. of Est. of her husb. JOHN TORREY of Barr., dtd. 20 Jan. 1740 [10:4/5].

Will of JOHN TORREY of Barr., Yeoman, "being very sick," dtd. 10 Dec. 1740, prob. 20 Jan. 1740. Wife Sarah. Sons: Josiah, Wilson, Nathan, Jonathan & David Torrey. Daus: Ann Torrey & Unice Torrey. Wife to be Exec. Witns: James Adams, Ebenezer Adams & John Adams [10:5/6].

Order to Benjamin Jones & Elnathan Jones, both of Rayn., Yeomen, Execs. of Est. of their father JOSEPH JONES of Rayn., dtd. 20 1740 [10:6].

Will of JOSEPH JONES of Rayn., "Being advanced In years," dtd. 18 Dec. 1740, prob. 20 Jan. 1740. Wife Mary. Mentions "all the Household Stuff that She Brough att the time of marraige with me." Sons: Joseph, Benjamin, Nathan & Elnathan Jones. Daus: Submit Partridge, Sarah Jones, Lidiah Bosworth, Rebecca Dyer dcd. & Mary Jones. Mentions chldn. [not named] of my dcd. dau. Rebecca Dyer. Incl. "my Brother Abraham Jones." Sons Ben-jamin & Elnathan to be Execs. Witns: Nehemiah Cambil, James Dean & Zephinia Leonard [10:6/7/8].

Appt. of Nathan Mason of Swan., Yeoman, to be guard. as chosen by Nathaniel Mason (minor over 14), son of SAMPSON MASON of Swan., dtd. 20 Jan. 1740 [10:8].

Inv. of Est. of BENJAMIN MASON of Swan., Yeoman, dtd. 19 Sept. 1740, pres. by Christopher Mason & Charles Mason, Execs. Pers. est. 1299-11-6; no real est. Apprs: Peres Bradford, Richard Harding & John Seamans [10:8/9].

Inv. of Est. of JOSEPH JONES of Rayn., dtd. 12 Jan. 1740, pres. by Benjamin Jones & Elnathan Jones, sons & Execs. Pers. est. 151-4-0; no real est. Apprs: John White, Zephaniah Leonard & Jonah Dean [10:9/10].

Inv. of Est. of HENRY FINCH of Reho., dtd. 10 March 1740, pres. by Elizebeth Finch, widow & Adm. Pers. est. 200-9-9; real est. 469-0-0. Apprs: Samuel Bulloch, Philip Wheler & Richard Whitiker [10:10/11].

Appt. of Comfort Bailey, widow, as Adm. of Est. of her husb.
WILLIAM BAILEY of Lit. Comp. dcd. intest., dtd. 4 March 1740
[10:11].

Appts. of John Fisher of Nort. to be guard. as chosen by Andrew
Starkey & Gemima Starkey (minors over 14) & of Thomas Starkey
(under 14), chldn. of ANDREW STARKEY of Attl., dtd. 18 March
1740 [10:11/2].

Appt. of Stephen Cook of Tiv., Yeoman, to be guard. of Mary
Cook (under 14), dau. of CHAPLIN COOK of Tiv., dtd. 21 Apr.
1740 [10:13].

Appt. of Joseph Wheaten of Reho., Yeoman, to be guard. as chosen
by his wife Abigail Wheaten (minor over 14), dau. of NATHANIEL
PAINE of Brist. [sic], dtd. 21 Apr. 1741 [10:13].

Appt. of Timothey Ide of Reho., Yeoman, to be guard. as chosen
by Dorothey Paine (minor over 14), dau. of NATHANIEL PAINE of
Reho., dtd. 21 Apr. 1741 [10:14].

Appt. of Benjamin Buffington of Swan. to be guard. as chosen by
Eber Chace (minor over 14), son of EBER CHACE of Swan., dtd.
21 Apr. 1741 [10:14/5].

Order to Mary Bailey & John Bailey of Lit. Comp., Execs. of Est.
of THOMAS BAILEY of Lit. Comp., dtd. 21 Apr. 1741 [10:15].

Will of THOMAS BAILEY of Lit. Comp., Gentleman, dtd. 31 Jan. 17-
40/1, prob. 21 Apr. 1741. Wife Mary. Sons: John (eldest), Thomas, Constant, Joseph, Oliver, James, Barzilla, William & Lemuel Bailey. Dau. Mary (unmar.). Wife & son John to be Execs.
Mentions lands in Tiv. Witns: Joseph Ward, Joseph Burges &
Richard Billings, Jr. [10:15/6/7].

Inv. of Est. of Lewt. THOMAS BAILEY of Lit. Comp., dtd. 14 Apr.
1741, pres. by Mary Bailey & John Bailey, Execs. Mentions Negro women Violet & Phillis, Negro boy Crawco. Pers. est. 6250-
18-3; real est. 10650-0-0. Apprs: William Richmond, William
Hall & Joseph Wood [10:17/8/9].

Acct. of Abigail Paine, widow & Adm. of Est. of NATHANIEL PAINE
of Reho., dtd. 21 Apr. 1741 [10:19/20].

Inv. of Est. of JAMES WILSON of Attl., Mariner, dtd. 28 Aug.
1740, pres. by Samuel Wilson, brother & Adm. Pers. est. 164-
10-8; no real est. Apprs: Noah Carpenter, Benjamin Day & Ebenezer Robinson [10:20].

Rcpt. by George & Mary Duggles of North Kingston, R.I. for legacy from Est. of her father JOHN HATHAWAY of Dart., paid by
her bro. John Hathaway, dtd. 10 Oct. 1737 [10:21].

Rcpt. by Sarah & John Cannon of Dart. for legacy from Est. of
her father JOHN HATHAWAY of Dart., paid by her bro. John Hathaway, dtd. 4 Aug. 1736 [10:21].

Rcpt. by Joannah & Nathaniel Blackwell of Dart. for legacy from
Est. of her father JOHN HATHAWAY of Dart., paid by her bro.
John Hathaway of Dart., dtd. ___ July 1736 [10:21].

Inv. of Est. of THOMAS READ of Digh., dtd. 19 Feb. 1740/1, pres.
by Sarah Read, widow, & Thomas Read, son, Adms. Pers. est.

238-18-6; real est. 45-0-0. Apprs: Ephraim Atwood, David Whitmarsh & Nathan Walker, Jr. [10:21/2].

Order for Nathaniel Millard of Reho., Exec. of Est. of his father NATHANIEL MILLARD of Reho., dtd. 21 Apr. 1741 [10:22].

Will of NATHANIEL MILLARD of Reho., Yeoman, "Being very Sick and weak of body," dtd. 14 March 1740/1, prob. 21 Apr. 1741. Wife Rebeccah. Sons: Nathaniel, Josiah, John, Joseph & Noah Millard. Daus: Sarah Andreas, Hannah Garnsey, Ann Horton, Mary, Elizebeth, Rebeccah & Mehetibel [no surnames]. Last 4 daus. to share 300 acres in Ashford, Windham Co., Ct. Son Nathaniel to be Exec. Witns: Henry West, Ephraim Martin & John Webber [10:22/3/4].

Appt. of Mary Coe of Lit. Comp., widow, to be Adm. of Est. of her husb. SAMUEL COE of Lit. Comp., Yeoman, dcd. intest., dtd. 19 May 1741 [10:24/5].

Appt. of Mary Coe of Lit. Comp., widow, to be guard. of John Coe & Elizebeth Coe (under 14), chldn. of SAMUEL COE of Lit. Comp., dtd. 19 May 1741 [10:25].

Appt. of Joseph Peckcom of Lit. Comp., Yeoman, to be guard. of his son John Peckcom (under 14), nephew of RUBEN PECKCOM of Newport, R.I., Yeoman, dtd. 15 May 1741 [10:26].

Inv. of Est. of BENJAMIN BOSWORTH of Brist., dtd. 15 Nov. 1740, pres. by Ruth Bosworth, widow & Adm. Pers. est. 1670-9-0; real est. 4832-0-0. Apprs: Thomas Lawton, Joseph Russel & William Munroe, Jr. [10:26/7/8].

Inv. of Est. of WILLIAM BAILEY of Lit. Comp. dcd. intest., dtd. 22 Jan. 1740/1, pres. by Comfort Bailey, widow & Adm. Pers. est. 1886-3-10; real est. 2000-0-0. Apprs: Samuel Gray, William Richmond & Joseph Wood [10:28].

Appt. of William Wilbour of Lit. Comp., Yeoman, to be guard. as chosen by Priscilla Coe & Sarah Coe (minors over 14), daus. of SAMUEL COE of Lit. Comp., dtd. 19 May 1741 [10:29].

Appt. of John Chandler, Esq., of Worchester, Co. of Worchester, to be guard. as chosen by Dorothey Paine now Dorothey Chandler (minor over 14), dau. of NATHANIEL PAINE, Esq., of Brist., dtd. 17 Apr. 1741 [10:29/30].

Appt. of John Chandler, Esq., of Worchester, to be guard. of Samuel Clerk Paine & Timothey Paine (both under 14), sons of NATHANIEL PAINE, Esq., of Brist., at the prayer of Madam Chandler, mother [sic] of said minors, dtd. 17 Apr. 1741 [10:30].

Appt. of Abigail Paine of Reho., widow, to be guard. of her son John Paine (under 14), son of NATHANIEL PAINE of Reho., dtd. 21 Apr. 1741 [10:30/1].

Acct. of Hannah Chace, late widow & Adm. of Est. of CHAPLIN COOK of Tiv., dtd. 19 May 1741 [10:31/2].

Appt. of Stephen Cook of Tiv., Yeoman, to be guard. of Thomas Cook (under 14), son of CHAPLIN COOK of Tiv., "att the prayer of the mother Hannah Chace," dtd. 21 Apr. 1741 [10:32/3].

Order to Nathaniel Bosworth of Brist., Exec. of Est. of GRACE WARDWEL of Brist., widow, dtd. 27 May 1741 [10:33].

Will of GRACE WARDWEL of Brist., widow, "Being Aged and Infirm
of Body," dtd. 19 Oct. 1739, prob. 27 May 1741. Sons: Uzal
(eldest), James, Joseph, Benjamin (dcd.) & William Wardwel.
Daus: Mary Barker, Grace Giddins & Sarah Bosworth. Grson. Uzal
Wardwel son of my son Benjamin dcd. Daus-in-law [sic] Abigail Green, Hannah Coumpton & Mary Lawles. Son-in-law Nathaniel Bosworth to be Exec. Witns: Elisha May, Hannah Diman &
Nathaniel Lindal [10:33/4].

Appt. of Nathaniel Cooper of Reho., Yeoman, to be Adm. of Est.
of his bro. NOAH COOPER of Reho. dcd. intest., dtd. 16 June
1741 [10:35].

Inv. of Est. of NOAH COOPER of Reho., dtd. 15 May 1741, pres.
by Nathaniel Cooper, bro. & Adm. Pers. est. 542-16-10; real
est. 1269-10-0. Apprs: Ephraim Carpenter, John Humphrey & Edward Glover [10:35/6].

Acct. of Comfort Taylor, Exec. of Est. of her husb. PHILLIP TAY-
LOR of Lit. Comp., dtd. 16 June 1741. Incl. item "for Record-
ing the Childrens Names 0-1-9" [10:36/7].

Appt. of Mrs. Elisabeth Davenport of Tiv., widow, to be Adm. of
Est. of her husb. JOHN DAVENPORT of Tiv. dcd. intest., dtd. 3
July 1741 [10:37/8].

Inv. of Est. of JOHN DAVENPORT of Tiv. who "Deceased April 20th
1741," dtd. 23 June 1741, pres. by Elisebeth Davenport, Adm.
Pers. est. 1065-6-1; real est. 2793-0-0. Incl. farm in Lit.
Comp. Apprs: Capt. John Manchester, Capt. William Wilcocks
& Phillip Corey [10:38/9].

Acct of Josiah Hathaway, Exec. of Est. of JOHN HATHAWAY of Dart.,
dtd. 16 June 1741. Incl. item for legacy by the dcd. "to his
Wife Alice Hathaway" [10:40/1].

Acct. of John Brown of Newport, R.I., Exec. of Est. of his fa-
ther NATHANIEL BROWNE of Reho. Incl. item "to my Mother in Law
Mary Brown by a Contract made before Marriage with my Honoured
Father." Legacies per will to: Esther Sweeting, Sarah Bullock,
Penelope Butterworth, Lydia Chapman, Kezia Brown, Elisabeth
Thurston & "to Benjamin Brown Guardian unto Peleg Brown A Leg-
acy given to said Peleg by his Grandfather's Will"[10:41].

Rcpt. by Henry Sweeting for legacy to his wife Esther from Est.
of her father NATHANIEL BROWN, paid by her bro. John Brown,
std. at Providence 17 Dec. 1739 [10:41].

Rcpt. by Benjamin Brown, guard. of Peleg Brown son of Mary Brown
for legacy from Est. of Peleg's grfather NATHANIEL BROWN, paid
by Benjamin's bro-in-law John Brown, dtd. REho. 15 March 17/
39/40 [10:42].

Rcpt. by Israel Bullock for legacy to his wife [not named] from
Est. of her father NATHANIEL BROWN, paid by John Brown, dtd.
Barr. 13 March 1739/40 [10:42].

Rcpt. by Benjamin Brown for legacy to his wife Kezia Brown from
Est. of her father NATHANIEL BROWN of Reho., paid by Benjamin's
bro-in-law John Brown of Newport, dtd. Reho. 25 May 1740[10:42]

Rcpt. by Luke Thurston for legacy to his wife Elisabeth from Est.
of her father NATHANIEL BROWN of Reho., paid by John Brown,
dtd. Newport 23 Sept. 1740 [10:42].

Rcpt. by Benjamin & Lydia Chapman for legacy from Est. of her
father NATHANIEL BROWN of Reho., paid by her bro. John Brown,
dtd. Newport 16 Dec. 1740 [10:42].

Rcpt. by Ales Hathaway, widow, for legacy from Est. of her husb.
JOHN HATHAWAY of Dart., paid by Josiah Hathaway of Dart., Exec.
dtd. 29 Apr. 1741 [10:42].

Appt. of Thomas Church of Lit. Comp. to be guard. as chosen by
Constant Church (minor over 14), son of Capt. CONSTANT CHURCH
of Free., dtd. 3 July 1741 [10:43].

Order to Barnabas Tisdale of Free., Exec. of Est. of his mother
ABIGAIL TISDALE of Free., dtd. 16 June 1741 [10:43].

Will of ABIGAIL TISDALE of Free., Widow & relict of Joshua Tisdale of Free., "Being sick and weak," dtd. 16 Apr. 1741, prob.
16 June 1741. Sons: Samuel, Henry, Barnabas, Joshua (dcd.) &
Ephraim Tisdale. Daus: Elizebeth Winslow, Hepzebeth Gibbs &
Mercy Palmer. "My son Edward Palmer." Abigail & Mary daus.
of my son Samuel Tisdale. Son Barnabas to be Exec. Witns: Andrew Pickens, Content [called "Constant" at time of probate]
Pray & Mercy Pitts [10:44/5].

Order for div. of Est. of NATHANIEL PAINE, Esq., of Brist., dtd.
16 Apr. 1741 [10:45/6].

Div. of Est. of Col. NATHANIEL PAINE of Brist., dcd. intest.,
btwn. his late widow Madam Sarah Chandler & his chldn: Edward
Paine (eldest son), Nathaniel Paine (son), Sarah Drown (dau.),
Samuel Clerk Paine (son), Timothey Paine (son) & Dorothy Chand-
ler (dau.), dtd. 16 June 1741. Incl. lands in Attl. & Brist.
Comm: John Throope, Samuel Royal, Thomas Throope, Allen Cary
& Thomas Lawton [10:46/7].

Appt. of William Dean of Nort. to be guard of Nathan Dean & Sarah Dean (both under 14), chldn. of NATHAN DEAN of Nort., dtd.
18 Aug. 1741 [10:48].

Appt. of John Manchester of Dart., Cordwainer, to be guard. of
Lemuel, Thomas & Mary Manchester (all under 14), chldn. of
THOMAS MANCHESTER of Dart., dtd. 21 July 1741 [10:48/9].

Appt. of John Manchester of Dart., Corwainer, to be Adm. of Est.
of his mother MARAH MANCHESTER of Dart., Widow, dcd. intest.,
dtd. 21 July 1741 [10:49].

Appt. of Ebenezer Cowel of Wrentham, Co. of Suffolk, Locksmith,
to be guard. of Jonathan Titus (over 14), son of ROBERT TITUS
of Attl., Yeoman, dtd. 21 July 1741 [10:49/50].

Order to John Shrieff of Lit. Compt., Husbandman, Exec. of Est.
of his father DANIEL SHRIEFF of Lit. Comp., dtd. 21 July 1741
[10:50/1].

Order to Sarah Huddleston, widow, & Darias Talman, Weaver, both
of Dart., Execs. of Est. of RICHARD HUDDLESTON of Dart., dtd.
21 July 1741 [10:51].

Will of RICHARD HUDDLESTON of Dart., "being very weak," dtd. 7
May 1741, prob. 21 July 1741. Wife Sarah. Dau. Judith (under
21 & unmar.). Wife Sarah, "Darius Talman her Brother" & "my
Uncle Isaac Case" to be Execs. Witns: Jonathan Talman, Jr.,
Samuel Maccomber & Peleg Huddleston [10:51/2].
Will of DANIEL SHRIEFF of Lit. Comp., Yeoman, "Being Weak and
Low in Body," dtd. 2 May 1741, prob. 21 July 1741. No wife
mentioned. Sons: John & Abial Shrieff. Witns: Nathaniel
Searl, Jr., John Salsbury & Edward Manchester [10:52/3].
Inv. of Est. of DANIEL SHRIEFF of Lit. Comp., dtd. 15 July 1741,
pres. by John Shrieff, Exec. Pers. est. 582-7-4; no real est.
Apprs: Henry Head, Nathaniel Searl, Jr. & Eliphelet Davenport
[10:53/4].
Inv. of Est. of NATHANIEL MILLARD of Reho., "Malster," dtd. 15
May 1741, pres. by Nathaniel Millard, son & Exec. Pers. est.
1217-11-9; real est. 4220-10-0. Mentions lands given by will
to Josiah Millard, to John Millard & to Joseph Millard. Apprs:
Azarikim Pearce, Philip Wheler & Henry West [10:54/5/6].
Inv. of Est. of MARY MANCHESTER of Dart., dtd. 26 June 1741,
pres. by John Manchester, Adm. Pers. est. 339-15-00; no real
est. Apprs: Nathaniel Soule, Ichabod Potter & John Potter
[10:56/7].
Inv. of Est. of BENJAMIN WARDWEL of Brist., dtd. 25 Oct. 1739
[Entry is only 5 lines long, running to the bottom of the page,
and is not continued on the next page. The following entry is
totally different. See 10:61][10:57].
Inv. of Est. of SAMUEL COE of Lit. Comp., dtd. 10 July 1741,
pres. by Mary Coe, Adm. Incl. item for land "given by his father to him and his Brother Joseph." Pers. est. 125-17-0;
real est. 875-0-0. Apprs: William Richmond, John Peabodye &
Joseph Wood [10:58].
Acct. of Hannah Slade of Swan., Adm. of Est. of her husb. WIL-
LIAM SLADE of Swan., dtd. 21 July 1741. Mentions items "used
in the familey" [10:58/9].
Inv. of Est. of RICHARD HUDDLESTON of Dart., dtd. 29 June 1741,
pres. by Sarah Huddleston & Darias Talman, Execs. Pers. est.
471-1-10; no real est. Apprs: Jacob Anthoney, Joseph Wingg
& Peleg Huddleston [10:59/60].
Inv. of Est. of GRACE WARDWEL of Brist., dtd. 27 May 1741, pres.
by Nathaniel Bosworth, Exec. Pers. est. 123-16-6; no real
est. Apprs: Joseph Russell, Samuel Smith & Joshua Bailey
[10:60/1].
Inv. of Est. of BENJAMIN WARDWEL of Brist., dtd. 25 Oct. 1739,
pres. by Nathaniel Bosworth, Exec. Incl. item abt. bond due
from Joseph Wardwel to his brother Benjamin. Pers. est. 27-
11-6; no real est. Apprs: Samuel Royal, Joshua Bailey & Samuel Smith [10:61/2].
Order to div. Est. of ROBERT TITUS of Attl., dtd. 20 March 1738/9
[10:62].

Div. of Est. of ROBERT TITUS of Attl. btwn. his widow "Sarah present Wife of John Stephens" & his chldn: Robert (eldest son), Noah (2nd son), Jonathan (youngest son), Sarah (eldest dau.) & Hannah (youngest dau.), dtd. 18 Aug. 1741. Comm: Daniel Carpenter, Daniel Chaffey & Zachariah Carpenter [10:62/3/4].

Acct. of John & Sarah Stephens of Attl., guards. of Jonathan Titus (under 14), son of ROBERT TITUS of Attl., dtd. 18 Aug. 1741. Mentions 5 yrs. & 5 mos. of interest on money "which Belonged to the Said minor." Pres. by John Stephens [10:64/5].

Appt. of Mary Wood of Dart., Widow, to be Adm. of Est. of her husb. ISAAC WOOD of Dart., Yeoman, dcd. intest., dtd. 18 Aug. 1741 [10:65/6].

Inv. of Est. of ISAAC WOOD of Dart., dtd. 6 Aug. 1741, pres. by Mary Wood, Adm. Incl. var. shoe hammers & knives and 116 lasts. Pers. est. 801-18-4; real est. 102-0-0. Apprs: Philip Tabor, Nathaniel Soule & Jacob Soule [10:66/7/8].

Acct. of Jael Chace, Exec. of Est. of HEZEKIAH CHACE of Swan., dtd. 15 Sept. 1741. Incl. item "to her Daughter Barsheba Chace" [10:69].

Appt. of Obediah Papillion of Brist., "Shipwrite," to be Adm. of Est. of his son JOHN PAPILLION of Brist., "Shipwrite," dcd. intest., dtd. 18 Aug. 1741 [10:70].

Appt. of Obediah Papillion of Brist., "Shipwrite," to be guard. of his sons John & Peter Papillion (minors over 14), grsons. of MARY BOSWORTH of Brist., not dated [10:70/1].

Appt. of William Dean of Norton, Yeoman, to be Adm. of Est. of his bro. NATHAN DEAN of Nort. dcd. intest., dtd. 18 Aug. 1741 [10:71].

Acct. of Katherine Hodges, Adm. of Est. of her husb. THOMAS HODGES of Taun., dtd. 15 Sept. 1741. Incl. items: "Lying in Charges," "toward finishing the Dweling house" & "to father Hodges on Bond." Mentions small sums to: Henery Hodges, Joseph Hodges, William Hodges & Ensign Hodges [10:71/2].

Acct. of Mary Paul, widow & Adm. of Est. of JAMES PAUL of Digh., dtd. 15 Sept. 1741. Mentions sale of 30 acres to William Paul & 64 acres to James Paul [10:72/3].

Order to Samuel Smith of Brist., Cordwainer, Exec. of Est. of his bro. DANIEL SMITH of Brist., Bricklayer, dtd. 24 Aug. 1741 [10:73].

Will of DANIEL SMITH of Brist., Bricklayer, "Being Sick and weak of Body," dtd. 17 Aug. 1741, prob. 24 Aug. 1741. Wife Elizebeth. Sons: Daniel (eldest), John, David, William & Nathan Smith. Daus: Elizabeth James & Joyce [no surname]. Negro man named Will. Brother Samuel Smith to be Exec. Witns: Benjamin Raynolds,Samuel Howland & Benjamin Smith [10:73/4/5].

Order to Caleb Walker of Reho., Yeoman, Exec. of Est. of his mother DOROTHEY READ of Reho., dtd. 21 Aug. 1741 [10:75/6].

Will of DOROTHEY READ of Reho., "Present Wife of John Read of Said Rehoboth...widdow and Relict of Ebenezer Walker Late of

Rehoboth," dtd. 14 Dec. 1737, prob. 21 Aug. 1741. 2 sons: Caleb & Ebenezer Walker. 4 daus: Elizebeth Shorey, Joannah, Dorothey, & Martha [no surnames]. Mentions items that "were my
father Abels." Incl. depos. by husb. John Read of a written
agreement they signed before marriage "baring Date January the
Eaigth 1724." Son Caleb to be Exec. Mentions lands & rights
in Attl., Reho. & Barr. Witns: Daniel Carpenter, John Bair-
stow & Elezebeth Carpenter [10:76/7].
Appraisal of "Torreys farm," part of real est. of NATHANIEL
PAINE of Brist., being 84½ acres at 21 pounds per acre, dtd.
17 Apr. 1741. Comm:. John Throop,. Thomas Throope & Thomas Lawton [10:77].
Div. & settl. of part of real est. of NATHANIEL PAINE of Brist.
on eldest son Edward Paine, provided he "pay the other five
Children": Nathaniel Paine (son), Samuel Clerk Paine (son),
Timothey Paine (son), Sarah Drown (dau.) & Dorothey Chandler
(dau.), dtd. 19 May 1741 [10:77/8/9].
Inv. of Est. of DOROTHEY READ of Reho. "which She Brought with
her to the House of John Read...to be Returned to her heirs,"
shown by her husb. John Read, dtd. 13 Aug. 1741, pres. by Caleb Walker, son & Exec. Pers. est. 252-18-5; real est. 152-
0-0. Apprs: Daniel Carpenter, Edward Glover & Noah Sabin
[10:79/80].
Inv. of Est. of NATHAN DEAN of Nort., Yeoman, dtd. 7,8 & 9 Sept.
1741, pres. by William Dean, Adm. Pers. est. 365-3-0; real
est. 1823-15-6. Apprs: Nicholas White, William Stone & Benjamin Williams [10:81/2].
Order to Phillip King of Rayn., Yeoman, Exec. of Est. of his father JOHN KING of Rayn., Gentleman, dtd. 20 Oct. 1741[10:82].
Will of Capt. JOHN KING of Rayn., Gentleman, dtd. 24 July 1741,
prob. 20 Oct. 1741. Wife Alice. Sons: Philip, John, David, Jonathan & Benjamin King. Daus: Hannah Leonard wife of Zephiniah
Leonard of Rayn. & Abigail Williams wife of John Williams of
Easton. Mentions lands & rights in Dorchester, Norton & Middleborough. Son Philip to be Exec. Witns: Samuel Williams, William Wair & Samuel White [10:83/4/5].
Appt. of Mercy Ingols of Reho., widow, to be Adm. of Est. of her
husb. BENJAMIN INGOLS of Reho. dcd. intest., dtd. 20 Oct. 1741
[10:85/6].
Appt. of Mary Brownel wife of Thomas Brownel son of George Brownel, & Leah Clap wife of Elisha Clap of Lit. Comp. to be Adms.
of Est. of their grmother. LEAH BLACKMAN of Lit. Comp., widow,
dcd. intest., dtd. 20 Oct. 1741 [10:86].
Order to William Woodwel & Gershom Woodwel of Tiv., Yeoman & Execs. of Est. of their father GERSHOM WOODWEL of Tiv., Yeoman,
dtd. 20 Oct. 1741 [10:87].
Will of GERSHOM WOODWEL of Tiv., Yeoman, dtd. 30 Dec. 1738, prob.
20 Oct. 1741. Wife Sarah. Sons: William & Gershom Woodwel.
Daus: Elizebeth Woodwel, Ruth Phinias, Patiance Crandel, Alce

Butts & Innocent Shearman. 2 sons to be Execs. Witns: Jonathan Bennet, John Jennings & Silvanus Soule [10:87/8/9].
Acct. of Comfort Bailey, widow & Adm. of Est. of WILLIAM BAILEY
of Lit. Comp., dtd. 20 Oct. 1741 [10:89/90].
Appt. of Jerusha King of Nort., widow, to be Adm. of Est. of
her husb. HEZEKIAH KING of Nort. dcd. intest., dtd. 20 Oct.
1741 [10:90/1].
Inv. of Est. of HEZEKIAH KING, Esq., of Nort., dtd. 25 Aug. 17-
41, pres. by Jerusha King, widow & Adm. Pers. est. 124-3-0;
real est. 275-0-0. Mentions "his brother Samuel King of Norton" & "His Honoured mother Sarah Hore." Apprs: Daniel Brayman, Joseph Hodges & Benjamin Hodges [10:91/2].
Acct. of John Williams of Easton, Adm. of Est. of his mother RE-
BECAH LEONARD of Rayn., dtd. 20 Oct. 1741 [10:92/3].
Inv. of Est. of INCREASE ROBINSON of Taun., dtd. 2 Apr. 1739,
pres. by William Robinson, son & Adm. Incl. lands & rights in
Taun., Taun. No. Purch. & Rayn. Pers. est. 174-2-2; real est.
1410-0-0. Apprs: Benjamin Wilbour, Samuel Pitts & John God-
frey [10:93/4].
Appt. of Joseph Anthoney of Tiv., Yeoman, to be Adm. Cum Testi-
mento Annexo of Est. of JOHN TALMAN of Tiv., "Surgeion," since
Caleb Bennit who was appt. Exec. in the will has relinquished
& "Sarah Talman his Widdow" has also refused Adm., dtd. 29
Oct. 1741 [10:94/5].
Will of JOHN TALMAN of Tiv., Surgeon, "very Weak and Sick of
Body," dtd. 11 Aug. 1741, prob. 18 Aug. 1741. Wife Sarah.
Chldn: Mary Cook (eldest dau.), Hannah Chace (2nd dau.) & "Sev-
en other Childreen...Ann Talman Elizebeth Talman Joseph Talman
Rebeccah Talman Sarah Talman Ruth Talman and John Talman."
Bro-in-law Caleb Bennit of Portsmouth, R.I. to be Exec. Witns:
Joseph Anthoney, Isaac Howland & Samuel Borden [10:95/6].
Acct. of Isaac Howland of Dart., Exec. in the 2nd degree of Est.
of JOHN GATCHEL of Dart., dtd. 20 Oct. 1741. Incl. rcpts. for
rent of the farm from 1731 to 1737. Mentions: money to Thomas
Hicks for his wife's [not named] legacy; John Akin guard. of
Mary & Susanah Gatchel; & widow Mary Gatchel[10:96/7/8/9/100/1].
Appt. of William Hall, Esq., of Lit. Comp. to be guard. of Mat-
hew Coe (minor over 14), son of SAMUEL COE of Lit. Comp., Yeo-
man, dtd. 3 Nov. 1741 [10:101/2].
Appt. of William Wilbour of Lit. Comp., Yeoman, to be guard. of
John Coe (under 14), son of SAMUEL COE of Lit. Comp., dtd. 3
Nov. 1741 [10:102].
Acct. of John Kinicut, Adm. of Est. of JOANNAH PHINEY of Swan.,
dtd. 17 Nov. 1741. Incl. payms. to chldn: Jeremiah Clark,
Elizebeth Luden, Hopestill Potter, Joannah Clerk & Mercy Phiney
"in Right of her Two Childreen as her Late Husbands Double Por-
tion of his mothers Estate" [10:102/3].
Appt. of Edward Slade, Yeoman, Jonathan Slade, Gentleman & Han-
nah Slade, widow, all of Swan., to be guards. of Edward, Charles,
Obediah, John, Peleg & Jonathan Slade (all under 14), sons of

WILLIAM SLADE of Swan., dtd. 17 Nov. 1741 [10:104].

Appt. of Hannah Slade of Swan., widow, to be guard. of Mary Slade & Ruth Slade (minors over 14), daus. of WILLIAM SLADE of Swan., dtd. 17 Nov. 1741 [10:104/5].

Appt. of William Wilbour of Lit. Comp., Yeoman, to be guard. of Elizebeth Coe (under 14), dau. of SAMUEL COE of Lit. Comp., dtd. 3 Nov. 1741 [10:105/6].

Appt. of Job Mason of Swan., Tanner, to be guard. of Benjamin Slade (minor over 14), son of WILLIAM SLADE of Swan., dtd. 17 Nov. 1741 [10:106].

Acct. of Mercy Phiney, widow & Adm. of Est. of JONATHAN PHINEY of Swan., dtd. 17 Nov. 1741 [10:106/7].

Acct. of Samuel Willis, Adm. of Est. of SAMUEL HALL of Taun. dcd. intest., dtd. 17 Nov. 1741. Mentions items to Samuel Blake & wife of Taun. & to Barnibas Crossman & wife of Middleborough for legacies from the "Last Will of the Said Deceaseds father" [10:107/8/9].

Acct. of Mary Coe, widow & Adm. of Est. of SAMUEL COE of Lit. Comp., dtd. 18 Nov. 1741 [10:109/10].

Appt. of Henry West of Reho., Yeoman, to be guard. of Noah Millard (under 14), son of NATHANIEL MILLARD of Reho., dtd. 3 Nov. 1741 [10:110].

Order to Seth Richmond of Taun., Yeoman, Exec. of Est. of his father EDWARD RICHMOND of Taun., dtd. 9 Dec. 1741 [10:111],

Will of EDWARD RICHMOND of Taun., dtd. 3 June 1738, prob. 9 Dec. 1741. Wife Mary. Sons: Edward [*once called "Richard," probably erroneously*], Josiah, Nathaniel & Seth Richmond. Daus: Mary Burt, Mercy Walker, Pricilla Hacket, Sarah Crane & Phebe Eliot. My brother John Richmond. Lands in Taun. & Middleboro. Son Seth to be Exec. Witns: John Richmond, John Richmond, Jr. & Elkanah Leonard [10:111.2.3].

Inv. of Est. of Capt. JOHN KING of Rayn., Gentleman, dtd. 13 Nov. 1741, pres. by Philip King, son & Exec. Pers. est. 749-9-9; no real est. Apprs: Jonathan Shaw, Samuel Leonard & Samuel White [10:113/4].

Order to Daniel Wilbour of Swan., Yeoman, Exec. of Est. of his father DANIEL WILBOUR of Swan., dtd. 15 Dec. 1741 [10:114/5].

Will of DANIEL WILBOUR of Swan., Husbandman, dtd. 4 May 1740, prob. 15 Dec. 1741. Wife Ann. Sons: William, John (dcd.), Peleg, Daniel & Thomas Wilbour. Daus: Martha, Lidia, Elizebeth [*no surnames*] & Ann Carpenter. Grson. John Wilbour son of my son Peleg. Grson. Wilbour Carpenter. Indian slave Jane. "Two mollato Slaves" Jacob & Rose. Lands at Narraganset in East Greenwich, R.I. to go to Peleg & then his son John. Witns: James Anthoney (a Quaker), John Chace & William Hart[10:114/5/6/7].

Order to Josiah Fuller of Reho., Yeoman, Exec. of Est. of his grfather SILAS TITUS of Reho., dtd. 15 Dec. 1741 [10:117].

Will of SILAS TITUS of Reho., Yeoman, dtd. 22 Feb. 1727/8, prob. 15 Dec. 1741. Wife Mehetibel given the "moveable Estate She

Brought with her to my house." Sons: Silas (eldest) & Paul Ti-
tus. Daus: Martha Titus & Esther Hill wife of John Hill. Grdau.
Sarah Newell. Grson. Josiah Fuller to be Exec. Witns: Daniel
Carpenter, Peter Walker & Bithiah Lyon [10:118/9].
Inv. of Est. of DANIEL WILBOUR of Swan., pres. 15 Dec. 1741 by
Daniel Wilbour, son & Exec. Mentions: "the farm where Thomas
Wilbour Lives," "the Land Next to Job Carpenters" & "The Land
given to Wilbour Carpenter." Pers. est. 1647-11-6; real est.
9213-0-0. Apprs: Edward Slade, Job Chase & William Hart [10:
119/20].
Order to div. real est. of JAMES PAUL of Digh. dcd. intest., dtd.
3 Nov. 1741 [10:120].
Div. of real est. of JAMES PAUL of Digh. btwn. his widow [not
named] & his chldn: James Paul (son), Lidiah Paul (dau.) &
Elizebeth Briggs (dau.), dtd. 16 Nov. 1741. Comm: Abraham
Shaw, David Walker, Ephraim Atwood, David Whitmarsh & Ephraim
Emerson [10:121].
Order to div. Est. of ANDREW STARKEY of Attl., dtd. 1 March 17-
40/1 [10:122].
Div. of Est. of ANDREW STARKEY of Attl. btwn. his widow [not
named] & his chldn: John Starkey (eldest son), Andrew Starkey
(2nd son), Thomas Starkey (3rd son), Mehetibel Waite (eldest
dau.) & Jemima Starkey, dtd. 19 Sept. 1741. Comm: Samuel Ty-
ler, Obediah Fuller, Josiah Maxey & Thomas Wilmouth [10:122/
3/4/5/6].
Inv. of Est. of JOHN TORREY, dtd. 22 Jan. 1740. Pers. est. 547-
19-9; real est. 1000-0-0. Apprs: James Smith, James Adams &
Ebenezer Adams [10:126].
Appt. of George Rouse of Lit. Comp., Yeoman, to be Adm. of Est.
of his father JAMES ROUSE of Lit. Comp. dcd. intest., dtd. 8
March 1741 [10:127].
Appt. of Jonathan Woodbury, Esq., of Brist. to be guard. of Peter Norton (minor over 14), son of SHUBAL NORTON of Brist.,
Mariner, dtd. 12 March 1741 [10:127/8].
Appt. of Joseph Russell of Brist., Gentleman, to be guard. of
Elizebeth Walker of Brist., a widow who is non compus mentis,
dtd. 12 March 1741 [10:128].
Appt. of Sarah Mosher of Dart, widow, to be Adm. of Est. of her
husb. BENJAMIN MOSHER of Dart. dcd. intest., dtd. 16 March
1741 [10:129].
Order to Oliver Mason of Swan., Housewright, Exec. of Est. of
his father ISAAC MASON of Swan., dtd. 16 March 1741 [10:129/
30].
Will of ISAAC MASON of Swan., Yeoman, "being advanced in age,"
dtd. 7 March 1741, prob. 16 March 1741. Wife Hannah. Sons:
Isaac, Samson, Nathan, Hezekiah (dcd.) & Oliver ("that Liveth
with me") Mason. Daus. Hannah Luis & Mary Bowen. Grchldn.
Malatiah Mason, Hezekiah Mason & Phebe Mason chldn. of my son
Hezekiah (dcd.). Witns: Elisha Mason, Israel Cole & Joseph
Mason [10:130/1].

Inv. of Est. of JOHN TALMAN of Tiv., Surgeon, dtd. 14 Jan. 17-
41/2, pres. by Joseph Anthoney, Exec. Incl. item for "Goods
that Were his Wifes Before marriage." Pers. est. 537-15-10;
no real est. Apprs: John Howland, Samuel Durfey & Samuel Borden [10:131/2].
Inv. of Est. of BENJAMIN MOSHER of Dart., dtd. 7 Jan. 1741/2,
pres. by Sarah Mosher, widow & Adm. Pers. est. not totalled;
real est. 459-0-0. Apprs: George Lawton, Ichabod Potter &
Nathaniel Soule [10:134][page numbering error].
Appt. of Hannah Peck of Reho., widow, to be Adm. of Est. of her
husb. JOSEPH PECK of Reho. dcd. intest., dtd. 20 Apr. 1742
[10:135].
Appt. of Philip Whelar of Reho., Yeoman, to be guard. of John
Whelar (minor over 14), son of JAMES WHELAR of Reho., dtd. 20
Apr. 1742 [10:135/6].
Order to Ebenezer Fish of Dart., Yeoman, Exec. of Est. of his
father JOHN FISH of Dart., Yeoman, dtd. 20 Apr. 1742[10:136].
Will of JOHN FISH of Dart., Yeoman, dtd. 4 Apr. 1737, prob. 20
Apr. 1742. Wife Joan. Sons: Ebenezer & John Fish. Daus: Mary
Potter wife of William Potter, Abigail Case wife of John Case,
Mehetibel Cornel wife of William Cornel, Joana Fisher wife of
John Fisher, Hope Phillips wife of James Phillips, Susanah
Boyce wife of Benjamin Boyce, Elizebeth Fish, Sarah Arnold
wife of Anthoney Arnold, Alce Phillips (dcd.) & Patiance Rath-
bone (dcd.). 4 grchldn: Sarah, William, John & Thomas Phill-
lips (all minors), chldn. of my dau. Alce dcd. Grson Joshua
Rathbone son of my dau. Patiance dcd. Son Ebenezer to be Exec:
Witns: William Richetson, Benjamin Gifford & William Bowdish
[10:136/7/8/9].
Order to Lemuel Pope of Dart., Gentleman, Exec. of Est. of his
mother REBECAH POPE of Dart., dtd. 20 Apr. 1742 [10:139/40].
Will of REBEKAH POPE of Dart., widow, dtd. 8 Jan. 1741, prob.
20 Apr. 1742. Son Lemuel Pope. 4 grdaus: Rebekah Pope dau. of
my son Lemuel, Rebekah Peabody dau. of David Peabody (dcd.)
of Boxford, Rebekah Williams dau. of Samuel Hunt (dcd.) of
Dart. & Rebekah Church dau. of Charles Church (dcd.) of Free.
Grson. Lewin Pope son of Lemuel Pope. Grson. Seth Pope son of
Lemuel Pope. Dau[-in-law?] Elizebeth Pope wife of Lemuel Pope.
Patience Jenne [no relationship stated]. Grdau. Mercy Pope.
Son Lemuel to be Exec. Witns: Richard Pearce, Meribah Roon
& Gideon Southworth [10:140/1].
Inv. of Est. of ISAAC MASON of Swan., dtd. 31 March 1742, pres.
by Oliver Mason, son & Exec. Pers. est. 148-4-0; no real est.
Apprs: Israel Cole, Martin Luther & John Wood, Jr. [10:141/2].
Inv. of Est. of JOSEPH PECK of Reho., pres. 20 Apr. 1742 by Han-
nah Peck, widow & Adm. Pers. est. 401-11-6; real est. 1080-0-
0. Apprs: Jabiz Bosworth, Jonathan Chaiffe & Samuel Mason
[10:142/3].
Appt. of Richard Godfrey of Taun., Yeoman, to be guard. of Bethiah Richmond, dau. of WILLIAM RICHMOND of Taun., dtd. 3 May

1742 [10:143/4].

Appt. of Samuel Pitts of Taun., Gentleman, to be guard. of Ruth
Richmond (minor over 14), dau. of WILLIAM RICHMOND of Taun.,
dtd. 7 May 1742 [10:144].

Order to Jerusha Jenne of Dart., widow & Exec. of Est. of her
husb. SAMUEL JENNE of Dart., dtd. 18 May 1742 [10:146][*page
numbering error*].

Will of SAMUEL JENNE of Dart., Yeoman, "Being Sick and Weak of
Body," dtd. 24 Apr. 1742, prob. 18 May 1742. Wife Jerusha.
Sons: Sympson & Aron Jenne. Daus: Anne Jenne, Ruth Jenne, Eliz-
ebeth Jenne & Experiance (youngest dau., under 7) Jenne. Wife
to be Exec. Witns: Benjamin Burges, Ephraim Hunt & Richard
Pearce [10:146/7/8].

Inv. of Est. of SAMUEL JENNE of Dart., Yeoman, dtd. 17 May 1742,
pres. by Jerusha Jenne, widow & Exec. Pers. est. 185-17-0;
real est. 700-0-0. Apprs: Nathaniel Blackwell, Ephraim Hunt
& Christopher Turner [10:148/9].

Acct. of Anna Devil, widow & Exec. of Est. of BENJAMIN DEVIL of
Dart., dtd. 18 May 1742 [10:149].

Appt. of Hannah Delino of Dart., widow, to be guard. of Stephen
Delino, Hannah Delino & Sarah Delino (all under 14), chldn.
of JABIZ DELINO of Dart., dtd. 18 May 1742 [10:150].

Inv. of Est. of JAMES ROUSE of Lit. Comp., dtd. 15 May 1742,
pres. by George Rouse, son & Adm. Pers. est. 355-19-0; real
est. 930-0-0. Apprs: Fobes Little, William Richmond & John
Brown [10:150/1].

Acct. of Hannah Delino, widow & Adm. of Est. of her husb. JABIZ
DELINO of Dart. dcd. intest., dtd. 18 May 1742 [10:152/3].

Appt. of Abraham Shearman of Dart., Cooper, to be guard. of Eu-
nice Delino (minor over 14), dau. of JABIZ DELINO of Dart.,
Yeoman, dtd. 18 May 1742 [10:153/4].

Appt. of Abiel Simmons of Swan., Yeoman, to be Adm. of Est. of
his brother JOSEPH SIMMONS of Swan., Yeoman, dcd. intest.,
dtd. 18 May 1742 [10:154/5].

Appt. of Benjamin Brown of Reho., Yeoman, to be guard. of Win-
chester Peck & Jerusha Peck (minors over 14), chldn. of JO-
SEPH PECK of Reho., dtd. 18 May 1742 [10:155].

Appt. of Abraham Shearman of Dart., Yeoman, to be guard. of Mercy Delino (minor over 14), dau. of JABIZ DELINO of Dart., dtd.
18 May 1742 [10:156].

Report of claims against Est. of JAMES WHELER, Jr. of Reho. dcd.
intest., dtd. 18 May 1742. Comm: Jonathan Woodbury, Samuel
Royal & Joseph Russell. Mentions his widow Elizebeth Wheler.
Philip Wheler, Adm. [10:156/7/8/9].

Order to Benjamin Brown, Yeoman, Exec. of Est. of his mother
MARGARET BROWN of Barr., widow, dtd. 18 May 1742 [10:159].

Will of MARGARET BROWN of Barr., Spinster, dtd. 6 Feb. 1733/4,
prob. 18 May 1742, Chldn. [*not named*] of my son James Brown
dcd. Chldn. [*not named*] of my son William Brown dcd. Grson.

William Carpenter. Chldn. [*not named*] of my son Isaac Brown
dcd. My son Benjamin Brown. Nathan son of my son Benjamin.
My 4 daus: Mary Angil, Ann Hill, Dorothey Medbury & Mercy Carpenter. Son Benjamin to be Exec. Witns: John Aplin, Hezekiah
Brown & Charles Brown [10:159/60/1].

Appt. of Sarah Spooner of Dart., widow, to be Adm. of Est. of
her husb. SIMPSON SPOONER of Dart. dcd. intest., dtd. 18 May
1742 [10:161].

Inv. of Est. of JOSEPH SIMMONS of Swan., dtd. 10 May 1742, pres.
by Abiel Simmons, brother & Adm. Pers. est. 83-0-0; real est.
75-0-0. Apprs: Benjamin Buffington, Ephraim Hathaway & Henry
Hoar [10:162

Order to Jonathan Records of Lit. Comp., Yeoman, Exec. of Est.
of his father JONATHAN RECORDS of Lit. Comp., Setwork Cooper,
dtd. 15 June 1742 [10:162].

Will of JONATHAN RECORDS of Lit. Comp., Setwork Cooper, "being
Sick," dtd. 10 May 1742, prob. 15 June 1742. Wife Mary. Sons
Jonathan Records & John Records ("if he be in the Land of the
Living...if he ever Returns home again"). Daus: Hannah Wilbour
Mary Church, Martha Wilbour, Comfort Tabor & Abishad Briggs.
Son Jonathan to be Exec. Witns: Richard Brownel, Thomas
Brownel & Nathaniel Searl [10:163/4].

Inv. of Est. of JONATHAN RECORDS of Lit. Comp., dtd. 11 June
1742, pres. by Jonathan Records, son & Exec. Pers. est. 722-
6-5; real est. 360-0-0. Apprs: Thomas Brownel, William Richmond & Charles Brownel [10:164/5].

Appt. of Experiance Lee of Reho., widow, to be Adm. of Est. of
her husb. RICHARD LEE of Reho., Husbandman, dcd. intest., dtd.
15 June 1742 [10:165/6].

Inv. of Est. of RICHARD LEE of Reho., dtd. 25 May 1742, pres. by
Experiance Lee, widow & Adm. Pers. est. 88-8-9; no real est.
Apprs: Daniel Ormsbee, Samuel Peck & Samuel Atherton [10:166/
7].

Appt. of Martha Read of Reho., widow, to be guard. of Ruth Read
(minor over 14), dau. of ZACHARIAH READ of Reho., dtd. 15 June
1742 [10:167].

Appt. of Thomas French of Attl., Yeoman, to be guard. of Martha
Read (minor over 14), dau. of ZACHARIAH READ of Reho., dtd.
15 June 1742 [10:167/8].

Appt. of Martha Read of Reho., widow, to be guard. of Hipzebeth
Read (under 14), dau. of ZACHARIAH READ of Reho., dtd. 15 June
1742 [10:168/9].

Appt. of Mary Gofe of Reho., widow, to be Adm. of Est. of her
husb. JAMES GOFE of Reho. dcd. intest., dtd. 15 June 1742
[10:169].

Inv. of Est. of JAMES GOFE of Reho., dtd. 25 May 1742, pres. by
Mary Gofe, widow & Adm. Pers. est. 29-8-3; real est. 74-7-6.
Apprs: John Wilmouth, Abial Carpenter & Ephraim Hunt [10:169/
70].

Acct. of Ebenezer Carpenter, Exec. of Est. of his father JAMES
CARPENTER of Reho., dtd. 15 June 1742. Incl. legacies per
will to: Dorothey Mansfield & Susanah Carpenter [10:170/1].
Acct. of Martha Read, Adm. of Est. of her husb. ZACHARIAH READ
of Reho., dtd. 15 June 1742. Incl. items "worn out by the
Childreen" [10:171].
Acct. of Hannah Brittain, Adm. of Est. of JAMES BRITTAIN of
Digh., dtd. 15 June 1742. Incl. items: to Lydia Brittain, to
Ebenezer Brittain [10:172/3].
Appt. of Sarah Howland of Tiv., widow, to be Adm. of Est. of
her husb. BENJAMIN HOWLAND of Tiv. dcd. intest., dtd. 8 June
1742 [10:173/4].
Appt. of Thomas Church, Esq., of Lit. Comp. to be guard. of Eliz-
ebeth Head of Lit. Comp., widow, who is non compus mentis, dtd.
11 June 1742 [10:174/5].
Inv. of Est. of ELIZEBETH HEAD of Lit. Comp., widow, "Who is Now
non Compus," dtd. 20 July 1742. Pers. Est. 13-17-0; no real
est. Apprs: John Hunt, John Brown & William Davis [10:175].
Inv. of Est. of BENJAMIN HOWLAND of Tiv., Mariner, dtd. June 1742
pres. by Sarah Howland, widow & Adm. Pers. est. 134-16-0; real
est. 300-0-0. Apprs: Joseph Anthoney, Thomas Anthoney & George
Westgeats [10:175/6].
Appt. of Sarah Briggs of Reho., widow, to be Adm. of Est. of her
husb. NATHANIEL BRIGGS of Reho., Yeoman, dcd. intest., dtd. 20
July 1742 [10:176].
Acct. of Elizbeth Davenport, widow & Adm. of Est. of JOHN DAVEN-
PORT of Tiv., dtd. 20 July 1742 [10:177].
Acct. of Mary Welman & Isaac Welman, Adms. of Est. of ISAAC WEL-
MAN of Nort. dcd. intest., dtd. 20 July 1742. Incl. item: "Paid
for mourning for his Daughter" [10:177/8].
Will of JOHN ANDREWS of Taun., "being Aged," dtd. 30 Sept. 1736,
prob. 17 Aug. 1742. 4 daus: Alice Linkon, Hannah Linkon, Mar-
tha Jones & Susannah (youngest) Andrews. 4 sons: John, Edmond,
Samuel & Seth Andrews. No wife mentioned. Of dau. Susannah
is said: "Seing She have Lived Longist [sic] and Don most for
her two mothers." Son John to be Exec. Witns: Seth Williams,
Seth Sumner & John Sumner [10:179].
Order to John Andrews of Nort., Yeoman, Exec. of Est. of his
father JOHN ANDREWS of Taun., dtd. 17 Aug. 1742 [10:180].
Acct. of Mary Coe of Lit. Comp., widow & Adm. of Est. of SAMUEL
COE of Lit. Comp., dtd. 17 Aug. 1742. Incl. var. items "spent
in the Familey" [10:180/1/2].
Appt. of Samuel Eddy of Swan., Yeoman, to be guard. of James Mil-
lard, son of JOHN MILLARD of Swan., dtd. 17 Aug. 1742 [10:182].
Inv. of Est. of SIMPSON SPOONER of Dart., House Carpenter, dtd.
17 June 1742, pres. by Sarah Spooner, widow & Adm. Pers. est.
180-6-10; real est. 226-0-0. Apprs: Jabiz Shearman, Eliakim
Willis & Seth Spooner [10:183/4].
Order to Jacob Taber of Dart., Yeoman, Exec. of Est. of JOHN WAL-
KER of Dart., Blacksmith, dtd. 19 Oct. 1742 [10:184].

Will of JOHN WALKER of Dart., Blacksmith, dtd. 22 Apr. 1742,
prob. 19 Oct. 1742. Wife Sarah. Son John Walker. Daus: Jene-
very Walker, Mary Walker, Hannah Walker & Keziah Walker. Friend
Jacob Taber to be Exec. Witns: Jareth Swift, Deborah Spooner
& Stephen West, Jr. [10:185/6].

Appt. of George Weastgeat of Tiv., Cordwainer, to be guard. of
his chldn. George Wastgeat, John Weastgeat, Earl Weastgeat &
Pricilla Weastgeat (all under 14), chldn. of ELIZEBETH WEAST-
GEAT of Tiv., dtd. 19 Oct. 1742 [10:186].

Appt. of George Badcock of Dart., Wheelwright, to be guard. of
Moses Spooner (minor over 14), son of BARNABAS SPOONER of Dart.
dtd. 19 Oct. 1742 [10:186/7].

Acct. of Elizebeth Brown of Attl., widow & Exec. of Est. of JOHN
BROWN of Attl., dtd. 19 Oct. 1742 [10:187/8].

Inv. of Est. of JOHN WALKER of Dart., Blacksmith, dtd. 21 June
1742, pres. by Jacob Taber, Exec. Pers. est. 266-4-0; real
est. 300-0-0. Apprs: Nathaniel Blackwell, Jareth Swift & Eliakim Willis [10:188].

Inv. of Est. of Capt. JOHN ANDREWS of Taun., dtd. 2 Sept. 1742,
pres. by John Andrews, Exec. Pers. est. 177-5-2¼; no real est.
Apprs: Seth Williams, Benjamin Wilbour & Samuel White [10:189].

Inv. of Est. of NATHANIEL BRIGGS of Reho., Yeoman, dtd. 13 Aug.
1742, pres. by Sarah Briggs, widow & Adm. Pers. est. 128-13-6;
real est. 212-0-0. Apprs: not listed [10:189/90].

Order to Elizebeth Brownel, widow, & William Brownel, son, both
of Dart., Execs. of Est. of GEORGE BROWNEL of Dart., dtd. 19
Oct. 1742 [10:190/1].

Will of GEORGE BROWNEL of Dart., Yeoman, "Being Sick of Body,"
dtd. 27 Sept. 1742, prob. 19 Oct. 1742. Wife Elizebeth. Sons:
William (Wheelwright, Joyner & Carpenter), Jonathan, George,
Benjamin, Timothey & Elijah Brownel (last five under 21). Daus:
Hannah, Sarah, Elizebeth & Phebe (under 18) (all unmar.). Wife
& son William to be Execs. Witns: Benjamin Burgis, John Rouse
& William Palmer [10:191/2/3].

Order to Sarah Brown of Attl., widow & Exec. of Est. of her husb.
BENJAMIN BROWN of Attl., Husbandman, dtd. 19 Oct. 1742 [10:
193/4].

Will of BENJAMIN BROWN of Attl., Husbandman, "Being very Sick
and Weak," dtd. 23 Aug. 1742, prob. 19 Oct. 1742. Wife Sarah.
Son Benjamin Brown, son Jeremiah Brown (under age) & "my four
youngest sons," [not named]. "My Seven Daughters"[not named]
(all under age & unmar.). Witns: Noah Carpenter, Ebenezer
Robinson & Thomas Bowen [10:194/5/6].

Acct. of Sarah Read, widow & Adm. of Est. of THOMAS READ of
Digh., dtd. Oct. 1742. Calls Est. insolvent [10:196/7].

Order to Barzillia Hammond of Rochester, Co. of Plimouth, Yeoman, Exec. of Est. of SAMUEL HIX of Dart., Yeoman, dtd. 29
Oct. 1742 [10:197].

Will of SAMUEL HIX of Dart., Yeoman, "Being in health," dtd. 1

Oct. 1741, prob. 29 Oct. 1742. Wife Ruth. Mary Cocklen [*re-lationship not stated*]. Friend Barzillia Hammond of Rochester, Co. of Plimouth, to be Exec. Witns: Nathaniel Church, Israel Hammond & Roger Hammond [10:198].
Order to Barsheba Brown of Attl., widow & Exec. of Est. of her husb. JOHN BROWN of Attl., Cooper, dtd. 16 Nov. 1742 [10:199].
Will of JOHN BROWN of Attl., Cooper, "Being Very Sick and Weak," dtd. 15 Oct. 1742, prob. 16 Nov. 1742. Wife Barsheba to be Exec. & appt. to be guard. of his one child, a son [*not named*]. Witns: Noah Carpenter, Ebenezer Robinson & Jonathan Ormsbee [10:199/200].
Appt. of Ruth Joy of Reho., widow, to be guard. of David, Deborah, Tabitha, Obediah & Loes Joy (all under 14), chldn. of DAVID JOY of Reho., dtd. 16 Nov. 1742 [10:201].
Appt. of Thomas Bowen of Attl., Yeoman, to be guard. of Philip Brown (minor over 14), son of JOHN BROWN of Attl., dtd. 16 Nov. 1742 [10:201/2].
Appt. of Joseph Bowen of Attl., Blacksmith, to be guard. of Abeal Brown (minor over 14), son of JOHN BROWN of Attl., dtd. 16 Nov. 1742 [10:202].
Inv. of Est. of BENJAMIN BROWN of Attl., dtd. 14 Oct. 1742, pres. by Sarah Brown, widow & Exec. Pers. est. 109-15-6; real est. 200-0-0. Apprs: Noah Carpenter, Ebenezer Robinson & Jonathan Ormsbee [10:202/3].
Acct. of Sarah Briggs, widow & Adm. of Est. of NATHANIEL BRIGGS of Reho., dtd. 21 Oct. 1742. Incl. payms. to: Eliger Briggs, Noah Briggs, James Briggs, Abiel Briggs & Thomas Briggs [10: 203/4].
Acct. of Sarah Pope "Late Sarah Torrey," Exec. of Est. of her former husb. JOHN TORREY of Barr., dtd. 29 Oct. 1742. Incl. items: "Legacy given to the widow and two Daughters by Will." Paym. to "Mrs Sarah Chandler formerly Sarah Paine" [10:204/5/6].
Order for div. of Est. of EDWARD WING of Dart. dcd. intest., dtd. 25 Sept. 1741 [10:206].
Div. of Est. of EDWARD WING of Dart. dcd. intest., btwn. his widow now Patience Wood (wife of William Wood, Glazier) & his chldn: Abraham Wing (eldest son), Jemima Wing (dau.), Sarah Wing (dau.), Edward Wing (son), Deborah Wing (dau.), Mary Wing (dau.) & Hannah (dau.) wife of George Moshier, dtd. 8 June 1742 Comm: William Wood, Jabez Shearman & Stephen Shearman [10:206/ 7/8/9/10/1].
Acct. of Ruth Joy, widow & Adm. of Est. of DAVID JOY of Reho., dtd. 16 Nov. 1742 [10:211/2].
Appt. of Sarah Shove of Digh., widow, to be Adm. of Est. of her husb. GEORGE SHOVE of Digh. dcd. intest., dtd. 21 Dec. 1742 [10:213].
Appt. of Edward Glover of Reho., Yeoman, to be guard. of Timothey, Jesse & Elizebeth Perrin (minors over 14), chldn. of JOHN PERRIN of Reho., not dtd. [10:213].

Appt. of Ann Walker of Reho., widow, to be guard. of Munroe Walker & Joseph Walker (both under 14), chldn. of PHILIP WALKER of Reho., dtd. 21 Dec. 1742 [10:214].

Appt. of Mary Paul of Digh., widow, to be guard. as chosen by James Paul (minor over 14), son of JAMES PAUL of Digh., dtd. 15 Sept. 1741 [sic][10:214/5].

Appt. of William Jemeson of Lit. Comp., "Taylor," to be guard. of William, Rebecah, Joanah & Mary Jemeson (all under 14), grchldn. of JAMES ROUSE of Lit. Comp., dtd. 21 Dec. 1742 [10: 215].

Appt. of Mary Walker of Reho., widow, to be guard. of Martha, Lidia & Ann Walker (all under 14), daus. of EPHRAIM WALKER of Reho., dtd. 21 Dec. 1742 [10:215/6].

Appt. of Abial Carpenter of Reho., Yeoman, to be guard. of Philip Walker (minor over 14), son of PHILIP WALKER of Reho., dtd. 21 Dec. 1742 [10:216].

Appt. of Samuel Newman of Reho., Yeoman, to be guard. of Oliver Walker (minor over 14), son of PHILIP WALKER of Reho., dtd. 21 Dec. 1742 [10:216/7].

Appt. of Daniel Salsbury of Swan., Cordwainer, to be guard. of his wife Ann Salsbury (minor over 14), dau. of JOHN HAIL of Swan., dtd. 21 Dec. 1742 [10:217].

Appt. of Elisha Mason of Swan., Tanner, to be guard. of John Hail (minor over 14), son of JOHN HAIL of Swan., dtd. 21 Dec. 1742 [10:218].

Appt. of David Carpenter of Reho., Tanner, to be guard. of Sarah Abel (minor over 14), dau. of JOSHUA ABEL of Reho., dtd. 21 Dec. 1742 [10:218/9].

Order to Samuel Hix of Tiv., Yeoman, Exec. of Est. of his father SAMUEL HIX of Tiv., dtd. 21 Dec. 1742 [10:219].

Agrmt. abt. div. of real est. of SIMON DAVIS, Esq., of Brist. into 6 equal parts among his heirs, signed by: Capt. Nicholas Davis of Boston, Co. of Suffolk, Merchant; Capt. Simon Davis of Brist., Mariner; Shubal Norton of Brist., Mariner and his wife Sarah; John Newton of Brist., Mariner, and his wife Ann; Henry Bragg of Brist., Merchant, and his wife Elizebeth; & Capt. Jonathan Woodbury, Esq., of Brist. as attorney for Francis Throope of Woodstock, Co. of Worcester, widow, dtd. 1 Feb. 1736/7 [10:219/20/1].

Div. of real est. of SIMON DAVIS, Esq., of Brist. into 6 equal shares, dtd. 9 Feb. 1736/7. Comm: Samuel Royal, Joseph Russell & Samuel Smith [10:221/2/3].

Final agrmt. abt. drawing of the 6 shares of the div. of real est. of SIMON DAVIS, signed by his heirs: Capt. Nicholas Davis of Boston, Merchant; Capt. Simon Davis of Brist., Mariner; Shubal Norton of Brist., Mariner, & his wife Sarah; John Newton of Brist., Mariner, & his wife Ann; Henry Bragg of Brist., Merchant, & his wife Elizebeth; & Francis Throope of Woodstock, County of Worcester, widow, dtd. 30 March 1737. Witns: Samuel Howland, Tabitha Howland & Charles Church. On 2nd Tue. of

June 1738 Samuel Howland swore he saw Shubal Norton (since dcd.)
sign the above agrmt. [10:223/4/5].

Order to Ann Wood of Dart., widow & Exec. of Est. of her husb.
GEORGE WOOD of Dart., dtd. 21 Dec. 1742 [10:227].

Order to James Day of Boston, Co. of Suffolk, Distiller, Exec.
of Est. of his father JOSEPH DAY of Attl., Husbandman, dtd. 21
Dec. 1742 [10:227/8].

Appt. of Abia Follet of Attl., widow, to be Adm. of Est. of her
husb. JONATHAN FOLLET of Attl., Husbandman, dcd. intest., dtd.
18 Jan. 1742 [10:228].

Appt. of Abigail Follet. of Attl., widow, to be Adm. of Est. of
her husb. ROBERT FOLLET of Attl., Husbandman, dcd. intest.,
dtd. 18 Jan. 1742 [10:228/9].

Order to James Wheaton of Nedham, Co. of Suffolk, Housewright,
Exec. of Est. of his father JAMES WHEATON of Reho., dtd. 18
Jan. 1742 [10:229].

Will of JOSEPH DAY of Attl., Husbandman, dtd. 5 May 1739, prob.
21 Dec. 1742. Wife Martha. Son James to be Exec. Calls for later equal div. of remaining Est. "Among all my Childreen Excepting my son Joseph and my Daughter Rebeccah." Witns: Samuel Day, Aron Davis & John Foster [10:230].

Will of SAMUEL HICKS of Tiv., Yeoman, dtd. 20 June 1736, prob.
21 Dec. 1742. Wife Susanah. Son Samuel Hicks. 6 daus: Sarah
Peckham (eldest), Alce Hicks, Leah Hicks, Susanah Hicks, Abigail Hicks & Mary Hicks. Son to be Exec. Witns: John Anthoney
Joseph Anthoney & Joseph Borden [10:230/1/2].

Inv. of Est. of SAMUEL HICKS of Dart., dtd. 12 Jan. 1742/3, pres.
by Barzillia Hammond, Exec. Pers. est. 130-18-6; no real est.
Apprs: Nathaniel Church, Israel Hammond & Archelus Hammond
[10:233].

Acct. of Rachel Perrin now Rachel Glover, Adm. of Est. of JOHN
PERRIN of Reho., dtd. 21 Dec. 1742. Incl. item for "fitting
Two Apprintices with Clothing." Mentions "Provisions Spent in
the familey" [10:233/4].

Inv. of Est. of GEORGE SHOVE of Digh., dtd. 6 Jan. 1741, pres.
by Sarah Shove, widow & Adm. Pers. est. 272-16-0; no real est.
Apprs: Benjamin Jones, James Dean & Isaac Hathaway [10:235].

Will of PHILIP WALKER of Reho., Yeoman, "Being sick and weak,"
dtd. 9 Oct. 1742, prob. 21 Dec. 1742. Wife Anne. Sons: Munroo
Walker (under 21), Oliver Walker (under 21), Philip Walker,
Joseph Walker & Elijah Walker. Wife to be Exec. Witns: Josiah
Cushing, Thomas Allen & David Turner [10:235/6/7].

Will of GEORGE WOOD of Dart., dtd. 28 Oct. 1742, prob. 21 Dec.
1742. Wife Ann. Sons: William (eldest) & George Wood. Mentions
lands in Dart. & Lit. Comp. Wife to be Exec. Witns: Ruben
Peckcom, Samuel Irish & Philip Tabor [10:237/8].

Inv. of Est. of GEORGE WOOD of Dart., dtd. 25 Nov. 1742, pres.
by Ann Wood, widow & Exec. Pers. est. 454-14-10; real est.
1380-0-0. Apprs: Philip Tabor, John Wilbour & Ichabon [sic]
Potter [10:239].

Inv. of Est. of SAMUEL HICKS of Tiv., Yeoman, dtd. 20 Dec. 1742,
pres. by Samuel Hix, son & Exec. Pers. est. not totalled; real
est. 1500-0-0. Apprs: Joseph Anthoney, Samuel Durphey & Samuel Borden [10:240/1].

Inv. of Est. of JOSEPH DAY of Attl., dtd. 7 Jan. 1742, pres. by
Joseph Day, Exec. Pers. est. 219-10-6; real est. 355-0-0.
Apprs: John Robbins, Benjamin Day & Nathaniel Robinson [10:
241/2].

Will of JAMES WHEATON of Reho., Housewright, "Being in a good
measure of health," dtd. 4 Sept. 1740, prob. 18 Jan. 1742. Wife
Mary. Sons: Caleb (eldest), James, Comfort, Constant & Mason
Wheaton (some under 21). 3 daus: Christian Wheaton alias Wood,
Mary Wheaton (unmar.) & Hannah Wheaton. Wife to be "Guardian
to my Childreen under age." My 3 brothers: Robert, Ephraim &
Daniel Wheaton. Son James to be Exec. Witns: Seth Bullock,
Hezekiah Bullock & Samuel Bullock [10:242/3/4].

Acct. of Mary Wood Walker [sic], Adm. of Est. of ISAAC WOOD of
Dart., dtd. 21 Dec. 1742. At time it was presented she was
called "Mary Walker Widdow and Adminstratrix to the Estate of
Ephraim Walker Late of Rehoboth," with no reference then to
Isaac Wood. The amt. of the Inv. with which the "accomptant"
was charged was 481-13-6 "taken into the Registers Office,"
is not the amount of the Inv. for Isaac Wood, listed in 10:
66/7/8, above [This entry may be an inadvertent mixture of
portions of entries for two different persons][10:245/6].

Appt. of Enos Gifford of Lit. Comp., Yeoman, to be guard. of
Christopher Borden (minor over 14), son of THOMAS BORDEN of
Tiv., dtd. 15 Feb. 1742 [10:246].

Appt. of Obediah Read of Reho., Yeoman, to be guard. of Joshua
Abel (under 14), son of JOSHUA ABEL of Reho., dtd. 15 Feb.
1742/3 [10:246/7].

Appt. of Esther Brown of Barr., widow, to be guard. of Thomas
Brown & Mary Brown (both under 14), chldn. of ISAAC BROWN of
Barr., dtd. 15 Feb. 1742/3 [10:247].

Appt. of Benjamin Brown of Reho., Gentleman, to be guard. of
Peleg Brown(minor over 14), son of ISAAC BROWN of Barr., dtd.
15 Feb. 1742/3 [10:248].

Appt. of John Newman of Reho., Yeoman, to be guard. of Joannah
Abel (under 14), dau. of JOSHUA ABEL of Reho., dtd. 15 Feb.
1742/3 [10:248/9].

Appt. of Seth Mackpeice of Nort., Yeoman, to be Adm. of Est. of
his bro. WILLIAM MACKPEICE of Nort., since Experiance Mackpeice his widow is since dcd., dtd. 15 Feb. 1742 [10:249].

Acct. of Patiance Butterworth, widow & Adm. of Est. of her husb.
SAMUEL BUTTERWORTH of Reho., dtd. 15 Feb. 1742/3. Incl. item
for "Provisions Spent in the familey" [10:250].

Appt. of James Brown of Barr., Yeoman, to be guard. of Enoch
Remington (minor over 14), son of THOMAS REMINGTON of Barr.,
dtd. 15 March 1742/3 [10:251].

Appt. of William Peck of Digh., Saddler, to be guard. of Rebec-
cah Talbut & Jamima Talbut (both under 14), daus. of SETH TAL-
BUT of Digh., dtd. 15 March 1742/3 [10:251/2].
Acct. of Huldah Carpenter, Adm. of Est. of Widow ELIZEBETH CAR-
PENTER of Reho., dtd. 15 Feb. 1742/3. Mentions her Inv. dtd.
12 July 1740 [10:252].
Acct. of Esther Brown, widow & Adm. of Est. of ISAAC BROWN of
Barr., dtd. 15 Feb. 1742/3 [10:253].
Order for div. of Est. of JOHN PERRIN of Reho. dcd. intest., dtd.
21 Dec. 1742 [10:254].
Div. of Est. of JOHN PERRIN of Reho. btwn. his widow Rachel now
wife of Edward Glover & his chldn: John Perrin (eldest son),
Ezra Perrin (2nd son), Timothey Perrin (3rd son), Jesse Perrin
(youngest son), Rachel Perrin (eldest dau.), & Elizebeth Per-
rin (youngest dau.), dtd. 28 Dec. 1742. Comm: Capt. Daniel Car-
penter, Ephraim Carpenter, Samuel Mason, John Humphrey & Capt.
Benjamin Brown [10:254/5/6/7].
Acct. of Rebeccah Abel, widow & Adm. of Est. of her husb. JOSHUA
ABEL of Reho. dcd. intest., dtd. 15 Feb. 1742/3. Mentions his
Inv. which was dtd. 12 May 1732. Incl. item "to Cloth the
Childreen" [10:257].
Order for div. of Est. of WILLIAM SLADE of Swan. dcd. intest.,
dtd. 17 Nov. 1741 [10:258].
Div. of Est. of WILLIAM SLADE of Swan. btwn. his widow [not nam-
ed] & his chldn: William Slade (eldest son), Benjamin Slead
(2nd son), Jonathan Slade (3rd son), Peleg Slade (4th son),
Obediah Slead (5th son), Richard [? Unclear; written over]
Slade (6th son), John Slead (7th son), Charles Slead (8th son)
Mary Slead (eldest dau.) & Ruth Slead(2nd dau.), dtd. 2 Apr.
1742. Comm: Hezekiah Luther, William Anthoney, Samuel Gardner, Hezekiah Kingsley & Abraham Waldroon [10:259/60/1/2/3].
Petition by Esther Brown, widow of ISAAC BROWN of Barr., asking
for div. of his real est. btwn. herself & the chldn. Order de-
nied, it not appearing to the court that he had any real est.
at death, dtd. 15 March 1742/3 [10:263].
Acct. of Mary Wood, widow & Adm. of Est. of ISAAC WOOD of Dart.
dcd. intest., dtd. 15 March 1742/3. Incl. item "for Provisions Spent in the familey " [10:263/4].
Appts. of Isaac Wellman of Nort., Cooper, to be guard. of Timothey Wellman & Hannah Wellman (minors over 14), chldn. of
ISAAC WELLMAN of Nort., Husbandman, dtd. 15 March 1742/3 [10:
265].
Appt. of Hezekiah Brown of Barr., Yeoman, to be guard. of Rebeccah Brown (minor over 14), dau. of OLIVER BROWN of Barr., dtd.
15 Feb. 1742 [10:266].
Appt. of Josiah Howland of Brist., Yeoman, to be guard. of ED-
WARD SHOVE of Digh., Gentleman, "who is non Compus mentis,"
dtd. 22 March 1742 [10:266/7].
Appt. of Seth Mackpeice of Nort., Yeoman, to be guard. of George,

William & Abigail Mackpeice (all under 14), chldn. of WILLIAM MACKPEICE of Nort., dtd. 19 Apr. 1743 [10:267].

Appt. of Caleb Eddy of Swan., Yeoman, to be guard. of Simion Read (minor over 14), son of STEPHEN READ of Swan., dtd. 19 Apr. 1743 [10:267/8].

Order to John Freelove of Free., Yeoman, Exec. of Est. of his father [sic; but should say "grandfather"] MORRIS FREELOVE of Free., dtd. 19 Apr. 1743 [10:268].

Rcpt. from John Perrin & his wife Elizabeth of Reho., Elizabeth being dau. of BENJAMIN LYON of Reho., dtd. 21 Feb. 1742/3, for legacies paid by her uncle & guard. Daniel Carpenter of Reho. Incl. item, "part of the Rent of the farme at Providence for the year 1741." Witns: Abigail Lyon & Elizabeth Carpenter [10:269].

Will of MORRIS FREELOVE of Free., Yeoman, "Now Being very aged," dtd. 13 June 1740, prob. 19 Apr. 1742/3. Wife Elizebeth. Sons: Samuel Freelove & Thomas (dcd.) Freelove. Daus: Rebeccah Burrington (eldest dau.) wife of William Burrington, Abigail Burrington (2nd dau.) wife of John Burrington, Hannah Borman [sic] (3rd dau.) & Mary Brownel dcd. (youngest dau.). Grsons: Thomas Freelove & John Freelove sons of my son Thomas dcd. Grson William Brownel son of my dau. Mary Brownel dcd. Dau. [sic] Sarah Soul [Notation in later hand above this line inserts "Grand" before "Daughter," stating "See deed of John Freelove"]. Grson. John Freelove to be Exec. Son-in-law Capt. John Burrington of Portsmouth. R.I. & Samuel Forman [sic] to be overseers. Witns: Benjamin Quithell, Joseph Read & Hannah Read. Followed by widow Elizebeth Freelove's resignation of all rights to land in Free., dtd. 14 Jan. 1742/3 [10:269/70/1/2].

Inv. of Est. of MORRIS FREELOVE of Free., Yeoman, dtd. 1 Jan. 1742/3, pres. by John Freelove, Exec. Pers. est. 182-13-0; real est. 2200-0-0. Apprs: Daniel Lawton, Jr., Joshua Bomer & John Turner [10:272/3].

Inv. of Est. of GERSHOM WOODWEL of Tiv., Yeoman, dtd. 15 Jan. 1741/2, pres. by William & Gershom Woodwel, Execs. Pers. est. 44-8-6; real est. 1850-0-0. Apprs: Joseph Anthoney, Samuel Forman & Samuel Borden [10:273].

Order to Joseph Anthoney of Tiv., Yeoman, Exec. of Est. of JOSIAH STAFFORD of Tiv., dtd. 17 May 1743 [10:273/4].

Acct. of William Robinson of Taun., Yeoman, Adm. of Est. of his father INCREASE ROBINSON of Taun. now Rayn., dtd. 19 Apr. 1743 [10:274/5].

Inv. of Est. of WILLIAM MACKPEICE of Nort. that "was in the Possetion of Experiance Mackpeice Late Deceased," dtd. 3 March 1742/3, pres. by Seth Mackpeice, Adm. de bonis non. Pers. est. 124-4-6; no real est. Apprs; John Briggs, Benjamin Cobb & William Dean [10:275/6].

Inv. of Est. of JOHN FISH of Dart., dtd. 8 March 1741/2, pres. by Ebenezer Fish, Exec. Pers. est. 721-1-1; no real est.

Apprs: Ebenezer Slocum, James Allen & Timothey Gifford [10: 276/7].

Acct. of Jonathan Woodbury, Adm. "Cum Testimento Annexo," of Est. of SIMON DAVIS, Esq., of Brist., dtd. 19 Apr. 1743. Incl. items: "Delivered him his mothers Picture as by Will," & "Delivered Simon his fathers Picture" [10:277/8/9].

Order to Joseph Anthoney of Tiv., Yeoman, Exec. of Est. of JOSIAH STAFFORD of Tiv., dtd. 17 May 1743 [10:279/80].

Appt. of Mary Talbut of Digh., widow, to be Adm. of Est. of her husb. JARED TALBUT of Digh., Yeoman, dcd. intest., dtd. 19 Apr. 1740 [10:280].

Appt. of Elizebeth Lane of Attl., widow, to be Adm. of Est. of her husb. EBENEZER LANE of Attl., Yeoman, dcd. intest., dtd. 21 June 1743 [10:281].

Acct. of Sarah Blanding, widow & Adm. of Est. of her husb. JOHN BLANDING of Reho., dtd. 20 Apr. 1743. Mentions "Charges in Lying in With a Posthumus Child Born After the fathers Decease" [10:281/2].

Order to Samuel Bartlet of Attl., Yeoman, Exec. of Est. of his father SAMUEL BARTLET of Attl., Yeoman, dtd. 21 June 1743 [10: 282].

Order to Martha Carpenter of Reho., widow & Exec. of Est. of her husb. EPHRAIM CARPENTER of Reho., dtd. 21 June 1743 [10: 283].

Order to Thankful Bowen of Swan., widow & Exec. of Est. of her husb. THOMAS BOWEN of Swan., Yeoman, dtd. 21 June 1743 [10: 283/4].

Appt. of Joseph Greenhil of Brist., Merchant, to be guard. of Daniel Dorgello (minor over 14), son of HENERY DORGELLO "of Amsterdam in Holland," dtd. 23 Nov. 1743 [10:284].

Will of JOSIAH STAFFORD of Tiv., Yeoman, "Being Aged Yet in Good health," dtd. 1 June 1742, prob. 17 May 1743. Wife Sarah. Sons: Joseph (eldest son), David & Abraham Stafford. 8 daus: Pricilla Lowdin, Sarah, Elizebeth, Bethiah, Bathsheba, Phebe, Hannah & Patiance [no surnames]. Grson Samuel son of my dau. Sarah. Friend & neighbor Joseph Anthoney of Tiv. to be Exec. Witns: George Weastgate, Bathsheba Howland & Ebenezer Mousher [10: 285/6/7].

Will of THOMAS BOWEN of Swan., Yeoman, "Being Grown Aged," dtd. 25 Dec. 1736, prob. 21 June 1743. Wife Thankful. Sons: Josiah (eldest son), Isaac, Stephen, Samuel, Nathaniel, Richard & John Bowen. Daus: "Mary and Hannah Wives of Gilbert & Charles Seamans," Katherine [Carter?] & Mercy Luther dcd. Grdau. Lydia Luther (under 18) dau. of my dcd. dau. Mercy. Grson Constant Luther. Witns: Thomas Wood, Jr., Rebeca Wood & Joseph Mason [10:287/8/9].

Will of SAMUEL BARTLET of Attl. Gore, Yeoman, "Being Very Sick and Weak," dtd. 24 Feb. 1742/3, prob. 21 June 1743. No wife mentioned. Sons: Noah & Samuel Bartlet. Grdau. Mary Smith &

grson Noah Smith, their mother being dcd. Son Samuel to be
Exec. Witns: Mark Peters, Job Bartlet & Richard Aldrich, Jr.
[10:289/90].

Inv. of Est. of JOSIAH STAFFORD of Tiv., dtd. 24 May 1743, pres.
by Joseph Anthoney, Exec. Pers. est. not totalled; no real
est. Apprs: Samuel Borden, Job Durphey & Weston Hicks [10:
290/1/2].

Inv. of Est. of JOHN BROWN of Attl., dtd. 22 Nov. 1742, pres.
by Bathsheba Brown, Exec. Pers. est. 37-6-19; real est. 45-
0-0. Apprs: Ebenezer Robinson, Thomas Bowen & Jonathan Ormsbe [10:292].

Acct. of Bathsheba Brown, widow & Exec. of Est. of her husb.
JOHN BROWN of Attl., dtd. 17 June 1743 [10:292/3].

Will of EPHRAIM CARPENTER of Reho., Yeoman, dtd. 28 Dec. 1732
[sic], prob. 21 June 1743. Wife Martha. Sons: Ephraim (eldest) & Eliphilet (under 21) Carpenter. Dau. Hannah Carpenter
(under 18). Wife to be Exec. Incl. lands & rights in Barr.,
Reho. & Attl. Witns: Daniel Perrin, Ezekiel Read & Daniel
Carpenter [10:293/4/5].

Acct. of Lidia Brintnal, Adm. of Est. of SAMUEL BRINTNAL of Nort.
dtd. 21 June 1743. Incl. item for "Necessarys in her familey
Since her Husbands Decease" [10:295].

Acct. of George Rouse, Adm. of Est. of JAMES ROUSE of Lit. Comp.
dtd. 21 June 1743 [10:296].

Inv. of Est. of EBENEZER LANE of Attl., dtd. 9 Feb. 1742/3, pres.
by Elizebeth Lane, widow & Adm. Pers. est. 85-8-9; real est.
140-0-0. Apprs: Obediah Fuller, Samuel Tyler & Hezekiah Peck
[10:296/7].

Order for div. of Est. of SAMUEL HALL of Taun. now Rayn. dcd.
intest., dtd. 22 Apr. 1743 [10:297/8].

Div. of Est. of SAMUEL HALL of Taun. now Rayn. btwn. his widow
Mercy Hall & his chldn: Amariah Hall (only son), Hannah Alden
(eldest dau.), Mercy Hall (2nd dau.) & Patiance Hall (youngest
dau.), dtd. 7 June 1743. Comm: Jonathan Shaw, John White,
Samuel Leonard & Samuel White [10:298/9/300].

Order for div. of Est. of JAMES WALKER of Taun., Yeoman, dcd.
intest., dtd. 18 May 1742 [10:300].

Div. of Est. of JAMES WALKER of Taun. btwn. his widow [not nam-
ed] & his only child Elisha Walker, dtd. 6 Dec. 1742. Comm:
Abraham Waldroon, Thomas Eliot, Thomas Briggs & Ephraim Atwood
[10:300/1/2].

Order for div. of Est. of EPHRAIM WALKER of Reho. dcd. intest.,
dtd. 15 Feb. 1742/3 [10:302].

Div. of Est. of EPHRAIM WALKER of Reho. btwn. his widow Mary Walker & his chldn: Mary Walker (eldest dau.), Lydia Walker (2nd
dau.), Anna Walker (3rd dau.) & Martha (youngest dau.), dtd.
29 March 1743. Widow Mary Walker surrendered her rights in
the shares of the Ests. of her daus. Sarah Walker & Freelove,
"Both Said Daughters Being Living att my s^d Husbands Decease

and Since Deceased." Comm: Capt. Daniel Carpenter, Edward
Glover, Timothey Ide & Samuel Mason [10:302/3/4/5/6].
Inv. of Est. of SAMUEL BRINTNAL of Nort., Yeoman, dtd. 4 Sept.
1741, pres. by Lidia Brintnal, widow & Adm. Pers. est. 92-
18-9; real est. 407-10-0. Apprs: William Dean, John Grover
& Benjamin Williams [10:306/7].
Inv. of Est. of EPHRAIM CARPENTER of Reho., dtd. 3 June 1743,
pres. by Martha Carpenter, widow & Exec. Pers. est. 117-16-
6; real est. 200-0-0. Apprs: Daniel Perrin, Daniel Carpenter
& Ephraim French [10:307/8].
Acct. of Mary Fuller wife of Moses Fuller, late widow of JOSEPH
PECK, Jr. of Reho. dcd. intest., dtd. 17 May 1743 [10:308/9].
Order for div. of Est. of ZACHARIAH READ of Reho., dtd. 18 Nov.
1742 [10:309/10].
Div. of Est. of ZACHARIAH READ of Reho. dcd. intest., btwn. his
widow Martha Read & his chldn: Moses (only son), Martha (el-
dest dau.), Ruth (2nd) & Hepzibeth (youngest dau.), dtd. 26
Feb. 1742/3. Comm: Ephraim Carpenter, Noah Sabin, Daniel Car-
penter & William Brown [10:310/1/2/3].
Will of ELIZEBETH WALKER of Brist., widow. "Being aged and Infirm," dtd. 23 June 1735, prob. 8 Apr. 1743. Son William Walker. Dau. Mary wife of Edward Little. Grdaus. Mary Little &
Elizebeth Little (both under 18 & unmar.). Grchldn: John &
Thomas Bowen, Sarah & Esther & Elizebeth chldn. of my dau.
Elizebeth Bowen dcd. Grdau. Jane Walker of Barbados dau. of
my son Thomas Walker dcd. Sarah Little (under 18 & unmar.)
eldest dau. of Edward Little. Friend Samuel Howland of Brist.
to be Exec. & guard. of my grchldn. Witns: Samuel Royal, Sam-
uel Smith & Martha Durfee [10:313/4].
Appt. of William Hall of Lit. Comp., Esq., to be guard. of Ann
Mercy Irish (minor over 14), dau. of JONATHAN IRISH of Lit.
Comp., dtd. 27 June 1743 [10:315].
Appt. of Samuel Eddy of Swan., Yeoman, to be Adm. of Est. of his
bro. SETH EDDY of Swan., Shipwright, since his widow & Adm.
Patiance Eddy is now dcd., dtd. 19 July 1743 [10:315/6].
Order to Lidia Manley, widow, & Abiah Manley, son, both of East.
Execs. of Est. of [not named], dtd. 19 June 1743 [10:316/7].
Will of THOMAS MANLEY, Sr. of East., dtd. 6 Apr. 1743, prob. 19
July 1743. Wife Lidia. Sons: Thomas (eldest son), John (2nd),
Abiah (3rd), Daniel (4th), Timothey (5th) & Seth (6th & young-
est son, under 21) Manley. Daus: Lidia Hayward (eldest), Pri-
cilla Kingsley (2nd), Ruth Keith (3rd), Jehannah Keith (4th),
Hannah Drake, Susanah Manley & Silance Manley (last 3 called
"my three youngest Daughters"). Incl. "my Negro boy George."
Wife & son Abiah to be Execs. Witns: Samuel Philips, William
Bailey & John Manley [10:317/8/9].
Acct. of Sarah Read, widow & Adm. of Est. of THOMAS READ of Digh.
dtd. 19 July 1743, it being insolvent. Mentions former acct.
dtd. Oct. 1742 [10:318/20].

Order to Mary Burt, widow, & William Burt, both of Taun., Execs.
of Est. of JAMES BURT, Sr. of Taun., Yeoman, dtd. 19 July 1743
[10:320/1].

Will of JAMES BURT, Sr. of Taun., Husbandman, "Being aged," dtd.
5 July 1733 [sic], prob. 19 July 1743. Wife Mary. Sons: James,
Thomas, Nathaniel & William Burt. Daus: Mary Burt, Mehetibel
Badcock, Tabitha Sprage, Abigail Burt & Charity Burt. "My
Cusen William French." Wife & son William to be Execs. Witns:
Morgan Cobb, 2nd, Nathan Dean & Sarah Thayer [10:321/2/3].

Appt. of Martha Gofe of Reho., widow, to be Adm. of Est. of her
husb. RICHARD GOFE of Reho. dcd. intest., dtd. 19 July 1743
[10:323].

Inv. of Est. of RICHARD GOFE of Reho., dtd. 14 May 1743, pres.
by Martha Gofe, widow & Adm. Pers. est. not totalled; real
est. 125-0-0. Apprs: Philip Wheeler, Israel Cole & Jonathan
Cole [10:324].

Order to Hannah Royal of Brist., widow & Exec. of Est. of her
husb. SAMUEL ROYAL of Brist., dtd. 7 July 1743 [10:324/5].

Will of SAMUEL ROYAL of Brist., House Carpenter, dtd. 10 Dec.
1739, prob. 27 July 1743. Wife Hannah. Dau. Prisilla Paine.
Grsons. Royal Paine & Stephen Paine (both under 21). Wife to
be Exec. Witns: Samuel Smith, Benjamin Bosworth & Joseph Russel [10:325/6].

Acct. of Abigail Dean of Taun., widow & Adm. of Est. of her husb.
EZRA DEAN of Taun., dtd. 19 July 1743. Incl. "the Charge of
Lying in and Paying the Nurse" [10:326/7/8].

Appt. of Samuel Eddy of Swan., Yeoman, to be Adm. of Est. of
his bro. SETH EDDY of Brist., since his widow & Adm. Patiance
Eddy is now dcd., dtd. 19 July 1743 [identical to entry in
10:315/6, above][10:328].

Acct. of Joseph Russel, guard. of ELIZEBETH WALKER who was non
Compus mentis & is now dcd., dtd. 3 Aug. 1743. Incl. items:
to John Walker, to Hannah Walker for board & from Est. of
Capt. William Walker [10:329].

Appt. of James Smith of Barr., Yeoman, to be guard. of Josiah
Torrey (minor over 14), son of JOHN TORREY of Barr., dtd. 20
Sept. 1743 [10:330].

Order to div. Est. of EPHRAIM GREEN of Attl. dcd. intest., dtd.
16 Aug. 1743 [10:330/1].

Div. of Est. of EPHRAIM GREEN of Attl. btwn. his widow Hannah
Green & his chldn: Ephraim Green (eldest son), Hannah Green,
Sarah Green & Mary Green, dtd. 18 Oct. 1743. Comm: Capt. Mathew Dagget, Hezekiah Peck, Thomas Wilmouth & Jonathan Caproon
[10:331/2].

Order to John Hunt of Lit. Comp., Gentleman, Exec. of Est. of
MARY IRISH of Lit. Comp., widow, dtd. 20 Sept. 1743 [10:332/3].

Will of MARY IRISH of Lit. Comp., widow, dtd. 13 May 1743, prob.
20 Sept. 1743. Sons Jese Irish & Samuel Irish. Daus: Mary Davis, Hannah Vigneson & Anna Mercy. Grchldn: George, Jonathan

& Joseph Wilbour chldn. of my dau. Susanah Wilbour. Grchldn:
Job, Abner & Anna Wilbour chldn. of my dau. Pricilla Wilbor
dcd. Friend Capt. John Hunt to be Exec. Witns: John Irish,
George Rouse & William Richmond [10:333/4].

Appt. of James Lee of Reho., Husbandman, to be Adm. of Est. of
his father RICHARD LEE of Reho. dcd. intest., dtd. 20 Sept.
1743 [10:334/5].

Inv. of Est. of MARY IRISH, widow, of Lit. Comp., dtd. 19 Sept.
1743, pres. by John Hunt, Exec. Pers. est. 129-0-0; no real
est. Apprs: John Irish, George Rouse & Fobes Little [10:335].

Inv. of Est. of THOMAS MANLEY of East., dtd. 5, 9 & 10 Sept.
1743, pres. by Lidia & Abiah Manley, Execs. Pers. est. 162-
9-1; real est. 432-0-1. Apprs: John Phillips, Eliphilet Leonard & Robert Randall [10:336/7/8].

Inv. of Est. of PHILIP WALKER of Reho., dtd. 15 Jan. 1742/3,
pres. by Ann Allen late Ann Walker, Exec. Pers. est. 393-7-6;
real est. 1030-0-0. Apprs: Josiah Cushing, Abiah Carpenter &
Thomas Allen [10:338/9].

Order to Nicholas White & Jacob White, Yeomen of Nort., Execs.
of Est. of their father NICHOLAS WHITE of Nort., Yeoman, dtd.
3 Oct. 1743 [10:339].

Will of NICHOLAS WHITE of Nort., "Being Now in the Sixty Ninth
year of my Age and Being att This Time of A Poor and Weak
State," dtd. 8 Aug. 1743, prob. 3 Oct. 1743. Wife Experiance.
Sons: Nicholas (eldest), Jonathan (2nd), Jacob (3rd), Isaac
(4th) & Phillip (dcd.) White. Daus: Ursley Caswel wife of Samuel Caswel of Nort., Judith Williams wife of Nathaniel Williams
of Nort., & Mercy White. Grdau. Lidia White (under 18 & unmar.) dau. of my son Phillip White dcd. Sons Nicholas & Jacob
to be Execs. Witns: Seth White, Benjamin White & George Leonard, Esq. [10:339/40/1/2/3].

Inv. of Est. of NICHOLAS WHITE of Nort., dtd. 28 Sept. 1743, pres.
by Nicholas & Jacob White, sons & Execs. Pers. est. 83-8-6;
no real est. [10:344].

Order to Abiah Carpenter of Reho., Yeoman, Exec. of Est. of his
father ABIAH CARPENTER of Reho., Gentleman, dtd. 16 Aug. 1743
[10:345].

Will of ABIAH CARPENTER of Reho., Yeoman, dtd. 18 Feb. 1742/3,
prob. 16 Aug. 1743. Wife Experiance. Sons: Abiah (eldest) &
Abel (youngest) Carpenter. Daus: Mehetibel (eldest), Experiance (2nd), Lidia (3rd), Huldah (4th), Sarah [? written over]
(5th), Hannah (6th) & Esther (7th)[no surnames]. Negro man
Boswain. My bro. Thomas Carpenter. Wife to be guard. "to all
my Childreen that are under Age." Son Abiah to be Exec. Witns:
Thomas Carpenter, David Carpenter & Daniel Carpenter [10:345/
6/7/8].

Order to Mary Whiple of Attl., widow & Exec. of Est. of her husb.
WILLIAM WHIPLE of Attl., Cooper, dtd. 16 Aug. 1743 [10:348/9].

Will of WILLIAM WHIPLE of Attl., Cooper, dtd. 29 March 1740,

prob. 16 Aug. 1743. Wife Mary. Sons: Peter, Samuel, John,
Brook & Israel. Daus: Jemimah, Abigail, Penelope & Mary [*no
surnames*]. Wife to be Exec. Witns: Gideon Bisshop, Esther
Tower & John Foster [10:349/50].
Appt. of Elinor Huddleston of Dart., widow, to be Adm. "Cum Tes-
timento Annexo" of Est. of ISAAC HUDDLESTON of Dart., since
the appt. Exec. Peleg Huddleston refuses to serve, dtd. 16
Aug. 1743 [10:350/1].
Will of ISAAC HUDDLESTON of Dart., Cordwainer, "Being Very Sick
and Weak," dtd. 12 July 1743, prob. 16 Aug. 1743. Wife Elinor.
Son George Huddleston. "Unto all the Rest of my Daughters"
[*not named*]. My cousin Peleg Huddleston to be Exec. Witns:
Thomas Venes, Maxson Mosheir & Phillip Mosheir, Jr.[10:351/2].
Order to Deborah Tower of Attl, widow & Exec. of Est. of her
husb. BENJAMIN TOWER of Attl., Yeoman, dtd. 16 Aug. 1743 [10:
352].
Will of BENJAMIN TOWER of Attl., dtd. 22 Dec. 1742, prob. 16
Aug. 1743. Wife Deborah. Sons: Gideon, John, Benjamin & Joseph. Daus: Sarah, Margaret, Ziporah, Hannah & Hesther [*no
surnames*]. Grson. Nathan Carpenter "that Lives with me."
Incl. lands in Attl. & in Wrentham, Co. of Suffolk. Wife to
be Exec. Witns: Samuel Whiple, John Foster & Abigail Bigford
[10:352/3/4].
Inv. of Est. of WILLIAM WHIPLE of Attl., dtd. 12 Aug. 1743, pres.
by Mary Whiple, widow & Exec. Pers. est. 61-8-6; no real est.
Apprs: Ichabod Peck, Israel Whiple & David Whiple [10:354].
Inv. of Est. of BENJAMIN TOWER of Attl., dtd. 2 Aug. 1743, pres.
by Deborah Tower, widow & Exec. Pers. est. not totalled; no
real est. Apprs: David Whiple, Israel Whiple & Ichabod Peck
[10:354/5].
Inv. of Est. of SAMUEL BARTLET of Attl., dtd. 23 June 1743, pres.
by Samuel Bartlet, Exec. Pers. est. 351-3-8; no real est.
Apprs: Daniel Peck, Joseph Staples & Jeremiah Bartlet [10:
355/6].
Inv. of Est. of Capt. ABIAH CARPENTER of Reho, dtd. 10 Aug. 1743
pres. by Abiah Carpenter, Exec. Incl. negro man Boswain. Pers.
est. 480-15-11; real est. 761-1-0. Apprs: John Wilmouth, David Carpenter & Daniel Carpenter [10:356/7].
Order to Edward & Thomas Burges, Yeomen of Lit. Comp., Execs. of
Est. of their father THOMAS BURGES of Lit. Comp., dtd. 16 Aug.
1743 [10:357/7½].
Will of THOMAS BURGES of Lit. Comp., Yeoman, dtd. 10 May 1743,
prob. 16 Aug. 1743. Wife Patiance. Sons: Edward, Joseph, John,
Thomas, Jacob & Nathaniel (under 21). Daus: Deborah Brownel,
Lidia Collins, Abigail Thomas, Hesther Wilbour, Mercy Thurston, Rebecah & Martha [*no surnames*]. Grson. Burges Thomas
(under 21). Grchldn: Thomas Wood, Constant Wood, Martha Wood,
Abigail Wood, Content Wood, Mary Wood & Avis Wood, chldn. of
my dau. Mary Wood. Gives to son Edward "one desk called father

Richmonds desk." Sons Edward & Thomas to be Execs. Witns: William Richmond, John Peabody & Joseph Coe [10:357½/8/9/60].

Inv. of Est. of THOMAS BURGES of Lit. Comp., dtd. 4 Aug. 1743, pres. by Edward & Thomas Burges, Execs. Pers. est. 1955-5-0; real est. 5700-0-0. Apprs: William Richmond, John Peabody & Edward Gray [10:361/2].

Order for div. of Est. of SAMUEL BUTTERWORTH of Reho. dcd. intest., dtd. 21 March 1742/3 [10:362].

Div. of Est. of SAMUEL BUTTERWORTH of Reho. btwn. his widow Patiance & his chldn: Samuel Butterworth (only son), Patiance (eldest dau.), Hannah (youngest dau.) & "Late Deceased Daughter Rachel who was Liveing att her fathers Decease," dtd. 15 Apr. 1743. Comm: Daniel Carpenter, John Wilmouth, Edward Glover, Jonathan Ormsbee & John Jacobs [10:362/3/4/5/6].

Order for div. of Est. of JOSHUA ABEL of Reho., dtd. 15 Feb. 1743 [10:366].

Div. of the Est.of JOSHUA ABEL of Reho. dcd. intest. btwn. his widow Rebecka & his chldn: Robert Abel (eldest son), Joshua Abel (youngest son), Sarah Abel (eldest dau.), Abigail Abel (2nd dau.) & Joanna Abel (youngest dau.), dtd. 1 Apr. 1743. Comm: Daniel Carpenter, Edward Glover, Samuel Mason & Timothy Ide [10:366/7/8/9].

Order to Sarah Read, Adm. of insolvent Est. of THOMAS READ of Digh. dcd. intest., dtd. 30 Sept. 1743 [10:370].

Acct. of debts due from Est. of THOMAS READ of Digh., not dated [10:370/1].

Order to Gershom Dodson of Free., Yeoman, Exec. of Est. of his father JONATHAN DODSON of Free., dtd. 18 Oct. 1743 [10:371].

Will of JONATHAN DODSON of Free., Husbandman, dtd. 8 June 1741, prob. 18 Oct. 1743. Wife not mentioned. Sons: Gershom, Jonathan & Anthoney Dodson. My 2 daus. that live with me: Deborah Dodson & Mary Dodson. Other 3 daus: Sarah wife of Richard Collins, Hannah wife of Edward Thurston & Margaret wife of John Blunt. Son Gershom to be Exec. Witns: Thomas Durfe, Ambrose Barnaby & Robert Millard [10:371/2/3/4].

Inv. of JONATHAN DODSON of Free., Yeoman, dtd. Oct. 1743, pres. by Gershom Dodson, son & Exec. Pers. est. 259-2-6; real est. 1230-0-0. Apprs: Samuel Borman, Robert Millard & Ambrose Barnaby [10:374/5].

Appt. of Dorothy Wilcox of Dart., widow, to be Adm. of Est. of her husb. WILLIAM WILCOX of Dart. dcd. intest., dtd. 18 Oct. 1743 [10:375/6].

Inv. of Est. of RICHARD LEE of Reho., dtd. 5 Oct. 1743, pres. by James Lee, Adm. Pers. est. 55-2-0; real est. 150-0-0. Apprs: Hezekiah Kingsley, Martin Luther & Oliver Mason [10:376].

Appt. of Phebe Davis of Attl., widow, to be Adm. of Est. of her husb. ARON DAVIS of Attl. dcd. intest., dtd. 18 Oct. 1743 [10:376/7].

Inv. of Est. of ARON DAVIS of Attl., dtd. 17 Oct. 1743, pres.
by Phebe Davis, widow & Adm. Pers. est. 201-6-0; real est.
225-0-0. Apprs: Mayhew Dagget, Jacob Stanley & Elihu Dagget [10:377/8].

Acct. of Samuel Bartlet of Attl., Exec. of Est. of SAMUEL BART-
LET of Attl., dtd. 18 Oct. 1743. Incl. moveables "given By
my father Samuel Bartlet to my Brother Noah Bartlet" by his
will [10:378].

Acct. of Sarah Howland, widow & Adm. of Est. of BENJAMIN HOW-
LAND of Tiv. dcd. intest., dtd. Oct. 1743. Incl. item for
paym. "To John Franlen of Barbados" [10:279].

Acct. of James Lee late [sic] of Reho. & son & Adm. of Est. of
RICHARD LEE of Reho. Incl. item "for Housekeeping to the widdow." Incl. debts to: Nathaniel Lee, John Lee & Stephen Lee
[10:380].

Acct. of Sarah Spooner, widow & Adm. of Est. of SIMPSON SPOONER
of Dart., dtd. 27 Oct. 1743 [10:380/1].

Inv. of Est. of SETH EDDY of Swan., Shipwright, dtd. 17 Aug.
1743, pres. by Samuel Eddy, brother & Adm. De Bonis Non. Pers.
est. 126-11-0; real est. "in the first Inventory" 700-0-0.
Apprs: John Cummins, Thomas Wilbour & Stephen Cornel [10:381/2].

Acct. of Samuel Eddy, Adm. De Bonis Non of Est. of his bro. SETH
EDDY, Shipwright, since Patiance Martin, late widow of her 1st
husb. Seth Eddy, is also now dcd., dtd. 15 Nov. 1743. Mentions
cost for widow Patiance "In Supporting and Bringing up the
Orphan Children of the Said Seth Eddy" [10:382/3/4].

Appts. of Samuel Miller of Swan., Gentleman, to be guard. of
Jesse Eddy (minor over 14) & of Seth Eddy & Thomas Eddy (both
under 14), all sons of SETH EDDY of Swan., Shipwright, dtd.
15 Nov. 1743 [10:385/6].

Appts. of Samuel Eddy of Swan., Blacksmith, to be guard. of Enos
Eddy (minor over 14) & of Mercy Eddy (under 14), chldn. of
SETH EDDY of Swan., dtd. 15 Nov. 1743 [10:386/7].

Appt. of Mary Crane of Bartley [sic], Co. of Brist., widow, to
be Adm. of Est. of BENJAMIN CRANE of Bartley dcd. intest.,
dtd. 15 Nov. 1743 [10:387/8].

Appt. of James Cole of Swan., Yeoman, to be guard. of James Wood
(minor over 14), son of GEORGE WOOD of Swan., dtd. 17 Jan.
1743/4 [10:388/9].

Order to John Anthoney & James Anthoney, Yeomen of Swan., Execs.
of [line omitted], dtd. 17 Jan. 1743/4 [10:389].

Will of WILLIAM ANTHONEY of Swan., Farmer, "Being Antiant and
Weakly of Body," dtd. 26 May 1739, prob. 17 Jan. 1743/4. Wife
Mary. Sons: Abraham, John, James,Benjamin, William, Job & Dan-
iel (dcd.) Anthoney. Grson. William Slade (under 21) to re-
ceive,in lieu of his mother's portion. Daus: Alce Chase, Ann
Wilbour & Amy Chase. Grson. William Anthoney son of my son
William. Grson. Daniel Anthoney son of my son Abraham. Sons
John & James to be Execs. Incl. "my Negro Jack" & lands in

Swan., in Taun. & in Rhode Island. Witns: Martin Luther, John
Thurber & Esek Luther [10:389/90/1/2].
Inv. of Est. of WILLIAM ANTHONEY of Swan., dtd. 6 Jan. 1743/4,
pres. by John & James Anthoney, Execs. Pers. est. 2929-19-0;
real est. 20,650-0-0. Apprs: Esek Brown, Samuel Gardner &
William Hart [10:292/2½/3].
Acct. of Hannah Peck, widow & Adm. of Est. of JOSEPH PECK of
Reho. dcd. intest., dtd. 27 Oct. 1743 [10:393/3½].
Order to Edmun [sic] Hodges of Nort., Yeoman, Exec. of Est. of
his father JOHN HODGES of Nort., dtd. 16 Feb. 1743/4 [10:393½/4].
Will of JOHN HODGES of Nort., "Being now in the Seventy first
year of my Age," dtd. 7 Jan. 1743/4, prob. 16 Feb. 1743/4. Wife
Mary. Sons: Ebenezer (eldest), Eliphelit (2nd) & Edmun (3rd)
Hodges. Daus: Elizabeth wife of George Morey, Anna wife of
William Ware of Nort. & Marcy wife of Silas Titus. Son Edmun
to be Exec. John Hodges son of my son Eliphelit. Negroes: Fil-
lis (woman), Boston (boy), Tower Hill (boy) & Newport (boy).
Witns: George Leonard, Samuel Caswel & Jeremiah Fisher [10:
394/5/6].
Codicil by JOHN HODGES, dtd. 13 Jan. 1743/4. Mentions his negroes:
Brum or Brumswick (man), Fillis (woman) & chldn. Prince (boy)
& Louis (boy). Witns: George Leonard, William Coddington & Jon-
athan Knapp [10:397].
Inv. of Est. of JOHN HODGES of Nort., dtd. 2 Feb. 1743/4, pres.
by Edmun Hodges, Exec. Pers. est. 1048-17-9; no real est. Apprs:
George Leonard, Joseph Hodges & Benjamin Hodges [10:397/8/9].
Order to James Mason of Swan., Gentleman, Exec. of Est. of his
father SAMUEL MASON of Swan., dtd. 21 Feb. 1743/4 [10:399/400].
Will of SAMUEL MASON of Swan., Cordwainer, dtd. 24 July 1742,
prob. 21 Feb. 1743/4. No wife mentioned. Sons: Samuel (eldest)
& James Mason. Dau. Elizebeth Luther. Grdaus. Rebecca, Elize-
beth, Mary, Lidia & Susanah daus. of my son Samuel Mason. Grdau.
Hannah Brown. Grson. Moses Mason son of my son Samuel. Grson.
Samuel Mason. Grsons. John Mason & James Mason. Mentions "my
Brother Joseph Mason" & "my Cosen Elisha Mason Son of Peletiah
Mason". Son James to be Exec. Witns: Samuel Reed, John Earl
& Job Mason [10:400/1/2].
Inv. of Est. of GEORGE BROWNEL of Dart., pres. 15 Nov. 1743 by
Elizebeth Brownel & William Brownel, Execs. Pers. est. not
totalled; real est. 2212-0-0. Apprs. not named [10:402/3].
Acct. of John Russel, Benjamin Russel & Jabiz Barker, Execs. of
Est. of JOSEPH RUSSEL of Dart., dtd. 15 Nov. 1743. Incl. leg-
acies per will to: Joseph Russel; John Russel; Jabiz Barker;
John Lapham; Benjamin Allen as guard. of Elizebeth Russel,
Constant Russel & Ruth Russel; Benjamin Russel; Rebecca Barker
wife of Jabiz [10:403/4].
Appt. of David Day of Attl., Yeoman, to be guard. of Anne & Rebekah Carpenter (minors over 14), daus. of JEDEDIAH CARPENTER
of Reho., dtd. 21 Feb. 1743/4 [10:404/5].

Appt. of Benjamin Day of Attl. to be guard. of Caleb & Patience
Carpenter (both under 14), chldn. of JEDEDIAH CARPENTER of
Reho., dtd. 21 Feb. 1743/4 [10:405].
Appt. of Nathaniel Miller of Reho., Yeoman, to be guard. of Noah
Miller (minor over 14), son of NATHANIEL MILLER of Reho., dtd.
21 Feb. 1743/4 [10:405/6].
Appt. of Richard Round of Reho., Yeoman, to be guard. of Record
Franklen (minor over 14), son of JOHN FRANKLEN of Swan., dtd.
21 Feb. 1743/4 [10:406].
Appt. of Hannah Peck of Reho., widow, to be guard. of Mary Peck
(under 14), dau. of JOSEPH PECK of Reho., dtd. 20 March 1743/4
[10:407].
Appt. of Seth Leonard of Taun., Yeoman, to be Adm. of Est. of
JOHN LEACH of Taun., since Susanah Gatchel "Late widdow of
John Leach" has relinquished adm., dtd. 20 March 1743/4 [10:
407/8].
Order to Joshua Boomer of Free., Yeoman, Exec. of Est. of his
father MATHEW BOOMER of Free., Yeoman, dtd. 20 March 1743/4
[10:408/9].
Order to Hannah Carpenter of Reho., widow & Exec. of Est. of her
husb. CHARLES CARPENTER of Reho., dtd. 20 March 1743/4 [10:
409].
Will of CHARLES CARPENTER of Reho., Yeoman, dtd. 24 Dec. 1743,
prob. 20 March 1743/4. Wife Hannah. Sons: Jedediah, Charles
& Samuel Carpenter (all under age). Dau.: Susanah Carpenter
(under 18 & unmar.). "My father Jabiz Bosworth." Wife to be
Exec. Witns: Edward Glover, Ebenezer Titus & John Perrin
[10:409/10/1].
Will of MATHEW BOOMER of Free., Yeoman, dtd. 8 Oct. 1732 [sic],
prob. 20 March 1743/4. Wife Hannah. Sons: Mathew (eldest),
Caleb & Joshua Boomer. Daus: Lidia (eldest, unmar.) Boomer,
Mercy Luther, Deborah Mason, Ruth Salsbury, Mary Elsberry &
Hannah Jenks (dcd.). Grchldn. Benjamin Jenks, Lidia Jenks &
Joseph Jenks chldn. of my dcd. dau. Hannah Jenks. Grson.
Mathew Luther. Mentions his lands in Westerly, R.I. Wife &
son Joshua to be Execs. Witns: John Read, Samuel Forman,
Thomas Gaige & Mary Gaige [10:411/2/3/4].
Order to set off widow's thirds to Margaret Rouse from Est. of
her late husb. JAMES ROUSE of Lit. Comp., dtd. 30 Sept. 1743
[10:414].
Div. of 1/3rd of real est. of JAMES ROUSE of Lit. Comp. set off
to his widow, Margaret Rouse, dtd. 29 Nov. 1743. Comm: William Richmond, John Hunt, Fobes Little, Samuel Gray & William
Wilbour [10:415/6].
Inv. of Est. of CHARLES CARPENTER of Reho., dtd. 9 March 1743/4,
pres. by Hannah Carpenter, widow & Exec. Pers. est. 464-14-0;
real est. 1400-0-0. Apprs: Timothey Ide, Edward Glover & Joseph Wheaton [10:416].
Acct. of Martha Cooper, widow & Adm. of Est. of NATHANIEL COOPER

of Reho., dtd. 20 March 1743/4. Mentions paym. for mourning clothes "for my Self and Daughter" [10:417].

Appt. of Sarah Gladding of Brist., widow, to be Adm. of Est. of her husb. JONATHAN GLADDING of Brist., Housewright, dcd. intest., dtd. 20 March 1743/4 [10:418].

Appt. of Elizebeth Fuller of Attl., widow, to be Adm. of Est. her husb. JONATHAN FULLER of Attl. dcd. intest., dtd. 17 Apr. 1744 [10:418/9].

Inv. of Est. of JONATHAN FULLER of Attl., dtd. 26 March 1744, pres. by Elizebeth Fuller, widow & Adm. Pers. est. 46-2-0; real est. 325-0-0. Apprs: Obediah Fuller, Benjamin Wise & Francis Fuller [10:419/20].

Inv. of Est. of MATHEW BOOMER of Free., dtd. 8 March 1743/4, pres. by Joshua Boomer, Exec. Pers. est. 231-13-6; real est. 550-0-0. Apprs: Ambrose Barnaby, John Read & Daniel Lawton, Jr. [10:420].

Order to Deborah Dennis & Mary Dennis, both of Tiv., Spinsters, Execs. of Est. of their mother SUSANAH DENNIS of Tiv., widow, dtd. 15 May 1744 [10:421].

Will of SUSANNA DENNIS, widow, of Tiv., dtd. 20 Jan. 1743, prob. 15 May 1744. Son John Dennis. Daus: Tabitha Dennis, Lydia Dennis, Deborah Dennis, Mary Dennis (these 4 unmar.), Comfort Taylor, Ann Sanford, Sarah Soul & Elizebeth Dennis. Grson. Robert Dennis. Negros: Jenne (girl), Dinah (woman), Pero (boy) & Newport (man). Daus. Deborah & Mary to be Execs. Witns: James Pears, William Pears & William Sanford [10:421/2/3].

Inv. of Est. of SUSANNAH DENNIS of Tiv., widow, dtd. 4 May 1744, pres. by Deborah Dennis & Mary Dennis, daus. & Execs. Pers. est. 4513-0-9; real est. 1350-0-0. Apprs: Joseph Anthoney, William Richmond & John Hunt [10:423/4/5].

Acct. of Sarah Brown [*Signature & record of appearance say "Sarah," but first sentence erroneously has "Rebecca*.], widow & Exec. of Est. of OLIVER BROWN of Barr., dtd. 15 May 1744. Mentions land sold to Jabiz Brown, Benjamin Brown & John Brown. Incl. legacies to: Hezekiah Brown, Jabiz Brown, John Brown, John Bullock & Ann Brown (dau., under 18) [10:426/7].

Acct. of Hope Dagget, widow & Adm. of Est. of JOHN DAGGET of Reho., dtd. 19 June 1744. Incl. items for care and nursing "when I Lay in," & expenses for "Childs funeral Coffin and Diging the Grave." Incl. "charge for Sickness of three of my Childreen" [10:427/8].

Inv. of Est. of BENJAMIN CRANE of Berk., dtd. 11 Nov. 1743, pres. by Mary Crane, his widow & Adm. Pers. est. 187-5-4; real est. 600-0-0. Apprs: John Crane, Daniel Atwel & Benajah Babbit [10:428/9].

Appts. of Abigail Dean of Taun., widow, to be guard. of Elisha, William, George & Esther Dean (all under 14) & of Seth, Elkanah & Prudence Dean (minors over 14), all chldn. of EZRA DEAN of Taun., dtd. 13 June 1744 [10:429/30].

338   BRISTOL COUNTY, MASSACHUSETTS PROBATE RECORDS

Appt. of Nathaniel Hubbard, Esq. to be Judge of Probate for Brist.
Co., made by King George II, signed by William Shirley, Esq.,
Gov. of Prov. of Mass. Bay, dtd. 2 Aug. 1744 [10:431].
Order to Joseph Greenhil, Merchant, Mary Emmerson, widow, & Jon-
athan Woodbury, Esq., all of Brist., Execs. of Est. of NATHAN-
AEL BLAGROVE, Esq. of Brist., dtd. 23 Aug. 1744 [10:431/2].
Will of NATHANIEL BLAGROVE of Brist., dtd. 30 Dec. 1742, prob.
23 Aug. 1744. Only wife mentioned is in: "the Remains of my
first wife with the Remains of her former Husband Capt Nathan
Hayman" to be put in a coffin together & buried in Nathaniel's
grave. Dau-in-law Mrs. Grace Otis. Grson-in-law John Otis.
Grdau-in-law Mrs. Alce Vunice [or Uunice] dau. of Capt. Thomas
Church. Grson-in-law William Brattle, Esq. & his wife. Son-in-
law John Otis. The Rev. Mr. John Burt, Pastor of the Church of
Christ in Brist. Niece Mrs. Mary Emmerson & "my Negro Girl Dinah now in her Possession." Nephew Joseph Greenhil. My sister
Mrs. Sarah Chandler, widow. Niece Sarah Roffey [or Rottey].
Nephew Joseph Greenhil, niece Mary Emmerson & friend Jonathan
Woodbury, Esq. to be Execs. Witns: Samuel Smith, Charles Mun-
roe & Richard Smith [10:432/3/4].
Appt. of Sarah Cole of Swan., widow, to be Adm. of Est. of her
husb. EDWARD COLE of Swan. dcd. intest., dtd. 13 Sept. 1744
[10:434/5].
Appt. of Hannah Little of Swan., widow, to be Adm. of Est. of
her husb. SAMUEL LITTLE, Mariner, of Swan., dcd. intest., dtd.
10 Sept. 1744 [10:435].
Order to postpone one week proving of will of ELISHA MAY of
Barr., requested by Elizebeth May & Benjamin May, widow & son
of the dcd. Elisha [10:436].
Order to Elisha May of Brist., Blockmaker & Simon Burr of Swan.,
Setwork Cooper, Execs. of Est. of ELISHA MAY of Barr., Yeoman,
dtd. 10 Sept. 1744 [10:436].
Will of ELISHA MAY of Barr., Yeoman, dtd. 3 March 1742/3, prob.
17 Sept. 1744. Wife Elizebeth. Sons: Elisha (eldest), Elijah
(2nd son) & Benjamin May. Daus: Sarah Allen (dcd.) & Ruth Burr.
5 grchldn "which my Daughter Sarah Allen Left" (all under 21),
one of whom is Sarah Allen (under 18). Mentions lands in Reho.
& Barr. Son Elisha May & "my Son Simon Burr" to be Execs.
Witns: Elizabeth Luther, Daniel Salsbury & Edward Luther [10:
436/7/8].
Appt. of Rachel Whittiker of Reho., widow, to be Adm. of Est. of
her husb. JOSEPH WHITTIKER of Reho. dcd. intest., dtd. 8 Oct.
1744 [10:438].
Appt. of Jemima Myrick of Berk., widow, to be Adm. of Est. of
her husb. SAMUEL MYRICK of Berk. dcd. intest., dtd. 8 Oct.
1744 [10:438/9].
Inv. of Est. of EDWARD COLE of Swan., Yeoman, dtd. 6 Oct. 1744,
pres. by Sarah Cole, widow & Adm. Pers. est. 728-15-0; real
est. 1025-0-0. Mentions Mrs. Mehetibel Cole "mother of ye

Deceased." Apprs: Joseph Butterworth, John Kinnicut & John
Child [110:439/40].

Acct. of Mary Crane, widow & Adm. of Est. of BENJAMIN CRANE of
Berk., dtd. 9 Oct. 1744. Incl. small payms. to Temperance
Crane & Ziperah Crane & debts owed to Seth Crane & Gershom
Crane, Esq. [10:441].

Acct. of Lidiah Manley & Abiah Manley, Execs. of Est. of THOMAS
MANLEY of East., dtd. 8 Oct. 1744. Incl. legacies by will to:
Lydia, Pricilla & Ruth [no surnames] [10:442/3].

Rcpt. by Benjamin Kingsley & wife Pricilla of East. for legacy
from Est. of her father THOMAS MANLEY, paid by Lydia Manley &
Abiah Manley of East., Execs., dtd. 26 Jan. 1743/4 [10:443].

Rcpt. of Josiah Keith & wife Ruth of East. for legacy from Est.
of her father THOMAS MANLEY, paid by Lydia Manley & Abiah Manley, dtd. 26 Jan. 1743 [10:443].

Rcpt. by William Hayward & wife Lydia of East. for legacy from
Est. of her father THOMAS MANLEY, paid by Lydia Manley & Abiah
Manley, Execs., dtd. 26 Jan. 1743 [10:443/4].

Order to Simon Munroo of Brist., Cordwainer, Exec. of Est. of
his father GEORGE MUNROO of Brist., Cordwainer, dtd. 8 Oct.
1744 [10:444].

Will of GEORGE MUNROO of Brist., Cordwainer, dtd. 25 Aug. 1744,
prob. 8 Oct. 1744. No wife mentioned. Sons: Benjamin (eldest),
Simeon & Thomas Munroo. Daus: Hannah James & Sarah Eddy. Grdaus. Phebe Eddy, Mary Eddy & Martha (under 18, unmar.) Eddy.
Grdau. Mary Munroo dau. of son Simeon. Grson. Thomas Munroo
son of son Benjamin. Grdau. Hannah James. Son Simeon to be
Exec. Witns: John Walker, Martha Martin & Joseph Munroo [10:
444/5/6].

Order to John & William Pabodie, Yeomen of Lit. Comp., Execs. of
Est. of WILLIAM PABODIE of Lit. Comp., dtd. 12 Nov. 1745 [10:
446/7].

Will of WILLIAM PABODIE of Lit. Comp., "Being Aged and weak in
Body," dtd. 7 Aug. 1743, prob. 12 Nov. 1744. Wife Mary. Sons:
John, William (these called eldest 2 sons), Joseph & Benjamin
Pabodie. Daus: Elizebeth wife of Edward Gray, Rebecah wife of
Joseph Fish [sic], Pricilla wife of William Wilcox, Judith wife
of Benjamin Church & Mary wife of Nathaniel Fish [sic]. Leaves
to wife Mary "all the Household Stuff that was hers Before I
marryed her." Sons John & William to be Execs. Witns: William
Wilbour, John Coe & Joseph Coe [10:447/8].

Order to Nathanael Willis & Ebenezer Willis, Yeomen of Taun.,
Execs. of Est. of JOHN WILLIS of Taun., Yeoman, dtd. 12 Nov.
1744 [10:448/9].

Will of JOHN WILLIS of Taun., Husbandman, "Being Sick & Weak
and in Grait Pain," dtd. 12 Sept. 1744, prob. 12 Nov. 1744.
No wife mentioned. Sons: Nathaniel, Ebenezer & John (dcd.)
Willis. Daus: Sarah Willis (unmar.) & Elezebeth Wardwell (dcd.)
My dcd. son John's chldn: Mehetibel Willis (eldest dau.) &
Abiah Willia (3rd dau.). My dcd. dau. Elizebeth's chldn:

Samuel Holmes & Elizabeth Holmes chldn. of the marriage of
said Elizabeth & Samuel Holmes. Sons Nathaniel & Ebenezer to
be Execs. Witns: William Hodges, Morgan Cobb 2nd & Jacob
Cobb [10:449/50].
Order to Robert Carr of Lit. Comp., Exec. of Est. of ESEK CARR
of Lit. Comp., Yeoman, dtd. 12 Nov. 1744 [10:450/1].
Will of ESEK CARR of Lit. Comp., Yeoman, dtd. 16 May 1739, prob.
12 Nov. 1744. No wife mentioned. Sons: Esek (dcd.) & Robert
Carr. Daus: Mary (dcd.) late wife of John Brownel, Sarah Thurston, Elizabeth wife of Samuel Wilbour, Anne wife of Jonathan
Wood, Susanah wife of Thomas Wilbour, Margaret (dcd.) Dossan
[sic; but is it Closson?] & Thankful wife of William Lake.
Grdau. Deborah Carr (under 18) dau. of my son Esek dcd. Chldn.
of my dau. Mary Brownel dcd. Chldn. of my dau. Margaret Dossan
(dcd.). Witns: William Head, Joseph Peckcom & James Fisher
[10:451/2].
Acct. of Joshua & Uriah Atherton of Nort., Adms. of Est. of their
father JOSHUA ATHERTON of Nort. dcd. intest., dtd. 12 Nov.
1744 [10:452/3].
Inv. of Est. of JONATHAN FOLLET of Attl., dtd. 10 Feb. 1742/3,
pres. by Abiah Follet, widow & Adm. Pers. est. 58-16-4; real
est. 100-0-0. Apprs: Obediah Fuller, Samuel Tyler & Hezekiah
Peck [10:454].
Acct. of Elizebeth Lane, Adm. of Est. of EBENEZER LANE of Attl.,
dtd. 12 Nov. 1744. Incl. debt for "money Spent in Looking After
the Deceased when he was Drowned and Burying him." Incl. paym.
for "Expenses att her Lying in with a Posthumus Child After
the Death of her Husband" [10:454/5].
Acct. of Abigail Fuller, late widow & Adm. of Est. of ROBERT
FOLLET [sic] of Attl. dcd. intest., dtd. 12 Nov. 1744 [10:
455/6].
Order to John Mason of Reho., Yeoman, Exec. of Est. of NOAH MA-
SON of Reho., dtd. Nov. 1744 [10:456].
Will of NOAH MASON of Reho., Yeoman, dtd. 23 Aug. 1744, prob.
12 Nov. 1744. No wife mentioned. Sons: John & Noah Mason.
Daus: Mary Bairsto wife of Samuel Bairsto, Lydia Kindrick &
Hannah (unmar.) Mason. Incl. his "Tanyard and Stock of
Leathers." Son Noah to be Exec. Witns: Thomas Read, Na-
thaniel Bosworth & Edward Glover [10:457/8].
Inv. of Est. of Deacon WILLIAM PEABODY of Lit. Comp., dtd. 12
Oct. 1744, pres. by John & William Pabodie, Execs. Pers. est.
312-0-0; real est. 4600-0-0. Apprs: William Richmond, Joseph
Wood & William Wilbour [10:458/9].
Acct. of Martha Carpenter, widow & Exec. of Est. of her husb.
EPHRAIM CARPENTER of Reho., dtd. 12 Nov. 1744 [10:459/60].
Inv. of Est. of JOSEPH WHITAKER of Reho. dcd. intest., dtd. 4
Oct. 1744. Pers. est. 278-3-0; no real est. Apprs: John
Bucklen, Nathaniel Smith & Thomas Reading [10:460].
Appt. of Dorothey Wilcox of Dart., widow, to be Adm. of Est. of

her husb. WILLIAM WILCOX of Dart. dcd. intest., dtd. 12 Nov.
1744 [10:460/1].

Order to Jeremiah Read of Attl. [sic; both this name & name of
deceased are written on top of some previously written names],
Exec. of Est. of JEREMIAH READ of Attl., dtd. 12 Nov. 1744
[10:461/2].

Inv. of Est. of ROBERT FOLLET of Attl., dtd. 10 Feb. 1742/3,
pres. by "Abiah Follet widow and Administratrix to the Estate
of Jonathan Follet Late of Attleborough" [sic; but probably a
clerk's error, confusing this estate with the one below of
Jonathan Follet]. Pers. est. 29-11-12; real est. 50-0-0. Apprs:
Obediah Fuller, Samuel Tyler & Hezekiah Peck [10:462].

Acct. of Abiah Follet, widow & Adm. of Est. of JONATHAN FOLLET
of Attl. dcd. intest., dtd. 12 Nov. 1744. Incl. paym. "for Provisions Spent in the Family" [10:462/3].

Appts. of Margaret Pope of Dart., widow of ELNATHAN POPE, to be
guard. of Seth Pope & Deborah Pope (minors over 14) & of Margaret Pope & Hannah Pope (both under 14), chldn. of said Elnathan, dtd. 13 Nov. 1744 [10:463/4].

Appt. of Elizebeth Hunt of Reho., widow, to be Adm. of Est. of
her husb. NATHANAEL HUNT of Reho. dcd. intest., dtd. 17 Nov.
1744 [10:464/5].

Appt. of Katherine Hodges of Taun., widow, to be guard. of Katherine Hodges (under 14), dau. of THOMAS HODGES of Taun., dtd.
12 Nov. 1744 [10:465].

Acct. of Margaret Pope, widow & Adm. of Est. of ELNATHAN POPE of
Dart., dtd. 20 Nov. 1744. Incl. item "Memorandum the Use and
Improvement of Two thirds of the Estate of Elnathan Pope Late
of Dartmouth Deceased in the Hands of the Administratrix Being
Eaight years and Nine months att thirty Pound old Tenour per
year...which is for Educating the young Childreen" [10:465/6].

Inv. of Est. of Madam REBECA POPE late widow of Dart., dtd. 5
March 1743, pres. by Lemuel Pope, Exec. Pers. est. 186-16-0;
no real est. Apprs: William Wood, Alexander Torrance & Gideon
Southworth [10:466/7].

Order to Ebenezer Fish of Dart., Exec. of Est. of JOAN FISH of
Dart., dtd. 10 Dec. 1744 [10:467/8].

Will of JOAN FISH of Dart., widow, dtd. 5 Apr. 1744, prob. 10
Dec. 1744. Son Ebenezer Fish. Daus: Mary Potter, Abigail Case
wife of John Case, Johannah Fisher wife of John Fisher, Susan-
nah Boyse wife of Benjamin Boyse, Mehetibel Cornil wife of Wil-
liam Cornil, Hope Phillips wife of James Phillips & Elizebeth
Huddleston wife of Seth Huddleston. Grson. John Wickham. Grson.
Thomas Phillips. Grson. John Fisher son of John Fisher. Witns:
Jeremiah Wilcox, Jonathan Wood & Thomas Trafford [10:468/9].

Petition by Peter Makepeace, son of WILLIAM MAKEPEACE of Nort.
dcd., "being Come to the age of fourteen years of Age," asking
that Seth Makepeace be appt. as his guard., dtd. 10 Dec. 1744.
Witns: Benjamin Fairbank & Anne Fairbank [10:469].

Appt. of Thomas Peck of Reho. to be guard. of Darias Paine "about
the age of fourteen years," son of JONATHAN PAINE of Reho.,
dtd. 10 Dec. 1744 [10:469/70].

Inv. of Est. of SAMUEL LITTLE of Swan., Yeoman, dtd. 8 Oct. 1744
pres. by Hannah Little, widow & Adm. Pers. est. 424-15-0; real
est. 254-16-0. Incl. lands at Brist. & Swan. Apprs: John Child,
Edward Luther & Thomas Jolls [10:470/1].

Inv. of Est. of ELISHA MAY of Barr., Yeoman, dtd. 5 Nov. 1744,
pres. by Elisha May & Simon Burr., Execs. Pers. est. 252-14-3;
real est. 1100-0-0. Apprs: Peres Bradford, William Turner &
Job Mason [10:471/2].

Inv. of Est. of WILLIAM WILCOX of Dart., dtd. 15 Sept. 1743, pres.
by Dorothy Wilcox, widow & Adm. Pers. est. 260-5-6; no real
est. Apprs: James Howland, Jonathan Shermen & William Bowdish
[10:473/4].

Inv. of Est. of NOAH MASON of Reho., dtd. 5 Oct. 1744, pres. by
John Mason, his son & Exec. Pers. est. 1351-11-8; real est.
3599-0-0. Apprs: Edward Glover, Nathaniel Smith & Richard
Till [10:474/5].

Inv. of Est. of BENJAMIN BRIGGS of Digh., dtd. 3 Dec. 1744, pres.
by Sarah Briggs, widow & Adm. Pers. est. 21-19-17; real est.
176-7-6. Apprs: Ephraim Atwood, Samuel Talbert & David King
[10:475].

Order to Nathaniel Pearce & William Pearce, Execs. of Est. of
RICHARD PEARCE of Brist., dtd. 14 Jan. 1744 [10:475/6].

Will of RICHARD PEARCE of Brist., Yeoman, dtd. 19 Feb. 1740,
prob. 14 Jan. 1744. Wife Susanah. Sons: Nathaniel & William
Pearce. Daus: Sarah Pearce, Experiance Simmons wife of Ichabod
Simmons, Mary Pearce, Susanah Pearce, Ann Pearce & Elizabeth
Pearce. In speaking of the 3 eldest daus. (Sarah, Experiance
& Mary), reference is made to "Their Grandfather Samuel Hum-
phrey Late of Barrington Deceased," who left them legacies.
Sons Nathaniel & William to be Execs. Witns: Edward Paine,
Priscilla Paine & Stephen Paine [10:476/7].

Rcpt. & discharge by Samuel Howland, Daniel Howland, Job Howland, Benjamin Howland, Benjamin Russel who mar. Abigail Howland, William Wood who mar. Hannah Howland, Joseph Tucker who
mar. Mary Howland, William Sandford who mar. Rebekah Howland
& Daniel Russel who mar. Edith Howland, all chldn. of HANNAH
HOWLAND of Dart., for legacies from her Est. as paid by "our
brother Nicholas Howland Sole Executor," not dated [10:477].

Order to David Chaiffey of Attl., Yeoman, Exec. of Est. of JER-
EMIAH READ of Attl., dtd. 10 Dec. 1744 [10:478].

Will of JEREMIAH READ of Attl., Husbandman, "Being very Sick &
weak," dtd. 19 Nov. 1744, prob. 20 Dec. 1744. Wife Patience.
Mentions "all my Children." Cozen Noah Read of Reho. to be
guard. of my dau. Patience. Cozen Samuel Robinson to be guard.
of my dau. Lidda. Friend David Chaffee of Attl. to be Exec.
Witns: John Ide, Samuel Robinson & Noah Carpenter [10:478/9].

Order to James Smith of Barr., Yeoman, Exec. of Est. of his fa-
ther JAMES SMITH of Barr., dtd. 14 Jan. 1744 [10:479].
Will of JAMES SMITH of Barr., Yeoman, dtd. 15 Jan. 1739/40,
prob. 14 Jan. 1744. Wife Elizabeth. Sons: Ebenezer (eldest),
Joshua & James Smith. Daus: Leah Paine, Lydia Paine, Abigail
Paine, Elizabeth Tiffiny & Ruth Bicknal. Witns: Thomas Kin-
nicutt, Thomas Jolls & David Turner [10:479/80].
Order to Mary Shepard of Dart., widow & Exec. of Est. of DANIEL
SHIPPERD of Dart., Yeoman, dtd. 14 Jan. 1744 [10:481].
Will of DANIEL SHEPARD of Dart., "Being grown Into years and
under Decay of Body," dtd. 21 June 1744, prob. 15 Jan. 1744.
Wife Mary. Sons: Daniel & Benjamin Sheperd (both under 21).
7 daus: Mary Hart wife of William Hart, Abigail Gifford wife
of Peleg Gifford, Martha Sheperd, Virtue Sheperd, Elisabeth
Sheperd, Hannah Sheperd & Ruth Sheperd. Wife to be Exec. Bro-
in-law Peleg Shearman to assist my widow. Witns: John Russel,
Houlder Slocum & Abraham Butt [sic][10:481/2].
Appt. of Seth Makepeace of Nort., Yeoman, to be guard. of Peter
Makepeace (minor over 14), son of WILLIAM MAKEPEACE of Nort.,
dtd. 11 Dec. 1744 [10:482/3].
Appt. of John Wood, Jr. of Swan., Yeoman, to be guard. of Nathan
Dagget (minor over 14), son of JOHN DAGGET of Reho., dtd. 11
Feb. 1744 [10:483].
Appt. of John Bowen of Tiv., Shipwright, to be guard. of Hannah
Bourden (minor over 14), dau. of STEPHEN BOURDEN of Tiv., dtd.
11 Feb. 1744 [10:484].
Appt. of Sarah Briggs of Digh., widow, to be guard. of William
Briggs & Thankful Briggs (minors over 14), chldn. of BENJAMIN
BRIGGS of Digh., dtd. 11 Feb. 1744 [10:484].
Will of SAMUEL ATHERTON of Reho., Sadler, "Being Very Sick and
Weak In Body," dtd. 9 Oct. 1744, prob. 11 Feb. 1744. Wife Eliz-
abeth. Son Samuel Atherton. Mentions "the Rest of my Childreen"
& "all my Childreen." Friend Daniel Millard of Reho. to be
Exec. Witns: Daniel Ormsbee, Ezra Read & Edward Martin [10:
485].
Inv. of Est. of NATHANAEL HUNT of Reho. dcd. intest., dtd. 23
Nov. 1744, pres. by Elizebeth Hunt, widow & Adm. Pers. est.
245-4-8; real est. 524-0-0. Apprs: Jabiz Bosworth, Jonathan
Chaiffe & Edward Glover [10:486].
Appt. of Mary Razey of Attl., widow, to be Adm. of Est. of her
husb. JOSEPH RAZEY of Attl. dcd. intest., dtd. 12 March 1744
[10:486/7].
Order to Thomas Bowen of Reho. & Jabez Bowen of Providence,
Esqs., Execs. of Est. of DAMARIS PECK of Reho., widow, dtd.
12 March 1744 [10:487].
Will of DAMARAS PECK of Reho., widow, dtd. 28 May 1743, prob. 11
March 1744. To Michall Brown son of James Brown late of Barr.
To Caleb Bowen & Elijah Bowen (both under 21) sons of brother
Ebenezer Bowen. To my sister Vraine [sic; meaning Uraine or
Urania?] Bush. To son-in-law Simeon Horton. My sister Elize-

beth Brown. To my maid Leah Haskin. My brothers Thomas Bowen,
Esq. & Jabiz Bowen, Esq., to be Execs. Witns: Samuel Peck,
Daniel Millard & Mary Whiteker [10:487/8].
Appt. of William Hall [or *Hatt; unclear*] of Lit. Comp., Esq.
to be guard. of John Bennit (minor over 14), son of JAMES
BENNIT of Lit. Comp. [10:488/9].
Order to Barnard Cole of Swan., Yeoman, Exec. of Est. of NATH-
ANIEL COLE of Swan., Yeoman, dtd. 12 March 1744 [10:489].
Will of NATHANIEL COLE of Swan., Yeoman, dtd. 28 May 1744, prob.
15 March 1744. Wife Elizabeth. Sons: Nathaniel (eldest, now
non compos mentis) & Caleb Cole. Dau. Patience wife of Aaron
Kingsley. Sarah the wife of my son Nathaniel. Grsons. Barnard,
Ephraim & Nathaniel Cole the sons & only chldn. of my son Na-
thaniel by Sarah his wife. Grson. Barnard Cole to be Exec.
Witns: Benjamin Cole, Daniel Salsbury, Andrew Cole & Benjamin
Herrington [10:489/90].
Appt. of [*no name given*] to be guard. of Elijah Walker (minor
over 14), son of PHILLIP WALKER of Reho., dtd. 11 Feb. 1744
[10:491].
Will of PENTICOST BLACKINGTON of Attl., dtd. 12 Nov. 1744, prob.
11 March 1744. Wife Rebeckah. Sons: Penticost, George, John
(these called my 3 eldest sons), Othaniell (under 21), Peter
& Oliver Blackington. 3 daus: Rebeckah Everet, Anne & Mary
[*no surnames for last 2*]. Wife & son George to be Execs. Incl.
lands in Attl. & in Stoughton. Witns: Josiah Maxcey, Joshua
Everett & John Foster [10:491/2].
Order to Rebeckah Blackington & George Blackington, Execs. of
Est. of PENTICOST BLACKINGTON of Attl., dtd. 12 March 1744
[10:492].
2nd Acct. of Hannah Peck, widow & Adm. of Est. of JOSEPH PECK
of Reho., dtd. 12 March 1744. Incl. items "To Nursing and Tending Jabez Peck Son of Joseph Peck Deceased and funerall Charges"
& "To Keeping the said Jabez Peck with victualls and Clothes
Two years wanting six Days" [10:492/3].
Appt. of Ebenezer Mireck of Berk., Husbandman, to be Adm. of Est.
of his bro. SAMUEL MIRECK of Berk., Husbandman, dcd. intest.,
dtd. 13 March 1744 [10:493/4].
Appt. of Rebeckah Harvey of Berk., widow, to be Adm. of Est. of
her husb. SETH HARVEY of Berk. dcd. intest., dtd. 13 March
1744 [10:494].
Inv. of Est. of SETH HARVEY of Berk., dtd. 9 Feb. 1744, pres.
by Rebeckah Harvey, widow & Exec. Pers. est. 209-12-2; real
est. 340-0-0. Apprs: John Crane, Chr. Paull & Jacob French
[10:494/5].
Appt. of Marcey Razey of Attl., widow, to be Adm. of Est. of her
husb. JOSEPH RAZEY of Attl. dcd. intest., dtd. 12 March 1744
[10:495/6].
Inv. of Est. of JOSEPH RAZEY of Attl., dtd. 17 Dec. 1744, pres.
by Marcy Razey, widow & Adm. Pers. est. 109-18-6; real est.

302-5-15. Incl. lands in Attl. & in Wrentham. Apprs: Noah
Carpenter, Daniel Peck & Joseph Staples [10:496].
Order to Samuel Read of Free., Yeoman, Exec. of Est. of his
father JOSEPH READ of Free., Yeoman, dtd. 8 Apr. 1745 [10:
496/7].
Will of JOSEPH READ of Free., Yeoman, dtd. 21 June 1742, prob.
8 Apr. 1745. Wife Hannah (Incl. items about "the agreement
We made before our marrage"). Sons: Joseph & Samuel Read.
Daus: Elizebeth P[icken? faded], Dorothey Hunt, Phebe Read,
Hannah Read, Sarah Read & Mary Read (last 4 under age & un-
mar.). Dau-in-law Sarah Hunt. My Negro boy Nero & my Indian
fellow Moses. Son Samuel to be Exec. Witns: Joshua [Boomer?
faded], Benjamin Jencks & Richard [Pearce? faded][10:497/8/9].
Appt. of [faded] W[faded], Esq. of Brist. to be Adm. of Est. of
SARAH NORTON of Brist., widow, dcd. intest., dtd. 8 Apr. 1745
[10:499/500].
Appt. of Mathew Allen of Barr., Gentleman, to be guard. of Mary
Brown (minor over 14), dau. of ISAAC BROWN of Barr., dtd. 8
Apr. 1745 [10:500].
Appt. of Ann Hix of Dart., widow, to be Adm. of Est. of her husb.
WILLIAM HIX of Dart. dcd. intest., dtd. 8 Apr. 1745 [10:500/1].
Inv. of Est. of WILLIAM HIX of Dart., dtd. 6 Apr. 1745, pres. by
Ann Hix, widow & Adm. Pers. est. 1601-3-0; real est. 4000-0-0.
Apprs: Ichabod Potter, Nathanael Potter & Restcome Sandford
[10:501/2].
Order to Penelope Allen of Dart., Exec. of Est. of JEDEDIAH AL-
LEN of Dart., dtd. 8 Apr. 1745 [10:502/3].
Will of JEDEDIAH ALLEN of Dart., Yeoman, dtd. 25 Dec. 1744, prob.
8 Apr. 1745. Wife Penelope. Sons: Increase, Othniel & Jedediah
Allen. 8 daus: Mehetibel Allen, Naomi Allen, Susanah Allen,
Penelope Allen, Mary Allen, Elizebeth Allen, Bridget Allen &
Wait Allen. Wife to be Exec. Cousin Jonathan Wood to assist my
Exec. Witns: Jedediah Wood (a Quaker), Gabriel Hix & John
Wood [10:503/4].
Inv. of Est. of JEDEDIAH ALLEN of Dart., dtd. 17 Jan. 1744/5,
pres. by Penelope Allen of Dart., his widow & Exec. Pers. est.
1013-1-4; real est. 3550-0-0. Apprs: Ebenezer Slocum, Timo-
they Gifford & James Allen [10:504/5/6].
Will of RICHARD SISSON of Dart., Yeoman, dtd. 29 Sept. 1744,
prob. 12 Nov. 1744. Wife Mehetibel. Sons: Richard, James, Tho-
mas, George & Lemuel Sisson. Daus: Susanah Sisson, Lidia Soul &
Avis Shearman. Son Richard to be Exec. My bro. Jonathan Sisson. Witns: Thomas Sisson, Prince Goddard (a Quaker) & Beriah
Goddard [10:506/7].
Order to Richard Sisson of Dart., Exec. of Est. of his father
RICHARD SISSON of Dart., dtd. 12 Nov. 1744 [10:508].
Inv. of Est. of RICHARD SISSON of Dart., dtd. 18 Oct. 1744, pres.
by Richard Sisson, son & Exec. Pers. est. 669-0-4; real est.
811-0-0. Apprs: Beriah Goddard, George White & Prince Goddard
[10:508/9].

Inv. of Est. of JEREMIAH READ of Attl., dtd. 12 Dec. 1744, pres.
by David Chaiffe, Exec. Pers. est. 25-14-6; real est. 50-0-0.
Apprs: Beniah Barrus, John Ide & Noah Carpenter [10:509].
Inv. of Est. of JOAN FISH of Dart., widow, dtd. 18 Jan. 1744/5,
pres. by Ebenezer Fish, Exec. Pers. est. 197-2-0; no real
est. Apprs: Ebenezer Slocum, Timothey Gifford & James Allen
[10:510].
Appt. of Ruth Church of Brist., widow, to be Adm. of Est. of
her husb. NATHANIEL CHURCH of Brist. dcd. intest., dtd. 26
Apr. 1745 [10:510/1].
Order to Ezekiel Carpenter, Exec. of Est. of ELIZEBETH IDE of
Reho., widow, dtd. 13 May 1745 [10:511].
Will of ELIZABETH IDE, widow of Timothey Ide late of Reho.,
Gentleman, dtd. 30 Sept. 1735, prob. 13 May 1745. Sons: Tim-
othey, Daniel & Josiah (dcd.?) Ide. Daus: Elizebeth Read,
Mary [Read? One name written over another], Sarah Carpenter,
Rachel Perrin & Experiance Lindley. My son Josiah Ide's chldn.
Ezekiel Carpenter to be Exec. Dau. Experiance Lindley's por-
tion be only for her and for her chldn., with Thomas Lindley
to have no part of it due to his "Bad and Undutiful carrage."
Witns: John Bucklen, Jonathan Bucklen & George Allen [10:511/2].
Appt. of Thomas Lawton of Brist., Gentleman, to be Adm. of Est.
of his son THOMAS LAWTON, Jr. of Brist., Mariner, dcd. intest.,
dtd. 13 May 1745 [10:513].
Order to Obediah Carpenter [sic; clerk erred in surname, since
the will names son Obediah Baker], Exec. of Est. of DANIEL
BAKER of Swan., dtd. 13 May 1745 [10:513/4].
Rcpt. dtd. 21 Nov. 1744 by Noah Read, Hannah Read, Samuel Drown
& Sarah his wife for legacy from Est. of THOMAS READ of Reho.,
father of Noah, Hannah & Sarah, as paid to them "by our father
in law Peter Walker of Rehoboth Guardian to us," as recorded
in the div. in Probate office bearing date 18 Apr. 1734 [10:
514].
Will of DANIEL BAKER of Swan., Yeoman, dtd. 6 March 1743/4,
prob. 13 May 1745. Wife Mary. Sons: Samuel, Ebenezer & Obediah Baker. Daus: Martha Smith, Mary Chase, Phebe Weaver &
Sarah Baker. Son Obediah to be Exec. Witns: Edward Slead (a
Quaker), David Perce & William Hart [10:514/5/6].
Inv. of Est. of NATHANIEL BLAGROVE, Esq., of Brist., dtd. Dec.
1744. Pers. est. 2883-17-1; real est. 1595-0-0. Incl. memo.
of 400 acres in Town of Stafford, Town of Hartford, Conn. &
half a thousand acres in Mass. Apprs: Timothey Fales, Joseph Russel & Samuel Smith [10:517/8/9].
Inv. of Est. of BENJAMIN INGOLLS of Reho., Yeoman, dtd. 11 Dec.
1744, pres. by Mercy Ingolls, widow & Adm. Pers. est. 161-
13-0; real est. 700-0-0. Apprs: Peres Bradford, Richard Harding & William Turner [10:519/20].
Acct. of Mercy Ingolls, widow & Adm. of Est. of BENJAMIN INGOLLS
of Reho., dtd. 13 May 1745. Incl. item "to provisions spent

in the family ye first year" [10:520/1].

Inv. of Est. of JOSEPH READ of Free., Gentleman, dtd. 11 Apr.
1745, pres. by Samuel Read, Exec. Pers. est. 481-15-0; real
est. 70-0-0. Also gives list of "Goods of the Widdow...brought
by her" that were supposed to be inventoried "before marrage."
Apprs: Ambrose Barnaby, Daniel Lawton, Jr. & Joshua Boumer
[10:521/2].

Acct. of Elizabeth Fuller of Attl., widow & Adm. of Est. of
JONATHAN FULLER of Attl., dtd. 13 May 1745 [10:523].

Appt. of Jonathan Woodbury of Brist., Esq., to be Adm. of Est.
of SHUBALL NORTON of Brist., Mariner, dcd. intest., the former
Adm., widow Sarah Norton, having since died, dtd. 15 May 1745
[10:523/4].

Appt. of John Pearce of Tiv., Gentleman, to be guard. of Stephen
Burden (minor over 14), son of STEPHEN BURDEN of Free., dtd.
13 May 1745 [10:524].

Will of WILLIAM COLE of Reho., Tanner, dtd. 2 March 1744/5, prob.
13 May 1745. Wife Ann. My grson. William Cole to be Exec.
Witns: Noah Newman, Daniel Bowen & John Greenwood [10:524/5].

Summons to James Leonard of Taun., Gentleman, to settle his acct.
as the guard. of Mary Paddock, now Mary Rawson, wife of Elijah
Rawson, dtd. 18 March 1744, served by Ebenezer Richmond, Depu-
ty Sheriff [10:525].

Order to William Cole of Reho., Yeoman, Exec. of Est. of WILLIAM
COLE of Reho., Tanner, dtd. 13 May 1745 [10:525].

End of Volume 10

* Signifies two or more entries on that page

[ ] Indicates an entry regarding an estate of that person

366

HERIDON (See HARADON)
HERINDEN/HERRINGTON
  Benjamin 344
HERSIN (Also see HEWINS)
  Judith (Porter) 205
HEWES (See HUGHES)
HEWETT/HUET
  Elizabeth 229
  Ephraim [224]*[225]*[226]*
    227* [229]*[259]
  Hannah 229
  Henry 229
  Mercy 226 229
  Ruth 226 229 [259]
  Solomon 226 229 [259]
  Susanna 229
HEWINS (Also see HERSIN)
  Judith (Porter) 215
HEWLETT
  John 217
HICKS/HIX
  Abigail 39 323
  Alices 323
  Ann (___) 345*
  Elizabeth 39
  Ephraim 39 176 215 223* 226
  Experience 182
  Freelove 226 235
  Gabriel 217 255* 345
  Hezekiah 223 235
  James 83 [186][215][223]*
    [226][235]*
  Jane 182
  Joseph [46][78] 95
  Judith (___)(Gatchel) 199
  Leah 323
  Lois 226 235
  Lydia 182
  Mary 78 226 235 323
  Mary (___) 39* 46 182 186
    188 215 235 240
  Mary (Garnzey) 89* 92 256
  Nathaniel 182
  Patience (Wheaton) 261
  Priscilla (Wheaton) 261
  Ruth 321
  Samuel 39 89* 92 124 [182]*
    [188][240] 256 [320]*
    [322]*[323]*[324]*
  Sarah 323
  Sarah (Manchester) 232
  Susanna 38 323
  Susanna (___) 323*
  Thomas [39]* 313
  Weston 328
  William 261 291 293 294
    [345]*
HILL
  Ann/Anna (___) 206 207 283*
    285
  Ann (Brown) 318
  Barnard 266* 269
  Benjamin 283
  Caleb 266
  Elizabeth 266
  Elizabeth (___) 266* 269
  Elizabeth (Allen) 266
  Esther (Titus) 315
  James 285
  John [275]* 315
  Jonathan 196 198* [266]*
    [269]
  Joseph 42 251
  Martha 266
  Mary 166
  Nathaniel 266
  Phebe 283
  Rebeckah 283

HILL (cont.)
  Rebeckah (Allen)(Cole) 267
  Samuel 7 8 89* 92 124 [182]
    [188][207] 247 [283]*[285]
  Sarah 266
  Thomas 266* 267
  William 283
HILLIARD/HILLAR
  Abigail 62
  Abigail (Wilbour) 271
  Daniel 194
  David 23 62 78 93 155 281
  Deborah 62 [78]
  Deborah (___) 62 78*
  Esther 62
  Jabez 186
  Joanna (Andrews) 262 263
  Mary 62
  Richard 78
  Sarah 62
  William [62]*
HILLMAN/HILMON
  Benjamin 297
  Susanna (Sampson) 297
HINTON
  John [1]*
HIX (See HICKS)
HIXON/HIXSON
  John 208
HOAR/HOARD
  Hannah (___) 6 25
  Henry 162 318
  Mary (Talbut) 274
  Nathaniel 3 18
  Sarah (___) 3 313
  Sarah (Brightman) 162
  Sarah (Wilbour) 18 23 26
  William 3 [6][25] 255
HODGE(S)
  Abigail 84
  Ann/Anna 335
  Benjamin 118 201 202 235
    272 279 313 335
  Ebenezer 335
  Edmund 335*
  Eliphalet 66* 335
  Elizabeth 25 335
  Elizabeth (Macey) 7 12
  Ensign 311
  Ephraim 99 107 155 166
  Experience 119
  Experience (Leonard) 57
  George 84
  Hannah 156
  Hannah (Dean) 47
  Hannah (Tisdale) 84 180
  Henry 3* 4* 6* 8* 9 11* 13*
    14 15 18* 19* 22 23 26 27
    33 35 41 42 44 47 51* 62
    63 64 68 69 72 [78]*[99]
    187 188 192 298 311
  James [193][195][197]*[198]
    [218]
  John 6 25 65 66 [78] 106
    119 217 [335]*
  Joseph 104 119 122 145 180
    191 194 201 275 311 313
    335
  Katherine (___) 265 272
    311 341
  Lydia 119
  Martha 122 156
  Martha (Tisdale) 65
  Mary 198
  Mary (___) 335
  Mercy 335
  Miriam 125
  Nathan 116 123 156 189 254

HODGE(S)
  Nathan (cont.) 276
  Nathaniel [115]* 127 275
  Ruth 335
  Samuel 7 12 57 69 106 107
    117 [119]*[122][123] 145
    [156]
  Sarah 25 122
  Sarah (Leonard) 145
  Seth 122 156 197
  Silence 119
  Susanna (Gilbert) 136
  Thomas [265][272][311][341]
  William [25]* 63 84 105 123
    136* 156 180 204 210* 311
    340
HOLBROOK
  Alice (Godfrey) 4
  Peter 4
  Sarah 131
HOLDRIDGE
  Sarah (Walker) 292
HOLLODAY (See HALLODAY)
HOLLAWAY (See also HALLOWWAY)
  Elizabeth (Babbitt) 246
  Malachi 246
  Timothy 52
HOLLET
  Samuel 218
HOLMES
  Abraham [89][91]*[129]*
  Bathsheba 89 129
  Cornelius 110
  Ebenezer 85
  Elizabeth 89 129* 340
  Elizabeth (Willis) 340
  Experience [69]*[91][129]*
  John [301]
  Patience (___) 69 [91] 129*
  Rose 89
  Samuel 284 301 340*
  Sarah 129
  Susanna 89
HOMAN/HOLMAN
  Hannah (Hall) 151
HONAR
  William 61
HOPING (See HOPPING)
HOPKINS
  Abigail (Godfrey) 127
  Deborah (Allen) 97
  Elizabeth (Jenckes) 258
  Susanna (Jenckes) 258
HORSEE (Also see HOXIE)
  Sarah (Tucker) 11*
HORSEWELL/HOSWELL
  Elizabeth 60
  James 216
  John 156 208 213 215 222
    248
  Peter 60 90 [218][222]
HORTON
  Ann/Anna 128
  Ann (Millard) 307
  Daniel 128 243
  David 140
  Hannah 128 140
  Hannah (Garnzey) 89* 92 256
  Hester 128
  John 69* 83 89* 92 125 128
    140 166 256
  Kezia (___) 217
  Kezia (Carpenter) 155
  Mehetabel (Garnzey) 89* 92
    256
  Mehetabel (Richmond) 251
  Moses 128
  Patience 128

HORTON (cont.)
  Richard 27
  Simeon 128 343
  Solomon [114][116][125]
    [128]*[140][243]
  Susanna (___) 114 116
  Thomas [69]* 89* 92 128
    [218] 243 256
HOSKINS/HASKINS
  Abiah 187*
  Amy 78
  Ann/Anna 187
  Elizabeth (___) 71
  Hannah [133] 187 209 [260]
  Henry 151 161 187 217*
  Jacob [197][207][208]
  John 7 18* 35 [71] 187*
    192 228
  Joshua 209
  Josiah 187
  Leah 344
  Lydia 209
  Mary 65 66* 187*
  Mary (___) 187* 188
  Mary (Tisdale) 65
  Mercy 209
  Mercy (___) 188 209
  Nehemiah 209*
  Rebeckah 12 13
  Richard 35 66 70 78
  Samuel 187 [209]*
  Sarah 187
  Sarah (___) 187
  Stephen [187]*[188]
  William 123 [187]* 188
    [192] 202 217
HOSWELL (See HORSEWELL)
HOUSE
  Hannah (Davenport) 172
HOWARD (See HAYWARD)
HOWE
  Eleanor (___) 43
  Eleanor (Dye) 186 191 204
  Nicholas [43]
HOWLAND
  Abigail 45 57 87 143 162
    166 180* 279 342
  Abigail (Cary) 180
  Abraham 70
  Alice 70
  Barnabas 142 143 144 199
    223 230
  Bathsheba 327
  Benjamin 5 87 [142][143]
    279 [319]*[334] 342
  Bithia 210 214 229 230
  Bithia (___) 55 60 61 68
  Content 70 102 126 127*
  Daniel 22 47 [53] 87 [255]*
    278 279 342
  Deborah 176
  Deborah (Cook) 262
  Desire 143
  Edith 87 279 342
  Elizabeth 1 68 210 214 229
    230
  Elizabeth (___) [1]* 176
  Freelove (Wood) 229
  George 54 102* 126 127 143
    147 230
  Gershom 70
  Hannah 1 87 176 279 343
  Hannah (___) 85 86* 107*
    176 [279]*[342]
  Hannah (Allen) 121
  Hannah (Woodman) 60* 63*
  Henry 87* 91 144 147 153
    154 [176]* 182 217 230 279

HOWLAND (cont.)
  Isaac 1 53 70 133 134 143
    182 199 213 223 313*
  Jabez 1 17 27 [55]*[60]*
    [61][68]* 102* 170 [210]
    [211]*[213][214][229]*
    [230]*
  James 102* 126 127 133 176*
    183 217 262* 271* 274 279
    296 300 342
  Job 87 279 342
  John [1]* 70* 102 120 127
    137 159 239 255 262* 316
  Joseph 1* 68 87 166 170 235
    243 263 [265]
  Joshua 70
  Josiah [78][169] 325
  Judith (___) 143
  Lydia 1 143
  Mary 70 87 102 126 127*
    176* 279 342
  Mary (___) 53 70 255
  Mary (Cook) 262
  Mercy 230
  Meribah 176
  Nathaniel 1 11 54* 78 [102]*
    [126]*[127]* 147
  Nicholas 57 60* 63* [85] 86*
    [87]*[98]* 143 279* 342
  Patience 213 230
  Rebeckah 87 102 126 127*
    279 342
  Rose (___) 102
  Rose (Allen) 31
  Samuel 1 61 68 [70]* 86 109
    113 119 128 129 130* 132
    138 140 162* 164* 166 168*
    169 170 177* 180* 210 235
    236 240* 241 245 247 253
    255* 257 259 265 278 279*
    284 294 295 297 301 311
    322 323 329 342
  Sarah 102 126 127* 230
  Sarah (___) 318* 334
  Stephen 176
  Tabitha 322
  Thomas 176 213 229 230
  William 176
  Yetmercy (___) 169
  Yetmercy (___)(Palmer) 230
  Zachariah 57
  Zoeth 176
HOXIE/HAXSE
  Joseph 11
  Sarah (Tucker) 11
HUBBARD
  John 265 275
  Nathaniel 188 189 192 249
    338
HUDDLESTON
  Eleanor (___) 332*
  Elizabeth 227
  Elizabeth (___) 227*
  Elizabeth (Fish) 341
  George 332
  Isaac [332]*
  Judith 310
  Peleg 221 222 227 310*
    332*
  Richard [309][310]*
  Sarah 309
  Sarah (Tallman) 310*
  Seth 341
  Valentine 5* 6 11 47*
  William 221 [222][227]*
HUES (See HUGHES)
HUET (See HEWETT)

HUGHES/HUES
  Dr. 9
  William 10
HULET (See HEWLET)
HULL
  Samuel 212
HUMPHREY
  James 205
  John 55 64 108 109 114 115
    116 123 205* 210 244 287
    308 325
  Jonas 205
  Josiah 205 226 293
  Martha 205
  Mary 204 222
  Samuel 37 164 [205]*[210]*
    222 342
  Sarah 205
  Sarah (Cooper 55 64 109
HUNT
  Adam 140*
  Bartholomew [78]
  Benjamin 5 23 34 47 49* 58
    60 69 94 194* [208]*
  Capt. 25
  Daniel 13 14 157 [278][280]
    [286][287]
  Deborah 72 302
  Dorothy 302
  Dorothy (___) 278 280 286
  Dorothy (Read) 345
  Elizabeth 72
  Elizabeth (___) 5 341 343
  Enoch 5 10 13 21 23* 28 30
    [56]*
  Ephraim 5 [8][13][14]* 303
    317*
  Hannah 13 14 72
  Hannah (___) 263*
  Hannah (Pope) 144
  Huldah 208
  Joanna 303
  John 5 13 14 21 23 29 30 36
    38 50 54 [72]* 107 160 195*
    209 252 256 263 287 319 330
    331* 336 337
  Joseph 143*
  Judith 5
  Martha 72
  Martha (___) 298 300
  Mary 56 72 73 88*
  Mary (___) 72 208*
  Mary (Peck) 34
  Nathaniel 56* [78]*[191]*
    [213][341][343]
  Oliver 287
  Peter [5] 23 72* [78] 85 86
    110 124 172 176
  Rebeckah 191* 263 303 316
  Rebeckah (___) 8 13 14
  Samuel 144 145 146* [196]
    [262]*[273][303]* 316
  Sarah 13 14 263 303 345
  Stephen 56* [78]
  Susanna (Sweeting) 160 195*
  Sybil 208
  Tabitha 208
  Thomas 302
  William 277 [298][300]
HUTCHENSON
  Margaret (Sandford) 251 252
  Thomas 251 252
IDE
  Benjamin 95
  Daniel 215 240* 241 243 271
    292* 346
  Elizabeth 153 215 240* 271
    346

www.ingramcontent.com/pod-product-compliance
Lightning Source LLC
Chambersburg PA
CBHW060134280326
41932CB00012B/1510